Principles of Information Security

Sixth Edition

Michael E. Whitman, *Ph.D., CISM, CISSP*

Herbert J. Mattord, *Ph.D., CISM, CISSP*

Kennesaw State University

CENGAGE
Learning·

Australia · Brazil · Mexico · Singapore · United Kingdom · United States

CENGAGE
Learning·

Principles of Information Security,
Sixth Edition
Michael E. Whitman and
Herbert J. Mattord

GM, Science, Technology, & Math: Balraj Kalsi

Sr. Product Director, Computing: Kathleen McMahon

Product Team Manager: Kristin McNary

Associate Product Manager: Amy Savino

Director, Development: Julia Caballero

Content Development Manager: Leigh Hefferon

Managing Content Developer: Alyssa Pratt

Senior Content Developer: Natalie Pashoukos

Product Assistant: Jake Toth

Marketing Director: Michele McTighe

Marketing Managers: Stephanie Albracht and Jeff Tousignant

Marketing Coordinator: Cassie Cloutier

Executive Director, Production: Martin Rabinowitz

Production Director: Patty Stephan

Senior Content Project Manager: Brooke Greenhouse

Senior Designer: Diana Graham

Cover image(s): iStockPhoto.com/maciek905

For product information and technology assistance, contact us at
Cengage Learning Customer & Sales Support, 1-800-354-9706
For permission to use material from this text or product, submit all requests online at **www.cengage.com/permissions.**
Further permissions questions can be e-mailed to
permissionrequest@cengage.com

Library of Congress Control Number: 2017930059

ISBN: 978-1-337-10206-3

Cengage Learning
20 Channel Center Street
Boston, MA 02210
USA

Cengage Learning is a leading provider of customized learning solutions with employees residing in nearly 40 different countries and sales in more than 125 countries around the world. Find your local representative at **www.cengage.com**.

Cengage Learning products are represented in Canada by Nelson Education, Ltd.

To learn more about Cengage Learning, visit **www.cengage.com**

Purchase any of our products at your local college store or at our preferred online store **www.cengagebrain.com**

Notice to the Reader

Publisher does not warrant or guarantee any of the products described herein or perform any independent analysis in connection with any of the product information contained herein. Publisher does not assume, and expressly disclaims, any obligation to obtain and include information other than that provided to it by the manufacturer. The reader is expressly warned to consider and adopt all safety precautions that might be indicated by the activities described herein and to avoid all potential hazards. By following the instructions contained herein, the reader willingly assumes all risks in connection with such instructions. The publisher makes no representations or warranties of any kind, including but not limited to, the warranties of fitness for particular purpose or merchantability, nor are any such representations implied with respect to the material set forth herein, and the publisher takes no responsibility with respect to such material. The publisher shall not be liable for any special, consequential, or exemplary damages resulting, in whole or part, from the readers' use of, or reliance upon, this material.

Printed in the United States of America
Print Number: 04   Print Year: 2018

Table of Contents

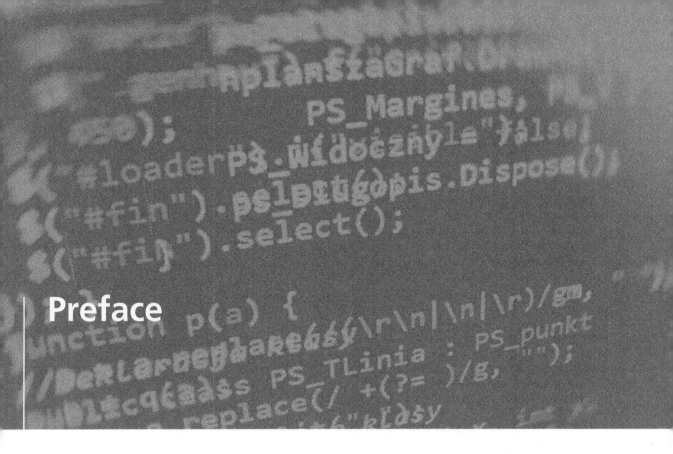

Preface

As global networks expand, the interconnection of the world's information systems and devices of every description becomes vital, as does the smooth operation of communication, computing, and automation solutions. However, ever-evolving threats such as malware and phishing attacks and the success of criminal attackers illustrate the weaknesses in current information technologies and the need to provide heightened security for these systems.

When attempting to secure current and planned systems and networks, organizations must draw on the current pool of information security practitioners. However, to develop more secure computing environments in the future, these same organizations are counting on the next generation of professionals to have the correct mix of skills and experience to anticipate and manage the complex information security issues that will arise. Thus, improved texts with supporting materials, along with the efforts of college and university faculty, are needed to prepare students of technology to recognize the threats and vulnerabilities in existing systems and to learn to design and develop the secure systems needed.

The purpose of *Principles of Information Security, Sixth Edition,* is to continue to meet the need for a current, high-quality academic textbook that surveys the breadth of the information security discipline. Even today, there remains a lack of textbooks that provide students with a *balanced* introduction to the managerial and technical aspects of information security. By creating a book specifically focused on the information security common body of knowledge, we hope to close this gap. Further, there is a clear need to include principles from criminal justice, political science, computer science, information systems, and other related disciplines to gain a clear understanding of information security principles and formulate interdisciplinary solutions for systems vulnerabilities. The essential tenet of this textbook is that information security in the modern organization is a problem for management to solve, and not one that technology alone can address. In other words, an organization's information security has important economic consequences for which management will be held accountable.

Approach

Principles of Information Security, Sixth Edition, provides a broad review of the entire field of information security, background on many related elements, and enough detail to facilitate an understanding of the topic as a whole. The book covers the terminology of the field, the history of the discipline, and strategies for managing an information security program.

Structure and Chapter Descriptions

Principles of Information Security, Sixth Edition, is structured to follow an approach that moves from the strategic aspects of information security to the operational—beginning with the external impetus for information security, moving through the organization's governance, risk management, and regulatory compliance strategic approaches, and continuing with the technical and operational implementation of security in the organization. This textbook's use of this approach is intended to provide a supportive but not overly dominant foundation that will guide instructors and students through the information domains of information security. To serve this end, the book is organized into 12 chapters.

⟩ Chapter 1—Introduction to Information Security

The opening chapter establishes the foundation for understanding the broader field of information security. This is accomplished by defining key terms, explaining essential concepts, and reviewing the origins of the field and its impact on the understanding of information security.

⟩ Chapter 2—The Need for Security

Chapter 2 examines the business drivers behind the design process of information security analysis. It examines current organizational and technological security needs while emphasizing and building on the concepts presented in Chapter 1. One principal concept presented in this chapter is that information security is primarily a management issue rather than a technological one. To put it another way, the best practices within the field of information security involve applying technology only after considering the business needs.

The chapter also examines the various threats facing organizations and presents methods for ranking and prioritizing these threats as organizations begin their security planning process. The chapter continues with a detailed examination of the types of attacks that could result from these threats, and how these attacks could affect the organization's information systems. Chapter 2 also provides further discussion of the key principles of information security, some of which were introduced in Chapter 1: confidentiality, integrity, availability, authentication and identification, authorization, accountability, and privacy.

❯ Chapter 3—Legal, Ethical, and Professional Issues in Information Security

A critical aspect of the field is the inclusion of a careful examination of current legislation, regulation, and common ethical expectations of both national and international entities that provides important insights into the regulatory constraints that govern business. This chapter examines several key laws that shape the field of information security and examines the computer ethics to which those who implement security must adhere. This chapter also presents several common legal and ethical issues found in today's organizations, as well as formal and professional organizations that promote ethics and legal responsibility.

❯ Chapter 4—Planning for Security

This chapter presents a number of widely accepted security models and frameworks. It examines best business practices and standards of due care and due diligence, and offers an overview of the development of security policy. This chapter details the major components, scope, and target audience for each level of security policy. This chapter also explains data classification schemes, both military and private, as well as the security education training and awareness (SETA) program. The chapter examines the planning process that supports business continuity, disaster recovery, and incident response; it also describes the organization's role during incidents and specifies when the organization should involve outside law enforcement agencies.

❯ Chapter 5—Risk Management

Before the design of a new information security solution can begin, information security analysts must first understand the current state of the organization and its relationship to information security. Does the organization have any formal information security mechanisms in place? How effective are they? What policies and procedures have been published and distributed to security managers and end users? This chapter describes how to conduct a fundamental information security assessment by describing procedures for identifying and prioritizing threats and assets as well as procedures for identifying what controls are in place to protect these assets from threats. The chapter also discusses the various types of control mechanisms and identifies the steps involved in performing the initial risk assessment. The chapter continues by defining risk management as the process of identifying, assessing, and reducing risk to an acceptable level and implementing effective control measures to maintain that level of risk. Chapter 5 concludes with a discussion of risk analysis and various types of feasibility analyses.

❯ Chapter 6—Security Technology: Access Controls, Firewalls, and VPNs

Chapter 6 provides a detailed overview of the configuration and use of technologies designed to segregate the organization's systems from the insecure Internet. This chapter examines the various definitions and categorizations of firewall technologies and the architectures under which firewalls may be deployed. The chapter discusses the rules and guidelines associated with the proper configuration and use of firewalls. Chapter 6 also discusses remote dial-up services and the security precautions necessary to secure access points for organizations still deploying this older technology. The chapter continues by presenting content filtering capabilities and considerations, and concludes by examining technologies designed to provide remote access to authorized users through virtual private networks.

〉 Chapter 7—Security Technology: Intrusion Detection and Prevention Systems, and Other Security Tools

Chapter 7 continues the discussion of security technologies by examining the concept of intrusion and the technologies necessary to prevent, detect, react, and recover from intrusions. Specific types of intrusion detection and prevention systems (IDPSs)—the host IDPS, network IDPS, and application IDPS—and their respective configurations and uses are presented and discussed. The chapter examines specialized detection technologies that are designed to entice attackers into decoy systems (and thus away from critical systems) or simply to identify the attackers' entry into these decoy areas. Such systems are known as honeypots, honeynets, and padded cell systems. The discussion also examines trace-back systems, which are designed to track down the true address of attackers who were lured into decoy systems. The chapter then examines key security tools that information security professionals can use to examine the current state of their organization's systems and identify potential vulnerabilities or weaknesses in the organization's overall security posture. Chapter 7 concludes with a discussion of access control devices commonly deployed by modern operating systems and new technologies in the area of biometrics that can provide strong authentication to existing implementations.

〉 Chapter 8—Cryptography

Chapter 8 continues the section on security technologies by describing the underlying foundations of modern cryptosystems as well as their architectures and implementations. The chapter begins by summarizing the history of modern cryptography and discussing the various types of ciphers that played key roles in that history. The chapter also examines some of the mathematical techniques that comprise cryptosystems, including hash functions. The chapter then extends this discussion by comparing traditional symmetric encryption systems with more modern asymmetric encryption systems and examining the role of asymmetric systems as the foundation of public-key encryption systems. Also covered are the cryptography-based protocols used in secure communications, including S-HTTP, S/MIME, SET, and SSH. The chapter then discusses steganography and its emerging role as an effective means of hiding information. Chapter 8 concludes by revisiting attacks on information security that are specifically targeted at cryptosystems.

〉 Chapter 9—Physical Security

A vital part of any information security process, physical security includes the management of physical facilities, the implementation of physical access control, and the oversight of environmental controls. Physical security involves a wide range of special considerations that encompass designing a secure data center, assessing the relative value of guards and watchdogs, and resolving technical issues in fire suppression and power conditioning. Chapter 9 examines these considerations by factoring in the physical security threats that modern organizations face.

❯ Chapter 10—Implementing Information Security

The preceding chapters provide guidelines for how an organization might design its information security program. Chapter 10 examines the elements critical to *implementing* this design. Key areas in this chapter include the bull's-eye model for implementing information security and a discussion of whether an organization should outsource components of its information security program. The chapter also discusses change management, program improvement, and additional planning for business continuity efforts.

❯ Chapter 11—Security and Personnel

The next area in the implementation stage addresses personnel issues. Chapter 11 examines both sides of the personnel coin: security personnel and security of personnel. It examines staffing issues, professional security credentials, and the implementation of employment policies and practices. The chapter also discusses how information security policy affects and is affected by consultants, temporary workers, and outside business partners.

❯ Chapter 12—Information Security Maintenance

Last and most important is the discussion of maintenance and change. Chapter 12 describes the ongoing technical and administrative evaluation of the information security program that an organization must perform to maintain the security of its information systems. This chapter explores the controlled administration of changes to modern information systems to prevent the introduction of new security vulnerabilities. Special considerations needed for the varieties of vulnerability analysis in modern organizations are explored, from Internet penetration testing to wireless network risk assessment. The chapter and the book conclude by covering the subject of digital forensics.

Features

Here are some features of the book's approach to information security:

Information Security Professionals' Common Bodies of Knowledge—Because the authors hold both the Certified Information Security Manager (CISM) and Certified Information Systems Security Professional (CISSP) credentials, those knowledge domains have had an influence in the design of the text. Although care was taken to avoid producing a certification study guide, the authors' backgrounds ensure that the book's treatment of information security integrates the CISM and CISSP Common Bodies of Knowledge (CBKs).

Chapter Scenarios—Each chapter opens and closes with a short story that features the same fictional company as it encounters information security issues commonly found in real-life organizations. At the end of each chapter, a set of discussion questions provides students and instructors with opportunities to discuss the issues suggested by the story as well as offering an opportunity to explore the ethical dimensions of those issues.

Clearly Defined Key Terms Boxes—At the start of every major section, the key terms for that section are listed and defined. While the terms are referenced in the body of the text, the isolation of the definitions from the discussion allows a smoother presentation of the key terms and supports their standardization throughout all Whitman and Mattord books.

Offline and Technical Details Boxes—Interspersed throughout the textbook, these sections highlight interesting topics and detailed technical issues, giving students the option of delving into information security topics more deeply.

Hands-On Learning—At the end of each chapter, students will find a chapter summary and review questions as well as exercises. In the exercises, students are asked to research, analyze, and write responses to reinforce learning objectives, deepen their understanding of the text, and examine the information security arena outside the classroom.

New to This Edition

- Coverage of the newest laws and industry trends
- Increased visibility for terminology used in the industry through Key Terms text boxes and integration of this terminology across the Whitman and Mattord textbook series
- Updated and additional "For More Information" callouts that provide Web locations where students can find more information about the subject covered

Instructor Resources

❯ MindTap

MindTap® activities for Whitman and Mattord's *Principles of Information Security, Sixth Edition*, are designed to help students master the skills they need in today's workforce. Research shows employers need critical thinkers, troubleshooters, and creative problem-solvers to stay relevant in our fast-paced, technology-driven world. MindTap helps you achieve this with assignments and activities that provide hands-on practice, real-life relevance, and mastery of difficult concepts. Students are guided through assignments that progress from basic knowledge and understanding to more challenging problems.

All MindTap activities and assignments are tied to learning objectives. The hands-on exercises provide real-life application and practice. Readings and "Whiteboard Shorts" support the lecture, while "In the News" assignments encourage students to stay current. Pre- and post-course assessments allow you to measure how much students have learned using analytics and reporting that makes it easy to see where the class stands in terms of progress, engagement, and completion rates. Use the content and learning path as is, or pick and choose how our material will wrap around yours. You control what the students see and when they see it. Learn more at *www.cengage.com/mindtap/*.

❯ Instructor Companion Site

Free to all instructors who adopt *Principles of Information Security, Sixth Edition*, for their courses is a complete package of instructor resources. These resources are available from the Cengage Web site, *www.cengagebrain.com*. Go to the product page for this book in the online catalog and choose "Instructor Downloads."

Resources include:

- *Instructor's Manual*: This manual includes course objectives and additional information to help your instruction.

- *Cengage Testing Powered by Cognero*: A flexible, online system that allows you to import, edit, and manipulate content from the text's test bank or elsewhere, including your own favorite test questions; create multiple test versions in an instant; and deliver tests from your LMS, your classroom, or wherever you want.

- *PowerPoint Presentations*: A set of Microsoft PowerPoint slides is included for each chapter. These slides are meant to be used as a teaching aid for classroom presentations, to be made available to students for chapter review, or to be printed for classroom distribution. Some tables and figures are included in the PowerPoint slides; however, all are available in the online instructor resources. Instructors are also at liberty to add their own slides.

- *Lab Manual*: Cengage has produced a lab manual (*Hands-On Information Security Lab Manual, Fourth Edition*) written by the authors that can be used to provide technical experiential exercises in conjunction with this book. Contact your Cengage learning consultant for more information.

- *Readings and Cases*: Cengage also produced two texts—*Readings and Cases in the Management of Information Security* (ISBN-13: 9780619216276) and *Readings & Cases in Information Security: Law & Ethics* (ISBN-13: 9781435441576)—by the authors, which make excellent companion texts. Contact your Cengage learning consultant for more information.

- *Curriculum Model for Programs of Study in Information Security*: In addition to the texts authored by this team, a curriculum model for programs of study in Information Security and Assurance is available from the Kennesaw State University Center for Information Security Education (*http://infosec.kennesaw.edu*). This document provides details on designing and implementing security coursework and curricula in academic institutions, as well as guidance and lessons learned from the authors' perspective.

Author Team

Michael Whitman and Herbert Mattord have jointly developed this text to merge knowledge from the world of academic study with practical experience from the business world.

Michael E. Whitman, Ph.D., CISM, CISSP is a Professor of Information Security and Assurance in the Information Systems Department, Michael J. Coles College of Business at Kennesaw State University, Kennesaw, Georgia, where he is also the Executive Director of the KSU Center for Information Security Education (*infosec.kennesaw.edu*). Dr. Whitman is an active researcher in Information Security, Fair and Responsible Use Policies, Ethical Computing, and Curriculum Development Methodologies. He currently teaches graduate and undergraduate courses in Information Security Management. He has published articles in the top journals in his field, including *Information Systems Research, Communications of the ACM, Information and Management, Journal of International Business Studies,* and *Journal of Computer Information Systems.* Dr. Whitman is also the Co-Editor-in-Chief of the Journal of Cybersecurity Education, Research and Practice. He is a member of the Information Systems Security Association, the Association for Computing Machinery, and the Association for Information Systems. Dr. Whitman is also the co-author of *Management of Information Security, Principles of Incident Response and Disaster Recovery, Readings and Cases in the Management of Information Security, The Guide to Firewalls and VPNs, The Guide to Network Security*, and *The Hands-On Information Security Lab Manual*, among others, all published by Cengage. Prior to his career in academia, Dr. Whitman was an Armored Cavalry Officer in the United States Army, which included duties as Automated Data Processing Systems Security Officer (ADPSSO).

Herbert J. Mattord, Ph.D., CISM, CISSP completed 24 years of IT industry experience as an application developer, database administrator, project manager, and information security practitioner before joining the faculty of Kennesaw State University in 2002. Dr. Mattord is the Assistant Chair of the Information Systems Department and the Associate Director of the KSU Center for Information Security Education and Awareness *(infosec.kennesaw.edu)*. Dr. Mattord is also the Co-Editor-in-Chief of the Journal of Cybersecurity Education, Research and Practice. During his career as an IT practitioner, he has been an adjunct professor at Kennesaw State University, Southern Polytechnic State University in Marietta, Georgia, Austin Community College in Austin, Texas, and Texas State University: San Marcos. He currently teaches undergraduate courses in Information Security. He was formerly the Manager of Corporate Information Technology Security at Georgia-Pacific Corporation, where much of the practical knowledge found in this textbook was acquired. Dr. Mattord is also the co-author of *Management of Information Security, Principles of Incident Response and Disaster Recovery, Readings and Cases in the Management of Information Security, The Guide to Firewalls and VPNs, The Guide to Network Security*, and *The Hands-On Information Security Lab Manual*, among others, all published by Cengage.

Acknowledgments

The authors would like to thank their families for their support and understanding for the many hours dedicated to this project—hours taken away, in many cases, from family activities.

❯ Contributors

Several people and organizations also provided materials for this textbook, and we thank them for their contributions:

- The National Institute of Standards and Technology (NIST) is the source of many references, tables, figures, and other content used in many places in the textbook.

❯ Reviewers

- We are indebted to Paul Witman, California Lutheran University, for his perceptive feedback during the chapter-by-chapter reviews of the text.

❯ Special Thanks

The authors wish to thank the editorial and production teams at Cengage. Their diligent and professional efforts greatly enhanced the final product:

- Natalie Pashoukos, Senior Content Developer
- Dan Seiter, Development Editor

- Kristin McNary, Product Team Manager
- Amy Savino, Associate Product Manager
- Brooke Baker, Senior Content Project Manager

In addition, several professional organizations, commercial organizations, and individuals aided the development of the textbook by providing information and inspiration. The authors wish to acknowledge their contributions:

- Dave Lineman
- Donn Parker
- Our colleagues in the Department of Information Systems and the Coles College of Business at Kennesaw State University

〉 Our Commitment

The authors are committed to serving the needs of adopters and readers of this book. We would be pleased and honored to receive feedback on the textbook and its supporting materials. You can contact us at *infosec@kennesaw.edu*.

Foreword

Information security is an art more than a science, and the mastery of protecting information requires multidisciplinary knowledge of a huge quantity of information plus experience and skill. You will find much of what you need here in this book as the authors take you through the security systems development life cycle using real-life scenarios to introduce each topic. The authors provide their perspective from many years of real-life experience, combined with their academic approach for a rich learning experience expertly presented in this book. You have chosen the authors and the book well.

Since you are reading this book, you are most likely working toward a career in information security or at least have serious interest in information security. You must anticipate that just about everybody hates the constraints that security puts on their work. This includes both the good guys and the bad guys—except for malicious hackers who love the security we install as a challenge to be beaten. We concentrate on stopping the intentional wrongdoers because it applies to stopping the accidental ones as well. Security to protect against accidental wrongdoers is not good enough against those with intent.

I have spent 40 years of my life in a field that I found to be exciting and rewarding, working with computers and pitting my wits against malicious people, and you will too. Security controls and practices include logging on and off, using passwords, encrypting and backing up vital information, locking doors and drawers, motivating stakeholders to support security, and installing antivirus software. These means of protection have no benefit except rarely, when adversities occur. Good security is in effect when nothing bad happens, and when nothing bad happens, who needs security? Nowadays, in addition to loss experience, we need it because the law, regulations, and auditors say so—especially if we deal with the personal information of others, electronic money, intellectual property, and keeping ahead of the competition.

There is great satisfaction in knowing that your employer's information and systems are reasonably secure and that you are paid a good salary, are the center of attention in emergencies, and are applying your wits against the bad guys. This makes up for the downside of your security work. It is no job for perfectionists because you will almost never be fully successful, and there will always be vulnerabilities that you aren't aware of or that the bad guys discover first. Our enemies have a great advantage over us. They have to find only one vulnerability and one target to attack in a known place, electronically or physically at a time of their choosing, while we must defend from potentially millions of attacks against assets and vulnerabilities that are no longer in one computer room but are spread all over the world. It's like playing a game in which you don't know your opponents and where they are, what they are doing, or why they are doing it, and they are secretly changing the rules as they play. You must be highly ethical, defensive, secretive, and cautious. Bragging about the great security you are employing might tip off the enemy. Enjoy the few successes that you experience, for you will not even know about some of them.

There is a story that describes the kind of war you are entering into. A small country inducted a young man into its ill-equipped army. The army had no guns, so it issued a broom to the new recruit for training purposes. In basic training, the young man asked, "What do I do with this broom?"

The instructor took him to the rifle range and told him to pretend the broom is a gun, aim it at the target, and say, "Bang, bang, bang." He did that. Then the instructor took him to bayonet practice, and the recruit said, "What do I do with this broom?"

The instructor said, "Pretend it is a gun with a bayonet and say, 'Stab, stab, stab.'"

The recruit did that as well. Then the war started and the army still didn't have guns; the young man found himself on the front line with enemy soldiers running toward him across a field. All he had was his trusty broom, so he could only do what he was trained to do. He aimed the broom at the enemy soldiers and said, "Bang, bang, bang." Some of the enemy soldiers fell down, but many kept coming. Some got so close that he had to say "Stab, stab, stab," and more enemy soldiers fell down. However, there was one stubborn enemy soldier (there always is in these stories) running toward him. The recruit said, "Bang, bang, bang," but to no effect. The enemy continued to get closer and the recruit said, "Stab, stab, stab," but it still had no effect. In fact, the enemy soldier ran right over the recruit, broke his broom in half, and left him lying in the dirt. As the enemy soldier ran by, the recruit heard him muttering under his breath, "Tank, tank, tank."

I tell this story at the end of my many lectures on computer crime and security to impress on my audience that if you are going to win against crime, you must know the rules, and it is the criminals who are making up their own secret rules as they go along. This makes winning very difficult.

When I was lecturing in Rio de Janeiro, a young woman performed simultaneous translation into Portuguese for my audience of several hundred people, all with earphones clapped over their ears. In such situations, I have no idea what my audience is hearing, and after telling my joke nobody laughed. They just sat there with puzzled looks on their faces. After the lecture, I asked the translator what had happened. She had translated "tank, tank, tank" into "water tank, water tank, water tank." I and the recruit were both deceived that time.

Three weeks later, I was lecturing to an audience of French bankers at the George V Hotel in Paris. I had a bilingual friend listen to the translation of my talk. The same thing happened as in Rio. Nobody laughed. Afterwards, I asked my friend what had happened. He said, "You will never believe this, but the translator translated 'tank, tank, tank' into 'merci, merci, merci' (thanks)." Even in telling the joke, like the recruit, I didn't know the rules to the game.

Remember that when working in security, you are in a virtual army defending your employer and stakeholders from their enemies. From your point of view, the enemies will probably think and act irrationally, but from their perspective they are perfectly rational, with serious personal problems to solve and gains to be made by violating your security. You are no longer just a techie with the challenging job of installing technological controls in systems and networks. Most of your work should be in assisting potential victims to protect themselves from information adversities and dealing with your smart but often irrational enemies, even though you rarely see or even identify them. I spent a major part of my security career hunting down computer criminals and interviewing them and their victims, trying to obtain insights to do a better job of defending from their attacks. Likewise, you should use every opportunity to seek them out and get to know them. This experience gives you great cachet as a real and unique expert, even with minimal exposure to only a few enemies.

Comprehensiveness is an important part of the game you play for real stakes because the enemy will likely seek the easiest way to attack vulnerabilities and assets that you haven't fully protected yet or even know exist. For example, a threat that is rarely found on threat lists is endangerment of assets—putting information assets in harm's way. Endangerment is also one of the most common violations by security professionals when they reveal too much about their security and loss experience.

You must be thorough and meticulous and document everything pertinent, in case your competence is questioned and to meet the requirements of the Sarbanes-Oxley Law. Keep your documents safely locked away. Documentation is important so that when an adversity hits and you lose the game, you will have proof of being diligent in spite of the loss. Otherwise, your career could be damaged, or at least your effectiveness will be diminished. For example, if the loss occurred because management failed to give you an adequate budget and support for security you knew you required, you need to have documented that failure before the incident occurred. Don't brag about how great your security is, because it can always be beaten. Keep and expand checklists for everything: threats, vulnerabilities, assets, key potential victims, suspects of wrongdoing, security supporters and nonsupporters, attacks, enemies, criminal justice resources, auditors, regulators, and legal counsel. To assist your stakeholders, who are the front-line defenders of their information and systems, identify what they must protect and know the real extent of their security. Make sure that upper management and other people to whom you report understand the nature of your job and its limitations.

Use the best possible security practices yourself to set a good example. You will have a huge collection of sensitive passwords to do your job. Write them down, and keep the list safely in your wallet next to your credit card. Know as much as possible about the systems and networks in your organization and have access to experts who know the rest. Make good friends of local and national criminal justice officials, your organization's lawyers, insurance risk managers, human resources people, facilities managers, and auditors. Audits are one of the most powerful controls your organization has. Remember that people hate security and must be properly motivated by penalties and rewards to make it work. Seek ways to make security invisible or transparent to stakeholders while keeping it effective. Don't recommend or install controls or practices that stakeholders won't support, because they will beat you every time by making it look like the controls are effective when they are not—a situation worse than no security at all.

One of the most exciting parts of the job is the insight you gain about the inner workings and secrets of your organization, its business, and its culture. As an information security consultant, I was privileged to learn about the culture and secrets of more than 250 of the largest corporations throughout the world. I had the opportunity to interview and advise the most powerful business executives, if only for a few minutes of their valuable time. You should always be ready with a "silver bullet" to use in your short time with top management for the greatest benefit of enterprise security. Carefully learn the limits of management's security appetites. Know the nature of the business, whether it is a government department or a hotly competitive business. I once found myself in a meeting with a board of directors intensely discussing the protection of their greatest trade secret, the manufacturing process of their new disposable diapers.

Finally, we come to the last important bit of advice. Be trustworthy and develop mutual trust among your peers. Your most important objectives are not just risk reduction and increased security. They also include diligence to avoid negligence and endangerment, compliance with all of the laws and standards, and enablement when security becomes a competitive or budget issue. To achieve these objectives, you must develop a trusting exchange of the most sensitive security intelligence among your peers so you'll know where your organization stands relative to other enterprises. But be discreet and careful about it. You need to know the generally accepted and current security solutions. If the information you exchange is exposed, it could ruin your career and others, and could create a disaster for your organization. Your personal and ethical performance must be spotless, and you must protect your reputation at all costs. Pay particular attention to the ethics section of this book. I recommend that you join the Information Systems Security Association, become active in it, and become professionally certified as soon as you are qualified. My favorite certification is the Certified Information Systems Security Professional (CISSP) from the International Information Systems Security Certification Consortium.

Donn B. Parker, CISSP *Retired*
Los Altos, California

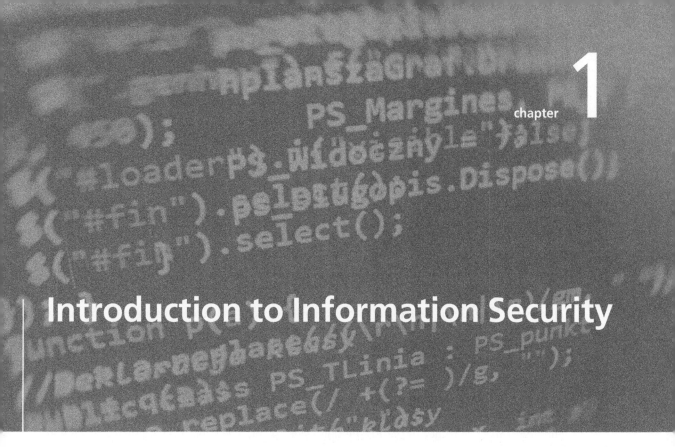

chapter 1

Introduction to Information Security

Do not figure on opponents not attacking; worry about your own lack of preparation.

BOOK OF THE FIVE RINGS

For Amy, the day began like any other at the Sequential Label and Supply Company (SLS) help desk. Taking calls and helping office workers with computer problems was not glamorous, but she enjoyed the work; it was challenging and paid well enough. Some of her friends in the industry worked at bigger companies, some at cutting-edge tech companies, but they all agreed that jobs in information technology were a good way to pay the bills.

The phone rang, as it did about four times an hour. The first call of the day, from a worried user hoping Amy could help him out of a jam, seemed typical. The call display on her monitor showed some of the facts: the user's name, his phone number and department, where his office was on the company campus, and a list of his past calls to the help desk.

"Hi, Bob," she said. "Did you get that document formatting problem squared away?"

"Sure did, Amy. Hope we can figure out what's going on this time."

"We'll try, Bob. Tell me about it."

"Well, my PC is acting weird," Bob said. "When I go to the screen that has my e-mail program running, it doesn't respond to the mouse or the keyboard."

"Did you try a reboot yet?"

"Sure did. But the window wouldn't close, and I had to turn my PC off. After it restarted, I opened the e-mail program, and it's just like it was before—no response at all. The other stuff is working OK, but really, really slowly. Even my Internet browser is sluggish."

"OK, Bob. We've tried the usual stuff we can do over the phone. Let me open a case, and I'll dispatch a tech over as soon as possible."

Amy looked up at the help desk ticket status monitor on the wall at the end of the room. She saw that only two technicians were dispatched to user support at the moment, and since it was the day shift, four technicians were available. "Shouldn't be long at all, Bob."

She hung up and typed her notes into the company's trouble ticket tracking system. She assigned the newly generated case to the user dispatch queue, which would page the roving user support technician with the details in a few minutes.

A moment later, Amy looked up to see Charlie Moody, the senior manager of the server administration team, walking briskly down the hall. He was being trailed by three of his senior technicians as he made a beeline from his office to the room where the company servers were kept in a carefully controlled environment. They all looked worried.

Just then, Amy's screen beeped to alert her of a new e-mail. She glanced down. The screen beeped again—and again. It started beeping constantly. She clicked the envelope icon and, after a short delay, the mail window opened. She had 47 new e-mails in her inbox. She opened one from Davey Martinez in the Accounting Department. The subject line said, "Wait till you see this." The message body read, "Funniest joke you'll see today." Davey often sent her interesting and funny e-mails, and she clicked the file attachment icon to open the latest joke.

After that click, her PC showed the hourglass pointer icon for a second and then the normal pointer reappeared. Nothing happened. She clicked the next e-mail message in the queue. Nothing happened. Her phone rang again. She clicked the icon on her computer desktop to activate the call management software and activated her headset. "Hello, Help Desk, how can I help you?" She couldn't greet the caller by name because her computer had not responded.

"Hello, this is Erin Williams in Receiving."

Amy glanced down at her screen. Still no tracking system. She glanced up to the tally board and was surprised to see the inbound-call counter tallying up waiting calls like digits on a stopwatch. Amy had never seen so many calls come in at one time.

"Hi, Erin," Amy said. "What's up?"

"Nothing," Erin answered. "That's the problem." The rest of the call was a replay of Bob's, except that Amy had to jot notes down on a legal pad. She couldn't dispatch the user support team either. She looked at the ticket status monitor again. It had gone dark. No numbers at all.

Then she saw Charlie running down the hall from the server room. His expression had changed from worried to frantic.

Amy picked up the phone again. She wanted to check with her supervisor about what to do now. There was no dial tone.

LEARNING OBJECTIVES

Upon completion of this material, you should be able to:

- Define information security
- Recount the history of computer security, and explain how it evolved into information security
- Define key terms and critical concepts of information security
- Explain the role of security in the systems development life cycle
- Describe the information security roles of professionals within an organization

Introduction

Martin Fisher, IT Security Manager at Northside Hospital in Atlanta, believes that enterprise information security is a "critical business capability that needs to be aligned with corporate expectations and culture that provides the leadership and insight to identify risks and implement effective controls." He is not alone in his perspective. Many information security practitioners recognize that aligning information security needs with business objectives must be the top priority.

This chapter's opening scenario illustrates that information risks and controls may not be in balance at SLS. Though Amy works in a technical support role to help users with their problems, she did not recall her training about malicious e-mail attachments, such as worms or viruses, and fell victim to this form of attack herself. Understanding how malware might be the cause of a company's problems is an important skill for information technology (IT) support staff as well as users. SLS's management also shows signs of confusion and seems to have no idea how to contain this kind of incident. If you were in Amy's place and were faced with a similar situation, what would you do? How would you react? Would it occur to you that something far more insidious than a technical malfunction was happening at your company? As you explore the chapters of this book and learn more about information security, you will become more capable of answering these questions. But, before you can begin studying details about the discipline of information security, you must first know its history and evolution.

The History of Information Security

> **Key Term**
>
> **computer security** In the early days of computers, this term specified the need to secure the physical location of computer technology from outside threats. This term later came to represent all actions taken to preserve computer systems from losses. It has evolved into the current concept of information security as the scope of protecting information in an organization has expanded.

The history of information security begins with the concept of **computer security**. The need for computer security arose during World War II when the first mainframe computers were developed and used to aid computations for communication code breaking messages from enemy

Earlier versions of the German code machine Enigma were first broken by the Poles in the 1930s. The British and Americans managed to break later, more complex versions during World War II. The increasingly complex versions of the Enigma, especially the submarine or *Unterseeboot* version of the Enigma, caused considerable anguish to Allied forces before finally being cracked. The information gained from decrypted transmissions was used to anticipate the actions of German armed forces. "Some ask why, if we were reading the Enigma, we did not win the war earlier. One might ask, instead, when, if ever, we would have won the war if we hadn't read it."[1]

Figure 1-1 The Enigma

Source: Bletchley Park Trust. Used with permission.[2]

cryptographic devices like the Enigma, shown in Figure 1-1. Multiple levels of security were implemented to protect these devices and the missions they served. This required new processes as well as tried-and-true methods needed to maintain data confidentiality. Access to sensitive military locations, for example, was controlled by means of badges, keys, and the facial recognition of authorized personnel by security guards. The growing need to maintain national security eventually led to more complex and technologically sophisticated computer security safeguards.

During these early years, information security was a straightforward process composed predominantly of physical security and simple document classification schemes. The primary threats to security were physical theft of equipment, espionage against products of the systems, and sabotage. One of the first documented security problems that fell outside these categories occurred in the early 1960s, when a systems administrator was working on a MOTD (message of the day) file while another administrator was editing the password file. A software glitch mixed the two files, and the entire password file was printed on every output file.[3]

⟩ The 1960s

During the Cold War, many more mainframe computers were brought online to accomplish more complex and sophisticated tasks. These mainframes required a less cumbersome process of communication than mailing magnetic tapes between computer centers. In response to this need, the Department of Defense's Advanced Research Projects Agency (ARPA) began examining the feasibility of a redundant, networked communications system to support the military's exchange of information. In 1968, Dr. Larry Roberts developed the ARPANET

ARPANET Program Plan

June 3, 1968

In ARPA, the Program Plan is the master document describing a major program. This plan, which I wrote in 1968, had the following concepts:

1. Objectives – **Develop Networking and Resource Sharing**
2. Technical Need – **Linking Computers**
3. Military Need – **Resource Sharing** - Not Nuclear War
4. Prior Work – **MIT-SDC experiment**
5. Effect on ARPA – **Link 17 Computer Research Centers, Network Research**
6. Plan - **Develop IMP's and start 12/69**
7. Cost – **$3.4 M for 68-71**

ADVANCED RESEARCH PROJECTS AGENCY
Washington, D.C. 20301

Program Plan No. __723__

Date: ___3 June 1968___

RESOURCE SHARING COMPUTER NETWORKS

A. Objective of the Program.

The objective of this program is twofold: (1) To develop techniques and obtain experience on interconnecting computers in such a way that a very broad class of interactions are possible, and (2) To improve and increase computer research productivity through resource sharing. By establishing a network tying IPT's research centers together, both goals are achieved. In fact, the most efficient way to develop the techniques needed for an effective network is by involving the research talent at these centers in prototype activity.

Just as time-shared computer systems have permitted groups of hundreds of individual users to share hardware and software resources with one another, networks connecting dozens of such systems will permit resource sharing between thousands of users. Each system, by virtue of being time-shared, can offer any of its services to another computer system on demand. The most important criterion for the type of network interconnection desired is that any user or program on any of the networked computers can utilize any program or subsystem available on any other computer without having to modify the remote program.

Figure 1-2 Development of the ARPANET

Source: Courtesy of Dr. Lawrence Roberts. Used with permission.[4]

project. Figure 1-2 is an excerpt from his Program Plan. ARPANET evolved into what we now know as the Internet, and Roberts became known as its founder.

 For more information on Dr. Roberts and the history of the Internet, visit his Web site at www .packet.cc.

> The 1970s and 80s

During the next decade, ARPANET became more popular and saw wider use, increasing the potential for its misuse. In 1973, Internet pioneer Robert M. Metcalfe (pictured in Figure 1-3) identified fundamental problems with ARPANET security. As one of the creators of Ethernet, a dominant local area networking protocol, he knew that individual remote sites did not have sufficient controls and safeguards to protect data from unauthorized remote users. Other problems abounded: vulnerability of password structure and formats; lack of safety procedures for dial-up connections; and nonexistent user identification and authorizations. Phone numbers were widely distributed and openly publicized on the walls of phone booths, giving hackers easy access to ARPANET. Because of the range and frequency of computer security violations and the explosion in the numbers of hosts and users on ARPANET, network security was commonly referred to as network insecurity.[5] In 1978, Richard Bisbey and Dennis Hollingworth, two researchers in the Information Sciences Institute at the University of Southern California, published a study entitled "Protection Analysis: Final Report." It focused on a project undertaken by ARPA to understand and detect vulnerabilities in

Figure 1-3 Dr. Metcalfe receiving the National Medal of Technology

Source: U.S. Department of Commerce. Used with permission.

operating system security. For a timeline that includes this and other seminal studies of computer security, see Table 1-1.

Security that went beyond protecting the physical location of computing devices effectively began with a single paper published by the RAND Corporation in February 1970 for the Department of Defense. RAND Report R-609 attempted to define the multiple controls and mechanisms necessary for the protection of a computerized data processing system. The document was classified for almost ten years, and is now considered to be the paper that started the study of computer security.

The security—or lack thereof—of systems sharing resources inside the Department of Defense was brought to the attention of researchers in the spring and summer of 1967. At that time, systems were being acquired at a rapid rate and securing them was a pressing concern both for the military and defense contractors.

In June 1967, ARPA formed a task force to study the process of securing classified information systems. The task force was assembled in October 1967 and met regularly to formulate recommendations, which ultimately became the contents of RAND Report R-609.[6] The document was declassified in 1979 and released as Security Controls for Computer Systems: Report of Defense Science Board Task Force on Computer Security-RAND Report R-609-1. The content of the two documents is identical with the exception of two transmittal memorandums.

 For more information on the RAND Report, visit www.rand.org/pubs/reports/R609-1.html.

Date	Document
1968	Maurice Wilkes discusses password security in *Time-Sharing Computer Systems*.
1970	Willis H. Ware authors the report *Security Controls for Computer Systems: Report of Defense Science Board Task Force on Computer Security-RAND Report R-609*, which was not declassified until 1979. It became known as the seminal work identifying the need for computer security.
1973	Schell, Downey, and Popek examine the need for additional security in military systems in *Preliminary Notes on the Design of Secure Military Computer Systems*.
1975	The Federal Information Processing Standards (FIPS) examines DES (Digital Encryption Standard) in the *Federal Register*.
1978	Bisbey and Hollingworth publish their study "Protection Analysis: Final Report," which discussed the Protection Analysis project created by ARPA to better understand the vulnerabilities of operating system security and examine the possibility of automated vulnerability detection techniques in existing system software.[7]
1979	Morris and Thompson author "Password Security: A Case History," published in the *Communications of the Association for Computing Machinery* (ACM). The paper examined the design history of a password security scheme on a remotely accessed, time-sharing system.
1979	Dennis Ritchie publishes "On the Security of UNIX" and "Protection of Data File Contents," which discussed secure user IDs, secure group IDs, and the problems inherent in the systems.
1982	The U.S. Department of Defense Computer Security Evaluation Center publishes the first version of the Trusted Computer Security (TCSEC) documents, which came to be known as the Rainbow Series.
1984	Grampp and Morris write "The UNIX System: UNIX Operating System Security." In this report, the authors examined four "important handles to computer security": physical control of premises and computer facilities, management commitment to security objectives, education of employees, and administrative procedures aimed at increased security.[8]
1984	Reeds and Weinberger publish "File Security and the UNIX System Crypt Command." Their premise was: "No technique can be secure against wiretapping or its equivalent on the computer. Therefore no technique can be secure against the system administrator or other privileged users...the naive user has no chance."[9]
1992	Researchers for the Internet Engineering Task Force, working at the Naval Research Laboratory, develop the Simple Internet Protocol Plus (SIPP) Security protocols, creating what is now known as IPSEC security.

Table 1-1 Key Dates in Information Security

RAND Report R-609 was the first widely recognized published document to identify the role of management and policy issues in computer security. It noted that the wide use of networking components in military information systems introduced security risks that could not be mitigated by the routine practices then used to secure these systems. Figure 1-4 shows an illustration of computer network vulnerabilities from the 1979 release of this document. This paper signaled a pivotal moment in computer security history—the scope of computer security expanded significantly from the safety of physical locations and hardware to include:

- Securing the data
- Limiting random and unauthorized access to that data
- Involving personnel from multiple levels of the organization in information security

Computer Network Vulnerabilities

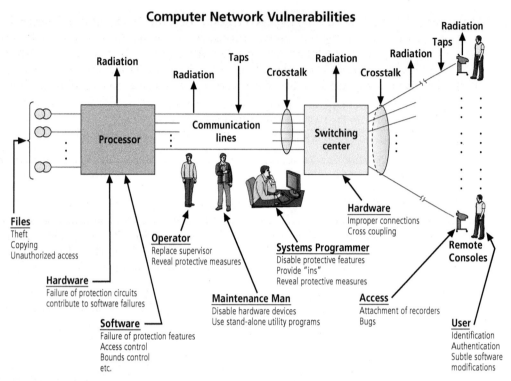

Figure 1-4 Illustration of computer network vulnerabilities from RAND Report R-609

Source: RAND Report R-609-1. Used with permission.[10]

MULTICS Much of the early research on computer security centered on a system called Multiplexed Information and Computing Service (MULTICS). Although it is now obsolete, MULTICS is noteworthy because it was the first operating system to integrate security into its core functions. It was a mainframe, time-sharing operating system developed in the mid-1960s by a consortium of General Electric (GE), Bell Labs, and the Massachusetts Institute of Technology (MIT).

 For more information on the MULTICS project, visit web.mit.edu/multics-history.

In 1969, not long after the restructuring of the MULTICS project, several of its developers (Ken Thompson, Dennis Ritchie, Rudd Canaday, and Doug McIlroy) created a new operating system called UNIX. While the MULTICS system implemented multiple security levels and passwords, the UNIX system did not. Its primary function, text processing, did not require the same level of security as that of its predecessor. Not until the early 1970s did even the simplest component of security, the password function, become a component of UNIX.

In the late 1970s, the microprocessor brought the personal computer (PC) and a new age of computing. The PC became the workhorse of modern computing, moving it out of the data center. This decentralization of data processing systems in the 1980s gave rise to networking—the interconnecting of PCs and mainframe computers, which enabled the entire computing community to make all its resources work together.

In the early 1980s, TCP (the Transmission Control Protocol) and IP (the Internet Protocol) were developed and became the primary protocols for the ARPANET, eventually becoming the protocols we use on the Internet to this day. Also during this time frame, DNS, the hierarchical Domain Name System, was developed. The first dial-up Internet service provider (ISP)—The World, operated by Standard Tool & Die—came online, allowing home users to access the Internet. Prior to that, vendors like CompuServe, GEnie, Prodigy, and Delphi had provided dial-up access for online computer services, while independent Bulletin Board Systems (BBSs) became popular for sharing information among their subscribers.

 For more information on the history of the Internet, visit www.livescience.com/20727-internet-history.html.

In the mid-1980s, the U.S. Government passed several key pieces of legislation that formalized the recognition of computer security as a critical issue for federal information systems. The Computer Fraud and Abuse Act of 1986 and the Computer Security Act of 1987 defined computer security and specified responsibilities and associated penalties. These laws and others are covered in Chapter 3, "Legal, Ethical, and Professional Issues in Information Security."

In 1988, the Defense Advanced Research Projects Agency (DARPA) within the Department of Defense created the Computer Emergency Response Team (CERT) to address network security.

❯ The 1990s

At the close of the 20th century, networks of computers became more common, as did the need to connect them to each other. This gave rise to the Internet, the first global network of networks. The Internet was made available to the general public in the 1990s after decades of being the domain of government, academia, and dedicated industry professionals. The Internet brought connectivity to virtually all computers that could reach a phone line or an Internet-connected local area network (LAN). After the Internet was commercialized, the technology became pervasive, reaching almost every corner of the globe with an expanding array of uses.

Since its inception as ARPANET, a tool for sharing Defense Department information, the Internet has become an interconnection of millions of networks. At first, these connections were based on de facto standards because industry standards for interconnected networks did not exist. These de facto standards did little to ensure the security of information, though some degree of security was introduced as precursor technologies were widely adopted and became industry standards. However, early Internet deployment treated security as a low priority. In fact, many problems that plague e-mail on the Internet today result from this early lack of security. At that time, when all Internet and e-mail users were presumably trustworthy computer scientists, mail server authentication and e-mail encryption did not seem necessary. Early computing approaches relied on security that was built into the physical environment of the data center that housed the computers. As networked computers became the dominant style of computing, the ability to physically secure a networked computer was lost, and the stored information became more exposed to security threats.

In 1993, the first DEFCON conference was held in Las Vegas. Originally it was established as a gathering for people interested in information security, including authors, lawyers, government employees, and law enforcement officials. A compelling topic was the involvement of hackers in creating an interesting venue for the exchange of information between two adversarial groups—the "white hats" of law enforcement and security professionals and the "black hats" of hackers and computer criminals.

In the late 1990s and into the 2000s, many large corporations began publicly integrating security into their organizations. Antivirus products became extremely popular, and information security began to emerge as an independent discipline.

❯ 2000 to Present

Today, the Internet brings millions of unsecured computer networks and billions of computer systems into continuous communication with each other. The security of each computer's stored information is contingent on the security level of every other computer to which it is connected. Recent years have seen a growing awareness of the need to improve information security, as well as a realization that information security is important to national defense. The growing threat of cyberattacks has made governments and companies more aware of the need to defend the computerized control systems of utilities and other critical infrastructure. Another growing concern is the threat of nation-states engaging in information warfare, and the possibility that business and personal information systems could become casualties if they are undefended. Since 2000, Sarbanes-Oxley and other laws related to privacy and corporate responsibility have affected computer security.

The attack on the World Trade Centers on September 11, 2001 resulted in major legislation changes related to computer security, specifically to facilitate law enforcement's ability to collect information about terrorism. The USA PATRIOT Act of 2001 and its follow-up laws, the USA PATRIOT Improvement and Reauthorization Act of 2005, the PATRIOT Sunsets Act of 2011, and the USA FREEDOM Act, are discussed in Chapter 3.

 For more information on the history of computer security, visit the NIST Computer Security site at http: //csrc.nist.gov/publications/history/. NIST is the National Institute of Standards and Technology.

What Is Security?

Key Terms

C.I.A. triad The industry standard for computer security since the development of the mainframe. The standard is based on three characteristics that describe the utility of information: confidentiality, integrity, and availability.

communications security The protection of all communications media, technology, and content.

information security Protection of the confidentiality, integrity, and availability of information assets, whether in storage, processing, or transmission, via the application of policy, education, training and awareness, and technology.

network security A subset of **communications security**; the protection of voice and data networking components, connections, and content.

security A state of being secure and free from danger or harm. Also, the actions taken to make someone or something secure.

Security is protection. Protection from adversaries—those who would do harm, intentionally or otherwise—is the ultimate objective of security. National security, for example, is a multilayered system that protects the sovereignty of a state, its assets, its resources, and its people. Achieving the appropriate level of security for an organization also requires a multifaceted system. A successful organization should have multiple layers of security in place to protect its operations, physical infrastructure, people, functions, communications, and information.

1

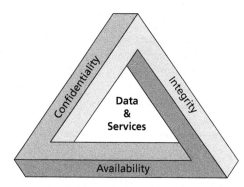

Figure 1-5 Components of information security

Figure 1-6 The C.I.A. triad

The Committee on National Security Systems (CNSS) defines **information security** as the protection of information and its critical elements, including the systems and hardware that use, store, and transmit the information.[11] Figure 1-5 shows that information security includes the broad areas of information security management, data security, and **network security**. The CNSS model of information security evolved from a concept developed by the computer security industry called the C.I.A. triad. The **C.I.A. triad** (see Figure 1-6) has been the standard for computer security in both industry and government since the development of the mainframe. This standard is based on the three characteristics of information that give it value to organizations: confidentiality, integrity, and availability. The security of these three characteristics is as important today as it has always been, but the C.I.A. triad model is generally viewed as no longer adequate in addressing the constantly changing environment. The threats to the confidentiality, integrity, and availability of information have evolved into a vast collection of events, including accidental or intentional damage, destruction, theft, unintended or unauthorized modification, or other misuse from human or nonhuman threats. This vast array of constantly evolving threats has prompted the development of a more robust model that addresses the complexities of the current information security environment. The expanded model consists of a list of critical characteristics of information, which are described in the next section. C.I.A. triad terminology is used in this chapter because of the breadth of material that is based on it.

 For more information on CNSS, visit www.cnss.gov and click the About link, then select "History of CNSS."

› Key Information Security Concepts

This book uses many terms and concepts that are essential to any discussion of information security. Some of these terms are illustrated in Figure 1-7; all are covered in greater detail in subsequent chapters.

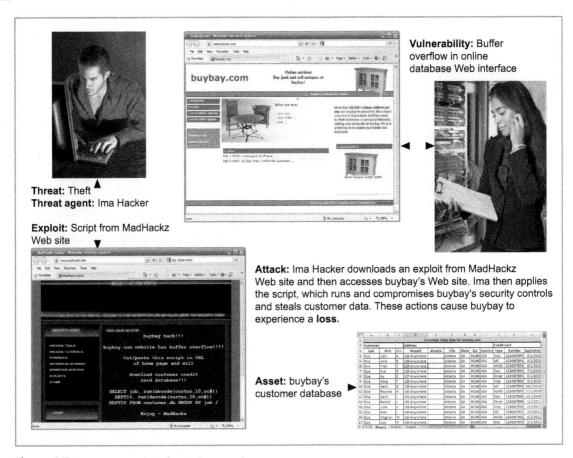

Figure 1-7 Key concepts in information security

Sources (top left to bottom right): © iStockphoto/tadija, Internet Explorer, © iStockphoto/darrenwise, Internet Explorer, Microsoft Excel.

- **Access:** A subject or object's ability to use, manipulate, modify, or affect another subject or object. Authorized users have legal access to a system, whereas hackers must gain illegal access to a system. Access controls regulate this ability.

- **Asset:** The organizational resource that is being protected. An asset can be logical, such as a Web site, software information, or data; or an asset can be physical, such as a person, computer system, hardware, or other tangible object. Assets, particularly information assets, are the focus of what security efforts are attempting to protect.

- **Attack:** An intentional or unintentional act that can damage or otherwise compromise information and the systems that support it. Attacks can be active or passive, intentional or unintentional, and direct or indirect. Someone who casually reads sensitive information not intended for his or her use is committing a passive attack. A hacker attempting to break into an information system is an intentional attack. A lightning strike that causes a building fire is an unintentional attack. A direct attack is perpetrated by a hacker using a PC to break into a system. An indirect attack is a hacker compromising a system and using it to attack other systems—for example, as part of a botnet (slang for *robot network*). This group of compromised computers, running software of the attacker's choosing, can operate autonomously or under the attacker's direct control to attack systems and steal user information or conduct distributed denial-of-service attacks. Direct attacks originate from the threat itself. Indirect attacks originate from a compromised system or resource that is malfunctioning or working under the control of a threat.

- **Control, safeguard,** or **countermeasure:** Security mechanisms, policies, or procedures that can successfully counter attacks, reduce risk, resolve vulnerabilities, and otherwise improve security within an organization. The various levels and types of controls are discussed more fully in the following chapters.

- **Exploit:** A technique used to compromise a system. This term can be a verb or a noun. Threat agents may attempt to exploit a system or other information asset by using it illegally for their personal gain. Or, an exploit can be a documented process to take advantage of a vulnerability or exposure, usually in software, that is either inherent in the software or created by the attacker. Exploits make use of existing software tools or custom-made software components.

- **Exposure:** A condition or state of being exposed; in information security, exposure exists when a vulnerability is known to an attacker.

- **Loss:** A single instance of an information asset suffering damage or destruction, unintended or unauthorized modification or disclosure, or denial of use. When an organization's information is stolen, it has suffered a loss.

- **Protection profile** or **security posture:** The entire set of controls and safeguards, including policy, education, training and awareness, and technology, that the organization implements to protect the asset. The terms are sometimes used interchangeably with the term *security program*, although a security program often comprises managerial aspects of security, including planning, personnel, and subordinate programs.

- **Risk:** The probability of an unwanted occurrence, such as an adverse event or loss. Organizations must minimize risk to match their risk appetite—the quantity and nature of risk they are willing to accept.

- **Subjects** and **objects of attack:** A computer can be either the subject of an attack—an agent entity used to conduct the attack—or the object of an attack: the target entity, as shown in Figure 1-8. A computer can also be both the subject and object of an attack. For example, it can be compromised by an attack (object) and then used to attack other systems (subject).

- **Threat:** Any event or circumstance that has the potential to adversely affect operations and assets. The term *threat source* is commonly used interchangeably with the more generic term *threat*. While the two terms are technically distinct, in order to simplify discussion, the text will continue to use the term *threat* to describe threat sources.

- **Threat agent:** The specific instance or a component of a threat. For example, the threat source of "trespass or espionage" is a category of potential danger to information assets, while "external professional hacker" (like Kevin Mitnick, who was convicted of hacking into phone systems) is a specific threat agent. A lightning strike, hailstorm, or tornado is a threat agent that is part of the threat source known as "acts of God/acts of nature."

- **Threat event:** An occurrence of an event caused by a threat agent. An example of a threat event might be damage caused by a storm. This term is commonly used interchangeably with the term *attack*.

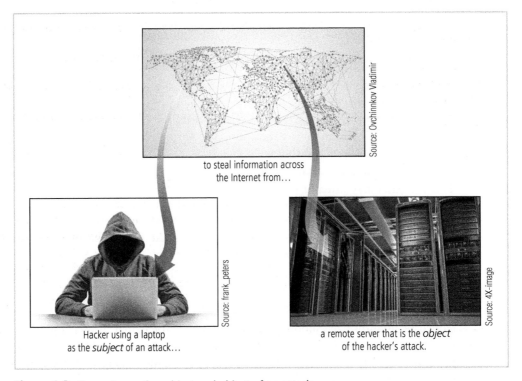

Source: Ovchinnkov Vladimir

to steal information across
the Internet from...

Source: frank_peters

Hacker using a laptop
as the *subject* of an attack...

Source: 4X-image

a remote server that is the *object*
of the hacker's attack.

Figure 1-8 Computer as the subject and object of an attack

- **Threat source:** A category of objects, people, or other entities that represents the origin of danger to an asset—in other words, a category of threat agents. Threat sources are always present and can be purposeful or undirected. For example, threat agent "hackers," as part of the threat source "acts of trespass or espionage," purposely threaten unprotected information systems, while threat agent "severe storms," as part of the threat source "acts of God/acts of nature," incidentally threaten buildings and their contents.

- **Vulnerability:** A potential weakness in an asset or its defensive control system(s). Some examples of vulnerabilities are a flaw in a software package, an unprotected system port, and an unlocked door. Some well-known vulnerabilities have been examined, documented, and published; others remain latent (or undiscovered).

❯ Critical Characteristics of Information

Key Terms

accuracy An attribute of information that describes how data is free of errors and has the value that the user expects.

authenticity An attribute of information that describes how data is genuine or original rather than reproduced or fabricated.

availability An attribute of information that describes how data is accessible and correctly formatted for use without interference or obstruction.

> **confidentiality** An attribute of information that describes how data is protected from disclosure or exposure to unauthorized individuals or systems.
>
> **integrity** An attribute of information that describes how data is whole, complete, and uncorrupted.
>
> **personally identifiable information (PII)** A set of information that could uniquely identify an individual.
>
> **possession** An attribute of information that describes how the data's ownership or control is legitimate or authorized.
>
> **utility** An attribute of information that describes how data has value or usefulness for an end purpose.

The value of information comes from the characteristics it possesses. When a characteristic of information changes, the value of that information either increases or, more commonly, decreases. Some characteristics affect information's value to users more than others, depending on circumstances. For example, timeliness of information can be a critical factor because information loses much or all of its value when delivered too late. Though information security professionals and end users share an understanding of the characteristics of information, tensions can arise when the need to secure information from threats conflicts with the end users' need for unhindered access to it. For instance, end users may perceive a .1-second delay in the computation of data to be an unnecessary annoyance. Information security professionals, however, may perceive .1 seconds as a minor delay that enables an important task, like data encryption. Each critical characteristic of information—that is, the expanded C.I.A. triad—is defined in the following sections.

Availability Availability enables authorized users—people or computer systems—to access information without interference or obstruction and to receive it in the required format. Consider, for example, research libraries that require identification before entrance. Librarians protect the contents of the library so that they are available only to authorized patrons. The librarian must accept a patron's identification before the patron has free access to the book stacks. Once authorized patrons have access to the stacks, they expect to find the information they need in a usable format and familiar language. In this case, the information is bound in a book that is written in English.

Accuracy Information has **accuracy** when it is free from mistakes or errors and has the value that the end user expects. If information has been intentionally or unintentionally modified, it is no longer accurate. Consider a checking account, for example. You assume that the information in your account is an accurate representation of your finances. Incorrect information in the account can result from external or internal errors. If a bank teller, for instance, mistakenly adds or subtracts too much money from your account, the value of the information is changed. Or, you may accidentally enter an incorrect amount into your account register. Either way, an inaccurate bank balance could cause you to make other mistakes, such as bouncing a check.

Authenticity Authenticity of information is the quality or state of being genuine or original, rather than a reproduction or fabrication. Information is authentic when it is in the same state in which it was created, placed, stored, or transferred. Consider for a moment some common assumptions about e-mail. When you receive e-mail, you assume that a specific individual or group created and transmitted the e-mail—you assume you know its origin. This is not always the case. E-mail spoofing, the act of sending an e-mail message with a modified field, is a problem for many people today because the modified field often is the address of the originator. Spoofing the sender's address can fool e-mail recipients into thinking that the messages are legitimate traffic, thus inducing them to open e-mail they otherwise might not have.

Confidentiality Information has **confidentiality** when it is protected from disclosure or exposure to unauthorized individuals or systems. Confidentiality ensures that *only* users with the rights, privileges, and need to access information are able to do so. When unauthorized individuals or systems view information, its confidentiality is breached. To protect the confidentiality of information, you can use several measures, including the following:

- Information classification
- Secure document storage
- Application of general security policies
- Education of information custodians and end users

Confidentiality, like most characteristics of information, is interdependent with other characteristics and is closely related to the characteristic known as privacy. The relationship between these two characteristics is covered in more detail in Chapter 3, "Legal, Ethical, and Professional Issues in Information Security."

The value of confidentiality is especially high for personal information about employees, customers, or patients. People who transact with an organization expect that their personal information will remain confidential, whether the organization is a federal agency, such as the Internal Revenue Service, a healthcare facility, or a business. Problems arise when companies disclose confidential information. Sometimes this disclosure is intentional, but disclosure of confidential information also happens by mistake—for example, when confidential information is mistakenly e-mailed to someone *outside* the organization rather than to someone *inside* it.

Other examples of confidentiality breaches include an employee throwing away a document containing critical information without shredding it, or a hacker who successfully breaks into an internal database of a Web-based organization and steals sensitive information about their clients, such as names, addresses, and credit card numbers.

As a consumer, you give up pieces of personal information in exchange for convenience or value almost daily. By using a "members" card at a grocery store, you disclose some of your spending habits. When you fill out an online survey, you exchange pieces of your personal history for access to online privileges. When you sign up for a free magazine, Web resource, or free software application, you provide **personally identifiable information (PII)**. The bits and pieces of personal information you disclose may be copied, sold, replicated, distributed, and eventually coalesced into profiles and even complete dossiers of you and your life.

Integrity Information has **integrity** when it is whole, complete, and uncorrupted. The integrity of information is threatened when it is exposed to corruption, damage, destruction, or other disruption of its authentic state. Corruption can occur while information is being stored or transmitted. Many computer viruses and worms are designed with the explicit purpose of corrupting data. For this reason, a key method for detecting a virus or worm is to look for changes in file integrity, as shown by the file size. Another key method of assuring information integrity is file hashing, in which a file is read by a special algorithm that uses the bit values in the file to compute a single large number called a hash value. The hash value for any combination of bits is unique.

OFFLINE

Unintentional Disclosures

The number of unintentional information releases due to malicious attacks is substantial. Millions of people lose information to hackers and malware-focused attacks annually. However, organizations occasionally lose, misplace, or inadvertently release information in an event not caused by hackers or other electronic attacks.

The Georgia Secretary of State gave out more than 6 million voters' private information, including Social Security numbers, in a breach that occurred in late 2015. The breach was found to have been caused by an employee who failed to follow established policies and procedures, and resulted in the employee being fired. While the agency claimed it recovered all copies of the data that were sent to 12 separate organizations, it was still considered a data breach.

In January 2008, GE Money, a division of General Electric, revealed that a data backup tape with credit card data from approximately 650,000 customers and over 150,000 Social Security numbers went missing from a records management company's storage facility. Approximately 230 retailers were affected when Iron Mountain, Inc., announced it couldn't find a magnetic tape.[12]

In February 2005, the data aggregation and brokerage firm ChoicePoint revealed that it had been duped into releasing personal information about 145,000 people to identity thieves during 2004. The perpetrators used stolen identities to create ostensibly legitimate business entities, which then subscribed to ChoicePoint to acquire the data fraudulently. The company reported that the criminals opened many accounts and recorded personal information, including names, addresses, and identification numbers. They did so without using any network or computer-based attacks; it was simple fraud. The fraud was feared to have allowed the perpetrators to arrange hundreds of identity thefts.

The giant pharmaceutical organization Eli Lilly and Co. released the e-mail addresses of 600 patients to one another in 2001. The American Civil Liberties Union (ACLU) denounced this breach of privacy, and information technology industry analysts noted that it was likely to influence the public debate on privacy legislation. The company claimed the mishap was caused by a programming error that occurred when patients who used a specific drug produced by Lilly signed up for an e-mail service to access company support materials.

If a computer system performs the same hashing algorithm on a file and obtains a different number than the file's recorded hash value, the file has been compromised and the integrity of the information is lost. Information integrity is the cornerstone of information systems because information is of no value or use if users cannot verify its integrity. File hashing and hash values are examined in detail in Chapter 8, "Cryptography."

 For more details on information losses caused by attacks, visit Wikipedia.org and search on the terms "Data breach" and "Timeline of Computer Security Hacker History."

File corruption is not necessarily the result of external forces, such as hackers. Noise in the transmission media, for instance, can also cause data to lose its integrity. Transmitting data on a circuit with a low voltage level can alter and corrupt the data. Redundancy bits and check bits can compensate for internal and external threats to the integrity of information. During each transmission, algorithms, hash values, and error-correcting codes ensure the integrity of the information. Data whose integrity has been compromised is retransmitted.

Utility The **utility** of information is the quality or state of having value for some purpose or end. In other words, information has value when it can serve a purpose. If information is available but is not in a meaningful format to the end user, it is not useful. For example, U.S. Census data can quickly become overwhelming and difficult for a private citizen to interpret; however, for a politician, the same data reveals information about residents in a district, such as their race, gender, and age. This information can help form a politician's next campaign strategy.

Possession The **possession** of information is the quality or state of ownership or control. Information is said to be in one's possession if one obtains it, independent of format or other characteristics. While a breach of confidentiality always results in a breach of possession, a breach of possession does not always lead to a breach of confidentiality. For example, assume a company stores its critical customer data using an encrypted file system. An employee who has quit decides to take a copy of the tape backups and sell the customer records to the competition. The removal of the tapes from their secure environment is a breach of possession. But, because the data is encrypted, neither the former employee nor anyone else can read it without the proper decryption methods; therefore, there is no breach of confidentiality. Today, people who are caught selling company secrets face increasingly stiff fines and a strong likelihood of jail time. Also, companies are growing more reluctant to hire people who have demonstrated dishonesty in their past. Another example might be that of a ransomware attack in which a hacker encrypts important information and offers to provide the decryption key for a fee. The attack would result in a breach of possession because the owner would no longer have possession of the information.

CNSS Security Model

Key Term

McCumber Cube A graphical representation of the architectural approach widely used in computer and information security; commonly shown as a cube composed of 3×3×3 cells, similar to a Rubik's Cube.

The definition of information security in this text is based in part on the CNSS document called the National Training Standard for Information Systems Security Professionals, NSTISSI No. 4011 (1994). The hosting organization is the Committee on National Security Systems, which is responsible for coordinating the evaluation and publication of standards related to the protection of National Security Systems (NSS). CNSS was originally called the National Security Telecommunications and Information Systems Security Committee (NSTISSC) when established in 1990 by National Security Directive (NSD) 42, *National Policy for the Security of National Security Telecommunications and Information Systems*. The outdated CNSS standards are expected to be replaced by the newer NIST SP 800-16 Rev. 1 (2014), "A Role-Based Model for Federal Information Technology/Cyber Security Training," in the near future.

 For more information on CNSS and its standards, see www.cnss.gov/CNSS/issuances/Instructions .cfm.

The model, which was created by John McCumber in 1991, provides a graphical representation of the architectural approach widely used in computer and information security; it is now known as the **McCumber Cube**.[13] As shown in Figure 1-9, the McCumber Cube shows three dimensions. When extrapolated, the three dimensions of each axis become a $3 \times 3 \times 3$ cube with 27 cells representing areas that must be addressed to secure today's information systems. To ensure comprehensive system security, each of the 27 areas must be properly addressed during the security process. For example, the intersection of technology, integrity, and storage requires a set of controls or safeguards that address the need to use *technology* to protect the *integrity* of information while in *storage*. One such control might be a system for detecting host intrusion that protects the integrity of information by alerting security administrators to the potential modification of a critical file. A common omission from such a model is the need for guidelines and policies that provide direction for the practices and implementations of technologies. The need for policy is discussed in subsequent chapters of this book.

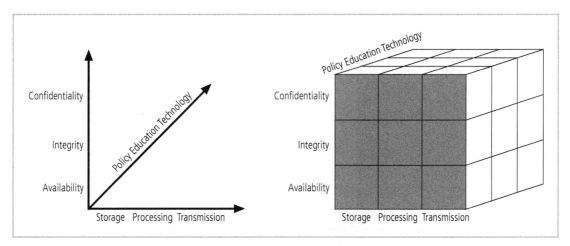

Figure 1-9 The McCumber Cube[14]

Components of an Information System

As shown in Figure 1-10, an **information system (IS)** is much more than computer hardware; it is the entire set of people, procedures, and technology that enable business to use information. The six critical components of hardware, software, networks, people, procedures, and data enable information to be input, processed, output, and stored. Each of these IS components has its own strengths and weaknesses, as well as its own characteristics and uses. Each component of the IS also has its own security requirements.

❯ Software

The software component of an IS includes applications (programs), operating systems, and assorted command utilities. Software is perhaps the most difficult IS component to secure. The exploitation of errors in software programming accounts for a substantial portion of the attacks on information. The information technology (IT) industry is rife with reports warning of holes, bugs, weaknesses, or other fundamental problems in software. In fact, many facets of daily life are affected by buggy software, from smartphones that crash to flawed automotive control computers that lead to recalls.

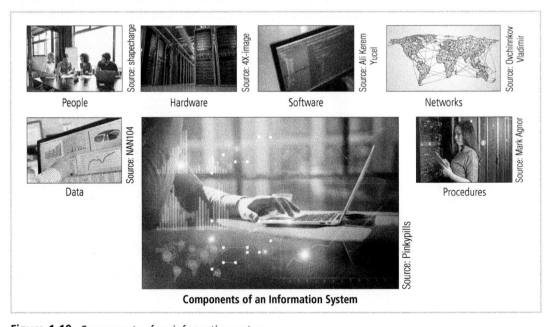

People — Source: shapecharge
Hardware — Source: 4X-image
Software — Source: Ali Kerem Yucel
Networks — Source: Ovchinnkov Vladimir
Data — Source: NAN104
Procedures — Source: Mark Agnor
Source: Pinkypills

Components of an Information System

Figure 1-10 Components of an information system

Software carries the lifeblood of information through an organization. Unfortunately, software programs are often created under the constraints of project management, which limit time, costs, and manpower. Information security is all too often implemented as an afterthought rather than developed as an integral component from the beginning. In this way, software programs become an easy target of accidental or intentional attacks.

❭ Hardware

Hardware is the physical technology that houses and executes the software, stores and transports the data, and provides interfaces for the entry and removal of information from the system. **Physical security** policies deal with hardware as a physical asset and with the protection of physical assets from harm or theft. Applying the traditional tools of physical security, such as locks and keys, restricts access to and interaction with the hardware components of an information system. Securing the physical location of computers and the computers themselves is important because a breach of physical security can result in a loss of information. Unfortunately, most information systems are built on hardware platforms that cannot guarantee any level of information security if unrestricted hardware access is possible.

Before September 11, 2001, laptop thefts in airports were common. A two-person team worked to steal a computer as its owner passed it through the conveyor scanning devices. The first perpetrator entered the security area ahead of an unsuspecting target and quickly went through. Then, the second perpetrator waited behind until the target placed the computer on the baggage scanner. As the computer was whisked through, the second perpetrator slipped ahead of the victim and entered the metal detector with a substantial collection of keys, coins, and the like, slowing the detection process and allowing the first perpetrator to grab the computer and disappear in a crowded walkway.

While the security response to September 11 did tighten the security process at airports, hardware can still be stolen in airports and other public places. Although laptops and notebook computers might be worth a few thousand dollars, the information stored on them can be worth a great deal more to disreputable organizations and individuals. Consider that unless plans and procedures are in place to quickly revoke privileges on stolen devices like laptops, tablets, and smartphones, the privileged access that these devices have to cloud-based data stores could be used to steal information that is many times more valuable than the device itself.

❭ Data

Data stored, processed, and transmitted by a computer system must be protected. Data is often the most valuable asset of an organization and therefore is the main target of intentional attacks. Systems developed in recent years are likely to make use of database management systems. When used properly, they should improve the security of the data and the applications that rely on the data. Unfortunately, many system development projects do not make full use of the database management system's security capabilities, and in some cases the database is implemented in ways that make them less secure than traditional file systems. Because data and information exist in physical form in many organizations as paper reports, handwritten notes, and computer printouts, the protection of physical information is as important as the protection of electronic, computer-based information. As an aside, the terms *data* and *information* are used interchangeably today. Information was originally defined as *data with meaning,* such as a report or statistical analysis. For our purposes, we will use the term *information* to represent both unprocessed data and actual information.

❯ People

Though often overlooked in computer security considerations, people have always been a threat to information security. Legend has it that around 200 B.C., a great army threatened the security and stability of the Chinese empire. So ferocious were the Hun invaders that the Chinese emperor commanded the construction of a great wall that would defend against them. Around 1275 A.D., Kublai Khan finally achieved what the Huns had been trying for more than a thousand years. Initially, the Khan's army tried to climb over, dig under, and break through the wall.

In the end, the Khan simply bribed the gatekeeper—and the rest is history. Whether this event actually occurred or not, the moral of the story is that people can be the weakest link in an organization's information security program. Unless policy, education and training, awareness, and technology are properly employed to prevent people from accidentally or intentionally damaging or losing information, they will remain the weakest link. Social engineering can prey on the tendency to cut corners and the commonplace nature of human error. It can be used to manipulate people to obtain access information about a system. This topic is discussed in more detail in Chapter 2, "The Need for Security."

❯ Procedures

Procedures are another frequently overlooked component of an IS. Procedures are written instructions for accomplishing a specific task. When an unauthorized user obtains an organization's procedures, it poses a threat to the integrity of the information. For example, a consultant to a bank learned how to wire funds by using the computer center's procedures, which were readily available. By taking advantage of a security weakness (lack of authentication), the bank consultant ordered millions of dollars to be transferred by wire to his own account. Lax security procedures caused the loss of more than $10 million before the situation was corrected. Most organizations distribute procedures to employees so they can access the information system, but many of these companies often fail to provide proper education for using the procedures safely. Educating employees about safeguarding procedures is as important as physically securing the information system. After all, procedures are information in their own right. Therefore, knowledge of procedures, as with all critical information, should be disseminated among members of an organization on a need-to-know basis.

❯ Networks

Networking is the IS component that created much of the need for increased computer and information security. When information systems are connected to each other to form LANs, and these LANs are connected to other networks such as the Internet, new security challenges rapidly emerge. The physical technology that enables network functions is becoming more accessible to organizations of every size. Applying the traditional tools of physical security, such as locks and keys, to restrict access to the system's hardware components is still important. However, when computer systems are networked, this approach is no longer enough. Steps to provide network security such as installing and configuring firewalls are essential, as is implementing intrusion detection systems to make system owners aware of ongoing compromises.

Balancing Information Security and Access

Even with the best planning and implementation, it is impossible to obtain perfect information security. Information security cannot be absolute: it is a process, not a goal. You can make a system available to anyone, anywhere, anytime, through any means. However, such unrestricted access poses a danger to the security of the information. On the other hand, a completely secure information system would not allow anyone access. For instance, when challenged to achieve a TCSEC C-2 level security certification for its Windows operating system, Microsoft had to remove all networking components and operate the computer only from the console in a secured room.[15]

To achieve balance—that is, to operate an information system that satisfies the user and the security professional—the security level must allow reasonable access, yet protect against threats. Figure 1-11 shows some of the competing voices that must be considered when balancing information security and access.

Because of today's security concerns and issues, an information system or data processing department can get too entrenched in the management and protection of systems. An imbalance can occur when the needs of the end user are undermined by obsessive focus on protecting and administering the information systems. Information security technologists and end users must recognize that both groups share the same overall goals of the organization—to ensure that data is available when, where, and how it is needed, with minimal delays or obstacles. In an ideal world, this level of availability can be met even after addressing concerns about loss, damage, interception, or destruction.

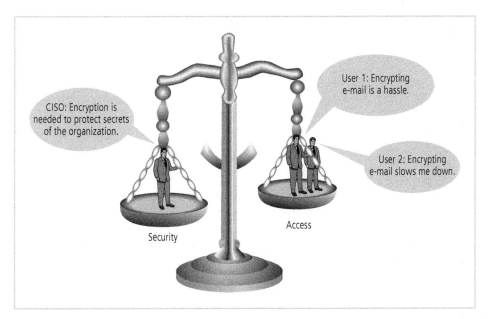

Figure 1-11 Balancing information security and access

Approaches to Information Security Implementation

Key Terms

bottom-up approach A method of establishing security policies and/or practices that begins as a grassroots effort in which systems administrators attempt to improve the security of their systems.

top-down approach A methodology of establishing security policies and/or practices that is initiated by upper management.

The implementation of information security in an organization must begin somewhere, and cannot happen overnight. Securing information assets is an incremental process that requires coordination, time, and patience. Information security can begin as a grassroots effort in which systems administrators attempt to improve the security of their systems. This is often referred to as a **bottom-up approach**. The key advantage of the bottom-up approach is the technical expertise of individual administrators. By working with information systems on a day-to-day basis, these administrators possess in-depth knowledge that can greatly enhance the development of an information security system. They know and understand the threats to their systems and the mechanisms needed to protect them successfully. Unfortunately, the bottom-up approach seldom works because it lacks critical features such as participant support and organizational staying power.

The **top-down approach** has a higher probability of success. With this approach, the project is initiated by upper-level managers who issue policies, procedures, and processes; dictate the goals and expected outcomes; and determine accountability for each required action. This approach has strong upper-management support, a dedicated champion, usually dedicated funding, a clear planning and implementation process, and the means of influencing organizational culture. The most successful kind of top-down approach also involves a formal development strategy known as a systems development life cycle.

For any organization-wide effort to succeed, management must buy into and fully support it. The champion's role in this effort cannot be overstated. Typically, the champion is an executive, such as a chief information officer (CIO) or the vice president of information technology (VP-IT), who moves the project forward, ensures that it is properly managed, and pushes for acceptance throughout the organization. Without this high-level support, many mid-level administrators fail to make time for the project or dismiss it as a low priority. The involvement and support of end users is also critical to the success of this type of project. Users are most directly affected by the process and outcome of the project and must be included in the information security process. Key end users should be assigned to a developmental team known as the joint application development (or design) team (JAD). To succeed, the JAD must have staying power. It must be able to survive employee turnover and should not be vulnerable to changes in the personnel team that is developing the information security system. This means the processes and procedures must be documented and integrated into the organizational culture. They must be adopted *and promoted* by the organization's management.

The organizational hierarchy and its relationship to the bottom-up and top-down approaches are illustrated in Figure 1-12.

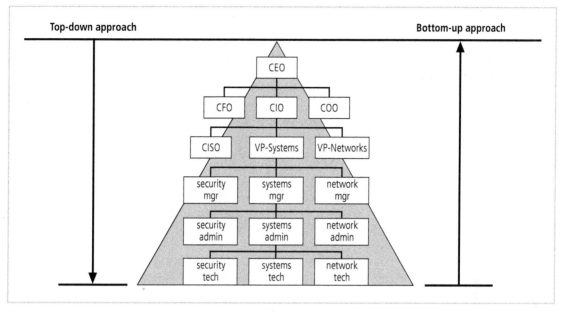

Figure 1-12 Approaches to information security implementation

Security in the Systems Development Life Cycle

> **Key Term**
>
> **systems development life cycle (SDLC)** A methodology for the design and implementation of an information system. The SDLC contains different phases depending on the methodology deployed, but generally the phases address the investigation, analysis, design, implementation, and maintenance of an information system.

Information security should be implemented into every major system in an organization. One approach for implementing information security into an organization's information systems is to ensure that security is a fundamental part of the organization's **systems development life cycle (SDLC)**. To understand how *security* is integrated into the systems development life cycle, you must first understand the foundations of systems development.

Each organization has a unique set of needs when it comes to how they might develop information (and security) systems. The organization's culture will dictate the nature and types of systems development activities that will be used. Many organizations do not develop a significant proprietary system, choosing instead to use off-the-shelf applications or work with other forms that specialize in the development and deployment of information systems. When organizations need to develop systems in-house, they can choose from a variety of approaches that have emerged over time. The traditional approach to software development (discussed in the next section) has given rise to a number of variations, including RAD, JAD, Agile, and one of the newest approaches, DevOps.

An early innovation in systems development was the inclusion of a broader cross-section of the organization in the development process. Whereas in early development projects, systems owners and software developers would collaborate to define specifications and create systems, an approach known as joint application development (JAD) added members of the management team from the supported business unit and in some cases, future users of the systems being created. Another innovation that often occurred with the JAD approach was to increase the speed at which requirements were collected and software was prototyped, thus allowing more iterations in the design process—an approach called rapid application development (RAD). This type of development later evolved into a combined approach known as the spiral method, in which each stage of development was completed in smaller increments, with delivery of working software components occurring more frequently and the software under development coming closer to its intended finished state with each pass through the development process.

Taking the objectives of JAD and RAD even further is the collective approach to systems development known as agile or extreme programming (XP), including aspects of systems development known as Kanban and scrum. As the need to reduce the time taken in the systems development cycle from gathering requirements to testing software continued to evolve, even faster feedback cycles were required to reduce time to market and shorten feature rollout times. When coupled with a need to better integrate the effort of the development team and the operations team to improve the functionality and security of applications, another model known as DevOps has begun to emerge.

DevOps focuses on integrating the need for the development team to provide iterative and rapid improvements to system functionality and the need for the operations team to improve security and minimize the disruption from software release cycles. By collaborating across the entire software/service lifecycle, DevOps uses a continuous development model that relies on systems thinking, short feedback loops, and continuous experimentation and learning.

Each of these approaches has its advantages and disadvantages, and each can be effective under the right circumstances. People who work in software development and some specialty areas of information security that support the software assurance process must be conversant with each of these methodologies.

An emerging development has been called SecOps by some. This is a process of using the DevOps methodologies of an integrated development and operations approach that is applied to the specification, creation, and implementation of security control systems.

❯ The Systems Development Life Cycle

Key Term

methodology A formal approach to solving a problem based on a structured sequence of procedures.

An SDLC is a **methodology** for the design and implementation of an information system. Using a methodology ensures a rigorous process with a clearly defined goal and increases the probability of success. Once a methodology has been adopted, the key milestones are established and a team is selected and made accountable for accomplishing the project goals.

> Traditional Development Methods

> **Key Term**
>
> **waterfall model** A type of SDLC in which each phase of the process "flows from" the information gained in the previous phase, with multiple opportunities to return to previous phases and make adjustments.

The traditional SDLC approach consists of six general phases. If you have taken a system analysis and design course, you may have been exposed to a model consisting of a different number of phases. SDLC models range from three to twelve phases, all of which have been mapped into the six presented here. The **waterfall model** pictured in Figure 1-13 illustrates that each phase begins with the results and information gained from the previous phase.

At the end of each phase of the traditional SDLC comes a structured review or reality check, during which the team determines if the project should be continued, discontinued, outsourced, postponed, or returned to an earlier phase. This determination depends on whether the project is proceeding as expected and whether it needs additional expertise, organizational knowledge, or other resources.

Once the system is implemented, it is maintained and modified over the remainder of its working life. Any information systems implementation may have multiple iterations as the cycle is repeated over time. Only by constant examination and renewal can any system, especially an information security program, perform up to expectations in a constantly changing environment.

The following sections describe each phase of a traditional SDLC.[16]

Investigation The first phase, investigation, is the most important. What problem is the system being developed to solve? The investigation phase begins by examining the

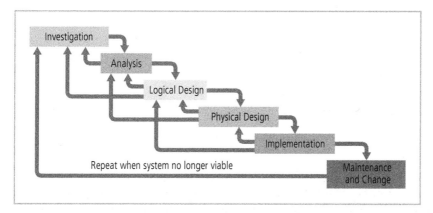

Figure 1-13 SDLC waterfall methodology

event or plan that initiates the process. During this phase, the objectives, constraints, and scope of the project are specified. A preliminary cost-benefit analysis evaluates the perceived benefits and their appropriate levels of cost. At the conclusion of this phase and at every phase afterward, a process will be undertaken to assess economic, technical, and behavioral feasibilities and ensure that implementation is worth the organization's time and effort.

Analysis The analysis phase begins with the information gained during the investigation phase. This phase consists primarily of assessments of the organization, its current systems, and its capability to support the proposed systems. Analysts begin by determining what the new system is expected to do and how it will interact with existing systems. This phase ends with documentation of the findings and an update of the feasibility analysis.

Logical Design In the logical design phase, the information gained from the analysis phase is used to begin creating a systems solution for a business problem. In any systems solution, the first and driving factor must be the business need. Based on the business need, applications are selected to provide needed services, and then the team chooses data support and structures capable of providing the needed inputs. Finally, based on all of this, specific technologies are delineated to implement the physical solution. The logical design, therefore, is the blueprint for the desired solution. The logical design is implementation independent, meaning that it contains no reference to specific technologies, vendors, or products. Instead, it addresses how the proposed system will solve the problem at hand. In this stage, analysts generate estimates of costs and benefits to allow for a general comparison of available options. At the end of this phase, another feasibility analysis is performed.

Physical Design During the physical design phase, specific technologies are selected to support the alternatives identified and evaluated in the logical design. The selected components are evaluated based on a make-or-buy decision—the option to develop components in-house or purchase them from a vendor. Final designs integrate various components and technologies. After yet another feasibility analysis, the entire solution is presented to the organization's management for approval.

Implementation In the implementation phase, any needed software is created. Components are ordered, received, and tested. Afterward, users are trained and supporting documentation created. Once all components are tested individually, they are installed and tested as a system. A feasibility analysis is again prepared, and the sponsors are then presented with the system for a performance review and acceptance test.

Maintenance and Change The maintenance and change phase is the longest and most expensive of the process. This phase consists of the tasks necessary to support and modify the system for the remainder of its useful life cycle. Even though formal development may conclude during this phase, the life cycle of the project continues until the team determines that the process should begin again from the investigation phase. At periodic points, the system is tested for compliance, and the feasibility of continuance versus discontinuance is evaluated. Upgrades, updates, and patches are managed. As the needs of the organization change, the systems that support the organization must also change. The people who manage and support the systems must continually monitor their effectiveness in relation to the organization's environment. When a current system can no longer support the evolving mission of the organization, the project is terminated and a new project is implemented.

 For more information on SDLCs, see Appendix E of NIST Special Publication 800-64, Rev. 2 at http://nvlpubs.nist.gov/nistpubs/Legacy/SP/nistspecialpublication800-64r2.pdf.

〉 Software Assurance

> **Key Term**
>
> **software assurance (SA)** A methodological approach to the development of software that seeks to build security into the development life cycle rather than address it at later stages. SA attempts to intentionally create software free of vulnerabilities and provide effective, efficient software that users can deploy with confidence.

Many of the information security issues facing modern information systems have their root cause in the software elements of the system. Secure systems require secure or at least securable software. The development of systems and the software they use is often accomplished using a methodology, such as the SDLC described earlier. Many organizations recognize the need to include planning for security objectives in the SDLC they use to create systems, and have established procedures to create software that is more capable of being deployed in a secure fashion. This approach to software development is known as **software assurance**, or SA.

Organizations are increasingly working to build security into the SDLC to prevent security problems before they begin. A national effort is underway to create a common body of knowledge focused on secure software development. The U.S. Department of Defense launched a Software Assurance Initiative in 2003. This initial process was led by Joe Jarzombek and was endorsed and supported by the Department of Homeland Security (DHS), which joined the program in 2004. This program initiative resulted in the publication of the Secure Software Assurance (SwA) Common Body of Knowledge (CBK).[17] A working group drawn from industry, government, and academia was formed to examine two key questions:

1. What are the engineering activities or aspects of activities that are relevant to achieving secure software?

2. What knowledge is needed to perform these activities or aspects?

Based on the findings of this working group and a host of existing external documents and standards, the SwA CBK was developed and published to serve as a guideline. While this work has not yet been adopted as a standard or even a policy requirement of government agencies, it serves as a strongly recommended guide to developing more secure applications.

The SwA CBK, which is a work in progress, contains the following sections:

- Nature of Dangers
- Fundamental Concepts and Principles
- Ethics, Law, and Governance
- Secure Software Requirements
- Secure Software Design
- Secure Software Construction
- Secure Software Verification, Validation, and Evaluation
- Secure Software Tools and Methods
- Secure Software Processes
- Secure Software Project Management
- Acquisition of Secure Software
- Secure Software Sustainment[18]

The following sections provide insight into the stages that should be incorporated into the software SDLC.

〉 Software Design Principles

Good software development should result in a finished product that meets all of its design specifications. Information security considerations are a critical component of those specifications, though that has not always been true. Leaders in software development J. H. Saltzer and M. D. Schroeder note that:

> *The protection of information in computer systems [... and] the usefulness of a set of protection mechanisms depends upon the ability of a system to prevent security violations. In practice, producing a system at any level of functionality that actually does prevent all such unauthorized acts has proved to be extremely difficult. Sophisticated users of most systems are aware of at least one way to crash the system, denying other users authorized access to stored information. Penetration exercises involving a large number of different general-purpose systems all have shown that users can construct programs that can obtain unauthorized access to information stored within. Even in systems designed and implemented with security as an important objective, design and implementation flaws provide paths that circumvent the intended access constraints. Design and construction techniques that systematically exclude flaws are the topic of much research activity, but no complete method applicable to the construction of large general-purpose systems exists yet...[19]*

This statement could be about software development in the early part of the 21st century, but it actually dates back to 1975, before information security and software assurance became critical factors for many organizations. In the same article, the authors provide insight into what are now commonplace security principles:

- *Economy of mechanism: Keep the design as simple and small as possible.*
- *Fail-safe defaults: Base access decisions on permission rather than exclusion.*
- *Complete mediation: Every access to every object must be checked for authority.*
- *Open design: The design should not be secret, but rather depend on the possession of keys or passwords.*
- *Separation of privilege: Where feasible, a protection mechanism should require two keys to unlock, rather than one.*
- *Least privilege: Every program and every user of the system should operate using the least set of privileges necessary to complete the job.*
- *Least common mechanism: Minimize mechanisms (or shared variables) common to more than one user and depended on by all users.*
- *Psychological acceptability: It is essential that the human interface be designed for ease of use, so that users routinely and automatically apply the protection mechanisms correctly.*[20]

Many of the common problems associated with programming approaches that don't follow the software assurance methodology are discussed in Chapter 2, "The Need for Security."

 For more information on software assurance and the national effort to develop an SA common body of knowledge and supporting curriculum, visit https://buildsecurityin.us-cert.gov/dhs /dhs-software-assurance-resources.

❯ The NIST Approach to Securing the SDLC

NIST has adopted a simplified SLDC for their approach, based on five phases: initiation, development/acquisition, implementation/assessment, operation/maintenance, and disposal. These loosely map to the SDLC approach described earlier, as shown in Table 1-2.

Each phase of the SDLC should include consideration for the security of the system being assembled as well the information it uses. Whether the system is custom-made and built

Waterfall SDLC Phase	Equivalent NIST SDLC Phase
Investigation	Initiation
Analysis	
Logical Design	Development/Acquisition
Physical Design	
Implementation	Implementation/Assessment
Maintenance and Change	Operation/Maintenance
	Disposal

Table 1-2 Comparison of Waterfall and NIST SDLC Phases

from scratch, purchased and then customized, or commercial off-the-shelf software (COTS), the implementing organization is responsible for ensuring its secure use. This means that each implementation of a system is secure and does not risk compromising the confidentiality, integrity, and availability of the organization's information assets. The following section, adapted from NIST Special Publication 800-64, rev. 2, provides an overview of the security considerations for each phase of the SDLC.

While the following section offers advice from NIST expressed in the context of traditional methods (the waterfall methodology), note that these principles are equally valid when the effort uses RAD, JAD, Agile, XP, and other approaches to systems development. Development projects that make use of nontraditional development methodologies must still build in the requirements dictated by sound security practices. Software development should always include meeting security requirements.

> *To be most effective, information security must be integrated into the SDLC from system inception. Early integration of security in the SDLC enables agencies to maximize return on investment in their security programs, through:*
>
> - *Early identification and mitigation of security vulnerabilities and misconfigurations, resulting in lower cost of security control implementation and vulnerability mitigation;*
>
> - *Awareness of potential engineering challenges caused by mandatory security controls;*
>
> - *Identification of shared security services and reuse of security strategies and tools to reduce development cost and schedule while improving security posture through proven methods and techniques; and*
>
> - *Facilitation of informed executive decision making through comprehensive risk management in a timely manner. […]*

Initiation

> *During this first phase of the development life cycle, security considerations are key to diligent and early integration, thereby ensuring that threats, requirements, and potential constraints in functionality and integration are considered. At this point, security is looked at more in terms of business risks with input from the information security office. For example, an agency may identify a political risk resulting from a prominent Web site being modified or made unavailable during a critical business period, resulting in decreased trust by citizens.*

> *Key security activities for this phase include:*
>
> - *Initial delineation of business requirements in terms of confidentiality, integrity, and availability;*
>
> - *Determination of information categorization and identification of known special handling requirements to transmit, store, or create information such as personally identifiable information; and*
>
> - *Determination of any privacy requirements.*

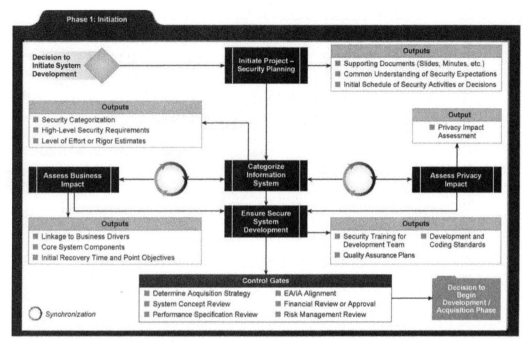

Figure 1-14 Relating security considerations in the Initiation phase

Source: NIST SP 800-64 Rev. 2: Security Considerations in the System Development Life Cycle.

Early planning and awareness will result in cost and time saving through proper risk management planning. Security discussions should be performed as part of (not separately from) the development project to ensure solid understandings among project personnel of business decisions and their risk implications to the overall development project. [...]

These activities and their related outputs are illustrated in Figure 1-14.

Development/Acquisition

This section addresses security considerations unique to the second SDLC phase.

Key security activities for this phase include:

- *Conduct the risk assessment and use the results to supplement the baseline security controls;*

- *Analyze security requirements;*

- *Perform functional and security testing;*

- *Prepare initial documents for system certification and accreditation; and*

- *Design security architecture.*

Although this section presents the information security components in a sequential top-down manner, the order of completion is not necessarily fixed. Security

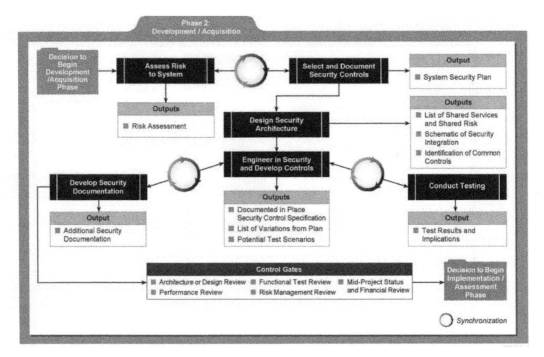

Figure 1-15 Relating security considerations in the Development/Acquisition phase

Source: NIST SP 800-64 Rev. 2: Security Considerations in the System Development Life Cycle.

analysis of complex systems will need to be iterated until consistency and completeness is achieved. [...]

These activities and their related outputs are illustrated in Figure 1-15.

Implementation/Assessment

Implementation/Assessment is the third phase of the SDLC. During this phase, the system will be installed and evaluated in the organization's operational environment.

Key security activities for this phase include:

- *Integrate the information system into its environment;*
- *Plan and conduct system certification activities in synchronization with testing of security controls; and*
- *Complete system accreditation activities. [...]*

Note that the Certification and Authorization (C&A) approach to systems formerly used by the federal government (discussed in later chapters in this text) has evolved into a comprehensive Risk Management Framework (RMF). As such, the performance of a risk assessment on the system under development would replace the C&A process. These activities and their related outputs are illustrated in Figure 1-16.

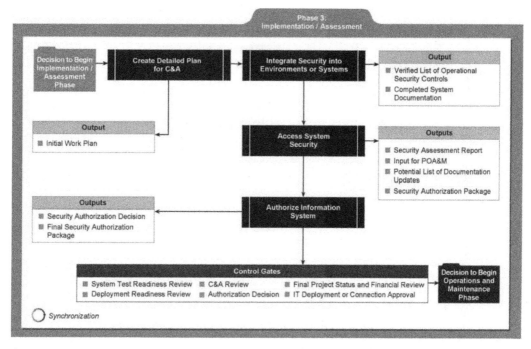

Figure 1-16 Relating security considerations in the Implementation/Assessment phase

Source: NIST SP 800-64 Rev. 2: Security Considerations in the System Development Life Cycle.

Operations and Maintenance

Operations and Maintenance is the fourth phase of the SDLC. In this phase, systems are in place and operating, enhancements and/or modifications to the system are developed and tested, and hardware and/or software is added or replaced. The system is monitored for continued performance in accordance with security requirements and needed system modifications are incorporated. The operational system is periodically assessed to determine how the system can be made more effective, secure, and efficient. Operations continue as long as the system can be effectively adapted to respond to an organization's needs while maintaining an agreed-upon risk level. When necessary modifications or changes are identified, the system may reenter a previous phase of the SDLC.

Key security activities for this phase include:

- *Conduct an operational readiness review;*
- *Manage the configuration of the system;*
- *Institute processes and procedures for assured operations and continuous monitoring of the information system's security controls; and*
- *Perform reauthorization as required. [...]*

These activities and their related outputs are illustrated in Figure 1-17.

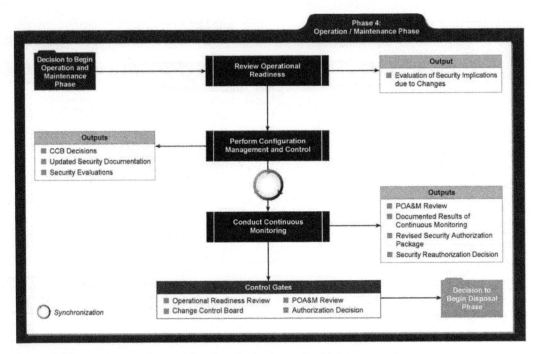

Figure 1-17   Relating security considerations in the Operation/Maintenance phase

Source: NIST SP 800-64 Rev. 2: Security Considerations in the System Development Life Cycle.

Disposal

Disposal, the final phase in the SDLC, provides for disposal of a system and closeout of any contracts in place. Information security issues associated with information and system disposal should be addressed explicitly. When information systems are transferred, become obsolete, or are no longer usable, it is important to ensure that government resources and assets are protected.

Usually, there is no definitive end to a system. Systems normally evolve or transition to the next generation because of changing requirements or improvements in technology. System security plans should continually evolve with the system. Much of the environmental, management, and operational information should still be relevant and useful in developing the security plan for the follow-on system.

The disposal activities ensure the orderly termination of the system and preserve the vital information about the system so that some or all of the information may be reactivated in the future, if necessary. Particular emphasis is given to proper preservation of the data processed by the system so that the data is effectively migrated to another system or archived in accordance with applicable records management regulations and policies for potential future access.

Key security activities for this phase include:

- *Building and executing a disposal/transition plan;*
- *Archival of critical information;*

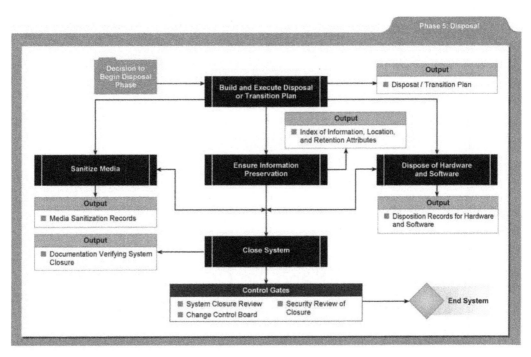

Figure 1-18 Relating security considerations in the Disposal phase

Source: NIST SP 800-64 Rev. 2: Security Considerations in the System Development Life Cycle.

- *Sanitization of media; and*
- *Disposal of hardware and software.*[21]

These activities and their related outputs are illustrated in Figure 1-18.

It is imperative that information security be designed into a system from its inception, rather than being added during or after the implementation phase. Information systems that were designed with no security functionality, or with security functions added as an afterthought, often require constant patching, updating, and maintenance to prevent risk to the systems and information. A well-known adage holds that "an ounce of prevention is worth a pound of cure." With this in mind, organizations are moving toward more security-focused development approaches, seeking to improve not only the functionality of existing systems but consumer confidence in their products. In early 2002, Microsoft effectively suspended development work on many of its products to put its OS developers, testers, and program managers through an intensive program that focused on secure software development. It also delayed release of its flagship server operating system to address critical security issues. Many other organizations are following Microsoft's recent lead in putting security into the development process. Since that time, Microsoft has developed its own Security Development Lifecycle, which uses a seven-phase, 16-step methodology that culminates in an executed incident response plan, as shown in Figure 1-19.

 For more information on the Microsoft SDL, visit the Web site at www.microsoft.com/en-us/sdl.

Training	Requirements	Design	Implementation	Verification	Release	Response
	2. Establish security requirements	5. Establish design requirements	8. Use approved tools	11. Perform dynamic analysis	14. Create an incident response plan	
1. Core security training	3. Create quality gates/bug bars	6. Perform attack surface analysis/ reduction	9. Deprecate unsafe functions	12. Perform fuzz testing	15. Conduct final security review	Execute incident response plan
	4. Perform security and privacy risk assessments	7. Use threat modeling	10. Perform static analysis	13. Conduct attack surface review	16. Certify release and archive	

Figure 1-19 Microsoft's SDL[22]

Source: Microsoft. Used with permission.

Security Professionals and the Organization

It takes a wide range of professionals to support a diverse information security program. As noted earlier in this chapter, information security is best initiated from the top down. Senior management is the key component and the vital force for a successful implementation of an information security program. However, administrative support is also essential to developing and executing specific security policies and procedures, and of course technical expertise is essential to implementing the details of the information security program. The following sections describe typical information security responsibilities of various professional roles in an organization.

⟩ Senior Management

Key Terms

chief information officer (CIO) An executive-level position that oversees the organization's computing technology and strives to create efficiency in the processing and access of the organization's information.

chief information security officer (CISO) Typically considered the top information security officer in an organization. The CISO is usually not an executive-level position, and frequently the person in this role reports to the CIO.

The senior technology officer is typically the **chief information officer** (CIO), although other titles such as vice president of information, VP of information technology, and VP of systems may be used. The CIO is primarily responsible for advising the chief executive officer, president, or company owner on strategic planning that affects the management of information in the organization. The CIO translates the strategic plans of the organization as a whole into strategic information plans for the information systems or data processing division of the organization. Once this is accomplished, CIOs work with subordinate managers to develop tactical and operational plans for the division and to enable planning and management of the systems that support the organization.

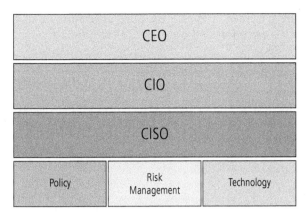

Figure 1-20 The CISO's place and roles

The **chief information security officer (CISO)** has primary responsibility for the assessment, management, and implementation of information security in the organization. The CISO may also be referred to as the manager for IT security, the security administrator, or by a similar title. The CISO usually reports directly to the CIO, although in larger organizations, one or more layers of management might exist between the two. However, the recommendations of the CISO to the CIO must be given equal if not greater priority than other technology and information-related proposals. The most common placement of CISOs in organizational hierarchies, along with their assigned roles and responsibilities, is illustrated in Figure 1-20. Note that such placement and accountabilities are the subject of current debate across the industry.[23]

❯ Information Security Project Team

> **Key Term**
>
> **project team** A small functional team of people who are experienced in one or multiple facets of the required technical and nontechnical areas for the project to which they are assigned.

The information security **project team** should consist of people who are experienced in one or multiple facets of the required technical and nontechnical areas. Many of the same skills needed to manage and implement security are also needed to design it. Members of the security project team fill the following roles:

- Champion: A senior executive who promotes the project and ensures its support, both financially and administratively, at the highest levels of the organization.
- Team leader: A project manager who may also be a departmental line manager or staff unit manager, and who understands project management, personnel management, and information security technical requirements.
- Security policy developers: People who understand the organizational culture, existing policies, and requirements for developing and implementing successful policies.
- Risk assessment specialists: People who understand financial risk assessment techniques, the value of organizational assets, and the security methods to be used.

- Security professionals: Dedicated, trained, and well-educated specialists in all aspects of information security from both a technical and nontechnical standpoint.

- Systems administrators: People with the primary responsibility for administering systems that house the information used by the organization.

- End users: Those whom the new system will most directly affect. Ideally, a selection of users from various departments, levels, and degrees of technical knowledge assist the team in focusing on the application of realistic controls that do not disrupt the essential business activities they seek to safeguard.

❯ Data Responsibilities

Key Terms

data custodians Individuals who work directly with data owners and are responsible for storage, maintenance, and protection of information.

data owners Individuals who control, and are therefore responsible for, the security and use of a particular set of information; data owners may rely on custodians for the practical aspects of protecting their information, specifying which users are authorized to access it, but they are ultimately responsible for it.

data users Internal and external stakeholders (customers, suppliers, and employees) who interact with information in support of their organization's planning and operations.

The three types of data ownership and their respective responsibilities are outlined below:

- **Data owners:** Members of senior management who are responsible for the security and use of a particular set of information. The data owners usually determine the level of data classification (discussed later), as well as the changes to that classification required by organizational change. The data owners work with subordinate managers to oversee the day-to-day administration of the data.

- **Data custodians:** Working directly with data owners, data custodians are responsible for the information and the systems that process, transmit, and store it. Depending on the size of the organization, this may be a dedicated position, such as the CISO, or it may be an additional responsibility of a systems administrator or other technology manager. The duties of a data custodian often include overseeing data storage and backups, implementing the specific procedures and policies laid out in the security policies and plans, and reporting to the data owner.

- **Data users:** Everyone in the organization is responsible for the security of data, so data users are included here as individuals with an information security role.

Communities of Interest

Key Term

community of interest A group of individuals who are united by similar interests or values within an organization and who share a common goal of helping the organization to meet its objectives.

Each organization develops and maintains its own unique culture and values. Within each organizational culture, there are **communities of interest** that develop and evolve. While an organization can have many different communities of interest, this book identifies the three that are most common and that have roles and responsibilities in information security. In theory, each role must complement the other, but this is often not the case in practice.

> Information Security Management and Professionals

The roles of information security professionals are aligned with the goals and mission of the information security community of interest. These job functions and organizational roles focus on protecting the organization's information systems and stored information from attacks.

> Information Technology Management and Professionals

The community of interest made up of IT managers and skilled professionals in systems design, programming, networks, and other related disciplines has many of the same objectives as the information security community. However, its members focus more on costs of system creation and operation, ease of use for system users, and timeliness of system creation, as well as transaction response time. The goals of the IT community and the information security community are not always in complete alignment, and depending on the organizational structure, this may cause conflict.

> Organizational Management and Professionals

The organization's general management team and the rest of the personnel in the organization make up the other major community of interest. This large group is almost always made up of subsets of other interests as well, including executive management, production management, human resources, accounting, and legal staff, to name just a few. The IT community often categorizes these groups as users of information technology systems, while the information security community categorizes them as security subjects. In fact, this community serves as the greatest reminder that all IT systems and information security objectives exist to further the objectives of the broad organizational community. The most efficient IT systems operated in the most secure fashion ever devised have no value if they are not useful to the organization as a whole.

Information Security: Is It an Art or a Science?

Given the level of complexity in today's information systems, the implementation of information security has often been described as a combination of art and science. System technologists, especially those with a gift for managing and operating computers and computer-based systems, have long been suspected of using more than a little magic to keep the systems running as expected. In information security, such technologists are sometimes called *security artisans*.[24] Everyone who has studied computer systems can appreciate the anxiety most people feel when faced with complex technology. Consider the inner workings of the computer: with the mind-boggling functions performed by the 1.4 billion transistors found in a CPU, the interaction of the various digital devices over the local networks and the Internet, and the memory storage units on the circuit boards, it's a miracle they work at all.

❭ Security as Art

The administrators and technicians who implement security can be compared to a painter applying oils to canvas. A touch of color here, a brush stroke there, just enough to represent the image the artist wants to convey without overwhelming the viewer—or in security terms, without overly restricting user access. There are no hard and fast rules regulating the installation of various security mechanisms, nor are there many universally accepted complete solutions. While many manuals exist to support individual systems, no manual can help implement security throughout an entire interconnected system. This is especially true given the complex levels of interaction among users, policy, and technology controls.

❭ Security as Science

Technology developed by computer scientists and engineers—which is designed for rigorous performance levels—makes information security a science as well as an art. Most scientists agree that specific conditions cause virtually all actions in computer systems. Almost every fault, security hole, and systems malfunction is a result of the interaction of specific hardware and software. If the developers had sufficient time, they could resolve and eliminate all of these faults.

The faults that remain are usually the result of technology malfunctioning for any of a thousand reasons. There are many sources of recognized and approved security methods and techniques that provide sound technical security advice. Best practices, standards of due care, and other tried-and-true methods can minimize the level of guesswork necessary to secure an organization's information and systems.

❭ Security as a Social Science

A third view to consider is information security as a social science, which integrates components of art and science and adds another dimension to the discussion. Social science examines the behavior of people as they interact with systems, whether they are societal systems or, as in this context, information systems. Information security begins and ends with the people inside the organization and the people who interact with the system, intentionally or otherwise.

What remains are those faults that are not really faults. There is a long-standing joke in IT that is sometimes told when a user has a system that is not performing as expected: "It's not a bug, it's a feature!" This situation occurs when a system performs as designed but not as expected, or when a user simply doesn't have the skills to use the system effectively. The same is true when an attacker learns of unintended ways to use systems, not by taking advantage of defects in a system, but by taking advantage of unintended functions or operations. Although the science of the system may be exact, its use—the human side of systems—is not.

End users who need the very information that security personnel are trying to protect may be the weakest link in the security chain. By understanding some behavioral aspects of organizational science and change management, security administrators can greatly reduce the levels of risk caused by end users and create more acceptable and supportable security profiles. These measures, coupled with appropriate policy and training issues, can substantially improve the performance of end users and result in a more secure information system.

Selected Readings

- *Beyond Fear* by Bruce Schneier, 2006, Springer-Verlag, New York. This book is an excellent look at the broader areas of security. Of special note is Chapter 4, "Systems and How They Fail," which describes how systems are often implemented and how they might be vulnerable to threats and attacks.
- *Fighting Computer Crime* by Donn B. Parker, 1983, Macmillan Library Reference.
- *Seizing the Enigma: The Race to Break the German U-Boat Codes, 1939–1943* by David Kahn, 1991, Houghton Mifflin.
- Glossary of Terms Used in Security and Intrusion Detection by SANS Institute. This glossary can be accessed online at *www.sans.org/resources/glossary.php*.
- RFC 2828–Internet Security Glossary from the Internet RFC/STD/FYI/BCP Archives. This glossary can be accessed online at *www.faqs.org/rfcs/rfc2828.html*.
- SP 800-12: An Introduction to Computer Security: The NIST Handbook. This document can be accessed online at *http://csrc.nist.gov/publications/nistpubs/800-12/handbook.pdf*.

Chapter Summary

- Information security evolved from the early field of computer security.
- Security is protection from danger. There are many types of security: physical security, personal security, operations security, communications security, national security, and network security, to name a few.
- Information security is the protection of information assets that use, store, or transmit information through the application of policy, education, and technology.
- The critical characteristics of information, including confidentiality, integrity, and availability (the C.I.A. triad), must be protected at all times. This protection is implemented by multiple measures that include policies, education, training and awareness, and technology.
- Information systems are made up of the major components of hardware, software, data, people, procedures, and networks.
- Upper management drives the top-down approach to security implementation, in contrast with the bottom-up approach or grassroots effort, in which individuals choose security implementation strategies.
- Information security should be implemented in every major system. One approach is to ensure that security is a part of the organization's system development methodology. DevOps and SecOps are emerging accelerated development models that merge development and operational skills.
- Software assurance is a methodological approach to the development of software that seeks to build security into the development life cycle rather than address it at later stages.

- The control and use of data in the organization is accomplished by:
  - Data owners, who are responsible for the security and use of a particular set of information
  - Data custodians, who are responsible for the storage, maintenance, and protection of the information
  - Data users, who work with the information to perform their daily jobs and support the mission of the organization
- Each organization has a culture in which communities of interest are united by similar values and share common objectives. The three communities in information security are general management, IT management, and information security management.
- Information security has been described as both an art and a science, and it comprises many aspects of social science as well.

Review Questions

1. What is the difference between a threat agent and a threat?
2. What is the difference between vulnerability and exposure?
3. How is infrastructure protection (assuring the security of utility services) related to information security?
4. What type of security was dominant in the early years of computing?
5. What are the three components of the C.I.A. triad? What are they used for?
6. If the C.I.A. triad is incomplete, why is it so commonly used in security?
7. Describe the critical characteristics of information. How are they used in the study of computer security?
8. Identify the six components of an information system. Which are most directly affected by the study of computer security? Which are most commonly associated with its study?
9. What system is the predecessor of almost all modern multiuser systems?
10. Which paper is the foundation of all subsequent studies of computer security?
11. Why is the top-down approach to information security superior to the bottom-up approach?
12. Why is a methodology important in the implementation of information security? How does a methodology improve the process?
13. Which members of an organization are involved in the security systems development life cycle? Who leads the process?
14. How can the practice of information security be described as both an art and a science? How does the view of security as a social science influence its practice?
15. Who is ultimately responsible for the security of information in the organization?
16. What is the relationship between the MULTICS project and the early development of computer security?

17. How has computer security evolved into modern information security?

18. What was important about RAND Report R-609?

19. Who decides how and when data in an organization will be used or controlled? Who is responsible for seeing that these decisions are carried out?

20. Who should lead a security team? Should the approach to security be more managerial or technical?

Exercises

1. Look up "the paper that started the study of computer security." Prepare a summary of the key points. What in this paper specifically addresses security in previously unexamined areas?

2. Assume that a security model is needed for the protection of information in your class. Using the CNSS model, examine each of the cells and write a brief statement on how you would address the three components of each cell.

3. Using the Web, identify the chief information officer (CIO), chief information security officer (CISO), and systems administrator for your school. Which of these people represents the data owner? Which represents the data custodian?

4. Using the Web, find a large company or government agency that is familiar to you or located in your area. Try to find the name of the chief executive officer (CEO), the CIO, and the CISO. Which was easiest to find? Which was hardest?

5. Using the Web, find out more about Kevin Mitnick. What did he do? Who caught him? Write a short summary of his activities and explain why he is infamous.

6. Using the Web, explore the technique known as "iterative and incremental development." Then, investigate "agile development." How are they related?

Case Exercises

The next day at SLS found everyone in technical support busy restoring computer systems to their former state and installing new virus and worm control software. Amy found herself learning how to re-install desktop computer operating systems and applications as SLS made a heroic effort to recover from the attack of the previous day.

Discussion Questions

1. Do you think this event was caused by an insider or outsider? Explain your answer.

2. Other than installing virus and worm control software, what can SLS do to prepare for the next incident?

3. Do you think this attack was the result of a virus or a worm? Explain your answer.

Ethical Decision Making

Often an attacker crafts e-mail attacks containing malware designed to take advantage of the curiosity or even greed of the recipients. Imagine that the message body Amy saw on the e-mail from Davey had been "See our managers' salaries and SSNs" instead of "Funniest joke you'll see today."

1. Would it be ethical for Amy to open such a file?

2. If such an e-mail came in, what would be the best action to take?

Endnotes

1. Churchwell. "Bletchley Park—Home of the Enigma Machine." Accessed 20 January 2014 from *http://churchwell.co.uk/bletchley-park-enigma.htm*.

2. Bletchley Park Trust.

3. Salus, Peter. "Net Insecurity: Then and Now (1969–1998)." *Sane '98 Online*. 19 November 1998. Accessed 20 January 2014 from *www.sane.nl/events/sane98/after math/salus.html*.

4. Roberts, Larry. "Program Plan for the ARPANET." Accessed 18 January 2014 from *www.packet.cc*.

5. Roberts, Larry. "Program Plan for the ARPANET." Accessed 18 January 2014 from *www.packet.cc*.

6. Ware, Willis. "Security Controls for Computer Systems: Report of Defense Science Board Task Force on Computer Security." *RAND Online*. 10 October 1979. Accessed 11 May 2016 from *www.rand.org/pubs/reports/R609-1.html*.

7. Bisbey, Richard II, and Hollingworth, Dennis. *Protection Analysis: Final Report*. May 1978. ISI/SR-78-13, USC/Information Sciences Institute. Marina Del Rey, CA 90291.

8. Grampp, F. T., and Morris, R. H. "UNIX Operating System Security." *AT&T Bell Laboratories Technical Journal* 63, no. 8 (1984): 1649–1672.

9. Salus, Peter. "Net Insecurity: Then and Now (1969–1998)." *Sane '98 Online*. 19 November 1998. Accessed 11 May 2016 from *www.sane.nl/events/sane98/after math/salus.html*.

10. Ware, Willis. "Security Controls for Computer Systems: Report of Defense Science Board Task Force on Computer Security." *RAND Online*. 10 October 1979. Accessed 11 May 2016 from *www.rand.org/pubs/reports/R609-1.html*.

11. National Security Telecommunications and Information Systems Security. *National Training Standard for Information Systems Security (Infosec) Professionals*. File 4011. 20 June 1994. Accessed 11 May 2016 from *www.cnss.gov/CNSS/issuances/Instruc tions.cfm*.

12. Claburn, Thomas. "GE Money Backup Tape with 650,000 Records Missing at Iron Mountain." Accessed 11 May 2016 from *www.informationweek.com/ge-money-backup-tape-with-650000-records-missing-at-iron-mountain/d/d-id/1063500?*.

13. McCumber, John. "Information Systems Security: A Comprehensive Model." Proceedings of the 14th National Computer Security Conference, National Institute of Standards and Technology, Baltimore, MD, October 1991.

14. Wikipedia. "The McCumber Cube." Accessed 11 May 2016 from *http://en.wikipedia .org/wiki/McCumber_cube*.

15. Microsoft. "C2 Evaluation and Certification for Windows NT (Q93362)." *Microsoft Online*. 1 November 2006. Accessed 11 May 2016 from *https://support.microsoft .com/en-us/kb/93362*.

16. Adapted from Dewitz, Sandra D. *Systems Analysis and Design and the Transition to Objects*. 1996. New York: McGraw Hill Publishers, 94.

17. Redwine, Samuel T., Jr. (Editor). *Software Assurance: A Guide to the Common Body of Knowledge to Produce, Acquire, and Sustain Secure Software Version 1.1*. U.S. Department of Homeland Security, September 2006.

18. Redwine, Samuel T., Jr. (Editor). *Software Assurance: A Guide to the Common Body of Knowledge to Produce, Acquire, and Sustain Secure Software Version 1.1*. U.S. Department of Homeland Security, September 2006.

19. Saltzer, J. H., and Schroeder, M. D. "The Protection of Information in Computer Systems." Proceedings of the IEEE, vol. 63, no. 9 (1975), pp. 1278–1308. Accessed 11 May 2016 from *http://cap-lore.com/CapTheory/ProtInf/*.

20. Martin, J. *Security, Accuracy, and Privacy in Computer Systems*. 1973. Englewood Cliffs, NJ: Prentice Hall.

21. Kissel, R., Stine, K., Scholl, M., Rossman, H., Fahlsing, J., and Gulick, J. *Security Considerations in the System Development Life Cycle*. NIST Special Publication 800-64, rev. 2. Accessed 11 May 2016 from *http://csrc.nist.gov/publications/nistpubs/800-64-Rev2/SP800-64-Revision2.pdf*.

22. Microsoft. "Microsoft Security Development Lifecycle." Accessed 11 May 2016 from *www.microsoft.com/security/sdl/default.aspx*.

23. Hayes, Mary. "Where the Chief Security Officer Belongs." *InformationWeek*, no. 877 (25 February 2002): 38.

24. Parker, D. B. *Fighting Computer Crime*. 1998. New York: Wiley Publishing, 189.

chapter 2

The Need for Security

Our bad neighbor makes us early stirrers, which is both healthful and good husbandry.

WILLIAM SHAKESPEARE (1564–1616),
KING HENRY, IN HENRY V, ACT 4, SC. 1, L. 6-7.

Fred Chin, CEO of Sequential Label and Supply (SLS), leaned back in his leather chair and propped his feet up on the long mahogany table in the conference room where the SLS Board of Directors had just adjourned from their quarterly meeting.

"What do you think about our computer security problem?" he asked Gladys Williams, the company's chief information officer (CIO). He was referring to the outbreak of a malicious worm on the company's computer network the previous month.

Gladys replied, "I think we have a real problem, and we need to put together a real solution. We can't sidestep this with a quick patch like last time." Six months ago, most of the systems on the company network had been infected with a different worm program that came from an employee's personal USB drive. To prevent this from happening again, all users in the company were now prohibited from using personal devices on corporate systems and networks.

Fred wasn't convinced. "Can't we just allocate additional funds to the next training budget?"

Gladys shook her head. "You've known for some time now that this business runs on technology. That's why you hired me as CIO. I've seen this same problem at other companies and I've been looking into our information security issues. My staff and I have some ideas to discuss with you. I've asked Charlie Moody to come in today to talk about it. He's waiting to speak with us."

When Charlie joined the meeting, Fred said, "Hello, Charlie. As you know, the Board of Directors met today. They received a report on the costs and lost production from the malware outbreak last month, and they directed us to improve the security of our technology. Gladys says you can help me understand what we need to do about it."

"To start with," Charlie said, "Instead of simply ramping up our antivirus solution, we need to develop a formal information security program. We need a thorough review of our policies and practices, and we need to establish an ongoing risk management program. There are some other things that are part of the process as well, but this is where I think we should start."

"Sounds like it is going to be complicated ... and expensive," said Fred.

Charlie looked at Gladys, then answered, "Well, there will probably be some extra expenses for specialized hardware and software, and we may have to slow down some of our product development projects a bit, but this approach will call more for a change in our attitude about security than just a spending spree. I don't have accurate estimates yet, but you can be sure we'll put cost-benefit worksheets in front of you before we commit any funds."

Fred thought about this for a few seconds. "OK. What's our next step?"

Gladys answered, "First, we need to initiate a project plan to develop our new information security program. We'll use our usual systems development and project management approach. There are a few differences, but we can easily adapt our current models. We'll also need to reassign a few administrators to help Charlie with the new program. We'd also like a formal statement to the entire company identifying Charlie as our new chief information security officer, and asking all of the department heads to cooperate with his new information security initiatives."

"Information security? What about computer security?" asked Fred.

Charlie responded, "Information security includes computer security, plus all the other things we use to do business: securing our networks, operations, communications, personnel, and intellectual property. Even our paper records need to be factored in."

"I see," Fred said. "Okay, Mr. Chief Information Security Officer." Fred held out his hand for a congratulatory handshake. "Bring me the draft project plan and budget in two weeks. The audit committee of the Board meets in four weeks, and we'll need to report our progress then."

LEARNING OBJECTIVES

Upon completion of this material, you should be able to:

- Discuss the organizational need for information security
- Explain why a successful information security program is the shared responsibility of an organization's three communities of interest
- List and describe the threats posed to information security and common attacks associated with those threats
- List the common development failures and errors that result from poor software security efforts

Introduction

> **Key Terms**
>
> **data** Items of fact collected by an organization. Data includes raw numbers, facts, and words. Student quiz scores are a simple example of data.
>
> **information** Data that has been organized, structured, and presented to provide additional insight into its context, worth, and usefulness. For example, a student's class average can be presented in the context of its value, as in "90 = A."
>
> **information asset** The focus of information security; information that has value to the organization, and the systems that store, process, and transmit the information.
>
> **media** As a subset of information assets, the systems and networks that store, process, and transmit information.

Unlike any other business or information technology program, the primary mission of an information security program is to ensure that **information assets**—information and the systems that house them—remain safe and useful. Organizations expend a lot of money and thousands of hours to maintain their information assets. If threats to these assets didn't exist, those resources could be used exclusively to improve the systems that contain, use, and transmit the information. However, the threat of attacks on information assets is a constant concern, and the need for information security grows along with the sophistication of the attacks. While some organizations lump both information and systems under their definition of an information asset, others prefer to separate the true information-based assets (data, databases, data sets, and the applications that may use data) from **media**—the systems and networks that store and transmit data. For our purposes, we will include both data and systems assets in our use of the term.

Organizations must understand the environment in which information assets reside so their information security programs can address actual and potential problems. This chapter describes the environment and identifies the threats to it, the organization, and its information.

Information security performs four important functions for an organization:

- Protecting the organization's ability to function
- Protecting the **data** and **information** the organization collects and uses, whether physical or electronic
- Enabling the safe operation of applications running on the organization's IT systems
- Safeguarding the organization's technology assets

❭ Business Needs First

> **Key Terms**
>
> **data security** Commonly used as a surrogate for information security, data security is the focus of protecting data or information in its various states—at rest (in storage), in processing, and in transmission (over networks).

database A collection of related data stored in a structured form and usually managed by a database management system.

database security A subset of information security that focuses on the assessment and protection of information stored in data repositories like database management systems and storage media.

Protecting Functionality The three communities of interest—general management, IT management, and information security management—are each responsible for facilitating the information security program that protects the organization's ability to function. Although many business and government managers shy away from addressing information security because they perceive it to be a technically complex task, implementing information security actually has more to do with *management* than *technology*. Just as managing payroll involves management more than mathematical wage computations, managing information security has more to do with risk management, policy, and its enforcement than the technology of its implementation. As the noted information security author Charles Cresson Wood writes:

> In fact, a lot of [information security] is good management for information technology. Many people think that a solution to a technology problem is more technology. Well, not necessarily.... So a lot of my work, out of necessity, has been trying to get my clients to pay more attention to information security as a management issue in addition to a technical issue, information security as a people issue in addition to the technical issue.[1]

Each of an organization's communities of interest must address information security in terms of business impact and the cost of business interruption, rather than isolating security as a technical problem.

Protecting Data That Organizations Collect and Use Without data, an organization loses its record of transactions and its ability to deliver value to customers. Any business, educational institution, or government agency that operates within the modern context of connected and responsive services relies on information systems. Even when transactions are not online, information systems and the data they process enable the creation and movement of goods and services. Therefore, **data security**—protecting data *in transmission, in processing*, and *at rest (storage)*—is a critical aspect of information security. The value of data motivates attackers to steal, sabotage, or corrupt it. An effective information security program implemented by management protects the integrity and value of the organization's data.

Organizations store much of the data they deem critical in **databases**, managed by specialized data management software known as a database management system (DBMS). The process of maintaining the confidentiality, integrity, and availability of data managed by a DBMS is known as **database security**. Database security is accomplished by applying a broad range of control approaches common to many areas of information security. Securing databases encompasses most of the topics you will cover in this textbook, including managerial, technical, and physical controls. Managerial controls include policy, procedure, and governance. Technical controls used to secure databases rely on knowledge of access control, authentication, auditing, application security, backup and recovery, encryption, and integrity controls. Physical controls include the use of data centers with locking doors, fire suppression systems, video monitoring, and physical security guards.

The fundamental practices of information security have broad applicability in the area of database security. One indicator of this strong degree of overlap is that the International Information Systems Security Certification Consortium (ISC)[2], the organization that evaluates candidates for many prestigious information security certification programs, allows experience as a database administrator to count toward the experience requirement for the Certified Information Systems Security Professional (CISSP).

Enabling the Safe Operation of Applications Today's organizations are under immense pressure to acquire and operate integrated, efficient, and capable applications. A modern organization needs to create an environment that safeguards these applications, particularly those that are important elements of the organization's infrastructure—operating system platforms, certain operational applications, electronic mail (e-mail), and instant messaging (IM) applications, like text messaging (short message service, or SMS). Organizations acquire these elements from a service provider or they implement their own. Once an organization's infrastructure is in place, management must continue to oversee it and not relegate its management to the IT department.

Safeguarding Technology Assets in Organizations To perform effectively, organizations must employ secure infrastructure hardware appropriate to the size and scope of the enterprise. For instance, a small business may get by in its startup phase using a small-scale firewall, such as a small office/home office (SOHO) device.

In general, as an organization grows to accommodate changing needs, more robust technology solutions should replace security technologies the organization has outgrown. An example of a robust solution is a commercial-grade, unified security architecture device complete with intrusion detection and prevention systems, public key infrastructure (PKI), and virtual private network (VPN) capabilities. Chapters 6 through 8 describe these technologies in more detail.

Information technology continues to add new capabilities and methods that allow organizations to solve business information management challenges. In recent years we have seen the emergence of the Internet and the Web as new markets. Cloud-based services, which have created new ways to deliver IT services, have also brought new risks to organizational information, additional concerns about the ways these assets can be threatened, and concern for how they must be defended.

Threats and Attacks

Key Terms

attack An intentional or unintentional act that can damage or otherwise compromise information and the systems that support it. Attacks can be active or passive and direct or indirect.

exploit A technique used to compromise a system.

vulnerability A potential weakness in an asset or its defensive control system(s).

Around 500 B.C., the Chinese general Sun Tzu Wu wrote *The Art of War*, a military treatise that emphasizes the importance of knowing yourself as well as the threats you face.[2] To protect your organization's information, you must: (1) know yourself; that is, be familiar with the information to be protected and the systems that store, transport, and process it; and (2) know the threats you face. To make sound decisions about information security, management must be informed about the various threats to an organization's people, applications, data, and information systems. As discussed in Chapter 1, a threat represents a *potential* risk to an information asset, whereas an **attack** represents an ongoing act against the asset that could result in a loss. Threat agents damage or steal an organization's information or physical assets by using **exploits** to take advantage of **vulnerabilities** where controls are not present or no longer effective. Unlike threats, which are always present, attacks exist only when a specific act may cause a loss. For example, the *threat* of damage from a thunderstorm is present throughout the summer in many places, but an *attack* and its associated risk of loss exist only for the duration of an actual thunderstorm. The following sections discuss each of the major types of threats and corresponding attacks facing modern information assets.

 For more information on The Art of War, check out MIT's Classics page at http://classics.mit.edu/ Tzu/artwar.html.

To investigate the wide range of threats that pervade the interconnected world, many researchers have collected information on threats and attacks from practicing information security personnel and their organizations. While the categorizations may vary, threats are relatively well researched and fairly well understood.

❯ 3.6 Billion Potential Hackers

There is wide agreement that the threat from external sources increases when an organization connects to the Internet. The number of Internet users continues to grow; about 49.2 percent of the world's 7.34 billion people—that is, more than 3.6 billion people—have some form of Internet access, a dramatic increase over the 25.6 percent reported as recently as 2009. Figure 2-1 shows Internet usage by continent. Since the time this data was collected in early 2015, the world population has continued to grow, with an expected increase in Internet usage. Therefore, a typical organization with an online connection to its systems and information faces an ever-increasing pool of potential hackers.

❯ Other Studies of Threats

Several studies in recent years have examined the threats and attacks to information security. The most recent study and survey, conducted in 2015, found that 67.1 percent of responding organizations suffered malware infections.

More than 98 percent of responding organizations identified malware attacks as a threat, with 58.7 percent indicating it was a significant or severe threat. Malware was identified as the second highest threat source behind electronic phishing/spoofing.[3]

Table 2-1 shows a summary of survey data since 2000.

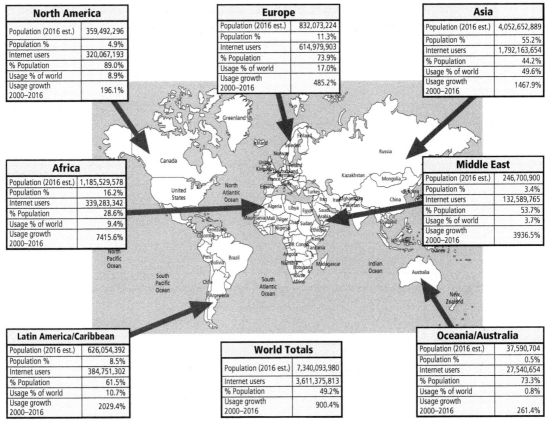

North America	
Population (2016 est.)	359,492,296
Population %	4.9%
Internet users	320,067,193
% Population	89.0%
Usage % of world	8.9%
Usage growth 2000–2016	196.1%

Europe	
Population (2016 est.)	832,073,224
Population %	11.3%
Internet users	614,979,903
% Population	73.9%
Usage % of world	17.0%
Usage growth 2000–2016	485.2%

Asia	
Population (2016 est.)	4,052,652,889
Population %	55.2%
Internet users	1,792,163,654
% Population	44.2%
Usage % of world	49.6%
Usage growth 2000–2016	1467.9%

Africa	
Population (2016 est.)	1,185,529,578
Population %	16.2%
Internet users	339,283,342
% Population	28.6%
Usage % of world	9.4%
Usage growth 2000–2016	7415.6%

Middle East	
Population (2016 est.)	246,700,900
Population %	3.4%
Internet users	132,589,765
% Population	53.7%
Usage % of world	3.7%
Usage growth 2000–2016	3936.5%

Latin America/Caribbean	
Population (2016 est.)	626,054,392
Population %	8.5%
Internet users	384,751,302
% Population	61.5%
Usage % of world	10.7%
Usage growth 2000–2016	2029.4%

World Totals	
Population (2016 est.)	7,340,093,980
Internet users	3,611,375,813
% Population	49.2%
Usage growth 2000–2016	900.4%

Oceania/Australia	
Population (2016 est.)	37,590,704
Population %	0.5%
Internet users	27,540,654
% Population	73.3%
Usage % of world	0.8%
Usage growth 2000–2016	261.4%

Figure 2-1 World Internet usage[4]

Type of Attack or Misuse	2010/11	2008	2006	2004	2002	2000
Malware infection (revised after 2008)	67%	50%	65%	78%	85%	85%
Being fraudulently represented as sender of phishing message	39%	31%	(new category)			
Laptop/mobile hardware theft/loss	34%	42%	47%	49%	55%	60%
Bots/zombies in organization	29%	20%	(new category)			
Insider abuse of Internet access or e-mail	25%	44%	42%	59%	78%	79%
Denial of service	17%	21%	25%	39%	40%	27%
Unauthorized access or privilege escalation by insider	13%	15%	(revised category)			
Password sniffing	11%	9%	(new category)			
System penetration by outsider	11%	(revised category)				
Exploit of client Web browser	10%	(new category)				

Table 2-1 Compiled Survey Results for Types of Attack or Misuse (2000–2011)[5] *(continues)*

Attack/Misuse Categories with Less Than 10% Responses (Listed in Decreasing Order):
Financial fraud
Web site defacement
Exploit of wireless network
Other exploit of public-facing Web site
Theft of or unauthorized access to PII or PHI due to all other causes
Instant Messaging misuse
Theft of or unauthorized access to IP due to all other causes
Exploit of user's social network profile
Theft of or unauthorized access to IP due to mobile device theft/loss
Theft of or unauthorized access to PII or PHI due to mobile device theft/loss
Exploit of DNS server
Extortion or blackmail associated with threat of attack or release of stolen data

Table 2-1   Compiled Survey Results for Types of Attack or Misuse (2000–2011)[5] (continued)

Source: Whitman and Mattord, 2015 SEC/CISE Threats to Information Protection Report.

OFFLINE

The 2015 SEC/CISE Survey of Threats to Information Protection[6]

In 2015, the Center for Information Security Education at Kennesaw State University conducted a survey on behalf of the Security Executive Council. The primary purpose of the survey was to collect and report on current threats to information protection. The survey asked respondents, *"For each of the following, please indicate the extent to which you view the item as a current threat to your information assets."* Respondents first rated threats from internal sources, as shown in Table 2-2.

From Employees or Internal Stakeholders	Not a Threat 1	2	3	4	A Severe Threat 5	Comp. Rank
Inability/unwillingness to follow established policy	6.6%	17.2%	**33.6%**	26.2%	16.4%	66%
Disclosure due to insufficient training	8.1%	23.6%	**29.3%**	25.2%	13.8%	63%
Unauthorized access or escalation of privileges	4.8%	24.0%	**31.2%**	**31.2%**	8.8%	63%

Table 2-2   Rated Threats from Internal Sources in 2015 SEC/CISE Survey of Threats to Information Protection

From Employees or Internal Stakeholders	Not a Threat 1	2	3	4	A Severe Threat 5	Comp. Rank
Unauthorized information collection/ data sniffing	6.4%	26.4%	**40.0%**	17.6%	9.6%	60%
Theft of on-site organizational information assets	10.6%	32.5%	**34.1%**	12.2%	10.6%	56%
Theft of mobile/laptop/tablet and related/connected information assets	15.4%	**29.3%**	28.5%	17.9%	8.9%	55%
Intentional damage or destruction of information assets	22.3%	**43.0%**	18.2%	13.2%	3.3%	46%
Theft or misuse of organizationally leased, purchased, or developed software	29.6%	**33.6%**	21.6%	10.4%	4.8%	45%
Web site defacement	**43.4%**	33.6%	16.4%	4.9%	1.6%	38%
Blackmail of information release or sales	**43.5%**	37.1%	10.5%	6.5%	2.4%	37%

Table 2-2 Rated Threats from Internal Sources in 2015 SEC/CISE Survey of Threats to Information Protection (*continued*)

Respondents then rated threats from external sources, as shown in Table 2-3.

From Outsiders or External Stakeholders	Not a Threat 1	2	3	4	A Severe Threat 5	Comp. Rank
Unauthorized information collection/ data sniffing	6.4%	14.4%	21.6%	**32.8%**	24.8%	71%
Unauthorized access or escalation of privileges	7.4%	14.0%	26.4%	**31.4%**	20.7%	69%
Web site defacement	8.9%	23.6%	22.8%	**26.8%**	17.9%	64%
Intentional damage or destruction of information assets	14.0%	**32.2%**	18.2%	24.8%	10.7%	57%
Theft of mobile/laptop/tablet and related/connected information assets	20.5%	25.4%	**26.2%**	15.6%	12.3%	55%
Theft of on-site organizational information assets	21.1%	24.4%	**25.2%**	17.9%	11.4%	55%
Blackmail of information release or sales	**31.1%**	30.3%	14.8%	14.8%	9.0%	48%
Disclosure due to insufficient training	**34.5%**	21.8%	22.7%	13.4%	7.6%	48%
Inability/unwillingness to follow established policy	**33.6%**	29.4%	18.5%	6.7%	11.8%	47%
Theft or misuse of organizationally leased, purchased, or developed software	**31.7%**	30.1%	22.8%	9.8%	5.7%	46%

Table 2-3 Rated Threats from External Sources in 2015 SEC/CISE Survey of Threats to Information Protection

(*continues*)

Respondents were then asked to specify the extent to which a list of items were viewed as threats to information assets, as shown in Table 2-4.

General Threats to Information Assets	Not a Threat 1	2	3	4	A Severe Threat 5	Comp. Rank
Electronic phishing/spoofing attacks	0.8%	13.1%	16.4%	32.0%	**37.7%**	79%
Malware attacks	1.7%	12.4%	27.3%	**36.4%**	22.3%	73%
Unintentional employee/insider mistakes	2.4%	17.1%	26.8%	**35.8%**	17.9%	70%
Loss of trust due to information loss	4.1%	18.9%	27.0%	22.1%	**27.9%**	70%
Software failures or errors due to unknown vulnerabilities in externally acquired software	5.6%	18.5%	28.2%	**33.9%**	13.7%	66%
Social engineering of employees/insiders based on social media information	8.1%	14.6%	32.5%	**34.1%**	10.6%	65%
Social engineering of employees/insiders based on other published information	8.9%	19.5%	24.4%	**32.5%**	14.6%	65%
Software failures or errors due to poorly developed, internally created applications	7.2%	21.6%	24.0%	**32.0%**	15.2%	65%
SQL injections	7.6%	17.6%	**31.9%**	29.4%	13.4%	65%
Social engineering of employees/insiders based on organization's Web sites	11.4%	19.5%	23.6%	**31.7%**	13.8%	63%
Denial of service (and distributed DoS) attacks	8.2%	23.0%	27.9%	**32.8%**	8.2%	62%
Software failures or errors due to known vulnerabilities in externally acquired software	8.9%	23.6%	26.8%	**35.8%**	4.9%	61%
Outdated organizational software	8.1%	**28.2%**	26.6%	26.6%	10.5%	61%
Loss of trust due to representation as source of phishing/spoofing attack	9.8%	23.8%	**30.3%**	23.0%	13.1%	61%
Loss of trust due to Web defacement	12.4%	30.6%	**31.4%**	19.8%	5.8%	55%
Outdated organizational hardware	17.2%	**34.4%**	32.8%	12.3%	3.3%	50%
Outdated organization data format	18.7%	**35.8%**	26.8%	13.8%	4.9%	50%
Inability/unwillingness to establish effective policy by management	**30.4%**	26.4%	24.0%	13.6%	5.6%	48%
Hardware failures or errors due to aging equipment	19.5%	**39.8%**	24.4%	14.6%	1.6%	48%
Hardware failures or errors due to defective equipment	17.9%	**48.0%**	24.4%	8.1%	1.6%	46%

Table 2-4   Perceived Threats to Information Assets in 2015 SEC/CISE Survey of Threats to Information Protection

General Threats to Information Assets	Not a Threat 1	2	3	4	A Severe Threat 5	Comp. Rank
Deviations in quality of service from other provider	25.2%	**38.7%**	25.2%	7.6%	3.4%	45%
Deviations in quality of service from data communications provider/ISP	26.4%	**39.7%**	23.1%	7.4%	3.3%	44%
Deviations in quality of service from telecommunications provider/ISP (if different from data provider)	29.9%	**38.5%**	18.8%	9.4%	3.4%	44%
Loss due to other natural disaster	31.0%	**37.9%**	23.3%	6.9%	0.9%	42%
Loss due to fire	26.2%	**49.2%**	21.3%	3.3%	0.0%	40%
Deviations in quality of service from power provider	36.1%	**43.4%**	12.3%	5.7%	2.5%	39%
Loss due to flood	33.9%	**43.8%**	19.8%	1.7%	0.8%	38%
Loss due to earthquake	**41.7%**	35.8%	15.0%	6.7%	0.8%	38%

Table 2-4 Perceived Threats to Information Assets in 2015 SEC/CISE Survey of Threats to Information Protection (*continued*)

In each case, a comparative ranking (Comp. Rank) was calculated based on the aggregate value of the number of responses for that value, multiplied by five points for a "severe threat" selection down to one point for "not a threat," and then converted to a percentage of the maximum possible points. This value is a weighted average that provides a basis of comparison for each threat.

❯ Common Attack Pattern Enumeration and Classification (CAPEC)

A tool that security professionals can use to understand attacks is the Common Attack Pattern Enumeration and Classification (CAPEC) Web site hosted by Mitre—a nonprofit research and development organization sponsored by the U.S. government. This online repository can be searched for characteristics of a particular attack or simply browsed by professionals who want additional knowledge of how attacks occur procedurally.

 For more information on CAPEC, visit http://capec.mitre.org, where the contents can be downloaded or viewed online.

❯ The 12 Categories of Threats

The scheme shown in Table 2-5 consists of 12 general categories of threats that represent a clear and present danger to an organization's people, information, and systems. Each organization must prioritize the threats it faces based on the particular security situation in which it operates, its organizational strategy regarding risk, and the exposure levels of its assets. Chapter 4 covers these topics in more detail. You may notice that many of the attack examples in Table 2-5 could be listed in more than one category. For example, theft performed by a hacker falls into the category of "theft," but it can also be preceded

Category of Threat	Attack Examples
Compromises to intellectual property	Piracy, copyright infringement
Deviations in quality of service	Internet service provider (ISP), power, or WAN service problems
Espionage or trespass	Unauthorized access and/or data collection
Forces of nature	Fire, floods, earthquakes, lightning
Human error or failure	Accidents, employee mistakes
Information extortion	Blackmail, information disclosure
Sabotage or vandalism	Destruction of systems or information
Software attacks	Viruses, worms, macros, denial of service
Technical hardware failures or errors	Equipment failure
Technical software failures or errors	Bugs, code problems, unknown loopholes
Technological obsolescence	Antiquated or outdated technologies
Theft	Illegal confiscation of equipment or information

Table 2-5   The 12 Categories of Threats to Information Security[7]

by "espionage or trespass" as the hacker illegally accesses the information. The theft may also be accompanied by defacement actions to delay discovery, qualifying it for the category of "sabotage or vandalism." As mentioned in Chapter 1, these are technically threat sources, but for simplicity's sake, they are described here as threats.

Compromises to Intellectual Property

Key Term

intellectual property (IP) The creation, ownership, and control of original ideas as well as the representation of those ideas.

Many organizations create or support the development of **intellectual property (IP)** as part of their business operations. (You will learn more about IP in Chapter 3.) IP includes trade secrets, copyrights, trademarks, and patents. IP is protected by copyright law and other laws, carries the expectation of proper attribution or credit to its source, and potentially requires the acquisition of permission for its use, as specified in those laws. For example, use of some IP may require specific payments or royalties before a song can be used in a movie or before the distribution of a photo in a publication. The unauthorized appropriation of IP constitutes a threat to information security. Employees may have access privileges to a variety of IP, including purchased and developed software and organizational information, as many employees typically need to use IP to conduct day-to-day business.

❯ Software Piracy

Organizations often purchase or lease the IP of other organizations, and must abide by a purchase or licensing agreement for its fair and responsible use. The most common IP breach is the unlawful use or duplication of software-based intellectual property, more commonly known as **software piracy**. Because most software is licensed to a particular purchaser, its use is restricted to a single user or to a designated user in an organization. If a user copies the program to another computer without securing another license or transferring the license, the user has violated the copyright. The nearby Offline feature describes a classic case of this type of copyright violation. While you may note that the example is from 1997, which seems a long time ago, it illustrates that the issue remains significant today.

Software licenses are strictly enforced by regulatory and private organizations, and software publishers use several control mechanisms to prevent copyright infringement. In addition to laws against software piracy, two watchdog organizations investigate allegations of software abuse: the Software & Information Industry Association (SIIA) at *www.siia.net*, formerly known as the Software Publishers Association, and the Business Software Alliance (BSA) at *www.bsa.org*. BSA estimates that approximately 39 percent of software installed on computers globally in 2015 was not properly licensed. This number is only slightly lower than the 43 percent reported in the 2013 BSA global study. Furthermore, about 26 percent of employees who responded to the 2015 study admitted installing unauthorized software on computers at work; over 84 percent of those employees installed two or more software packages. BSA also reports a modest global decline in the use of unlicensed software—down 4 percent from 2013 to an estimated commercial value of $52.2 billion.[8] Figure 2-2 shows the BSA's software piracy reporting Web site.

❯ Copyright Protection and User Registration

A number of technical mechanisms—digital watermarks, embedded code, copyright codes, and even the intentional placement of bad sectors on software media—have been used to enforce copyright laws. The most common tool is a unique software registration code in combination with an end-user license agreement (EULA) that usually pops up during the installation of new software, requiring users to indicate that they have read and agree to conditions of the software's use. Figure 2-3 shows a license agreement from Microsoft Office.

Another effort to combat piracy is online registration. Users who install software are often asked or even required to register their software to complete the installation, obtain technical support, or gain the use of all features. Some users believe that this process compromises personal privacy because they never know exactly what information is obtained from their

REPORT SOFTWARE PIRACY NOW!

YOUR REPORT IS CONFIDENTIAL.

ABOUT SSL CERTIFICATES

1 IN 5 PIECES OF SOFTWARE IN THE US ARE UNLICENSED. BE PART OF THE SOLUTION.

▶FILE YOUR REPORT NOW

In order to investigate your software piracy report, you will need to provide the name and address of the company being reported, what software is being pirated, and how you know the software is pirated. All information provided to BSA will be kept confidential.

I want to report: (hover for more detail)*

○ An organization or business that is using or installing more software than it has licenses for

○ A physical distributor who markets or sells unlicensed software

○ Someone who sells/distributes unlicensed copies of software via the Internet

* required field

Company you are reporting*

What type of company is it?*

A WORD ON CONFIDENTIALITY

It is BSA | The Software Alliance's strict policy to keep all information about you confidential. We thank you for your report and will not disclose your information unless required by law to do so.

HAVE A QUESTION?

CHAT LIVE NOW

Email: NoPiracy.org

1.888.NO.PIRACY

WHAT IS PIRACY

What Constitutes Software Piracy?

Figure 2-2 BSA's software piracy reporting Web site

Source: Business Software Alliance. Used with permission.

Microsoft Office Professional Plus 2013

Read the Microsoft Software License Terms

To continue you must accept the terms of this agreement. If you do not want to accept the Microsoft Software License Terms, close this window to cancel the installation.

PLEASE NOTE: Your use of this software is subject to the terms and conditions of the license agreement by which you acquired this software. For instance, if you are:

• a volume license customer, use of this software is subject to your volume license agreement.
• a MSDN customer, use of this software is subject to the MSDN agreement.

You may not use this software if you have not validly acquired a license for the software from Microsoft or its licensed distributors.

EULAID:O15_RTM_VL.1_RTM_EN

☐ I accept the terms of this agreement

Continue

Figure 2-3 Microsoft Office software license terms

Source: Microsoft. Used with permission.

Figure 2-4 Steam Online software registration and product activation

Source: Steam Online. Used with permission.

computers and sent to the software manufacturer. Figure 2-4 shows an example of online software registration from the Steam game client. Steam requires the user to create an account and log into it before registering software.

Intellectual property losses may result from the successful exploitation of vulnerabilities in asset protection controls. Many of the threats against these controls are described in this chapter.

OFFLINE

Violating Software Licenses

Adapted from "Bootlegged Software Could Cost Community College"[9]

By Natalie Patton, *Las Vegas Review Journal*, September 18, 1997.

Ever heard of the software police? The Washington-based Software Publishers Association (SPA) copyright watchdogs were tipped off that a community college in Las Vegas, Nevada, was using copyrighted software in violation of the software licenses. The SPA spent months investigating the report. Academic Affairs Vice President Robert Silverman said the college was prepared to pay some license violation fines, but was unable to estimate the total amount of the fines. The college cut back on new faculty hires and set aside more than $1.3 million in anticipation of the total cost.

The audit was intensive, and it examined every computer on campus, including faculty machines, lab machines, and the college president's computer. Peter Beruk, SPA's

(continues)

director of domestic antipiracy cases, said the decision to audit a reported violation is only made when there is overwhelming evidence to win a lawsuit, as the SPA has no policing authority and can only bring civil actions. Most of the investigated organizations settle out of court and agree to pay the fines to avoid costly court battles.

The process begins with an anonymous tip, usually from someone inside the organization. Of the hundreds of tips the SPA receives each week, only a handful are selected for onsite visits. If the audited organizations have license violations, they are required to destroy illegal software copies, repurchase software they want to keep (at double the retail price), and pay the proper licensing fees for the software they used illegally.

In this case, the community college president suggested the blame for the college's violations belonged to faculty and students who may have downloaded illegal copies of software from the Internet or installed software on campus computers without permission. Some of the faculty suspected that the problem lay with the qualifications and credibility of the campus technology staff. The president promised to put additional staff and rules in place to prevent future license violations.

Deviations in Quality of Service

Key Terms

availability disruption An interruption in service, usually from a service provider, which causes an adverse event within an organization.

downtime The percentage of time a particular service is not available; the opposite of uptime.

service level agreement (SLA) A document or part of a document that specifies the expected level of service from a service provider. An SLA usually contains provisions for minimum acceptable availability and penalties or remediation procedures for downtime.

uptime The percentage of time a particular service is available; the opposite of downtime.

An organization's information system depends on the successful operation of many interdependent support systems, including power grids, data and telecommunications networks, parts suppliers, service vendors, and even janitorial staff and garbage haulers. Any of these support systems can be interrupted by severe weather, employee illnesses, or other unforeseen events. Deviations in quality of service can result from such accidents as a backhoe taking out an ISP's fiber-optic link. The backup provider may be online and in service, but may be able to supply only a fraction of the bandwidth the organization needs for full service. This degradation of service is a form of **availability disruption**. Irregularities in Internet service, communications, and power supplies can dramatically affect the availability of information and systems.

❯ Internet Service Issues

In organizations that rely heavily on the Internet and the World Wide Web to support continued operations, ISP failures can considerably undermine the availability of information. Many organizations have sales staff and telecommuters working at remote locations. When these off-site employees cannot contact the host systems, they must use manual procedures

2

to continue operations. The U.S. government's Federal Communications Commission (FCC) maintains a Network Outage Reporting System (NORS), which according to FCC regulation 47 C.F.R. Part 4, requires communications providers to report outages that disrupt communications at certain facilities, like emergency services and airports.

When an organization places its Web servers in the care of a Web hosting provider, that provider assumes responsibility for all Internet services and for the hardware and operating system software used to operate the Web site. These Web hosting services are usually arranged with a **service level agreement (SLA)**. When a service provider fails to meet the terms of the SLA, the provider may accrue fines to cover losses incurred by the client, but these payments seldom cover the losses generated by the outage. Vendors may promote high availability or **uptime** (or low **downtime**), but Figure 2-5 shows even an availability that seems acceptably high can cost the average organization a great deal. In August 2013, the Amazon.com Web site went down for 30 to 40 minutes, costing the company between $3 million and $4 million.

❯ Communications and Other Service Provider Issues

Other utility services can affect organizations as well. Among these are telephone, water, wastewater, trash pickup, cable television, natural or propane gas, and custodial services. The loss of these services can impair the ability of an organization to function. For instance, most facilities require water service to operate an air-conditioning system. Even in Minnesota in February, air-conditioning systems help keep a modern facility operating. If a wastewater

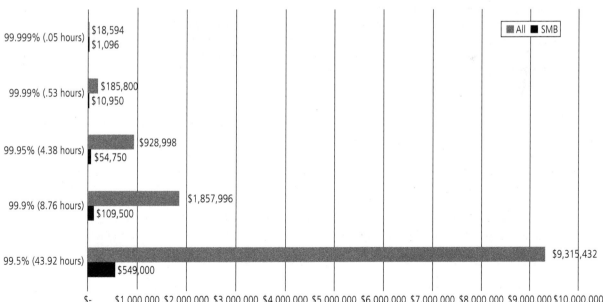

Figure 2-5 Cost of online service provider downtime[10]

Source: MegaPath. Used with permission.

system fails, an organization might be prevented from allowing employees into the building. While several online utilities allow an organization to compare pricing options from various service providers, only a few show a comparative analysis of availability or downtime.

❯ Power Irregularities

Key Terms

blackout A long-term interruption (outage) in electrical power availability.
brownout A long-term decrease in electrical power availability.
fault A short-term interruption in electrical power availability.
noise The presence of additional and disruptive signals in network communications or electrical power delivery.
sag A short-term decrease in electrical power availability.
spike A short-term increase in electrical power availability, also known as a swell.
surge A long-term increase in electrical power availability.

Irregularities from power utilities are common and can lead to fluctuations such as power excesses, power shortages, and power losses. These fluctuations can pose problems for organizations that provide inadequately conditioned power for their information systems equipment. In the United States, we are supplied 120-volt, 60-cycle power, usually through 15- and 20-amp circuits. Europe as well as most of Africa, Asia, South America, and Australia use 230-volt, 50-cycle power. With the prevalence of global travel by organizational employees, failure to properly adapt to different voltage levels can damage computing equipment, resulting in a loss. When power voltage levels vary from normal, expected levels, such as during a **spike, surge, sag, fault, noise, brownout,** or **blackout,** an organization's sensitive electronic equipment—especially networking equipment, computers, and computer-based systems, which are vulnerable to fluctuations—can be easily damaged or destroyed. With small computers and network systems, quality power-conditioning options such as surge suppressors can smooth out spikes. The more expensive uninterruptible power supply (UPS) can protect against spikes and surges as well as sags and even blackouts of limited duration. UPSs are discussed in additional detail in Chapter 9, "Physical Security."

Espionage or Trespass

Key Terms

competitive intelligence The collection and analysis of information about an organization's business competitors through legal and ethical means to gain business intelligence and competitive advantage.
industrial espionage The collection and analysis of information about an organization's business competitors, often through illegal or unethical means, to gain an unfair competitive advantage. Also known as corporate spying, which is distinguished from espionage for national security reasons.
shoulder surfing The direct, covert observation of individual information or system use.

Espionage or trespass is a well-known and broad category of electronic and human activities that can breach the confidentiality of information. When an unauthorized person gains access to information an organization is trying to protect, the act is categorized as espionage or trespass. Attackers can use many different methods to access the information stored in an information system. Some information-gathering techniques are legal—for example, using a Web browser to perform market research. These legal techniques are collectively called **competitive intelligence**. When information gatherers employ techniques that cross a legal or ethical threshold, they are conducting **industrial espionage**. Many countries that are considered allies of the United States engage in industrial espionage against American organizations. When foreign governments are involved, these activities are considered espionage and a threat to national security.

 For more information about industrial espionage in the United States, visit the National Counterintelligence and Security Center at www.ncsc.gov. Look through the resources for additional information on top issues like economic espionage and insider threats.

Some forms of espionage are relatively low tech. One example, called **shoulder surfing**, is pictured in Figure 2-6. This technique is used in public or semipublic settings when people gather information they are not authorized to have. Instances of shoulder surfing occur at computer terminals, desks, and ATMs; on a bus, airplane, or subway, where people use smartphones and tablet PCs; and in other places where employees may access confidential information.

Figure 2-6 Shoulder surfing

Shoulder surfing flies in the face of the unwritten etiquette among professionals who address information security in the workplace: If you can see another person entering personal or private information into a system, look away as the information is entered. Failure to do so constitutes not only a breach of etiquette, but an affront to privacy and a threat to the security of confidential information.

⟩ Hackers

Key Terms

expert hacker A hacker who uses extensive knowledge of the inner workings of computer hardware and software to gain unauthorized access to systems and information. Also known as elite hackers, expert hackers often create automated exploits, scripts, and tools used by other hackers.

hacker A person who accesses systems and information without authorization and often illegally.

jailbreaking Escalating privileges to gain administrator-level or root access control over a smartphone operating system (typically associated with Apple iOS smartphones). See also *rooting*.

novice hacker A relatively unskilled hacker who uses the work of expert hackers to perform attacks. Also known as a neophyte, n00b, or newbie. This category of hackers includes script kiddies and packet monkeys.

packet monkey A script kiddie who uses automated exploits to engage in denial-of-service attacks.

penetration tester An information security professional with authorization to attempt to gain system access in an effort to identify and recommend resolutions for vulnerabilities in those systems.

privilege escalation The unauthorized modification of an authorized or unauthorized system user account to gain advanced access and control over system resources.

professional hacker A hacker who conducts attacks for personal financial benefit or for a crime organization or foreign government. Not to be confused with a penetration tester.

rooting Escalating privileges to gain administrator-level control over a computer system (including smartphones). Typically associated with Android OS smartphones. See also *jailbreaking*.

script kiddie A hacker of limited skill who uses expertly written software to attack a system. Also known as skids, skiddies, or script bunnies.

trespass Unauthorized entry into the real or virtual property of another party.

Acts of **trespass** can lead to unauthorized real or virtual actions that enable information gatherers to enter premises or systems without permission. Controls sometimes mark the boundaries of an organization's virtual territory. These boundaries give notice to trespassers that they are encroaching on the organization's cyberspace. Sound principles of authentication and authorization can help organizations protect valuable information and systems. These control methods and technologies employ multiple layers or factors to protect against unauthorized access and trespass.

The classic perpetrator of espionage or trespass is the **hacker,** who is frequently glamorized in fictional accounts as a person who stealthily manipulates a maze of computer networks, systems, and data to find information that solves the mystery and heroically saves the day. However, the true life of the hacker is far more mundane. The profile of the typical hacker has shifted from that of a 13- to 18-year-old male with limited parental supervision who spends all of his free time on the computer to a person with fewer known attributes (see Figure 2-7). In the real world, a hacker frequently spends long hours examining the types and structures of targeted systems and uses skill, guile, or fraud to attempt to bypass controls placed on information owned by someone else.

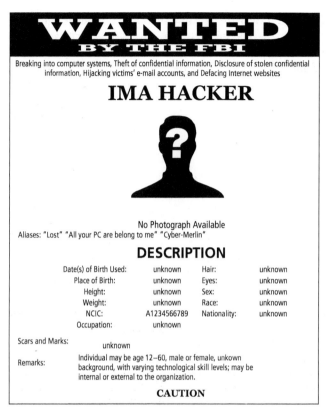

Figure 2-7 Contemporary hacker profile

Hacker Skills and Abilities

Hackers possess a wide range of skill levels, as with most technology users. However, most hackers are grouped into two general categories: the **expert hacker** and the **novice hacker**. The expert hacker is usually a master of several programming languages, networking protocols, and operating systems, and exhibits a mastery of the technical environment of the chosen targeted system. As described in the nearby Offline feature *Hack PCWeek*, expert hackers are extremely talented and usually devote extensive time and energy attempting to break into other people's information systems. Even though this example occurred several years ago, it illustrates that systems and networks are still attacked and compromised using the same techniques.

In March 2016, General Motors (GM) invited computer researchers to look for vulnerabilities in the software used in its vehicles and Web site, offering a reward to anyone who found an undocumented issue. In April 2015, the U.S. government did the same thing, inviting hackers to attack the Pentagon, of all places. This type of "bug bounty" program is an effort to convince both ethical and unethical hackers to help rather than hinder organizations in their security efforts. Other recent companies that invited such attacks include Tesla Motors, Inc., the ride-share company Uber, and Google.

Once an expert hacker chooses a target system, the likelihood is high that he or she will successfully enter the system. Fortunately for the many poorly protected organizations in the world, there are substantially fewer expert hackers than novice hackers.

A new category of hacker has emerged over the last few years. The **professional hacker** seeks to conduct attacks for personal benefit or the benefit of an employer, which is typically a crime organization or illegal government operation (see the section on cyberterrorism). The professional hacker should not be confused with the **penetration tester**, who has authorization from an organization to test its information systems and network defense, and is expected to provide detailed reports of the findings. The primary differences between professional hackers and penetration testers are the authorization provided and the ethical professionalism displayed.

 For more information about hacking, see the master's thesis of Steven Kleinknecht, "Hacking hackers: Ethnographic insights into the hacker subculture—Definition, ideology and argot," which you can find online either by searching on the title or linking to https://macsphere .mcmaster.ca/handle/11375/10956.

Expert hackers often become dissatisfied with attacking systems directly and turn their attention to writing software. These programs are automated exploits that allow novice hackers to act as **script kiddies** or **packet monkeys**. The good news is that if an expert hacker can post a script tool where a script kiddie or packet monkey can find it, then systems and security administrators can find it, too. The developers of protection software and hardware and the service providers who keep defensive systems up to date also stay informed about the latest in exploit scripts. As a result of preparation and continued vigilance, attacks conducted by scripts are usually predictable and can be adequately defended against.

OFFLINE

Hack PCWeek

On September 20, 1999, PCWeek did the unthinkable: It set up two computers, one Linux-based, one Windows NT-based, and challenged members of the hacking community to be the first to crack either system, deface the posted Web page, and claim a $1,000 reward. Four days later, the Linux-based computer was hacked. Figure 2-8 shows the configuration of *www.hackpcweek.com*, which is no longer functional. The following article provides the technical details of how the hack was accomplished not by a compromise of the root operating system, but by the exploitation of an add-on CGI script with improper security checks.

In just under 20 hours, the hacker, known as JFS and hailing from Gibraltar (a.k.a. the Rock), used his advanced knowledge of the Common Gateway Interface protocol (CGI) to gain control over the target server. He began as most attackers do, with a standard port scan, finding only the HTTP port 80 open. A more detailed analysis of the Web servers revealed no additional information.

"Port scanning reveals TCP-based servers, such as telnet, FTP, DNS, and Apache, any of which are potential access points for an attacker," wrote Pankaj Chowdhry in PCWeek. "Further testing revealed that most of the potentially interesting services refused connections, with JFS speculating that TCP Wrappers was used to provide access control. The Web server port, 80/TCP, had to be open for Web access to succeed. JFS next used a simple trick. If you send GET X HTTP/1.0 to a Web server, it

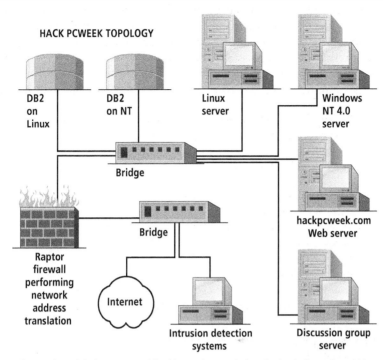

HACK PCWEEK TOPOLOGY

The topology of the honeynet used for this exercise was designed to be similar to that which an administrator might put into a real production site. It was built without esoteric defenses, sticking to standard firewall and network approaches.

Figure 2-8 Hack PCWeek

will send back an error message (unless there is a file named X) along with the standard Web server header. The header contains interesting facts, such as the type and version of the Web server, and sometimes the host operating system and architecture.... As the header information is part of the Web server standard, you can get this from just about any Web server, including IIS."[11]

He then methodically mapped out the target, starting with the directory server, using the publicly offered WWW pages. He identified commercial applications and scripts. Because he had learned nothing useful with the networking protocol analyses, he focused on vulnerabilities in the dominant commercial application served on the system, PhotoAds. He was able to access the source code, as it was offered with the product's sale. With this knowledge, JFS was able to find, identify, and look at the environment configuration script, but little else.

JFS then started his effort to exploit known server-side vulnerabilities such as the use of script includes and mod_PERL embedded commands. When that did not pan out with his first attempt, he kept on, trying the process with every field to find that a PERL regexp was in place to filter out most input before it was processed.

(continues)

JFS was able to locate just one user-assigned variable that wasn't being screened properly for malformed content. This single flaw encouraged him to keep up his effort.

JFS had located an ENV variable in the HTTP REFERER that was left unprotected. He first tried to use it with a server-side include or mod_PERL embedded command to launch some code of his choosing. However, these services were not configured on the machine.

JFS continued to poke and prod through the system configuration, looking specifically for vulnerabilities in the PhotoAds CGI scripts. He then turned his attention to looking at open() and system() calls. Dead end.

JFS tried post commands, but it stripped out one of the necessary components of the hack string, the % sign, making the code fail to function. He then tried uploading files, but the file name variable was again being filtered by a regexp, and they were just placed into a different directory and renamed anyway. He eventually gave up trying to get around the rename function.

After extensive work to create a C-based executable and smuggle it into the server, constantly battling to minimize the file size to the 8,190-byte restriction imposed on the get command, JFS hit another dead end, and turned his attention to gaining root access.

"Using the bugtraq service, he found a cron exploit for which patches hadn't been applied," Chowdhry wrote. "He modified the hack to get a suidroot. This got him root access—and the ability to change the home page to the chilling: 'This site has been hacked. JFS was here.'"[12]

Game over.

There are a few well-documented cases of unskilled hackers getting caught. In February 2000, Michael Calce, a.k.a. Mafiaboy, a 15-year-old Canadian, was responsible for a series of widely publicized denial-of-service attacks on prominent Web sites. He pleaded guilty to 56 counts of computer mischief and was sentenced to eight months of open custody (house arrest), one year of probation with restricted Internet access, and to pay $250 to charity.[13] His downfall came from his inability to delete the system logs that tracked his activity and his need to brag about his exploits in chat rooms.

The most notorious hacker in recent times is Kevin Mitnick, whose history is highlighted in the nearby Offline feature. While Mitnick was considered an expert hacker by most, he often used social engineering rather than technical skills to collect information for his attacks.

 For more information on Kevin Mitnick and his "pro-security" consulting practice, visit http:// mitnicksecurity.com/.

Escalation of Privileges Once an attacker gains access to a system, the next step is to increase his or her privileges (**privilege escalation**). While most accounts associated with a system have only rudimentary "use" permissions and capabilities, the attacker needs administrative or "root" privileges. These privileges allow attackers to access information, modify the system itself to view all information in it, and hide their activities by modifying system logs. The escalation of privileges is a skill set in and of itself. However, just as novice hackers can use tools to gain access, they can use tools to escalate privileges.

A common example of privilege escalation is called **jailbreaking** or **rooting**. Owners of certain smartphones can download and use particular tools to gain control over system functions, often against the original intentions of the designers. The term *jailbreaking* is more commonly associated with Apple's iOS devices, while the term *rooting* is more common with Android-based devices. Apple's tight controls over its iOS operating system prohibited other developers from creating applications for iOS devices. In 2010, the U.S. Copyright office issued a statement specifying that jailbreaking a smartphone was legal as a special exemption under the Digital Millennium Copyright Act, but jailbreaking a tablet (such as the iPad) was not.[14] Apple continues to insist that jailbreaking its devices violates the warranty and thus should not be attempted.

❯ Hacker Variants

Key Terms

cracker A hacker who intentionally removes or bypasses software copyright protection designed to prevent unauthorized duplication or use.

phreaker A hacker who manipulates the public telephone system to make free calls or disrupt services.

Other terms for system rule breakers may be less familiar. The term **cracker** is now commonly associated with software copyright bypassing and password decryption. With the removal of the copyright protection, software can be easily distributed and installed. With the decryption of user passwords from stolen system files, user accounts can be illegally accessed. In current usage, the terms *hacker* and *cracker* both denote criminal intent.

OFFLINE

Notorious Outlaws: Mitnick and Snowden

Among the most notorious hackers to date is Kevin Mitnick. The son of divorced parents, Mitnick grew up in an unremarkable middle-class environment. He got his start as a phreaker, later expanding his malicious activities to target computer companies. After physically breaking into the Pacific Bell Computer Center for Mainframe Operations, he was arrested. Mitnick, then 17, was convicted of the destruction of data and theft of equipment, and sentenced to three months in

(continues)

juvenile detention and a year's probation. He was arrested again in 1983 at the University of Southern California, where he was caught breaking into Pentagon computers. His next hacking battle pitched him against the FBI, where his unusual defense of computer addiction resulted in a one-year prison sentence and six months of counseling. In 1992 an FBI search of his residence resulted in charges of illegally accessing a phone company's computer, but this time Mitnick disappeared before his trial. In 1995, he was finally tracked down and arrested. Because he was a known flight risk, he was held without bail for nearly five years, eight months of it in solitary confinement. Afraid he would never get to trial, he eventually pleaded guilty to wire fraud, computer fraud, and intercepting communications. He was required to get permission to travel or use any technology until January 2003. His newest job is on the lecture circuit, where he speaks out in support of information security and against hacking.[15]

Another notorious case involved Edward Snowden and the leak of a significantly large trove of classified intelligence. In 2009, Snowden began working as a contractor for Dell in service to a contract with the National Security Agency. In April 2012, Snowden began collecting classified documents that described the U.S. government's activities in amassing intelligence that purportedly included proscribed surveillance of the domestic activities of U.S. citizens. After consulting with several journalists in early 2013, he changed employers, working at the NSA as a contractor for Booz Allen Hamilton. He began sending copies of these and other documents to the journalists. In June 2013, Snowden was fired by Booz Allen Hamilton and fled from Hawaii to Hong Kong, and the government charges against him began to mount. The public debate about Snowden and NSA wiretap and surveillance activities continues—some perceive Snowden as a traitor, releasing critical national intelligence to the nation's adversaries, while others view him as a patriot, pursuing an ideal in uncovering unconstitutional government misadventure.[16]

Phreakers grew in fame in the 1970s when they developed devices called blue boxes that enabled them to make free calls from pay phones. Later, red boxes were developed to simulate the tones of coins falling in a pay phone, and finally black boxes emulated the line voltage. With the advent of digital communications, these boxes became practically obsolete. Even with the loss of the colored box technologies, however, phreakers continue to cause problems for all telephone systems.

In addition to the Hack PCWeek competition described earlier in this chapter, numerous other "hacker challenges" are designed to provide targets to people who want to test their hacking abilities. For example, *www.hackthissite.org* promotes a "free, safe, and legal training ground for hackers to test and expand their hacking skills."[17] Interestingly, a site designed to support hacking requires user registration and compliance with a legal disclaimer.

❯ Password Attacks

> **Key Terms**
>
> **10.4 password rule** An industry recommendation for password structure and strength that specifies passwords should be at least 10 characters long and contain at least one uppercase letter, one lowercase letter, one number, and one special character.
>
> **brute force password attack** An attempt to guess a password by attempting every possible combination of characters and numbers in it.
>
> **cracking** Attempting to reverse-engineer, remove, or bypass a password or other access control protection, such as the copyright protection on software. See *cracker*.
>
> **dictionary password attack** A variation of the brute force password attack that attempts to narrow the range of possible passwords guessed by using a list of common passwords and possibly including attempts based on the target's personal information.
>
> **rainbow table** A table of hash values and their corresponding plaintext values that can be used to look up password values if an attacker is able to steal a system's encrypted password file.

Password attacks fall under the category of espionage or trespass just as lock-picking falls under breaking and entering. Attempting to guess or reverse-calculate a password is often called **cracking**. There are a number of alternative approaches to password cracking:

- Brute force
- Dictionary
- Rainbow tables
- Social engineering

Brute Force The application of computing and network resources to try every possible password combination is called a **brute force password attack**. If attackers can narrow the field of target accounts, they can devote more time and resources to these accounts. This is one reason to always change the password of the manufacturer's default administrator account.

Brute force password attacks are rarely successful against systems that have adopted the manufacturer's recommended security practices. Controls that limit the number of unsuccessful access attempts within a certain time are very effective against brute force attacks. As shown in Table 2-6, the strength of a password determines its ability to withstand a brute force attack. Using best practice policies like the **10.4 password rule** and systems that allow case-sensitive passwords can greatly enhance their strength.

Dictionary Attacks The **dictionary password attack**, or simply dictionary attack, is a variation of the brute force attack that narrows the field by using a dictionary of common passwords and includes information related to the target user, such as names of relatives or pets, and familiar numbers such as phone numbers, addresses, and even Social Security numbers. Organizations can use similar dictionaries to disallow passwords during the reset process and thus guard against passwords that are easy to guess. In addition, rules requiring numbers and special characters in passwords make the dictionary attack less effective.

Case-Insensitive Passwords Using a Standard Alphabet Set (No Numbers or Special Characters)		
Password Length	**Odds of Cracking: 1 in (Based on Number of Characters ^ Password Length):**	**Estimated Time to Crack***
8	208,827,064,576	1.01 seconds
9	5,429,503,678,976	26.2 seconds
10	141,167,095,653,376	11.4 minutes
11	3,670,344,486,987,780	4.9 hours
12	95,428,956,661,682,200	5.3 days
13	2,481,152,873,203,740,000	138.6 days
14	64,509,974,703,297,200,000	9.9 years
15	1,677,259,342,285,730,000,000	256.6 years
16	43,608,742,899,428,900,000,000	6,672.9 years

Case-Sensitive Passwords Using a Standard Alphabet Set (with Numbers and 20 Special Characters)		
Password Length	**Odds of Cracking: 1 in (Based on Number of Characters ^ Password Length):**	**Estimated Time to Crack***
8	2,044,140,858,654,980	2.7 hours
9	167,619,550,409,708,000	9.4 days
10	13,744,803,133,596,100,000	2.1 years
11	1,127,073,856,954,880,000,000	172.5 years
12	92,420,056,270,299,900,000,000	14,141.9 years
13	7,578,444,614,164,590,000,000,000	1,159,633.8 years
14	621,432,458,361,496,000,000,000,000	95,089,967.6 years
15	50,957,461,585,642,700,000,000,000,000	7,797,377,343.5 years
16	4,178,511,850,022,700,000,000,000,000,000	639,384,942,170.1 years

Table 2-6 Password Power

*Estimated Time to Crack is based on a 2015-era PC with an Intel i7-6700K Quad Core CPU performing 207.23 Dhrystone GIPS (giga/billion instructions per second) at 4.0 GHz.

Rainbow Tables A far more sophisticated and potentially much faster password attack is possible if the attacker can gain access to an encrypted password file, such as the Security Account Manager (SAM) data file. While these password files contain hashed representations of users' passwords—not the actual passwords, and thus cannot be used by themselves—the hash values for a wide variety of passwords can be looked up in a database known as a **rainbow table**. These plain text files can be quickly searched, and a hash value and its corresponding plaintext value can be easily located. Chapter 8, "Cryptography," describes plaintext, ciphertext, and hash values in greater detail.

Did you know that a space can change how a word is used? For example, plaintext is a special term from the field of cryptography that refers to textual information a cryptosystem will transmit securely as ciphertext. It is plaintext before it is encrypted, and it is plaintext after it is decrypted, but it is ciphertext in between. However, the phrase plain text is a term from the field of information systems that differentiates the text characters you type from the formatted text you see in a document. For more information about cryptosystems and cryptography, see Chapter 8.

Social Engineering Password Attacks While social engineering is discussed in detail later in the section called "Human Error or Failure," it is worth mentioning here as a mechanism to gain password information. Attackers posing as an organization's IT professionals may attempt to gain access to systems information by contacting low-level employees and offering to help with their computer issues. After all, what employee doesn't have issues with computers? By posing as a friendly helpdesk or repair technician, the attacker asks employees for their usernames and passwords, then uses the information to gain access to organizational systems. Some even go so far as to actually resolve the user's issues. Social engineering is much easier than hacking servers for password files.

Forces of Nature

Forces of nature, sometimes called acts of God, can present some of the most dangerous threats because they usually occur with little warning and are beyond the control of people. These threats, which include events such as fires, floods, earthquakes, landslides, mudslides, windstorms, sandstorms, solar flares, and lightning as well as volcanic eruptions and insect infestations, can disrupt not only people's lives but the storage, transmission, and use of information. Severe weather was suspected in three 2008 outages in the Mediterranean that affected Internet access to the Middle East and India. Knowing a region's susceptibility to certain natural disasters is a critical planning component when selecting new facilities for an organization or considering the location of off-site data backup.

Because it is not possible to avoid threats from forces of nature, organizations must implement controls to limit damage and prepare contingency plans for continued operations, such as disaster recovery plans, business continuity plans, and incident response plans. These threats and plans are discussed in detail in Chapter 5, "Planning for Security." Protection mechanisms are discussed in additional detail in Chapter 9, "Physical Security."

Another term you may encounter, *force majeure*, can be translated as "superior force," which includes forces of nature as well as civil disorder and acts of war.

> Fire

A structural fire can damage a building with computing equipment that comprises all or part of an information system. Damage can also be caused by smoke or by water from sprinkler systems or firefighters. This threat can usually be mitigated with fire casualty insurance or business interruption insurance.

❯ Floods

Water can overflow into an area that is normally dry, causing direct damage to all or part of the information system or the building that houses it. A flood might also disrupt operations by interrupting access to the buildings that house the information system. This threat can sometimes be mitigated with flood insurance or business interruption insurance.

❯ Earthquakes

An earthquake is a sudden movement of the earth's crust caused by volcanic activity or the release of stress accumulated along geologic faults. Earthquakes can cause direct damage to the information system or, more often, to the building that houses it. They can also disrupt operations by interrupting access to the buildings that house the information system. In 2006, a large earthquake just off the coast of Taiwan severed several underwater communications cables, shutting down Internet access for more than a month in China, Hong Kong, Taiwan, Singapore, and other countries throughout the Pacific Rim. In 2013, major earthquakes and the resulting tsunami severed cables around Japan. In 2016, several undersea cables around Singapore were damaged, resulting in substantial loss of communications capacity to the island. Losses due to earthquakes can sometimes be mitigated with casualty insurance or business interruption insurance, but earthquakes usually are covered by a separate policy.

❯ Lightning

Lightning is an abrupt, discontinuous natural electric discharge in the atmosphere. Lightning usually damages all or part of the information system and its power distribution components. It can also cause fires or other damage to the building that houses the information system, and it can disrupt operations by interfering with access to those buildings. In 2012, a lightning strike to a communications cable near Fort Wayne, Indiana, left almost 100,000 residents without phone and Internet access. Damage from lightning can usually be prevented with specialized lightning rods placed strategically on and around the organization's facilities and by installing special circuit protectors in the organization's electrical service. Losses from lightning may be mitigated with multipurpose casualty insurance or business interruption insurance.

❯ Landslides or Mudslides

The downward slide of a mass of earth and rock can directly damage the information system or, more likely, the building that houses it. Landslides or mudslides also disrupt operations by interfering with access to the buildings that house the information system. This threat can sometimes be mitigated with casualty insurance or business interruption insurance.

❯ Tornados or Severe Windstorms

A tornado is a rotating column of air that can be more than a mile wide and whirl at destructively high speeds. Usually accompanied by a funnel-shaped downward extension of a cumulonimbus cloud, tornados can directly damage all or part of the information system or, more likely, the building that houses it. Tornadoes can also interrupt access to the buildings that house the information system. Wind shear is a much smaller and linear wind effect, but it can have similar devastating consequences. These threats can sometimes be mitigated with casualty insurance or business interruption insurance.

› Hurricanes, Typhoons, and Tropical Depressions

A severe tropical cyclone that originates in equatorial regions of the Atlantic Ocean or Caribbean Sea is referred to as a hurricane, and one that originates in eastern regions of the Pacific Ocean is called a typhoon. Many hurricanes and typhoons originate as tropical depressions—collections of multiple thunderstorms under specific atmospheric conditions. Excessive rainfall and high winds from these storms can directly damage all or part of the information system or, more likely, the building that houses it. Organizations in coastal or low-lying areas may suffer flooding as well. These storms may also disrupt operations by interrupting access to the buildings that house the information system. This threat can sometimes be mitigated with casualty insurance or business interruption insurance.

› Tsunamis

A tsunami is a very large ocean wave caused by an underwater earthquake or volcanic eruption. These events can directly damage the information system or the building that houses it. Organizations in coastal areas may experience tsunamis. They may also disrupt operations through interruptions in access or electrical power to the buildings that house the information system. This threat can sometimes be mitigated with casualty insurance or business interruption insurance.

While you might think a tsunami is a remote threat, much of the world's coastal area is under some threat from such an event. In 2011, the Fukushima Daiichi nuclear disaster resulted from an earthquake and subsequent tsunami; the disruption to the Japanese economy directly and indirectly affected much of the world. The United States coastline has exposure to tsunamis caused by severe earthquakes or landslides that might begin across the Atlantic Ocean, Pacific Ocean, or the Gulf of Mexico.

To read about technology used to save lives after tsunamis, visit the Web site of NOAA's National Weather Service Pacific Tsunami Warning Center. From there you can find out how state-of-the-art satellite, computer, and network systems are used to notify people in the Pacific Rim about emergency tsunami events. You can see the Web page at ptwc.weather.gov/.

› Electrostatic Discharge

Electrostatic discharge (ESD), also known as static electricity, is usually little more than a nuisance. However, the mild static shock we receive when walking across a carpet can be costly or dangerous when it ignites flammable mixtures and damages costly electronic components. An employee walking across a carpet on a cool, dry day can generate up to 12,000 volts of electricity. Humans cannot detect static electricity until it reaches around 1,500 volts. When it comes into contact with technology, especially computer hard drives, ESD can be catastrophic; damage can be caused by as little as 10 volts.[18]

Static electricity can draw dust into clean-room environments or cause products to stick together. The cost of ESD-damaged electronic devices and interruptions to service can be millions of dollars for critical systems. ESD can also cause significant loss of production time in information processing. Although ESD can disrupt information systems, it is not usually an insurable loss unless covered by business interruption insurance.

> Dust Contamination

Some environments are not friendly to the hardware components of information systems. Accumulation of dust and debris inside systems can dramatically reduce the effectiveness of cooling mechanisms and potentially cause components to overheat. Some specialized technology, such as CD or DVD optical drives, can suffer failures due to excessive dust contamination. Because it can shorten the life of information systems or cause unplanned downtime, this threat can disrupt normal operations.

> Solar Activity

While most of us are protected by the earth's atmosphere from the more dramatic effects of solar activity, such as radiation and solar flares, our communications satellites bear the brunt of such exposure. Extreme solar activity can affect the power grids, however, as in Quebec in 1989, when "high currents in the magnetosphere induced high currents in power lines, blowing out electric transformers and power stations." Business communications that are heavily dependent on satellites should consider the potential for disruption.

Human Error or Failure

This category includes acts performed without intent or malicious purpose or in ignorance by an authorized user. When people use information systems, mistakes happen. Similar errors happen when people fail to follow established policy. Inexperience, improper training, and incorrect assumptions are just a few things that can cause human error or failure. Regardless of the cause, even innocuous mistakes can produce extensive damage. For example, a simple keyboarding error can cause worldwide Internet outages:

> *In April 1997, the core of the Internet suffered a disaster. Internet service providers lost connectivity with other ISPs due to an error in a routine Internet router-table update process. The resulting outage effectively shut down a major portion of the Internet for at least twenty minutes. It has been estimated that about 45 percent of Internet users were affected. In July 1997, the Internet went through yet another more critical global shutdown for millions of users. An accidental upload of a corrupt database to the Internet's root domain servers occurred. Since this provides the ability to address hosts on the net by name (i.e., eds.com), it was impossible to send e-mail or access Web sites within the .com and .net domains for several hours. The .com domain comprises a majority of the commercial enterprise users of the Internet.*[19]

One of the greatest threats to an organization's information security is its own employees, as they are the threat agents closest to the information. Because employees use data and information in everyday activities to conduct the organization's business, their mistakes represent a serious threat to the confidentiality, integrity, and availability of data—even, as Figure 2-9 suggests, relative to threats from outsiders. Employee mistakes can easily lead to revelation of

Tommy Twostory,
convicted burglar

Elite Skillz,
wannabe hacker

Harriett Allthumbs,
confused the copier with the shredder
when preparing the annual sales report

Figure 2-9 The biggest threat—acts of human error or failure

Source: © iStockphoto/BartCo, © iStockphoto/sdominick, © iStockphoto/mikkelwilliam.

classified data, entry of erroneous data, accidental deletion or modification of data, storage of data in unprotected areas, and failure to protect information. Leaving classified information in unprotected areas, such as on a desktop, on a Web site, or even in the trash can, is as much a threat as a person who seeks to exploit the information, because the carelessness can create a vulnerability and thus an opportunity for an attacker. However, if someone damages or destroys data on purpose, the act belongs to a different threat category.

In 2014, New York's Metro-North railroad lost power when one of the two power supply units was taken offline for repairs. Repair technicians apparently failed to note the interconnection between the systems, resulting in a two-hour power loss. Similarly, in 2016, Telstra customers in several major cities across Australia lost communications for more than two hours due to an undisclosed human error.

Human error or failure often can be prevented with training, ongoing awareness activities, and controls. These controls range from simple activities, such as requiring the user to type a critical command twice, to more complex procedures, such as verifying commands by a second party. An example of the latter is the performance of key recovery actions in PKI systems. Many military applications have robust, dual-approval controls built in. Some systems that have a high potential for data loss or system outages use expert systems to monitor human actions and request confirmation of critical inputs.

Humorous acronyms are commonly used when attributing problems to human error. They include PEBKAC (problem exists between keyboard and chair), PICNIC (problem in chair, not in computer), and ID-10-T error (idiot).

❯ Social Engineering

In the context of information security, **social engineering** is used by attackers to gain system access or information that may lead to system access. There are several social engineering techniques, which usually involve a perpetrator posing as a person who is higher in the organizational hierarchy than the victim. To prepare for this false representation, the perpetrator already may have used social engineering tactics against others in the organization to collect seemingly unrelated information that, when used together, makes the false representation more credible. For instance, anyone can check a company's Web site or even call the main switchboard to get the name of the CIO; an attacker may then obtain even more information by calling others in the company and falsely asserting his or her authority by mentioning the CIO's name. Social engineering attacks may involve people posing as new employees or as current employees requesting assistance to prevent getting fired. Sometimes attackers threaten, cajole, or beg to sway the target. The infamous hacker Kevin Mitnick, whose exploits are detailed earlier in this chapter, once stated:

> *People are the weakest link. You can have the best technology; firewalls, intrusion-detection systems, biometric devices ... and somebody can call an unsuspecting employee. That's all she wrote, baby. They got everything.*[20]

Advance-fee Fraud Another social engineering attack called the **advance-fee fraud** (AFF), internationally known as the 4-1-9 fraud, is named after a section of the Nigerian penal code. The perpetrators of 4-1-9 schemes often use the names of fictitious companies, such as the Nigerian National Petroleum Company. Alternatively, they may invent other entities, such as a bank, government agency, long-lost relative, lottery, or other nongovernmental organization. See Figure 2-10 for a sample letter used for this type of scheme.

The scam is notorious for stealing funds from credulous people, first by requiring them to participate in a proposed money-making venture by sending money up front, and then by

2

NIGERIA NATIONAL PETROLEUM CORPORATION
PETROLEUM AND PROJECT DIVISION
TEL: +234-80-33084057, 234-1-4805653, FAX: +234-1-2882183,234-1-7591061
P.M.B 2071, LAGOS – NIGERIA.

29TH JANUARY, 2002

DEAR SIR

This letter is not intended to cause any embarrassment in whatever form, rather is compelled to contact your esteemed self, following the knowledge of your high repute and trustworthiness. Firstly, I must solicit your confidentiality, this is by the virtue of its' nature as being utterly confidential and top secret though I know that a transaction of this magnitude will make anyone apprehensive and worried, but I am assuring you that all will be well at the end of the day. A bold step taken shall not be regretted I assure you.

I am Mr. Tony Okeke and I head a seven man tender board in charge of contract awards and payment approvals, I came to know of you in search of a reliable and reputable person to handle a very confidential business transaction which involves the transfer of a huge sum of money to foreign account requiring maximum confidence. My colleagues and I are top officials of the NIGERIA NATIONAL PETROLEUM CORPORATION (NNPC). OUR DUTIES INCLUDE VETTING, EVALUATION AND FORESEEING THE MAINTENANCE OF THE REFINERIES IN ALL THE DESIGNATED OIL PIPELINES. We are therefore soliciting for your assistance to enable us transfer into your account the said funds. Our country loses a lot of money everyday that is why the international community is very careful and warning their citizens to be careful but I tell you "A TRIAL WILL CONVINCE YOU".

The source of the fund is as follows; during the last military regime here in Nigeria this committee awarded a contract of US$400million to a group of five construction companies on behalf of the NIGERIA NATIONAL PETROLEUM CORPORATION for the construction of the oil pipelines in Kaduna, Port-Harcourt, Warri refineries. During this process my colleagues and I deliberately inflated the total contract sum to the tune US$428million with the intention of sharing the inflated sum of US$28. The government has since approved the sum of US$428 for us as the contract sum, but since the contract is only worth US$400million, the remaining US$28million is what we intend to transfer to reliable and safe offshore account, we are prohibited to operate foreign account in our names since we are still in government. Thus, making it impossible for us to acquire the money in our name right now, I have therefore been delegated as a matter of trust by my colleagues to look for an oversea partner into whose account we can transfer the sum of US$28million.

My colleagues and I have decided that if you/your company can be the beneficiary of this funds on our behalf, you or your company will retain 20% of the total sum US$28million while 75% will be for us the officials and remaining 5% will be used for offsetting all debts/expenses incurred during this transaction.

We have decided that this transaction can only proceed under the following conditions:
1. That you treat this transaction with utmost secrecy and confidentiality and conviction of your transparent honesty.
2. That upon the receipt of the funds you will release the funds as instructed by us after you have removed your share of 20%. Please acknowledge the receipt of this letter using the above telephone and fax numbers. I will bring you into the nomenclature of this transaction when I have heard from you.

Your urgent response will be highly appreciated as we catching on the next payment schedule for the financial quarter. Please be assured that this transaction is 100% legal/risk free, only trust can make the reality of this transaction.

Best Regards,

Tony Okeke
MR. TONY OKEKE

Figure 2-10 Example of a Nigerian 4-1-9 fraud letter

soliciting an endless series of fees. These 4-1-9 schemes are even suspected to involve kidnapping, extortion, and murder. According to Ultrascan Advanced Global Investigations, more than $82 billion had been swindled from victims as of 2014.

For more information on AFF, go to the Advance Fee Fraud Coalition's Web site at http:// affcoalition.org.

Phishing Many other attacks involve social engineering. One such attack is described by the Computer Emergency Response Team/Coordination Center (CERT/CC):

CERT/CC has received several incident reports concerning users receiving requests to take an action that results in the capturing of their password. The request could come in the form of an e-mail message, a broadcast, or a telephone call. The latest ploy instructs the user to run a "test" program, previously installed by the intruder, which will prompt the user for his or her password.

> *When the user executes the program, the user's name and password are e-mailed to a remote site. These messages can appear to be from a site administrator or root. In reality, they may have been sent by an individual at a remote site, who is trying to gain access or additional access to the local machine via the user's account.*[21]

While this attack may seem crude to experienced users, the fact is that *many* e-mail users have fallen for it (refer to CERT Advisory CA-91.03). These tricks and similar variants are called **phishing** attacks. They gained national recognition with the AOL phishing attacks that were widely reported in the late 1990s, in which attackers posing as AOL technicians attempted to get logon credentials from AOL subscribers. The practice became so widespread that AOL added a warning to all official correspondence that no AOL employee would ever ask for password or billing information. Variants of phishing attacks can leverage their purely social engineering aspects with a technical angle, such as that used in pharming, spoofing, and redirection attacks, as discussed later in this chapter.

Another variant is **spear phishing**. While normal phishing attacks target as many recipients as possible, a spear phisher sends a message to a small group or even one person. The message appears to be from an employer, a colleague, or other legitimate correspondent. This attack sometimes targets users of a certain product or Web site. When this attack is directed at a specific person, it is called spear phishing. When the intended victim is a senior executive, it may be called whaling or whale phishing.

Phishing attacks use two primary techniques, often in combination with one another: URL manipulation and Web site forgery. In Uniform Resource Locator (URL) manipulation, attackers send an HTML embedded e-mail message or a hyperlink whose HTML code opens a forged Web site. For example, Figure 2-11 shows an e-mail that appears to have come from Regions Bank. Phishers typically use the names of large banks or retailers

Figure 2-11 Phishing example: lure

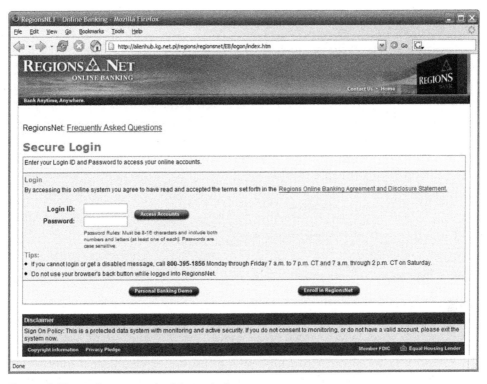

Figure 2-12 Phishing example: fake Web site

because potential targets are more likely to have accounts with them. In Figure 2-12, the link appears to be to RegionsNetOnline, but the HTML code actually links the user to a Web site in Poland. This is a very simple example; many phishing attackers use sophisticated simulated Web sites in their e-mails, usually copied from actual Web sites. Companies that are commonly used in phishing attacks include AOL, Bank of America, Microsoft, and Wachovia.

In the forged Web site shown in Figure 2-12, the page looks legitimate; when users click either of the bottom two buttons—*Personal Banking Demo* or *Enroll in RegionsNet*—they are directed to the authentic bank Web page. The *Access Accounts* button, however, links to another simulated page that looks just like the real bank login Web page. When victims type their banking ID and password, the attacker records that information and displays a message that the Web site is now offline. The attackers can use the recorded credentials to perform transactions, including fund transfers, bill payments, or loan requests.

People can use their Web browsers to report suspicious Web sites that might have been used in phishing attacks. Figure 2-13 shows the method to report these suspicious sites using Microsoft's Internet Explorer.

Pretexting, sometimes referred to as phone phishing or voice phishing (vishing), is pure social engineering. The attacker calls a potential victim on the telephone and pretends to be

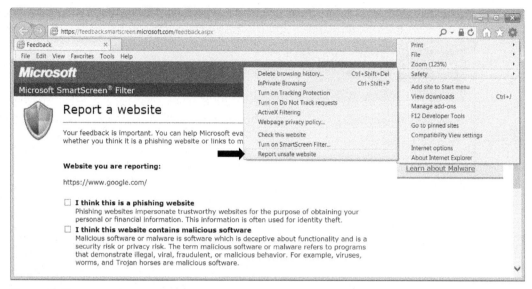

Figure 2-13   Microsoft's unsafe Web site reporting feature in Internet Explorer

Source: Microsoft. Used with permission.

an authority figure in order to gain access to private or confidential information, such as health, employment, or financial records. The attacker may impersonate someone who is known to the potential victim only by reputation. If your telephone rings and the caller ID feature shows the name of your bank, you might be more likely to reveal your account number. Likewise, if your phone displays the name of your doctor, you may be more inclined to reveal personal information than you might otherwise. Be careful; VOIP phone services have made it easy to spoof caller ID, and you can never be sure who you are talking to. Pretexting is generally considered pretending to be a person you are not, whereas phishing is pretending to represent an organization via a Web site or HTML e-mail. This can be a blurry distinction.

Information Extortion

Key Terms

information extortion The act of an attacker or trusted insider who steals or interrupts access to information from a computer system and demands compensation for its return or for an agreement not to disclose the information.

ransomware Computer software specifically designed to identify and encrypt valuable information in a victim's system in order to extort payment for the key needed to unlock the encryption.

Information extortion, also known as cyberextortion, is common in the theft of credit card numbers. For example, Web-based retailer CD Universe was victimized by a theft of data files that contained customer credit card information. The culprit was a Russian hacker named Maxus who hacked the online vendor and stole several hundred thousand credit card numbers. When the company refused to pay the $100,000 blackmail, he posted the card numbers to a Web site, offering them to the criminal community. His Web site became so popular he had to restrict access.[22]

Another incident of extortion occurred in 2008 when pharmacy benefits manager Express Scripts, Inc. fell victim to a hacker who demonstrated that he had access to 75 customer records and claimed to have access to millions more. The perpetrator demanded an undisclosed amount of money. The company notified the FBI and offered a $1 million reward for the arrest of the perpetrator. Express Scripts notified the affected customers, as required by various state laws. The company was obliged to pay undisclosed expenses for the notifications, and was required to buy credit monitoring services for its customers in some states.[23]

In 2010, Anthony Digati allegedly threatened to conduct a spam attack on the insurance company New York Life. He reportedly sent dozens of e-mails to company executives threatening to conduct a negative image campaign by sending over 6 million e-mails to people throughout the country. He then demanded approximately $200,000 to stop the attack, and next threatened to increase the demand to more than $3 million if the company ignored him. His arrest thwarted the spam attack.

In 2012, a programmer from Walachi Innovation Technologies allegedly broke into the organization's systems and changed the access passwords and codes, locking legitimate users out of the system. He then reportedly demanded $300,000 in exchange for the new codes. A court order eventually forced him to surrender the information to the organization. In Russia, a talented hacker created malware that installed inappropriate materials on an unsuspecting user's system, along with a banner threatening to notify the authorities if a bribe was not paid. At 500 rubles (about $17), victims in Russia and other countries were more willing to pay the bribe than risk prosecution by less considerate law enforcement.[24]

The latest type of attack in this category is known as **ransomware**. Ransomware is a malware attack on the host system that denies access to the user and then offers to provide a key to allow access back to the user's system and data for a fee. There are two types of ransomware: lockscreen and encryption. Lockscreen ransomware denies access to the user's system simply by disabling access to the desktop and preventing the user from bypassing the ransom screen that demands payment. Encryption ransomware is far worse, in that it encrypts some or all of a user's hard drive and then demands payment. Common phishing mechanisms to get a user to download ransomware include popups indicating that illegal information or malware was detected on the user's system, threatening to notify law enforcement, or offering to delete the offending material if the user clicks a link or button.

Sabotage or Vandalism

This category of threat involves the deliberate sabotage of a computer system or business, or acts of vandalism to destroy an asset or damage the image of an organization. These acts can range from petty vandalism by employees to organized sabotage against an organization.

Although they might not be financially devastating, attacks on the image of an organization are serious. Vandalism to a Web site can erode consumer confidence, diminishing an organization's sales, net worth, and reputation. For example, in the early hours of July 13, 2001, a group known as Fluffi Bunni left its mark on the front page of the SysAdmin, Audit, Network, Security (SANS) Institute, a cooperative research and education organization. This event was particularly embarrassing to SANS Institute management because the organization provides security instruction and certification. The defacement read, "Would you really trust these guys to teach you security?"[25] At least one member of the group was subsequently arrested by British authorities.

> Online Activism

Key Terms

cyberactivist See *hacktivist*.

cyberterrorist A hacker who attacks systems to conduct terrorist activities via networks or Internet pathways.

cyberwarfare Formally sanctioned offensive operations conducted by a government or state against information or systems of another government or state. Sometimes called information warfare.

hacktivist A hacker who seeks to interfere with or disrupt systems to protest the operations, policies, or actions of an organization or government agency.

There are innumerable reports of hackers accessing systems and damaging or destroying critical data. Hacked Web sites once made front-page news, as the perpetrators intended. The impact of these acts has lessened as the volume has increased. The Web site that acts as the clearinghouse for many hacking reports, *Attrition.org*, has stopped cataloging all Web site defacements because the frequency of such acts has outstripped the ability of the volunteers to keep the site up to date.[26]

Compared to Web site defacement, vandalism within a network is more malicious in intent and less public. Today, security experts are noticing a rise in another form of online vandalism, **hacktivist** or **cyberactivist** operations. For example, in November 2009, a group calling itself "anti-fascist hackers" defaced the Web site of Holocaust denier and Nazi sympathizer David Irving. They also released his private e-mail correspondence, secret locations of events on his speaking tour, and detailed information about people attending those events, among them members of various white supremacist organizations. This information was posted on the Web site WikiLeaks, an organization that publishes sensitive and classified information provided by anonymous sources.[27]

Figure 2-14 illustrates how Greenpeace, a well-known environmental activist organization, once used its Web presence to recruit cyberactivists.

Cyberterrorism and Cyberwarfare A much more sinister form of hacking is **cyberterrorism**. The United States and other governments are developing security measures intended to protect critical computing and communications networks as well as physical and power utility infrastructures.

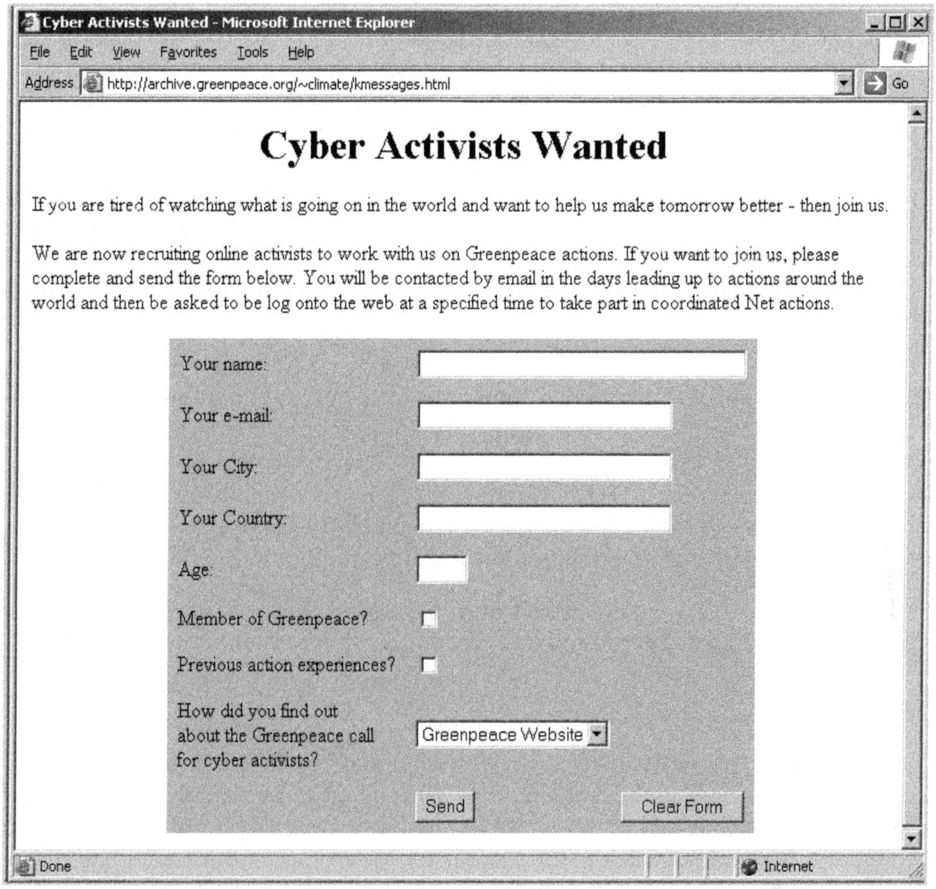

Figure 2-14 Cyberactivists wanted

> *In the 1980s, Barry Collin, a senior research fellow at the Institute for Security and Intelligence in California, coined the term "cyberterrorism" to refer to the convergence of cyberspace and terrorism. Mark Pollitt, special agent for the FBI, offers a working definition: "Cyberterrorism is the premeditated, politically motivated attacks against information, computer systems, computer programs, and data which result in violence against noncombatant targets by subnational groups or clandestine agents."*[28]

Cyberterrorism has thus far been largely limited to acts such as the defacement of NATO Web pages during the war in Kosovo. Some industry observers have taken the position that cyberterrorism is not a real threat, but instead is merely hype that distracts from more concrete and pressing information security issues that do need attention.

However, further instances of cyberterrorism have begun to surface. According to Dr. Mudawi Mukhtar Elmusharaf at the Computer Crime Research Center, "on Oct. 21, 2002, a distributed denial-of-service (DDoS) attack struck the 13 root servers that provide the primary road map for all Internet communications. Nine servers out of these thirteen were jammed. The problem was taken care of in a short period of time."[29] While this attack was significant, the results were not noticeable to most users of the Internet. A news report shortly after the event noted that "the attack, at its peak, only caused 6 percent of domain name service requests to go unanswered [... and the global] DNS system normally responds almost 100 percent of the time."[30]

Internet servers were again attacked on February 6, 2007, with four Domain Name System (DNS) servers targeted. However, the servers managed to contain the attack. It was reported that the U.S. Department of Defense was on standby to conduct a military counterattack if the cyberattack had succeeded.[31] In 2011, China confirmed the existence of a nation-sponsored cyberterrorism organization known as the Cyber Blue Team, which is used to infiltrate the systems of foreign governments.

Government officials are concerned that certain foreign countries are "pursuing cyberweapons the same way they are pursuing nuclear weapons."[32] Some of these cyberterrorist attacks are aimed at disrupting government agencies, while others seem designed to create mass havoc with civilian and commercial industry targets. However, the U.S. government conducts its own **cyberwarfare** actions, having reportedly targeted overseas efforts to develop nuclear enrichment plants by hacking into and destroying critical equipment.[33]

 For more information about the evolving threat of cyberwarfare, visit a leading think tank, the RAND Corporation, to read research reports and commentary from leaders in the field (www .rand.org/topics/cyber-warfare.html.)

Positive Online Activism Not all online activism is negative. Social media outlets, such as Facebook, MySpace, Twitter, and YouTube, are commonly used to perform fundraising, raise awareness of social issues, gather support for legitimate causes, and promote involvement. Modern business organizations try to leverage social media and online activism to improve their public image and increase awareness of socially responsible actions.

Software Attacks

Deliberate software attacks occur when an individual or group designs and deploys software to attack a system. This attack can consist of specially crafted software that attackers trick users into installing on their systems. This software can be used to overwhelm the processing capabilities of online systems or to gain access to protected systems by hidden means.

❯ Malware

Key Terms

adware Malware intended to provide undesired marketing and advertising, including popups and banners on a user's screens.

boot virus Also known as a boot sector virus, a type of virus that targets the boot sector or Master Boot Record (MBR) of a computer system's hard drive or removable storage media.

macro virus A type of virus written in a specific macro language to target applications that use the language. The virus is activated when the application's product is opened. A macro virus typically affects documents, slideshows, e-mails, or spreadsheets created by office suite applications.

malicious code See *malware*.

malicious software See *malware*.

malware Computer software specifically designed to perform malicious or unwanted actions.

memory-resident virus A virus that is capable of installing itself in a computer's operating system, starting when the computer is activated, and residing in the system's memory even after the host application is terminated. Also known as a resident virus.

non-memory-resident virus A virus that terminates after it has been activated, infected its host system, and replicated itself. NMR viruses do not reside in an operating system or memory after executing. Also known as a non-resident virus.

polymorphic threat Malware (a virus or worm) that over time changes the way it appears to antivirus software programs, making it undetectable by techniques that look for preconfigured signatures.

spyware Any technology that aids in gathering information about people or organizations without their knowledge.

Trojan horse A malware program that hides its true nature and reveals its designed behavior only when activated.

virus A type of malware that is attached to other executable programs. When activated, it replicates and propagates itself to multiple systems, spreading by multiple communications vectors. For example, a virus might send copies of itself to all users in the infected system's e-mail program.

virus hoax A message that reports the presence of a nonexistent virus or worm and wastes valuable time as employees share the message.

worm A type of malware that is capable of activation and replication without being attached to an existing program.

zero-day attack An attack that makes use of malware that is not yet known by the anti-malware software companies.

Malware is referred to as **malicious code** or **malicious software**. Other attacks that use software, like redirect attacks and denial-of-service attacks, also fall under this threat. These software components or programs are designed to damage, destroy, or deny service to targeted systems. Note that the terminology used to describe malware is often not mutually exclusive; for instance, Trojan horse malware may be delivered as a virus, a worm, or both.

Malicious code attacks include the execution of viruses, worms, Trojan horses, and active Web scripts with the intent to destroy or steal information. The most state-of-the-art malicious code attack is the polymorphic worm, or multivector worm. These attack programs use up to six known attack vectors to exploit a variety of vulnerabilities in common information system devices. Many successful malware attacks are completed using techniques that are widely known; some have been in use for years. When an attack makes use of malware that is not yet known by the anti-malware software companies, it is said to be a **zero-day attack**.

Other forms of malware include covert software applications—bots, spyware, and **adware**—that are designed to work out of users' sight or be triggered by an apparently innocuous user action. Bots are often the technology used to implement Trojan horses, logic bombs, back doors, and spyware.[34] **Spyware** is placed on a computer to secretly gather information about the user and report it. One type of spyware is a Web bug, a tiny graphic that is referenced within the Hypertext Markup Language (HTML) content of a Web page or e-mail to collect information about the user viewing the content. Another form of spyware is a tracking cookie, which is placed on users' computers to track their activity on different Web sites and create a detailed profile of their behavior.[35] Each of these hidden code components can be used to collect user information that could then be used in a social engineering or identity theft attack.

 For more information about current events in malware, visit the U.S. Computer Emergency Readiness Team (US-CERT) Web site and go to its Current Activity page, www.us-cert.gov/ncas/current-activity. US-CERT is part of the Department of Homeland Security.

Table 2-7 draws on two recent studies to list some of the malware that has had the biggest impact on computer users to date. While this table may seem out of date, the values still hold up as of mid-2016. It seems that newer malware cannot break into the all-time top 10, possibly because of the proliferation of malware variants and do-it-yourself malware kits. One security firm, Panda Security, has reported that over 27 percent of all malware ever reported was produced in 2015. It's hard for any one new malware to "break out" when so many variations are in play. It seems we are entering the days of precisely targeted malware.

Virus A computer **virus** consists of code segments (programming instructions) that perform malicious actions. This code behaves much like a virus pathogen that attacks animals

Malware	Type	Year	Estimated Number of Systems Infected	Estimated Financial Damage
MyDoom	Worm	2004	2 million	$38 billion
Klez (and variants)	Virus	2001	7.2% of Internet	$19.8 billion
ILOVEYOU	Virus	2000	10% of Internet	$5.5 billion
Sobig F	Worm	2003	1 million	$3 billion
Code Red (and CR II)	Worm	2001	400,000 servers	$2.6 billion
SQL Slammer, a.k.a. Sapphire	Worm	2003	75,000	$950 million to $1.2 billion
Melissa	Macro virus	1999	Unknown	$300 million to $600 million
CIH, a.k.a. Chernobyl	Memory-resident virus	1998	Unknown	$250 million
Storm Worm	Trojan horse virus	2006	10 million	Unknown
Conficker	Worm	2009	15 million	Unknown
Nimda	Multivector worm	2001	Unknown	Unknown
Sasser	Worm	2004	500,000 to 700,000	Unknown
Nesky	Virus	2004	Under 100,000	Unknown
Leap-A/Oompa-A	Virus	2006	Unknown (Apple)	Unknown

Table 2-7   The Most Dangerous Malware Attacks to Date[36,37]

and plants, using the cell's own replication machinery to propagate the attack beyond the initial target. The code attaches itself to an existing program and takes control of the program's access to the targeted computer. The virus-controlled target program then carries out the virus plan by replicating itself into additional targeted systems. Often, users unwittingly help viruses get into a system. Opening infected e-mail or some other seemingly trivial action can cause anything from random messages appearing on a user's screen to the destruction of entire hard drives. Just as their namesakes are passed among living bodies, computer viruses are passed from machine to machine via physical media, e-mail, or other forms of computer data transmission. When these viruses infect a machine, they may immediately scan it for e-mail applications or even send themselves to every user in the e-mail address book.

One of the most common methods of virus transmission is via e-mail attachment files. Most organizations block e-mail attachments of certain types and filter all e-mail for known viruses. Years ago, viruses were slow-moving creatures that transferred viral payloads through the cumbersome movement of diskettes from system to system. Now computers are networked, and e-mail programs prove to be fertile ground for computer viruses unless suitable controls are in place. The current software marketplace has several established vendors, such as Symantec Norton AntiVirus, Kaspersky Antivirus, AVG AntiVirus, and McAfee VirusScan, which provide applications to help control computer viruses. Microsoft's Malicious Software Removal Tools is freely available to help users of Windows operating systems remove viruses and other types of malware. Many vendors are moving to software suites that include antivirus applications and provide other malware and nonmalware protection, such as firewall protection programs.

Viruses can be classified by how they spread themselves. Among the most common types of information system viruses are the **macro virus**, which is embedded in automatically executing macro code used by word processors, spreadsheets, and database applications, and the **boot virus**, which infects the key operating system files in a computer's boot sector. Viruses can also be described by how their programming is stored and moved. Some are found as binary executables, including .exe or .com files; or as interpretable data files, such as command scripts or a specific application's document files; or both.

Alternatively, viruses may be classified as **memory-resident viruses** or **non-memory-resident viruses**, depending on whether they persist in a computer system's memory after they have been executed. Resident viruses are capable of reactivating when the computer is booted and continuing their actions until the system is shut down, only to restart the next time the system is booted.

In 2002, the author of the Melissa virus, David L. Smith of New Jersey, was convicted in U.S. federal court and sentenced to 20 months in prison, a $5,000 fine, and 100 hours of community service upon release.[38]

 For more information on computer criminals and their crimes and confections, visit http://en .wikipedia.org and search on "List of Computer Criminals."

Viruses and worms can use several attack vectors to spread copies of themselves to networked peer computers, as illustrated in Table 2-8.

Vector	Description
IP scan and attack	The infected system scans a range of IP addresses and service ports and targets several vulnerabilities known to hackers or left over from previous exploits, such as Code Red, Back Orifice, or PoizonBox.
Web browsing	If the infected system has write access to any Web pages, it makes all Web content files infectious, including .html, .asp, .cgi, and other files. Users who browse to those pages infect their machines.
Virus	Each affected machine infects common executable or script files on all computers to which it can write, which spreads the virus code to cause further infection.
Unprotected shares	Using vulnerabilities in file systems and in the way many organizations configure them, the infected machine copies the viral component to all locations it can reach.
Mass mail	By sending e-mail infections to addresses found in the address book, the affected machine infects many other users, whose mail-reading programs automatically run the virus program and infect even more systems.
Simple Network Management Protocol (SNMP)	SNMP is used for remote management of network and computer devices. By using the widely known and common passwords that were employed in early versions of this protocol, the attacking program can gain control of the device. Most vendors have closed these vulnerabilities with software upgrades.

Table 2-8 **Attack Replication Vectors**

Worms Named for the tapeworm in John Brunner's novel *The Shockwave Rider*, **worms** can continue replicating themselves until they completely fill available resources, such as memory, hard drive space, and network bandwidth. Read the nearby Offline feature about Robert Morris to learn how much damage a worm can cause. Code Red, Sircam, Nimda ("admin" spelled backwards), and Klez are examples of a class of worms that combine multiple modes of attack into a single package. Figure 2-15 shows sample

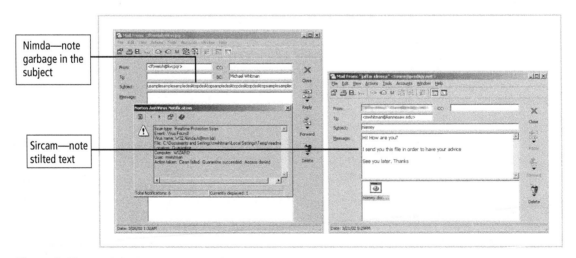

Figure 2-15 Nimda and Sircam worms

e-mails that contain the Nimda and Sircam worms. These newer worm variants contain multiple exploits that can use any predefined distribution vector to programmatically distribute the worm. (See the section on polymorphic threats later in this chapter for more details.)

Even though it happened long ago, the outbreak of Nimda in September 2001 still serves as an example of how quickly and widely malware can spread. It used five of the six vectors shown in Table 2-8 to spread itself with startling speed. TruSecure Corporation, an industry source for information security statistics and solutions, reports that Nimda spread across the Internet address space of 14 countries in less than 25 minutes.[39]

The Klez worm, shown in Figure 2-16, delivers a double-barreled payload: It has an attachment that contains the worm, and if the e-mail is viewed on an HTML-enabled browser, it attempts to deliver a macro virus. News-making attacks, such as MyDoom and Netsky, are variants of the multifaceted attack worms and viruses that exploit weaknesses in leading operating systems and applications.

The complex behavior of worms can be initiated with or without the user downloading or executing the file. Once the worm has infected a computer, it can redistribute itself to all e-mail addresses found on the infected system. Furthermore, a worm can deposit copies of itself onto all Web servers that the infected system can reach; users who subsequently visit those sites become infected. Worms also take advantage of open shares

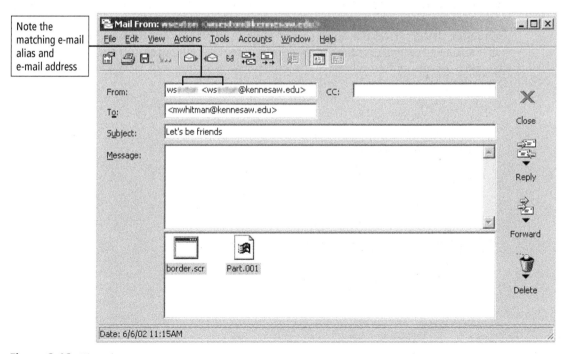

Figure 2-16 Klez worm

found on the network in which an infected system is located. The worms place working copies of their code onto the server so that users of the open shares are likely to become infected.

In 2003, Jeffrey Lee Parson, an 18-year-old high school student from Minnesota, was arrested for creating and distributing a variant of the Blaster worm called W32.Blaster-B. He was sentenced to 18 months in prison, 3 years of supervised release, and 100 hours of community service.[40] The original Blaster worm was reportedly created by a Chinese hacker group.

Trojan Horses Trojan horses are frequently disguised as helpful, interesting, or necessary pieces of software, such as the readme.exe files often included with shareware or freeware packages. Like their namesake in Greek legend, once Trojan horses are brought into a system, they become activated and can wreak havoc on the unsuspecting user. Figure 2-17 outlines a typical Trojan horse attack. Around January 20, 1999, Internet e-mail users began receiving messages with an attachment of a Trojan horse program named Happy99.exe. When the e-mail attachment was opened, a brief multimedia program displayed fireworks and the message "Happy 1999." While the fireworks display was running, the Trojan horse program was installing itself into the user's system. The program continued to propagate itself by following up every e-mail the user sent with a second e-mail to the same recipient and with the same attack program attached. A newer variant of the Trojan horse is an attack known as SMiShing, in which the victim is tricked into downloading malware onto a mobile phone via a text message. SMiShing is short for SMS phishing.

Polymorphic Threats One of the biggest challenges to fighting viruses and worms has been the emergence of polymorphic threats. A **polymorphic threat** actually evolves, changing its size and other external file characteristics to elude detection by antivirus software programs.

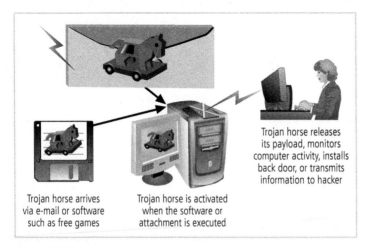

Trojan horse releases its payload, monitors computer activity, installs back door, or transmits information to hacker

Trojan horse arrives via e-mail or software such as free games

Trojan horse is activated when the software or attachment is executed

Figure 2-17 Trojan horse attacks

OFFLINE

Robert Morris and the Internet Worm[41]

In November 1988, Robert Morris, Jr. made history. He was a postgraduate student at Cornell who invented a self-propagating program called a worm. He released it onto the Internet, choosing to send it from the Massachusetts Institute of Technology (MIT) to conceal the fact that the worm was designed and created at Cornell. Morris soon discovered that the program was reproducing itself and then infecting other machines at a much greater speed than he had envisaged. The worm had a bug.

Many machines across the United States and the world stopped working or became unresponsive. When Morris realized what was occurring, he reached out for help. He contacted a friend at Harvard, and they sent a message to system administrators at Harvard that described the problem and requested guidance for how to disable the worm. However, because the networks involved were jammed from the worm infection, the message was delayed and had no effect. It was too little too late. Morris' worm had infected many computers, including those at academic institutions, military sites, and commercial concerns. The estimated cost of the infection and the aftermath was estimated at roughly $200 per site.

The worm that Morris created took advantage of flaws in the sendmail program. These widely known faults allowed debug features to be exploited, but few organizations had taken the trouble to update or patch the flaws. Staff at the University of California at Berkeley and MIT had copies of the program and reverse-engineered them to determine how it functioned. After working nonstop for about 12 hours, the teams of programmers devised a method to slow down the infection. Another method was discovered at Purdue University and widely published. Ironically, the response was hampered by the clogged state of the e-mail infrastructure caused by the worm. After a few days, things slowly started to regain normalcy and everyone wondered where the worm had originated. Morris was identified as its author in an article in the *New York Times*, even though his identity was not confirmed at that time.

Morris was convicted under the Computer Fraud and Abuse Act and sentenced to a fine, probation, community service, and court costs. His appeal was rejected in March 1991.

Virus and Worm Hoaxes As frustrating as viruses and worms are, perhaps more time and money are spent resolving **virus hoaxes**. Well-meaning people can disrupt the harmony and flow of an organization when they send group e-mails warning of supposedly dangerous viruses that don't exist. When people fail to follow virus-reporting procedures in response to a hoax, the network becomes overloaded and users waste time and energy forwarding the warning message to everyone they know, posting the message on bulletin boards, and trying to update their antivirus protection software. Some hoaxes are the chain letters or chain e-mails of the day, which are designed to annoy or bemuse the reader. They are known as "weapons of mass distraction." One of the most prominent virus hoaxes was the 1994 "Goodtimes virus," which reportedly was transmitted in an e-mail with the header "Good Times" or "goodtimes."[42] The virus never existed, and thousands of hours of employee time were wasted retransmitting the e-mail, effectively creating a denial of service.

At one time, hoaxes amounted to little more than pranks, although occasionally a sting was attached. For example, the Teddy Bear hoax tricked users into deleting necessary operating system files, which made their systems stop working. Recently, criminals have been able to monetize the hoax virus by claiming that systems are infected with malware and then selling a cure for a problem that does not exist. The perpetrator of the hoax may then offer to sell a fake antivirus program to correct the fake malware.

Several Internet resources enable people to research viruses and determine if they are fact or fiction.

 *For the latest information on real, threatening viruses and hoaxes, along with other relevant and current security information, visit the CERT Coordination Center at www.cert.org.*

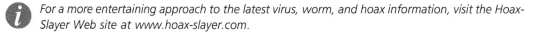 *For a more entertaining approach to the latest virus, worm, and hoax information, visit the Hoax-Slayer Web site at www.hoax-slayer.com.*

❯ Back Doors

Key Terms
_____

back door A malware payload that provides access to a system by bypassing normal access controls. A back door may also be an intentional access control bypass left by a system designer to facilitate development.
maintenance hook See *back door.*
trap door See *back door.*

Using a known or newly discovered access mechanism, an attacker can gain access to a system or network resource through a **back door**. Viruses and worms can have a payload that installs a back door or **trap door** component in a system, allowing the attacker to access the system at will with special privileges. Examples of such payloads include Subseven and Back Orifice.

Sometimes these doors are left behind by system designers or maintenance staff; such a door is referred to as a **maintenance hook**.[43] More often, attackers place a back door into a system or network they have compromised, making their return to the system that much easier the next time. A trap door is hard to detect because the person or program that places it often makes the access exempt from the system's usual audit logging features and makes every attempt to keep the back door hidden from the system's legitimate owners.

❯ Denial-of-Service (DoS) and Distributed Denial-of-Service (DDoS) Attacks

Key Terms

bot An abbreviation of *robot*, an automated software program that executes certain commands when it receives a specific input. See also *zombie*.

denial-of-service (DoS) attack An attack that attempts to overwhelm a computer target's ability to handle incoming communications, prohibiting legitimate users from accessing those systems.

distributed denial-of-service (DDoS) attack A form of DoS attack in which a coordinated stream of requests is launched against a target from many locations at the same time using bots or zombies.

zombie See *bot*.

In a **denial-of-service (DoS) attack,** the attacker sends a large number of connection or information requests to a target (see Figure 2-18). So many requests are made that the target system becomes overloaded and cannot respond to legitimate requests for service. The system may crash or simply become unable to perform ordinary functions. In a **distributed denial-of-service (DDoS) attack,** a coordinated stream of requests is launched against a target from many locations at the same time. Most DDoS attacks are preceded by a preparation phase in which many systems, perhaps thousands, are compromised. The compromised machines are turned into **bots** or **zombies,** machines that are directed remotely by the attacker (usually via a transmitted command) to participate in the

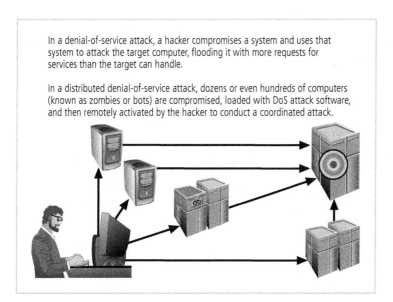

In a denial-of-service attack, a hacker compromises a system and uses that system to attack the target computer, flooding it with more requests for services than the target can handle.

In a distributed denial-of-service attack, dozens or even hundreds of computers (known as zombies or bots) are compromised, loaded with DoS attack software, and then remotely activated by the hacker to conduct a coordinated attack.

Figure 2-18 Denial-of-service attack

attack. DDoS attacks are more difficult to defend against, and currently there are no controls that any single organization can apply. There are, however, some cooperative efforts to enable DDoS defenses among groups of service providers; an example is the Consensus Roadmap for Defeating Distributed Denial of Service Attacks.[44] To use a popular metaphor, DDoS is considered a weapon of mass destruction on the Internet. The MyDoom worm attack in February 2004 was intended to be a DDoS attack against *www.sco.com*, the Web site of a vendor for a UNIX operating system. Allegedly, the attack was payback for the SCO Group's perceived hostility toward the open-source Linux community.[45]

Any system connected to the Internet and providing TCP-based network services (such as a Web server, FTP server, or mail server) is vulnerable to DoS attacks. DoS attacks can also be launched against routers or other network server systems if these hosts enable other TCP services, such as echo.

Prominent in the history of notable DoS attacks are those conducted by Michael Calce (a.k.a. Mafiaboy) on Amazon.com, CNN.com, ETrade.com, ebay.com, Yahoo.com, Excite.com, and Dell.com. These software-based attacks lasted approximately four hours and reportedly resulted in millions of dollars in lost revenue.[46] The British ISP CloudNine is believed to be the first business "hacked out of existence" by a DoS attack in January 2002. This attack was similar to the DoS attacks launched by Mafiaboy in February 2000.[47] In January 2016, a group calling itself New World Hacking attacked the BBC's Web site. If the scope of the attack is verified, it would qualify as the largest DDoS attack in history, with an attack rate of 602 Gbps (gigabits per second). The group also hit Donald Trump's campaign Web site on the same day.[48]

❯ E-mail Attacks

Key Terms

mail bomb An attack designed to overwhelm the receiver with excessive quantities of e-mail.
spam Undesired e-mail, typically commercial advertising transmitted in bulk.

Spam is unsolicited commercial e-mail. While many consider spam a trivial nuisance rather than an attack, it has been used as a means of enhancing malicious code attacks. In March 2002, there were reports of malicious code embedded in MP3 files that were included as attachments to spam.[49] The most significant consequence of spam, however, is the waste of computer and human resources. Many organizations attempt to cope with the flood of spam by using e-mail filtering technologies. Other organizations simply tell users of the mail system to delete unwanted messages.

A form of e-mail attack that is also a DoS attack is called a **mail bomb**. It can be accomplished using traditional e-mailing techniques or by exploiting various technical flaws in the Simple Mail Transport Protocol (SMTP). The target of the attack receives an unmanageably large volume of unsolicited e-mail. By sending large e-mails with forged header information, attackers can take advantage of poorly configured e-mail systems on the Internet and trick them into sending many e-mails to an address of the attackers' choice. If many such systems are tricked into participating, the target e-mail address is buried under thousands or even millions of unwanted e-mails.

Although phishing attacks occur via e-mail, they are much more commonly associated with a method of social engineering designed to trick users to perform an action, rather than simply making the user a target of a DoS e-mail attack.

❯ Communications Interception Attacks

Key Terms

Domain Name System (DNS) cache poisoning The intentional hacking and modification of a DNS database to redirect legitimate traffic to illegitimate Internet locations. Also known as DNS spoofing.

man-in-the-middle A group of attacks whereby a person intercepts a communications stream and inserts himself in the conversation to convince each of the legitimate parties that he is the other communications partner. Some man-in-the-middle attacks involve encryption functions.

packet sniffer A software program or hardware appliance that can intercept, copy, and interpret network traffic.

pharming The redirection of legitimate user Web traffic to illegitimate Web sites with the intent to collect personal information.

session hijacking See *TCP hijacking*.

sniffer See *packet sniffer*.

spoofing A technique for gaining unauthorized access to computers using a forged or modified source IP address to give the perception that messages are coming from a trusted host.

TCP hijacking A form of man-in-the-middle attack whereby the attacker inserts himself into TCP/IP-based communications. TCP/IP is short for Transmission Control Protocol/Internet Protocol.

Common software-based communications attacks include several subcategories designed to intercept and collect information in transit. These types of attacks include sniffers, spoofing, pharming, and man-in-the-middle attacks. The emergence of the Internet of Things (IoT)—the addition of communications and interactivity to everyday objects—increases the possibility of these types of attacks. Our automobiles, appliances, and entertainment devices have joined our smartphones in being interconnected and remotely controlled. The security of these devices has not always been a primary concern.

Packet Sniffer A **packet sniffer** (or simply **sniffer**) can monitor data traveling over a network. Sniffers can be used both for legitimate network management functions and for stealing information. Unauthorized sniffers can be extremely dangerous to a network's security because they are virtually impossible to detect and can be inserted almost anywhere. This feature makes them a favorite weapon in the hacker's arsenal. Sniffers often work on TCP/IP networks. Sniffers add risk to network communications because many systems and users send information on local networks in clear text. A sniffer program shows all the data going by, including passwords, the data inside files (such as word-processing documents), and sensitive data from applications.

Spoofing To engage in IP **spoofing**, hackers use a variety of techniques to obtain trusted IP addresses and then modify the packet headers (see Figure 2-19) to insert these forged addresses.[50] Newer routers and firewall arrangements can offer protection against IP spoofing.

Pharming Pharming attacks often use Trojans, worms, or other virus technologies to attack an Internet browser's address bar so that the valid URL the user types is modified to be that of an illegitimate Web site. A form of pharming called **Domain Name System (DNS) cache poisoning** targets the Internet DNS system, corrupting legitimate data tables.

The key difference between pharming and the social engineering attack called phishing is that the latter requires the user to actively click a link or button to redirect to the illegitimate site, whereas pharming attacks modify the user's traffic without the user's knowledge or active participation.

Man-in-the-Middle In the well-known **man-in-the-middle** attack, an attacker monitors (or sniffs) packets from the network, modifies them, and inserts them back into the network. In a **TCP hijacking** attack, also known as **session hijacking**, the attacker uses address spoofing to impersonate other legitimate entities on the network. It allows the attacker to eavesdrop as well as to change, delete, reroute, add, forge, or divert data. A variant of TCP hijacking involves the interception of an encryption key exchange, which enables the hacker to act as an invisible man in the middle—that is, an eavesdropper—on encrypted

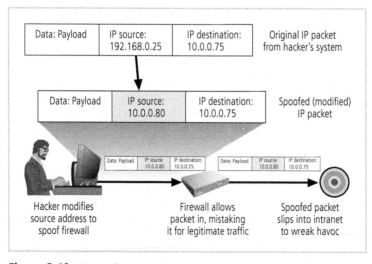

Figure 2-19 IP spoofing attack

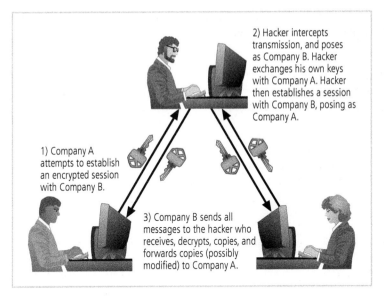

2) Hacker intercepts transmission, and poses as Company B. Hacker exchanges his own keys with Company A. Hacker then establishes a session with Company B, posing as Company A.

1) Company A attempts to establish an encrypted session with Company B.

3) Company B sends all messages to the hacker who receives, decrypts, copies, and forwards copies (possibly modified) to Company A.

Figure 2-20 Man-in-the-middle attack

communications. Figure 2-20 illustrates these attacks by showing how a hacker uses public and private encryption keys to intercept messages. You will learn more about encryption keys in Chapter 8.

Technical Hardware Failures or Errors

Technical hardware failures or errors occur when a manufacturer distributes equipment containing a known or unknown flaw. These defects can cause the system to perform outside of expected parameters, resulting in unreliable service or lack of availability. Some errors are terminal—that is, they result in the unrecoverable loss of the equipment. Some errors are intermittent in that they only manifest themselves periodically, resulting in faults that are not easily repeated. Thus, equipment can sometimes stop working or work in unexpected ways. Murphy's Law (yes, there really was a Murphy) holds that if something can possibly go wrong, it will.[51] In other words, it's not a question *if* something will fail, but *when*.

❯ The Intel Pentium CPU Failure

One of the best-known hardware failures is that of the Intel Pentium II chip (similar to the one shown in Figure 2-21), which had a defect that resulted in a calculation error under certain circumstances. Intel initially expressed little concern for the defect, and stated that it would take an inordinate amount of time to identify a calculation that would interfere with the reliability of the results. Yet, within days after the chip's defect was announced, popular computing journals were publishing a simple calculation (the division of 4195835 by 3145727 within a spreadsheet) that determined whether a machine contained the defective chip and thus the floating-point operation bug. The Pentium floating-point division bug

Figure 2-21 Intel chip

(FDIV) led to a public-relations disaster for Intel that resulted in its first-ever chip recall and a loss of over $475 million. A few months later, disclosure of another bug, known as the Dan-0411 flag erratum, further eroded the chip manufacturer's public image.[52] In 1998, Intel released its Xeon chip and discovered it also had hardware errors. Intel said, "All new chips have bugs, and the process of debugging and improving performance inevitably continues even after a product is in the market."[53]

❯ Mean Time Between Failure

Key Terms
---

mean time between failure (MTBF) The average amount of time between hardware failures, calculated as the total amount of operation time for a specified number of units divided by the total number of failures.

mean time to diagnose (MTTD) The average amount of time a computer repair technician needs to determine the cause of a failure.

mean time to failure (MTTF) The average amount of time until the next hardware failure.

mean time to repair (MTTR) The average amount of time a computer repair technician needs to resolve the cause of a failure through replacement or repair of a faulty unit.

In hardware terms, failures are measured in **mean time between failure (MTBF)** and **mean time to failure (MTTF)**. While MTBF and MTTF are sometimes used interchangeably, MTBF presumes that the item can be repaired or returned to service, whereas MTTF presumes the item must be replaced. From a repair standpoint, MTBF = MTTF + MTTD +

MTTR, where **MTTD** examines diagnosis time and **MTTR** calculates repair time.[54] The most commonly failing piece of computer hardware is the hard drive, which currently has an average MTBF of approximately 500,000 hours.

Technical Software Failures or Errors

Large quantities of computer code are written, debugged, published, and sold before all their bugs are detected and resolved. Sometimes, combinations of certain software and hardware reveal new failures that range from bugs to untested failure conditions. Sometimes these bugs are not errors, but purposeful shortcuts left by programmers for benign or malign reasons. Collectively, shortcut access routes into programs that bypass security checks are called trap doors, and they can cause serious security breaches.

Software bugs are so commonplace that entire Web sites are dedicated to documenting them. Among the most popular is Bugtraq, found at *www.securityfocus.com*, which provides up-to-the-minute information on the latest security vulnerabilities as well as a thorough archive of past bugs.

❯ The OWASP Top 10

The Open Web Application Security Project (OWASP) was founded in 2001 as a nonprofit consortium dedicated to helping organizations create and operate software applications they could trust. Every three years or so, OWASP publishes a list of "The Ten Most Critical Web Application Security Risks" along with an OWASP Developer's Guide. The OWASP Top 10 for 2013 was:

1. Injection
2. Broken authentication and session management
3. Cross-site scripting (XSS)
4. Insecure direct object references
5. Security misconfiguration
6. Sensitive data exposure
7. Missing function level access control
8. Cross-site request forgery (CSRF)
9. Using components with known vulnerabilities
10. Unvalidated redirects and forwards[55]

This list is virtually unchanged since 2010, although CSRF dropped from fifth in 2010 to eighth in 2013. Many of these items are described in detail in the following section.

 For more information on the top 10 software vulnerabilities or the OWASP project, visit www.owasp.org.

❯ The Deadly Sins in Software Security

Key Terms

---

buffer overrun (or buffer overflow) An application error that occurs when more data is sent to a program buffer than it is designed to handle.

command injection An application error that occurs when user input is passed directly to a compiler or interpreter without screening for content that may disrupt or compromise the intended function.

cross-site scripting (XSS) A Web application fault that occurs when an application running on a Web server inserts commands into a user's browser session and causes information to be sent to a hostile server.

integer bug A class of computational error caused by methods that computers use to store and manipulate integer numbers; this bug can be exploited by attackers.

Some software development failures and errors result in software that is difficult or impossible to deploy in a secure fashion. The most common of these failures have been identified as "deadly sins in software security."[56] These 24 problem areas in software development were originally categorized by John Viega, upon request of Amit Youran, who at the time was the Director of the Department of Homeland Security's National Cyber Security Division. These problem areas are described in the following sections.

Buffer Overruns Buffers are used to manage mismatches in the processing rates between two entities involved in a communication process. During a **buffer overrun**, an attacker can make the target system execute instructions or take advantage of some other unintended consequence of the failure. Sometimes this is limited to a DoS attack. In any case, data on the attacked system loses integrity.[57] In 1998, Microsoft encountered the following buffer overflow problem:

> *Microsoft acknowledged that if you type a res:// URL (a Microsoft-devised type of URL) which is longer than 256 characters in Internet Explorer 4.0, the browser will crash. No big deal, except that anything after the 256th character can be executed on the computer. This maneuver, known as a buffer overrun, is just about the oldest hacker trick in the book. Tack some malicious code (say, an executable version of the Pentium-crashing FooF code) onto the end of the URL, and you have the makings of a disaster.[58]*

Catching Exceptions One of the marks of effective software is the ability to catch and resolve exceptions—unusual situations that require special processing. If the program doesn't manage exceptions correctly, the software may not perform as expected. Exceptions differ from errors (as in the "failure to handle errors" category presented in a subsequent section) in that exceptions are considered "expected but irregular situations at runtime," while errors are "mistakes in the running program that can be resolved only by fixing the program."

Command Injection The problem of **command injection** is caused by a developer's failure to ensure that command input is validated before it is used in the program. Perhaps the simplest example can be demonstrated using the Windows command shell:

```
@echo off
set /p myVar="Enter the string>"
set someVar=%myVar%
echo
```

These commands ask the user to provide a string and then simply set another variable to the value and display it. However, an attacker could use the command chaining character "&" to append other commands to the string the user provides (Hello&del*.*).[59]

Cross-Site Scripting (XSS) **Cross-site scripting** allows the attacker to acquire valuable information, such as account credentials, account numbers, or other critical data. Often an attacker encodes a malicious link and places it in the target server, making it look less suspicious. After the data is collected by the hostile application, it sends what appears to be a valid response from the intended server.[60]

Failure to Handle Errors What happens when a system or application encounters a scenario that it is not prepared to handle? Does it attempt to complete the operation (reading or writing data or performing calculations)? Does it issue a cryptic message that only a programmer could understand? Or does it simply stop functioning? Failure to handle errors can cause a variety of unexpected system behaviors. Programmers are expected to anticipate problems and prepare their application code to handle them.

Failure to Protect Network Traffic With the growing popularity of wireless networking comes a corresponding increase in the risk that wirelessly transmitted data will be intercepted. Most wireless networks are installed and operated with little or no protection for the information that is broadcast between the client and the network wireless access point. This is especially true of public networks found in coffee shops, bookstores, and hotels. Without appropriate encryption such as that afforded by WPA, attackers can intercept and view your data.

Traffic on a wired network is also vulnerable to interception in some situations. On networks using hubs instead of switches, any user can install a packet sniffer and collect communications to and from users on that network. Periodic scans for unauthorized packet sniffers and unauthorized connections to the network, as well as general awareness of the threat, can mitigate this problem.

Failure to Store and Protect Data Securely Storing and protecting data securely is a large enough issue to be the core subject of this entire text. Programmers are responsible for integrating access controls into programs and keeping secret information out of them. Access controls, the subject of later chapters, regulate who, what, when, where, and how users and systems interact with data. Failure to properly implement sufficiently strong access controls makes the data vulnerable. Overly strict access controls hinder business users in the performance of their duties, and as a result the controls may be administratively removed or bypassed.

The integration of secret information—such as the "hard coding" of passwords, encryption keys, or other sensitive information—can put that information at risk of disclosure.

Failure to Use Cryptographically Strong Random Numbers Most modern cryptosystems, like many other computer systems, use random number generators. However, a decision support system that uses random and pseudorandom numbers for Monte Carlo method forecasting does not require the same degree of rigor and the same need for true randomness as a system that seeks to implement cryptographic procedures. These "random" number generators use a mathematical algorithm based on a seed value and another system component (such as the computer clock) to simulate a random number. Those who understand the workings of such a "random" number generator can predict particular values at particular times.

Format String Problems Computer languages often are equipped with built-in capabilities to reformat data while they output it. The formatting instructions are usually written as a "format string." Unfortunately, some programmers may use data from untrusted sources as a format string.[61] An attacker may embed characters that are meaningful as formatting directives (such as %x, %d, %p, etc.) into malicious input. If this input is then interpreted by the program as formatting directives (such as an argument to the C printf function), the attacker may be able to access information or overwrite very targeted portions of the program's stack with data of the attacker's choosing.[62]

Improper File Access If an attacker changes the expected location of a file by intercepting and modifying a program code call, the attacker can force a program to use files other than the ones it is supposed to use. This type of attack could be used either to substitute a bogus file for a legitimate file (as in password files) or trick the system into running a malware executable. The potential for damage or disclosure is great, so it is critical to protect not only the location of the files but the method and communications channels by which these files are accessed.

Improper Use of SSL Programmers use Secure Sockets Layer (SSL) to transfer sensitive data, such as credit card numbers and other personal information, between a client and server. While most programmers assume that using SSL guarantees security, they often mishandle this technology. SSL and its successor, Transport Layer Security (TLS), both need certificate validation to be truly secure. Failure to use Hypertext Transfer Protocol Secure (HTTPS) to validate the certificate authority and then the certificate itself, or failure to validate the information against a certificate revocation list (CRL), can compromise the security of SSL traffic. You will learn much more about cryptographic controls in Chapter 8.

Information Leakage One of the most common methods of obtaining inside and classified information is directly or indirectly from one person, usually an employee. A famous

World War II military poster warned that "loose lips sink ships," emphasizing the risk to naval deployments from enemy attack if sailors, marines, or their families disclosed the movements of U.S. vessels. A widely shared fear was that the enemy had civilian operatives waiting in bars and shops at common Navy ports of call, just waiting for the troops to drop hints about where they were going and when. By warning employees against disclosing information, organizations can protect the secrecy of their operation.

Integer Bugs (Overflows/Underflows) Although mathematical calculation theoretically can deal with numbers that contain an arbitrary number of digits, the binary representations used by computers are of a particular fixed length. The programmer must anticipate the size of the numbers to be calculated in any given part of the program. An **integer bug** can result when a programmer does not validate the inputs to a calculation to verify that the integers are of the expected size. For example, adding 1 to 32,767 should produce 32,768, but in computer arithmetic with 16-bit signed integers, the erroneous result is −32,768. An underflow can occur, for example, when you subtract 5 from negative 32,767, which returns the incorrect result +32,764, because the largest negative integer that can be represented in 16 bits is negative 32,768.

> *Integer bugs fall into four broad classes: overflows, underflows, truncations, and signedness errors. Integer bugs are usually exploited indirectly—that is, triggering an integer bug enables an attacker to corrupt other areas of memory, gaining control of an application. The memory allocated for a value could be exceeded, if that value is greater than expected, with the extra bits written into other locations. The system may then experience unexpected consequences, which could be miscalculations, errors, crashing or other problems. Even though integer bugs are often used to build a buffer overflow or other memory corruption attack, integer bugs are not just a special case of memory corruption bugs.*[63]

Neglecting Change Control Developers use a process known as change control to ensure that the working system delivered to users represents the intent of the developers. Early in the development process, change control ensures that developers do not work at cross purposes by altering the same programs or parts of programs at the same time. Once the system is in production, change control processes ensure that only authorized changes are introduced and that all changes are adequately tested before being released.

Poor Usability Employees prefer doing things the easy way. When faced with an "official way" of performing a task and an "unofficial way"—which is easier—they prefer the latter. The best solution to address this issue is to provide only one way—the secure way! Integrating security and usability, adding training and awareness, and ensuring solid controls all contribute to the security of information. Allowing users to choose easier solutions by default will inevitably lead to loss.

Race Conditions A race condition is a failure of a program that occurs when an unexpected ordering of events in its execution results in a conflict over access to the same system resource. This conflict does not need to involve streams of code inside the program because current operating systems and processor technology automatically break a program into multiple threads that can be executed simultaneously. If the threads that result from this process share any resources, they may interfere with each other.[64]

A race condition occurs, for example, when a program creates a temporary file and an attacker is able to replace it between the time it is created and the time it is used. A race condition can also occur when information is stored in multiple memory threads if one thread stores information in the wrong memory location, by accident or intent.

SQL Injection SQL injection occurs when developers fail to properly validate user input before using it to query a relational database. For example, a fairly innocuous program fragment might expect the user to input a user ID and then perform a SQL query against the USERS table to retrieve the associated name:

```
Accept USER-ID from console;

SELECT USERID, NAME FROM USERS WHERE USERID = USER-ID;
```

This is very straightforward SQL syntax; when used correctly, it displays the user ID and name. The problem is that the string accepted from the user is passed directly to the SQL database server as part of the SQL command. What if an attacker enters the string "JOE OR 1 = 1"? This string includes some valid SQL syntax that will return all rows from the table where the user ID is either "JOE" or "1 = 1." Because one is always equal to one, the system returns all user IDs and names. The possible effects of the hacker's "injection" of SQL code into the program are not limited to improper access to information—what if the attacker included SQL commands to drop the USERS table, or even shut down the database?[65]

Trusting Network Address Resolution The DNS is a function of the World Wide Web that converts a URL like *www.course.com* into the IP address of the Web server host. This distributed model is vulnerable to attack or "poisoning." DNS cache poisoning involves compromising a DNS server and then changing the valid IP address associated with a domain name into one the attacker chooses, usually a fake Web site designed to obtain personal information or one that accrues a benefit to the attacker—for example, redirecting shoppers from a competitor's Web site. Such attacks are usually more sinister, however; for instance, a simulated banking site used for a phishing attack might harvest online banking information.

How does someone get this fake information into the DNS server? Aside from a direct attack against a root DNS server, most attempts are made against primary and secondary DNS servers, which are local to an organization and part of the distributed DNS system. Other attacks attempt to compromise the DNS servers further up the DNS distribution mode—those of ISPs or backbone connectivity providers. The DNS relies on a process of automated updates that can be exploited. Attackers most commonly compromise segments of the DNS by attacking the name of the name server and substituting their own DNS primary name server, by incorrectly updating an individual record, or by responding before an actual DNS can. In the last type of attack, the attacker tries to discover a delay in a name server or to introduce a delay, as in a DoS attack. When the delay is in place, the attacker can set up another server to respond as if it were the actual DNS server, before the real DNS server can. The client accepts the first set of information it receives and is directed to that IP address.

Unauthenticated Key Exchange One of the biggest challenges in private key systems, which involve two users sharing the same key, is securely getting the key to the other party. Sometimes an "out of band" courier is used, but at other times a public key system, which uses both a public and private key, is used to exchange the key. However, an unauthorized person might receive a key that was copied onto a USB device and shipped. This person might not work for the company, but was simply expecting the delivery and intercepted it. The same scenario can occur on the Internet, where an attacker writes a variant of a public key system and makes it available as "freeware," or corrupts or intercepts the function of someone else's public key encryption system, perhaps by posing as a public key repository.

Use of Magic URLs and Hidden Forms HTTP is a stateless protocol in which computer programs on either end of the communication channel cannot rely on a guaranteed delivery of any message. This makes it difficult for software developers to track a user's exchanges with a Web site over multiple interactions. Too often, sensitive state information is included in hidden form fields on the HTML page or simply included in a "magic" URL (for example, the authentication ID is passed as a parameter in the URL for the exchanges that will follow). If this information is stored as plain text, an attacker can harvest the information from a magic URL as it travels across the network, or use scripts on the client to modify information in hidden form fields. Depending on the structure of the application, the harvested or modified information can be used in spoofing or hijacking attacks, or to change the way the application operates. For example, if an item's price is kept in a hidden form field, the attacker could arrange to buy that item for one cent.[66]

Use of Weak Password-Based Systems Failure to require sufficient password strength and to control incorrect password entry is a serious security issue. Password policy can specify the acceptable number and type of characters, the frequency of mandatory changes, and even the reusability of old passwords. Similarly, a system administrator can regulate the permitted number of incorrect password entries that are submitted and further improve the level of protection. Systems that do not validate passwords, or that store passwords in easily accessible locations, are ripe for attack.

Web Client-Related Vulnerability (XSS) One of the issues in programming Web-based applications is bugs that affect either the client side or the server side. Client-side cross-site scripting errors can cause problems that allow an attacker to send malicious code to the user's computer by inserting the script into an otherwise normal Web site. The user's Web browser, not knowing the code is malicious, runs it and inadvertently infects the client system. Some code can read a user's Web information, such as his or her Web history, stored cookies or session tokens, or even stored passwords.

Web Server-Related Vulnerabilities (XSS, XSRF, and Response Splitting)

The same cross-site scripting attacks that can infect a client system can also be used to attack Web servers. Cross-site request forgery (XSRF or CSRF) attacks cause users to attack servers they access legitimately, on behalf of an outside attacker. For example, on banking Web sites, this could include changing a fund transfer account number to the attacker's account number. "HTTP response splitting occurs when data enters a Web application through an untrusted source, most frequently an HTTP request, or data is included in an HTTP response header sent to a Web user without being validated for malicious characters."

Technological Obsolescence

Antiquated or outdated infrastructure can lead to unreliable and untrustworthy systems. Management must recognize that when technology becomes outdated, there is a risk of losing data integrity from attacks. Management's strategic planning should always include an analysis of the technology currently in use. Ideally, proper planning by management should prevent technology from becoming obsolete, but when obsolescence is clear, management must take immediate action. IT professionals play a large role in the identification of probable obsolescence.

Recently, the software vendor Symantec retired support for a legacy version of its popular antivirus software, and organizations that wanted continued product support were obliged to upgrade immediately to a different version of antivirus software. In organizations where IT personnel had kept management informed of the coming retirement, these replacements were made more promptly and at lower cost than in organizations where the software was allowed to become obsolete.

Perhaps the most significant case of technology obsolescence in recent years is Microsoft's Windows XP. This desktop operating system was dominant in the market for many years, beginning in 2001. The OS evolved over time to be used in multiple variations such as XP Pro and XP Home, it had feature and capability upgrades in three service packs, and it even made the transition to new processors with a 64-bit edition. It was superseded in the corporation's lineup of desktop operating systems by Microsoft Vista in January 2007. However, it has retained a large following of users and remained in widespread use for many years. Microsoft discontinued support for Windows XP in April 2014. This removal of support was expected to cause concern and perhaps even disruptions in some business sectors, notably the utility industry. Many industries and organizations have built critical elements of their business systems and even their infrastructure control systems on top of Windows XP, or they have used it as an embedded operating system inside other systems, such as automated teller machines and power generating and control systems.

Figure 2-22 shows other examples of obsolete technology, including removable storage media in 8-inch, 5-inch, and 3.5-inch formats as well as open-reel magnetic tape.

2

Figure 2-22 Obsolete technology

Theft

The threat of **theft** is a constant. The value of information is diminished when it is copied without the owner's knowledge. Physical theft can be controlled easily using a wide variety of measures, from locked doors to trained security personnel and the installation of alarm systems. Electronic theft, however, is a more complex problem to manage and control. When someone steals a physical object, the loss is easily detected; if it has any importance at all, its absence is noted. When electronic information is stolen, the crime is not always readily apparent. If thieves are clever and cover their tracks carefully, the crime may remain undiscovered until it is too late.

Theft is often an overlapping category with software attacks, espionage or trespass, information extortion, and compromises to intellectual property. A hacker or other individual threat agent could access a system and commit most of these offenses by downloading a company's information and then threatening to publish it if not paid.

The increasing use of mobile technology, including smartphones, tablet PCs, and laptops, increases the risk of data theft. More disconcerting than the loss of data is the chance that the user has allowed the mobile device to retain account credentials, allowing the thief to use legitimate access to get into business or personal accounts that belong to the victim.

Selected Readings

- The journal article "Enemy at the Gates: Threats to Information Security," by Michael Whitman, was published in *Communications of the ACM* in August 2003, on pages 91–96. An abstract is available from the ACM Digital Library at *www.acm.org*. Journal access may be available through your local library.
- *The Art of War* by Sun Tzu. Many translations and editions are widely available, both print and online.
- *24 Deadly Sins of Software Security—Programming Flaws and How to Fix Them*, by M. Howard, D. LeBlanc, and J. Viega, is published by McGraw-Hill/Osborne Publishing.

Chapter Summary

- Information security performs four important functions to ensure that information assets remain safe and useful:
  - Protecting the organization's ability to function
  - Enabling the safe operation of applications implemented on the organization's IT systems

- Protecting the data an organization collects and uses
- Safeguarding the organization's technology assets

- To make sound decisions about information security, management must be informed about threats to its people, applications, data, and information systems and the attacks they face.

- Threats are any events or circumstances that have the potential to adversely affect operations and assets. An attack is an intentional or unintentional act that can damage or otherwise compromise information and the systems that support it. A vulnerability is a potential weakness in an asset or its defensive controls.

- Threats or dangers facing an organization's people, information, and systems fall into the following categories:

  - Compromises to intellectual property: Intellectual property, such as trade secrets, copyrights, trademarks, or patents, are intangible assets that may be attacked via software piracy or the exploitation of asset protection controls.

  - Deviations in quality of service: Organizations rely on services provided by others. Losses can come from interruptions to those services.

  - Espionage or trespass: Asset losses may result when electronic and human activities breach the confidentiality of information.

  - Forces of nature: A wide range of natural events can overwhelm control systems and preparations to cause losses to data and availability.

  - Human error or failure: Losses to assets may come from intentional or accidental actions by people inside and outside the organization.

  - Information extortion: Stolen or inactivated assets may be held hostage to extract payment of ransom.

  - Sabotage or vandalism: Losses may result from the deliberate sabotage of a computer system or business, or from acts of vandalism. These acts can either destroy an asset or damage the image of an organization.

  - Software attacks: Losses may result when attackers use software to gain unauthorized access to systems or cause disruptions in systems availability.

  - Technical hardware failures or errors: Technical defects in hardware systems can cause unexpected results, including unreliable service or lack of availability.

  - Technical software failures or errors: Software used by systems may have purposeful or unintentional errors that result in failures, which can lead to loss of availability or unauthorized access to information.

  - Technological obsolescence: Antiquated or outdated infrastructure can lead to unreliable and untrustworthy systems that may result in loss of availability or unauthorized access to information.

  - Theft: Theft of information can result from a wide variety of attacks.

Review Questions

1. Why is information security a management problem? What can management do that technology cannot?

2. Why is data the most important asset an organization possesses? What other assets in the organization require protection?

3. Which management groups are responsible for implementing information security to protect the organization's ability to function?

4. Has the implementation of networking technology created more or less risk for businesses that use information technology? Why?

5. What is information extortion? Describe how such an attack can cause losses, using an example not found in the text.

6. Why are employees one of the greatest threats to information security?

7. How can you protect against shoulder surfing?

8. How has the perception of the hacker changed over recent years? What is the profile of a hacker today?

9. What is the difference between a skilled hacker and an unskilled hacker, other than skill levels? How does the protection against each differ?

10. What are the various types of malware? How do worms differ from viruses? Do Trojan horses carry viruses or worms?

11. Why does polymorphism cause greater concern than traditional malware? How does it affect detection?

12. What is the most common violation of intellectual property? How does an organization protect against it? What agencies fight it?

13. What are the various forces of nature? Which type might be of greatest concern to an organization in Las Vegas? Jakarta? Oklahoma City? Amsterdam? Miami? Tokyo?

14. How is technological obsolescence a threat to information security? How can an organization protect against it?

15. Does the intellectual property owned by an organization usually have value? If so, how can attackers threaten that value?

16. What are the types of password attacks? What can a systems administrator do to protect against them?

17. What is the difference between a denial-of-service attack and a distributed denial-of-service attack? Which is more dangerous? Why?

18. For a sniffer attack to succeed, what must the attacker do? How can an attacker gain access to a network to use the sniffer system?

19. What methods does a social engineering hacker use to gain information about a user's login ID and password? How would this method differ if it targeted an administrator's assistant versus a data-entry clerk?

20. What is a buffer overflow, and how is it used against a Web server?

Exercises

1. Consider that an individual threat agent, like a hacker, can be a factor in more than one threat category. If a hacker breaks into a network, copies a few files, defaces a Web page, and steals credit card numbers, how many different threat categories does the attack fall into?

2. Using the Web, research Mafiaboy's exploits. When and how did he compromise sites? How was he caught?

3. Search the Web for "The Official Phreaker's Manual." What information in this manual might help a security administrator to protect a communications system?

4. The chapter discussed many threats and vulnerabilities to information security. Using the Web, find at least two other sources of information about threats and vulnerabilities. Begin with *www.securityfocus.com* and use a keyword search on "threats."

5. Using the categories of threats mentioned in this chapter and the various attacks described, review several current media sources and identify examples of each threat.

Case Exercises

Shortly after the Board of Directors meeting, Charlie was named chief information security officer to fill a new leadership position that reports to the CIO, Gladys Williams. The primary role of the new position is to provide leadership for SLS's efforts to improve its information security profile.

Discussion Questions

1. Before the discussion at the start of this chapter, how do Fred, Gladys, and Charlie each perceive the scope and scale of the new information security effort? Did Fred's perception change after that?

2. How should Fred measure success when he evaluates Gladys' performance for this project? How should he evaluate Charlie's performance?

3. Which of the threats discussed in this chapter should receive Charlie's attention early in his planning process?

Ethical Decision Making

Instead of Charlie being named CISO, suppose instead that Fred hired his son-in-law, an unemployed accountant, to fill the role. Assuming the person had no prior experience or preparation for a job in information security, did Fred make an ethical choice? Explain your answer.

Suppose that SLS has implemented the policy prohibiting use of personal USB drives at work. Also, suppose that Davey Martinez brought in the USB drive he had used to store last month's accounting worksheet. When he plugged in the drive, the worm outbreak started again and infected two servers. It's obvious that Davey violated policy, but did he commit ethical violations as well?

Endnotes

1. Levine, Daniel S. "One on One with Charles Cresson Wood of InfoSecurity Infrastructure." *Techbiz Online.* 12 October 2001. Accessed 25 January 2014 from *www.biz journals.com/sanfrancisco/stories/2001/10/15/newscolumn7.html.*

2. Sun-Tzu. "Sun Tzu's The Art of War." Translation by the Sonshi Group. Accessed 31 May 2016 from *www.sonshi.com/original-the-art-of-war-translation-not-giles.html.*

3. Whitman, M., Mattord, H. 2015 SEC/CISE Threats to Information Protection Report. Security Executive Council. *www.securityexecutivecouncil.com.*

4. Internet World Stats. "Internet Usage Statistics: The Internet Big Picture, World Internet Users and Population Stats." Accessed 3 October 2016 from *www.internetworld stats.com/stats.htm.*

5. Whitman, M., Mattord, H. 2015 SEC/CISE Threats to Information Protection Report. Security Executive Council. *www.securityexecutivecouncil.com.*

6. Ibid.

7. Whitman, M., Mattord, H. "Threats to Information Security Revisited." *Journal of Information Systems Security* 8, no. 1 (2012): 21, 41. *www.jissec.org/.*

8. Business Software Alliance. "Seizing Opportunity Through License Compliance." 2015. Accessed 24 May 2016 from *http://globalstudy.bsa.org/2016/downloads/studies /BSA_GSS_US.pdf.*

9. Patton, Natalie. "Bootlegged Software Could Cost Community College." *Las Vegas Review Journal Online.* 18 September 1997. Accessed 24 May 2016 from *www.review journal.com/archive/search.*

10. MegaPath. "The Cost of Downtime." Accessed 24 May 2016 from *www.megapath .com/blog/blog-archive/infographic-the-cost-of-downtime/.*

11. Chowdhry, Pankaj. "The Gibraltar Hack: Anatomy of a Break-in." *PCWeek* 16, no. 41 (1999): 1, 22.

12. Ibid.

13. Rosencrance, Linda. "Teen Hacker 'Mafiaboy' Sentenced." *ComputerWorld Online.* Accessed 24 May 2016 from *www.computerworld.com/article/2583318/security0 /teen-hacker—mafiaboy—sentenced.html.*

14. Goldman, David. "Jailbreaking iPhone Apps is Now Legal." *CNN Money.* 26 July 2010. Accessed 24 May 2016 from *http://money.cnn.com/2010/07/26/technology /iphone_jailbreaking/.*

15. Mitnick, K., and Simon, W. *The Art of Deception: Controlling the Human Element of Security.* Wiley Publishing, Inc., Indianapolis, 2002.

16. Edward Snowden: A Timeline. NBC News. Accessed 23 May 2016 from *www .nbcnews.com/feature/edward-snowden-interview/edward-snowden-timeline-n114871.*

17. Hackthissite.org. Accessed 24 May 2016 from *www.hackthissite.org/.*

18. Webopedia. "Static Electricity and Computers." Accessed 24 May 2016 from *www .webopedia.com/DidYouKnow/Computer_Science/static.asp.*

19. Kennedy, James T. "Internet Intricacies: Don't Get Caught in the Net." *Contingency Planning & Management* 3, no. 1: 12.

20. Abreu, Elinor. "Kevin Mitnick Bares All." *ComputerWorld*. 28 September 2000. Accessed 24 May 2016 from *www.computerworld.com.au/article/78440/kevin_mit nick_bares_all/*.

21. CERT Advisory CA-1991-03. Unauthorized Password Change Requests Via Email Messages.

22. "Rebuffed Internet Extortionist Posts Stolen Credit Card Data." *CNN Online*. 10 January 2000.

23. Lewis, Truman. "Express Scripts Extortion Scheme Widens." *Consumer Affairs*. 30 September 2009. Accessed 24 May 2016 from *www.consumeraffairs.com/news04/ 2009/09/express_scripts_breach.html*.

24. Wlasuk, Alan. "Cyber-Extortion–Huge Profits, Low Risk." *Security Week*. 13 July 2012. Accessed 24 May 2016 from *www.securityweek.com/cyber-extortion-huge-prof its-low-risk*.

25. Bridis, Ted. "British Authorities Arrest Hacker Wanted as 'Fluffi Bunni.'" 29 April 2003. Accessed 24 May 2016 from *www.securityfocus.com/news/4320*.

26. Costello, Sam. "Attrition.org Stops Mirroring Web Site Defacements." *Computer-World Online*. 22 May 2001. Accessed 24 May 2016 from *www.computerworld .com/s/article/60769/Attrition.org_stops_mirroring_Web_site_defacements*.

27. Infoshop News. "Fighting the Fascists Using Direct Action Hacktivism." 28 March 2010. Accessed 24 May 2016 from *www.anarchistnews.org/content/fighting-fascists -using-direct-action-hacktivism*.

28. Denning, Dorothy E. "Activism, Hacktivism, and Cyberterrorism: The Internet as a Tool for Influencing Foreign Policy." *Info War Online*. 4 February 2000. Accessed 24 May 2016 from *www.iwar.org.uk/cyberterror/resources/denning.htm*.

29. Elmusharaf, M. "Cyber Terrorism: The New Kind of Terrorism." *Computer Crime Research Center Online*. 8 April 2004. Accessed 24 May 2016 from *www.crime -research.org/articles/Cyber_Terrorism_new_kind_Terrorism*.

30. Lemos, R. "Assault on Net Servers Fails." *C|Net News.com*. 22 October 2002. Accessed 24 May 2016 from *http://news.com/Assault+on+Net+servers+fails/2100 -1001_3-963005.html*.

31. Messmer, Ellen. "U.S. Cyber Counterattack: Bomb 'em One Way or the Other." 8 February 2007. Accessed 24 May 2016 from *www.networkworld.com/news/2007/ 020807-rsa-cyber-attacks.html*.

32. Perlroth, Nicole, and Sanger, David. "Cyberattacks Seem Meant to Destroy, Not Just Disrupt." 28 March 2013. Accessed 24 May 2016 from *www.nytimes.com/2013/03 /29/technology/corporate-cyberattackers-possibly-state-backed-now-seek-to-destroy -data.html?pagewanted=2&_r=2&hp&pagewanted=all&*.

33. Perlroth, Nicole, and Sanger, David. "Cyberattacks Seem Meant to Destroy, Not Just Disrupt." 28 March 2013. Accessed 24 May 2016 from *www.nytimes.com/2013/03 /29/technology/corporate-cyberattackers-possibly-state-backed-now-seek-to-destroy -data.html*.

34. Redwine, Samuel T., Jr. (Editor). *Software Assurance: A Guide to the Common Body of Knowledge to Produce, Acquire, and Sustain Secure Software*. Version 1.1. U.S. Department of Homeland Security. September 2006.

35. Ibid.

36. Strickland, Jonathon. "10 Worst Computer Viruses of All Time." *How Stuff Works*. Accessed 24 May 2016 from *http://computer.howstuffworks.com/worst-computer -viruses2.htm#page=1*.

37. Agrawal, Sakshi. "Top 10 Most Dangerous Computer Viruses Ever." 10 August 2013. Accessed 24 May 2016 from *http://listdose.com/top-10-most-dangerous-computer -viruses-ever/*.

38. U.S. Department of Justice Press Release. "Creator of Melissa Computer Virus Sentenced to 20 Months in Federal Prison." Accessed 24 May 2016 from *www.justice .gov/archive/criminal/cybercrime/press-releases/2002/melissaSent.htm*.

39. TruSecure. "TruSecure Successfully Defends Customers Against Goner Virus." *TruSecure Online*. 18 December 2001. Accessed 24 May 2016 from *www.thefreelibrary .com/TruSecure+Successfully+Defends+Customers+Against+Goner+Virus.-a080877835*.

40. McCarthy, Jack. "Blaster Worm Author Gets Jail Time." *InfoWorld*. 28 January 2005. Accessed 24 May 2016 from *www.infoworld.com/t/business/blaster-worm -author-gets-jail-time-441*.

41. Kehoe, Brendan P. *Zen and the Art of the Internet*, 1st Edition. January 1992. Accessed 24 May 2016 from *www.cs.indiana.edu/docproject/zen/zen-1.0_10.html#SEC91*.

42. Jones, Les. "GoodTimes Virus Hoax Frequently Asked Questions." 12 December 1998. Accessed 24 May 2016 from *http://fgouget.free.fr/goodtimes/goodtimes.html*.

43. SANS Institute. "Back Door, NSA Glossary of Terms Used in Security and Intrusion Detection." *SANS Institute Online*. Accessed 24 May 2016 from *www.sans.org /resources/glossary.php*.

44. SANS Institute. "Consensus Roadmap for Defeating Distributed Denial of Service Attacks: A Project of the Partnership for Critical Infrastructure Security." *SANS Institute Online*. 23 February 2000. Accessed 24 May 2016 from *www.sans.org/dosstep /roadmap.php*.

45. Trend Micro. "WORM_MYDOOM.A." Accessed 24 May 2016 from *www.trendmicro .com/vinfo/virusencyclo/default5.asp?VName=WORM_MYDOOM.A*.

46. Richtel, Matt. "Canada Arrests 15-Year-Old In Web Attack." *The New York Times*. 20 April 2000.

47. "How CloudNine Wound Up in Hell." *Wired Online*. 1 February 2002. Accessed 24 May 2016 from *http://archive.wired.com/techbiz/media/news/2002/02/50171*.

48. Korolov, M. "Last week's DDoS against the BBC may have been the largest in history." CSO Online. Accessed 31 May 2016 from *www.csoonline.com/article/3020292 /cyber-attacks-espionage/ddos-attack-on-bbc-may-have-been-biggest-in-history.html*.

49. Pearce, James. "Security Expert Warns of MP3 Danger." *ZDNet News Online*. 18 March 2002. Accessed 24 May 2016 from *www.zdnet.com/article/security-expert- warns-of-mp3-danger/*.

50. Webopedia. "IP Spoofing." *Webopedia Online*. 4 June 2002. Accessed 24 May 2016 from *www.webopedia.com/TERM/I/IP_spoofing.html*.

51. "Murphy's Laws Site." Accessed 24 May 2016 from *www.murphys-laws.com/*.

52. Wolfe, Alexander. "Intel Preps Plan to Bust Bugs in Pentium MPUs." *Electronic Engineering Times*, no. 960 (June 1997): 1.

53. Taylor, Roger. "Intel to Launch New Chip Despite Bug Reports." *Financial Times (London)*, no. 25 (June 1998): 52.

54. Russ, Kay. "QuickStudy: Mean Time Between Failures (MTBF)." *ComputerWorld*. 31 October 2005. Accessed 24 May 2016 from *www.computerworld.com/s/article/105781/MTBF*.

55. OWASP. "OWASP Top 10–2013 The Ten Most Critical Web Application Security Risks." Accessed 24 May 2016 from *http://owasptop10.googlecode.com/files/OWASP%20Top%2010%20-%202013.pdf*.

56. Howard, M., LeBlanc, D., and Viega, J. *19 Deadly Sins of Software Security–Programming Flaws and How to Fix Them*. 2005. New York: McGraw-Hill/Osborne.

57. Webopedia. "Buffer Overflow." *Webopedia Online*. 29 July 2003. Accessed 24 May 2016 from *www.webopedia.com/TERM/b/buffer_overflow.html*.

58. Spanbauer, Scott. "Pentium Bug, Meet the IE 4.0 Flaw." *PC World* 16, no. 2 (February 1998): 55.

59. Austin, Richard. *Conversations on 19 Deadly Sins of Software Security–Programming Flaws and How to Fix Them*. 28 February 2007.

60. cgisecurity.com. "The Cross Site Scripting FAQ." Accessed 24 May 2016 from *www.cgisecurity.com/articles/xss-faq.shtml*.

61. Wheeler, D. "Write It Secure: Format Strings and Locale Filtering." Accessed 24 May 2016 from *www.dwheeler.com/essays/write_it_secure_1.html*.

62. Austin, Richard. *Conversations on 19 Deadly Sins of Software Security–Programming Flaws and How to Fix Them*. 28 February 2007.

63. Brumley, D., Tzi-cker, C., Johnson, R., Lin, H., and Song, D. "RICH: Automatically Protecting Against Integer-Based Vulnerabilities." Accessed 24 May 2016 from *http://people.csail.mit.edu/huijia/papers/Rich.pdf*.

64. Wheeler, D. A. "Secure Programmer: Prevent Race Conditions." *Institute for Defense Analyses*. Accessed 24 May 2016 from *www.google.com/url?sa=t&rct=j&q=&esrc=s&source=web&cd=1&cad=rja&uact=8&ved=0ahUKEwjCsdSw-PPMAhUXFlIKHbMiDbwQFggcMAA&url=http%3A%2F%2Fwww.ida.liu.se%2F~TDDC90%2Fliterature%2Fpapers%2FSP-race-conditions.pdf&usg=AFQjCNE85s800x1Q34TiEG51mKkfpLnDSA&sig2=n5gJRNftL0qiJu74LHUDDA&bvm=bv.122676328,d.aXo*.

65. Austin, Richard. *Conversations on 19 Deadly Sins of Software Security–Programming Flaws and How to Fix Them*. 28 February 2007.

66. Ibid.

chapter 3

Legal, Ethical, and Professional Issues in Information Security

In civilized life, law floats in a sea of ethics.

EARL WARREN, CHIEF JUSTICE OF
THE UNITED STATES, 12 NOVEMBER 1962

Henry Magruder made a mistake—he left a flash drive at the coffee station. Later, when Iris Majwubu was topping off her mug with fresh tea while taking a breather from her current project, she saw the unlabeled drive on the counter. Being the helpful sort, she picked it up, intending to return it to the person who'd left it behind.

Expecting to find a program from someone on the development team or a project management schedule, Iris slotted the drive in her computer. The system automatically ran a virus scan before opening the file explorer program. She had been correct in assuming the drive contained SLS company data files. There were lots of them. She opened a file at random: names, addresses, and Social Security numbers appeared on her screen. These were not the test records she expected; they looked more like confidential payroll data. The next file she picked was full of what seemed to be customers' credit card numbers. Concerned, she found a readme.txt file and opened it. It read:

```
Jill, see files on this drive. Hope they meet your expectations. Wire
money to account as arranged. Rest of data sent on payment.
```

Iris realized that someone was selling sensitive company data. She looked back at the directory listing and saw that the files spanned the range of every department at Sequential Label and Supply—everything from customer financial records to shipping invoices. She opened another file and saw that it contained only a sampling of the relevant data. Whoever did this had split the data into two parts. That made sense: just a sample to see the type of data and then payment on delivery.

Now, who did the drive belong to? She opened the file properties option of the readme.txt file. The file owner was listed as "hmagruder." That must be Henry Magruder, the developer two cubes over in the next aisle. Iris pondered her next action.

LEARNING OBJECTIVES

Upon completion of this material, you should be able to:

- Describe the functions of and relationships among laws, regulations, and professional organizations in information security
- Explain the differences between laws and ethics
- Identify major national laws that affect the practice of information security
- Discuss the role of privacy as it applies to law and ethics in information security

Introduction

As a future information security professional, or an IT professional with security responsibilities, you must understand the scope of an organization's legal and ethical responsibilities. The information security professional plays an important role in an organization's approach to managing responsibility and liability for privacy and security risks. In modern litigious societies around the world, laws are sometimes enforced in civil courts, where large damages can be awarded to plaintiffs who bring suits against organizations. Sometimes these damages are punitive—a punishment assessed as a deterrent to future transgressions. To minimize liability and reduce risks from electronic and physical threats, and to reduce all losses from legal action, information security practitioners must thoroughly understand the current legal environment, stay current with laws and regulations, and watch for new and emerging issues. By educating the management and employees of an organization on their legal and ethical obligations and the proper use of information technology and information security, security professionals can help keep an organization focused on its primary business objectives.

In the first part of this chapter, you will learn about the legislation and regulations that affect the management of information in an organization. In the second part, you will learn about the ethical issues related to information security, and about several professional organizations with established codes of ethics. Use this chapter both as a reference to the legal aspects of information security and as an aid in planning your professional career.

Law and Ethics in Information Security

> **Key Terms**
>
> **cultural mores** The fixed moral attitudes or customs of a particular group.
> **ethics** The branch of philosophy that considers nature, criteria, sources, logic, and the validity of moral judgment.
> **laws** Rules that mandate or prohibit certain behavior and are enforced by the state.

In general, people elect to trade some aspects of personal freedom for social order. It is often a necessary but somewhat ironic proposition, as Benjamin Franklin asserted: "Those who would give up essential Liberty, to purchase a little temporary Safety, deserve neither Liberty nor Safety."[1] As Jean-Jacques Rousseau explained in *The Social Contract, or Principles of Political Right*,[2] the rules that members of a society create to balance the individual rights to self-determination against the needs of the society as a whole are called **laws**. The key difference between laws and **ethics** is that laws carry the authority of a governing body and ethics do not. Ethics in turn are based on **cultural mores**. Some ethical standards are universal. For example, murder, theft, assault, and arson are generally prohibited in ethical and legal codes throughout the world.

❯ Organizational Liability and the Need for Counsel

> **Key Terms**
>
> **due care** Measures that an organization takes to ensure every employee knows what is acceptable and what is not.
> **due diligence** Reasonable steps taken by people or organizations to meet the obligations imposed by laws or regulations.
> **jurisdiction** The power to make legal decisions and judgments; typically an area within which an entity such as a court or law enforcement agency is empowered to make legal decisions.
> **liability** An entity's legal obligation or responsibility.
> **long-arm jurisdiction** The ability of a legal entity to exercise its influence beyond its normal boundaries by asserting a connection between an out-of-jurisdiction entity and a local legal case.
> **restitution** A legal requirement to make compensation or payment resulting from a loss or injury.

What if an organization does not demand or even encourage strong ethical behavior from its employees? What if an organization does not behave ethically? Even if there is no breach of criminal law, there can still be **liability**—legal responsibility. Liability includes the legal obligation to make **restitution** for wrongs committed. The bottom line is that if an employee performs an illegal or unethical act that causes some degree of harm, the employer can be held financially liable for that action, regardless of whether the employer authorized the act. An organization increases its liability if it refuses to take measures known as **due care** (or a standard of due care). Similarly, **due diligence** requires that an organization make a valid attempt to *continually maintain* this level of effort. Whereas due care means the organization *acts* legally and ethically, due diligence means it *ensures compliance* with this level of expected behavior. Given the Internet's global reach, those who could be injured or wronged by an organization's employees might live anywhere in the world. Under the U.S. legal system, any court can assert its authority over an individual or organization if it can establish **jurisdiction**. This is sometimes referred to as **long-arm jurisdiction** when laws are stretched to apply to parties in distant locations. Trying a case in the injured party's home area is usually favorable to the injured party.[3]

> Policy Versus Law

> **Key Term**
>
> **policy** Guidelines that dictate certain behavior within the organization.

Within an organization, information security professionals help maintain security via the establishment and enforcement of **policy**. As discussed in greater detail in Chapter 4, "Planning for Security," these policies function as organizational laws, complete with penalties, judicial practices, and sanctions to require compliance. Because these policies function as laws, they must be crafted and implemented with the same care to ensure that they are complete, appropriate, and fairly applied to everyone in the workplace. The difference between a policy and a law, however, is that ignorance of a policy is an acceptable defense. Policies must be able to stand up in court if challenged, because if an employee is fired based on a policy violation, rest assured it will be challenged. Thus, for a policy to be enforceable, it must meet the following five criteria:

- Dissemination (distribution): The organization must be able to demonstrate that the relevant policy has been made readily available for review by the employee. Common dissemination techniques include hard copy and electronic distribution.

- Review (reading): The organization must be able to demonstrate that it disseminated the document in an intelligible form, including versions for employees who are illiterate, reading-impaired, and unable to read English. Common techniques include recordings of the policy in English and alternate languages.

- Comprehension (understanding): The organization must be able to demonstrate that the employee understands the requirements and content of the policy. Common techniques include quizzes and other assessments.

- Compliance (agreement): The organization must be able to demonstrate that the employee agreed to comply with the policy through act or affirmation. Common techniques include logon banners, which require a specific action (mouse click or keystroke) to acknowledge agreement, or a signed document clearly indicating the employee has read, understood, and agreed to comply with the policy.

- Uniform enforcement: The organization must be able to demonstrate that the policy has been uniformly enforced, regardless of employee status or assignment.

Only when all of these conditions are met can an organization penalize employees who violate a policy without fear of legal retribution.

❭ Types of Law

There are a number of ways to categorize laws within the United States. In addition to the hierarchical perspective of local, state, federal, and international laws, most U.S. laws can be categorized based on their origins:

- Constitutional Law: Originates with the U.S. Constitution, a state constitution, or local constitution, bylaws, or charter.
- Statutory Law: Originates from a legislative branch specifically tasked with the creation and publication of laws and statutes.
- Regulatory or Administrative Law: Originates from an executive branch or authorized regulatory agency, and includes executive orders and regulations.
- Common Law, Case Law, and Precedent: Originates from a judicial branch or oversight board and involves the interpretation of law based on the actions of a previous and/or higher court or board.

Within statutory law, one can further divide laws into their association with individuals, groups, and the "state":

- *Civil law* embodies a wide variety of laws pertaining to relationships between and among individuals and organizations. Civil law includes contract law, employment law, family law, and tort law. *Tort law* is the subset of civil law that allows individuals to seek redress in the event of personal, physical, or financial injury. Perceived damages within civil law are pursued in civil court and are not prosecuted by the state.
- *Criminal law* addresses violations harmful to society and is actively enforced and prosecuted by the state. Criminal law addresses statutes associated with traffic law, public order, property damage, and personal damage, where the state takes on the responsibility of seeking retribution on behalf of the plaintiff, or injured party.

Yet another distinction addresses how legislation affects individuals in society, and is categorized as private law or public law. *Private law* is considered a subset of civil law, and regulates the relationships among individuals as well as relationships between individuals and organizations; it encompasses family law, commercial law, and labor law. *Public law* regulates the structure and administration of government agencies and their relationships with citizens, employees, and other governments. Public law includes criminal law, administrative law, and constitutional law.

Regardless of how you categorize laws, it is important to understand which laws and regulations are relevant to your organization and what the organization needs to do to comply.

Relevant U.S. Laws

Historically, the United States has been a leader in the development and implementation of information security legislation to prevent misuse and exploitation of information and information technology. Information security legislation contributes to a more reliable business environment, which in turn enables a stable economy. In its global leadership capacity, the United States has demonstrated a clear understanding of the importance of securing information and has specified penalties for people and organizations that breach U.S. civil statutes. The sections that follow present the most important U.S. laws that apply to information security.

〉 General Computer Crime Laws

Several key laws are relevant to the field of information security and are of particular interest to those who live or work in the United States. The *Computer Fraud and Abuse Act of 1986 (CFA Act or CFAA)* is the cornerstone of many computer-related federal laws and enforcement efforts. It was originally written as an extension and clarification to the *Comprehensive Crime Control Act of 1984*. The CFAA was amended by the *National Information Infrastructure Protection Act of 1996*, which modified several sections of the previous act and increased the penalties for selected crimes. The punishment for offenses prosecuted under this statute includes fines, imprisonment of up to 20 years, or both. The severity of the penalty depends on the value of the information obtained and whether the offense is judged to have been committed for the following reasons:

- For purposes of commercial advantage
- For private financial gain
- In furtherance of a criminal act

The preceding law and many others were further modified by the *USA PATRIOT Act of 2001*, which provides law enforcement agencies with broader latitude to combat terrorism-related activities. The full title of this act is the Uniting and Strengthening America by Providing Appropriate Tools Required to Intercept and Obstruct Terrorism Act of 2001. In 2006, this act was amended by the *USA PATRIOT Improvement and Reauthorization Act*, which made permanent 14 of the 16 expanded powers of the Department of Homeland Security and the FBI in investigating terrorist activity. The act also reset an expiration date written into the law as a so-called sunset clause for certain wiretaps under the Foreign Intelligence Surveillance Act of 1978 (FISA), and revised many of the criminal penalties and procedures associated with criminal and terrorist activities.[4]

In 2011, President Obama signed the *PATRIOT Sunset Extension Act of 2011*, which provided yet another extension of certain provisions of the USA PATRIOT Act, specifically those related to wiretaps, searching of business records, and the surveillance of people with suspected ties to terrorism. Some of the laws modified by the USA PATRIOT Act are among the earliest laws created to deal with electronic technology. Certain portions of the USA PATRIOT Act were extended in 2006, 2010, and 2011.

In May 2015, the U.S. Senate failed to extend the Act, resulting in its expiration on June 1, 2015. The controversy over Section 215, which allowed the National Security Agency (NSA) to collect metadata (the to: and from: information from phone records), initially resulted in an attempt to transfer the responsibility for collecting and reporting this information to the telecommunications companies involved as part of the *USA FREEDOM Act*, an abbreviation of "Uniting and Strengthening America by Fulfilling Rights and Ending Eavesdropping, Dragnet-collection and Online Monitoring Act." However, this act met with similar resistance, until the stalemate in Congress resulted in the sunset of key components of the USA PATRIOT Act. The complex issues within the political context of this law were eventually resolved and the USA FREEDOM Act was signed into law by President Obama in June 2015.

Another key law, the *Computer Security Act of 1987*, was one of the first attempts to protect federal computer systems by establishing minimum acceptable security practices. The National Institute of Standards and Technology (NIST)—known as the National Bureau of Standards prior to 1988—is responsible for developing these security standards and guidelines in cooperation with the National Security Agency.

In 2002, Congress passed the *Federal Information Security Management Act (FISMA)*, which mandates that all federal agencies establish information security programs to protect their information assets. The act effectively brought the federal government into alignment with the private sector. FISMA extended NIST's responsibilities, along with those of the Office of Management and Budget. The document also provided many of the definitions used today in information security. FISMA requires the following:

> *Each agency shall develop, document, and implement an agency-wide information security program, approved by the Director to provide information security for the information and information systems that support the operations and assets of the agency, including those provided or managed by another agency, contractor, or other source, that includes—*
>
> *(1) periodic assessments of the risk and magnitude of the harm that could result from the unauthorized access, use, disclosure, disruption, modification, or destruction of information and information systems that support the operations and assets of the agency;*
>
> *(2) policies and procedures that are based on the risk assessments; cost-effectively reduce information security risks to an acceptable level; ensure that information security is addressed throughout the life cycle of each agency information system; and ensure compliance with this act and other standards and regulations;*
>
> *(3) subordinate plans for providing adequate information security for networks, facilities, and systems or groups of information systems, as appropriate;*
>
> *(4) security awareness training to inform personnel, including contractors and other users of information systems that support the operations and assets of the agency, of information security risks associated with their activities; and their responsibilities in complying with agency policies and procedures designed to reduce these risks;*
>
> *(5) periodic testing and evaluation of the effectiveness of information security policies, procedures, and practices, to be performed with a frequency depending on risk, but no less than annually, of which such testing shall include testing of management, operational, and technical controls of every information system identified in the inventory required under [this document]; and may include testing relied on in an evaluation;*
>
> *(6) a process for planning, implementing, evaluating, and documenting remedial action to address any deficiencies in the information security policies, procedures, and practices of the agency;*
>
> *(7) procedures for detecting, reporting, and responding to security incidents, consistent with standards and guidelines issued pursuant to section 3546(b), including mitigating risks associated with such incidents before substantial*

> *damage is done; notifying and consulting with the Federal information secu-*
> *rity incident center referred to in section 3546; and notifying and consulting*
> *with, relevant agencies and federal offices as appropriate;*
>
> (8) *plans and procedures to ensure continuity of operations for information systems*
> *that support the operations and assets of the agency.*[5]

 For more information on FISMA, visit NIST's FISMA Implementation Project at http://csrc.nist.gov /groups/SMA/fisma/index.html.

Privacy

Key Terms

aggregate information Collective data that relates to a group or category of people and that has been altered to remove characteristics or components that make it possible to identify individuals within the group. Not to be confused with *information aggregation*.

information aggregation Pieces of nonprivate data that, when combined, may create information that violates privacy. Not to be confused with *aggregate information*.

privacy In the context of information security, the right of individuals or groups to protect themselves and their information from unauthorized access, providing confidentiality.

Privacy has become one of the hottest topics in information security at the beginning of the 21st century. Many organizations collect, swap, and sell personal information as a commodity, and as a result many people are looking to governments to protect their privacy from such organizations. The ability to collect information, combine facts from separate sources, and merge it all with other information has resulted in databases that were previously impossible to create. One technology that was proposed to monitor private communications, known as the Clipper chip (see Figure 3-1), used an algorithm with a two-part key that was to be managed by two separate government agencies. The chip was reportedly designed to protect individual communications while allowing the government to decrypt suspect trans-missions.[6] This technology was the focus of intense discussion between advocates for personal privacy and people who believed the chip would enable more effective law enforcement. Ulti-mately, the technology was not implemented by the U.S. government.

In response to the pressure for privacy protection, the number of statutes that address indi-vidual rights to privacy has grown. To help you better understand this rapidly evolving issue, some of the more relevant privacy laws are presented here.

Some regulations in the U.S. legal code stipulate responsibilities of common carriers (organiza-tions that process or move data for hire) to protect the confidentiality of customer information. The *Privacy of Customer Information Section* of the common carrier regulation states that any proprietary information shall be used explicitly for providing services, and not for marketing purposes. Carriers cannot disclose this information except when it is necessary to provide their services. The only other exception is applied when a customer requests the disclosure of infor-mation, in which case the disclosure is restricted to that customer's information only. This law does allow for the use of **aggregate information** as long as the same information is provided to all common carriers and all of them engage in fair competitive business practices. Note that

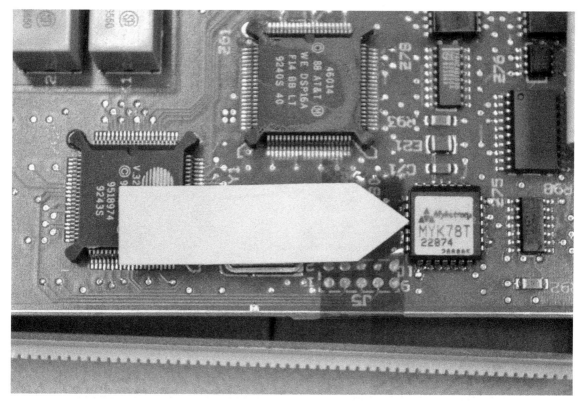

Figure 3-1 The Clipper chip[7]

aggregate information—the "blinding" of data collected for the purposes of managing networks or systems—is different from **information aggregation,** which is the development of individual profiles by combining information collected from multiple sources (see Figure 3-2).

While common carrier regulation oversees public carriers to protect individual privacy, the *Federal Privacy Act of 1974* regulates government agencies and holds them accountable if they release private information about individuals or businesses without permission. The following agencies, regulated businesses, and individuals are exempt from some of the regulations so they can perform their duties:

- Bureau of the Census
- National Archives and Records Administration
- Congress
- Comptroller General
- Federal courts with regard to specific issues using appropriate court orders
- Credit reporting agencies
- Individuals or organizations that demonstrate information is necessary to protect the health or safety of an individual party

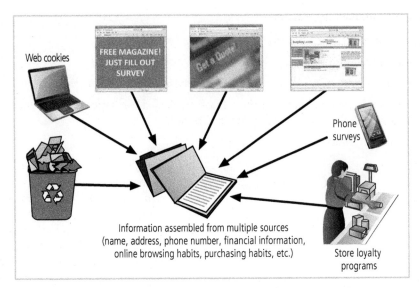

Web cookies

FREE MAGAZINE! JUST FILL OUT SURVEY

Phone surveys

Information assembled from multiple sources
(name, address, phone number, financial information,
online browsing habits, purchasing habits, etc.)

Store loyalty programs

Figure 3-2 Information aggregation

The *Electronic Communications Privacy Act (ECPA) of 1986*, informally referred to as the wiretapping act, is a collection of statutes that regulates the interception of wire, electronic, and oral communications. These statutes work in conjunction with the *Fourth Amendment of the U.S. Constitution*, which protects individual citizens from unlawful search and seizure.

The *Health Insurance Portability and Accountability Act of 1996 (HIPAA)*, also known as the *Kennedy-Kassebaum Act*, protects the confidentiality and security of healthcare data by establishing and enforcing standards and by standardizing electronic data interchange. HIPAA affects all healthcare organizations, including doctors' practices, health clinics, life insurers, and universities, as well as some organizations that have self-insured employee health programs. HIPAA specifies stiff penalties for organizations that fail to comply with the law, with fines of up to $250,000 and 10 years imprisonment for knowingly misusing client information.

How does HIPAA affect the field of information security? Beyond the basic privacy guidelines, the act requires organizations to use information security mechanisms as well as policies and procedures to protect healthcare information. It also requires a comprehensive assessment of information security systems, policies, and procedures in which healthcare information is handled or maintained. Electronic signatures have become more common, and HIPAA provides guidelines for the use of these signatures based on security standards that ensure message integrity, user authentication, and non-repudiation. There is no specification of particular security technologies for each of the security requirements, except that security must be implemented to ensure the privacy of the healthcare information.

The privacy standards of HIPAA severely restrict the dissemination and distribution of private health information without documented consent. The standards provide patients with the right to know who has access to their information and who has accessed it. The standards also restrict the use of health information to the minimum necessary for the healthcare services required.

HIPAA has five fundamental principles:

1. Consumer control of medical information
2. Boundaries on the use of medical information
3. Accountability to maintain the privacy of specified types of information
4. Balance of public responsibility for the use of medical information for the greater good measured against its impact to the individual patient
5. Security of health information

In 2009, an act that attempted to stimulate the American economy, *the American Recovery and Reinvestment Act of 2009 (ARRA)*, updated and broadened the scope of HIPAA in a section referred to as the *Health Information Technology for Economic and Clinical Health Act (HITECH)*. The update also provided "bounties" for investigators—financial monetary incentives to pursue violators. HIPAA only covered healthcare organizations (HCOs), but HITECH expanded HIPAA to include businesses associated with HCOs, including legal and accounting firms as well as IT firms or any business partners. These business partners must now comply with HIPAA regulations in protecting patient healthcare information (PHI) as if they were HCOs themselves.[8]

> *Effective February 2010, organizations face the same civil and legal penalties that doctors, hospitals, and insurance companies face for violating the HIPAA Privacy Rule. HITECH not only changes how fines will be levied, it also raises the upper limit on the fines that can be imposed. An HCO or business partner who violates HIPAA may have to pay fines reaching as high as $1.5 million per calendar year. In addition, private citizens and lawyers can now sue to collect fines for security breaches. Overall, HITECH considerably increases the potential financial liability of any organization that mishandles the PHI that passes through its IT infrastructure.*
>
> *The HITECH Act also includes new data breach notification rules that apply to HCOs and business partners. If an employee discovers a PHI security breach, the employee's organization has only 60 days in which to notify each individual whose privacy has been compromised. If the organization is unable to contact ten or more of the affected individuals, it must either report the security breach on its Web site or issue a press release about the breach to broadcast and print media. If the breach affects 500 or more individuals, the organization must additionally notify the Security of the HHS, along with major media outlets. The HHS will then report the breach on its own Web site.[9]*

HIPAA was again updated in 2013 with a Department of Health and Human Services Regulatory Action intended to strengthen the act's privacy and security protections. The changes increased liability for the protection of patient information, strengthened penalties for noncompliance, increased the requirements for notifying patients about breaches of confidentiality of their information, and other related PHI protection practices.[10]

- The *Financial Services Modernization Act* or *Gramm-Leach-Bliley Act of 1999* contains many provisions that focus on facilitating affiliation among banks, securities firms, and insurance companies. Specifically, this act requires all financial institutions to disclose their privacy policies on the sharing of nonpublic personal information. It also requires due notice to customers so they can request that their information not be shared with third parties. In addition, the act ensures that an organization's privacy policies are fully disclosed when a customer initiates a business relationship and then distributed at least annually for the duration of the professional association.

See Table 3-1 for a summary of information security-related laws.

Area	Act	Date	Description
Online commerce and information protection	Federal Trade Commission Act (FTCA)	1914	Recently used to challenge organizations with deceptive claims regarding the privacy and security of customers' personal information
Telecommunications	Communications Act (47 USC 151 et seq.)	1934	Includes amendments found in the Telecommunications Deregulation and Competition Act of 1996; this law regulates interstate and foreign telecommunications (amended 1996 and 2001)
Freedom of information	Freedom of Information Act (FOIA)	1966	Allows for the disclosure of previously unreleased information and documents controlled by the U.S. government
Protection of credit information	Fair Credit Reporting Act (FCRA)	1970	Regulates the collection and use of consumer credit information
Privacy	Federal Privacy Act	1974	Governs federal agency use of personal information
Privacy of student information	Family Educational Rights and Privacy Act (FERPA) (20 U.S.C. § 1232g; 34 CFR Part 99)	1974	Also known as the Buckley Amendment; protects the privacy of student education records
Copyright	Copyright Act (update to U.S. Copyright Law (17 USC))	1976	Protects intellectual property, including publications and software
Cryptography	Electronic Communications Privacy Act (update to 18 USC)	1986	Regulates interception and disclosure of electronic information; also referred to as the Federal Wiretapping Act
Access to stored communications	Unlawful Access to Stored Communications (18 USC 2701)	1986	Provides penalties for illegally accessing communications (such as e-mail and voice mail) stored by a service provider
Threats to computers	Computer Fraud and Abuse (CFA) Act (also known as Fraud and Related Activity in Connection with Computers) (18 USC 1030)	1986	Defines and formalizes laws to counter threats from computer-related acts and offenses (amended 1996, 2001, and 2006)
Federal agency information security	Computer Security Act (CSA)	1987	Requires all federal computer systems that contain classified information to have security plans in place, and requires periodic security training for all individuals who operate, design, or manage such systems
Trap and trace restrictions	General prohibition on pen register and trap-and-trace device use; exception (18 USC 3121 et seq.)	1993	Prohibits the use of electronic "pen registers" and trap-and-trace devices without a court order

Table 3-1 Key U.S. Laws of Interest to Information Security Professionals

Area	Act	Date	Description
Criminal intent	National Information Infrastructure Protection Act (update to 18 USC 1030)	1996	Categorizes crimes based on defendant's authority to access a protected computer system and criminal intent
Trade secrets	Economic Espionage Act	1996	Prevents abuse of information gained while employed elsewhere
Personal health information protection	Health Insurance Portability and Accountability Act (HIPAA)	1996	Requires medical practices to ensure the privacy of personal medical information
Encryption and digital signatures	Security and Freedom Through Encryption Act	1997	Affirms the rights of persons in the United States to use and sell products that include encryption and to relax export controls on such products
IP	No Electronic Theft Act amends 17 USC 506(a)—copyright infringement, and 18 USC 2319—criminal infringement of copyright (Public Law 105-147)	1997	These parts of the U.S. Code amend copyright and criminal statutes to provide greater copyright protection and penalties for electronic copyright infringement
Copy protection	Digital Millennium Copyright Act (DMCA) (update to 17 USC 101)	1998	Provides specific penalties for removing copyright protection from media
Identity theft	Identity Theft and Assumption Deterrence Act (18 USC 1028)	1998	Attempts to instigate specific penalties for identity theft by identifying the individual who loses their identity as the true victim, not just those commercial and financial credit entities who suffered losses
Child privacy protection	Children's Online Privacy Protection Act (COPPA)	1998	Provides requirements for online service and Web site providers to ensure the privacy of children under 13 is protected
Banking	Gramm-Leach-Bliley (GLB) Act (also known as the Financial Services Modernization Act)	1999	Repeals the restrictions on banks affiliating with insurance and securities firms; has significant impact on the privacy of personal information used by these industries
Accountability	Sarbanes-Oxley (SOX) Act (also known as the Public Company Accounting Reform and Investor Protection Act)	2002	Enforces accountability for executives at publicly traded companies; is having ripple effects throughout the accounting, IT, and related units of many organizations
General InfoSec	Federal Information Security Management Act, or FISMA (44 USC § 3541, et seq.)	2002	Requires each federal agency to develop, document, and implement an agency-wide program to provide InfoSec for the information and information systems that support the operations and assets of the agency, including those provided or managed by another agency, contractor, or other source
Spam	Controlling the Assault of Non-Solicited Pornography and Marketing (CAN-SPAM) Act (15 USC 7701 et seq.)	2003	Sets the first national standards for regulating the distribution of commercial e-mail, including mobile phone spam

Table 3-1 Key U.S. Laws of Interest to Information Security Professionals *(continues)*

Area	Act	Date	Description
Fraud with access devices	Fraud and Related Activity in Connection with Access Devices (18 USC 1029)	2004	Defines and formalizes law to counter threats from counterfeit access devices like ID cards, credit cards, telecom equipment, mobile or electronic serial numbers, and the equipment that creates them
Terrorism and extreme drug trafficking	USA PATRIOT Improvement and Reauthorization Act (update to 18 USC 1030)	2006	Renews critical sections of the USA PATRIOT Act
Privacy of PHI	American Recovery and Reinvestment Act	2009	In the privacy and security area, requires new reporting requirements and penalties for breach of Protected Health Information (PHI)
Privacy of PHI	Health Information Technology for Economic and Clinical Health (HITECH) Act (part of ARRA-2009)	2009	Addresses privacy and security concerns associated with the electronic transmission of PHI, in part, through several provisions that strengthen HIPAA rules for civil and criminal enforcement
Defense information protection	International Traffic in Arms Regulations (ITAR) Act	2012	Restricts the exportation of technology and information related to defense and military-related services and materiel including research and development information
National cyber infrastructure protection	National Cybersecurity Protection Act	2014	Updates the Homeland Security Act of 2002, which established the Department of Homeland Security, to include a national cybersecurity and communications integration center to share information and facilitate coordination between agencies, and perform analysis of cybersecurity incidents and risks
Federal information security updates	Federal Information Security Modernization Act	2014	Updates many outdated federal information security practices, updating FISMA, providing a framework for ensuring effectiveness in information security controls over federal information systems, and centralizing cybersecurity management within DHS
National information security employee assessment	Cybersecurity Workforce Assessment Act	2014	Tasks DHS to perform an evaluation of the national cybersecurity employee workforce at least every three years, and to develop a plan to improve recruiting and training of cybersecurity employees
Terrorist tracking	USA FREEDOM Act	2015	Updates the Foreign Intelligence Surveillance Act (FISA); transfers the requirement to collect and report communications to/from known terrorist phone numbers to communications carriers, to be provided to select federal agencies upon request, among other updates to surveillance activities

Table 3-1 Key U.S. Laws of Interest to Information Security Professionals *(continued)*

To learn more about laws that are not specifically discussed in this chapter, visit CSO Magazine's directory of security laws, regulations, and guidelines at www.csoonline.com/article/632218/the -security-laws-regulations-and-guidelines-directory.

Identity Theft

> **Key Terms**
>
> **identity theft** The unauthorized taking of personally identifiable information with the intent of committing fraud and abuse of a person's financial and personal reputation, purchasing goods and services without authorization, and generally impersonating the victim for illegal or unethical purposes.
>
> **personally identifiable information (PII)** Information about a person's history, background, and attributes that can be used to commit identity theft. This information typically includes a person's name, address, Social Security number, family information, employment history, and financial information.

Related to privacy legislation is the growing body of law on **identity theft.** Identity theft can occur when someone steals a victim's **personally identifiable information (PII)** and uses it to purchase goods and services, or conduct other actions while posing as the victim. According to a report from the U.S. Department of Justice, "approximately 17.6 million persons or 7% of all U.S. residents age 16 or older, were victims of one or more incidents of identity theft in 2014."[11] As shown in Figure 3-3, the bulk of this theft occurred with payment card

Persons age 16 or older who experienced at least one identity theft incident in the past 12 months, by type of theft, 2012 and 2014

	Anytime during the past 12 months[a]				Most recent incident					
	Number of victims		Percent of all persons		Number of victims		Percent of all persons		Percent of all victims	
Type of identity theft	2012	2014*	2012	2014*	2012	2014*	2012	2014*	2012	2014*
Total	16,580,500	17,576,200	6.7%	7.0%	16,580,500	17,576,200	6.7%	7.0%	100%	100%
Existing account	15,323,500	16,392,600	6.2%	6.6%	14,022,100	15,045,200	5.7%	6.0%	84.6%	85.6%
Credit card	7,698,500‡	8,598,600	3.1%	3.4%	6,676,300	7,329,100	2.7%	2.9%	40.3%	41.7%
Bank	7,470,700	8,082,600	3.0%	3.2%	6,191,500	6,735,800	2.5%	2.7%	37.3%	38.3%
Other	1,696,400	1,452,300	0.7%	0.6%	1,154,300	980,300	0.5%	0.4%	7.0%‡	5.6%
New account	1,125,100	1,077,100	0.5%	0.4%	683,400	683,300	0.3%	0.3%	4.1%	3.9%
Personal information	833,600	713,000	0.3%	0.3%	622,900	546,400	0.3%	0.2%	3.8%	3.1%
Multiple types	~	~	~	~	1,252,000	1,297,700	0.5%	0.6%	7.6%	7.4%
Existing account[b]	~	~	~	~	824,700	921,500	0.3%	0.4%	5.0%	5.2%
Other[c]	~	~	~	~	427,400	376,200	0.2%	0.2%	2.6%	2.1%

~Not applicable.
*Comparison year.
‡Significant difference from comparison year at the 90% confidence level.
[a]Identity theft classified as a single type.
[b]Includes victims who experienced two or more of the following: unauthorized use of a credit card, bank account, or other existing account.
[c]Includes victims who experienced two or more of the following: unauthorized use of an existing account, misuse of personal information to open a new account, or misuse of personal information for other fraudulent purposes.
Source: Bureau of Justice Statistics, National Crime Victimization Survey, Identity Theft Supplement, 2012 and 2014.

Figure 3-3 U.S. Department of Justice report on victims of identity theft in 2012 and 2014

Source: U.S. Federal Trade Commission.

accounts. Organizations can also be victims of identity theft by means of URL manipulation or DNS redirection, as described in Chapter 2.

In May 2006, President Bush signed an executive order creating the Identity Theft Task Force. On April 27, 2007, it issued a strategic plan to improve efforts by the government, private organizations, and individuals in combating identity theft. The U.S. Federal Trade Commission (FTC) now oversees efforts to foster coordination among groups, more effective prosecution of criminals engaged in identify theft, and methods to increase restitution made to victims.[12]

While numerous states have passed identity theft laws, the legislation at the federal level primarily began in 1997 with the passing of the Identity Theft and Assumption Deterrence Act of 1998 (Public Law 105-318). This law was later revised by the *Fraud and Related Activity in Connection with Identification Documents, Authentication Features, and Information Act* (Title 18, U.S.C. § 1028), which criminalizes the creation, reproduction, transfer, possession, or use of unauthorized or false identification documents or document-making equipment. The penalties for such offenses range from 1 to 25 years in prison and fines as determined by the courts.

The FTC recommends that people take the following four steps when they suspect they are victims of identity theft:

1. Place an initial fraud alert: Report to one of the three national credit reporting companies and ask for an initial fraud alert on your credit report. This makes it harder for an identity thief to open more accounts in your name.

2. Order your credit reports: Filing an initial fraud alert entitles you to a free credit report from *each* of the three credit reporting companies. Examine the reports for fraud activity and contact the fraud department in the organization that holds the suspect account.

3. Create an identity theft report: Filing a complaint with the FTC will generate an identity theft affidavit, which can be used to file a police report and create an identity theft report. This report helps when dealing with credit reporting companies, debt collectors, and any businesses with whom the identity thief has interacted.

4. Monitor your progress: Document all calls, letters, and communications during the process.[13]

In 2008, Congress passed another update to the CFAA titled the *Identity Theft Enforcement and Restitution Act of 2008*, which specifically addressed the malicious use of spyware or keyloggers to steal PII. This act also created a new designation of a level of identity theft that provided much stronger penalties for violators who used 10 or more computers to commit theft. The new law also created a mechanism by which victims of identity theft may receive restitution from criminals convicted under the act. The penalties that may be levied under this act include substantial fines, from which the restitution is paid, and prison terms of up to 10 or 20 years, depending on the severity of the crime.[14] Increasingly, consumers who recognize the increased threat of identity theft elect to buy credit protection insurance products that offset the expenses associated with such theft.

For more information on privacy and identity theft, visit the FTC's Web site at www.consumer.ftc .gov/topics/privacy-identity and the U.S. Department of Justice Web site at www.justice.gov /criminal-fraud/identity-theft.

❯ Export and Espionage Laws

To meet national security needs and to protect trade secrets and other state and private assets, several laws restrict which information, information management resources, and security resources may be exported from the United States. These laws attempt to stem the theft of information by establishing strong penalties for such crimes. Such laws have limited effectiveness in many cases because the theft is initiated from offshore and the ability to apply the law is reduced when perpetrators are from another jurisdiction.

To protect American ingenuity, intellectual property, and competitive advantage, Congress passed the *Economic Espionage Act* in 1996. This law attempts to prevent trade secrets from being illegally shared.

The *Security and Freedom through Encryption Act of 1999* provides guidance for the use of encryption and provides protection from government intervention. The acts include provisions that:

- Reinforce a person's right to use or sell encryption algorithms without concern for regulations requiring some form of key registration. Key registration is the storage of a cryptographic key (or its text equivalent) with another party for breaking the encryption of data. This is often called "key escrow."

- Prohibit the federal government from requiring the use of encryption for contracts, grants, and other official documents and correspondence.

- State that the use of encryption is not probable cause to suspect criminal activity. Relax export restrictions by amending the Export Administration Act of 1979.

- Provide additional penalties for the use of encryption in the commission of a criminal act.

As illustrated in Figure 3-4, which shows restrictions on the shipment of Microsoft products, the distribution of many software packages is restricted to approved organizations, governments, and countries.

❯ U.S. Copyright Law

Intellectual property is a protected asset in the United States. The *U.S. Copyright Law* extends this privilege to published works, including electronic formats. Fair use allows copyrighted materials to be used to support news reporting, teaching, scholarship, and similar activities, as long as the use is for educational or library purposes, is not for profit, and is not excessive. As long as proper acknowledgment is provided to the original author of such works, including a proper citation of the location of source materials, and the work is not represented as one's own, it is entirely permissible to include portions of someone else's work as reference.

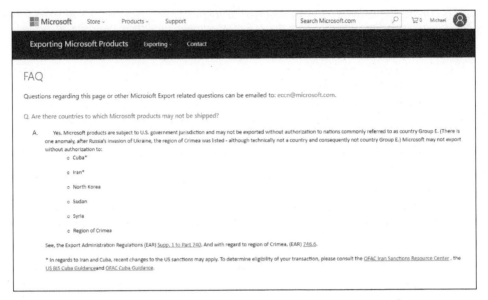

Figure 3-4 Export restrictions on Microsoft products

Source: www.microsoft.com/en-us/exporting/faq.aspx.

 For more information on the U.S. Copyright Law, visit the U.S. Copyright Office's Web site at www.copyright.gov/. You can view the law in its entirety at www.copyright.gov/title17/.

❯ Financial Reporting

The *Sarbanes-Oxley Act of 2002*, also known as SOX or the *Corporate and Auditing Accountability and Responsibility Act*, is a critical piece of legislation that affects the executive management of publicly traded corporations and public accounting firms. The law seeks to improve the reliability and accuracy of financial reporting, as well as increase the accountability of corporate governance, in publicly traded companies. Penalties for noncompliance range from fines to jail terms. Executives in firms covered by this law seek assurance for the reliability and quality of information systems from senior information technology managers. In turn, IT managers will likely ask information security managers to verify the confidentiality and integrity of the information systems in a process known as subcertification.

The two sections of SOX that most affect information security are Section 302 and Section 404. Section 302 of SOX requires an organization's executives to personally certify the accuracy and completeness of their financial reports as well as assess and report on the effectiveness of internal controls for their financial reporting. Section 404 complements the requirement to assess and report on internal controls, mandating that these assessment reports must be audited by an outside firm. Because SOX does not delineate IT from non-IT internal controls, and because most modern financial systems and their controls are based on IT and information security technologies, the expectation of effective controls trickles through the organization to the Information Security department.

❯ Freedom of Information Act of 1966

The *Freedom of Information Act (FOIA)* allows any person to request access to federal agency records or information not determined to be a matter of national security. Agencies of the federal government are required to disclose requested information upon receipt of a written request. This requirement is enforceable in court. However, some information is protected from disclosure, and the act does not apply to state or local government agencies or to private businesses or individuals, although many states have their own version of the FOIA. Figure 3-5 illustrates the number of FOIA requests received by the U.S. government between 2008 and 2012, and their disposition.

❯ Payment Card Industry Data Security Standards (PCI DSS)

For organizations that process payment cards, such as credit cards, debit cards, ATM cards, store-value cards, gift cards, or other related items, the Payment Card Industry (PCI) Security Standards Council offers a standard of performance to which participating organizations must comply. While not a law, per se, this standard has proven to be very effective in improving industry practices. The PCI Standards Council was founded in 2006 by a group of industry businesses that include American Express, Visa, Discover Financial Services, JCB, and MasterCard Worldwide. The Security Standards Council established a set of regulatory mandates with which organizations must comply to be certified by the PCI Council. These regulations, the *Payment Card Industry Data Security Standards (PCI DSS)*, are designed to enhance the security of customers' account data. The regulations include requirements for information security policies, procedures, and management, as well as technical software and networking specifications.

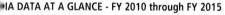

IA DATA AT A GLANCE - FY 2010 through FY 2015

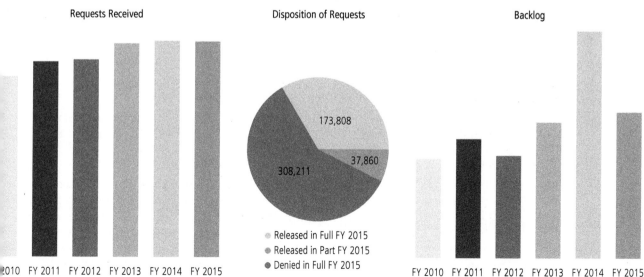

Figure 3-5 U.S. government FOIA requests and processing

Source: www.foia.gov.

PCI DSS "was developed to encourage and enhance cardholder data security and facilitate the broad adoption of consistent data security measures globally. PCI DSS provides a baseline of technical and operational requirements designed to protect cardholder data. PCI DSS applies to all entities involved in payment card processing—including merchants, processors, acquirers, issuers, and service providers, as well as all other entities that store, process or transmit cardholder data (CHD) and/or sensitive authentication data (SAD)."[15]

PCI DSS addresses the following six areas with 12 requirements:

Area 1: "Build and maintain a secure network and systems.

1. Install and maintain a firewall configuration to protect cardholder data.

2. Do not use vendor-supplied defaults for system passwords and other security parameters."

Area 2: "Protect cardholder data.

3. Protect stored cardholder data.

4. Encrypt transmission of cardholder data across open, public networks."

Area 3: "Maintain a vulnerability management program.

5. Protect all systems against malware and regularly update antivirus software or programs.

6. Develop and maintain secure systems and applications."

Area 4: "Implement strong access control measures.

7. Restrict access to cardholder data by a business need to know.

8. Identify and authenticate access to system components.

9. Restrict physical access to cardholder data."

Area 5: "Regularly monitor and test networks.

10. Track and monitor all access to network resources and cardholder data.

11. Regularly test security systems and processes."

Area 6: "Maintain an information security policy.

12. Maintain a policy that addresses information security for all personnel."[16]

The Council has also issued requirements called the Payment Application Data Security Standard (PA DSS) and PCI Pin Transaction Security (PCI PTS), which provide additional specifications for components of payment card processing.

 For more information on PCI DSS, visit www.pcisecuritystandards.org/.

❯ State and Local Regulations

A critical fact to keep in mind when reading federal computer laws is that the majority of them are written specifically to protect federal information systems. The laws have little applicability to private organizations. Thus, such organizations must be cognizant of the state and local laws that protect and apply to them. Information security professionals must understand state laws and regulations and ensure that their organizations' security policies and procedures are in compliance.

For example, in 1991, the state of Georgia passed the *Georgia Computer Systems Protection Act*, which protects information and established penalties for the use of information technology to attack or exploit information systems. In 1998, Georgia passed its Identity Fraud Act (updated in 2002), which established strong penalties for identity theft and the inappropriate disposal of customer confidential information.

 For more information on state security laws, visit the National Conference of State Legislatures Web site at www.ncsl.org. Use the search box to find your state's security breach notification laws, data disposal laws, and identity theft statutes.

3

International Laws and Legal Bodies

IT professionals and information security practitioners must realize that when their organizations do business on the Internet, they do business globally. As a result, these professionals must be sensitive to the laws and ethical values of many different cultures, societies, and countries. When it comes to certain ethical values, you may be unable to please all of the people all of the time, but the laws of other nations is one area in which it is certainly *not* easier to ask for forgiveness than for permission.

Several security bodies and laws are described in this section. Because of the political complexities of relationships among nations and differences in culture, few current international laws cover privacy and information security. The laws discussed in this section are important, but they are limited in their enforceability. The American Society of International Law is one example of an American institution that deals with international law (see *www.asil.org).*

❭ U.K. Computer Security Laws

The following laws are in force in the United Kingdom and are similar to those described earlier for the United States:

- Computer Misuse Act 1990: Defined three "computer misuse offenses":

    1. Unauthorized access to computer material.

    2. Unauthorized access with intent to commit or facilitate commission of further offenses.

    3. Unauthorized acts with intent to impair, or with recklessness as to impairing, operation of computer, etc.[17]

- Privacy and Electronic Communications (EC Directive) Regulations 2003: Revoked the Data Protection and Privacy Regulations of 1999, and focuses on protection against unwanted or harassing phone, e-mail, and SMS messages.

- Police and Justice Act 2006: Updated the Computer Misuse Act, modified the penalties, and created new crimes defined as the "unauthorized acts with intent to impair operation of computer, etc.,"[18] and the manufacture or provision of materials used in computer misuse offenses.

- Personal Internet Safety 2007: A report published by the House of Lords Science and Technology Committee provided a public service, and criticized the U.K. government's lack of action in protecting personal Internet safety.

> Australian Computer Security Laws

The following laws are in force in Australia and its territories, and are similar to those described earlier for the United States:

- Privacy Act 1988: Regulates the collection, storage, use, and disclosure of personal information. Applies both to private and public sectors. Contains 11 information privacy principles for handling personal information by most public sector agencies, and 10 national privacy principles for handling of personal information by nongovernment agencies.[19]

- Telecommunications Act 1997: Updated as of October 2013; contains regulation related to the collection and storage of privacy data held by telecommunications service providers.

- Corporations Act 2001: Updated by the Corporations Regulations of 2001 and 2002; focuses on business relationships, but similar to SOX, contains provisions related to financial reporting and audits.

- Spam Act 2003: Legislation designed to regulate the amount of unwanted commercial marketing materials, especially via e-mail. Requires businesses to obtain *consent* of recipients, ensure that businesses accurately *identify* the recipients, and provide a mechanism by which the recipients may *unsubscribe* from commercial messages.

- Cybercrime Legislation Amendment Bill 2011: Designed to align Australian laws with the European Convention on Cybercrime (see next section); the bill specifies information that communications carriers and Internet service providers must retain and surrender when requested by law enforcement.

> Council of Europe Convention on Cybercrime

The Council of Europe adopted the *Convention on Cybercrime* in 2001. It created an international task force to oversee a range of security functions associated with Internet activities and standardized technology laws across international borders. It also attempts to improve the effectiveness of international investigations into breaches of technology law. This convention has been well received by advocates of intellectual property rights because it emphasizes prosecution for copyright infringement. However, many supporters of individual rights oppose the convention because they think it unduly infringes on freedom of speech and threatens the civil liberties of U.S. residents.

Thirty-four countries attended the convention signing in November 2001, and 41 nations, including the United States and the United Kingdom, have ratified the convention as of January 2014.[20] The United States is technically not a member state of the Council of Europe, but it does participate in the convention.

As with much complex international legislation, the Convention on Cybercrime lacks any realistic provisions for enforcement. The overall goal of the convention is to simplify the acquisition of information for law enforcement agencies in certain types of international crimes. It also simplifies the extradition process. The convention has more than its share of skeptics, who see it as an overly simplistic attempt to control a complex problem.

 For more information on the Council of Europe Convention on Cybercrime, visit its Web site at www.coe.int/cybercrime.

3

❯ World Trade Organization and the Agreement on Trade-Related Aspects of Intellectual Property Rights

The *Agreement on Trade-Related Aspects of Intellectual Property Rights (TRIPS)*, created by the World Trade Organization (WTO) and negotiated from 1986 to 1994, introduced intellectual property rules into the multilateral trade system. It is the first significant international effort to protect intellectual property rights. It outlines requirements for governmental oversight and legislation of WTO member countries to provide minimum levels of protection for intellectual property. The WTO TRIPS agreement covers five issues:

- How basic principles of the trading system and other international intellectual property agreements should be applied
- How to give adequate protection to intellectual property rights
- How countries should enforce those rights adequately within their own borders
- How to settle disputes on intellectual property between members of the WTO
- Special transitional arrangements during the period when the new system is being introduced[21]

❯ Digital Millennium Copyright Act

The *Digital Millennium Copyright Act (DMCA)* is the American contribution to an international effort by the World Intellectual Properties Organization (WIPO) to reduce the impact of copyright, trademark, and privacy infringement, especially when accomplished via the removal of technological copyright protection measures. This law was created in response to the 1995 adoption of *Directive 95/46/EC* by the European Union, which added protection for individual citizens with regard to the processing of personal data and its use and movement. The United Kingdom has implemented a version of this law called the *Database Right* to comply with Directive 95/46/EC.

The DMCA includes the following provisions:

- Prohibits the circumvention of protections and countermeasures implemented by copyright owners to control access to protected content
- Prohibits the manufacture of devices to circumvent protections and countermeasures that control access to protected content
- Bans trafficking in devices manufactured to circumvent protections and countermeasures that control access to protected content
- Prohibits the altering of information attached or embedded into copyrighted material
- Excludes Internet service providers from certain forms of contributory copyright infringement

In June 2016, the United States and the European Union (EU) signed an agreement that superseded the prior agreement known as "Safe Harbor." The new agreement serves as a data privacy umbrella for EU citizens and allows cooperation between American and European law enforcement agencies in criminal investigations. It is the latest attempt to implement a solution for the issues that emerged when the Safe Harbor data-sharing agreement was ruled invalid by a Court of Justice of the European Union in October 2015. Industry observers had warned of economic consequences that the lack of certainty involving data sharing agreements could create. Even this agreement may not have the desired effect. Some organizations have responded to this uncertainty by avoiding simple compliance with specific government policies and moving to use more stringent standards. Some companies are considering adopting Binding Corporate Rules (BCRs) accreditation. That standard enables companies that obtain BCR accreditation to transfer personal data outside of the EU in a secure manner and in accordance with local laws and regulations. Security practitioners are closely monitoring this policy spat between the United States and the EU to find ways to meet important policy compliance demands.

Ethics and Information Security

Many professionally regulated disciplines have explicit rules that govern the ethical behavior of their members. For example, doctors and lawyers who commit egregious violations of their professions' canons of conduct can have their legal ability to practice revoked. Unlike the medical and legal fields, however, the information technology and information security fields do not have binding codes of ethics. Instead, professional associations such as the ACM and ISSA, and certification agencies such as (ISC)² and ISACA, work to maintain ethical codes of conduct for their respective memberships. While these professional organizations can prescribe ethical conduct, they do not have the authority to banish violators from practicing their trade. To begin exploring some of the ethical issues of information security, take a look at the Ten Commandments of Computer Ethics in the nearby Offline feature.

OFFLINE

The Ten Commandments of Computer Ethics[22] from the Computer Ethics Institute

1. Thou shalt not use a computer to harm other people.

2. Thou shalt not interfere with other people's computer work.

3. Thou shalt not snoop around in other people's computer files.

4. Thou shalt not use a computer to steal.

5. Thou shalt not use a computer to bear false witness.

6. Thou shalt not copy or use proprietary software for which you have not paid.

7. Thou shalt not use other people's computer resources without authorization or proper compensation.

8. Thou shalt not appropriate other people's intellectual output.

9. Thou shalt think about the social consequences of the program you are writing or the system you are designing.

10. Thou shalt always use a computer in ways that ensure consideration and respect for your fellow humans.

❯ Ethical Differences Across Cultures

Cultural differences can make it difficult to determine what is ethical and what is not—especially when it comes to the use of computers. Studies on ethics and computer use reveal that people of different nationalities have different perspectives; difficulties arise when one nationality's ethical behavior violates the ethics of another national group. For example, to Western cultures, many of the ways in which Asian cultures use computer technology amount to software piracy. This ethical conflict arises out of Asian traditions of collective ownership, which clash with the protection of intellectual property.

Approximately 90 percent of all software is created in the United States. The Business Software Alliance's 2016 global software study found that in 2015, 39 percent of software installed on computers globally was not properly licensed. Table 3-2 shows the results from the most recent BSA study of the rates and commercial values of unlicensed PC software installations biennially between 2009 and 2015, both by world region and within G-20 countries.

Some countries are more relaxed than others when dealing with intellectual property copy restrictions. A study published in 1999 examined the computer-use ethics in several nations, including Singapore, Hong Kong, the United States, England, Australia, Sweden, Wales, and the Netherlands.[23] This study selected various computer-use vignettes (see the Offline feature titled "The Use of Scenarios in Computer Ethics Studies") and presented them to university students in the various nations. The study did not categorize or classify the responses as ethical or unethical. Instead, the responses only indicated a degree of ethical sensitivity or knowledge about the performance of the characters in the short case studies. The scenarios were grouped into three categories of ethical computer use: software license infringement, illicit use, and misuse of corporate resources.[24]

Software License Infringement The topic of software license infringement, or piracy, is routinely covered by the popular press. Among study participants, attitudes toward piracy were generally similar; however, participants from the United States and the Netherlands showed statistically significant differences in attitudes from those of the overall group. Participants from the United States were significantly less tolerant of piracy, while those from the Netherlands were significantly more permissive. Although other studies have reported that the Pacific Rim countries of Singapore and Hong Kong are hotbeds of software piracy, this study found tolerance for copyright infringement in those countries to be moderate, as were attitudes in England, Wales, Australia, and Sweden. This could mean that the people surveyed *understood* what software license infringement was, but felt either that certain use was not piracy or that their society permitted this piracy in some way. Peer pressure, the lack of legal disincentives, the lack of punitive measures, and other reasons could explain why users in these alleged piracy centers disregarded intellectual property laws despite their professed attitudes toward them. Even though participants from the Netherlands displayed a more permissive attitude toward piracy, that country only ranked third in piracy rates of the nations surveyed in the study.

Illicit Use The study respondents unilaterally condemned viruses, hacking, and other forms of system abuse. There were, however, different degrees of tolerance for such activities

Worldwide by Region								
	Rates of Unlicensed Software Installations				Commercial Value of Unlicensed Software ($M)			
	2015	2013	2011	2009	2015	2013	2011	2009
Asia Pacific	61%	62%	60%	59%	$19,064	$21,041	$20,998	$16,544
Central & Eastern Europe	58%	61%	62%	64%	$3,136	$5,318	$6,133	$4,673
Latin America	55%	59%	61%	63%	$5,787	$8,422	$7,459	$6,210
Middle East & Africa	57%	59%	58%	59%	$3,696	$4,309	$4,159	$2,887
North America	17%	19%	19%	21%	$10,016	$10,853	$10,958	$9,379
Western Europe	28%	29%	32%	34%	$10,543	$12,766	$13,749	$11,750
Total Worldwide	39%	43%	42%	43%	$52,242	$62,709	$63,456	$51,443
In G-20 Countries								
	Rates of Unlicensed Software Installations				Commercial Value of Unlicensed Software ($M)			
	2015	2013	2011	2009	2015	2013	2011	2009
Argentina	69%	69%	69%	71%	$554	$950	$657	$645
Australia	20%	21%	23%	25%	$579	$743	$763	$550
Brazil	47%	50%	53%	56%	$1,770	$2,851	$2,848	$2,254
Canada	24%	25%	27%	29%	$893	$1,089	$1,141	$943
China	70%	74%	77%	79%	$8,657	$8,767	$8,902	$7,583
France	34%	36%	37%	40%	$2,101	$2,685	$2,754	$2,544
Germany	22%	24%	26%	28%	$1,720	$2,158	$2,265	$2,023
India	58%	60%	63%	65%	$2,684	$2,911	$2,930	$2,003
Indonesia	84%	84%	86%	86%	$1,145	$1,463	$1,467	$886
Italy	45%	47%	48%	49%	$1,341	$1,747	$1,945	$1,733
Japan	18%	19%	21%	21%	$994	$1,349	$1,875	$1,838
Mexico	52%	54%	57%	60%	$980	$1,211	$1,249	$1,056
Russia	64%	62%	63%	67%	$1,341	$2,658	$3,227	$2,613
Saudi Arabia	49%	50%	51%	51%	$412	$421	$449	$304
South Africa	33%	34%	35%	35%	$274	$385	$564	$324
South Korea	35%	38%	40%	41%	$657	$712	$815	$575
Turkey	58%	60%	62%	63%	$291	$504	$526	$415
United Kingdom	22%	24%	26%	27%	$1,935	$2,019	$1,943	$1,581
United States	17%	18%	19%	20%	$9,095	$9,737	$9,773	$8,390
European Union	29%	31%	33%	35%	$11,060	$13,486	$14,433	$12,469

Table 3-2 Rates and Commercial Values of Unlicensed PC Software Installations Biennially from 2009 to 2015

Source: BSA, 2016.[25]

among the groups. Students from Singapore and Hong Kong proved to be significantly more tolerant than those from the United States, Wales, England, and Australia. Students from Sweden and the Netherlands were also significantly more tolerant than those from Wales and Australia, but significantly less tolerant than those from Hong Kong. The low overall degree of tolerance for illicit system use may be a function of the easy correspondence between the common crimes of breaking and entering, trespassing, theft, destruction of property, and their computer-related counterparts.

Misuse of Corporate Resources The scenarios examined levels of tolerance for misuse of corporate resources, and each presented a different situation in which corporate assets were used for nonbusiness purposes without specifying the company's policy on personal use of its resources. In general, participants displayed a rather lenient view of personal use of company equipment. Only students from Singapore and Hong Kong viewed this personal use as unethical. There were several substantial differences in this category, with students from the Netherlands revealing the most lenient views. With the exceptions of students from Singapore and Hong Kong, many people from many cultural backgrounds indicated that unless an organization explicitly forbids personal use of its computing resources, such use is acceptable.[26]

Larger organizations, especially those that operate in international markets, are faced with cultural differences in ethical perceptions and decision making. For example, the Boeing Company has a clear and well-developed Ethics and Business Conduct program. It seeks to communicate company standards of ethical business conduct to all employees, inform all stakeholders of the policy and procedure that governs ethical conduct, identify company processes that help stakeholders comply with corporate standards of conduct, and promote an ongoing awareness of ethical conduct within the company. Like other large organizations, Boeing takes its business values and corporate conduct program very seriously. The approach is best summarized as "Communicate, Educate, and Execute," in which Boeing seeks to inform all corporate stakeholders about ethically motivated actions and then implement programs to achieve its stated values in practice.

 To learn more about the Boeing ethics program, visit the Boeing Web site at www.boeing.com /boeing/companyoffices/aboutus/ethics/hotline.page.

In a nutshell, Boeing promotes the goal that all stakeholders will conduct business dealings fairly, impartially, and in an ethical and proper manner consistent with its code of conduct.

❭ Ethics and Education

Attitudes toward the ethics of computer use are affected by many factors other than nationality. Differences are found among people within the same country, within the same social class, and within the same company. Key studies reveal that education is the overriding factor in leveling ethical perceptions within a small population. Employees must be trained and kept aware of many topics related to information security, not the least of which is the expected behavior of an ethical employee. This education is especially important in information security, as many employees may not have the formal technical training to understand that their

OFFLINE

The Use of Scenarios in Computer Ethics Studies[27]

The following vignettes can be used in an open and frank discussion of computer ethics. Review each scenario carefully and respond to each question using a form of the following statement, choosing the description you consider most appropriate: *I feel the actions of this person were (very ethical/ethical/neither ethical nor unethical/unethical/very unethical).* Then, justify your response.

1. A scientist developed a theory that required proof through the construction of a computer model. He hired a computer programmer to build the model, and the theory was shown to be correct. The scientist won several awards for the development of the theory, but he never acknowledged the contribution of the computer programmer.

   The scientist's failure to acknowledge the computer programmer was:

2. The owner of a small business needed a computer-based accounting system. He identified the various inputs and outputs he felt were required to satisfy his needs. Then he showed his design to a computer programmer and asked if she could implement such a system. The programmer knew she could because she had developed much more sophisticated systems in the past. In fact, she thought the design was rather crude and would soon need several major revisions. But she didn't voice her thoughts because the business owner didn't ask, and she wanted to be hired to implement the needed revisions.

   The programmer's decision not to point out the design flaws was:

3. A student found a loophole in his university's computer system that allowed him access to other students' records. He told the system administrator about the loophole, but continued to access student records until the problem was corrected two weeks later.

   The student's action in searching for the loophole was:

   The student's action in continuing to access others' records for two weeks was:

   The system administrator's failure to correct the problem sooner was:

4. A computer user ordered an accounting system from a popular software vendor's Web site. When he received his order, he found that the store had accidentally sent him a very expensive word-processing program as well as the accounting package he had ordered. The invoice listed only the accounting package. The user decided to keep the word-processing program.

   The customer's decision to keep the word-processing program was:

5. A programmer at a bank realized that she had accidentally overdrawn her checking account. She made a small adjustment in the bank's accounting system so that her account would not incur a service charge. As soon as she deposited

funds that made her balance positive again, she corrected the bank's accounting system.

The programmer's modification of the accounting system was:

6. A computer programmer built and sold small computer applications to supplement his income. He worked for a moderately sized computer vendor, and would frequently go to his office on Saturdays when no one was working and use his employer's computer to develop the applications. He did not hide the fact that he was entering the building; he had to sign a register at a security desk each time he entered.

The programmer's weekend use of the company computer was:

7. A student in a computer class was also employed at a local business part-time. Frequently her class homework required using popular word-processing and spreadsheet packages. Occasionally she did her homework on the office computer at her part-time job during coffee or meal breaks.

The student's use of the company computer was:

If the student had done her homework during "company time" (not during a break), her use of the company computer would have been:

8. A university student learned to use an expensive accounting program in her accounting class. The student would go to the university computer lab and use the software to complete her assignment. Signs were posted in the lab indicating that copying software was forbidden. One day, she decided to copy the software anyway to complete her work assignments at home.

If the student destroyed her copy of the software at the end of the term, her action in copying the software was:

If the student forgot to destroy her copy of the software at the end of the term, her action in copying the software was:

If the student never intended to destroy her copy of the software at the end of the term, her action in copying the software was:

9. A university student found out that a fellow student's personal Web site contained a "pirate" section of illegally copied software programs. He accessed the Web site and proceeded to download several games and professional programs, which he then distributed to several of his friends.

The student's actions in downloading the games were:

The student's actions in downloading the programs were:

The student's actions in sharing the programs and games with his friends were:

10. An engineer needed a program to perform a series of complicated calculations. He found a computer programmer who was capable of writing the program, but would only hire the programmer if he agreed to share any liability that may result from an error in the engineer's calculations. The programmer was willing

(continues)

to assume any liability due to a program malfunction, but was unwilling to share liability due to an error in the engineer's calculations.

The programmer's position in this situation is:

The engineer's position in this situation is:

11. A manager of a company that sells Web hosting services bought similar services from a competitor. She used her access to the competitor's computer to try to break the security system, identify other customers, and cause the system to crash. She used the service for a year and always paid her bills promptly.

The manager's actions were:

12. A student programmer decided to write a virus program. Such programs usually spread automatically by making copies of themselves onto other users' media (like flash drives). The student wrote a program that caused the computer to ignore every fifth command entered by a user. The student took his program to the university computing lab and installed it on one of the computers. Before long, the virus had spread to hundreds of users.

The student's action of infecting hundreds of users' flash drives was:

If the virus program output the message "Have a nice day," then the student's action of infecting hundreds of users' flash drives would have been:

If the virus erased files, then the student's action of infecting hundreds of users' flash drives would have been:

behavior is unethical or even illegal. Proper ethical and legal training is vital to creating an informed and well-prepared system user.

❯ Deterring Unethical and Illegal Behavior

There are three general causes of unethical and illegal behavior:

- Ignorance: Ignorance of the law is no excuse; however, ignorance of policy and procedures is. The first method of deterrence is education, which is accomplished by designing, publishing, and disseminating an organization's policies and relevant laws, and obtaining agreement to comply with these policies and laws from all members of the organization. Reminders, training, and awareness programs keep policy information in front of employees to support retention and compliance.

- Accident: People who have authorization and privileges to manage information within the organization are most likely to cause harm or damage by accident. Careful planning and control help prevent accidental modification to systems and data.

- Intent: Criminal or unethical intent goes to the state of mind of the person performing the act; it is often necessary to establish criminal intent to successfully prosecute offenders. Protecting a system against those with intent to cause harm or damage is best accomplished by means of technical controls, and vigorous litigation or prosecution if these controls fail.

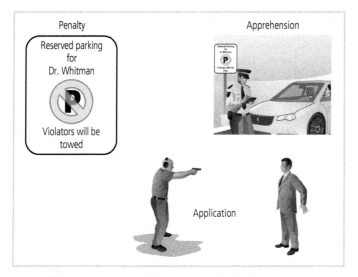

Figure 3-6 Deterrents to illegal or unethical behavior

Whatever the cause of illegal, immoral, or unethical behavior, one thing is certain: information security personnel must do everything in their power to deter these acts and to use policy, education and training, and technology to protect information and systems. Many security professionals understand the technology aspect of protection but underestimate the value of policy. However, laws, policies, and their associated penalties only provide deterrence if three conditions are present, as illustrated in Figure 3-6:

- Fear of penalty: Potential offenders must fear the penalty. Threats of informal reprimand or verbal warnings do not have the same impact as the threat of imprisonment or forfeiture of pay.

- Probability of being apprehended: Potential offenders must believe there is a strong possibility of being caught.

- Probability of penalty being applied: Potential offenders must believe that the penalty will be administered.

Codes of Ethics of Professional Organizations

Many professional organizations have established codes of conduct or codes of ethics that members are expected to follow. Codes of ethics can have a positive effect on people's judgment regarding computer use.[28] Unfortunately, many employers do not encourage their employees to join these professional organizations. But, employees who have earned some level of certification or professional accreditation can be deterred from ethical lapses if they fear losing that accreditation or certification by violating a code of conduct. Loss of certification or accreditation can dramatically reduce their marketability and earning power.

Security professionals have a responsibility to act ethically and according to the policies and procedures of their employers, their professional organizations, and the laws of society.

Professional Organization	Web Resource Location	Description	Focus
Association of Computing Machinery	www.acm.org	Code of 24 imperatives of personal and ethical responsibilities for security professionals	Ethics of security professionals
Information Systems Audit and Control Association	www.isaca.org	Focus on auditing, information security, business process analysis, and IS planning through the CISA and CISM certifications	Tasks and knowledge required of the information systems audit professional
Information Systems Security Association	www.issa.org	Professional association of information systems security professionals; provides education forums, publications, and peer networking for members	Professional security information sharing
International Information Systems Security Certification Consortium (ISC)²	www.isc2.org	International consortium dedicated to improving the quality of security professionals through SSCP and CISSP certifications	Requires certificants to follow its published code of ethics
SANS Institute's Global Information Assurance Certification	www.giac.org	GIAC certifications focus on four security areas: security administration, security management, IT audits, and software security; these areas have standard, gold, and expert levels	Requires certificants to follow its published code of ethics

Table 3-3 Professional Organizations of Interest to Information Security Professionals

Likewise, it is the organization's responsibility to develop, disseminate, and enforce its policies. The following discussion explains where professional organizations fit into the ethical landscape. Table 3-3 provides an overview of these organizations. Many of them offer certification programs that require applicants to subscribe formally to the ethical codes. Professional certification is discussed in Chapter 11.

〉 Major IT and InfoSec Professional Organizations

Many of the major IT and information security professional organizations maintain their own codes of ethics.

Association of Computing Machinery (ACM) The ACM is a respected professional society that was established in 1947 as "the world's first educational and scientific computing society." It is one of the few organizations that strongly promotes education and provides discounts for student members. The ACM's code of ethics requires its more than 100,000 members to perform their duties in a manner befitting an ethical computing professional. The code contains specific references to protecting the confidentiality of information, causing no harm (with specific references to viruses), protecting the privacy of others, and respecting the intellectual property and copyrights of others. The ACM (*www.acm.org*) also hosts more than 170 conferences annually and publishes a wide variety of professional computing publications, including the highly regarded *Communications of the ACM*.

3

International Information Systems Security Certification Consortium, Inc. (ISC)² (ISC)² is a nonprofit organization that focuses on the development and implementation of information security certifications and credentials. The organization manages a body of knowledge on information security and administers and evaluates examinations for information security certifications. The code of ethics put forth by (ISC)² is primarily designed for the more than 90,000 information security professionals who have earned an (ISC)² certification, and has four mandatory canons: "Protect society, the commonwealth, and the infrastructure; act honorably, honestly, justly, responsibly, and legally; provide diligent and competent service to principals; and advance and protect the profession."[29] This code enables (ISC)² to promote reliance on the ethicality and trustworthiness of information security professionals as the guardians of information and systems. For more information, visit *www.isc2.org*.

SANS Formerly known as the System Administration, Networking, and Security Institute, SANS was founded in 1989 as a professional research and education cooperative organization and has awarded certifications to more than 55,000 information security professionals. SANS offers a set of certifications called the Global Information Assurance Certification (GIAC). All GIAC-certified professionals are required to acknowledge that certification, and its privileges carry a corresponding obligation to uphold the GIAC code of ethics. Certificate holders who do not conform to this code face censure and may lose GIAC certification. For more information, visit *www.sans.org* and *www.giac.org*.

ISACA Originally known as the Information Systems Audit and Control Association, ISACA is a professional association that focuses on auditing, control, and security. The membership comprises both technical and managerial professionals. ISACA (*www.isaca.org*) provides IT control practices and standards, and includes many information security components within its areas of concentration, although it does not focus exclusively on information security. ISACA also has a code of ethics for its 110,000 constituents, and it requires many of the same high standards for ethical performance as the other organizations and certifications.

Information Systems Security Association (ISSA) ISSA is a nonprofit society of more than 10,000 information security professionals in over 100 countries. As a professional association, its primary mission is to bring together qualified information security practitioners for information exchange and educational development. ISSA (*www.issa.org*) provides scheduled conferences, meetings, publications, and information resources to promote information security awareness and education. ISSA also promotes a code of ethics, similar in content to those of (ISC)², ISACA, and the ACM, whose focus is "promoting management practices that will ensure the confidentiality, integrity, and availability of organizational information resources."[30]

Key U.S. Federal Agencies

Several key U.S. federal agencies are charged with the protection of American information resources and the investigation of threats or attacks against these resources. These organizations include the Department of Homeland Security (DHS) and its subordinate agencies—the U.S. Secret Service (USSS) and US-CERT, the National Security Agency, the Federal Bureau of Investigation (FBI), and the FBI's InfraGard program.

〉 Department of Homeland Security

The *Department of Homeland Security (DHS*, at *www.dhs.gov)* was created in 2003 by the Homeland Security Act of 2002, which was passed in response to the events of September 11, 2001. DHS is made up of several directorates and offices through which it carries out its mission of protecting American citizens as well as the physical and information assets of the United States. The National Protection and Programs Directorate creates and enhances resources used to discover and respond to attacks on national information systems and critical infrastructure. The Science and Technology Directorate is responsible for research and development activities in support of domestic defense. This effort is guided by an ongoing examination of vulnerabilities throughout the national infrastructure; the directorate sponsors the emerging best practices developed to counter threats and weaknesses in the system.

Table 3-4 describes the DHS departments and their functions.

DHS Department	Function
United States Citizenship and Immigration Services (USCIS)	Secures America's promise as a nation of immigrants by providing accurate and useful information to customers, granting immigration and citizenship benefits, promoting an awareness and understanding of citizenship, and ensuring the integrity of the immigration system
United States Customs and Border Protection (CBP)	One of DHS's largest and most complex components, with the mission of keeping terrorists and their weapons out of the United States; it also helps secure and facilitate trade and travel while enforcing hundreds of U.S. regulations, including immigration and drug laws
United States Coast Guard (USCG)	One of the five armed forces of the United States and the only military organization within DHS; the Coast Guard protects the maritime economy and the environment and defends maritime borders
United States Immigration and Customs Enforcement (ICE)	Promotes security and public safety through the criminal and civil enforcement of federal laws governing border control, customs, trade, and immigration
Federal Emergency Management Agency (FEMA)	Supports citizens and first responders by providing preparation for, protection against, response to, and recovery from national and regional emergency events
Federal Law Enforcement Training Center (FLETC)	Provides training for all levels of law enforcement professionals
Transportation Security Agency (TSA)	Protects the nation's transportation systems
United States Secret Service (USSS)	Safeguards the nation's financial infrastructure and payment systems to preserve the integrity of the economy, and protects national leaders, visiting heads of state and government, designated sites, and national special security events

Table 3-4 DHS Departments and Functions

DHS Department	Function
Directorate for Management	Responsible for DHS budgets and appropriations, expenditure of funds, accounting and finance, procurement, human resources, information technology systems, facilities and equipment, and the identification and tracking of performance measurements
National Protection and Programs Directorate (NPPD)	Works to advance DHS's risk-reduction mission; reducing risk requires an integrated approach that encompasses both physical and virtual threats and their associated human elements
Science and Technology Directorate (S&T)	The primary research and development arm of the DHS; it provides federal, state, and local officials with the technology and capabilities to protect the country
Domestic Nuclear Detection Office (DNDO)	Works to enhance the nuclear detection efforts of the private sector and federal, state, territorial, tribal, and local governments, and to ensure a coordinated response to such threats
Office of Health Affairs (OHA)	Coordinates all medical activities of DHS to ensure appropriate preparation for and response to incidents of medical significance
Office of Intelligence and Analysis (I&A)	Uses information and intelligence from multiple sources to identify and assess current and future threats to the United States
Office of Operations Coordination	Monitors national security on a daily basis and coordinates activities within DHS and with governors, Homeland Security advisors, law enforcement partners, and critical infrastructure operators in all 50 states and more than 50 major urban areas nationwide
Office of Policy	The primary policy formulation and coordination component of DHS; it provides a centralized, coordinated focus for developing long-range planning to protect the United States

Table 3-4 DHS Departments and Functions *(continued)*

Source: Department of Homeland Security.[31]

DHS works with academic campuses nationally, focusing on resilience, recruitment, internationalization, growing academic maturity, and academic research. Resilience calls for academic institutions to improve their own preparedness for unexpected events. Recruitment refers to the roles of academic organizations in preparing students and recent graduates to fill the increasing demand for workers and managers in the preparedness industry. Internationalization recognizes that students around the world can help meet the increased demand. Recently, information security and preparedness has become more recognized as a discrete area of academic study. Academic organizations conduct ongoing research to help develop solutions in the areas of information security and crisis preparedness.[32]

DHS's cybersecurity role extends from its National Protection and Programs Directorate, as shown in Figure 3-7.

US-CERT The U.S. Computer Emergency Readiness Team (US-CERT) is a division of DHS's National Cybersecurity and Communications Integration Center (NCCIC), which is focused on information security and response. Figure 3-8 shows the Web site for the DHS/US-CERT incident reporting system. DHS provides mechanisms to report the following attacks:

- Phishing (*www.us-cert.gov/report-phishing/*)
- Malware (*malware.us-cert.gov/*)

- DHS
  - National Protection and Programs Directorate
    - Office of Infrastructure Protection
    - Office of Biometric Identity Management
    - Office of Cyber and Infrastructure Analysis
    - Federal Protective Service
    - Office of Cybersecurity and Communications
      - The Office of Emergency Communications
      - Stakeholder Engagement and Cyber Infrastructure Resilience
      - Federal Network Resilience
      - Network Security Deployment
      - The National Cybersecurity and Communications Integration Center
        - NCCIC Operations and Integration (NO&I)
        - United States Computer Emergency Readiness Team (US-CERT)
        - Industrial Control Systems Cyber Emergency Response Team (ICS-CERT)
        - National Coordinating Center for Communications (NCC)

Figure 3-7 DHS cybersecurity organizational structure

Source: DHS.

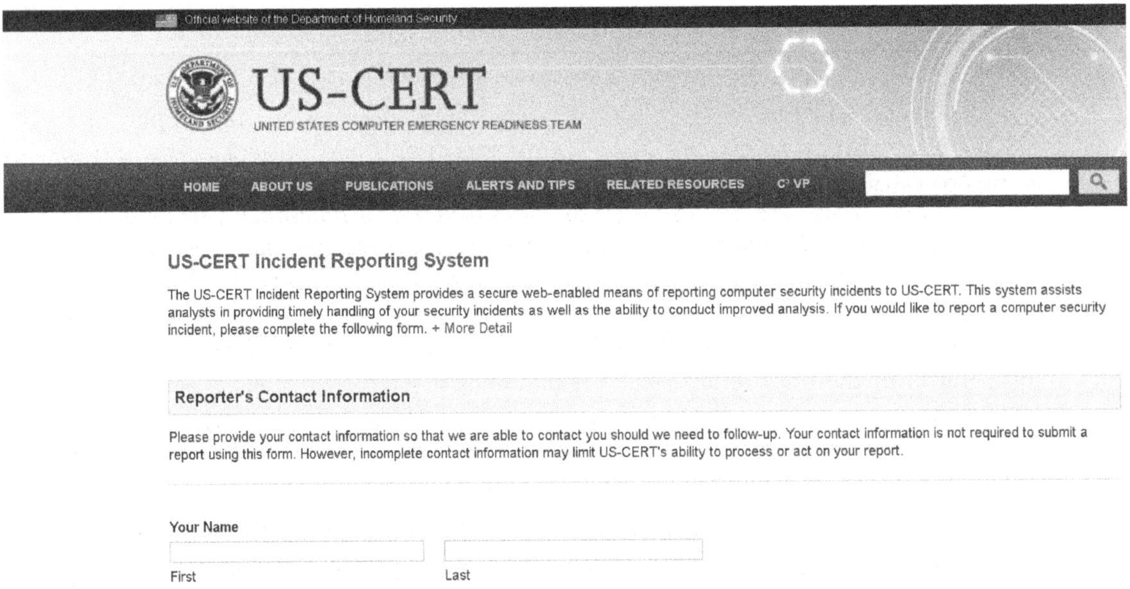
Official website of the Department of Homeland Security
US-CERT
UNITED STATES COMPUTER EMERGENCY READINESS TEAM
HOME
ABOUT US
PUBLICATIONS
ALERTS AND TIPS
RELATED RESOURCES
US-CERT Incident Reporting System
The US-CERT Incident Reporting System provides a secure web-enabled means of reporting computer security incidents to US-CERT. This system assists analysts in providing timely handling of your security incidents as well as the ability to conduct improved analysis. If you would like to report a computer security incident, please complete the following form. + More Detail
Reporter's Contact Information
Please provide your contact information so that we are able to contact you should we need to follow-up. Your contact information is not required to submit a report using this form. However, incomplete contact information may limit US-CERT's ability to process or act on your report.
Your Name
First
Last

Figure 3-8 DHS/US-CERT incident reporting system

Source: US-CERT.

- Software vulnerabilities (*www.kb.cert.org/vuls/html/report-a-vulnerability/*)—through CERT at the Software Engineering Institute at Carnegie Mellon (*https://forms.cert.org/VulReport/*)
- Other types of incidents (*www.us-cert.gov/forms/report*)

A cybersecurity career support program under US-CERT is the National Initiative for Cybersecurity Careers and Studies. "NICCS underscores the four components of The National Initiative for Cybersecurity Education (NICE) and serves as a national resource for government, industry, academia, and the general public in their quest to learn about cybersecurity awareness, education, careers, and workforce development opportunities."[33]

 For more information on NICCS and careers in cybersecurity, visit its Web site at http://niccs .us-cert.gov.

❭ U.S. Secret Service

The *U.S. Secret Service* was relocated from the Department of the Treasury to the DHS in 2002. In addition to its well-known mission of providing protective services for key members of the U.S. government, the Secret Service is charged with safeguarding the nation's financial infrastructure and payments systems to preserve the integrity of the economy. This charge is an extension of the agency's original mission to protect U.S. currency—a logical extension, given that the communications networks of the United States carry more funds than all the armored cars in the world combined. By protecting the networks and their data, the Secret Service protects money, stocks, and other financial transactions.

The Secret Service has several strategic objectives that address cybersecurity-related activity:

> *The following Mission Priorities represent the highest-priority efforts for the Department of Homeland Security within Mission 1. While the Department will continue to work on all of the mission goals and objectives laid out in the 2014 Quadrennial Homeland Security Review and the 2014-2018 Strategic Plan, these are the top areas of focus in terms of investment, strategic and operational planning, and stakeholder engagement, and will be addressed through actions undertaken in one or more of the following DHS foundational activities: Joint Requirements Council, joint operational plans and operations, enhanced budget and investment processes, and focused strategic and analytic efforts.*

> - *Prevent terrorist travel into the United States by enhancing information sharing, international cooperation, and risk-based targeting, including by focusing on foreign fighters.*

> - *Strengthen aviation security by implementing risk-based mitigation strategies.*

> - *Prevent the hostile use of nuclear materials against the homeland by deterring or preventing adversaries from smuggling nuclear weapons and materials, and enhancing the ability to detect nuclear weapons and materials out of regulatory control.*

> - *Protect key leaders, facilities, and National Special Security Events by deterring, minimizing, and responding to identified vulnerabilities and threats against the President, Vice President, other protected individuals, the White House Complex, and other sites.*[34]

Figure 3-9 U.S. Secret Service Operation Firewall

Source: USSS.[35]

Figure 3-9 shows the Secret Service's operating center during Operation Firewall, a joint task force of the USSS, the Department of Justice, domestic and foreign law enforcement, and financial industry investigators. The operation led to 28 arrests across the United States and six other countries; "the suspects [...] were involved in a global cyber organized crime network. Charges against the suspects include identity theft, computer fraud, credit card fraud and conspiracy."[36]

> Federal Bureau of Investigation (FBI)

The FBI is the primary U.S. law enforcement agency. As such, it investigates both traditional crimes and cybercrimes, and works with the U.S. Attorney's Office to prosecute suspects under federal law (the U.S. Code). The FBI's mission changed dramatically after the terrorist attacks of September 11, 2001.

> *On May 29, 2002, the attorney general issued revised investigative guidelines to assist the Bureau's counterterrorism efforts.*

> *To support the Bureau's change in mission and to meet newly articulated strategic priorities, Director Mueller called for a reengineering of FBI structure and operations to closely focus the Bureau on prevention of terrorist attacks, on countering foreign intelligence operations against the U.S., and on addressing*

cybercrime-based attacks and other high-technology crimes. In addition, the Bureau remains dedicated to protecting civil rights, combatting public corruption, organized crime, white-collar crime, and major acts of violent crime. The Bureau has also strengthened its support to federal, county, municipal, and international law enforcement partners and has dedicated itself to upgrading its technological infrastructure to successfully meet each of its priorities.[37]

One of the FBI's primary missions is to investigate cybercrime. Its key priorities include:

- Computer and network intrusions, through the FBI's Cyber Division (*www.fbi.gov/about-us/investigate/cyber/computer-intrusions*)

- Identity theft (*www.fbi.gov/about-us/investigate/cyber/identity_theft*)

- Fraud, in cooperation with the Internet Crime Complaint Center (*www.ic3.gov/default.aspx*)

The Internet Crime Complaint Center (IC3) is a partnership between the FBI and the National White Collar Crime Center (NW3C). The IC3 serves as a clearinghouse for cybercrime complaints. People may submit claims through the IC3 Web site, as shown in Figure 3-10.

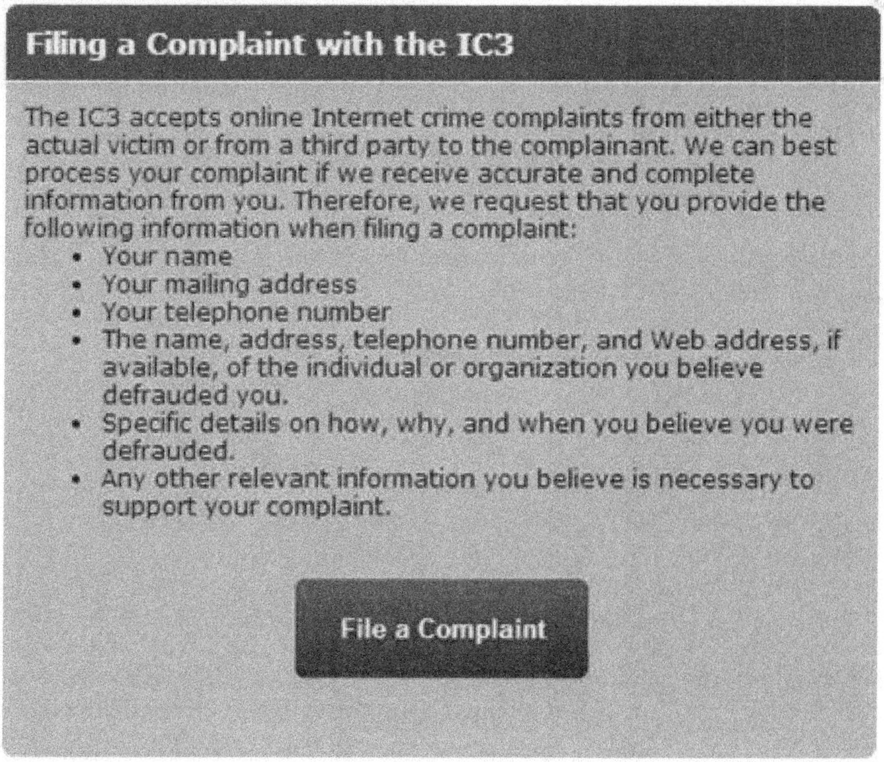

Filing a Complaint with the IC3

The IC3 accepts online Internet crime complaints from either the actual victim or from a third party to the complainant. We can best process your complaint if we receive accurate and complete information from you. Therefore, we request that you provide the following information when filing a complaint:
- Your name
- Your mailing address
- Your telephone number
- The name, address, telephone number, and Web address, if available, of the individual or organization you believe defrauded you.
- Specific details on how, why, and when you believe you were defrauded.
- Any other relevant information you believe is necessary to support your complaint.

File a Complaint

Figure 3-10 Filing a complaint with the IC3

Source: IC3.

Figure 3-11   FBI Cyber's Most Wanted list

Source: fbi.gov.

The FBI Cyber's Most Wanted list is shown in Figure 3-11.

 For more information on the U.S. Code, visit http://uscode.house.gov/.

National InfraGard Program   Established in January 2001, the *National InfraGard Program (www.infragard.org/)* began as a cooperative effort between the FBI's Cleveland field office and local technology professionals. The FBI sought assistance in determining a more effective method of protecting critical national information resources. The resulting cooperative, the first InfraGard chapter, was a formal effort to combat both cyber and physical threats. Since then, every FBI field office has established an InfraGard chapter to collaborate with public and private organizations and the academic community, and to share information about attacks, vulnerabilities, and threats. The National InfraGard Program serves its members in four basic ways:

- Maintains an intrusion alert network using encrypted e-mail
- Maintains a secure Web site for communication about suspicious activity or intrusions

- Sponsors local chapter activities
- Operates a help desk for questions

InfraGard's most significant contribution is the free exchange of information with the private sector in the areas of threats and attacks on information resources. InfraGard has more than 60 regional chapters (such as *http://infragardatlanta.org/*), which provide numerous opportunities for individuals and organizations to interact with the agency.

❯ National Security Agency (NSA)

Key Terms

information assurance The affirmation or guarantee of the confidentiality, integrity, and availability of information in storage, processing, and transmission. This term is often used synonymously with *information security.*

signals intelligence The collection, analysis, and distribution of information from foreign communications networks for intelligence and counterintelligence purposes and in support of military operations. In recent years, the debate around the collection and use of signals intelligence has grappled with the integration of domestic intelligence gathering.

Another key federal agency is the *National Security Agency (NSA)*:

> *The National Security Agency/Central Security Service (NSA/CSS) leads the U.S. Government in cryptology that encompasses both Signals Intelligence (SIGINT) and Information Assurance (IA) products and services, and enables Computer Network Operations (CNO) in order to gain a decision advantage for the Nation and our allies under all circumstances.*[38]

The director of the NSA is also the chief of the Central Security Service, which is tasked with providing "timely and accurate cryptologic support, knowledge, and assistance to the military cryptologic community."[39]

The NSA is responsible for **signals intelligence** and **information assurance** (the government term for information security). The NSA's Information Assurance Directorate (IAD) provides information security "solutions including the technologies, specifications and criteria, products, product configurations, tools, standards, operational doctrine, and support activities needed" for cyber defense.[40] The IAD also develops and promotes an Information Assurance Framework Forum in cooperation with commercial organizations and academic researchers. This framework provides strategic guidance as well as technical specifications for security solutions. IAD's Common Criteria provide a set of standards designed to promote understanding of information security.

The IAD is responsible for the protection of systems that store, process, and transmit classified information or information deemed to be of high national military or intelligence value. The IAD includes several outreach programs, including business, research, and academic outreach.

The NSA's IA academic program, called the National IA Education and Training Program (NIETP), supports IA education and training. As part of the NIETP, the NSA works with

DHS to recognize universities that offer information security education and that have integrated information security philosophies and efforts into their internal operations. These recognized "Centers of Excellence in Information Assurance/Cyber Defense" receive the honor of displaying the recognition as well as being acknowledged on the NSA's Web site. Graduates of these programs receive certificates that indicate their accreditation.

 For more information on the NSA's IA Directorate, visit the Web site at www.iad.gov. Information videos are available at www.nsa.gov/resources/everyone/digital-media-center/video-audio/information-assurance/index.shtml.

Selected Readings

- *The Digital Person: Technology and Privacy in the Information Age*, by Daniel Solove. 2004. New York University Press.
- *The Practical Guide to HIPAA Privacy and Security Compliance*, by Kevin Beaver and Rebecca Herold. 2003. Auerbach.
- *When Good Companies Do Bad Things*, by Peter Schwartz. 1999. John Wiley and Sons.

Chapter Summary

- Laws are formally adopted rules for acceptable behavior in modern society. Ethics are socially acceptable behavior. The key difference between laws and ethics is that laws carry the authority of a governing body and ethics do not.

- Organizations formalize desired behavior in documents called policies. Policies must be read and agreed to before they are binding.

- Civil law comprises a wide variety of laws that govern a nation or state. Criminal law addresses violations that harm society and are enforced by agents of the state or nation.

- Private law focuses on individual relationships, and public law governs regulatory agencies. Key U.S. laws to protect privacy include the Federal Privacy Act of 1974, the Electronic Communications Privacy Act of 1986, and the Health Insurance Portability and Accountability Act of 1996.

- The desire to protect national security, trade secrets, and a variety of other state and private assets has led to the passage of several laws that restrict what information, information management resources, and security resources may be exported from the United States.

- Intellectual property is recognized as a protected asset in this country. U.S. copyright law extends this privilege to published works, including electronic media.

- Studies have determined that people of differing nationalities have varying perspectives on ethical practices with the use of computer technology.

- Deterrence can prevent an illegal or unethical activity from occurring. Deterrence requires significant penalties, a high probability of apprehension, and an expectation that penalties will be enforced.

- As part of an effort to encourage ethical behavior, many professional organizations have established codes of conduct or codes of ethics that their members are expected to follow.

- Several U.S. federal agencies are responsible for protecting American information resources and investigating threats against them.

Review Questions

1. What is the difference between law and ethics?
2. What is civil law, and what does it accomplish?
3. What are the primary examples of public law?
4. Which law amended the Computer Fraud and Abuse Act of 1986, and what did it change?
5. Which law was created specifically to deal with encryption policy in the United States?
6. What is privacy in an information security context?
7. What is another name for the Kennedy-Kassebaum Act (1996), and why is it important to organizations that are not in the healthcare industry?
8. If you work for a financial services organization such as a bank or credit union, which 1999 law affects your use of customer data? What other effects does it have?
9. What is the primary purpose of the USA PATRIOT Act and how has it been revised since its original passage?
10. What is PCI DSS and why is it important for information security?
11. What is intellectual property (IP)? Is it afforded the same protection in every country of the world? What laws currently protect IP in the United States and Europe?
12. How does the Sarbanes-Oxley Act of 2002 affect information security managers?
13. What is due care? Why should an organization make sure to exercise due care in its usual course of operations?
14. How is due diligence different from due care? Why are both important?
15. What is a policy? How is it different from a law?
16. What are the three general categories of unethical and illegal behavior?
17. What is the best method for preventing an illegal or unethical activity?
18. Of the information security organizations listed in this chapter that have codes of ethics, which has been established for the longest time? When was it founded?
19. Of the organizations listed in this chapter that have codes of ethics, which is focused on auditing and control?
20. How do people from varying ethnic backgrounds differ in their views of computer ethics?

Exercises

1. What does CISSP stand for? Use the Internet to identify the ethical rules CISSP holders have agreed to follow.

2. For what kind of information security jobs does the NSA recruit? Use the Internet to visit its Web page and find out.

3. Using the resources in your library, find out what laws your state has passed to prosecute computer crime.

4. Using a Web browser, go to *www.eff.org*. What are the current top concerns of this organization?

5. Using the ethical scenarios presented earlier in this chapter in the Offline feature called "The Use of Scenarios in Computer Ethics Studies," finish each of the incomplete statements and bring your answers to class to compare them with those of your peers.

Case Exercises

Iris called the company's security hotline. The hotline is an anonymous way to report suspicious activity or abuse of company policy, although Iris chose to identify herself. The next morning, she was called to a meeting with an investigator from corporate security, which led to more meetings with others from corporate security and then with the director of human resources and Gladys Williams, the CIO of SLS.

Discussion Questions

1. Should Iris have approached Henry directly, or was the hotline the most effective way to take action? Why do you think so?

2. Should Gladys call the legal authorities? Which agency should she call?

3. Do you think this matter needs to be communicated elsewhere inside the company? Who should be informed and how? How about outside the company?

Ethical Decision Making

It seems obvious that Henry is doing something wrong. Do you think Henry acted in an ethical manner? Did Iris act in an ethical manner by determining the owner of the flash drive? Assuming that this incident took place in the United States, what law or laws has Henry violated? Suppose Iris had placed the flash drive back at the coffee station and forgotten the whole thing. Explain why her action would have been ethical or unethical.

Endnotes

1. Franklin, Benjamin. "Pennsylvania Assembly: Reply to the Governor." *The Franklin Papers*. Accessed 6 June 2016 from *http://franklinpapers.org/franklin/framedVolumes .jsp?vol=6&page=238a*.

2. Noone, John B. *Rousseau*'s *Social Contract: A Conceptual Analysis*. 1981. Athens: University of Georgia Press.

3. Aalberts, Robert J., Townsend, Anthony M., and Whitman, Michael E. "The Threat of Long-arm Jurisdiction to Electronic Commerce." *Communications of the ACM* 41, no. 12 (December 1998): 15–20.

4. Doyle, Charles. "The USA PATRIOT Act: A Legal Analysis." 15 April 2002. Accessed 6 June 2016 from *www.fas.org/irp/crs/RL31377.pdf*.

5. Federal Information Security Management Act of 2002. Accessed 6 June 2016 from *http://csrc.nist.gov/drivers/documents/FISMA-final.pdf*.

6. EPIC. "The Clipper Chip." 6 March 2004. Accessed 6 June 2016 from *http://epic.org/crypto/clipper/*.

7. Whitman, Michael. Original photograph.

8. Proofpoint. "Healthcare Email Security Regulations: HIPAA and Beyond." Accessed 6 June 2016 from *www.findwhitepapers.com/whitepaper8558*.

9. Ibid.

10. U.S. Government Federal Register "Rules and Regulations." Vol. 78, No 17. 25 January 2013. Accessed 6 June 2016 from *www.gpo.gov/fdsys/pkg/FR-2013-01-25/pdf/2013-01073.pdf*.

11. Harrell, E. "Victims of Identity Theft, 2014." Report prepared for the Department of Justice Bureau of Justice Statistics. 17 September 2015. Accessed 6 June 2016 from *www.bjs.gov/index.cfm?ty=pbdetail&iid=5408*.

12. Federal Trade Commission. "The President's Identity Theft Task Force Releases Comprehensive Strategic Plan to Combat Identity Theft." Accessed 6 June 2016 from *www.ftc.gov/news-events/press-releases/2007/04/presidents-identity-theft-task-force-releases-comprehensive*.

13. Federal Trade Commission. "Immediate Steps to Repair Identity Theft." Accessed 6 June 2016 from *www.identitytheft.gov/Steps*.

14. Krebs, Brian. "New Federal Law Targets ID Theft, Cybercrime." 1 October 2008. Accessed 6 June 2016 from *http://voices.washingtonpost.com/securityfix/2008/10/new_federal_law_targets_id_the.html*.

15. PCI Security Standards Council. "Payment Card Industry (PCI) Data Security Standard: Requirements and Security Assessment Procedures, V. 3.0." Accessed 6 June 2016 from *www.pcisecuritystandards.org/documents/PCI_DSS_v3.pdf*.

16. Ibid.

17. Computer Misuse Act of 1990. Accessed 6 June 2016 from *www.legislation.gov.uk/ukpga/1990/18/contents*.

18. Police and Justice Act of 2006. Accessed 6 June 2016 from *www.legislation.gov.uk/ukpga/2006/48/pdfs/ukpga_20060048_en.pdf*.

19. Australian Privacy Act of 1988. Accessed 6 June 2016 from *www.oaic.gov.au/privacy/privacy-act/the-privacy-act*.

20. Convention on Cybercrime CETS No. 185. Accessed 6 June 2016 from *http://conven tions.coe.int/Treaty/Commun/ChercheSig.asp?NT=185&CM=8&DF=&CL=ENG*.

21. World Trade Organization. "Understanding the WTO: The Agreements, Intellectual Property: Protection and Enforcement." Accessed 6 June 2016 from *www.wto.org /english/thewto_e/whatis_e/tif_e/agrm7_e.htm*.

22. The Computer Ethics Institute. "The 10 Commandments of Computer Ethics." Accessed 6 June 2016 from *http://cpsr.org/issues/ethics/cei/*.

23. Whitman, Michael E., Townsend, Anthony M., and Hendrickson, Anthony R. "Cross-National Differences in Computer-Use Ethics: A Nine Country Study." *The Journal of International Business Studies* 30, no. 4 (1999): 673–687.

24. Ibid.

25. Business Software Alliance. Seizing Opportunity through License Compliance: The BSA Global Software Survey 2016. Accessed 10 June 2016 from *http://globalstudy .bsa.org/2016*.

26. Whitman, Michael E., Townsend, Anthony M., and Hendrickson, Anthony R. "Cross-National Differences in Computer-Use Ethics: A Nine Country Study." *The Journal of International Business Studies* 30, no. 4 (1999): 673–687.

27. Ibid.

28. Harrington, Susan J. "The Effects of Codes of Ethics and Personal Denial of Responsibility on Computer Abuse Judgment and Intentions." *MIS Quarterly* 20, no. 3 (September 1996): 257–278.

29. International Information Systems Security Certification Consortium, Inc. "(ISC)[2] Code of Ethics." Accessed 6 June 2016 from *www.isc2.org/ethics/default.aspx?terms= code%20of%20ethics*.

30. Information Systems Security Association (ISSA). "ISSA Code of Ethics." *ISSA Online.* Accessed 6 June 2016 from *www.issa.org/?page=CodeofEthics*.

31. Department of Homeland Security Department Components. Accessed 6 June 2016 from *www.dhs.gov/department-components*.

32. Department of Homeland Security. "Academic Engagement Overview." Accessed 6 June 2016 from *www.dhs.gov/academic-engagement-overview*.

33. National Initiative for Cybersecurity Careers and Studies (NICCS). *About NICCS.* Accessed 6 June 2016 from *http://niccs.us-cert.gov/home/about-niccs*.

34. United States Secret Service Strategic Plan (FY 2008-2013). Accessed 6 June 2016 from *www.dhs.gov/sites/default/files/publications/FY14-18%20Strategic%20Plan.PDF*.

35. U.S. Secret Service's Operation Firewall Nets 28 Arrests. Accessed 6 June 2016 from *https://www.scribd.com/document/1220697/US-Treasury-pub2304*.

36. Ibid.

37. Federal Bureau of Investigation. "A Brief History of the FBI." Accessed 6 June 2016 from *www.fbi.gov/about-us/history/brief-history*.

38. National Security Agency. "Introduction to NSA/CSS." Accessed 6 June 2016 from *www.nsa.gov/about/mission-strategy/*.

39. Central Security Service (CSS). Accessed 6 June 2016 from *www.nsa.gov/about/central -security-service/*.

40. National Security Agency. "Information Assurance." Accessed 6 June 2016 from *www .nsa.gov/ia/*.

3

chapter 4

Planning for Security

> *Begin with the end in mind.*
> STEPHEN COVEY, AUTHOR OF *SEVEN HABITS OF HIGHLY EFFECTIVE PEOPLE*

Charlie Moody flipped up his jacket collar to cover his ears. The spray blowing over him from the fire hoses was icing the cars along the street where he stood watching his office building burn. The warehouse and shipping dock were not gone, but were severely damaged by smoke and water. He tried to hide his dismay by turning to speak to Fred Chin.

"Look at the bright side," said Charlie. "At least we can get the new servers that we've been putting off."

Fred shook his head. "Charlie, you must be dreaming. We don't have enough insurance for a full replacement of everything we've lost."

Charlie was stunned. The offices were gone, all the computer systems, servers, and desktops were melted slag, and he would have to try to rebuild without the resources he needed. At least he had good backups, or so he hoped. He thought hard, trying to remember the last time the off-site backup tapes had been tested.

He wondered where all the network design diagrams were. He knew he could call his network provider to order new circuits as soon as Fred found some new office space. But where were all the circuit specs? The only copy had been in a drawer in his office, which wasn't there anymore. This was not going to be fun. He would have to call directory assistance just to get the phone number for his boss, Gladys Williams, the chief information officer (CIO).

Charlie heard a buzzing noise to his left. He turned to see the flashing numbers of his alarm clock. Relief flooded him as he realized it was just a nightmare; Sequential Label and Supply (SLS) had not burned down. He turned on the light and started making notes for reviewing with his staff later that morning. Charlie would make some changes to the company contingency plans *today*.

LEARNING OBJECTIVES

Upon completion of this material, you should be able to:

- Describe management's role in the development, maintenance, and enforcement of information security policy, standards, practices, procedures, and guidelines
- Explain what an information security blueprint is, identify its major components, and explain how it supports the information security program
- Discuss how an organization institutionalizes its policies, standards, and practices using education, training, and awareness programs
- Describe what contingency planning is and how it relates to incident response planning, disaster recovery planning, and business continuity plans

Introduction

An organization's information security effort succeeds only when it operates in conjunction with the organization's information security policy. An information security program begins with policy, standards, and practices, which are the foundation for the information security architecture and blueprint. The creation and maintenance of these elements require coordinated planning. The role of planning in modern organizations is hard to overemphasize. All but the smallest organizations engage in some planning: strategic planning to manage the allocation of resources and contingency planning to prepare for the uncertainties of the business environment.

Information Security Planning and Governance

Key Terms

goals Sometimes used synonymously with *objectives*; the desired end of a planning cycle.

objectives Sometimes used synonymously with *goals*; the intermediate states obtained to achieve progress toward a goal or goals.

strategic plan The documented product of strategic planning; a plan for the organization's intended strategic efforts over the next several years.

strategic planning The process of defining and specifying the long-term direction (strategy) to be taken by an organization, and the allocation and acquisition of resources needed to pursue this effort.

Strategic planning sets the long-term direction to be taken by the organization and each of its component parts. Strategic planning should guide organizational efforts and focus resources toward specific, clearly defined **goals**. After an organization develops a general strategy, it generates an overall **strategic plan** by extending that general strategy into plans for major divisions. Each level of each division then translates those plan **objectives** into more specific objectives for the level below. To execute this broad strategy, the executive team must first define individual responsibilities. (The executive team is sometimes called the organization's C-level, as in CEO, COO, CFO, CIO, and so on.)

〉 Planning Levels

Key Terms

operational plan The documented product of operational planning; a plan for the organization's intended operational efforts on a day-to-day basis for the next several months.

operational planning The actions taken by management to specify the short-term goals and objectives of the organization in order to obtain specified tactical goals, followed by estimates and schedules for the allocation of resources necessary to achieve those goals and objectives.

tactical plan The documented product of tactical planning; a plan for the organization's intended tactical efforts over the next few years.

tactical planning The actions taken by management to specify the intermediate goals and objectives of the organization in order to obtain specified strategic goals, followed by estimates and schedules for the allocation of resources necessary to achieve those goals and objectives.

Once the organization's overall strategic plan is translated into strategic plans for each major division or operation, the next step is to translate these plans into tactical objectives that move toward reaching specific, measurable, achievable, and time-bound accomplishments. The process of strategic planning seeks to transform broad, general, sweeping statements into more specific and applied objectives. Strategic plans are used to create **tactical plans**, which in turn are used to develop **operational plans**.

Tactical planning focuses on short-term undertakings that will be completed within one or two years. The process of tactical planning breaks each strategic goal into a series of incremental objectives. Each objective in a tactical plan should be specific and should have a delivery date within a year of the plan's start. Budgeting, resource allocation, and personnel are critical components of the tactical plan. Tactical plans often include project plans and resource acquisition planning documents (such as product specifications), project budgets, project reviews, and monthly and annual reports. The chief information security officer (CISO) and security managers use the tactical plan to organize, prioritize, and acquire resources necessary for major projects and to provide support for the overall strategic plan.

Managers and employees use **operational planning** derived from tactical planning to organize the ongoing, day-to-day performance of tasks. An operational plan includes the necessary tasks for all relevant departments as well as communication and reporting requirements, which might include weekly meetings, progress reports, and other associated tasks. These plans must reflect the organizational structure, with each subunit, department, or project team conducting its own operational planning and reporting. Frequent communication and feedback from the teams to the project managers and/or team leaders, and then up to the various management levels, will make the planning process more manageable and successful.

❯ Planning and the CISO

The first priority of the CISO and the information security management team is the creation of a strategic plan to accomplish the organization's information security objectives. While each organization may have its own format for the design and distribution of a strategic plan, the fundamental elements of planning share characteristics across all types of enterprises. The plan is an evolving statement of how the CISO and various elements of the organization will implement the objectives of the information security charter, which is expressed in the enterprise information security policy (EISP). You will learn about EISPs later in this chapter.

As a clearly directed strategy flows from top to bottom, a systematic approach is required to translate it into a program that can inform and lead all members of the organization. Strategic plans formed at the highest levels of the organization are used to create an overall corporate strategy. As lower levels of the organizational hierarchy are involved (moving down the hierarchy), the plans from higher levels are evolved into more detailed, more concrete planning. So, higher-level plans are translated into more specific plans for intermediate layers of management. That layer of strategic planning by function (such as financial, IT, and operations strategies) is then converted into tactical planning for supervisory managers and eventually provides direction for the operational plans undertaken by non-management members of the organization. This multi-layered approach encompasses two key objectives: general strategy and overall strategic planning. First, general strategy is translated into specific strategy; second, overall strategic planning is translated into lower-level tactical and operational planning.

Information security, like information technology, must support more than its own functions. All organizational units will use information, not just IT-based information, so the Information Security group must understand and support the strategic plans (a.k.a. strategies) of all business units. This role may sometimes conflict with that of the IT department, as IT's role is the efficient and effective delivery of information and information resources, while the role of information security is the protection of all information assets.

 For more information on information security planning, read NIST Special Publication (SP) 800-18, Rev. 1, which is available from the NIST SP Web site at http://csrc.nist.gov/publications/PubsSPs.html.

❯ Information Security Governance

Key Terms

corporate governance Executive management's responsibility to provide strategic direction, ensure the accomplishment of objectives, oversee that risks are appropriately managed, and validate responsible resource use.

> **governance** "The set of responsibilities and practices exercised by the board and executive management with the goal of providing strategic direction, ensuring that objectives are achieved, ascertaining that risks are managed appropriately and verifying that the enterprise's resources are used responsibly."[1]
>
> **information security governance** The application of the principles of corporate governance to the information security function.

Governance describes the entire function of controlling, or governing, the processes used by a group to accomplish some objective. It represents the strategic controlling function of an organization's senior management, which is designed to ensure informed, prudent strategic decisions made in the best interest of the organization.

Just like governments, corporations and other organizations have guiding documents—corporate charters or partnership agreements—as well as appointed or elected leaders or officers, and planning and operating procedures. These elements in combination provide **corporate governance**. Each operating unit within an organization also has controlling customs, processes, committees, and practices. The information security group's leadership monitors and manages all of the organizational structures and processes that safeguard information. **Information security governance** then applies these principles and management structures to the information security function.

The governance of information security is a strategic planning responsibility whose importance has grown in recent years. To secure information assets, management must integrate information security practices into the fabric of the organization, expanding corporate governance policies and controls to encompass the objectives of the information security process. Information security objectives must be addressed at the highest levels of an organization's management team in order to be effective and sustainable. A broader view of information security encompasses all of an organization's information assets, including the knowledge managed by those IT assets.

According to the Information Technology Governance Institute (ITGI), information security governance includes all of the accountabilities and methods undertaken by the board of directors and executive management to provide:

- Strategic direction
- Establishment of objectives
- Measurement of progress toward those objectives
- Verification that risk management practices are appropriate
- Validation that the organization's assets are used properly

Figure 4-1 illustrates the responsibilities of various people within an organization for information security governance.

> Information Security Governance Outcomes

Effective communication among stakeholders is critical to the structures and processes used in governance at every level, especially in information security governance. This requires the

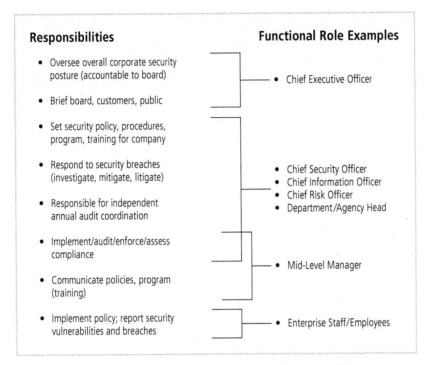

Responsibilities

- Oversee overall corporate security posture (accountable to board)

- Brief board, customers, public

- Set security policy, procedures, program, training for company

- Respond to security breaches (investigate, mitigate, litigate)

- Responsible for independent annual audit coordination

- Implement/audit/enforce/assess compliance

- Communicate policies, program (training)

- Implement policy; report security vulnerabilities and breaches

Functional Role Examples

- Chief Executive Officer

- Chief Security Officer
- Chief Information Officer
- Chief Risk Officer
- Department/Agency Head

- Mid-Level Manager

- Enterprise Staff/Employees

Figure 4-1 Information security governance roles and responsibilities

Source: This information is derived from the Corporate Governance Task Force Report, "Information Security Governance: A Call to Action," April 2004, National Cyber Security Task Force.

development of constructive relationships, a common language, and a commitment to the objectives of the organization.

The five goals of information security governance are:

1. *Strategic alignment of information security with business strategy to support organizational objectives*

2. *Risk management by executing appropriate measures to manage and mitigate threats to information resources*

3. *Resource management by using information security knowledge and infrastructure efficiently and effectively*

4. *Performance measurement by measuring, monitoring, and reporting information security governance metrics to ensure that organizational objectives are achieved*

5. *Value delivery by optimizing information security investments in support of organizational objectives*[2]

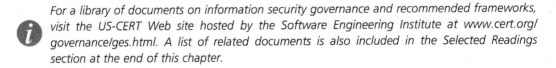

For a library of documents on information security governance and recommended frameworks, visit the US-CERT Web site hosted by the Software Engineering Institute at www.cert.org/ governance/ges.html. A list of related documents is also included in the Selected Readings section at the end of this chapter.

Information Security Policy, Standards, and Practices

Management from all communities of interest, including general staff, information technology, and information security, must make policies the basis for all information security planning, design, and deployment. Policies direct how issues should be addressed and how technologies should be used. Policies do not specify the proper operation of equipment or software—this information should be placed in the standards, procedures, and practices of users' manuals and systems documentation. In addition, *policy should never contradict law; policy must be able to stand up in court, if challenged; and policy must be properly administered through dissemination and documented acceptance.* Otherwise, an organization leaves itself exposed to significant liability. For a discussion of this issue, see the Offline feature on Arthur Andersen.

Good security programs begin and end with policy.[3] Information security is primarily a management problem, not a technical one, and policy is a management tool that obliges personnel to function in a manner that preserves the security of information assets. Security policies are the least expensive control to execute, but the most difficult to implement *properly*. They have the lowest cost in that their creation and dissemination require only the time and effort of the management team. Even if the management team hires an outside consultant to help develop policy, the costs are minimal compared to those of technical controls.

❭ Policy as the Foundation for Planning

Key Terms

de facto standard A standard that has been widely adopted or accepted by a public group rather than a formal standards organization. Contrast with a *de jure standard*.

de jure standard A standard that has been formally evaluated, approved, and ratified by a formal standards organization. Contrast with a *de facto standard*.

guidelines Nonmandatory recommendations the employee may use as a reference in complying with a policy. If the policy states to "use strong passwords, frequently changed," the guidelines might advise that "we recommend you don't use family or pet names, or parts of your Social Security number, employee number, or phone number in your password."

information security policy Written instructions provided by management that inform employees and others in the workplace about proper behavior regarding the use of information and information assets.

practices Examples of actions that illustrate compliance with policies. If the policy states to "use strong passwords, frequently changed," the practices might advise that "according to X, most organizations require employees to change passwords at least semi-annually."

procedures Step-by-step instructions designed to assist employees in following policies, standards, and guidelines. If the policy states to "use strong passwords, frequently changed," the procedure might advise that "in order to change your password, first click the Windows Start button, then...."

standard A detailed statement of what must be done to comply with policy, sometimes viewed as the rules governing policy compliance. If the policy states that employees must "use strong passwords, frequently changed," the standard might specify that the password "must be at least 8 characters, with at least one number, one letter, and one special character."

OFFLINE

Arthur Andersen and Enron

"I obstructed justice," testified David B. Duncan, the former chief outside auditor of Enron Corporation, an American energy company. He told a federal jury that he knew he had committed a crime when he instructed his colleagues at Arthur Andersen LLP to destroy documents as their energy client collapsed. "I instructed people on the engagement team to follow a document-retention policy which I knew would result in the destruction of documents." Duncan was fired by Andersen in January 2002 after an internal probe revealed that the world-renowned accounting company had shredded tons of financial documents and deleted Enron-related e-mail messages. He pleaded guilty to a single count of obstruction of justice.[4]

Enron Corporation was found to have lied about its financial records, specifically its reported profits. Enron was also accused of many dubious business practices, including concealing financial losses and debts. The depth and breadth of the fraud was so great that at least one executive committed suicide rather than face criminal charges. One of the company's accounting firms, Andersen, contributed to the fraud by shredding documents in an attempt to hide the problem. Andersen claimed this was its policy.

Policy that conflicts with law is by definition illegal; therefore, following such a policy is a criminal act. In the Enron/Arthur Andersen scandal, people went to jail claiming they had simply followed policy, although they might have gotten away with it if the policy had been enforced for legitimate and lawful purposes.

The Andersen policy for document retention stated that staff must keep work papers for six years before destroying them, but client-related files, such as correspondence or other records, were only kept "until not useful." Managers and individual partners who kept such material in client folders or other files should "purge" the documents, the policy stated. But, in cases of threatened litigation, Andersen staff were not supposed to destroy "related information."[5] A subsequent update to the policy was interpreted as a mandate to shred all but the most basic working papers as soon as possible unless precluded by an order for legal discovery.

So the shredding party began. A big part of the problem was that the policy was not followed consistently—that is, the shredding began right *after* Andersen found out that Enron was to be investigated for fraudulent business practices, which indicated that the consulting firm had decided to cover its tracks and those of its business partner.

In the end, people went to jail, one person is dead, and thousands of people's lives were disrupted because they lost their jobs, investments, or retirement accounts. A company with a tradition of integrity and trustworthiness is gone, and many claimed they were just following policy.

Policies function like laws in an organization because they dictate acceptable and unacceptable behavior there, as well as the penalties for failure to comply. Like laws, policies define what is right and wrong, the penalties for violating policy, and the appeal process. **Standards,** on the other hand, are more detailed statements of what must be done to comply with policy. They have the same requirements for compliance as policies. Standards may be informal or part of an organizational culture, as in **de facto standards.** Or, standards may be published, scrutinized, and ratified by a group, as in formal or **de jure standards.** Practices, procedures, and guidelines effectively explain how to comply with policy. Figure 4-2 shows the relationships among policies, standards, **guidelines, procedures,** and **practices.** This relationship is further examined in the nearby Offline feature.

The meaning of the term *security policy* depends on the context in which it is used. Governmental agencies view security policy in terms of national security and national policies to deal with foreign states. A security policy can also communicate a credit card agency's method for processing credit card numbers. In general, a security policy is a set of rules that protects an organization's assets. An **information security policy** provides rules for protection of the organization's information assets.

Management must define three types of security policy, according to Special Publication (SP) 800-14 of the National Institute of Standards and Technology (NIST):

1. Enterprise information security policies

2. Issue-specific security policies

3. Systems-specific security policies

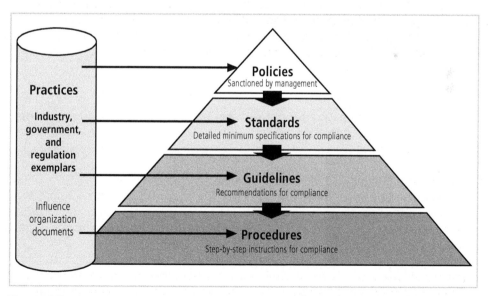

Figure 4-2 Policies, standards, guidelines, and procedures

OFFLINE

Policies, Practices, Standards, Guidelines, and Procedures

The relationships among these terms, even when carefully defined, sometimes confuse the reader. The following examples are provided for assistance. Note that many organizations may use the terms differently and publish documents they identify as policy, which may be a combination of what this text defines as policy, standards, or procedures.

The initial statement of intent is the policy.

Policy: Employees must use strong passwords on their accounts. Passwords must be changed regularly and protected against disclosure.

The standard provides specifics to help employees comply with the policy.

Standard: Passwords must be at least 10 characters long and incorporate at least one lowercase letter, one uppercase letter, one numerical digit (0–9), and one special character permitted by our system (&%$#@!). Passwords must be changed every 90 days, and must not be written down or stored on insecure media.

The practice identifies other reputable organizations and agencies that offer recommendations the organization may have adopted or adapted.

Practice: US-CERT recommends the following:

- *Use a minimum password length of 15 characters for administrator accounts.*
- *Require the use of alphanumeric passwords and symbols.*
- *Enable password history limits to prevent the reuse of previous passwords.*
- *Prevent the use of personal information as passwords, such as phone numbers and dates of birth.*
- *Use a minimum password length of 8 characters for standard users.*
- *Disable local machine credential caching if not required through the use of a Group Policy Object (GPO).*
- *Deploy a secure password storage policy that provides password encryption.*[6]

Guidelines provide examples and recommendations to assist users in complying with the new policy.

Guidelines: In order to create strong yet easy-to-remember passwords, consider the following recommendations from NIST SP 800-118: Guide to Enterprise Password Management (Draft), April 2009:

- *Mnemonic Method. A user selects a phrase and extracts a letter of each word in the phrase (such as the first letter or second letter of each word), adding numbers or special characters or both.*
  - *Example: "May the force be with you always, young Jedi" becomes Mtfbwya-yJ*

- *Altered Passphrases. A user selects a phrase and alters it to form a derivation of that phrase. This method supports the creation of long, complex passwords. Passphrases can be easy to remember due to the structure of the password: it is usually easier for the human mind to comprehend and remember phrases within a coherent structure than a string of random letters, numbers, and special characters.*
  - *Example: Never Give Up! Never Surrender! becomes Nv.G.Up!-Nv.Surr!*
- *Combining and Altering Words. A user can combine two or three unrelated words and change some of the letters to numbers or special characters.*
  - *Example: Jedi Tribble becomes J3d13bbl*

Finally, procedures are step-by-step instructions for accomplishing the task specified in the policy.

Procedures: To change your log-in password on our system, perform the following steps:

1) *Log in using your current (old) password.*

2) *On your organizational portal home page, click the [Tools] Menu option.*

3) *Select [Change Password].*

4) *Enter your old password in the first field and your new password in the second. The system will ask you to confirm your new password to prevent you from mis-typing it.*

5) *The system will then report that your password has been updated, and ask you to log out and log back in with your new password.*

   Do not write your new password down. If you own a smartphone, you may request that your department purchase an approved password management application like eWallet for storing passwords.

As stated earlier, many organizations combine their policy and standards in the same document, and then provide directions or a Web link to a page with guidelines and procedures.

SP 800-14 will be discussed in greater detail later in this chapter.

As introduced in Chapter 3, a policy must meet the following criteria to be effective and thus legally enforceable:

- Dissemination (distribution): The organization must be able to demonstrate that the policy has been made readily available for review by the employee. Common dissemination techniques include hard copy and electronic distribution.
- Review (reading): The organization must be able to demonstrate that it disseminated the document in an intelligible form, including versions for employees who are

illiterate, reading-impaired, and unable to read English. Common techniques include recording the policy in English and other languages.

- Comprehension (understanding): The organization must be able to demonstrate that the employee understands the requirements and content of the policy. Common techniques include quizzes and other assessments.

- Compliance (agreement): The organization must be able to demonstrate that the employee agrees to comply with the policy through act or affirmation. Common techniques include logon banners, which require a specific action (mouse click or keystroke) to acknowledge agreement, or a signed document clearly indicating the employee has read, understood, and agreed to comply with the policy.

- Uniform enforcement (fairness in application): The organization must be able to demonstrate that the policy has been uniformly enforced, regardless of employee status or assignment.

⟩ Enterprise Information Security Policy

Key Term

enterprise information security policy (EISP) The high-level information security policy that sets the strategic direction, scope, and tone for all of an organization's security efforts. An EISP is also known as a security program policy, general security policy, IT security policy, high-level InfoSec policy, or simply an InfoSec policy.

An **enterprise information security policy (EISP)** is also known as a general security policy, organizational security policy, IT security policy, or information security policy. The EISP is an executive-level document, usually drafted by or in cooperation with the organization's chief information officer. This policy is usually 2 to 10 pages long and shapes the philosophy of security in the IT environment. The EISP usually needs to be modified only when there is a change in the strategic direction of the organization.

The EISP guides the development, implementation, and management of the security program. It sets out the requirements that must be met by the information security blueprint or framework. It defines the purpose, scope, constraints, and applicability of the security program. It also assigns responsibilities for the various areas of security, including systems administration, maintenance of the information security policies, and the practices and responsibilities of users. Finally, it addresses legal compliance. According to NIST, the EISP typically addresses compliance in two areas:

1. General compliance to ensure that an organization meets the requirements for establishing a program and assigning responsibilities therein to various organizational components

2. The use of specified penalties and disciplinary action[7]

When the EISP has been developed, the CISO begins forming the security team and initiating necessary changes to the information security program.

EISP Elements Although the specifics of EISPs vary among organizations, most EISP documents should include the following elements:

- An overview of the corporate philosophy on security
- Information on the structure of the information security organization and people who fulfill the information security role
- Fully articulated responsibilities for security that are shared by all members of the organization (employees, contractors, consultants, partners, and visitors)
- Fully articulated responsibilities for security that are unique to each role within the organization

The components of a good EISP are shown in Table 4-1. For examples of EISP documents and recommendations for how to prepare them, we recommend using *Information Security Policies Made Easy* by Charles Cresson Wood, published by Information Shield. While the current version is relatively expensive, prior editions are widely available as used books and in libraries around the world.

Component	Description
Statement of Purpose	Answers the question "What is this policy for?" Provides a framework that helps the reader understand the intent of the document. Can include text such as the following: "This document will: • Identify the elements of a good security policy • Explain the need for information security • Specify the various categories of information security • Identify the information security responsibilities and roles • Identify appropriate levels of security through standards and guidelines This document establishes an overarching security policy and direction for our company. Individual departments are expected to establish standards, guidelines, and operating procedures that adhere to and reference this policy while addressing their specific and individual needs."[8]
Information Security Elements	Defines information security. For example: "Protecting the confidentiality, integrity, and availability of information while in processing, transmission, and storage, through the use of policy, education and training, and technology ..." This section can also lay out security definitions or philosophies to clarify the policy.
Need for Information Security	Provides information on the importance of information security in the organization and the legal and ethical obligation to protect critical information about customers, employees, and markets.
Information Security Responsibilities and Roles	Defines the organizational structure designed to support information security within the organization. Identifies categories of people with responsibility for information security (IT department, management, users) and those responsibilities, including maintenance of this document.
Reference to Other Information Standards and Guidelines	Lists other standards that influence this policy document and are influenced by it, perhaps including relevant federal laws, state laws, and other policies.

Table 4-1 Components of the EISP[9]

❯ Issue-Specific Security Policy

Key Term
_____

issue-specific security policy (ISSP) An organizational policy that provides detailed, targeted guidance to instruct all members of the organization in the use of a resource, such as one of its processes or technologies.

As an organization supports routine operations by executing various technologies and processes, it must instruct employees on their proper use. In general, the **issue-specific security policy**, or **ISSP**, (1) addresses specific areas of technology as listed below, (2) requires frequent updates, and (3) contains a statement about the organization's position on a specific issue.[10] An ISSP may cover the following topics, among others:

- E-mail
- Use of the Internet and World Wide Web
- Specific minimum configurations of computers to defend against worms and viruses
- Prohibitions against hacking or testing organization security controls
- Home use of company-owned computer equipment
- Use of personal equipment on company networks (BYOD: bring your own device)
- Use of telecommunications technologies, such as fax and phone
- Use of photocopy equipment
- Use of portable storage devices such as USB memory sticks, backpack drives, game players, music players, and any other device capable of storing digital files
- Use of cloud-based storage services that are not self-hosted by the organization or engaged under contract; such services include Google Drive, Dropbox, and Microsoft Live

For examples of ISSP policies and recommendations for how to prepare them, we recommend using _Information Security Policies Made Easy_ by Charles Cresson Wood, published by Information Shield. The book includes a wide variety of working policy documents and can assist in defining which are needed and how to create them.

Several approaches are used to create and manage ISSPs within an organization. Three of the most common are:

1. Independent ISSP documents, each tailored to a specific issue
2. A single comprehensive ISSP document that covers all issues
3. A modular ISSP document that unifies policy creation and administration while maintaining each specific issue's requirements

The independent ISSP document typically has a scattershot effect. Each department responsible for a particular application of technology creates a policy governing its use, management, and control. This approach may fail to cover all of the necessary issues and can lead to poor policy distribution, management, and enforcement.

The single comprehensive ISSP is centrally managed and controlled. With formal procedures for the management of ISSPs in place, the comprehensive policy approach establishes guidelines for overall coverage of necessary issues and clearly identifies processes for the dissemination, enforcement, and review of these guidelines. Usually, these policies are developed by the people responsible for managing the information technology resources. Unfortunately, these policies tend to overgeneralize the issues and skip over vulnerabilities.

The optimal balance between the independent and comprehensive ISSP is the modular ISSP. It is also centrally managed and controlled, but it is tailored to individual technology issues. The modular approach provides a balance between issue orientation and policy management. The policies created with this approach comprise individual modules, each created and updated by people responsible for the issues addressed. These people report to a central policy administration group that incorporates specific issues into an overall comprehensive policy.

Table 4-2 is an outline of a sample ISSP, which can be used as a model. An organization should start with this structure and add specific details that dictate security procedures not covered by these general guidelines.

The components of each major category presented in the sample ISSP in Table 4-2 are discussed after the table. Even though the details may vary from policy to policy and some sections of a modular policy may be combined, it is essential for management to address and complete each section.

Statement of Policy

The policy should begin with a clear statement of purpose—in other words, what exactly is this policy supposed to accomplish? Consider a policy that covers the issue of fair and responsible Internet use. The introductory section of this policy should address the following questions: What is the scope of this policy? Who is responsible and accountable for policy implementation? What technologies and issues does it address?

Authorized Access and Usage of Equipment

This section of the policy statement addresses *who* can use the technology governed by the policy, and *what* it can be used for. Remember that an organization's information systems are its exclusive property, and users have no particular rights of use. Each technology and process is provided for business operations. Use for any other purpose constitutes misuse of equipment. This section defines "fair and responsible use" of equipment and other organizational assets and should address key legal issues, such as protection of personal information and privacy.

Prohibited Use of Equipment

Unless a particular use is clearly prohibited, the organization cannot penalize its employees for misuse. For example, the following can be prohibited: personal use, disruptive use or misuse, criminal use, offensive or harassing materials, and infringement of copyrighted, licensed, or other intellectual property. As an alternative approach, categories 2 and 3 of Table 4-2 can be collapsed into a single category called "Appropriate Use." Many organizations use such an ISSP section to cover both categories.

Systems Management

The systems management section of the ISSP policy statement focuses on the users' relationship to systems management. Specific rules from management

Components of an ISSP

1. Statement of policy
  a. Scope and applicability
  b. Definition of technology addressed
  c. Responsibilities

2. Authorized access and usage of equipment
  a. User access
  b. Fair and responsible use
  c. Protection of privacy

3. Prohibited use of equipment
  a. Disruptive use or misuse
  b. Criminal use
  c. Offensive or harassing materials
  d. Copyrighted, licensed, or other intellectual property
  e. Other restrictions

4. Systems management
  a. Management of stored materials
  b. Employee monitoring
  c. Virus protection
  d. Physical security
  e. Encryption

5. Violations of policy
  a. Procedures for reporting violations
  b. Penalties for violations

6. Policy review and modification
  a. Scheduled review of policy procedures for modification
  b. Legal disclaimers

7. Limitations of liability
  a. Statements of liability
  b. Other disclaimers as needed

Table 4-2 Components of an ISSP[11]

Source: Whitman, Townsend, and Aalberts, Communications of the ACM.

include regulating the use of e-mail, the storage of materials, the authorized monitoring of employees, and the physical and electronic scrutiny of e-mail and other electronic documents. It is important that all such responsibilities are assigned either to the systems administrator or the users; otherwise, both parties may infer that the responsibility belongs to the other.

Violations of Policy The people to whom the policy applies must understand the penalties and repercussions of violating it. Violations of policy should carry penalties that are appropriate—neither draconian nor overly lenient. This section of the policy statement should contain not only specific penalties for each category of violation, but instructions for how people in the organization can report observed or suspected violations. Many people think that powerful employees in an organization can retaliate against someone who reports violations. Allowing anonymous submissions is often the only way to convince users to report the unauthorized activities of more influential employees.

Policy Review and Modification Because any document is only useful if it is up to date, each policy should contain procedures and a timetable for periodic review. As the organization's needs and technologies change, so must the policies that govern their use. This section should specify a methodology for reviewing and modifying the policy to ensure that users do not begin circumventing it as it grows obsolete.

Limitations of Liability If an employee is caught conducting illegal activities with the organization's equipment or assets, management does not want the organization held liable. The policy should state that if employees violate a company policy or any law using company technologies, the company will not protect them, and the company is not liable for their actions. In fact, many organizations assist in the prosecution of employees who violate laws when their actions violate policies. It is assumed that such violations occur without knowledge or authorization by the organization.

❯ Systems-Specific Security Policy (SysSP)

Key Terms

access control list (ACL) Specifications of authorization that govern the rights and privileges of users to a particular information asset. ACLs include user access lists, matrices, and capabilities tables.

access control matrix An integration of access control lists (focusing on assets) and capability tables (focusing on users) that results in a matrix with organizational assets listed in the column headings and users listed in the row headings. The matrix contains ACLs in columns for a particular device or asset and capability tables in rows for a particular user.

capabilities table A lattice-based access control with rows of attributes associated with a particular subject (such as a user).

configuration rules The instructions a system administrator codes into a server, networking device, or security device to specify how it operates.

managerial guidance SysSP A systems-specific security policy that expresses management's intent for the acquisition, implementation, configuration, and management of a particular technology, written from a business perspective.

systems-specific security policies (SysSPs) Organizational policies that often function as standards or procedures to be used when configuring or maintaining systems. SysSPs can be separated into two general groups—managerial guidance and technical specifications—but may be written as a single unified SysSP document.

technical specifications SysSP A type of systems-specific security policy that expresses technical details for the acquisition, implementation, configuration, and management of a particular technology, written from a technical perspective. Typically the policy includes details on configuration rules, systems policies, and access control.

While issue-specific policies are formalized as written documents readily identifiable as policy, **systems-specific security policies (SysSPs)** sometimes have a different look. SysSPs often function as standards or procedures to be used when configuring or maintaining systems. For example, a SysSP might describe the configuration and operation of a network firewall. This document could include a statement of managerial intent; guidance to network engineers on the selection, configuration, and operation of firewalls; and an access control list that defines levels of access for each authorized user. SysSPs can be separated into two general groups, **managerial guidance SysSPs** and **technical specifications SysSPs**, or they can be combined into a single policy document that contains elements of both.

Managerial Guidance SysSPs A managerial guidance SysSP document is created by management to guide the implementation and configuration of technology and to address the behavior of employees in ways that support information security. For example, while the method for implementing a firewall belongs in the technical specifications SysSP, the firewall's configuration must follow guidelines established by management. An organization might not want its employees to access the Internet via the organization's network, for instance; in that case, the firewall should be implemented accordingly.

Firewalls are not the only technology that may require systems-specific policies. Any system that affects the confidentiality, integrity, or availability of information must be assessed to evaluate the trade-off between improved security and restrictions.

Systems-specific policies can be developed at the same time as ISSPs, or they can be prepared in advance of their related ISSPs. Before management can craft a policy informing users what they can do with certain technology and how to do it, system administrators might have to configure and operate the system. Some organizations may prefer to develop ISSPs and SysSPs in tandem so that operational procedures and user guidelines are created simultaneously.

Technical Specifications SysSPs While a manager can work with a systems administrator to create managerial policy, as described in the preceding section, the systems administrator in turn might need to create a policy to implement the managerial policy. Each type of equipment requires its own set of policies, which are used to translate management's intent for the technical control into an enforceable technical approach. For example, an ISSP may require that user passwords be changed quarterly; a systems administrator can implement a technical control within a specific application to enforce this policy. There are two general methods of implementing such technical controls: access control lists and configuration rules.

Access Control Lists An **access control list (ACL)** consists of details about user access and use permissions and privileges for an organizational asset or resource, such as a file storage system, software component, or network communications device. ACLs focus on assets and the users who can access and use them. A **capabilities table** is similar to an ACL, but it focuses on users, the assets they can access, and what they can do with those assets. In some systems, capability tables are called user profiles or user policies.

These specifications frequently take the form of complex matrices rather than simple lists or tables, resulting in an **access control matrix** that combines the information in ACLs and capability tables.

As illustrated in Figures 4-3 and 4-4, both Microsoft Windows and Linux systems translate ACLs into sets of configurations that administrators use to control access to their systems.

The level of detail may differ from system to system, but in general ACLs can restrict access for a particular user, computer, time, or duration—even a particular file. This specificity provides powerful control to the administrator. In general, ACLs regulate the following:

- *Who* can use the system
- *What* authorized users can access
- *When* authorized users can access the system
- *Where* authorized users can access the system

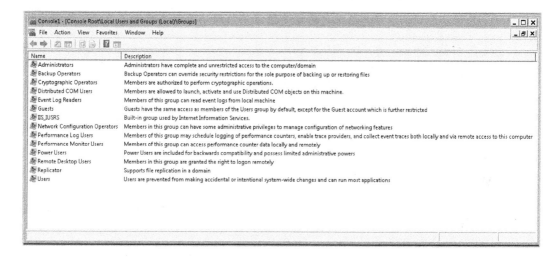

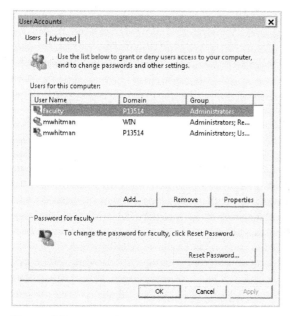

Figure 4-3 Microsoft Windows use of ACLs

Source: Microsoft.

Figure 4-4   Linux use of ACLs

Source: Ubuntu Linux.

The *who* of ACL access may be determined by a person's identity or membership in a group. Restricting *what* authorized users are permitted to access—whether by type (printers, files, communication devices, or applications), name, or location—is achieved by adjusting the resource privileges for a person or group to Read, Write, Create, Modify, Delete, Compare, or Copy. To control *when* access is allowed, some organizations implement time-of-day and day-of-week restrictions for certain network or system resources. To control *where* resources can be accessed, many network-connected assets block remote usage and have some levels of access that are restricted to locally connected users, such as restrictions by computer MAC address or network IP address. When these various ACL options are applied concurrently, the organization can govern how its resources can be used.

Configuration Rule Policies   Configuration rules (or policies) govern how a security system reacts to the data it receives. Rule-based policies are more specific to the operation of a system than ACLs, and they may or may not deal with users directly. Many security systems—for example, firewalls, intrusion detection and prevention systems (IDPSs), and proxy servers—use specific configuration scripts that represent the configuration rule policy to determine how the system handles each data element they process. The examples in Figures 4-5 and 4-6 show how network security policy has been implemented by a Check Point firewall's rule set and by Ionx Verisys (File Integrity Monitoring) in a host-based IDPS rule set.

Combination SysSPs   Many organizations create a single document that combines the managerial guidance SysSP and the technical specifications SysSP. While this document can be somewhat confusing to casual users, it is practical to have the guidance from managerial and technical perspectives in a single place. If this approach is used, care should be taken to clearly articulate the required actions. Some might consider this type of policy document a

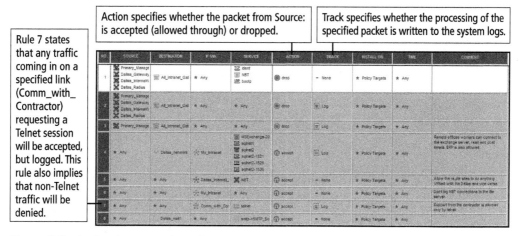

Action specifies whether the packet from Source: is accepted (allowed through) or dropped.

Track specifies whether the processing of the specified packet is written to the system logs.

Rule 7 states that any traffic coming in on a specified link (Comm_with_ Contractor) requesting a Telnet session will be accepted, but logged. This rule also implies that non-Telnet traffic will be denied.

Figure 4-5 Check Point VPN-1/Firewall-1 Policy Editor

Source: Check Point.

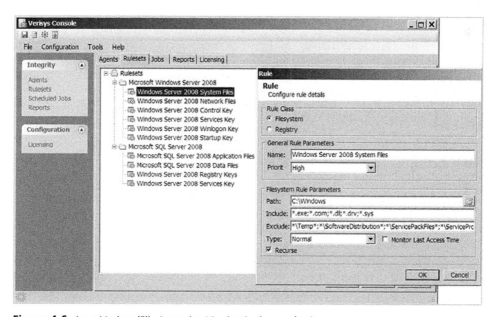

Figure 4-6 Ionx Verisys (File Integrity Monitoring) use of rules

Source: Ionx.

procedure, but it is actually a hybrid that combines policy with procedural guidance to assist implementers of the system being managed. This approach is best used by organizations that have multiple technical control systems of different types, and by smaller organizations that want to document policy and procedure in a compact format.

⟩ Policy Management

Policies are living documents that must be managed. It is unacceptable to create such an important set of documents and then shelve them. These documents must be properly distributed, read, understood, agreed to, uniformly applied, and managed. How they are managed should be specified in the policy management section of the issue-specific policy described earlier. Good management practices for policy development and maintenance make for a more resilient organization. For example, all policies, including security policies, undergo tremendous stress when corporate mergers and divestitures occur. In such situations, employees are faced with uncertainty and many distractions. System vulnerabilities can arise, for instance, if incongruent security policies are implemented in different parts of a newly merged organization. When two companies merge but retain separate policies, the difficulty of implementing security controls increases. Likewise, when one company with unified policies splits in two, each new company may require different policies.

To remain viable, security policies must have a responsible manager, a schedule of reviews, a method for making recommendations for reviews, and a policy issuance and revision date.

Responsible Manager Just as information systems and information security projects must have champions and managers, so must policies. The policy manager is often called the **policy administrator**. Note that the policy administrator does not necessarily have to be proficient in the relevant technology. While practicing information security professionals require extensive technical knowledge, policy management and policy administration require only a moderate technical background. It is good practice, however, for policy administrators to solicit input both from technically adept information security experts and from business-focused managers in each community of interest when making revisions to security policies. The administrator should also notify all affected members of the organization when the policy is modified.

It is disheartening when a policy that required hundreds of staff-hours to develop and document is ignored. Thus, someone must be responsible for placing the policy and all subsequent revisions into the hands of people who are accountable for its implementation. The policy administrator must be clearly identified in the policy document as the primary point of contact for additional information or suggested revisions to the policy.

Schedule of Reviews Policies can only retain their effectiveness in a changing environment if they are periodically reviewed for currency and accuracy and then modified accordingly. Policies that are not kept current can become liabilities as outdated rules are enforced (or not) and new requirements are ignored. To demonstrate due diligence, an organization must actively seek to meet the requirements of the market in which it operates. This applies to government, academic, and nonprofit organizations as well as private, for-profit organizations. A properly organized schedule of reviews should be defined and published as part of the document. Typically, a policy should be reviewed at least annually to ensure that it is still an effective control.

Review Procedures and Practices To facilitate policy reviews, the policy manager should implement a mechanism by which people can comfortably make recommendations for revisions, whether via e-mail, office mail, or an anonymous drop box. If the policy is controversial, anonymous submission of recommendations may be the best way to encourage staff opinions. Many employees are intimidated by management and hesitate to voice honest opinions about a policy unless they can do so anonymously. Once the policy has come up for review, all comments should be examined and management-approved improvements should be implemented. In reality, most policies are drafted by a single responsible employee and then reviewed by a higher-level manager. But, even this method does not preclude the collection and review of employee input.

Policy and Revision Date The simple action of dating the policy is often omitted. When policies are drafted and published without dates, confusion can arise. If policies are not reviewed and kept current, or if members of the organization are following undated versions, disastrous results and legal headaches can ensue. Such problems are particularly common in a high-turnover environment. Therefore, the policy must contain the date of origin and the date(s) of any revisions. Some policies may also need a **sunset clause** that indicates their expiration date, particularly if the policies govern information use in short-term business associations. Establishing a policy end date prevents a temporary policy from mistakenly becoming permanent, and it also enables an organization to gain experience with a given policy before adopting it permanently.

Automated Policy Management In recent years, a new category of software has emerged for the management of information security policies. This type of software was developed in response to the needs of information security practitioners. While many software products can meet the need for a specific technical control, software now can automate some of the busywork of policy management. Automation can streamline the repetitive steps of writing policy, tracking the workflow of policy approvals, publishing policy once it is written and approved, and tracking when employees have read the policy. Using techniques from computer-based training and testing, an organization can train staff members and improve its awareness program. To quote the VigilEnt Policy Center (VPC) user's guide from NetIQ Corporation:

> *Effective security policies are the cornerstone of any security effort. This effort includes writing policies, as well as communicating them to everyone who has access to and uses company information. Once you communicate the policies, you should measure how well the policies are communicated and understood by*

each employee. VigilEnt Policy Center (VPC) helps automate this entire process of security policy management.

Keeping policies up to date and making sure employees are aware of these changes is a complex but necessary procedure. As businesses grow and expand to include new companies, products, and regions, each with their own set of policies and standards, information security officers often ask themselves serious questions.

- *VigilEnt Policy Center helps educate employees about current policies and tests their knowledge through customized policy quizzes.*

- *You can easily update any existing policy document or create new policies as technology and regulations change throughout your company's life.*

- *Using a company's intranet, you can instantly send news items and alert users of sudden events.*

- *VPC lets you easily distribute policies around the world and verify that your users have received, read, and understood the current documents.*

VigilEnt Policy Center is the first product to address these issues with a comprehensive security management solution.[12]

The Information Security Blueprint

> ### Key Terms
>
> **information security blueprint** In information security, a framework or security model customized to an organization, including implementation details.
>
> **information security framework** In information security, a specification of a model to be followed during the design, selection, and initial and ongoing implementation of all subsequent security controls, including information security policies, security education and training programs, and technological controls. Also known as a security model.
>
> **information security model** See *information security framework*.

Once an organization has developed its information security policies and standards, the information security community can begin developing the blueprint for the information security program. If any policies, standards, or practices have not been completed, management must determine whether to proceed nonetheless with the development of the blueprint.

After the information security team has inventoried the organization's information assets and then assessed and prioritized threats to those assets, it must conduct a series of risk assessments using quantitative or qualitative analyses, feasibility studies, and cost-benefit analyses. These assessments, which include determining each asset's current protection level, are used to decide whether to proceed with any given control. Armed with a general idea of vulnerabilities in the organization's information technology systems, the security team develops a design blueprint that is used to implement the security program.

This **information security blueprint** is the basis for the design, selection, and implementation of all security program elements, including policy implementation, ongoing policy management, risk management programs, education and training programs, technological controls, and program maintenance. The security blueprint builds on top of the organization's information security policies. It is a detailed implementation of an **information security framework.** The blueprint specifies tasks and the order in which they are to be accomplished, just as an architect's blueprint serves as the design template for the construction of a building. The framework (also known as an information security model) is the philosophical foundation from which the blueprint is designed, like the style or methodology in which an architect was trained.

In choosing a methodology you might use to develop an information security blueprint, you should adapt or adopt a recognized or widely accepted **information security model** backed or promoted by an established security organization or agency. This exemplar framework can outline steps for designing and implementing information security in the organization. Several published information security frameworks from government agencies and other sources are presented later in this chapter. Because each information security environment is unique, the security team may need to modify or adapt pieces from several frameworks. Experience teaches that what works well for one organization may not precisely fit another.

⟩ The ISO 27000 Series

One of the most widely referenced security models is the *Information Technology—Code of Practice for Information Security Management,* which was originally published as British Standard BS7799. In 2000, this code of practice was adopted as ISO/IEC 17799, an international standard framework for information security by the International Organization for Standardization (ISO) and the International Electrotechnical Commission (IEC). The document was revised in 2005 to become ISO 17799:2005, and then it was renamed as ISO 27002 in 2007 to align it with ISO 27001, which is discussed later in this chapter. While the details of ISO/IEC 27002 are available only to those who purchase the standard, its structure and general organization are well known and are becoming increasingly significant for all who work in the area of information security. For a summary description of the structure of ISO 27002:2013, see Table 4-3.

The stated purpose of ISO/IEC 27002, as derived from its ISO/IEC 17799 origins, is to:

> *offer guidelines and voluntary directions for information security management. It is meant to provide a high level, general description of the areas currently considered important when initiating, implementing or maintaining information security in an organization.... The document specifically identifies itself as "a starting point for developing organization specific guidance." It states that not all of the guidance and controls it contains may be applicable and that additional controls not contained may be required. It is not intended to give definitive details or "how-to's."*[13]

ISO/IEC 27002:2013 is focused on a broad overview of the various areas of security. It provides information on 14 security control clauses and addresses 35 control objectives and more than 110 individual controls. Its companion document, ISO/IEC 27001:2013, provides information for how to implement ISO/IEC 27002 and set up an information security

ISO 27002:2013 Contents
Foreword
0. Introduction
1. Scope
2. Normative references
3. Terms and definitions
4. Structure of this standard
5. Information security policies
6. Organization of information security
7. Human resource security
8. Asset management
9. Access control
10. Cryptography
11. Physical and environmental security
12. Operations security
13. Communication security
14. System acquisition, development, and maintenance
15. Supplier relationships
16. Information security incident management
17. Information security aspects of business continuity management
18. Compliance
Bibliography

Table 4-3 The Sections of ISO/IEC 27002:2013[14]

Source: Compiled from various sources.

management system (ISMS). ISO/IEC 27001's primary purpose is to be used as a standard so organizations can adopt it to obtain certification and build an information security program; ISO 27001 serves better as an assessment tool than as an implementation framework. ISO 27002 is for organizations that want information about implementing security controls; it is not a standard used for certification. As shown in Figure 4-7, ISO 27001 has moved from its previous Plan-Do-Check-Act format to a more formal and comprehensive approach to implementing the ISO 27002 control structure.

In the United Kingdom, correct implementation of both volumes of these standards had to be determined by a BS7799 certified evaluator before organizations could obtain ISMS certification and accreditation. When the standard first came out, several countries, including the United States, Germany, and Japan, refused to adopt it, claiming that it had fundamental problems:

- The global information security community had not defined any justification for a code of practice identified in ISO/IEC 17799.

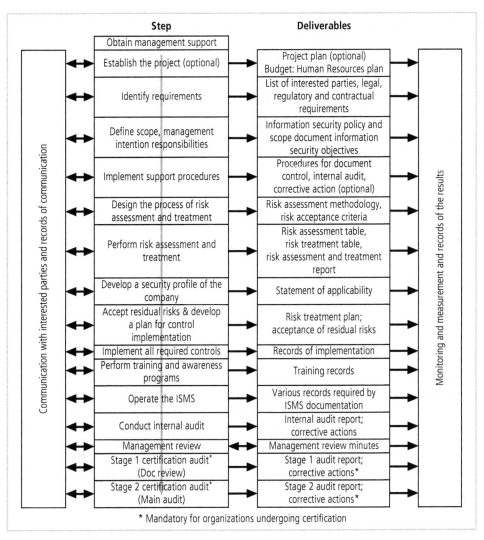

Figure 4-7 ISO/IEC 27001:2013 major process steps

Source: 27001 Academy: ISO 27001 and ISO 22301 Online Consultation Center[15]

- The standard lacked the measurement precision associated with a technical standard.
- There was no reason to believe that ISO/IEC 17799 was more useful than any other approach.
- It was not as complete as other frameworks.
- The standard was hurriedly prepared given the tremendous impact its adoption could have on industry information security controls.[16]

The ISO/IEC 27000 series is becoming increasingly important in the field, especially among global organizations. Many certification bodies and corporate organizations are complying with it or will someday be expected to comply with it.

For more details on ISO/IEC 27001 sections, see www.praxiom.com/iso-27001.htm or www .bsigroup.com/en-GB/iso-27001-information-security/ISOIEC-27001-Revision/.

The ISO has a roadmap for planned standards in the 27000 series related to information security issues and topics. Table 4-4 provides a list of ISO 27000 documents that are currently issued or were planned as of mid-2016.

ISO 27000 Series Standard	Title or Topic	Comment
27000	Series Overview and Terminology	Defines terminology and vocabulary for the standard series
27001:2013	Information Security Management System Specification	Drawn from BS7799:2
27002:2013	Code of Practice for Information Security Management	Renamed from ISO/IEC 17799; drawn from BS7799:1
27003:2010	Information Security Management Systems Implementation Guidelines	Guidelines for project planning requirements for implementing an ISMS
27004:2009	Information Security Measurements and Metrics	Performance measures and metrics for information security management decisions
27005:2011	ISMS Risk Management	Supports 27001, but doesn't recommend any specific risk method
27006:2011	Requirements for Bodies Providing Audit and Certification of an ISMS	Largely intended to support the accreditation of certification bodies providing ISMS certification
27007:2011	Guideline for ISMS Auditing	Focuses on management systems
27008:2011	Guideline for Information Security Auditing	Focuses on security controls
27009:Draft	Sector-specific application of ISO/IEC 27001	Guidance for those who develop "sector-specific" standards based on or relating to ISO/IEC 27001
27010:2015	Information security management for inter-sector and inter-organizational communications	Guidance for inter-sector and inter-organizational communications
27011:2008	Information security management guidelines for telecommunications organizations	Guidance in the application of ISO/IEC 27002 in telecommunications organizations
27013:2015	Guidance on the integrated implementation of ISO/IEC 27001 and ISO/IEC 20000-1	Support for implementing an integrated dual management system
27014:2013	Governance of information security	ISO's approach to security governance—guidance on evaluating, directing, monitoring, and communicating information security
27015:2012	Information Security Management Guidelines for Financial Services	Guidance for financial services organizations
27016:2014	Information security management – Organizational economics	Guidance for understanding the economical consequences of information protection decisions

Table 4-4 ISO 27000 Series Current and Planned Standards

ISO 27000 Series Standard	Title or Topic	Comment
27017:2015	Code of practice for information security controls based on ISO/IEC 27002 for cloud services	Guidance for practice in applying 27002 standards to cloud services
27018:2014	Code of practice for protection of personally identifiable information (PII) in public clouds acting as PII processors	Guidance for practice in applying 27002 standards to PII processed in cloud services
27019:2013	Information security management guidelines for process control systems specific to the energy industry	Focused on helping organizations in the energy industry implement ISO standards
27023:2015	Mapping the revised editions of ISO/IEC 27001 and ISO/IEC 27002	Guidance on the revised editions of ISO/IEC 27001 and ISO/IEC 27002
27031:2011	Guidelines for information and communication technology readiness for business continuity	Application of ISO/IEC 27002 to information and communication technology readiness for business continuity
27032:2012	Guidelines for cybersecurity	Guidance to achieve cybersecurity
27033-1:2015	Network security – Part 1: Overview and concepts	Overview and concepts of network security
27033-2:2012	Network security – Part 2: Design and implementation of network security	Guidance for the design and implementation of network security
27033-3:2010	Network security – Part 3: Reference networking scenarios – Threats, design techniques, and control issues	Networking scenarios
27033-4:2014	Network security – Part 4: Securing communications between networks using security gateways	Securing communications between networks using security gateways
27033-5:2013	Network security – Part 5: Securing communications across networks using virtual private networks (VPNs)	Securing communications across networks using VPNs
27034-1:2011	Application security – Part 1: Overview and concepts	Overview and concepts of application security
27034-2:2015	Application security – Part 2: Organization normative framework for application security	A framework for application security
27035:2011	Information security incident management	Guidance for information security incident management
27036-1:2014	Information security for supplier relationships – Part 1: Overview and concepts	Overview of information security for supplier relationships
27036-2:2014	Information security for supplier relationships – Part 2: Requirements	Requirements for information security for supplier relationships
27036-3:2013	Information security for supplier relationships – Part 3: Guidelines for information and communication technology supply chain security	Guidelines for information security for supplier relationships

Table 4-4 ISO 27000 Series Current and Planned Standards *(continues)*

ISO 27000 Series Standard	Title or Topic	Comment
27038:2014	Specification for digital redaction	Digital redaction specification
27039:2015	Selection, deployment, and operations of intrusion detection systems (IDPSs)	Guidance for IDPS selection, deployment, and operations
27040:2015	Storage security	Guidance on storage security
27041:2015	Guidance on assuring suitability and adequacy of incident investigative methods	Guidance on incident investigative methods
27042:2015	Guidelines for the analysis and interpretation of digital evidence	Guidelines for the analysis and interpretation of digital evidence
27043:2015	Incident investigation principles and processes	Incident investigation principles and processes
27799:2008	Health informatics – Information security management in health using ISO/IEC 27002	Provides guidance to health organizations and other holders of personal health information on how to protect such information via implementation of ISO/IEC 27002
Identified Future 27000 Series Standards (In Draft)		
27033-6	Network security – Part 6: Securing wireless IP network access	
27034-3	Application security – Part 3: Application security management process	
27034-5	Application security – Part 5: Protocols and application security controls data structure – XML schemas	
27034-7	Application security – Part 7: Application security assurance prediction	
27035-2	Information security incident management – Part 2: Guidelines to plan and prepare for incident response	
27035-3	Information security incident management – Part 3: Guidelines for CSIRT operations	
27036-4	Information security for supplier relationships – Part 4: Guidelines for security of cloud services	

Table 4-4 ISO 27000 Series Current and Planned Standards[17] *(continued)*

Note: Additional 27000 series documents are in preparation and are not included here.

Source: www.iso27001security.com/html/iso27000.html.

> NIST Security Models

Other approaches are described in the many documents available from the NIST Computer Security Resource Center (*http://csrc.nist.gov*). Because the NIST documents are publicly available at no charge and have been for some time, they have been broadly reviewed by government and industry professionals, and were among the references cited by the U.S. government when it decided not to select the ISO/IEC 17799 (now 27000 series) standards. The following NIST documents can assist in the design of a security framework:

- SP 800-12: *An Introduction to Computer Security: The NIST Handbook*
- SP 800-14: *Generally Accepted Principles and Practices for Securing Information Technology Systems*
- SP 800-18 Rev. 1: *Guide for Developing Security Plans for Federal Information Systems*

- SP 800-30 Rev. 1: *Guide for Conducting Risk Assessments*
- SP 800-37 Rev. 1: *Guide for Applying the Risk Management Framework to Federal Information Systems: A Security Life Cycle Approach*
- SP 800-39: *Managing Information Security Risk: Organization, Mission, and Information System View*
- SP 800-50: *Building an Information Technology Security Awareness and Training Program*
- SP 800-55 Rev. 1: *Performance Measurement Guide for Information Security*
- SP 800-100: *Information Security Handbook: A Guide for Managers*

Many of these documents have been referenced earlier in this book as sources of information for the management of security. The following sections examine these documents as they apply to the blueprint for information security.

NIST SP 800-12 SP 800-12, *An Introduction to Computer Security: The NIST Handbook*, is an excellent reference and guide for the security manager or administrator in the routine management of information security. It provides little guidance, however, for the design and implementation of new security systems, and therefore should be used only as a precursor to understanding an information security blueprint.

NIST SP 800-14 SP 800-14, *Generally Accepted Principles and Practices for Securing Information Technology Systems*, provides best practices and security principles that can direct the security team in the development of a security blueprint. In addition to detailing security best practices across the spectrum of security areas, it provides philosophical principles that the security team should integrate into the entire information security process. The document can guide the development of the security framework and should be combined with other NIST publications to provide the necessary structure for the entire security process. While the document itself is a bit aged, many of the principles and approaches to information security are timeless.

The scope of NIST SP 800-14 is broad, so you should consider each of the security principles it presents. The following sections examine some of its significant points in more detail.

- *2.1 Security supports the mission of the organization*: Failure to develop an information security system based on the organization's mission, vision, and culture guarantees the failure of the information security program.

- *2.2 Security is an integral element of sound management*: Effective management includes planning, organizing, leading, and controlling. Security enhances management functions by providing input during the planning process for organizational initiatives. Information security controls support sound management via the enforcement of managerial and security policies.

- *2.3 Security should be cost-effective*: The costs of information security should be considered part of the cost of doing business, much like the costs of computers, networks, and voice communications systems. Security is not a profit-generating area of the organization and may not lead to competitive advantages. Information security should justify its own costs. The use of security measures that do not justify their cost must have a strong business justification, such as a legal requirement.

- *2.4 Systems owners have security responsibilities outside their own organizations*: Whenever systems store and use information from customers, patients, clients, partners, or others, the security of this information becomes the responsibility of the systems' owners. These owners are expected to diligently work with each other to assure the confidentiality, integrity, and availability of the entire value chain of their interconnected systems.

- *2.5 Security responsibilities and accountability should be made explicit*: Policy documents should clearly identify the security responsibilities of users, administrators, and managers. To be legally binding, the policies must be documented, disseminated, read, understood, and agreed to by all involved members of the organization. As noted in Chapter 3, ignorance of the law is no excuse, but ignorance of policy is. Organizations should also provide information about relevant laws in issue-specific security policies.

- *2.6 Security requires a comprehensive and integrated approach*: Security personnel alone cannot effectively implement security. As emphasized throughout this textbook, *security is everyone's responsibility*. The three communities of interest—information technology management and professionals, information security management and professionals, and users, managers, administrators, and other stakeholders—should participate in the process of developing a comprehensive information security program.

- *2.7 Security should be periodically reassessed*: Information security that is implemented and then ignored is considered negligent because the organization has not demonstrated due diligence. Security is an ongoing process. To be effective against a constantly shifting set of threats and a changing user base, the security process must be periodically repeated. Continuous analyses of threats, assets, and controls must be conducted and new blueprints developed. Only thorough preparation, design, implementation, vigilance, and ongoing maintenance can secure the organization's information assets.

- *2.8 Security is constrained by societal factors*: Several factors influence the implementation and maintenance of security controls and safeguards, including legal demands, shareholder requirements, and even business practices. For example, security professionals generally prefer to isolate information assets from the Internet, which is the leading avenue of threats to the assets, but the business requirements of the organization may preclude this control measure.

Table 4-5 lists the principles for securing information technology systems, which is part of NIST SP 800-14. You can use this document to make sure the needed key elements of a successful effort are factored into the design of an information security program and to produce a blueprint for an effective security architecture.

NIST SP 800-18 Rev. 1 SP 800-18 Rev. 1, The *Guide for Developing Security Plans for Federal Information Systems,* can be used as the foundation for a comprehensive security blueprint and framework. This publication provides detailed methods for assessing, designing, and implementing controls and plans for applications of varying size. SP 800-18 Rev. 1 can serve as a useful guide to the activities described in this chapter and as an aid in the planning process. It also includes templates for major application security plans. As with any publication of this scope and magnitude, SP 800-18 Rev. 1 must be customized to fit the particular needs of an organization.

	Principles and Practices for Securing IT Systems
1.	Establish a sound security policy as the foundation for design.
2.	Treat security as an integral part of the overall system design.
3.	Clearly delineate the physical and logical security boundaries governed by associated security policies.
4.	Reduce risk to an acceptable level.
5.	Assume that external systems are insecure.
6.	Identify potential trade-offs among reducing risk, increased costs, and decreases in other aspects of operational effectiveness.
7.	Implement layered security to ensure there is no single point of vulnerability.
8.	Implement tailored system security measures to meet the organization's security goals.
9.	Strive for simplicity.
10.	Design and operate an IT system to limit vulnerability and to be resilient in response.
11.	Minimize the system elements to be trusted.
12.	Implement security through a combination of measures distributed physically and logically.
13.	Provide assurance that the system is, and continues to be, resilient in the face of expected threats.
14.	Limit or contain vulnerabilities.
15.	Formulate security measures to address multiple overlapping information domains.
16.	Isolate public access systems from mission-critical resources, such as data and processes.
17.	Use boundary mechanisms to separate computing systems and network infrastructures.
18.	Where possible, base security on open standards for portability and interoperability.
19.	Use common language in developing security requirements.
20.	Design and implement audit mechanisms to detect unauthorized use and to support incident investigations.
21.	Design security to allow for regular adoption of new technology, including a secure and logical technology upgrade process.
22.	Authenticate users and processes to ensure appropriate access control within and across domains.
23.	Use unique system identities that are tied to people who have defined relationships to the organization and are linked to specific data ownership and usage roles to ensure accountability.
24.	Implement least privilege.
25.	Do not implement unnecessary security mechanisms.
26.	Protect information while it is being processed, in transit, and in storage.
27.	Strive for operational ease of use.
28.	Develop and exercise contingency or disaster recovery procedures to ensure appropriate availability.
29.	Consider custom products to achieve adequate security.
30.	Ensure proper security in the shutdown or disposal of a system.
31.	Protect against all likely classes of attacks.
32.	Identify and prevent common errors and vulnerabilities.
33.	Ensure that developers are trained in how to develop secure software.

Table 4-5 Principles for Securing Information Technology Systems[18]

Source: NIST SP 800-14.

NIST and the Risk Management Framework NIST's approach to managing risk in the organization, titled the Risk Management Framework (RMF), emphasizes the following:

- *Building information security capabilities into federal information systems through the application of state-of-the-practice management, operational, and technical security controls*
- *Maintaining awareness of the security state of information systems on an ongoing basis through enhanced monitoring processes*
- *Providing essential information to help senior leaders make decisions about accepting risk to an organization's operations and assets, individuals, and other organizations arising from the use of information systems*

The RMF has the following characteristics:

- *Promotes the concept of near real-time risk management and ongoing information system authorization through the implementation of robust continuous monitoring*
- *Encourages the use of automation to provide senior leaders with necessary information to make cost-effective, risk-based decisions about information systems that support an organization's core missions and business functions*
- *Integrates information security into the enterprise architecture and system development life cycle*
- *Emphasizes the selection, implementation, assessment, and monitoring of security controls and the authorization of information systems*
- *Links risk management processes at the information system level to risk management processes at the organization level through a risk executive function*
- *Establishes responsibility and accountability for security controls deployed within an organization's information systems and inherited by those systems (i.e., common controls).*[19]

The NIST Risk Management Framework is discussed in detail in Chapter 5, "Risk Management."

The NIST Cybersecurity Framework In early 2014, NIST published a new Cybersecurity Framework in response to Executive Order 13636 from President Obama. NIST's mandate was to create a voluntary framework that provides an effective approach to "manage cybersecurity risk for those processes, information, and systems directly involved in the delivery of critical infrastructure services."[20] The resulting framework, which is designed specifically to be vendor-neutral, closely resembles the other approaches described in this textbook, but it provides additional structure to the process, if not detail. The NIST Framework builds on and works closely with the RMF described in the previous section. The Framework document represents the integration of previously discussed special publications from NIST, in a form that makes the Framework easier to understand and enables organizations to implement an information security improvement program.

The intent of the Framework is to allow organizations to: "1) Describe their current cybersecurity posture; 2) Describe their target state for cybersecurity; 3) Identify and prioritize opportunities for improvement within the context of a continuous and repeatable process; 4) Assess progress toward the target state; and 5) Communicate among internal and external stakeholders about cybersecurity risk."[21]

The NIST Framework consists of three fundamental components:

- The Framework core: This is a set of information security activities an organization is expected to perform, as well as their desired results. These core activities are:
    - "Identify: Develop the organizational understanding to manage cybersecurity risk to systems, assets, data, and capabilities.
    - Protect: Develop and implement the appropriate safeguards to ensure delivery of critical infrastructure services.
    - Detect: Develop and implement the appropriate activities to identify the occurrence of a cybersecurity event.
    - Respond: Develop and implement the appropriate activities to take action regarding a detected cybersecurity event.
    - Recover: Develop and implement the appropriate activities to maintain plans for resilience and to restore any capabilities or services that were impaired due to a cybersecurity event."[22]

- The Framework tiers: The Framework then provides a self-defined set of tiers so organizations can relate the maturity of their security programs and implement corresponding measures and functions. The four tiers include:
    - Tier 1: Partial: In this category, an organization does not have formal risk management practices, and security activities are relatively informal and ad hoc.
    - Tier 2: Risk Informed: Organizations in this category have developed but not fully implemented risk management practices, and have just begun their formal security programs, so security is not fully established across the organization.
    - Tier 3: Repeatable: Organizations in this category not only have risk management practices formally established, they also have documented policy implemented. The organization has begun a repeatable security program to improve its approach to information protection and proactively manage risk to information assets.
    - Tier 4: Adaptive: The most mature organization falls into this tier. The organization not only has well-established risk management and security programs, it can quickly adapt to new environments and threats. The organization is experienced at managing risk and responding to threats and has integrated security completely into its culture.

- The Framework profile: Organizations are expected to identify which tier their security programs most closely match and then use corresponding recommendations within the Framework to improve their programs. This Framework profile is then used to perform a gap analysis—comparing the current state of information security and risk management to a desired state, identifying the difference, and developing a plan to move the organization toward the desired state. This approach is identical to the approaches outlined elsewhere in this text.

Using the materials provided in the NIST Framework, organizations are encouraged to follow a seven-step approach to implementing or improving their risk management and information security programs:

- "Step 1: Prioritize and scope: The organization identifies its business/mission objectives and high-level organizational priorities. With this information, the organization makes strategic decisions regarding cybersecurity implementations and determines the scope of systems and assets that support the selected business line or process.

- Step 2: Orient: Once the scope of the cybersecurity program has been determined for the business line or process, the organization identifies related systems and assets, regulatory requirements, and overall risk approach. The organization then identifies threats to, and vulnerabilities of, those systems and assets.

- Step 3: Create a current profile: The organization develops a current profile by indicating which category and subcategory outcomes from the Framework core are currently being achieved.

- Step 4: Conduct a risk assessment: This assessment could be guided by the organization's overall risk management process or previous risk assessment activities. The organization analyzes the operational environment in order to discern the likelihood of a cybersecurity event and the impact that the event could have on the organization.

- Step 5: Create a target profile: The organization creates a target profile that focuses on the assessment of the Framework categories and subcategories describing the organization's desired cybersecurity outcomes.

- Step 6: Determine, analyze, and prioritize gaps: The organization compares the current profile and the target profile to determine gaps. Next it creates a prioritized action plan to address those gaps that draws upon mission drivers, a cost-benefit analysis, and understanding of risk to achieve the outcomes in the target profile. The organization then determines resources necessary to address the gaps.

- Step 7: Implement action plan: The organization determines which actions to take in regards to the gaps, if any, identified in the previous step. It then monitors its current cybersecurity practices against the target profile."[23]

As you learned in Chapter 1 while studying the SecSDLC waterfall methodology, the preceding steps are designed to be an iterative process that gradually moves the organization closer to a Tier 4 security level and results in a better approach to risk management and information protection.

NIST also provides a "Roadmap for Improving Critical Infrastructure Cybersecurity,"[24] which provides supplemental guidance for the Framework and insights into its future development and refinement as an evolutionary, living document.

 For more information on the NIST Cybersecurity Framework, visit the NIST Web site at www.nist .gov/cyberframework.

⟩ Other Sources of Security Frameworks

Many public and private organizations promote solid best security practices. A variety of public and semipublic institutions provide information on best practices—one is the Computer Emergency Response Team Coordination Center (CERT/CC) at Carnegie Mellon University (*www.cert.org*). CERT/CC provides detailed and specific assistance for how to implement a sound security methodology.

Professional societies often provide information on best practices for their members. The Technology Manager's Forum (*www.techforum.com*) has an annual best practice award in several areas, including information security. The Information Security Forum (*www.security forum.org*) has a free publication titled "Standard of Good Practice for Information Security," which outlines information security best practices.

Many organizations hold seminars and classes on best practices for implementing security; in particular, the Information Systems Audit and Control Association (*www.isaca.org*) hosts regular seminars. The International Association of Professional Security Consultants (*www .iapsc.org*) has a listing of best practices. At a minimum, information security professionals can peruse Web portals for posted security best practices. Several free portals dedicated to security have collections of best practices, such as SearchSecurity.com and NIST's Computer Resources Center.

⟩ Design of Security Architecture

Key Terms

defense in depth A strategy for the protection of information assets that uses multiple layers and different types of controls (managerial, operational, and technical) to provide optimal protection.

managerial controls Information security safeguards that focus on administrative planning, organizing, leading, and controlling, and that are designed by strategic planners and implemented by the organization's security administration. These safeguards include governance and risk management.

operational controls Information security safeguards focusing on lower-level planning that deals with the functionality of the organization's security. These safeguards include disaster recovery and incident response planning.

redundancy The use of multiple types and instances of technology that prevent the failure of one system from compromising the security of information.

security domain An area of trust within which information assets share the same level of protection. Each trusted network within an organization is a security domain. Communication between security domains requires evaluation of communications traffic.

security perimeter The boundary in the network within which an organization attempts to maintain security controls for securing information from threats from untrusted network areas. The advent of mobile and cloud information technologies makes the security perimeter increasingly difficult to define and secure.

technical controls Information security safeguards that focus on the application of modern technologies, systems, and processes to protect information assets. These safeguards include firewalls, virtual private networks, and IDPSs.

To inform the discussion of information security program architecture and to illustrate industry best practices, the following sections outline a few key components of security architecture. Many of these components are examined in detail in later chapters of the book, but this overview can help you assess whether a framework and blueprint are on target to meet an organization's needs.

Spheres of Security

The spheres of security, shown in Figure 4-8, are the foundation of the security framework. Generally speaking, the spheres of security illustrate how information is under attack from a variety of sources. The sphere of use, on the left side of Figure 4-8, illustrates the ways in which people access information. For example, people read hard copies of documents and access information through systems. Information, as the most important asset in this model, is at the center of the sphere. Information is always at risk from attacks whenever it is accessible by people or computer systems. Networks and the Internet are indirect threats, as exemplified by the fact that a person attempting to access information from the Internet must traverse local networks.

The sphere of protection, as shown by the shaded bands on the right side of Figure 4-8, illustrates that a layer of protection must exist between each layer of the sphere of use. For example, "Policy and law" and "Education and training" are protections placed between people and the information. Controls are also implemented between systems and the information, between networks and the computer systems, and between the Internet and internal networks. This reinforces the concept of defense in depth. A variety of controls can be used to protect the information. The items of control shown in the figure are not intended to be comprehensive, but they illustrate some of the safeguards that can protect the systems closer to the center of the sphere. Because people can directly access each ring as well as the information at the core of the model, the side of the sphere of protection that attempts to control

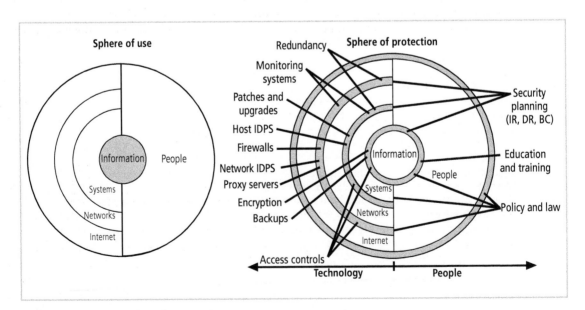

Figure 4-8 Spheres of security

access by relying on people requires a different approach to security than the side that uses technology. The members of the organization must become a safeguard that is effectively trained, implemented, and maintained, or they too will present a threat to the information.

Information security is designed and implemented in three layers: policies, people (education, training, and awareness programs), and technology. These layers are commonly referred to as PPT. Each layer contains controls and safeguards to protect the information and information system assets that the organization values. But, before any technical controls or other safeguards can be implemented, the policies that define the management philosophies behind the security process must be in place.

Levels of Controls Information security safeguards provide three levels of control: managerial, operational, and technical. **Managerial controls** set the direction and scope of the security process and provide detailed instructions for its conduct. In addition, these controls address the design and implementation of the security planning process and security program management. They also address risk management and security control reviews (as described in Chapter 5), describe the necessity and scope of legal compliance, and set guidelines for the maintenance of the entire security life cycle.

Operational controls address personnel security, physical security, and the protection of production inputs and outputs. In addition, operational controls guide the development of education, training, and awareness programs for users, administrators, and management. Finally, they address hardware and software systems maintenance and the integrity of data.

Technical controls are the tactical and technical implementations of security in the organization. While operational controls address specific operating issues, such as developing and integrating controls into the business functions, technical controls include logical access controls, such as identification, authentication, authorization, accountability (including audit trails), cryptography, and the classification of assets and users.

Defense in Depth A basic tenet of security architectures is the layered implementation of security. To achieve **defense in depth,** an organization must establish multiple layers of security controls and safeguards, which can be organized into policy, training and education, and technology, as shown in the CNSS model presented in Chapter 1. While policy itself may not prevent attacks, it certainly prepares the organization to handle them; when coupled with other layers, policy can deter attacks. For example, the layer of training and education can help defend against attacks enabled by employee ignorance and social engineering. Technology is also implemented in layers, with detection equipment working in tandem with reaction technology behind access control mechanisms. **Redundancy** can be implemented at several points throughout the security architecture, such as in firewalls, proxy servers, and access controls. Figure 4-9 illustrates the concept of building controls in multiple and sometimes redundant layers. The figure shows firewalls and prevention IDPSs that use both packet-level rules (shown as the packet header in the diagram) and content analysis (shown as a database icon with the caption 0100101011). More information on firewalls and intrusion detection systems is presented in Chapters 6 and 7, respectively.

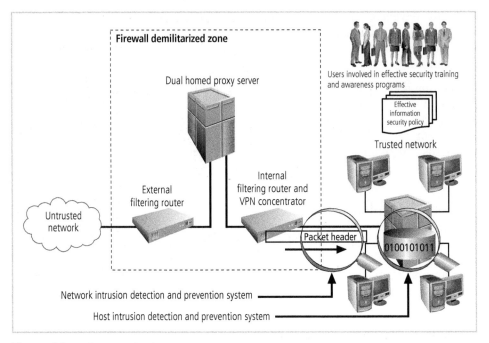

Figure 4-9 Defense in depth

Security Perimeter A perimeter is a boundary of an area. A **security perimeter** is the border of security that protects all internal systems from outside threats, as pictured in Figure 4-10. Unfortunately, the perimeter does not protect against internal attacks from employee threats or onsite physical threats. In addition, the emergence of mobile computing devices, telecommuting, and cloud-based functionality has made the definition and defense of the perimeter increasingly more difficult. This has led some security experts to declare the security perimeter extinct and call for an increased focus on improved system-level security and active policing of networked assets. An organization can have both an electronic security perimeter, usually at the exterior network or Internet connection, and a physical security perimeter, usually at the entrance to the organization's offices. Both require perimeter security. Security perimeters can effectively be implemented as multiple technologies that segregate the protected information from potential attackers. Within security perimeters the organization can establish **security domains**, each with differing levels of security, between which traffic must be screened. The assumption is that if people have access to one system within a security domain, they have authorized access to all systems within that domain. The security perimeter is an essential element of the overall security framework, and its implementation details are the core of the completed security blueprint. The key components of the security perimeter are firewalls, DMZs (demilitarized zones), proxy servers, and IDPSs. You will learn more about information security technologies in Chapters 6, 7, and 8.

Many security experts argue that the security perimeter is dead. With the dramatic growth in popularity of cloud-based computing and data storage, and the continued use of mobile

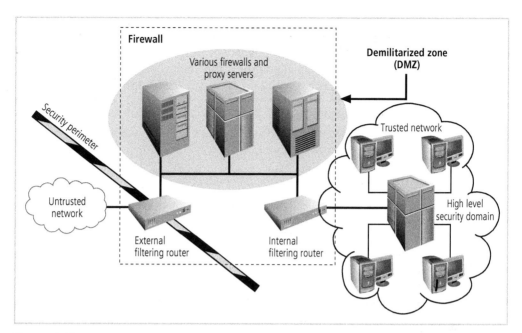

Figure 4-10 Security perimeters and domains

computing devices, they argue that there is no "inside" or "outside" to organizations' networks anymore. Whether this is true is the subject of much debate. With the extensive use of cloud-based services to deliver key systems capability, including security-related functions, there is a growing movement toward realizing that a security perimeter is the entirety of an organization's network presence, anywhere and everywhere the company's data is, and that the use of defense in depth is still a valid approach to protecting it. Whether you subscribe to the "perimeter is dead" philosophy or not, the responsibility for protecting the organization's data using every available resource is still alive and well.

Security Education, Training, and Awareness Program

Key Term

security education, training, and awareness (SETA) A managerial program designed to improve the security of information assets by providing targeted knowledge, skills, and guidance for an organization's employees.

Once your organization has defined the policies that will guide its security program and selected an overall security model by creating or adapting a security framework and a corresponding detailed implementation blueprint, it is time to implement a **security education, training, and awareness (SETA)** program. The SETA program is the responsibility of the

CISO and is a control measure designed to reduce incidents of accidental security breaches by employees. Employee errors are among the top threats to information assets, so it is well worth developing programs to combat this threat. SETA programs are designed to supplement the general education and training programs that many organizations use to educate staff about information security. For example, if an organization detects that many employees are opening questionable e-mail attachments, those employees must be retrained. As a matter of good practice, systems development life cycles must include user training during the implementation phase. Practices used to take control of the security and privacy of online data are sometimes called *cyber hygiene*.

The SETA program consists of three elements: security education, security training, and security awareness. An organization may not be able or willing to undertake all three of these elements, and it may outsource elements to local educational institutions. The purpose of SETA is to enhance security by doing the following:

- Improving awareness of the need to protect system resources
- Developing skills and knowledge so computer users can perform their jobs more securely
- Building in-depth knowledge as needed to design, implement, or operate security programs for organizations and systems[25]

Table 4-6 compares the features of security education, training, and awareness within the organization.

❯ Security Education

Everyone in an organization needs to be trained and made aware of information security, but not everyone needs a formal degree or certificate in information security. When management

	Education	Training	Awareness
Attribute	Why	How	What
Level	Insight	Knowledge	Information
Objective	Understanding	Skill	Exposure
Teaching method	Theoretical instruction • Discussion seminar • Background reading • Hands-on practice	Practical instruction • Lecture • Case study workshop • Posters	Media • Videos • Newsletters
Test measure	Essay (interpret learning)	Problem solving (apply learning)	• True or false • Multiple choice (identify learning)
Impact timeframe	Long term	Intermediate	Short term

Table 4-6 Comparative Framework of SETA[26]

Source: NIST SP 800-12.

agrees that formal education is appropriate, an employee can investigate courses in continuing education from local institutions of higher learning. Several universities have formal coursework in information security. For people who are interested in researching formal information security programs, resources are available, such as the DHS/NSA-identified National Centers of Academic Excellence program (see *www.iad.gov/NIETP/index.cfm*). This program identifies universities that offer coursework in information security and an integrated view of information security in the institution itself. Other local resources can also provide information on security education, such as Kennesaw State's Center for Information Security Education (*http://infosec.kennesaw.edu*).

❭ Security Training

Security training provides employees with detailed information and hands-on instruction to prepare them to perform their duties securely. Management of information security can develop customized in-house training or outsource the training program.

Alternatives to formal training programs are industry training conferences and programs offered through professional agencies such as SANS (*www.sans.org*), (ISC)[2] (*www.isc2.org*), and ISSA (*www.issa.org*). All of these agencies have been described in previous chapters. Many of these programs are too technical for the average employee, but they may be ideal for the continuing education requirements of information security professionals.

Several resources for conducting SETA programs offer assistance in the form of sample topics and structures for security classes. For organizations, the Computer Security Resource Center at NIST provides several useful documents free of charge in its special publications area (*http://csrc.nist.gov*).

❭ Security Awareness

A security awareness program is one of the least frequently implemented but most beneficial programs in an organization. A security awareness program is designed to keep information security at the forefront of users' minds. These programs don't have to be complicated or expensive. Good programs can include newsletters, security posters (see Figure 4-11 for an example), videos, bulletin boards, flyers, and trinkets. Trinkets can include security slogans printed on mouse pads, coffee cups, T-shirts, pens, or any object frequently used during the workday that reminds employees of security. In addition, a good security awareness program requires a dedicated person who is willing to invest time and effort to promoting the program, and a champion willing to provide the needed financial support.

The security newsletter is the most cost-effective method of disseminating security information and news to employees. Newsletters can be distributed via hard copy, e-mail, or intranet. Topics can include new threats to the organization's information assets, the schedule for upcoming security classes, and the addition of new security personnel. The goal is to keep the idea of information security in users' minds and to stimulate users to care about security. If a security awareness program is not actively implemented, employees may begin to neglect security matters and the risk of employee accidents and failures is likely to increase.

Figure 4-11   Information security awareness at Kennesaw State University

Continuity Strategies

> ### Key Terms
>
> **adverse event** An event with negative consequences that could threaten the organization's information assets or operations. Sometimes referred to as an incident candidate.
>
> **business continuity plan (BC plan)** The documented product of business continuity planning; a plan that shows the organization's intended efforts to continue critical functions when operations at the primary site are not feasible.
>
> **business continuity planning (BCP)** The actions taken by senior management to develop and implement the BC policy, plan, and continuity teams.
>
> **business resumption planning (BRP)** The actions taken by senior management to develop and implement a combined DR and BC policy, plan, and set of recovery teams.
>
> **contingency plan** The documented product of contingency planning; a plan that shows the organization's intended efforts in reaction to adverse events.
>
> **contingency planning (CP)** The actions taken by senior management to specify the organization's efforts and actions if an adverse event becomes an incident or disaster. This planning includes incident response, disaster recovery, and business continuity efforts, as well as preparatory business impact analysis.
>
> **contingency planning management team (CPMT)** The group of senior managers and project members organized to conduct and lead all CP efforts.
>
> **disaster** An adverse event that could threaten the viability of the entire organization. A disaster may either escalate from an incident or be initially classified as a disaster.

disaster recovery plan (DR plan) The documented product of disaster recovery planning; a plan that shows the organization's intended efforts in the event of a disaster.

disaster recovery planning (DRP) The actions taken by senior management to specify the organization's efforts in preparation for and recovery from a disaster.

incident An adverse event that could result in loss of an information asset or assets, but does not currently threaten the viability of the entire organization.

incident response plan (IR plan) The documented product of incident response planning; a plan that shows the organization's intended efforts in the event of an incident.

incident response planning (IRP) The actions taken by senior management to develop and implement the IR policy, plan, and computer security incident response team.

A key role for all managers is **contingency planning (CP)**. Managers in the IT and information security communities are usually called on to provide strategic planning to assure the continuous availability of information systems.[27] Unfortunately for managers, however, the probability that some form of attack will occur—from inside or outside, intentional or accidental, human or nonhuman, annoying or catastrophic—is very high. Thus, managers from each community of interest must be ready to act when a successful attack occurs.

Various types of contingency plans are available to respond to **adverse events**, including incident response plans, disaster recovery plans, and business continuity plans. In some organizations, these might be handled as a single integrated plan. In large, complex organizations, each of these plans may cover separate but related planning functions that differ in scope, applicability, and design. In a small organization, the security administrator or systems administrator may have one simple plan that consists of a straightforward set of media backup and recovery strategies and service agreements from the company's service providers. However, the sad reality is that many organizations have a level of planning that is woefully deficient.

Plans for incident response, disaster recovery, and business continuity are components of contingency planning, as shown in Figure 4-12. A **contingency plan** is prepared by the organization to anticipate, react to, and recover from events that threaten the security of information

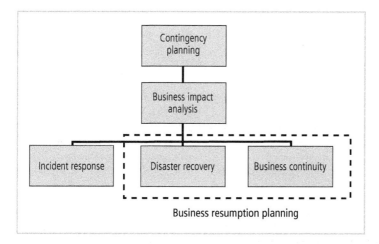

Figure 4-12 Components of contingency planning

and information assets in the organization. This plan also helps restore the organization to normal modes of business operations after an event. The discussion of contingency planning begins by explaining the differences among its various elements and examining the points at which each element is brought into play.

CP includes **incident response planning (IRP)**, **disaster recovery planning (DRP)**, and **business continuity planning (BCP)**, in preparation for adverse events that become **incidents** or **disasters**. The primary functions of these three types of planning are as follows:

- The **incident response plan (IR plan)** focuses on immediate response, but if the attack escalates or is disastrous (for example, a fire, flood, earthquake, or total blackout), the process moves on to disaster recovery and the BC plan.

- The **disaster recovery plan (DR plan)** typically focuses on restoring systems at the original site after disasters occur, and so is closely associated with the BC plan.

- The **business continuity plan (BC plan)** occurs concurrently with the DR plan when the damage is major or ongoing, and requires more than simple restoration of information and information resources. The BC plan establishes critical business functions at an alternate site.

Some experts argue that the DR and BC plans are so closely linked that they are indistinguishable (a.k.a. **business resumption planning, or BRP**). However, each has a distinct role and planning requirement. The following sections detail the tasks necessary for each of the three types of plans. You can also further distinguish among these types of planning by examining when each comes into play during the life of an incident. Figure 4-13 shows a sample

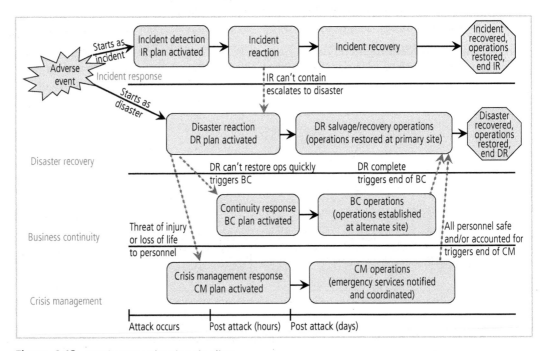

Figure 4-13 Contingency planning timeline

sequence of events and the overlap between when each plan comes into play. Disaster recovery activities typically continue even after the organization has resumed operations at the original site.

Before any planning can begin, an assigned person or a planning team has to get the process started. In the usual case, a **contingency planning management team (CPMT)** is assembled for that purpose. A roster for this team may consist of the following members:

- Champion: As with any strategic function, the contingency planning project must have a high-level manager to support, promote, and endorse the findings of the project. This could be the CIO or ideally the CEO.

- Project manager: A mid-level manager or even the CISO must lead the project and make sure a sound planning process is used, a complete and useful project plan is developed, and resources are prudently managed to reach the goals of the project.

- Team members: The team members should be managers or their representatives from the various communities of interest: business, information technology, and information security.

The CPMT is responsible for obtaining commitment and support from senior management, writing the contingency plan document, conducting the business impact analysis (BIA), and organizing the subordinate teams.

The overall CP process, which should integrate the BIA, IRP, and DRP efforts, includes the following steps, once the CPMT (and other subordinate teams) have been formed:

1. *Develop the CP policy statement. A formal policy provides the authority and guidance necessary to develop an effective contingency plan.*

2. *Conduct the BIA. The BIA helps identify and prioritize information systems and components critical to supporting the organization's mission/business processes. A template for developing the BIA is provided to assist the user.*

3. *Identify preventive controls. Measures taken to reduce the effects of system disruptions can increase system availability and reduce contingency life cycle costs.*

4. *Create contingency strategies. Thorough recovery strategies ensure that the system may be recovered quickly and effectively following a disruption.*

5. *Develop a contingency plan. The contingency plan should contain detailed guidance and procedures for restoring damaged organizational facilities unique to each business unit's impact level and recovery requirements.*

6. *Ensure plan testing, training, and exercises. Testing validates recovery capabilities, whereas training prepares recovery personnel for plan activation and exercising the plan identifies planning gaps; combined, the activities improve plan effectiveness and overall organization preparedness.*

7. *Ensure plan maintenance. The plan should be a living document that is updated regularly to remain current with system enhancements and organizational changes.*[28]

This seven-step methodology recommended by NIST for DRP and BCP has been expanded to include details of the BIA and IRP, resulting in the model shown in Figure 4-14. As you read the remainder of this chapter, you might want to refer back to this diagram because many

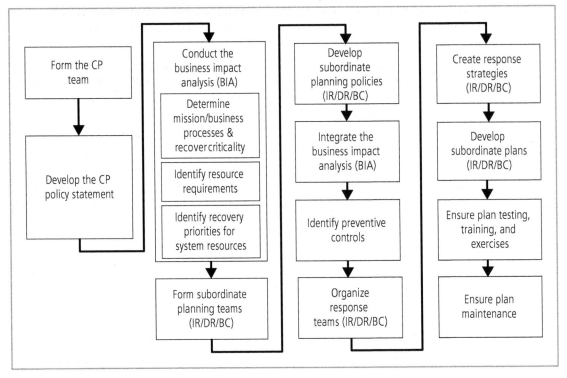

Figure 4-14 Major steps in contingency planning

upcoming sections correspond to the steps depicted in it. Note that each subordinate planning task begins with the creation (or update) of a corresponding policy document that specifies the purpose and scope of the plan and identifies roles and responsibilities for the plan's creation and implementation.

The stages of the CP development methodology are adapted from NIST's SP 800-34, Rev. 1, Contingency Planning Guide for Federal Information Systems (2010), and SP 800-61, Rev. 1, Computer Security Incident Handling Guide (2008). Including the formulation of the CPMT, these stages are:

1. "Form the CPMT. Assemble the management team that will guide CP planning and execution. This includes representatives from business management, operations, and the projected subordinate teams.

2. Develop the contingency planning policy statement. The CP policy is the formal policy that will guide the efforts of the subordinate teams in developing their plans, and the overall operations of the organization during contingency operations.

3. Conduct the business impact analysis (BIA). The BIA, described later in this chapter, helps identify and prioritize organizational functions, and the information systems and components critical to supporting the organization's mission/business processes.

4. Form subordinate planning teams. For each of the subordinate areas, organize a team to develop the IR, DR, and BC plans. These groups may or may not contain people responsible for implementing the plan.

5. Develop subordinate planning policies. Just as the CPMT develops an overall CP policy, the newly formed IR, DR, and BC planning teams will begin by developing an IR, DR, or BC planning policy, respectively.

6. Integrate the business impact analysis. Each of the subordinate planning teams will independently review and incorporate aspects of the BIA of importance to their planning efforts. As different teams may need different components, the actions and assessments of each team may vary.

7. Identify preventive controls. Assess those countermeasures and safeguards that mitigate the risk and impact of events on organizational data, operations, and personnel.

8. Organize response teams. Specify the skills needed on each subordinate response team (IR/DR/BC) and identify personnel needed. Ensure personnel rosters are exclusive (no personnel on two different teams) and that all needed skills are covered. These are the people who will be directly called up if a particular plan is activated in response to an actual incident or disaster.

9. Create contingency strategies. The CPMT, with input from the subordinate team leaders, will evaluate and invest in strategies that support the IR, DR, and BC efforts should an event affect business operations. These include data backup and recovery plans, off-site data storage, and alternate site occupancy strategies.

10. Develop subordinate plans. For each subordinate area, develop a plan to handle the corresponding actions and activities necessary to (a) respond to an incident, (b) recover from a disaster, and (c) establish operations at an alternate site following a disruptive event.

11. Ensure plan testing, training, and exercises. Ensure each subordinate plan is tested and the corresponding personnel are trained to handle any event that escalates into an incident or a disaster.

12. Ensure plan maintenance. Manage the plan, ensuring periodic review, evaluation, and update."

❭ The CP Policy

The CP policy should contain the following sections:

- An introductory statement of philosophical perspective by senior management that explains the importance of contingency planning to the strategic, long-term operations of the organization

- A statement of the scope and purpose of the CP operations, specifically the requirement to cover all critical business functions and activities

- A call for periodic risk assessment and business impact analysis by the CPMT to include identification and prioritization of critical business functions (while this is intuitive to the CPMT, the formal inclusion in policy reinforces the need for such studies in the remainder of the organization)

- A specification of the CP's major components to be designed by the CPMT, as described earlier

- A call for, and guidance in, the selection of recovery options and business continuity strategies

- A requirement to test the various plans on a regular basis, whether semiannually, annually, or more often as needed

- Identification of key regulations and standards that affect CP planning and a brief overview of their relevancy

- Identification of key people responsible for CP operations, such as establishment of the COO as CPMT champion, the deputy COO as CPMT team lead/project manager, CISO as IR team lead, manager of business operations as DR team lead, manager of marketing and services as BC team lead, and legal counsel as crisis management team lead

- A challenge to individual members of the organization that asks for their support and reinforces their importance as part of the overall CP process

- Additional administrative information, including the date of the document's original authorship, revisions, and a schedule for periodic review and maintenance

⟩ Business Impact Analysis

Key Terms

business impact analysis (BIA) An investigation and assessment of the various adverse events that can affect the organization, conducted as a preliminary phase of the contingency planning process, which includes a determination of how critical a system or set of information is to the organization's core processes and recovery priorities.

maximum tolerable downtime (MTD) The total amount of time the system owner or authorizing official is willing to accept for a mission/business process outage or disruption, including all impact considerations.

recovery point objective (RPO) The point in time prior to a disruption or system outage to which mission/business process data can be recovered after an outage (given the most recent backup copy of the data).

recovery time objective (RTO) The maximum amount of time that a system resource can remain unavailable before there is an unacceptable impact on other system resources, supported mission/business processes, and the MTD.

work recovery time (WRT) The amount of effort (expressed as elapsed time) necessary to make the business function operational after the technology element is recovered (as identified with RTO). Tasks include testing and validation of the system.

The next phase in developing the contingency planning process, after developing the CP policy, is the **business impact analysis (BIA)**. The BIA, a preparatory activity common to both CP and risk management, helps determine which business functions and information systems are the most critical to the success of the organization.

A fundamental difference between a BIA and the risk management processes discussed in Chapter 5 is that risk management focuses on identifying the threats, vulnerabilities, and attacks to determine which controls can protect the information. The BIA assumes that these controls have been bypassed, have failed, or have otherwise proved ineffective; that the attack succeeded; and that the adversity being defended against has come to fruition. By assuming the worst has happened and then assessing how that adversity will affect the organization, planners gain insight into how to respond to the adverse event, minimize the damage, recover from the effects, and return to normal operations. The BIA attempts to answer the question, "How will it affect us?"

When undertaking the BIA, the organization should consider the following:

1. Scope: The parts of the organization to be included in the BIA should be carefully considered to determine which business units to cover, which systems to include, and the nature of the risk being evaluated.

2. Plan: The needed data will likely be voluminous and complex, so work from a careful plan to ensure that the proper data is collected to enable a comprehensive analysis. Getting the correct information to address the needs of decision makers is important.

3. Balance: Some information may be objective in nature and other information may be available only as subjective or anecdotal references. Facts should be weighted properly against opinions; however, sometimes the knowledge and experience of key personnel can be invaluable.

4. Know the objective: Identify in advance what the key decision makers require for making choices. Structure the BIA so the information they need facilitates consideration of those choices.

5. Follow-up: Communicate periodically to ensure that process owners and decision makers will support the process and the end result of the BIA.[29]

According to NIST's SP 800-34, Rev. 1, the CPMT conducts the BIA in three stages, as described in the sections that follow:[30]

1. Determine mission/business processes and recovery criticality.

2. Identify resource requirements.

3. Identify recovery priorities for system resources.

Determine Mission/Business Processes and Recovery Criticality The first major BIA task is the analysis and prioritization of business processes within the organization, based on their relationship to the organization's mission. Each business department, unit, or division must be independently evaluated to determine how important its functions are to the organization as a whole. For example, recovery operations would probably focus on the IT Department and network operation before turning to the Personnel Department's hiring activities. Likewise, recovering a manufacturing company's assembly line is more urgent than recovering its maintenance tracking system. Personnel functions and assembly line maintenance are important, but unless the organization's main revenue-producing operations can be restored quickly, other functions are irrelevant.

It is important to collect critical information about each business unit before prioritizing the business units. Remember to avoid "turf wars" and instead focus on selecting business functions that must be sustained to continue business operations. While some managers or executives might feel that their function is the most critical to the organization, it might prove to be less critical in the event of a major incident or disaster. Senior management must arbitrate these inevitable conflicts about priority because it has the perspective to make such trade-off decisions.

When organizations consider recovery criticality, key recovery measures are usually described in terms of how much of the asset they must recover within a specified time frame. The terms most commonly used to describe these values are:

- **Maximum tolerable downtime (MTD)**
- **Recovery time objective (RTO)**
- **Recovery point objective (RPO)**
- **Work recovery time (WRT)**

Planners should determine the optimal point for recovering the information system to meet BIA-mandated recovery needs while balancing the cost of system inoperability against the cost of resources required for restoring systems. This work must be done in the context of critical business processes identified by the BIA, and can be shown with a simple chart (see Figure 4-15).

The longer system availability is interrupted, the more impact it will have on the organization and its operations. Costs will increase as well. When plans require a short RTO, the required solutions are usually more expensive to design and use. For example, if a system must be recovered immediately, it will have an RTO of 0. These types of solutions will require fully redundant alternative processing sites and will therefore have much higher costs. On the other hand, a longer RTO would allow a less expensive recovery system.[31]

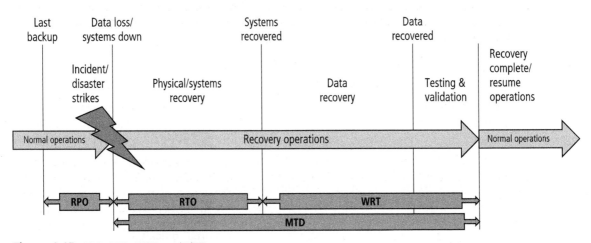

Figure 4-15 RPO, RTO, WRT, and MTD

Source: http://networksandservers.blogspot.com/2011/02/high-availability-terminology-ii.html.

Identify Resource Requirements Once the organization has created a prioritized list of its mission and business processes, it needs to determine which resources would be required to recover those processes and associated assets. Some processes are resource intensive, like IT functions. Supporting customer data, production data, and other organizational information requires extensive quantities of information processing, storage, and transmission (through networking). Other business production processes require complex or expensive components to operate. For each process and information asset identified in the previous BIA stage, the organization should identify and describe the relevant resources needed to provide or support that process.

Identify Recovery Priorities for System Resources As the CPMT conducts the BIA, it will assess priorities and relative values for mission/business processes. To do so, it needs to understand the information assets used by those processes. The presence of high-value information assets may influence the valuation of a particular business process. Normally, this task would be performed as part of the risk assessment function within the risk management process. The organization should identify, classify, and prioritize its information assets, placing classification labels on each collection or repository of information to better understand its value and prioritize its protection. If the organization has not performed this task, the BIA process is the appropriate time to do so.

❯ Incident Response Planning

Incident response planning includes the identification and classification of an incident and the response to it. The IR plan is made up of activities that must be performed when an incident has been identified. Before developing such a plan, you should understand the philosophical approach to incident response planning.

If an action that threatens information occurs and is completed, it is classified as an incident. All of the threats identified in earlier chapters could result in attacks that would be classified as information security incidents. For purposes of this discussion, however, adverse events are classified as incidents if they have the following characteristics:

- They are directed against information assets.
- They have a realistic chance of success.
- They could threaten the confidentiality, integrity, or availability of information resources.

Incident response planning focuses on detecting and correcting the impact of an incident on information assets. Prevention is purposefully omitted, as this activity is more a function of general information security than of incident response. In other words, IR is more reactive than proactive, with the exception of the planning that must occur to prepare Computer Security Incident Response Teams (CSIRTs) to react to an incident. While the IR planning team develops the plans to respond to an incident, the CSIRT carries them out, reacting to real-world incidents on a day-to-day basis.

IR consists of the following four phases:

1. Planning
2. Detection
3. Reaction
4. Recovery

Incident Response Policy An important early step for the IR team is to develop an IR policy. NIST's Special Publication 800-61, Rev. 2, *The Computer Security Incident Handling Guide*, identifies the following key components of a typical IR policy:

1. *Statement of management commitment*
2. *Purpose and objectives of the policy*
3. *Scope of the policy (to whom and what it applies and under what circumstances)*
4. *Definition of InfoSec incidents and related terms*
5. *Organizational structure and definition of roles, responsibilities, and levels of authority; should include the authority of the incident response team to confiscate or disconnect equipment and to monitor suspicious activity, and the requirements for reporting certain types of incidents, the requirements and guidelines for external communications and information sharing (what can be shared with whom, when, and over what channels), and the handoff and escalation points in the incident management process*
6. *Prioritization or severity ratings of incidents*
7. *Performance measures (discussed in Chapter 6)*
8. *Reporting and contact forms*[32]

Like all policies, IR policy must have the full support of top management and be clearly understood by all affected parties. It is especially important to gain the support of communities of interest that must alter business practices or make changes to their IT infrastructures. For example, if the IR team determines that the only way to stop a massive denial-of-service attack is to sever the organization's connection to the Internet, it should have a signed document locked in an appropriate filing cabinet to authorize such action. This document ensures that the IR team is performing authorized actions, and it protects IR team members and the organization from misunderstanding and potential liability.

Incident Planning Planning for an incident requires a detailed understanding of the scenarios developed for the BIA. With this information in hand, the IR planning team can develop a series of predefined responses that guide the organization's CSIRT and information security staff. These responses enable the organization to react quickly and effectively to the detected incident. This discussion assumes that the organization has a CSIRT and that the organization can detect the incident.

The CSIRT consists of people who must be present to handle systems and functional areas that can minimize the impact of an incident as it takes place. Picture a military movie in which U.S. forces have been attacked. If the movie is accurate in its portrayal of CSIRTs, you saw the military version of a CSIRT verifying the threat, determining the appropriate response, and coordinating the actions necessary to deal with the situation.

Incident Response Plan The idea of military team responses can be used to guide incident response planners. The planners should develop a set of documents that direct the actions of each person who must help the organization react to and recover from the incident. These plans must be properly organized and stored to be available when and where they are needed, and in a useful format.

Format and Content   The IR plan must be organized to support quick and easy access to required information. The simplest measure is to create a directory of incidents with tabbed sections for each incident. To respond to an incident, the responder simply opens the binder, flips to the appropriate section, and follows the clearly outlined procedures for an assigned role. This means that planners must develop the detailed procedures necessary to respond to each incident. These procedures must include the actions to take *during* the incident and *afterward* as well. In addition, the document should prepare the staff for the incident by providing procedures to perform *before* it occurs.

Storage   Information in the IR plan is sensitive and should be protected. If attackers learn how a company responds to a particular incident, they can improve their chances of success. On the other hand, the organization needs to have this information readily available to those who must respond to the incident. This typically means storing the IR plan within arm's reach of the information assets that must be modified or manipulated during or immediately after the attack. The organization could use physical binders stored adjacent to the administrator's workstation or in a bookcase in the server room. An even more effective solution is an encrypted file stored on an online resource. The bottom line is that the people who respond to the incident should not have to search frantically for the needed information.

Testing   An untested plan is not a useful plan. Or, in military vernacular, "Train as you fight, and fight as you train." Even if an organization has an effective IR plan on paper, the procedures may be ineffective unless the plan has been practiced or tested. A plan can be tested in many different ways using one or more testing strategies. Four common testing strategies are presented here.[33]

1. Checklist: Copies of the IR plan are distributed to each person who has a role to play during an actual incident. Each person reviews the plan and identifies any inaccurate components for correction. Although the checklist is not a true test, it is an important step in reviewing the document before it is actually needed.

2. Structured walk-through: In a walk-through, each involved person practices the steps he or she will take during an actual event. Team members can conduct an "on-the-ground" walk-through, in which everyone discusses required actions at each location and juncture, or they can conduct a "talk-through," in which all team members sit around a conference table and discuss how they would act as the incident unfolded.

3. Simulation: Here, each involved person works individually rather than in conference, simulating the performance of each task required to react to and recover from a simulated incident. The simulation stops short of the physical tasks required, such as installing a backup or disconnecting a communications circuit. The major difference between a walk-through and a simulation is the independence of individual performers as they work on their own tasks and assume responsibility for identifying faults in their own procedures.

4. Full interruption: The final, most comprehensive and realistic test is to react to a mock incident as if it were real. In a full interruption test, team members follow every procedure, including interruption of service, restoration of data from backups, and notification of appropriate people, as discussed in subsequent sections. This test is often performed after normal business hours in organizations that cannot afford to disrupt

business functions or simulate disruption. This test is the best practice the team can get, but it is too risky for most businesses.

At a minimum, organizations should conduct periodic walk-throughs or talk-throughs of the IR plan. Because business and information resources change quickly, a failure to update the IR plan can result in inability to react effectively to an incident or possibly cause greater damage than the incident itself. If this plan sounds like a major training effort, note the following sayings from author Richard Marcinko, a former Navy SEAL. These remarks have been paraphrased (and somewhat sanitized) for your edification.[34]

- The more you sweat in training, the less you bleed in combat.
- Training and preparation hurt.
- Lead from the front, not the rear.
- You don't have to like it, just do it.
- Keep it simple.
- Never assume.
- You are paid for your results, not your methods.

Incident Detection

Key Terms

incident candidate See *adverse event*.
incident classification The process of examining an incident candidate and determining whether it constitutes an actual incident.

Members of an organization sometimes notify systems administrators, security administrators, or their managers of an unusual occurrence. This occurrence most often causes a complaint to the help desk from one or more users about a technology service. Complaints are often collected by the help desk, and can include reports such as "the system is acting unusual," "programs are slow," "my computer is acting weird," or "data is not available." Incident detection relies on either a human or automated system (often the help desk staff) to identify an unusual occurrence and classify it properly. The mechanisms that might detect an incident include intrusion detection and prevention systems (both host-based and network-based), virus detection software, systems administrators, and even end users. Intrusion detection systems and virus detection software are examined in detail in later chapters. This chapter focuses on the human element.

Note that an incident, as previously defined, is any *clearly identified* attack on the organization's information assets. An ambiguously identified event could be an actual attack, a problem with heavy network traffic, or even a computer malfunction. Only by carefully training users, the help desk, and all security personnel to analyze and identify attacks can the organization hope to identify and classify an incident quickly. Once an attack is properly identified through **incident classification**, the organization can effectively execute the corresponding procedures from the IR plan. Anyone with the appropriate level of knowledge can classify an incident. Typically, a help desk operator brings the issue to a help desk supervisor, the security manager, or a designated incident watch manager. Once an adverse event (also known as an **incident candidate**) has been classified as an actual incident, the responsible manager must decide whether to implement the incident response plan.

Incident Indicators Several occurrences signal the presence of an incident candidate. Unfortunately, many of them are similar to the actions of an overloaded network, computer, or server, and some are similar to the normal operation of these information assets.

Other incident candidates resemble a misbehaving computing system, software package, or other less serious threat. Donald Pipkin, an IT security expert, identifies three categories of incident indicators: possible, probable, and definite.[35] The indicators identified by Pipkin are not exhaustive; each organization adds indicators based on its own context and experience.

The following four types of events are possible incident indicators:

1. Presence of unfamiliar files: If users discover new files in their home directories or on their office computers, or administrators find files that do not seem to have been placed in a logical location or were not created by an authorized user, an incident may have occurred.

2. Presence or execution of unknown programs or processes: If users or administrators detect unfamiliar programs running or processes executing on office machines or network servers, an incident may have occurred.

3. Unusual consumption of computing resources: Many computer operating systems can monitor the consumption of resources. Windows 2000 and XP, as well as many UNIX variants, allow users and administrators to monitor CPU and memory consumption. Most computers can monitor available hard drive space. Servers maintain logs of file creation and storage. The sudden consumption of resources can indicate a candidate incident.

4. Unusual system crashes: Some computer systems crash on a regular basis. Older operating systems running newer programs are notorious for locking up or rebooting when the OS is unable to execute a requested process or service. Many people are familiar with system error messages such as *Unrecoverable Application Error* and *General Protection Fault*, and many unfortunate users have seen the infamous NT Blue Screen of Death. However, if a computer system seems to be crashing, hanging, rebooting, or freezing more than usual, it could be a candidate incident.

The following four types of events are probable indicators of incidents:

1. Activities at unexpected times: If traffic levels on the organization's network exceed the measured baseline values, an incident is probably under way. If this surge in activity occurs when few members of the organization are at work, an incident is even more likely to be occurring. Similarly, if systems are accessing drives when the operator is not using them, an incident may be in progress.

2. Presence of new accounts: Periodic review can reveal an account (or accounts) that the administrator does not remember creating, or accounts that are not logged in the administrator's journal. Even one unlogged new account is a candidate incident. An

unlogged new account with root or other special privileges has an even higher probability of being an actual incident.

3. Reported attacks: If users of the system report a suspected attack, there is a high probability that an incident is under way or has already occurred. When considering the probability of an attack, you should consider the technical sophistication of the person making the report.

4. Notification from IDPS: If the organization has installed host-based or network-based intrusion detection and prevention systems, and they are correctly configured, a notification from the IDPS indicates a strong likelihood that an incident is in progress. The problem with most IDPSs is that they are seldom configured optimally, and even when they are, they tend to issue many false positives or false alarms. The administrator must determine whether the notification is significant or the result of a routine operation by a user or other administrator.

The following five types of events are definite indicators of incidents. Definite indicators are activities that clearly signal an incident is in progress or has occurred:

1. Use of dormant accounts: Many network servers maintain default accounts that came with the system from the manufacturer. Although industry best practices dictate that these accounts should be changed or removed, some organizations ignore these practices by making the default accounts inactive. In addition, systems may have any number of accounts that are not actively used, such as those for previous employees, employees on extended vacation or sabbatical, or dummy accounts set up to support system testing. If any of these dormant accounts suddenly becomes active without a change in user status, an incident has almost certainly occurred.

2. Changes to logs: The smart administrator backs up systems logs as well as systems data. As part of a routine incident scan, these logs may be compared to an online version to determine whether they have been modified. If logs have been modified and the systems administrator cannot determine explicitly that an authorized person modified them, an incident has occurred.

3. Presence of hacker tools: Hacker tools can be installed or stored on office computers so internal computers and networks can be scanned periodically to determine what a hacker can see. These tools are also used to support research into attack profiles. When a computer contains such tools, its antivirus program detects them as threats to the system every time the computer is booted. If users did not know they had installed the tools, their presence would constitute an incident. Many organizations have policies that explicitly prohibit the installation of such tools without the written permission of the CISO. Installing these tools without proper authorization is a policy violation and should result in disciplinary action. Most organizations that have sponsored and approved penetration-testing operations require all related tools in this category to be confined to specific systems that are not used on the general network unless active penetration testing is under way.

4. Notifications by partner or peer: Many organizations have business partners, upstream and downstream value-chain associations, and superior or subordinate organizations. If one of these organizations indicates that it is being attacked and that the attackers are using your computing systems, an incident has probably occurred or is likely in progress.

5. Notification by hacker: Some hackers enjoy taunting their victims. If your Web page suddenly begins displaying a "gotcha" from a hacker, an incident has occurred. If you receive an e-mail from a hacker that contains information from your "secured" corporate e-mail account, an incident has occurred. If you receive an extortion request for money in exchange for your customers' credit card files, an incident has occurred. Even if proof of loss is elusive, such claims can have an impact on an organization's reputation.

Several other situations are definite incident indicators:

1. Loss of availability: Information or information systems become unavailable.

2. Loss of integrity: Users report corrupt data files, garbage where data should be, or data that looks wrong.

3. Loss of confidentiality: You are notified of sensitive information leaks or informed that information you thought was protected has been disclosed.

4. Violation of policy: Organizational policies that address information or information security have been violated.

5. Violation of law: The law has been broken, and the organization's information assets are involved.

Incident Reaction

Key Terms

alert message A scripted description of the incident that usually contains just enough information so that each person knows what portion of the IR plan to implement without slowing down the notification process.

alert roster A document that contains contact information for people to be notified in the event of an incident.

hierarchical roster An alert roster in which the first person calls a few other people on the roster, who in turn call others. This method typically uses the organizational chart as a structure.

sequential roster An alert roster in which a single contact person calls each person on the roster.

Incident reaction consists of actions outlined in the IR plan that guide the organization in attempting to stop the incident, mitigate its impact, and provide information for recovery. These actions take place as soon as the incident is over. Several actions must occur quickly, including notification of key personnel and documentation of the incident. These actions should be prioritized and documented in the IR plan for quick use in the heat of the moment.

Notification of Key Personnel As soon as the help desk, a user, or a systems administrator determines that an incident is in progress, the right people must immediately be notified in the right order. Most organizations, including the military, maintain an **alert roster** for just such an emergency. There are two types of alert rosters: sequential and hierarchical. The **hierarchical roster** works faster, with more people calling at the same time, but the message may get distorted as it is passed from person to person. The **sequential roster** is more accurate because the contact person provides each person with the same **alert message**, but it takes longer.

As with any document, the alert roster must be maintained and tested to ensure accuracy. The notification process must be periodically rehearsed to ensure that it is effective and efficient.

Other personnel must also be notified in reaction to an incident, but they may not be part of the scripted alert notification because they are not needed until preliminary information has been collected and analyzed. Management must be notified, of course, but not so early that it causes undue alarm, especially if the incident is minor or turns out to be a false alarm. On the other hand, notification cannot be so late that the media or other external sources learn of the incident before management. Some incidents are disclosed to employees in general as a lesson in security, and some are not, as a measure of security. If the incident spreads beyond the target organization's information resources, or if the incident is part of a large-scale assault, it may be necessary to notify other organizations. An example of a large-scale assault is Mafiaboy's DDoS attack on multiple Web-based vendors in 1999. In such cases, the IR planning team must determine who to notify and when to offer guidance about additional notification steps.

Documenting an Incident As soon as an incident or disaster has been declared, key personnel must be notified and documentation of the unfolding event must begin. There are many reasons to document the event. First, it enables an organization to learn what happened, how it happened, and what actions were taken. The documentation records the *who, what, when, where, why,* and *how* of the event. Therefore, it can serve as a case study that the organization can use to determine if the right actions were taken and if they were effective. Second, documenting the event can prove that the organization did everything possible to prevent the spread of the incident if the response is questioned later. From a legal standpoint, the standards of due care protect the organization in cases where an incident affects people inside and outside the organization or other organizations that use the targeted systems. Finally, the documentation of an incident can be used to run a simulation in future training sessions.

Incident Containment Strategies

The first priority of incident reaction is to stop the incident or contain its scope or impact. Unfortunately, the most direct means of containment, sometimes known as "cutting the wire," is often not an option for an organization. Incident containment strategies vary depending on the incident and on the amount of damage it causes or may cause. Before an incident can be contained, an organization needs to determine which information and information systems have been affected. This is not the time to conduct a detailed analysis of the affected areas; such analysis is typically performed after the fact in the forensics process. Instead, the organization needs to determine what kind of containment strategy is best and which systems or networks need to be contained. In general, incident containment strategies focus on two tasks: stopping the incident and recovering control of the systems.

The organization can stop the incident and attempt to recover control using several strategies:

- If the incident originates outside the organization, the simplest and most straightforward approach is to sever the affected communication circuits. However, if the organization's lifeblood runs through those circuits, such a drastic measure may not be feasible. If the incident does not threaten the most critical functional areas, it may be more feasible to monitor the incident and contain it in another way. One approach is to apply filtering rules dynamically to limit certain types of network access. For example, if a threat agent is attacking a network by exploiting a vulnerability in the Simple Network Management Protocol (SNMP), applying a blocking filter for the commonly used IP ports stops the attack without compromising other network services. Depending on the nature of the attack and the organization's technical capabilities, such ad hoc controls can sometimes buy valuable time to devise a more permanent control strategy.

- If the incident involves the use of compromised accounts, those accounts can be disabled.
- If the incident involves bypassing a firewall, the firewall can be reconfigured to block that traffic.
- If the incident involves using a particular service or process, it can be disabled temporarily.
- If the incident involves using the organization's e-mail system to propagate itself, the application or server that supports e-mail can be taken down.

The ultimate containment option, which is reserved for only the most drastic scenarios, involves a full stop of all computers and network devices in the organization. Obviously, this step is taken only when all control of the infrastructure has been lost, and the only hope is to preserve the data stored on those computers so it can possibly be used in the future to restore operations.

The bottom line is that containment consists of isolating affected channels, processes, services, or computers; stopping the losses; and regaining control of affected systems. Taking down the entire system, servers, and network may accomplish this objective, but it is typically a measure of last resort. The incident response manager, with the guidance of the IR plan, determines the length of the interruption.

Incident Recovery

Key Terms

after-action review A detailed examination and discussion of the events that occurred, from first detection to final recovery.

computer forensics The process of collecting, analyzing, and preserving computer-related evidence.

evidence A physical object or documented information entered into a legal proceeding that proves an action occurred or identifies the intent of a perpetrator.

incident damage assessment The rapid determination of how seriously a breach of confidentiality, integrity, and availability affected information and information assets during an incident or just following one.

Once the incident has been contained and control of the systems is regained, the next stage of the IR plan is incident recovery. This stage of the plan must be executed immediately. As with incident reaction, the first task is to identify needed human resources and launch them into action. Almost simultaneously, the organization must assess the full extent of the damage to determine how to restore the system to a fully functional state. Next, the process of computer forensics determines how the incident occurred and what happened. These facts emerge from a reconstruction of the data recorded before and during the incident. Next, the organization repairs vulnerabilities, addresses any shortcomings in its safeguards, and restores systems data and services.

Prioritization of Efforts As the dust settles from the incident, a state of confusion and disbelief may follow. The fallout from stressful workplace activity is well-documented; the common view is that cyberattacks, like conflicts of all kinds, affect everyone involved. To recover from the incident, the organization must keep people focused on the task ahead and make sure that the necessary personnel begin recovery operations according to the IR plan.

Damage Assessment An **incident damage assessment** may take only moments, or it may take days or weeks, depending on the extent of the damage. The damage caused by an incident can range from the minor effects of a curious hacker snooping around to extremely severe—a credit card number theft or the infection of hundreds of computer systems by a worm or virus.

Several sources of information can be used to determine the type, scope, and extent of damage, including system logs, intrusion detection logs, configuration logs and documents, documentation from the incident response, and the results of a detailed assessment of systems and data storage. Using these logs and documentation as a basis for comparison, the IR team can evaluate the current state of the information and systems. A related part of incident damage assessment is the field of **computer forensics**. Computer **evidence** must be carefully collected, documented, and maintained to be usable in formal or informal proceedings. Legally speaking, an item is evidence only once it has been admitted in a legal proceeding. Prior to that time, it is also referred to as an item of potential evidentiary value or evidentiary material (EM). Organizations may conduct informal proceedings when dealing with internal violations of policy or standards of conduct. They may also need to use evidence in formal administrative or legal proceedings. Sometimes the fallout from an incident lands in a courtroom for a civil trial. In each of these circumstances, the people who examine the damage incurred must receive special training so that if an incident becomes part of a crime or civil action, they are adequately prepared to participate.

Recovery Once the extent of the damage has been determined, the recovery process can begin in earnest. Full recovery from an incident requires the following actions:

1. Identify the vulnerabilities that allowed the incident to occur and spread. Resolve them.

2. Address the safeguards that failed to stop or limit the incident, or that were missing from the system in the first place. Install, replace, or upgrade these safeguards.

3. Evaluate monitoring capabilities if they are present. Improve their detection and reporting methods or install new monitoring capabilities.

4. Restore the data from backups. See the following Technical Details features for more information on data storage and management, system backups and recovery, and redundant array of independent disks (RAID). Restoration requires the IR team to understand the organization's backup strategy, restore the data contained in backups, and then recreate the data that was created or modified since the last backup.

5. Restore the services and processes in use. Compromised services and processes must be examined, cleaned, and then restored. If services or processes were interrupted while regaining control of the systems, they need to be brought back online.

6. Continuously monitor the system. If an incident happened once, it can easily happen again. Just because the incident is over doesn't mean the organization is in the clear. Hackers frequently boast of their abilities in chat rooms and dare peers to match their efforts. If word gets out, others may be tempted to try their hands at similar attacks. Therefore, it is important to maintain vigilance during the entire IR process.

7. Restore confidence to the organization's communities of interest. It may be advisable to issue a short memorandum that outlines the incident and assures everyone that it was controlled with as little damage as possible. If the incident was minor, the organization should say so. If the incident was major or severely damaged the systems or data, users should be reassured that they can expect operations to return to normal shortly. The objective is not to placate or lie, but to prevent panic or confusion from causing additional disruptions to the organization's operations.

Before returning to routine duties, the IR team must conduct an **after-action review** or AAR. All key players review their notes and verify that the IR documentation is accurate and precise.

All team members review their actions during the incident and identify areas in which the IR plan worked, didn't work, or should be improved. This approach allows team members to update the IR plan while the needed changes are fresh in their minds. The AAR is documented and can serve as a training case for future staff. The finished AAR completes the actions of the IR team.

Backup Media The following Technical Details feature provides additional insight into backup management and strategies. The most common types of local backup media include digital audio tapes (DAT), quarter-inch cartridge drives (QIC), 8-mm tape, and digital linear tape (DLT). Each type of tape has its restrictions and advantages. Backups can also be performed with CD-ROM and DVD options (CD-R, CD-RW, and DVD-RW), specialized drives (solid state flash drives), or tape arrays.

Online and Cloud Backup Many organizations are abandoning physical, local backup media in favor of online or cloud backups. In fact, as part of some organizations' strategies to have improved performance and resilience as well as to shift operations risk to key suppliers, cloud-based architectures are being adopted. The approaches use network-based computing infrastructure to operate critical business functions. When this happens, much of the responsibility for backup and recovery capability, along with many other aspects of system operations, shifts to the supplier of the services. This means that all aspects of operational capability and security (specifically including backup and recovery) must be accounted for in contracts and audit requirements.

One of the newest forms of data backup is online backup to a third-party data storage vendor. Several backup software and service providers now offer multi-terabyte online data storage anywhere. Even for the home user, companies like Microsoft (OneDrive, at *onedrive.live.com*), Memeo (*www.memeo.com*), Dropbox (*www.dropbox.com*), and Google

(Google Drive, at *http://drive.google.com*) offer options that range from free accounts for minimal amounts of storage to inexpensive multi-gigabyte and terabyte solutions.

For the corporate user, this online storage is sometimes referred to as data storage *in the cloud*. This option is more commonly associated with the leasing of computing resources from a third party, as in cloud computing, but many organizations also lease data storage from cloud vendors. Cloud computing is most commonly described in three offerings:

- Software as a Service (SaaS), in which applications are provided for a fee but hosted on third-party systems and accessed over the Internet and the Web.

- Platform as a Service (PaaS), in which development platforms are available to developers for a fee and are hosted by third parties.

- Infrastructure as a Service (IaaS), which is informally known as Everything as a Service, provides hardware and operating systems resources to host whatever the organization wants to implement. Again, the service is hosted by a third party for a fee.

Organizations can easily lease SaaS online backup services and receive data storage as part of the package. From an ownership perspective, clouds can be public, community, private, or some combination of the three:

- Public clouds: The most common implementation, in which a third party makes services available via the Internet and Web to anyone who needs them.

- Community clouds: A collaboration between a few entities for their sole benefit.

- Private clouds: An extension of an organization's intranet applied to cloud computing; this option technically negates one of the benefits of cloud computing, which is that it requires little or no capital investment. Some larger organizations choose to deploy cloud architectures and implement the services across subordinate organizations.

From a security perspective, the leasing of third-party services is always a challenge. If the organization doesn't own the hardware, software, and infrastructure, it can't guarantee effective security. Therefore, security must be obtained through a warranty; the organization must scrutinize the service agreement and insist on minimal standards of due care.

Automated Response   New technologies are emerging in the field of incident response. Some of them build on existing technologies and extend their capabilities and functions. Traditional systems were configured to detect incidents and then notify a human administrator, but new systems can respond to the incident threat autonomously, based on preconfigured options. A more complete discussion of these technologies is presented in Chapter 7.

The disadvantages of current automated response systems may outweigh their benefits. For example, legal issues of tracking suspects with these systems have yet to be resolved. What if the "hacker" turns out to be a compromised system running an automated attack? What are the legal liabilities of a counterattack? How can security administrators condemn a hacker when they may have illegally hacked systems themselves to track the hacker? These issues are complex, but they must be resolved to give security professionals better tools to combat incidents.

TECHNICAL DETAILS

Data Storage and Management

Key Terms

differential backup The duplication of all files that have changed or been added since the last full backup.

full backup The duplication of all files for an entire system, including all applications, operating systems components, and data.

incremental backup The duplication of only the files that have been modified since the previous incremental backup.

To better understand what happens during data restoration in an incident response or disaster recovery, you should understand how system backups are created. Data backup is a complex operation that involves selecting the backup type, establishing backup schedules, and even duplicating data automatically using a redundant array of independent disks (see the next Technical Details feature).

There are three basic types of backups: full, differential, and incremental. The advantage of a **full backup** is that it takes a comprehensive snapshot of the organization's system. The primary disadvantages are that a lot of media are required to store such a large archive and the backup can be time consuming. The **differential backup** updates the backup set only with files that have changed since the last full backup. This method is faster and uses less storage space than the full backup, but each daily differential backup is larger and slower than that of the previous day. For example, if you conduct a full backup on Sunday, then Monday's backup contains all the files that have changed since Sunday, as does Tuesday's backup. By Friday, the file size will have grown substantially. Also, if one backup is corrupt, the previous day's backup contains almost all of the same information.

The third type of backup is the **incremental backup**. It captures files that have changed since the last incremental backup and requires less space and time than the differential method. The downside to incremental backups is that multiple backups would be needed to restore the full system if an incident occurs.

The first component of a backup and recovery system is scheduling and storing the backups. The most common schedule is a daily onsite incremental or differential backup and a weekly off-site full backup. Most backups are conducted overnight, when systems activity is lowest and the probability of user interruption is limited. There are many methods for selecting files to back up and determining where to store various versions of the backups. Organizations will choose methods that best balance security needs against allowing ready accessibility for less severe recovery needs.

(continues)

Regardless of the strategy employed, some fundamental principles remain the same. For example, all onsite and off-site storage must be secured. Fireproof safes or filing cabinets are commonly used to store tapes or external drives. Off-site storage in particular requires a safe location, such as a bank's safety deposit box or a professional backup and recovery service. (The trunk of the administrator's car is not secure off-site storage.) Most backup media (tape, hard drives, or optical drives) will likely require a conditioned environment—preferably an airtight, humidity-free, static-free storage container. Each device must be clearly labeled and write-protected. Because tapes frequently wear out, they should be retired periodically and replaced with new media.

TECHNICAL DETAILS

System Backups and Recovery—RAID

Key Terms

disk duplexing An approach to disk mirroring in which each drive has its own controller to provide additional redundancy.

disk mirroring A RAID implementation (typically referred to as RAID Level 1) in which the computer records all data to twin drives simultaneously, providing a backup if the primary drive fails.

disk striping A RAID implementation (typically referred to as RAID Level 0) in which one logical volume is created by storing data across several available hard drives in segments called stripes.

hot swap A hard drive feature that allows individual drives to be replaced without powering down the entire system and without causing a fault during the replacement.

redundant array of independent disks (RAID) A system of drives that stores information across multiple units to spread out data and minimize the impact of a single drive failure. By storing the data redundantly, the loss of a drive will not necessarily cause a loss of data. Also known as RAID.

server fault tolerance A level of redundancy provided by mirroring entire servers to provide redundant capacity for services.

One form of data backup for online usage is the **redundant array of independent disks (RAID)**, originally known as *redundant array of inexpensive disks*. Unlike tape backups, RAID uses several hard drives to store information across multiple units, which spreads out data and minimizes the impact of a single drive failure. There are nine established RAID configurations, many of which are illustrated in Figure 4-16.

RAID Level 0: RAID 0 is not actually a form of redundant storage—it creates one large logical volume and stores the data in segments called stripes across all available hard disk drives in the array. This method is also often called **disk striping** without

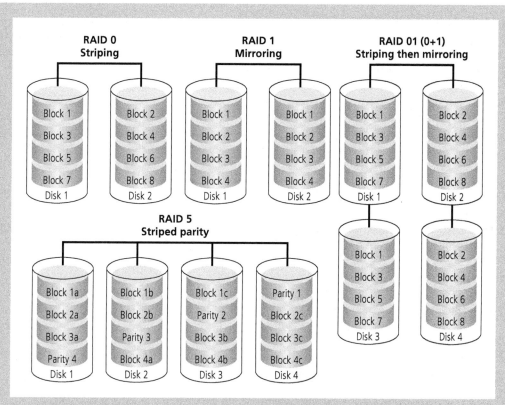

Figure 4-16 Common RAID implementations

parity, and it is frequently used to combine smaller drive volumes into fewer, larger volumes. Unfortunately, failure of one drive may make all data inaccessible. This type of RAID is useful when larger aggregate volume sizes are needed without regard for redundancy or reliability.

RAID Level 1: Commonly called **disk mirroring**, RAID Level 1 uses twin drives in a computer system. The computer records all data to both drives simultaneously, providing a backup if the primary drive fails. However, RAID 1 is a rather expensive and inefficient use of media. A variation of mirroring called **disk duplexing** provides additional redundancy by incorporating separate controllers for each drive. Mirroring is often used to create duplicate copies of operating system volumes for high-availability systems. This type of RAID is useful when a high degree of redundancy and improved access performance are required.

RAID Level 2: This specialized form of disk striping with parity is not widely employed. It uses a specialized parity coding mechanism known as the Hamming Code to store stripes of data on multiple data drives and corresponding redundant error correction on separate error-correcting drives. This approach allows the reconstruction of data if some of the data or redundant parity information is lost. There are no commercial implementations of RAID Level 2.

(continues)

RAID Levels 3 and 4: RAID 3 is byte-level striping of data and RAID 4 is block-level striping, in which data is stored in segments on dedicated data drives and parity information is stored on a separate drive. As with RAID 0, one large volume is used for the data, but the parity drive operates independently to provide error recovery.

This level of RAID is used when an organization requires a trade-off between disk capacity usage and reliability of recovery.

RAID Level 5: This form of RAID is most commonly used in organizations that balance safety and redundancy against the costs of acquiring and operating the systems. It is similar to RAID 3 and 4 in that it stripes the data across multiple drives, but there is no dedicated parity drive. Instead, segments of data are interleaved with parity data and are written across all of the drives in the set. RAID 5 drives can also be **hot swapped**, which improves the organization's chances of regaining full capability, compared with a RAID 3 or 4 implementation.

RAID Level 6: RAID 5 with two sets of parity for each parcel of data, which provides an additional level of protection.

RAID Level 7: This is a variation on RAID 5, in which the array works as a single virtual drive. RAID Level 7 is sometimes performed by running special software over RAID 5 hardware.

RAID Level 10: This is a combination of RAID 1 and RAID 0 (0+1: mirroring then striping).

Additional redundancy can be provided by mirroring entire servers called redundant servers or **server fault tolerance**.

❯ Disaster Recovery Planning

An event can be categorized as a disaster when an organization is unable to mitigate the impact of an incident while it is occurring and the level of damage or destruction is so severe that the organization is unable to recover quickly. The difference between an incident and a disaster may be subtle; the contingency planning team must make the distinction between the two, which may not be possible until an attack occurs. Often an event that is initially classified as an incident is later determined to be a disaster. When this happens, the organization must change its response and secure its most valuable assets to preserve their value for the long term, even at the risk of more short-term disruption.

Disaster recovery (DR) planning is the process of preparing an organization to handle a disaster and recover from it, whether the disaster is natural or man-made. The key emphasis of a DR plan is to reestablish operations at the primary site, the location at which the organization performs its business. The goal of the plan is to make things whole, or as they were before the disaster.

The Disaster Recovery Plan Similar in structure to the IR plan, the DR plan provides detailed guidance in the event of a disaster. It is organized by the type or nature of the disaster, and it specifies recovery procedures during and after each type of disaster. It also provides details about the roles and responsibilities of the people involved in the DR effort, and it identifies the personnel and agencies that must be notified. The DR plan must be tested using the same testing mechanisms as the IR plan. At a minimum, the DR plan must be reviewed periodically during a walk-through or talk-through. As with IR teams, the DR group consists of a planning team and a response team.

Many of the same precepts of incident response apply to disaster recovery:

- Priorities must be clearly established. The first priority is always the preservation of human life. The protection of data and systems immediately falls to the wayside if the disaster threatens the lives, health, or welfare of the organization's employees or community. Only after all employees and neighbors have been safeguarded can the disaster recovery team attend to protecting other assets.

- Roles and responsibilities must be clearly delineated. All members of the DR response team should be aware of their expected actions during a disaster. Some people are responsible for coordinating with local authorities, such as fire, police, and medical staff. Others are responsible for the evacuation of personnel, if required. Still others are tasked simply to pack up and leave.

- Someone must initiate the alert roster and notify key personnel, including the fire, police, or medical authorities mentioned earlier, as well as insurance agencies, disaster teams like the Red Cross, and management teams.

- Someone must be tasked with documenting the disaster. As with an IR reaction, some-one must begin recording what happened to serve as a basis for later determining why and how the event occurred.

- If possible, attempts must be made to mitigate the impact of the disaster on the organization's operations. If everyone is safe and all needed authorities have been notified, some employees can be tasked with the evacuation of physical assets. Some can be responsible for making sure all systems are securely shut down to prevent further loss of data.

Recovery Operations Reactions to a disaster can vary so widely that it is impossible to describe the process with any accuracy. Each organization must examine the scenarios developed at the start of contingency planning and determine how to respond.

Should the physical facilities be spared after the disaster, the disaster recovery response team should begin restoring systems and data to reestablish full operational capability. If the organization's facilities do not survive, alternative actions must be taken until new facilities can be acquired. When a disaster threatens the viability of the organization at the primary site, the disaster recovery process transitions into the process of business continuity planning.

> Business Continuity Planning

Business continuity planning prepares an organization to reestablish or relocate critical business operations during a disaster that affects operations at the primary site. If a disaster has rendered the current location unusable, a plan must be in place to allow the business to continue to function. Not every business needs such a plan or such facilities. Small companies or fiscally sound organizations may have the latitude to cease operations until the physical facilities can be restored. Manufacturing and retail organizations may not have this option because they depend on physical commerce and may not be able to relocate operations.

Developing Continuity Programs Once the incident response and disaster recovery plans are in place, the organization needs to consider finding temporary facilities to support its continued viability in a disaster. A BC plan is somewhat simpler to develop than an IR plan or DR plan because it consists primarily of selecting a continuity strategy and integrating the off-site data storage and recovery functions into this strategy. Some components of the BC plan, such as an off-site backup service, could already be integral to the organization's normal operations. Other components require special consideration and negotiation.

The first part of business continuity planning is performed when the joint DR/BC plan is developed. The identification of critical business functions and the resources needed to support them is the cornerstone of the BC plan. When a disaster strikes, these functions are the first to be reestablished at the alternate site. The contingency planning team needs to appoint a group of people to evaluate and compare various alternatives and recommend which strategy should be selected and implemented. The selected strategy usually involves some form of off-site facility, which should be inspected, configured, secured, and tested on a periodic basis. The selection should be reviewed periodically to determine if a superior alternative has emerged or if the organization needs a different solution.

Site and Data Contingency Strategies

Key Terms

cold site A facility that provides only rudimentary services, with no computer hardware or peripherals. Cold sites are used for BC operations.

database shadowing A backup strategy to store duplicate online transaction data along with duplicate databases at the remote site on a redundant server. This server combines electronic vaulting with remote journaling by writing multiple copies of the database simultaneously to two locations.

electronic vaulting A backup method that uses bulk batch transfer of data to an off-site facility; this transfer is usually conducted via leased lines or secure Internet connections.

hot site A fully configured computing facility that includes all services, communications links, and physical plant operations. Hot sites are used for BC operations.

mutual agreement A continuity strategy in which two organizations sign a contract to assist the other in a disaster by providing BC facilities, resources, and services until the organization in need can recover from the disaster.

remote journaling The backup of data to an off-site facility in close to real time based on transactions as they occur.

service bureau A continuity strategy in which an organization contracts with a service agency to provide a BC facility for a fee.

time-share A continuity strategy in which an organization co-leases facilities with a business partner or sister organization. A time-share allows the organization to have a BC option while reducing its overall costs.

warm site A facility that provides many of the same services and options as a hot site, but typically without installed and configured software applications. Warm sites are used for BC operations.

An organization can choose from several strategies when planning for business continuity. The determining factor when selecting a strategy is usually cost. In general, organizations have three exclusive options: hot sites, warm sites, and cold sites. Options are also available for three shared functions: time-shares, service bureaus, and mutual agreements.

Hot Sites A **hot site** is a fully configured computer facility with all services, communications links, and physical plant operations, including heating and air conditioning. Hot sites duplicate computing resources, peripherals, phone systems, applications, and workstations. A hot site is the pinnacle of contingency planning; it is a duplicate facility that needs only the latest data backups and personnel to become a fully operational twin of the original. A hot site can be operational in a matter of minutes, and in some cases it may be built to provide a process that is seamless to system users by picking up the processing load from a failing site. (This process is sometimes called a seamless fail-over.) The hot site is therefore the most expensive alternative available. Other disadvantages include the need to provide maintenance for all systems and equipment in the hot site, as well as physical and information security. However, if the organization needs a 24/7 capability for near real-time recovery, a hot site is the best option.

Warm Sites The next step down from the hot site is the warm site. A **warm site** provides many of the same services and options as the hot site. However, it typically does not include the actual applications the company needs, or the applications may not yet be installed and configured. A warm site frequently includes computing equipment and peripherals with servers, but not client workstations. A warm site has many of the advantages of a hot site, but at a lower cost. The downside is that a warm site requires hours, if not days, to become fully functional.

Cold Sites The final dedicated site option is the cold site. A **cold site** provides only rudimentary services and facilities. No computer hardware or peripherals are provided. All communications services must be installed after the site is occupied. Basically, a cold site is an empty room with heating, air conditioning, and electricity. Everything else is an option. Although the obvious disadvantages may preclude its selection, a cold site is better than nothing. The main advantage of cold sites over hot and warm sites is the cost. If the warm or hot site is a shared arrangement, not having to contend with other organizations and their equipment after a widespread disaster may make the cold site a better option, albeit slower. In spite of these advantages, some organizations feel it would be easier to lease a new space on short notice than pay maintenance fees on a cold site.

Time-shares A **time-share** allows the organization to maintain a disaster recovery and business continuity option by sharing the cost of a hot, warm, or cold site with one or more partners. The time-share has the same advantages as the type of site selected (hot, warm, or cold). The primary disadvantage is the possibility that more than one organization involved in the time-share may need the facility simultaneously. Other disadvantages include the need to stock the facility with equipment and data from all organizations involved, the negotiations for arranging the time-share, and additional agreements if one or more parties decide to cancel the agreement or sublease its options. A time-share is like agreeing to co-lease an apartment with a group of friends. The participating organizations need to remain on amiable terms because they would have physical access to each other's data.

Service Bureaus In case of a disaster, a **service bureau** agrees to provide physical facilities. These types of agencies also frequently provide off-site data storage for a fee. Contracts can be carefully created with service bureaus to specify exactly what the organization needs without having to reserve dedicated facilities. A service agreement usually guarantees space when needed, even if the service bureau has to acquire additional space in the event of a widespread disaster. This option is much like the rental car clause in your car insurance policy. The disadvantage is that the bureau is a service and must be renegotiated periodically. Also, using a service bureau can be quite expensive.

Mutual Agreements **Mutual agreements** stipulate that participating unaffected organizations are obligated to provide necessary facilities, resources, and services until the receiving organization can recover from the disaster. This type of arrangement is like moving in with relatives or friends: it doesn't take long to outstay your welcome. The problem with this approach is that many organizations balk at the idea of having to fund duplicate services and resources for other parties, even in the short term. The arrangement is ideal if you need the assistance, but not if you are the host. Still, mutual agreements between divisions of the same parent company, between subordinate and superior organizations, or between business partners can be a cost-effective solution.

Other Options Specialized alternatives are available, such as a rolling mobile site configured in the payload area of a tractor or trailer, or externally stored resources. These resources can consist of a rental storage area that contains duplicate or second-generation equipment to be extracted in an emergency. An organization can also contract with a prefabricated building company for immediate, temporary facilities (mobile offices) that can be placed onsite in the event of a disaster.

One of the newest options available as a specialized alternative is called Disaster Recovery as a Service (DRaaS). DRaaS involves the use of cloud-based computing services as part of a service agreement with a third party. With DRaaS, the organization only needs to access its data (which should have been backed up regularly off-site) in order to regain operations, while employees could literally begin work from anywhere, almost negating the need for expensive, temporary physical offices in organizations with little or no manufacturing functions. These alternatives should be considered when evaluating strategy options.

Off-site Disaster Data Storage To get continuity sites up and running quickly, the organization must be able to move data into the new site's systems. Besides the traditional backup methods mentioned earlier, several more options are available, and some can be used for purposes other than restoring continuity:

- **Electronic vaulting** transfers data off-site in batches, usually through leased lines or services provided for a fee. The receiving server archives the data until the next electronic vaulting process is received. Some disaster recovery companies specialize in electronic vaulting services.

- **Remote journaling** differs from electronic vaulting in that only transactions are transferred, not archived data; also, the transfer is in real time. Electronic vaulting is much like a traditional backup, with a dump of data to the off-site storage, but remote journaling involves activities at a systems level, much like server fault tolerance, with data written to two locations simultaneously.

- An improvement to the process of remote journaling, **database shadowing** combines the server fault tolerance mentioned earlier with remote journaling, writing three or more copies of the database simultaneously to backup systems locally and at one or more remote locations.

〉 Crisis Management

Key Term

crisis management An organization's set of planning and preparation efforts for dealing with potential human injury, emotional trauma, or loss of life as a result of a disaster.

Disasters, of course, are larger in scale and less manageable than incidents, but the planning processes for both are the same and in many cases are conducted simultaneously. What may truly distinguish an incident from a disaster are the actions of the response teams. An incident response team typically rushes to duty stations or to the office from home. The first act is to reach for the IR plan. A disaster recovery response team may not have the luxury of flipping through a binder to see what must be done. Disaster recovery response personnel must know their roles without any supporting documentation. This knowledge is a function of preparation, training, and rehearsal. You probably remember frequent fire, tornado, or hurricane drills—or even nuclear blast drills—from your school days. Moving from school to the business world doesn't lessen the threat of a fire or other disaster.

The actions taken during and after a disaster are referred to as **crisis management**. Crisis management differs dramatically from incident response, as it focuses first and foremost on the people involved. The disaster recovery team works closely with the crisis management team. According to Gartner Research, the crisis management response team is:

> *responsible for managing the event from an enterprise perspective and covers the following major activities:*
>
> - *Supporting personnel and their loved ones during the crisis*
> - *Determining the event's impact on normal business operations and, if necessary, making a disaster declaration*
> - *Keeping the public informed about the event and the actions being taken to ensure the recovery of personnel and the enterprise*
> - *Communicating with major customers, suppliers, partners, regulatory agencies, industry organizations, the media, and other interested parties.*[36]

The crisis management response team should establish a base of operations or command center to support communications until the disaster has ended. The crisis management response team includes people from all functional areas of the organization to facilitate communications and cooperation. Some key areas of crisis management include the following:

- Verifying personnel head count: Everyone must be accounted for, including people on vacations, leaves of absence, and business trips.
- Checking the alert roster: Alert rosters and general personnel phone lists are used to notify people whose assistance may be needed or simply to tell employees not to report to work until the crisis or event is over.
- Checking emergency information cards: It is important that each employee has two types of emergency information cards. The first is personal information that includes next of kin and other contacts in case of an emergency, medical conditions, and a form of identification. The second is a set of instructions for what to do in an emergency. This mini-snapshot of the disaster recovery plan should contain at least a contact number or hotline number; emergency services numbers for fire, police, and medical assistance; evacuation and assembly locations, such as storm shelters; the name and number of the disaster recovery coordinator; and any other needed information.

Crisis management must balance the needs of employees with the needs of the business in providing personnel with support at home during disasters.

❭ The Consolidated Contingency Plan

Using the strategy described earlier and illustrated in Figure 4-14, an organization can build a single document that combines all aspects of the contingency policy and plan, incorporating the IR, DR, and BC plans. In large organizations, such a document may be massive; because it would be unwieldy in physical form, it is often created and stored electronically in a safe and secure off-site location. The document should be online and easily accessible via the Internet by appropriate employees in time of need. The document may be stored in an encrypted file and within a password-protected repository.

Small and medium-sized organizations can use the same approach, but they may also store hard copies of the document both within and outside the organization, at the residences of people who may need them.

All contingency planners live by the following words: *plan for the worst and hope for the best*.

❭ Law Enforcement Involvement

Sometimes, an attack, breach of policy, or other incident constitutes a violation of law. Perhaps the incident was originally considered an accident, but turns out to have been an attempt at corporate espionage, sabotage, or theft. When an organization considers involving law enforcement in an incident, several questions must be answered. When should the organization get law enforcement involved? What level of law enforcement agency should be involved—local, state, or federal? What happens when a law enforcement agency is involved? Some of these questions are best answered by the organization's legal department, but organizations should be prepared to address them in the absence of legal staff. These incidents often occur under circumstances that do not allow for leisurely decision making. Some agencies that may be involved were discussed in detail in Chapter 3.

Benefits and Drawbacks of Law Enforcement Involvement The involvement of law enforcement agencies has advantages and disadvantages. The agencies may be much more capable of processing evidence than an organization. In fact, unless the organization's security forces have been trained in processing evidence and computer forensics, they may do more harm than good when extracting the necessary information to legally convict a suspected criminal. Law enforcement agencies can issue the warrants and subpoenas necessary to document a case, and are adept at obtaining statements from witnesses, affidavits, and other required documents. Law enforcement personnel can be a security administrator's greatest ally in the war on computer crime. Therefore, organizations should get to know the local and state officials charged with enforcing information security laws before having to make a call to report a suspected crime.

Once a law enforcement agency takes over a case, however, the organization cannot entirely control the chain of events, the collection of information and evidence, and the prosecution of suspects. A suspect who might face censure and dismissal by an organization may also face criminal charges and all the attendant publicity. The organization may not be informed about the case's progress for weeks or even months. Equipment that is vital to the organization's business may be tagged as evidence and then removed, stored, and preserved until it is no longer needed for the criminal case. In fact, the equipment may never be returned.

If an organization detects a criminal act, it is legally obligated to involve appropriate law enforcement officials. Failure to do so can subject the organization and its officers to prosecution as accessories to the crimes or as impediments to an investigation. The security administrator must ask law enforcement officials when their agencies need to become involved and which crimes need to be addressed by each agency.

Selected Readings

Many excellent sources of additional information are available in the area of information security. The following can add to your understanding of this chapter's content:

- Information Security Governance: Guidance for Boards of Directors and Executive Management, available by searching at *www.isaca.org*.

- Information Security Governance: A Call to Action, available from *www.cccure.org /Documents/Governance/InfoSecGov4_04.pdf*.

- *Information Security Policies Made Easy*, Version 12, by Charles Cresson Wood and Dave Lineman. 2012. Information Shield.

- *Management of Information Security*, by Michael E. Whitman and Herbert J. Mattord. 2016. Cengage Learning.

- *Principles of Incident Response and Disaster Recovery*, by Michael E. Whitman, Herbert J. Mattord, and Andrew Green. 2013. Cengage Learning.

Chapter Summary

- Information security governance is the application of the principles of corporate governance to the information security function. These principles include executive management's responsibility to provide strategic direction, ensure the accomplishment of objectives, oversee that risks are appropriately managed, and validate responsible resource use.

- Management must use policies as the basis for all information security planning, design, and deployment. Policies direct how issues should be addressed and technologies should be used.

- Standards are more detailed than policies and describe the steps that must be taken to conform to policies.

- Management must define three types of security policies: general or security program policies, issue-specific security policies, and systems-specific security policies.

- The enterprise information security policy (EISP) should be a driving force in the planning and governance activities of the organization as a whole.

- Several published information security frameworks by government organizations, private organizations, and professional societies supply information on best practices for their members.

- One of the foundations of security architectures is the layered implementation of security. This layered approach is referred to as defense in depth.

- Information security policy is best disseminated in a comprehensive security education, training, and awareness (SETA) program. A security awareness program is one of the least frequently implemented but most beneficial programs in an organization. A security awareness program is designed to keep information security at the forefront of users' minds.

- Contingency planning (CP) comprises a set of plans designed to ensure effective reactions to an attack and recovery from it. These plans also help restore an organization to normal modes of business operations.

- Organizations must develop disaster recovery plans, incident response plans, and business continuity plans using a business impact analysis (BIA). This process consists of five stages: identification and prioritization of the threat attack, business unit analysis and prioritization, attack success scenario development, potential damage assessment, and subordinate plan classification.

- Incident response planning consists of four phases: incident planning, incident detection, incident reaction, and incident recovery.

- Disaster recovery planning outlines the response to a disaster and recovery from it, whether the disaster is natural or man-made.

- Business continuity planning includes the steps organizations take so they can function when business cannot be resumed at the primary site.

- Crisis management refers to the actions an organization takes during and immediately after a disaster. Crisis management focuses first and foremost on the people involved.

- It is important to understand when and if to involve law enforcement in a corporate incident. Getting to know local and state law enforcement can assist organizations in these decisions.

Review Questions

1. How can a security framework assist in the design and implementation of a security infrastructure? What is information security governance? Who in the organization should plan for it?

2. Where can a security administrator find information on established security frameworks?

3. What is the ISO 27000 series of standards? Which individual standards make up the series?

4. What are the issues associated with adopting a formal framework or model?

5. What documents are available from the NIST Computer Security Resource Center, and how can they support the development of a security framework?

6. What benefit can a private, for-profit agency derive from best practices designed for federal agencies?

7. What Web resources can aid an organization in developing best practices as part of a security framework?

8. Briefly describe management, operational, and technical controls, and explain when each would be applied as part of a security framework.

9. What are the differences between a policy, a standard, and a practice? What are the three types of security policies? Where would each be used? What type of policy would be needed to guide use of the Web? E-mail? Office equipment for personal use?

10. Who is ultimately responsible for managing a technology? Who is responsible for enforcing policy that affects the use of a technology?

11. What is contingency planning? How is it different from routine management planning? What are the components of contingency planning?

12. When is the IR plan used?

13. When is the DR plan used?

14. When is the BC plan used? How do you determine when to use the IR, DR, and BC plans?

15. What are the elements of a business impact analysis?

16. What are Pipkin's three categories of incident indicators?

17. What is containment, and why is it part of the planning process?

18. When should law enforcement be involved in an IR or DR action? What are the issues associated with law enforcement involvement?

19. What is an after-action review? When is it performed? Why is it done?

20. List and describe the six site and data contingency strategies identified in the text.

Exercises

1. Using a graphics program, design several security awareness posters on the following themes: updating antivirus signatures, protecting sensitive information, watching out for e-mail viruses, prohibiting the personal use of company equipment, changing and protecting passwords, avoiding social engineering, and protecting software copyrights. What other themes can you imagine?

2. Search the Web for security education and training programs in your area. Keep a list and see which category has the most examples. See if you can determine the costs associated with each example. Which do you think would be more cost-effective in terms of both time and money?

3. Search the Web for examples of issue-specific security policies. What types of policies can you find? Using the format provided in this chapter, draft a simple issue-specific policy that outlines fair and responsible use of computers at your college, based on the rules and regulations of your institution. Does your school have a similar policy? Does it contain all the elements listed in the text?

4. Use your library or the Web to find a reported natural disaster that occurred at least six months ago. From the news accounts, determine whether local or national officials had prepared disaster plans and if the plans were used. See if you can determine how the plans helped officials improve disaster response. How do the plans help the recovery?

5. Classify each of the following occurrences as an incident or disaster. If an occurrence is a disaster, determine whether business continuity plans would be called into play.

   a. A hacker breaks into the company network and deletes files from a server.

   b. A fire breaks out in the storeroom and sets off sprinklers on that floor. Some computers are damaged, but the fire is contained.

   c. A tornado hits a local power station, and the company will be without power for three to five days.

   d. Employees go on strike, and the company could be without critical workers for weeks.

   e. A disgruntled employee takes a critical server home, sneaking it out after hours.

For each of the scenarios (a–e), describe the steps necessary to restore operations. Indicate whether law enforcement would be involved.

Case Exercises

Charlie sat at his desk the morning after his nightmare. He had answered the most pressing e-mails in his inbox and had a piping hot cup of coffee at his elbow. He looked down at a blank legal pad, ready to make notes about what to do in case his nightmare became reality.

Discussion Questions

1. What would be the first note you wrote down if you were Charlie?

2. What else should be on Charlie's list?

3. Suppose Charlie encountered resistance to his plans to improve continuity planning. What appeals could he use to sway opinions toward improved business continuity planning?

Ethical Decision Making

The policies that organizations put in place are similar to laws, in that they are directives for how to act properly. Like laws, policies should be impartial and fair, and are often founded on ethical and moral belief systems of the people who create them.

In some cases, especially when organizations expand into foreign countries, they experience a form of culture shock when the laws of their new host country conflict with their internal policies. Suppose that SLS has expanded its operations in France. Setting aside any legal requirements that SLS make its policies conform to French law, does SLS have an ethical imperative to modify its policies to better meet the needs of its stakeholders in the new country?

Suppose SLS has altered its policies for all operations in France and that the changes are much more favorable to employees—such as a requirement to provide child and elder-care services at no cost to the employee. Is SLS under any ethical burden to offer the same benefit to employees in its original country?

Endnotes

1. IT Governance Institute. *Board Briefing on IT Governance*, 2nd Edition. 2003. The Chartered Institute of Management Accountants (CIMA) and the International Federation of Accountants (IFAC) also adopted this definition in 2004. Accessed 5 July 2016 from *www.isaca.org*.

2. ITGI. "Information Security Governance: Guidance for Information Security Managers." Accessed 11 October 2016 from *www.isaca.org*.

3. Wood, Charles Cresson. "Integrated Approach Includes Information Security." *Security* 37, no. 2 (February 2000): 43–44.

4. "Former Andersen Auditor Admits to Breaking Law." 14 May 2002. Accessed 11 October 2016 from *www.pbs.org/newshour/updates/business-jan-june02-andersen_05-14/*.

5. Beltran, Luisa. "Andersen Exec: Shredding Began after E-mail." 21 January 2002. Accessed 4 July 2016 from *http://money.cnn.com/2002/01/21/companies/enron_odom/*.

6. US-CERT. "Security Recommendations to Prevent Cyber Intrusions." Accessed 4 July 2016 from *www.us-cert.gov/ncas/alerts/TA11-200A*.

7. National Institute of Standards and Technology. *An Introduction to Computer Security: The NIST Handbook.* SP 800-12. Gaithersburg, MD, 1996.

8. Whitman, Michael E., Anthony M. Townsend, and Robert J. Aalberts. "Considerations for an Effective Telecommunications Use Policy." *Communications of the ACM* 42, no. 6 (June 1999): 101–109.

9. Ibid.

10. Derived from a number of sources, the most notable of which was accessed 4 July 2016 from *www.wustl.edu/policies/infosecurity.html*.

11. National Institute of Standards and Technology. *An Introduction to Computer Security: The NIST Handbook.* SP 800-12. Gaithersburg, MD, 1996.

12. NetIQ Security Technologies, Inc. *User Guide, NetIQ.* August 2011. Accessed 4 July 2016 from *https://www.netiq.com/documentation/vigilent-policy-center/pdfdoc/vigilent -policy-center-user-guide/vigilent-policy-center-user-guide.pdf*

13. National Institute of Standards and Technology. *International Standard ISO/IEC 17799:2000 Code of Practice for Information Security Management.* November 2002. Accessed 4 July 2016 from *http://csrc.nist.gov/publications/secpubs/otherpubs/reviso -faq-110502.pdf*.

14. Compiled from a number of sources, including: "ISO/IEC 27002:2013 Information Technology—Security Techniques—Code of Practice for Information Security Controls." Accessed 4 July 2016 from *www.iso27001security.com/html/27002.html*; and "Introduction to ISO 27002." Accessed 4 July 2016 from *www.27000.org/iso-27002.htm*.

15. Adapted from diagram of ISO 27001:2013 implementation process. Accessed 4 July 2016 from *www.iso27001standard.com/en/free-downloads*.

16. National Institute of Standards and Technology. *Information Security Management, Code of Practice for Information Security Management.* ISO/IEC 17799. 6 December 2001. Geneva, Switzerland.

17. About the ISO27k standards. Accessed 4 July 2016 from *www.iso27001security.com/html/iso27000.html*.

18. National Institute of Standards and Technology. *Generally Accepted Principles and Practices for Securing Information Technology Systems*. SP 800-14. September 1996. Gaithersburg, MD.

19. National Institute of Standards and Technology. *Guide for Applying the Risk Management Framework to Federal Information Systems: A Security Life Cycle Approach*. Accessed 4 July 2016 at *http://csrc.nist.gov/publications/nistpubs/800-37-rev1/sp800-37-rev1-final.pdf*.

20. National Institute of Standards and Technology. "Framework for Improving Critical Infrastructure Cybersecurity, Version 1.0." 12 February 2014. Accessed 4 July 2016 from *www.nist.gov/cyberframework/upload/cybersecurity-framework-021214-final.pdf*.

21. Ibid.

22. Ibid.

23. Ibid.

24. National Institute of Standards and Technology. "Roadmap for Improving Critical Infrastructure Cybersecurity." 12 February 2014. Accessed 4 July 2016 from *www.nist.gov/cyberframework/upload/roadmap-021214.pdf*.

25. National Institute of Standards and Technology. *An Introduction to Computer Security: The NIST Handbook*. SP 800-12. Gaithersburg, MD, 1996.

26. Ibid.

27. King, William R., and Gray, Paul. *The Management of Information Systems*. 1989. Chicago: Dryden Press, 359.

28. Swanson, M., Bowen, P., Phillips, A., Gallup, D., and Lynes, D. National Institute of Standards and Technology. *Contingency Planning Guide for Federal Information Systems*. SP 800-34, Rev. 1. Accessed 4 July 2016 at *http://nvlpubs.nist.gov/nistpubs/Legacy/SP/nistspecialpublication800-34r1.pdf*.

29. Zawada, B., and Evans, L. "Creating a More Rigorous BIA." *CPM Group*. November/December 2002. Accessed 12 May 2005 at *www.contingencyplanning.com/archives/2002/novdec/4.aspx*.

30. Swanson, M., Bowen, P., Phillips, A., Gallup, D., and Lynes, D. National Institute of Standards and Technology. *Contingency Planning Guide for Federal Information Systems*. SP 800-34, Rev. 1. Accessed 4 July 2016 at *http://nvlpubs.nist.gov/nistpubs/Legacy/SP/nistspecialpublication800-34r1.pdf*.

31. Ibid.

32. Cichonski, P., Millar, T., Grance, T., and Scarfone, K. National Institute of Standards and Technology. *Computer Security Incident Handling Guide*. SP 800-61, Rev. 2. August 2012. Accessed 11 October 2016 at *http://nvlpubs.nist.gov/nistpubs/Special Publications/NIST.SP.800-61r2.pdf*.

33. Krutz, Ronald L., and Vines, Russell Dean. *The CISSP Prep Guide: Mastering the Ten Domains of Computer Security*. 2001. New York: John Wiley and Sons Inc., 288.

34. Marcinko, Richard, and Weisman, John. *Designation Gold*. 1998. New York: Pocket Books, preface.

35. Pipkin, D. L. *Information Security: Protecting the Global Enterprise*. 2000. Upper Saddle River, NJ: Prentice Hall, 256.

36. Witty, Roberta. "What is Crisis Management?" *Gartner Online*. 19 September 2001. Accessed 11 October 2016 from *www.gartner.com/DisplayDocument?id=340971*.

4

chapter 5

Risk Management

Once we know our weaknesses, they cease to do us any harm.
G.C. (GEORG CHRISTOPH) LICHTENBERG (1742–1799),
GERMAN PHYSICIST, PHILOSOPHER

Charlie Moody called the meeting to order. The conference room was full of developers, systems analysts, and IT managers, as well as staff and management from Sales and other departments.

"All right everyone, let's get started. Welcome to the kickoff meeting of our new risk management project team, the Sequential Label and Supply Information Security Task Force. We're here today to talk about our objectives and to review the initial work plan."

"Why is my department here?" asked the Sales manager. "Isn't security a problem for the IT department?"

Charlie explained, "Well, we used to think so, but we've come to realize that information security is about managing the risk of using information, which involves almost everyone in the company. In order to make our systems more secure, we need the participation of representatives from all departments."

Charlie continued, "I hope everyone read the packets I sent out last week describing the legal requirements we face in our industry and the background articles on threats and attacks. Today we'll begin the process of identifying and classifying all of the information technology risks that face our organization. This includes everything from fires and floods that could disrupt our business to hackers who might try to steal or destroy our data.

Once we identify and classify the risks facing our assets, we can discuss how to reduce or eliminate these risks by establishing controls. Which controls we actually apply will depend on the costs and benefits of each control."

"Wow, Charlie!" said Amy Windahl from the back of the room. "I'm sure we need to do it—I was hit by the last attack, just as everyone here was—but we have dozens of systems."

"It's more like hundreds," said Charlie. "That's why we have so many people on this team, and why the team includes members of every department."

Charlie continued, "Okay, everyone, please open your packets and take out the project plan with the work list showing teams, tasks, and schedules. Any questions before we start reviewing the work plan?"

LEARNING OBJECTIVES

Upon completion of this material, you should be able to:

- Define risk management, risk identification, risk assessment, and risk control
- Describe how risk is identified and assessed
- Assess risk based on probability of occurrence and likely expected impact
- Explain the fundamental aspects of documenting risk via the process of risk assessment
- Describe various options for a risk mitigation strategy
- Define risk appetite and explain how it relates to residual risk
- Discuss conceptual frameworks for evaluating risk controls and formulate a cost-benefit analysis

Introduction

> **Key Terms**
>
> **avoidance of competitive disadvantage** The adoption and implementation of a business model, method, technique, resource, or technology to prevent being outperformed by a competing organization; working to keep pace with the competition through innovation, rather than falling behind.
>
> **competitive advantage** The adoption and implementation of an innovative business model, method, technique, resource, or technology in order to outperform the competition.

The upper management of an organization is responsible for overseeing, enabling, and supporting the structuring of IT and information security functions to defend its information assets—information and data, hardware, software, procedures, networks, and people. Part of the information security governance requirement of upper management is the establishment and support of an effective risk management (RM) program. The IT community must serve the information technology needs of the entire organization and at the same time leverage the special skills and insights of the information security community in supporting the RM program. The information security team must lead the way with skill, professionalism, and flexibility as it works with other communities of interest to balance the usefulness and security of the information system, as well as identify, assess, and control the risks facing the organization's information assets.

In the early days of information technology, corporations used IT systems mainly to gain a definitive advantage over the competition. Establishing a superior business model, method, or technique enabled an organization to provide a product or service that created a **competitive advantage**. In the modern business environment, however, all competitors have reached a certain level of technological resilience. IT is now readily available to all organizations that make the investment, allowing them to react quickly to changes in the market. In this highly competitive environment, organizations cannot expect the implementation of new technologies to provide a competitive lead over others in the industry. Instead, the concept of **avoidance of competitive disadvantage**—working to prevent falling behind the competition—has emerged. Effective IT-enabled organizations quickly absorb relevant emerging technologies not just to gain or maintain competitive advantage, but to avoid loss of market share from an inability to maintain the highly responsive services required by their stakeholders.

To keep up with the competition, organizations must design and create safe environments in which their business processes and procedures can function. These environments must maintain confidentiality and privacy and assure the integrity of an organization's data—objectives that are met by applying the principles of risk management. As an aspiring information security professional, you will play a key role in risk management.

This chapter explores a variety of risk management approaches and provides a discussion of how risk is identified and assessed. The chapter finishes with a section on selecting and implementing effective control strategies for the protection of information assets in the modern organization.

An Overview of Risk Management

Key Terms

risk assessment A determination of the extent to which an organization's information assets are exposed to risk.

risk control The application of controls that reduce the risks to an organization's information assets to an acceptable level.

risk identification The recognition, enumeration, and documentation of risks to an organization's information assets.

risk management The process of identifying risk, assessing its relative magnitude, and taking steps to reduce it to an acceptable level.

In Chapter 1, you learned about the C.I.A. triangle. Each of the three elements in the triangle is an essential part of every IT organization's ability to sustain long-term competitiveness. When an organization depends on IT-based systems to remain viable, information security and the discipline of **risk management** must become an integral part of the economic basis for making business decisions. These decisions are based on trade-offs between the costs of applying information system controls and the benefits of using secured, available systems.

Risk management involves three major undertakings: **risk identification, risk assessment,** and **risk control.** Initially, the organization must identify and understand the risk it faces, especially the risk to information assets. Once identified, risk must be assessed, measured, and evaluated. The key determination is whether the risk an organization faces exceeds its comfort level. If not, the organization is satisfied with the risk management process. Otherwise, the organization needs to do something to reduce risk to an acceptable level. The various components of risk management and their relationships to each other are shown in Figure 5-1.

An observation made over 2,500 years ago by Chinese general Sun Tzu Wu has direct relevance to information security today (see Figure 5-2).

> *If you know the enemy and know yourself, you need not fear the result of a hundred battles. If you know yourself but not the enemy, for every victory gained you will also suffer a defeat. If you know neither the enemy nor yourself, you will succumb in every battle.*[1]

Consider the similarities between information security and warfare. Information security managers and technicians are the defenders of information. The many threats discussed in Chapter 2 constantly attack the defenses surrounding information assets. Defenses are built in layers by placing safeguards behind safeguards. The defenders attempt to prevent, protect,

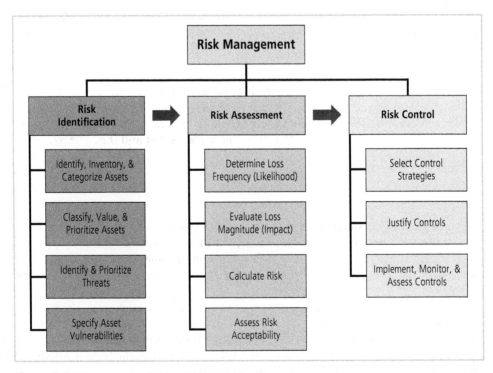

Figure 5-1 Components of risk management

5

Figure 5-2 Sun Tzu's *The Art of War*. Part of the University of California, Riverside Collection

Source: Wikimedia Commons.[2]

detect, and recover from a seemingly endless series of attacks. Moreover, those defenders are legally prohibited from deploying offensive tactics, so the attackers have no need to expend resources on defense. While the defenders need to win every battle, the attackers only need to win once. To be victorious, defenders must know themselves and their enemy.

 For more information on Sun Tzu's The Art of War, visit http://suntzusaid.com/.

❯ Know Yourself

You must identify, examine, and understand the current information and systems in your organization. To protect *information assets*, which were defined earlier in this book as information and the systems that use, store, and transmit information, you must know what those assets are, where they are, how they add value to the organization, and the vulnerabilities to which they are susceptible. Once you know what you have, you can identify what you are already doing to protect it. Just because a control is in place does not necessarily mean that the asset is protected. Frequently, organizations implement control mechanisms but then neglect the necessary periodic review, revision, and maintenance. The policies, education and training programs, and technologies that protect information must be carefully maintained and administered to ensure that they remain effective.

❯ Know the Enemy

Having identified your organization's assets and weaknesses, you move on to Sun Tzu's second step: Know the enemy. This means identifying, examining, and understanding the *threats* facing the organization. You must determine which threat aspects most directly affect the security of the organization and its information assets, and then use this information to create a list of threats, each one ranked according to the importance of the information assets that it threatens.

❯ The Roles of the Communities of Interest

Each community of interest has a role to play in managing the risks that an organization encounters. Because members of the information security community best understand the threats and attacks that introduce risk into the organization, they often take a leadership role in addressing risk to information assets. Management and users, when properly trained and kept aware of the threats the organization faces, play a part in early detection and response.

Management must also ensure that sufficient time, money, personnel, and other resources are allocated to the information security and information technology groups to meet the organization's security needs. Users work with systems and data and are therefore well positioned to understand the value these information assets offer the organization. Users also understand which assets are the most valuable. The information technology community of interest must build secure systems and operate them safely. For example, IT operations ensure good backups to control the risk of data loss due to hard drive failure. The IT community can provide both valuation and threat perspectives to management during the risk management process. The information security community of interest has to pull it all together in the risk management process.

All communities of interest must work together to address all levels of risk, which range from disasters that can devastate the whole organization to the smallest employee mistakes. The three communities of interest are also responsible for the following:

- Evaluating current and proposed risk controls
- Determining which control options are cost effective for the organization
- Acquiring or installing the needed controls
- Ensuring that the controls remain effective

All three communities of interest must conduct periodic managerial reviews or audits, with general management usually providing oversight and access to information retained outside the IT department. The first managerial review is of the asset inventory. On a regular basis, management must ensure that the completeness and accuracy of the asset inventory is verified, usually through an IT audit. In addition, IT and information security must review and verify threats and vulnerabilities in the asset inventory, as well as current controls and mitigation strategies. They must also review the cost effectiveness of each control and revisit decisions for deploying controls. Furthermore, managers at all levels must regularly verify the ongoing effectiveness of every deployed control. For example, a business manager might assess control procedures by periodically walking through the office after the workday ends, ensuring that all classified information is locked up, that all workstations are shut down, that all users are logged off, and that offices are secured. Managers may further ensure that no sensitive information is discarded in trash or recycling bins. Such controls are effective ways for managers and employees alike to ensure that no information assets are placed at risk. Other controls include following policy, promoting training and awareness, and employing appropriate technologies.

> Risk Appetite and Residual Risk

Key Terms

residual risk The risk to information assets that remains even after current controls have been applied.

risk appetite The quantity and nature of risk that organizations are willing to accept as they evaluate the trade-offs between perfect security and unlimited accessibility.

risk tolerance See *risk appetite*.

Risk appetite (also known as **risk tolerance**) defines the quantity and nature of risk that organizations are willing to accept as they evaluate the trade-offs between perfect security and unlimited accessibility. For instance, a financial services company that is regulated by government and conservative by nature may seek to apply every reasonable control and even some invasive controls to protect its information assets. Less regulated organizations may also be conservative by nature, and seek to avoid the negative publicity associated with the perceived loss of integrity from an exploited vulnerability. Thus, a firewall vendor may provide a default set of firewall rules that are far stricter than those needed by the average organization because the negative consequence of being hacked would be catastrophic in the eyes of its customers.

Other organizations may take on dangerous risks through ignorance. The reasoned approach to risk is one that balances the expense of controlling vulnerabilities against possible losses if the vulnerabilities are exploited. (Note that expenses in this context are considered both in terms of finance and the usability of information assets.) There is a well-known directive in information security: Never spend more to protect an asset than the asset is worth. James Anderson, an executive with a long history as a chief information security officer, believes that information security in today's enterprise is a "well-informed sense of assurance that the information risks and controls are in balance." The key for the organization is to find balance in its decision-making and feasibility analyses, which ensures that its risk appetite is based on experience and facts instead of ignorance or wishful thinking.

Residual Risk When vulnerabilities have been controlled as much as possible, any remaining risk that has not been removed, shifted, or planned for is called **residual risk**—the risk that is left over after the risk management process has concluded. To express the concept another way, "residual risk is a combined function of (1) a threat less the effect of threat-reducing safeguards, (2) a vulnerability less the effect of vulnerability-reducing safeguards, and (3) an asset less the effect of asset value-reducing safeguards."[3] Figure 5-3 illustrates how residual risk remains after safeguards are implemented.

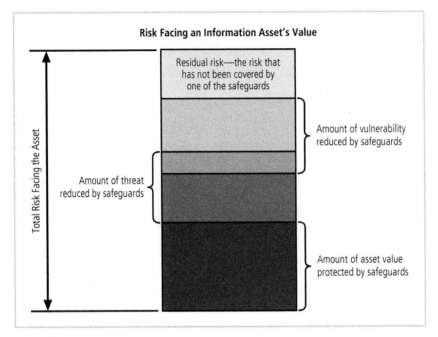

Figure 5-3 Residual risk

The significance of residual risk must be judged within the context of the organization. Although it might seem counterintuitive, the goal of information security is not to bring residual risk to zero; it is to bring residual risk into line with an organization's comfort zone or risk appetite. If decision makers have been informed of uncontrolled risks and the proper authorities within the communities of interest decide to leave residual risk in place, the information security program has accomplished its primary goal. To put it another way, if residual risk is less than or equal to the organization's risk appetite, then the risk management team has done its job.

Finally, when management requires details about a specific risk to the organization, risk assessment may be documented in a topic-specific report. These reports are usually prepared at the direction of senior management to focus on a narrow area of operational risk to an information system. For example, an emergent vulnerability might be reported to management, which then asks for a specific risk assessment. For a more complete treatment of documenting the results of risk management activities, see Chapter 12.

 For a list of risk management methods and tools, visit the ISO 27k FAQ site at http://www .iso27001security.com/html/risk_mgmt.html.

Risk Identification

A risk management strategy requires that information security professionals know their organizations' information assets—that is, how to identify, classify, and prioritize them. Once the

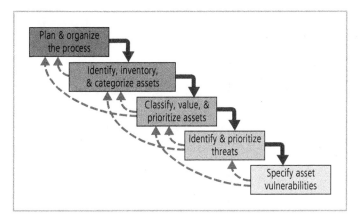

Figure 5-4 Components of risk identification

organizational assets have been identified, a threat assessment process is used to identify and quantify the risks facing each asset.

The components of risk identification are shown in Figure 5-4.

〉 Planning and Organizing the Process

As with any major undertaking in information security, the first step in risk identification is to follow your project management principles. You begin by organizing a team, which typically consists of representatives from all affected groups. Because risk can exist everywhere in the organization, representatives will come from every department and will include users, managers, IT groups, and information security groups. The process must then be planned, with periodic deliverables, reviews, and presentations to management. Once the project is ready to begin, the team can organize a meeting like the one Charlie is conducting in the opening case. Tasks are laid out, assignments are made, and timetables are discussed. Only then is the organization ready to begin the next step—identifying and categorizing assets.

〉 Identifying, Inventorying, and Categorizing Assets

This iterative process begins with the identification and inventory of assets, including all elements of an organization's system, such as people, procedures, data and information, software, hardware, and networking elements (see Table 5-1). Then, you categorize the assets, adding details as you dig deeper into the analysis. The objective of this process is to establish the relative priority of assets to the success of the organization. Some organizations will only focus on information assets, as defined earlier, or on a subset of information assets such as applications and their associated data repositories (data sets, databases), and define the remaining hardware and applications (such as operating systems and support applications and utilities) as media. Whatever approach is formally adopted, what is important is the selection of a formal risk management methodology, as described later in this chapter, and the rigorous adherence to its guidelines.

Traditional System Components	Information Asset Components	Risk Management System Components
People	Employees	Trusted employees Other staff
	Nonemployees	People at trusted organizations Strangers and visitors
Procedures	Procedures	IT and business standard procedures IT and business-sensitive procedures
Data	Information	Transmission Processing Storage
Software	Software	Applications Operating systems Security components
Hardware	System devices and peripherals	Systems and peripherals Security devices
	Networking components	Intranet components Internet or DMZ components

Table 5-1 Categorizing the Components of an Information System

People, Procedures, and Data Asset Identification Identifying assets for human resources, documentation, and data is more difficult than identifying hardware and software assets. People with knowledge, experience, and judgment should be assigned the task. As assets for people, procedures, and data are identified, they should be recorded using a reliable data-handling process. Regardless of the record keeping mechanism you use, make sure it has the flexibility to allow specification of attributes for a particular type of asset. Some attributes are unique to a class of elements. Most large organizations find that they can effectively track only a few valuable facts about the most critical devices. For instance, a company may only track the IP address, server name, and device type for its mission-critical servers. The company may forgo the tracking of additional details on all devices and completely forgo the tracking of desktop or laptop systems. Fortunately, automated applications are now available that can automatically investigate and catalog installed hardware, software, and in some cases, data. When deciding which information assets to track, consider the following asset attributes:

- People: Position name, number, or ID (avoid using people's names and stick to identifying positions, roles, or functions); supervisor; security clearance level; special skills

- Procedures: Description; intended purpose; relationship to software, hardware, and networking elements; storage location for reference; storage location for update

- Data: Classification; owner, creator, and manager; size of data structure; data structure used (sequential or relational); online or offline; location; backup procedures employed. As you develop the data-tracking process, consider carefully how much data should be tracked and for which specific assets.

Hardware, Software, and Network Asset Identification Which attributes of hardware, software, and network assets should be tracked? It depends on the needs of the organization and its risk management efforts, as well as the preferences and needs of the information security and information technology communities. You may want to consider including the following asset attributes:

- Name: Use the most common device or program name. Organizations may have several names for the same product. For example, a software product might have a nickname within the company while it is in development, as well as a formal name used by marketing staff and vendors. Make sure that the names you choose are meaningful to all the groups that use the information. You should adopt naming standards that do not convey information to potential system attackers. For instance, a server named CASH1 or HQ_FINANCE may entice attackers to take a shortcut to that system.

- IP address: This can be a useful identifier for network devices and servers, but it does not usually apply to software. You can, however, use a relational database to track software instances on specific servers or networking devices. Also, many organizations use the Dynamic Host Configuration Protocol (DHCP) within TCP/IP that reassigns IP numbers to devices as needed, which creates a problem for using IP numbers as part of the asset identification process. IP address use in inventory is usually limited to devices that use static IP addresses.

- Media access control (MAC) address: MAC addresses are sometimes called electronic serial numbers or hardware addresses. As part of the TCP/IP standard, all network interface hardware devices have a unique number. The MAC address number is used by the network operating system to identify a specific network device. It is used by the client's network software to recognize traffic that it must process. In most settings, MAC addresses can be a useful way to track connectivity. However, they can be spoofed by some hardware and software combinations.

- Element type: For hardware, you can develop a list of element types, such as servers, desktops, networking devices, or test equipment. The list can have any degree of detail you require. For software elements, you may develop a list of types that includes operating systems, custom applications by type (accounting, HR, or payroll, for example), packaged applications, and specialty applications, such as firewall programs. The needs of the organization determine the degree of specificity. For instance, types may need to be recorded at two or more levels of specificity. If so, record one attribute that classifies the asset at a high level and then add attributes for more detail. For example, one server might be listed as:

  - DeviceClass = S (server)

  - DeviceOS = W2K (Windows 2000)

  - DeviceCapacity = AS (advanced server)

- Serial number: For hardware devices, the serial number can uniquely identify a specific device. Some software vendors also assign a software serial number to each instance of the program licensed by the organization.

- Manufacturer name: Record the manufacturer of the device or software component. This can be useful when responding to incidents that involve the device or when certain manufacturers announce specific vulnerabilities.

- Manufacturer's model number or part number: Record the model or part number of the element. This exact record of the element can be very useful in later analysis of vulnerabilities, because some vulnerability instances apply only to specific models of certain devices and software components.

- Software version, update revision, or FCO number: Whenever possible, document the specific software or firmware revision number and, for hardware devices, the current *field change order (FCO)* number. An FCO is an authorization issued by an organization for the repair, modification, or update of a piece of equipment. The equipment is not returned to the manufacturer, but is usually repaired at the customer's location, often by a third party. Documenting the revision number and FCO is particularly important for networking devices that function mainly via the software running on them. For example, firewall devices often have three versions: an operating system (OS) version, a software version, and a basic input/output system (BIOS) firmware version. Depending on your needs, you may have to track all three version numbers.

- Physical location: Note the element's physical location. This information may not apply to software elements, but some organizations have license terms that specify where software can be used. This information falls under asset inventory, which can be performed once the identification process is started.

- Logical location: Note where the element can be found on the organization's network. The logical location is most useful for networking devices and indicates the logical network where the device is connected. Again, this information is an inventory item that is important to track for identification purposes.

- Controlling entity: Identify which organizational unit controls the element. Sometimes a remote location's onsite staff controls a networking device, and sometimes the central network team controls other devices of the same make and model. You should try to specify which group or unit controls each specific element because that group may want a voice in determining how much risk the device can tolerate and how much expense they can sustain to add controls.

For a listing of software that can assist in the asset management inventory, visit http://en .wikipedia.org and search on "Open source configuration management software." You can also go to www.techrepublic.com and search on "Top apps for managing inventory."

Information Asset Inventory Creating an inventory of information assets is a critical function of understanding what the organization is protecting. Unless the information assets are identified and inventoried, they cannot be effectively protected. The inventory process is critical in determining where information is located; most commonly it is in storage. Not all information is stored in networked databases. A great deal of an organization's information is stored in hard copy—in filing cabinets, desks, and in employee hands and briefcases. Even more information is stored on portable hard drives, flash drives, laptops, smartphones, and other mobile devices. While it may be impossible to completely control where information is located, policy and training programs can assist in informing employees where information should and should not be stored.

The inventory process involves formalizing the identification process in some form of organizational tool. At this point in the process, simple spreadsheets and database tools can provide effective record keeping. The inventory information can be updated later with classification and valuation data. Automated tools can sometimes identify the system elements that make up hardware, software, and network components. For example, many organizations use automated asset inventory systems. The inventory listing is usually available in a database, or it can be exported to a database for custom information about security assets. Once stored, the inventory listing must be kept current, often by means of a tool that periodically refreshes the data. When you move to the later steps of risk management, which involve calculations of loss and projections of costs, the case for using automated risk management tools to track information assets becomes stronger.

Asset Categorization Table 5-1, shown earlier, compares the categorizations of a standard information system (people, procedures, data and information, software, and hardware) with those in an enhanced version that incorporates risk management principles. As you can see, the risk management categorizations introduce several new subdivisions:

- People comprise employees and nonemployees. There are two subcategories of employees: those who hold trusted roles and have correspondingly greater authority and accountability, and other staff who have assignments without special privileges. Nonemployees include contractors and consultants, members of other trusted organizations, and strangers.

- Procedures essentially belong in one of two categories: procedures that do not expose knowledge a potential attacker might find useful, and sensitive procedures that could allow an adversary to gain an advantage or craft an attack against the organization's assets. These business-sensitive procedures may introduce risk to the organization if they are revealed to unauthorized people. For example, BellSouth discovered several years ago that someone had stolen the documentation for its E911 system.[4] This documentation revealed the inner workings of a critical phone system.

- Data components account for the management of information in all its states: transmission, processing, and storage. These expanded categories solve the problem posed by the term *data*, which is usually associated with databases and not the full range of modalities of data and information used by a modern organization.

- Software components are assigned to one of three categories: applications, operating systems, or security components. Security components can be applications or operating systems, but they are categorized as part of the information security control environment and must be protected more thoroughly than other system components.

- Hardware is assigned to one of two categories: the usual system devices and their peripherals, and devices that are part of information security control systems. The latter must be protected more thoroughly than the former because networking subsystems are often the focal point of attacks against the system; they should be considered special cases rather than combined with general hardware and software components.

❯ Classifying, Valuing, and Prioritizing Information Assets

Key Term

---

data classification scheme A formal access control methodology used to assign a level of confidentiality to an information asset and thus restrict the number of people who can access it.

Most organizations further subdivide the categories listed in Table 5-1. For example, the Hardware category can be subdivided into servers, networking devices (routers, hubs, switches), protection devices (firewalls, proxies), and cabling. Each of the other categories can be similarly subdivided as needed by the organization. You should also include a dimension to represent the sensitivity and security priority of the data and the devices that store, transmit, and process the data—that is, a **data classification scheme**. A simple data classification scheme could include levels of confidential, internal, and public. A data classification scheme generally requires a corresponding structure for personnel security clearance, which determines the level of information that employees are authorized to view based on what they need to know.

Any classification method must be specific enough to enable ease of understanding and assignment of priority levels, because the next step in risk assessment is to rank the components. It is also important that the categories be comprehensive and mutually exclusive. *Comprehensive* means that all information assets must fit in the list somewhere, and *mutually exclusive* means that an information asset should fit in only one category. For example, suppose an organization has a public key infrastructure certificate authority, which is a software application that provides cryptographic key management services. Using a purely technical standard, an analysis team could categorize the certificate authority as software in the asset list of Table 5-1. Then, within the software category, the certificate authority could be listed either as an application or as a security component. However, a certificate authority should actually be categorized as a software security component because it is part of the security infrastructure and must be protected carefully.

Data Classification and Management Corporate and government organizations use a variety of classification schemes. Many corporations use a data classification scheme to help secure the confidentiality and integrity of information.

A simplified information classification scheme would have three categories: confidential, internal, and external. Information owners must classify the information assets for which they are responsible. At least once a year, information owners must review their classifications to ensure that the information is still classified correctly and the appropriate access controls are in place.

The information classifications are as follows:

- Confidential: Used for the most sensitive corporate information that must be tightly controlled, even within the company. Access to information with this classification is strictly on a need-to-know basis or as required by the terms of a contract. Information with this classification may also be referred to as "sensitive" or "proprietary."

- Internal: Used for all internal information that does not meet the criteria for the confidential category. Internal information is to be viewed only by corporate employees, authorized contractors, and other third parties.

- External: All information that has been approved by management for public release.

As you might expect, the U.S. Classified National Security Information (NSI) system uses more complex categorization than most corporations. The U.S. government and the Department of Defense (DoD), with all of its military branches, are perhaps the best-known users of data classification schemes. To maintain protection of the confidentiality of information, the government and the DoD have invested heavily in INFOSEC (information security), OPSEC (operations security), and COMSEC (communications security). In fact, many developments in data communications and information security are the result of government-sponsored research and development. For most NSI, which is vital to the security of the nation, the government uses a three-level classification scheme: Top Secret, Secret, and Confidential.

- "'Top Secret' shall be applied to information, the unauthorized disclosure of which reasonably could be expected to cause exceptionally grave damage to the national security that the original classification authority is able to identify or describe.

- 'Secret' shall be applied to information, the unauthorized disclosure of which reasonably could be expected to cause serious damage to the national security that the original classification authority is able to identify or describe.

- 'Confidential' shall be applied to information, the unauthorized disclosure of which reasonably could be expected to cause damage to the national security that the original classification authority is able to identify or describe."[5]

This classification system comes with the general expectation of "crib-to-grave" protection, meaning that all people entrusted with classified information are expected to retain this level of confidence for their lifetimes, or at least until the information is officially unclassified. The government also has some specialty classification ratings, such as Personnel Information and Evaluation Reports, to protect related areas of information.

Federal agencies such as the NSA, FBI, and CIA also use specialty classification schemes, like Sensitive Compartmented Information (SCI; in other words, Named Projects or code word clearances). SCI represents clearance levels based on an extreme need-to-know basis. When an operation, project, or set of classified data is created, the project is assigned a security level such as "Secret" and a code name, such as *Operation Phoenix*. Next, a list of authorized people is created and assigned to the SCI category, and the list is maintained to restrict access to this category of material. Individuals must possess the assigned security level and be on the SCI list to access the information. The only way a person outside the original list can access this information is to be authorized by a top-level official to be "read in" to the information.

For non-NSI material, other classification schemes are employed. Each of these is defined below.

- Sensitive but Unclassified data (SBU): Information that if lost, misused, accessed without authorization, or modified might adversely affect U.S. interests, the conduct of DoD programs, or the privacy of DoD personnel. Common SBU categories include Restricted, For Official Use Only, Not for Public Release, and For Internal Use Only.[6]

- Unclassified data: Information that can generally be distributed to the public without any threat to U.S. interests.

In the United Kingdom, the Government Protective Marketing Scheme is a five-layer model that incorporates categories similar to those in the combined NSI and non-NSI U.S. government models. This scheme has recently been revised to a much simpler model known as the Government Security Classification Policy, with Confidential, Restricted (SBU), and Unclassified levels merged into a single Official category. The result is a simpler, three-layer model with Top-Secret, Secret, and Official categories for all U.K. government information.

Most organizations do not need the detailed level of classification used by the government or DoD agencies. However, a simple scheme that uses the Confidential, Internal, and External classifications discussed earlier can allow an organization to protect sensitive information such as marketing or research data, personnel data, customer data, and general internal communications. As a rule of thumb, when a set of information contains multiple classification levels, the information must be categorized at the highest level it contains.

 For a listing of federal statutes, regulations, and directives for data classification programs, visit http://energy.gov/hss/statutes-regulations-and-directives-classification-program.

Security Clearances

Key Term

security clearance A personnel security structure in which each user of an information asset is assigned an authorization level that identifies the level of classified information he or she is "cleared" to access.

Corresponding to the data classification scheme is the personnel **security clearance** structure. In organizations that require security clearances, all users of data must be assigned authorization levels that indicate what types of classified data they are authorized to view. This structure is usually accomplished by assigning each employee to a named role, such as data entry clerk, development programmer, information security analyst, or even CIO. Most organizations have a set of roles and associated security clearances. Overriding an employee's security clearance requires that the employee meet the need-to-know standard described earlier. In fact, this standard should be met regardless of an employee's security clearance. This extra level of protection ensures that confidentiality of information is properly maintained.

Management of Classified Data

Key Terms

clean desk policy An organizational policy that specifies employees must inspect their work areas and ensure that all classified information, documents, and materials are secured at the end of every work day.

dumpster diving An information attack that involves searching through a target organization's trash and recycling bins for sensitive information.

Management of classified data includes its storage, distribution, transportation, and destruction. All information that is not unclassified or public must be clearly marked as such, as shown in the government examples in Figure 5-5. The government also uses color-coordinated cover sheets to protect classified information from the casual observer, with Orange (Top Secret), Red (Secret), and Blue (Confidential) borders and fonts. In addition, each classified document should contain the appropriate designation at the top and bottom of each page. Two-sided documents are required to have the designation on both sides. When classified data is stored, it must be available only to authorized personnel. This

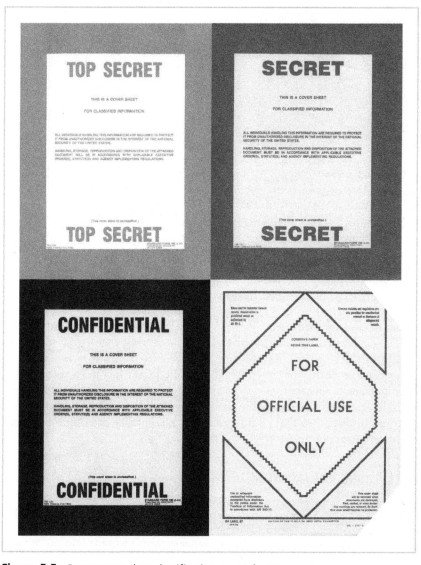

Figure 5-5 Government data classification cover sheets

Figure 5-6 Clean desk policy violation?

storage usually requires locking file cabinets, safes, or other protective devices for hard copies and systems. When a person carries classified information outside the organization, it should be inconspicuous, as in a locked briefcase or portfolio.

One important control policy that is often difficult to enforce is the **clean desk policy**, which is designed to ensure that all classified information is secured at the end of every day. When copies of classified information are no longer valuable or excess copies exist, proper care should be taken to destroy them, usually after double signature verification. Documents can be destroyed by means of shredding, burning, or transferring them to a service that offers authorized document destruction. As you can see in Figure 5-6, this type of policy does not mean the office itself is clean, but only that all classified data has been secured. It is important to enforce policies to ensure that no classified information is discarded in trash or recycling areas. Some attackers search trash and recycling bins—a practice known as **dumpster diving**—to retrieve information that could embarrass a company or compromise information security.

Information Asset Valuation

Key Term

asset valuation The process of assigning financial value or worth to each information asset.

One of the toughest tasks of information security in general and risk management in particular is information **asset valuation**. While most organizations have a general understanding of the relative worth of their information assets, it is much more difficult to place a specific financial value on an information asset. For example, what's the worth of the chemical formula for a drug that could cure cancer? What about an organization's strategic plan for the next five years? The Sales department's marketing plan for next quarter? As a result, many organizations use categorical values to provide ranges of values for assets (such as very low to very high), or they use other qualitative measures, as discussed later in the section on qualitative versus quantitative assessments.

To assist in the process of assigning values to information assets for risk assessment purposes, you can pose several questions and collect your answers on a worksheet (see Figure 5-7) for later analysis. Before beginning the inventory process, the organization should determine which criteria can best establish the value of the information assets.

Among the criteria to be considered are:

- Which information asset is most critical to the organization's success? When determining the relative importance of each asset, refer to the organization's mission statement or statement of objectives to determine which elements are essential, which are supportive, and which are merely adjuncts. For example, a manufacturing company that

System Name: SLS E-Commerce

Date Evaluated: February 2012

Evaluated By: D. Jones

Information assets	Data classification	Impact to profitability
Information Transmitted:		
EDI Document Set 1—Logistics BOL to outsourcer (outbound)	Confidential	High
EDI Document Set 2—Supplier orders (outbound)	Confidential	High
EDI Document Set 3—Supplier fulfillment advice (inbound)	Confidential	Medium
Customer order via SSL (inbound)	Confidential	Critical
Customer service request via e-mail (inbound)	Private	Medium
DMZ Assets:		
Edge router	Public	Critical
Web server #1—home page and core site	Public	Critical
Web server #2—Application server	Private	Critical

Notes: BOL: Bill of Lading
       DMZ: Demilitarized Zone
       EDI: Electronic Data Interchange
       SSL: Secure Sockets Layer

Figure 5-7 Sample inventory worksheet

makes aircraft engines might find that its process control systems for machine tools on the assembly line are of the first order of importance. Although shipping and receiving data-entry consoles are important, they are less critical because alternatives are available or can be easily arranged. Another example is an online sales organization such as Amazon.com. The Web servers that advertise Amazon's products and receive orders 24 hours a day are critical to the success of the business, whereas the desktop systems used by the customer service department to answer e-mails are less important.

- Which information asset generates the most revenue? You can also determine which information assets are critical by evaluating how much of the organization's revenue depends on a particular asset. For nonprofit organizations, you can determine which assets are most critical to service delivery. In some organizations, different systems are in place for each line of business or service offering.

- Which of these assets plays the biggest role in generating revenue or delivering services? Which information asset generates the most profitability? Organizations should evaluate how much of the organization's profitability depends on a particular asset. For instance, at Amazon.com, some servers support sales operations, others support the auction process, and others support the customer review database. Which of these servers contributes most to the profitability of the business? Although important, the customer review database server does not directly add to profitability, at least not to the same degree as the sales operations servers. Note that some services may have large revenue values, but are operating on such thin margins that they do not generate a profit. Nonprofit organizations can determine what percentage of their clientele receives services from the information asset being evaluated.

- Which information asset would be the most expensive to replace? Sometimes an information asset acquires special value because it is unique. For example, if an enterprise still uses a Model 129 keypunch machine to create special punch-card entries for a critical batch run, that machine may be worth more than its cost because spare parts or service providers may longer be available for it. Another example is a specialty device with a long acquisition lead time because of manufacturing or transportation requirements. After the organization has identified the unique value of this device, it can address ways to control the risk of losing access to the unique asset. An organization can also control the risk of loss for such an asset by buying and storing a backup device.

- Which information asset would be the most expensive to protect? In this case, you are determining the cost of providing controls. Some assets are difficult to protect by their nature. Finding a complete answer to this question may have to be delayed beyond the risk identification phase because the costs of controls cannot be computed until the controls are identified later in the risk management process. However, information about the difficulty of establishing controls should be collected in the identification phase.

- Which information asset would most expose the company to liability or embarrassment if revealed? Almost every organization is aware of its local, national, and international image. For many organizations, the compromise of certain assets could prove especially damaging to this image. The image of Microsoft, for example, was tarnished when one of its employees became a victim of the QAZ Trojan and the (then) latest version of Microsoft Office was stolen.[7]

When it is necessary to calculate, estimate, or derive values for information assets, you might give consideration to the following:

- The cost of creating the information asset: Information is created or acquired at some cost to the organization. This cost can be calculated or estimated. One category of this cost is software development, and another is data collection and processing. Many organizations have developed extensive accounting practices to capture the costs associated with the collection and processing of data as well as the costs of software development and maintenance.

- The cost associated with past maintenance of the information asset: It is estimated that for every dollar spent developing an application or acquiring and processing data, many more dollars are spent on maintenance over the useful life of the data or software. Such costs can be estimated by quantifying the human resources used to continually update, support, modify, and service the applications and systems associated with a particular information asset.

- The cost of replacing the information: Another important cost associated with the loss or damage to information is the cost of replacing or restoring it. This includes the human resource time needed to reconstruct, restore, or regenerate the information from backups, independent transaction logs, or even hard copies of data sources. Most organizations rely on routine media backups to protect their information, but lost real-time information may not be recoverable from a tape backup unless journaling capabilities are built into the system. To replace information in the system, it may have to be reconstructed, and the data might have to be reentered into the system and validated. This restoration can take longer than it took to create the data.

- The cost of providing the information: Separate from the cost of developing or maintaining information is the cost of providing it to the users who need it. This cost includes the value associated with delivery of information via databases, networks, and hardware and software systems. It also includes the cost of the infrastructure necessary to provide access and control of the information.

- The cost of protecting the information: This value is a recursive dilemma. In other words, the value of an asset is based in part on the cost of protecting it, while the amount of money spent to protect an asset is based in part on its value. While this is a seemingly unsolvable circle of logic, it is possible to estimate the value of protection for an information asset to better understand the value associated with its potential loss. The values listed previously are easier to calculate. This value and the following values are more likely to be estimates of cost.

- Value to owners: How much is your Social Security number or telephone number worth to you? Placing a value on information can be a daunting task. For example, a market researcher might collect data from a company's sales figures and determine that strong market potential exists for a new product within a certain age group and demographic group. The cost associated with the creation of this new information may be small, but it could be worth millions if it successfully defines a new market. The value of information to an organization, or how much of the organization's bottom line can be directly attributed to the information, may be impossible to estimate. However, it is vital to understand the overall cost of protecting this information in order to understand its value. Again, estimating value may be the only method.

- Value of intellectual property: Related to the value of information is the specific consideration of the value of intellectual property. The value of a new product or service to a customer may be unknowable. How much would a cancer patient pay for a cure? How much would a shopper pay for a new type of cheese? What is the value of an advertising jingle? All of these items could represent the intellectual property of an organization, yet their valuation is complex. A related but separate consideration is intellectual property known as trade secrets. These assets are so valuable that they are the primary assets of some organizations.

- Value to adversaries: How much would it be worth to an organization to know what the competition is doing? This valuation approach is often overlooked, but believing that an asset is unimportant just because it is not valuable to the organization is short-sighted and may result in losses from damage to reputation or another indirect reason. If an asset will attract an attacker's attention, it needs to be removed or protected. Many organizations have departments that deal in competitive intelligence and that assess and estimate the activities of their competition. Even organizations that are traditionally nonprofit can benefit from understanding developments in political, business, and competing organizations.

Other company-specific criteria might add value to the asset valuation process. They should be identified, documented, and added to the process. To finalize this step of information asset identification, each organization should assign a weight to each asset based on the answers to the chosen questions.

 For another perspective on information asset valuation, read ISO 27001 Implementer's Forum: Guideline for Information Asset Valuation, which is available from www.iso27001security.com /ISO27k_Guideline_on_information_asset_valuation.pdf.

Information Asset Prioritization Once the inventory and value assessment are complete, you can prioritize each asset using a straightforward process known as *weighted factor analysis* or simply using a weighted table, as shown in Table 5-2. In this process, each information asset is assigned scores for a set of assigned critical factors. In the example shown in Table 5-2, a score is assessed for each asset according to three assigned critical factors. In the example, the scores range from 0.1 to 1.0, which is the range of values recommended in NIST SP 800-30, *Risk Management for Information Technology Systems*. In addition, each critical factor is assigned a weight ranging from 1 to 100 to show the criterion's assigned importance for the organization.

A quick review of Table 5-2 shows that the customer order via SSL (inbound) data flow is the most important asset on this worksheet, with a weighted score of 100. EDI Document Set 2—Supplier fulfillment advice (inbound) is the least critical asset, with a score of 41.

❯ Identifying and Prioritizing Threats

Key Term

threat assessment An evaluation of the threats to information assets, including a determination of their potential to endanger the organization.

Information Asset	Criterion 1: Impact to Revenue	Criterion 2: Impact to Profitability	Criterion 3: Impact to Public Image	Weighted Score
Criteria weights must total 100	30	40	30	
EDI Document Set 1—Logistics BOL to outsourcer (outbound)	0.8	0.9	0.5	75
EDI Document Set 2—Supplier orders (outbound)	0.8	0.9	0.6	78
EDI Document Set 3—Supplier fulfillment advice (inbound)	0.4	0.5	0.3	41
Customer order via SSL (inbound)	1.0	1.0	1.0	100
Customer service request via e-mail (inbound)	0.4	0.4	0.9	55

Table 5-2 Example of a Weighted Factor Analysis Worksheet

Note: In the table, EDI stands for *electronic data interchange,* BOL stands for *bill of lading,* and SSL is Secure Sockets Layer.

After an organization identifies and performs the preliminary classification of its information assets, the analysis phase next examines threats to the organization. As you discovered in Chapter 2, a wide variety of threats face an organization, its information, and its information systems. The realistic threats must be investigated further, while the unimportant threats are set aside. If you assume that every threat can and will attack every information asset, the project's scope quickly becomes so complex that it overwhelms your ability to plan.

The threats to information security that you learned about in Chapter 2 are shown in Table 5-3.

Each threat in Table 5-3 must be examined to assess its potential to endanger the organization. This examination is known as a **threat assessment**. You can begin a threat assessment by answering a few basic questions, as follows:

- Which threats present a danger to an organization's assets in the given environment? Not all threats have the potential to affect every organization. While an entire category of threats probably cannot be eliminated, such elimination speeds up later steps of the process. (Read the Offline feature entitled *Threats to Information Security: Survey of Industry* to see which threats leading CIOs identified for their organizations.) Once an organization has determined which threats apply, the security team brainstorms for particular examples of threats within each category. These specific threats are examined to determine whether they apply to the organization. For example, a company with offices on the twelfth floor of a high-rise in Denver, Colorado, is not subject to flooding. Similarly, a firm with an office in Oklahoma City should not be concerned with landslides. Using this methodology, specific threats may be eliminated because of very low probability.

- Which threats represent the most danger to the organization's information? The degree of danger from a threat is difficult to assess. Danger may be the probability of a threat attacking the organization, or it can represent the amount of damage the threat could create. It can also represent the frequency with which an attack can occur. Because this analysis is a preliminary assessment, it is limited to examining the existing level of preparedness as well as

Threat	Examples
Compromises to intellectual property	Software piracy or other copyright infringement
Deviations in quality of service from service providers	Fluctuations in power, data, and other services
Espionage or trespass	Unauthorized access and/or data collection
Forces of nature	Fire, flood, earthquake, lightning, etc.
Human error or failure	Accidents, employee mistakes, failure to follow policy
Information extortion	Blackmail threat of information disclosure
Sabotage or vandalism	Damage to or destruction of systems or information
Software attacks	Malware: viruses, worms, macros, denial-of-services, or script injections
Technical hardware failures or errors	Hardware equipment failure
Technical software failures or errors	Bugs, code problems, loopholes, backdoors
Technological obsolescence	Antiquated or outdated technologies
Theft	Illegal confiscation of equipment or information

Table 5-3 Threats to Information Security

Source: Communications of the ACM, used with permission.

improving the information security strategy. The results represent a quick overview of the components involved. As you will learn later in this chapter, you can use both quantitative and qualitative measures to rank values. Because information in this case is preliminary, the security team may want to rank threats subjectively in order of danger. Alternatively, the organization may simply rate each of the threats on a scale of 1 to 5, with 1 representing insignificant threats and 5 representing threats that are highly significant.

- How much would it cost to recover from a successful attack? One calculation that guides corporate spending on controls is the cost of recovery operations in the event of a successful attack. At this preliminary phase, it is not necessary to conduct a detailed assessment of the costs associated with recovering from a particular attack. You might find a simpler technique sufficient to allow investigators to continue with the process. For example, you could subjectively rank or list the threats based on the cost to recover. Or, you could assign a rating for each of the threats on a scale of 1 to 5, with 5 representing the most expensive threats. If the information were available, you could assign a raw value to the cost, such as $5,000, $10,000, or $2 million. The goal of this phase is a rough assessment of the cost to recover operations if an attack interrupts normal business operations and requires recovery.

- Which of the threats would require the greatest expenditure to prevent? In addition to examining the previous cost of recovering from attacks, organizations must determine the cost of protecting against threats. The cost of protecting against some threats, such as malicious code, is nominal. The cost of protection from forces of nature, on the other hand, can be very great. As a result, the amount of time and money invested in protecting against a particular threat is moderated by the amount of time and money required to fully protect against that threat. Again, you can begin by ranking, rating, or attempting to quantify the level of effort or expense required to defend an asset from a particular threat. The ranking might use the same techniques outlined previously to calculate recovery costs. Read the Offline feature to see how some top executives handled this issue.

By answering the preceding questions, you establish a framework for discussing threat assessment. This list of questions may not cover everything that affects the information security threat assessment. If an organization has specific guidelines or policies, they should influence the process and require additional questions. This list can be easily expanded to include additional requirements.

OFFLINE

Threats to Information Security: Survey of Industry

What are the threats to InfoSec according to top computing executives?

Table 5-4 presents data collected in a study published in the *Journal of Information Systems Security* (JISSec) and based on a previous study published in the *Communications of the ACM* (CACM) that asked that very question. Based on the categories of threats presented earlier, more than 1,000 top computing executives were asked to rate each threat category on a scale ranging from "not significant" to "very significant." The results were converted to a five-point scale, where "5" represented "very significant," and are shown under the Rate heading in the following table.

2012 JISSec Ranking	Categories of Threats	Rate	Rank	Combined	2003 CACM Rank
1	Espionage or trespass	3.54	462	16.35	4
2	Software attacks	4.00	306	12.24	1
3	Human error or failure	4.30	222	9.55	3
4	Theft	3.61	162	5.85	7
5	Compromises to intellectual property	3.59	162	5.82	9
6	Sabotage or vandalism	3.11	111	3.45	5
7	Technical software failures or errors	3.17	105	3.33	2
8	Technical hardware failures or errors	2.88	87	2.51	6
9	Forces of nature	2.76	81	2.24	8
10	Deviations in quality of service from service providers	2.88	72	2.07	10
11	Technological obsolescence	2.66	57	1.52	11
12	Information extortion	2.68	18	0.48	12

Table 5-4 Weighted Ranks of Threats to InfoSec[8,9]

Source: Journal of Information Systems Security and Communications of the ACM.

(continues)

The executives were also asked to identify the top five threats to their organizations. Their responses were weighted, with five points assigned to a first-place vote and one point assigned to a fifth-place vote. The sum of weights is presented under the Rank heading in the table. The two ratings were then multiplied together and divided by 100 to calculate a combined score. The final column shows the same threat as ranked in the 2003 CACM study.

Another popular study that examines the threats to InfoSec is the annual survey of computer users conducted by the Computer Security Institute (CSI). Table 5-5 shows biannual results since 2000. (Note that the CSI ceased operations in 2011; thus, the survey was discontinued.)

Type of Attack or Misuse	2010/11	2008	2006	2004	2002	2000
Malware infection (revised after 2008)	67%	50%	65%	78%	85%	85%
Being fraudulently represented as sender of phishing message	39%	31%	(new category)			
Laptop/mobile hardware theft/loss	34%	42%	47%	49%	55%	60%
Bots/zombies in organization	29%	20%	(new category)			
Insider abuse of Internet access or e-mail	25%	44%	42%	59%	78%	79%
Denial-of-service	17%	21%	25%	39%	40%	27%
Unauthorized access or privilege escalation by insider	13%	15%	(revised category)			
Password sniffing	11%	9%	(new category)			
System penetration by outsider	11%		(revised category)			
Exploit of client Web browser	10%		(new category)			
Attack/misuse categories with less than 10% responses (listed in decreasing order):						
Financial fraud						
Web site defacement						
Exploit of wireless network						
Other exploit of public-facing Web site						
Theft of or unauthorized access to PII or PHI due to all other causes						
Instant Messaging misuse						
Theft of or unauthorized access to IP due to all other causes						
Exploit of user's social network profile						
Theft of or unauthorized access to IP due to mobile device theft/loss						
Theft of or unauthorized access to PII or PHI due to mobile device theft/loss						
Exploit of DNS server						
Extortion or blackmail associated with threat of attack or release of stolen data						

Table 5-5 CSI Survey Results for Types of Attack or Misuse (2000–2011)[10]

Source: CSI surveys 2000 to 2010 and 2011 (www.gocsi.com).

Note that these studies of threats do not reflect the most current threat environment. Some newer information technologies, such as the cloud and the Internet of Things (IoT), have not yet been evaluated for their relative importance on the threat landscape.

A recent survey of computing executives also asked the following question: "In your organization's risk management efforts, what basis do you use to assess threats? (Select all that apply.)" The percentages of respondents who selected each option are shown in Table 5-6.

Answer Options	Response Percentage
Probability of occurrence	85.4%
Reputation loss if successful	77.1%
Financial loss if successful	72.9%
Cost to protect against	64.6%
Cost to recover from successful attack	64.6%
Frequency of attack	52.1%
Competitive advantage loss if successful	35.4%
None of these	6.3%

Table 5-6 Means to Assess Threats

❯ Specifying Asset Vulnerabilities

Once you have identified the organization's information assets and documented some criteria for beginning to assess the threats it faces, you review each information asset for each relevant threat and create a list of vulnerabilities. Vulnerabilities are specific avenues that threat agents can exploit to attack an information asset. They are chinks in the armor—a flaw or weakness in an information asset, security procedure, design, or control that could be exploited accidentally or on purpose to breach security. For example, suppose the edge router in an organization's DMZ is the asset. The threats to the possible vulnerabilities of this router would be analyzed as shown in Table 5-7.

Next, you examine how each possible or likely threat could be perpetrated, and list the organization's assets and their vulnerabilities. At this point in the risk identification phase, the focus is simply on identifying assets that have a vulnerability, not determining *how* vulnerable they are. The list is usually long and shows all the vulnerabilities of the information asset. Some threats manifest themselves in multiple ways, yielding multiple vulnerabilities. The process of listing vulnerabilities is somewhat subjective and depends on the experience and knowledge of the people creating the list. Therefore, the process works best when groups of people with diverse backgrounds within the organization work iteratively in a series of brainstorming sessions. For instance, the team that reviews the vulnerabilities of networking

Threat	Possible Vulnerabilities
Compromises to intellectual property	• Copyrighted works developed in-house and stored on intranet servers can be copied without permission unless the router is configured to limit access from outsiders. • Works copyrighted by others can be stolen; your organization is liable for that loss to the copyright holder.
Espionage or trespass	• This information asset (router) may have little intrinsic value, but other assets protected by this device could be attacked if it does not perform correctly or is compromised.
Forces of nature	• All information assets in the organization are subject to forces of nature unless suitable controls are provided.
Human error or failure	• Employees or contractors may cause an outage if configuration errors are made.
Information extortion	• If attackers bypass the router or compromise it and then enter your network, they may encrypt your data in place. They may not have stolen it, but unless you pay them to acquire the encryption key, the data is inert and no longer of value to you.
Deviations in quality of service	• Power system failures are always possible. Unless suitable electrical power conditioning is provided, failure is probable over time. • ISP connectivity failures can interrupt Internet bandwidth.
Sabotage or vandalism	• The Internet protocol is vulnerable to denial of service. This device may be subject to defacement or cache poisoning.
Software attacks	• The Internet protocol is vulnerable to denial of service. Outsider IP fingerprinting activities can reveal sensitive information unless suitable controls are implemented.
Technical hardware failures or errors	• Hardware can fail and cause an outage.
Technical software failures or errors	• Vendor-supplied routing software could fail and cause an outage.
Technological obsolescence	• If this asset is not reviewed and periodically updated, it may fall too far behind its vendor support model to be kept in service.
Theft	• Data has value and can be stolen. Routers are important network devices; their controls are critical layers in your defense in depth. When data is copied in place, you may not know it has been stolen.

Table 5-7   Vulnerability Assessment of a Hypothetical DMZ Router

equipment should include networking specialists, the systems management team that operates the network, the information security risk specialist, and technically proficient users of the system.

 For additional information on system vulnerabilities, visit the databases at www.securityfocus .com and the Common Vulnerabilities and Exposure database at http://cve.mitre.org.

The TVA Worksheet

At the end of the risk identification process, you should have a prioritized list of assets and their vulnerabilities. You should also have a list that prioritizes the threats facing the organization based on the weighted table discussed earlier. These two lists can be combined into a **threats-vulnerabilities-assets (TVA) worksheet** in preparation for adding vulnerability and control information during risk assessment. Along with supporting documentation from the identification process, this worksheet serves as the starting point for the next step in the risk management process—risk assessment.

Table 5-8 shows the placement of assets along the horizontal axis, with the most important asset at the left. The prioritized list of threats is placed along the vertical axis, with the most

	Asset 1	Asset 2	...	...	...	...	...	...	...	Asset n
Threat 1	T1V1A1 T1V2A1	T1V1A2 T1V2A2								
Threat 2	T2V1A1 T2V2A1									
...										
...										
...										
...										
...										
...										
Threat n										
Priority of Controls	1		2		3		4		5	
These bands of controls should be continued through all asset–threat pairs.										

Table 5-8 Sample TVA Spreadsheet

important or most dangerous threat listed at the top. The resulting grid provides a convenient method of determining the exposure of assets and allows a simplistic vulnerability assessment. As you begin the risk assessment process, create a list of **threats-vulnerabilities-assets (TVA) triples** to help identify the severity of vulnerabilities. For example, there may or may not be a vulnerability between threat 1 and asset 1. Not all threats pose risk to all assets. If a pharmaceutical company's most important asset is its research and development database, which resides on a stand-alone network that is not connected to the Internet, then the database may have no vulnerability to external hackers. If the intersection of threat 1 and asset 1 has no vulnerability, then the risk assessment team simply crosses out that box. It is much more likely, however, that one or more vulnerabilities exist between the two. As these vulnerabilities are identified, they are categorized as follows:

> T1V1A1—Vulnerability 1 that exists between Threat 1 and Asset 1
> T1V2A1—Vulnerability 2 that exists between Threat 1 and Asset 1
> T2V1A1—Vulnerability 1 that exists between Threat 2 and Asset 1 ... and so on.

In the risk assessment phase, the assessment team examines not only vulnerabilities but any existing controls that protect the asset or mitigate possible losses. Cataloging and categorizing these controls is the next step in the TVA spreadsheet.

Risk Assessment

Now that you have identified the organization's information assets and its threats and vulnerabilities, you can evaluate the relative risk for each vulnerability. This process is called risk assessment. Risk assessment assigns a risk rating or score to each information asset. While this number does not mean anything in absolute terms, it is useful in gauging the relative risk to each vulnerable information asset and it facilitates the development of comparative ratings later in the risk control process. The major stages of risk assessment are shown in Figure 5-8.

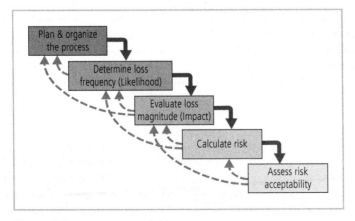

Figure 5-8 Major stages of risk assessment

> **RISK is**
> **the Probability of a Successful Attack on the Organization**
> (Loss Frequency = Likelihood * Attack Success Probability)
> *Multiplied by*
> **the Expected Loss from a Successful Attack**
> (Loss Magnitude = Asset Value * Probable Loss)
> *Plus*
> The *Uncertainty* of estimates of all stated values

Figure 5-9 Factors of risk

> Planning and Organizing Risk Assessment

Figure 5-9 shows a simplified perspective of the factors that go into the risk-rating estimate for each vulnerability. The goal at this point is to create a method for evaluating the relative risk of each listed vulnerability. The risk model described in Figure 5-9 is used to evaluate the risk for each information asset. The following sections itemize the factors that are used to calculate the relative risk for each vulnerability.

> Determining the Loss Frequency

Key Terms

attack success probability The number of successful attacks that are expected to occur within a specified time period.

likelihood The probability that a specific vulnerability within an organization will be the target of an attack.

loss frequency The calculation of the likelihood of an attack coupled with the attack frequency to determine the expected number of losses within a specified time range.

Loss frequency describes an assessment of the **likelihood** of an attack combined with its expected probability of success if it targets your organization (**attack success probability**). The resulting information will be coupled with an expected level of loss in evaluating risk. This calculation is also known as the annualized rate of occurrence, as you will see later in the chapter in the discussion of cost-benefit analysis. Note that some organizations calculate likelihood as the probability of a successful attack, using likelihood as a surrogate for loss frequency and automatically incorporating the definition of likelihood used here with the attack success probability. Which factor is more appropriate is a decision for your risk management team.

Likelihood In risk assessment, you assign a numeric value to the likelihood of an attack on your organization. For each threat, the organization must determine the expected likelihood of attack, which is typically converted to an annual value. For example, if an organization within a particular industry is targeted by hackers once every five years, the annualized likelihood of attack is 1/5, or 20 percent. This likelihood is often relayed as a 20 percent probability of an attack, given the current control structure. This probability is comparable to the fact that approximately one motorist in 1,500 is expected to be in a driving accident every day. The ratio doesn't apply to a particular motorist but to the overall group of drivers.

An event with a likelihood of more than once a year obviously has a higher probability of attack. For example, if organizations in a particular industry expect to be targeted by a malware attack at least four times per year, then the likelihood is 4/1, or 400 percent.

Where would an organization get this information? Provided that the organization does not have an extensive history of being successfully attacked, some values may be determined from published works like the CSI study mentioned earlier in this chapter. You can also search the Web to find and download other available studies that discuss attacks and their reported frequencies. Another resource may be the organization's insurance carrier. Not long ago, "hacker insurance" was not an option, but insurance companies are starting to recognize the value of offering cyber and privacy insurance, as described in the nearby Offline feature.

 For more information on cybersecurity insurance, visit the DHS Web site at www.dhs.gov/publication/cybersecurity-insurance.

Whenever possible, an organization should use external references for likelihood values that have been reviewed and adjusted for its specific circumstances. Many combinations

OFFLINE

Cyber and Privacy Insurance

Insurance has recently become more widely available to cover the costs of incident response after an event. This insurance might cover the costs of identity theft protection, forensic investigations, setting up call centers to deal with customer complaints and service requests, and other recovery expenses. According to David Derigiotis, a vice president at the insurance brokerage firm Burns & Wilcox, the Target Corporation employed such an insurance policy to help recover from its security breach in 2013. Target used benefits from the policy to deal with costs and fees associated with reissuing more than 2 million payment cards as well as monitoring credit and fraud alerts and freezes. The policy also included coverage for bringing in a forensic team to determine the cause of the incident and liability protection from affected customers and businesses.

Sales of these insurance policies have increased by 30 percent to 40 percent between 2012 and 2013, but they are still greatly underused. Policies can cost as little as $500 per year depending on the industry segment and type of information being protected.[11]

of assets and vulnerabilities have references for determining the likelihood of an attack. For example:

- The likelihood of a fire has been estimated by actuaries for any type of structure.
- The likelihood that any given e-mail contains a virus or worm has been researched.
- The number of network attacks against an organization can be forecast based on its number of assigned network addresses.

In its Special Publication 800-30, the National Institute of Standards and Technology recommends assigning a likelihood between 0.1 and 1.0, which provides a qualitative approach rather than the quantitative percentages shown previously. For example, the likelihood of an indoor asset being struck by a meteorite would be rated as 0.1. At the other extreme, the likelihood of receiving at least one e-mail that contains a virus or worm in the next year would be rated as 1.0. You could also choose to use a number between 1 and 100; note that 0 is not used because vulnerabilities with no likelihood have been removed from the asset/vulnerability list. Using a range is much simpler than attempting to determine specific probabilities. However, regardless of the rating system you choose, use professionalism, experience, and judgment—and use the rating system consistently.

Attack Success Probability The second half of the loss frequency calculation is determining the probability of an attack's *success* if the organization becomes a target.

The key component of this assessment is that the attack successfully compromises vulnerabilities in the organization's information asset. Another important part of the assessment is determining the organization's current level of protection, which further complicates the calculations and makes the "guestimates" that much more complex. An attack can be successful only if it gets by the current level of protection; determining that level of protection requires fully understanding the various controls and safeguards in place.

The person or team that performs the risk assessment calculations must work closely with the IT and information security groups to understand the current level of protection. Then, based on the probable threats, the responsible person or team develops an estimate for the probability of success of any attack in a particular threat category. For a poorly prepared organization, the probability is high that a professional hacker will successfully access protected information assets, so the organization may assign a quantitative value of 75 percent or a qualitative value of "very likely." For a well-protected organization that has up-to-date malware detection and a well-trained employee force, the probability of a successful malware attack may be poor. Therefore, the organization may assign a quantitative value of 10 percent or a qualitative value of "very unlikely."

Creating estimates for the probability of a successful attack is very difficult. IT and information security technical staffs may tend to overestimate their level of preparedness, and managers may overstate the skills and qualifications of their staffs. In general, the accuracy of any estimates in this category is susceptible to a great deal of uncertainty.

Loss Event Frequency Combining the likelihood and attack success probability results in an assessment of the loss frequency, also known as loss event frequency. To explain this assessment in other words, loss frequency is the probability that an organization will be the target of an attack, multiplied by the probability that the organization's information assets will be successfully compromised if attacked.

As an oversimplified example, let's say you have a 10 percent chance of getting caught in a hailstorm this year, and that you have a 5 percent chance of dying if you are hit by a hailstone. Therefore, you have a 2 percent chance of dying from a hailstone strike this year if you're caught outside during a hailstorm. Note that these calculations come with extensive conditions, but the gist is the same. The calculations must include the probability of an organization being the target of an attack and the probability of the attack being successful, given the vulnerabilities of the organization's information assets under its current protection mechanisms.

❯ Evaluating Loss Magnitude

Key Terms

asset exposure See *loss magnitude*.
loss magnitude Also known as event loss magnitude, the combination of an asset's value and the percentage of it that might be lost in an attack.

The next important step of risk assessment is to determine how much of an information asset could be lost in a successful attack. This quantity is known as the **loss magnitude** or **asset exposure**; its evaluation can be quantitative or qualitative. Organizations usually have some level of experience in creating best-case, worst-case, and most likely outcomes for various scenarios. The same types of calculations apply when determining loss magnitude.

The event loss magnitude combines the value of an information asset with the percentage of that asset that would be lost in the event of a successful attack. The difficulty of making these calculations is twofold:

- As mentioned earlier, valuating an information asset is extremely difficult, but if the organization can assess an asset to provide a working value, it is the first component of the loss magnitude.

- The second difficulty is estimating what percentage of an information asset might be lost during each of the best-case, worst-case, and most likely scenarios, given that the organization may have little or no experience in assessing such losses. Again, information from industry surveys, insurance organizations, and other sources may assist.

When all is said and done, the organization will probably "guestimate" these values in lieu of having authoritative data. This approach is widely used, and when done in good faith with a consistently applied process, it can yield results that meet the essential risk assessment requirements.

❯ Calculating Risk

If an organization can determine loss frequency and loss magnitude for an asset, it can then calculate the risk to the asset. For the purpose of relative and simplistic risk determination, risk *equals* loss frequency *times* loss magnitude *plus* an element of uncertainty, as illustrated in Figure 5-9 earlier. A few examples will help explain risk calculations:

- Information asset A is an online e-commerce database. Industry reports indicate a 10 percent chance of an attack this year, based on an estimate of one attack every 10 years. The information security and IT departments report that if the organization is attacked, the attack has a 50 percent chance of success based on current asset vulnerabilities and protection mechanisms. The asset is valued at a score of 50 on a scale of 0 to 100, and information security and IT staff expect that 100 percent of the asset would be lost or compromised by a successful attack. You estimate that the assumptions and data are 90 percent accurate.

- Information asset B is an internal personnel database behind a firewall. Industry reports indicate a 1 percent chance of an attack. The information security and IT departments report that if the organization is attacked, the attack has a 10 percent chance of success based on current asset vulnerabilities and protection mechanisms. The asset is valued at a score of 25 on a scale of 0 to 100, and information security and IT staff expect that 50 percent of the asset would be lost or compromised by a successful attack, because not all of the asset is stored in a single location. You estimate that the assumptions and data are 90 percent accurate.

Here are the risk ratings for the two vulnerabilities:

- Asset A's risk is $(10\% \times 50\%) \times (50 \times 100\%) + 10\%$, which is: $(5\% \times 50) + 10\% = 2.5 + 10\% = 2.75$
- Asset B's risk is $(1\% \times 10\%) \times (25 \times 50\%) + 10\%$, which is: $(0.1\% \times 12.5) + 10\% = 0.125 + 10\% = 0.1375$

Based on these calculations, the organization's asset A has a much higher level of risk than asset B.

❯ Assessing Risk Acceptability

For each threat and its associated vulnerabilities that have residual risk, you must create a ranking of their relative risk levels, as illustrated in the previous sections. These rankings provide a simplistic approach to documenting residual risk—the left-over risk after the organization has done everything feasible to protect its assets. Next, the organization must compare the residual risk to its risk appetite—the amount of risk the organization is willing to tolerate.

When the organization's risk appetite is less than an asset's residual risk, it must move to the next stage of risk control and look for additional strategies to further reduce the risk. Failure to do so indicates negligence on the part of the organization's security and management teams. When the organization's risk appetite is greater than the asset's residual risk, the organization should move to the latter stages of risk control and continue to monitor and assess its controls and assets.

As an extreme example, assume that a vicious new malware attack is occurring 100 times per year, with a 100 percent chance of success at your organization. A successful attack would result in a 100 percent loss of any asset it targets, including assets with a value of 100. You are 100 percent certain that your values are correct, meaning that you could have a maximum risk of $(100 \times 100\%) \times (100 \times 100\%) + 0\% = 10,000$. However, if you calculate the values of all your assets and find they range from less than 1 percent to 10 percent, then values between 2 and 5 may be significant enough to fall outside your risk appetite. It depends on what values the organization specifies for its calculations.

Documenting the Results of Risk Assessment By the end of the risk assessment process, you will probably have long lists of information assets and data about each of them. The goal so far has been to identify the information assets that have specific vulnerabilities, list them, and then rank them according to which need protection most. In preparing the list, you collected and preserved a wealth of information about the assets, the threats they face, and the vulnerabilities they expose. You should also have collected some information about the controls that are already in place.

The final summarized document is the ranked vulnerability risk worksheet, a sample of which is shown in Table 5-9. A review of this worksheet shows similarities to the approach used for the weighted factor analysis worksheet shown in Table 5-2. The worksheet shown in Table 5-9 is organized as follows:

- Asset: List each vulnerable asset.
- Asset relative value: Show the results for the asset from the weighted factor analysis worksheet. In Table 5-9, this is a number from 1 to 100.
- Vulnerability: List each uncontrolled vulnerability. Some assets might be listed more than once.

Asset	Asset Relative Value	Vulnerability	Loss Frequency	Loss Magnitude
Customer service request via e-mail (inbound)	55	E-mail disruption due to hardware failure	0.2	11
Customer order via SSL (inbound)	100	Lost orders due to Web server hardware failure	0.1	10
Customer order via SSL (inbound)	100	Lost orders due to Web server or ISP service failure	0.1	10
Customer service request via e-mail (inbound)	55	E-mail disruption due to SMTP mail relay attack	0.1	5.5
Customer service request via e-mail (inbound)	55	E-mail disruption due to ISP service failure	0.1	5.5
Customer order via SSL (inbound)	100	Lost orders due to Web server denial-of-service attack	0.025	2.5
Customer order via SSL (inbound)	100	Lost orders due to Web server software failure	0.01	1

Table 5-9 Ranked Vulnerability Risk Worksheet

- Loss frequency: Estimate the cumulative likelihood that the vulnerability will be successfully exploited by threat agents, as noted in the previous examples. In the table, the number ranges from 0 to 1.0 and corresponds to values of 0 percent to 100 percent.

- Loss magnitude: Calculate the estimated loss magnitude by multiplying the asset's relative value by the loss frequency. In this example, the calculation will yield a number from 0 to 100.

You may be surprised that the most pressing risk in Table 5-9 is the vulnerable mail server. Even though the customer service e-mail has an impact rating of only 55, the relatively high likelihood of a hardware failure makes it the most pressing problem.

Now that you have completed the risk identification process, what should its documentation package look like? In other words, what are the deliverables from this phase of the project? The process you develop for risk identification should include designating what function the reports serve, who is responsible for preparing the reports, and who reviews them. The ranked vulnerability risk worksheet is the initial working document for the next step in the risk management process: assessing and controlling risk. Table 5-10 shows a sample list of worksheets that might be prepared by the information security project team. Another method of presenting the results of the risk assessment process is provided in Chapter 12.

Deliverable	Purpose
Information asset classification worksheet	Assembles information about information assets and their value to the organization
Weighted criteria analysis worksheet	Assigns a ranked value or impact weight to each information asset
Ranked vulnerability risk worksheet	Assigns a ranked value or risk rating for each uncontrolled asset-vulnerability pair

Table 5-10   Risk Identification and Assessment Deliverables

> Likelihood and Impact: The Simpler Method

As stated earlier, some organizations assess risk using a simplified definition and calculation of likelihood and impact. This version, based on NIST SP 800-30 Rev. 1, views likelihood as the probability of a successful attack, as *loss frequency* was described earlier. It also views impact as the result of a successful attack, as *expected loss* was described earlier. This method is implemented in industry-leading software such as Clearwater Compliance's Analysis application within its Information Risk Management suite. As shown in Figure 5-10, this application is designed to support the entire risk management process from Asset Inventory (risk identification) through Risk Determination (risk assessment) to Risk Response (risk control).

As shown in Figure 5-11, impact is identified on a simple, qualitative six-point scale ranging from Not Applicable (0) to Almost Certain (5), while risk impact is assessed on a similar scale from Not applicable threat (0) to Disastrous (5). Risk is then calculated using a simple formula of Likelihood multiplied by Impact. All risk levels below the organization's risk appetite (for example, 10 on the resulting scale of 0 to 25) are automatically accepted. Levels

Figure 5-10 Risk questionnaire

Source: Clearwater Compliance with permission.

above the risk appetite are addressed through risk controls, as described elsewhere in this chapter.

 For more information on the Clearwater Compliance Information Risk Management suite, visit www.clearwatercompliance.com.

❯ The Open FAIR Approach to Risk Assessment

The FAIR methodology, which was developed by risk management consultant Jack Jones and promoted through his consulting agency Risk Management Insight and its parent company CXO Media, provides a qualitative approach to risk assessment. Recently, the Open Group selected FAIR as its international standard for risk management (see *www.fairinstitute.org/an-international-standard*). The major stages in the FAIR analysis consist of 10 steps in four stages:

"Stage 1—Identify scenario components

1. Identify the asset at risk

2. Identify the threat community under consideration

Figure 5-11 Likelihood and impact

Source: Clearwater Compliance with permission.

Stage 2—Evaluate loss event frequency (LEF)

3. Estimate the probable threat event frequency (TEF)

4. Estimate the threat capability (TCap)

5. Estimate control strength (CS)

6. Derive vulnerability (Vuln)

7. Derive loss event frequency (LEF)

Stage 3—Evaluate probable loss magnitude (PLM)

8. Estimate worst-case loss

9. Estimate probable loss

Stage 4—Derive and articulate risk

10. Derive and articulate risk"[12]

Note that the strategy recommended in the FAIR analysis generally aligns with the risk identification and risk assessment approach discussed thus far in this chapter. Stage 1 includes the tasks associated with risk identification, and Stages 2–4 include phases recommended under risk assessment. The FAIR approach includes specific range-based calculations to determine vulnerability and loss frequency for a single asset/threat pair as noted in Stage 2 above, as follows:

3. Estimate the probable threat event frequency (TEF) by ranking it on a scale of very low (such as less than 10 percent or once every 10 years) to very high (over 100 times a year).

4. Estimate the threat capability (TCap) by ranking it on a scale of very low (the bottom 2 percent of the overall threat population) to very high (the top 2 percent).

5. Estimate control strength (CS), which is an assessment of current protection capabilities of the organization's protection system. The CS can be a ranking from very low, which protects only against the bottom 2 percent of the average threat population, to very high, which protects against all but the top 2 percent of the average threat population.

6. Derive vulnerability (Vuln), which is the probability that an asset will be unable to resist the actions of a threat agency. The Vuln value is taken from a table that compares the TCap to the control strength, as shown in Table 5-11. Rankings are VL (very low), L (low), M (medium), H (high), and VH (very high).

7. Derive loss event frequency (LEF). Table 5-12 compares the Vuln values derived from Table 5-11 with the TEF specified during FAIR Step 3.

		Control Strength				
		VL	L	M	H	VH
TCap	VH	VH	VH	VH	H	M
	H	VH	VH	H	M	L
	M	VH	H	M	L	VL
	L	H	M	L	VL	VL
	VL	M	L	VL	VL	VL

Table 5-11 Vulnerability Assessment Definitions[13]

Source: FAIR Basic Risk Assessment Guide.

		Vulnerability				
		VL	L	M	H	VH
TEF	VH	M	H	VH	VH	VH
	H	L	M	H	H	H
	M	VL	L	M	M	M
	L	VL	VL	L	L	L
	VL	VL	VL	VL	VL	VL

Table 5-12 Loss Event Frequency Descriptions[14]

Source: FAIR Basic Risk Assessment Guide.

The result is the loss event frequency, which is rated on a scale of very low to very high. This value is used later to determine the overall risk present between the asset and its paired threat.

FAIR Stage 3 involves calculating the worst-case loss and most likely (probable) loss of an asset to its paired threat.

8. Estimating the worst-case loss involves determining the magnitude of loss to an asset if a threat becomes a successful attack. Assign values to each cell to represent the comparison between threat actions (rows) and forms of loss (columns), as illustrated in Table 5-13. Each column identifies the estimated impact of a form of loss. Some losses represent a direct impact on productivity; others include expenses from managing loss during the incident response process, costs for replacement of equipment or data, and payments to settle legal fines or regulatory judgments. Some losses stem from diminished competitive advantage (Comp. Adv.) if the organization becomes less capable of competing in the marketplace due to loss of trade secrets, R&D project information, and strategic plans. Other losses are estimates of damage to the organization's reputation.

   The cell values use sample loss estimate ranges derived from Table 5-14. Obviously, not every organization will experience losses in the multimillion-dollar range. Organizations may choose to adjust the values in any of these tables to suit their particular needs.

9. Estimate probable loss. Use the same process described in FAIR Step 8, but this time use the most likely outcome instead of the worst-case scenario.

Probable loss magnitude (PLM) is calculated by entering the correct Mid Range magnitude value from Table 5-14 into the corresponding cell in Table 5-15 for each form of loss, and then adding the losses to determine the total PLM that could result from a successful attack. In the example in Table 5-15, total losses for the Access attribute are an estimated $160,000, which qualifies as a Significant PLM.

The final stage of the FAIR method is to assess the level of risk within an asset/threat pair by comparing the PLM in Stage 3 to the loss frequency from Stage 2. Risk assessments are presented as Low, Medium, High, and Critical. The values from Table 5-16 are used to create an "outcome assessment of risk."[15]

Threat Action	Form of Loss						Worst Case Loss
	Productivity	Response	Replacement	Fine/ Judgment	Comp. Adv.	Reputation	
Access							
Misuse							
Disclosure							
Modification							
Deny Access							

Table 5-13 Worst-Case Loss Table for Information Assets and Threats[16]

Source: FAIR Basic Risk Assessment Guide.

Magnitude	Range Low End	Mid Range	Range High End
Severe (SV)	$10,000,000	$50,000,000	∞
High (H)	$1,000,000	$5,000,000	$9,999,999
Significant (Sg)	$100,000	$500,000	$999,999
Moderate (M)	$10,000	$50,000	$99,999
Low (L)	$1,000	$5,000	$9,999
Very Low (VL)	$0	$500	$999

Table 5-14 Worst-Case Loss Magnitude Definitions[17]

Source: FAIR Basic Risk Assessment Guide.

Threat Action	Form of Loss						Probable Loss
	Productivity	Response	Replacement	Fine/ Judgment	Comp. Adv.	Reputation	
Access	M ($50,000)	L ($5,000)	L ($5,000)	M ($50,000)	N/A	M ($50,000)	Sum = $160K

Table 5-15 Probable Losses for Information Assets and Threats[18]

Source: FAIR Basic Risk Assessment Guide.

		LEF				
		VL	L	M	H	VH
PLM	Severe	H	H	C	C	C
	VH	M	H	H	C	C
	H	M	M	H	H	C
	M	L	M	M	H	H
	L	L	L	M	M	M
	VL	L	L	M	M	M

Key	Risk Level
C	Critical
H	High
M	Medium
L	Low

Table 5-16 Risk Assessment Evaluation[19]

Source: FAIR Basic Risk Assessment Guide.

The resulting risk values provide the organization with an assessment it can use to create a ranking of asset/threat pairs. This information can help the organization determine whether the current level of risk is acceptable based on its risk appetite and establish priorities of effort for implementing new controls and safeguards.

 For more information on the FAIR methodology, visit www.fairinstitute.org.

Risk Control

When an organization's management determines that risks from information security threats are creating a competitive disadvantage, it empowers the information technology and information security communities of interest to control the risks.

Risk control involves three basic steps: selection of control strategies, justification of these strategies to upper management, and the implementation, monitoring, and ongoing assessment of the adopted controls.

❯ Selecting Control Strategies

Once the project team for information security development has created the ranked vulnerability risk worksheet, the team must choose a strategy for controlling each risk that results from these vulnerabilities. The five strategies are defense, transference, mitigation, acceptance, and termination. Table 5-17 summarizes the strategies defined here and how other risk management authorities refer to them.

Defense

> **Key Term**
>
> **defense risk control strategy** The risk control strategy that attempts to eliminate or reduce any remaining uncontrolled risk through the application of additional controls and safeguards. Also known as the avoidance strategy.

Risk Control Strategy	Categories Used by NIST SP 800-30, Rev. 1	Categories Used by ISACA and ISO/IEC 27001	Others
Defense	Research and Acknowledgement	Treat	Self-protection
Transference	Risk Transference	Transfer	Risk transfer
Mitigation	Risk Limitation and Risk Planning	Tolerate (partial)	Self-insurance (partial)
Acceptance	Risk Assumption	Tolerate (partial)	Self-insurance (partial)
Termination	Risk Avoidance	Terminate	Avoidance

Table 5-17 Summary of Risk Control Strategies

The **defense risk control strategy** attempts to prevent the exploitation of vulnerabilities. This strategy is the preferred approach to controlling risk. It is accomplished by countering threats, removing vulnerabilities from assets, limiting access to assets, and adding protective safeguards. The defense strategy includes three common methods:

- Application of policy
- Education and training
- Application of technology

Organizations can mitigate risk to an asset by countering the threats it faces or by eliminating its exposure. It is difficult, but possible, to eliminate a threat. For example, in 2002, McDonald's Corporation was being subjected to attacks by animal-rights cyberactivists, so it sought to reduce risks by imposing stricter conditions on egg suppliers that promoted the health and welfare of chickens.[20] This strategy was consistent with other changes made by McDonald's to meet demands from animal-rights activists and improve relationships with these groups.

Another defense strategy is to implement security controls and safeguards that deflect attacks on systems and therefore minimize the probability that an attack will be successful. As you learned in Chapter 1, controls, safeguards, and countermeasures are terms for security mechanisms, policies, and procedures, all of which serve to counter attacks, reduce risk, resolve vulnerabilities, and otherwise improve the general state of security within an organization. An organization with a dial-in access vulnerability, for example, can implement a control or safeguard for that service. An authentication procedure based on a cryptographic technology, such as Remote Authentication Dial-In User Service (RADIUS), would provide sufficient control. On the other hand, the organization may choose to eliminate the dial-in system and service to avoid the potential risk. (For details, see the Termination section later in this chapter.)

Transference

> **Key Term**
> _____
>
> **transference risk control strategy** The risk control strategy that attempts to shift risk to other assets, other processes, or other organizations.

The **transference risk control strategy** attempts to shift risk to other assets, other processes, or other organizations. These controls can be accomplished by rethinking how services are offered, revising deployment models, outsourcing to other organizations, purchasing insurance, or implementing service contracts with providers. In the popular book *In Search of Excellence*, management consultants Tom Peters and Robert Waterman presented a series of case studies of high-performing corporations. One of the eight characteristics of excellent organizations is that they "stick to their knitting.... They stay reasonably close to the business they know."[21] This means that Kodak focuses on digital printing while General Motors focuses on the design and construction of cars and trucks. Neither company spends strategic energy on the technology of Web site development—for this expertise, they rely on consultants or contractors.

This principle should be considered whenever an organization begins to expand its operations, including information and systems management and even information security. If an organization does not already have high-quality security management and administration experience, it should hire people or firms that provide such expertise. For example, many organizations want Web services, including Web presences, domain name registration, and domain and Web hosting. Rather than implementing their own servers and hiring their own Web site administrators, Web systems administrators, and specialized security experts, savvy organizations hire an ISP or a consulting organization to provide these products and services for them. This allows the organization to transfer the risks associated with managing these complex systems to another organization that has experience in dealing with such risks. A side benefit of such contract arrangements is that the provider is responsible for disaster recovery. Through service-level agreements, the provider is also responsible for guaranteeing server and Web site availability.

Outsourcing, however, is not without risks. The owner of the information asset, IT management, and the information security team must ensure that the disaster recovery requirements of the outsourcing contract are sufficient and have been met *before* they are needed. If the outsourcer fails to meet the contract terms, the consequences may be far worse than expected.

Mitigation

> **Key Term**
>
> **mitigation risk control strategy** The risk control strategy that attempts to reduce the impact of the loss caused by a realized incident, disaster, or attack through effective contingency planning and preparation.

The **mitigation risk control strategy** attempts to reduce the impact of an attack rather than reduce the success of the attack itself. This approach requires the creation of three types of contingency plans: the incident response plan, the disaster recovery plan, and the business continuity plan. Each of these plans relies on the quality of the other plans and depends on the organization's ability to detect an attack and respond to it as quickly as possible. Mitigation begins with the early detection of an attack in progress and a quick, efficient, and effective response.

The most common mitigation plans are contingency plans, as discussed in Chapter 4:

- Incident response (IR) plan: The actions an organization can and should take while an incident is in progress. The IR plan also enables the organization to take coordinated action that is either predefined and specific or ad hoc and reactive.
- Disaster recovery (DR) plan: The most common of the mitigation procedures, the DR plan includes all preparations for the recovery process, strategies to limit losses during a disaster, and detailed steps to follow in the aftermath.
- Business continuity (BC) plan: The most strategic and long-term plan of the three. The BC plan includes the steps necessary to ensure the continuation of the organization when the disaster's scope or scale exceeds the ability of the DR plan to restore operations, usually through relocation of critical business functions to an alternate location.

Acceptance

Key Term

acceptance risk control strategy The risk control strategy that indicates the organization is willing to accept the current level of risk. As a result, the organization makes a conscious decision to do nothing to protect an information asset from risk and to accept the outcome from any resulting exploitation.

The **acceptance risk control strategy** is the choice to do nothing more to protect a vulnerability based on the current residual risk and the organization's risk appetite. This strategy may or may not be a conscious business decision. The only recognized valid use of this strategy occurs when the organization has done the following:

- Determined the level of risk
- Assessed the probability of attack
- Estimated the potential damage that could occur from attacks
- Performed a thorough cost-benefit analysis
- Evaluated controls using each appropriate type of feasibility
- Decided that the particular function, service, information, or asset did not justify the cost of protection

This strategy is based on the conclusion that the cost of protecting an asset does not justify the security expenditure. For example, suppose it would cost an organization $100,000 per year to protect a server. The security assessment determined that for $10,000, the organization could replace the information contained on the server, replace the server itself, and cover associated recovery costs. In this case, management may be satisfied with taking its chances and saving the money that would otherwise be spent to protect the asset. However, if the acceptance strategy is used to handle every vulnerability in the organization, its managers may be unable to conduct proactive security activities and portray an apathetic approach to security in general. An organization cannot adopt a policy that ignorance is bliss and hope to avoid litigation by pleading ignorance of its obligation to protect employee and customer information. By the same token, management cannot hope that if it neglects to protect information, the opposition will assume that little is to be gained from an attack. The risks far outweigh the benefits of this approach. Acceptance as a strategy is often chosen based on the "school of fish" or "safety in numbers" justification—that the odds of being attacked by a shark are much smaller if you're swimming in a large school with many other fish. This reasoning can be very risky.

Termination

Key Term

termination risk control strategy The risk control strategy that eliminates all risk associated with an information asset by removing it from service.

The **termination risk control strategy** directs the organization to avoid business activities that introduce uncontrollable risks. For example, if an organization studies the risks of implementing business-to-consumer e-commerce operations and determines that the risks are not sufficiently offset by the potential benefits, the organization may seek an alternate mechanism to meet customer needs—perhaps developing new channels for product distribution or new partnership opportunities. By terminating the questionable activity, the organization reduces risk exposure.

Selecting a Risk Control Strategy Risk control involves selecting one of the five risk control strategies for each vulnerability. The flowchart in Figure 5-12 can guide you through the process of selecting one of the five strategies. After the information system is designed, you query whether the protected system has vulnerabilities that can be exploited. If the answer is yes and a viable threat exists, you begin to examine what the attacker would gain from a successful attack. To determine whether the risk is acceptable, you estimate the expected loss the organization might incur if the risk is exploited.

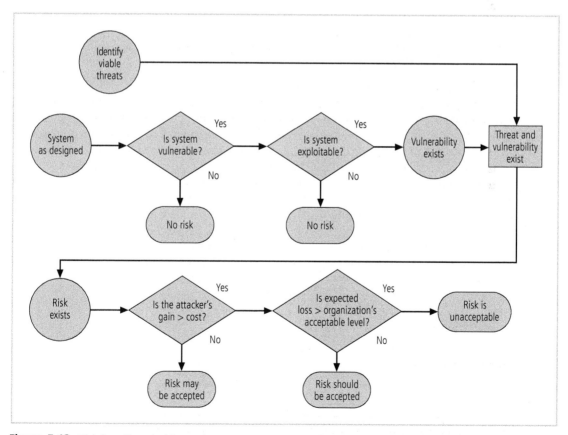

Figure 5-12 Risk handling decision points

The following list provides some rules of thumb for selecting a risk control strategy. When weighing the benefits of the different strategies, keep in mind that the level of threat and value of the asset should play a major role in the selection.

- When a vulnerability exists, implement security controls to reduce the likelihood of the vulnerability being exploited.

- When a vulnerability can be exploited, apply layered protections, architectural designs, and administrative controls to minimize risk or prevent occurrence.

- When the attacker's cost is less than his or her potential gain, apply protections to increase the attacker's cost. For example, use system controls to limit what a system user can access and do, which significantly reduces an attacker's gain.

- When potential loss is substantial, apply design principles, architectural designs, and other protections to limit the extent of the attack. These protections reduce the potential for loss.

The preceding risk control strategies are not designed to be implemented in isolation, but should be used to craft a portfolio approach to information security. Most organizations will choose a combination of strategies at this stage. The adoption of additional controls, such as an upgraded firewall, should be coupled with revised policy, improved mitigation planning, and even additional support from external security management and insurance organizations. By adopting all *reasonable and prudent* measures given its risk appetite, an organization can implement an effective security strategy. The primary purpose of risk management is to understand and then control an organization's risks in order to bring them within a level that is acceptable to the organization. Figure 5-13 illustrates how risk should be considered in relationship to threats, assets, and countermeasures used to reduce that risk.

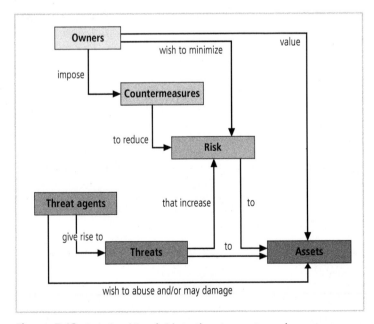

Figure 5-13 Relationship of risk to threats, assets, and countermeasures

❯ Justifying Controls

Key Terms

---

annualized cost of a safeguard (ACS) In a cost-benefit analysis, the total cost of a control or safeguard, including all purchase, maintenance, subscription, personnel, and support fees, divided by the total number of expected years of use.

annualized loss expectancy (ALE) In a cost-benefit analysis, the product of the annualized rate of occurrence and single loss expectancy.

annualized rate of occurrence (ARO) In a cost-benefit analysis, the expected frequency of an attack, expressed on a per-year basis.

cost avoidance The financial savings from using the defense risk control strategy to implement a control and eliminate the financial ramifications of an incident.

cost-benefit analysis (CBA) Also known as an economic feasibility study, the formal assessment and presentation of the economic expenditures needed for a particular security control, contrasted with its projected value to the organization.

exposure factor (EF) In a cost-benefit analysis, the expected percentage of loss that would occur from a particular attack.

single loss expectancy (SLE) In a cost-benefit analysis, the calculated value associated with the most likely loss from an attack. The SLE is the product of the asset's value and the exposure factor.

5

OFFLINE

Top 10 Information Security Mistakes Made by Employees

Adapted from "Top 10 Security Mistakes"[22]

By Alan S. Horowitz, *Computerworld*, July 9, 2001.

The following compilation was developed by security experts to represent the mistakes most commonly made by employees—often unknowingly—which put their organization's information assets at risk:

1. Passwords written down close to systems (such as on Post-it notes)
2. Computers allowed to stay running and connected to the Internet or LAN even when not needed
3. E-mail attachments opened when the content and/or sender is unknown
4. Creating weak passwords
5. Losing laptops that have not been properly secured to protect the data saved on them
6. Disclosing passwords

(continues)

7. Using systems configured to plug and play (technology that enables hardware devices to be installed and configured without the protection provided by people who perform installations)

8. Failing to report security violations or suspicious issues

9. Failing to keep system software and applications updated (the patch procrastinator)

10. Not watching for dangers *inside* the organization

Interestingly, this list was created in 2001 but has not changed significantly since then. Each of these mistakes is still being made by employees around the world.

Before implementing one of the five control strategies described in the previous section for a specific vulnerability, the organization must explore all consequences of the vulnerability to the information asset. To justify use of a control, the organization must determine the actual and perceived advantages of the control as opposed to its actual and perceived disadvantages.

An organization has several ways to determine the advantages and disadvantages of a specific control. The following sections discuss common techniques for making these choices. Note that some of these techniques use dollar expenses and savings implied from economic **cost avoidance**, and others use noneconomic feasibility criteria.

When justifying the acquisition of new controls or safeguards, the management of most organizations would expect to see a carefully developed business case that provides insight into the needs, costs, and values of these acquisitions. Aside from the "make or buy" decisions discussed in Chapter 1, business decision makers want to know clearly defined costs, benefits, and risks associated with acquisitions.

Anecdotally, information security is described as being in its third "FUD" era, where FUD stands for *fear, uncertainty,* and *doubt.* In the first FUD era, information security professionals were able to obtain needed controls and other resources simply by preying on the FUD of upper management and asserting, "If you don't buy this _____, you'll get hacked!" The fear of losing an information asset caused most organizations to overspend on information security, which resulted in inflated information security salaries and complex control implementations that were difficult to maintain.

Eventually, upper management became desensitized to this threat, leading to the second FUD era. This era was marked by the passage of numerous new standards and laws such as Sarbanes-Oxley, so information security demanded new resources by preying again on the FUD of upper management and asserting, "If you don't buy this _____, you'll go to jail!"

Again, upper management eventually became desensitized to these threats as the laws were challenged, revised, or became difficult to apply. In the third FUD era, information security professionals now must convince upper management to purchase security assets simply because it makes good business sense to do so.

Thus, information security staff must prepare effective business justifications for information security expenditures, illustrating the costs, benefits, and other reasons that upper management should make the additional investments. Some investments involve time and effort, but virtually all boil down to some form of economic feasibility, which organizations must consider when implementing information security controls and safeguards. Although several alternatives may exist for solving a problem, they may not have the same economic feasibility. Most organizations can spend only a certain amount of time and money on information security, and those amounts differ from organization to organization and even from manager to manager. Organizations are urged to evaluate the worth of the information assets to be protected and the loss in value if those assets are compromised by an exploited vulnerability. In short, organizations must gauge the cost of protecting an asset against the value of that asset. This formal decision-making process is called a **cost-benefit analysis (CBA)** or an economic feasibility study.

Just as it is difficult to determine the value of information, you might also discover during the process of justifying controls that it is difficult to determine the cost of implementing safeguards. The following list contains some of the items that affect the cost of a control or safeguard:

- Cost of development or acquisition of hardware, software, and services
- Training fees for personnel
- Cost of implementation, which includes the costs to install, configure, and test hardware, software, and services
- Service costs, which include vendor fees for maintenance and upgrades
- Cost of maintenance, which includes labor expenses to verify and continually test, maintain, and update

The amount of the benefit is usually determined by valuing the information asset(s) exposed by the vulnerability, determining how much of that value is at risk, and determining how much risk exists for the asset, as discussed earlier in this chapter.

As we've mentioned earlier, some people argue that it is virtually impossible to determine the true value of information and information-bearing assets. It is true that insurance underwriters currently have no definitive valuation tables for assigning worth to information assets. The value of information differs within and between organizations, depending both on the information's characteristics and perceived value. Much of the work of assigning value to assets can draw on the information asset inventory and assessment prepared for the risk identification process, as described earlier in this chapter.

The valuation of assets involves estimating real and perceived costs associated with design, development, installation, maintenance, protection, recovery, and defense against loss and litigation. These estimates are calculated for every set of information-bearing systems or information assets. Some component costs are easy to determine, such as the cost to replace a network switch or the hardware needed for a specific class of server. Other costs are almost impossible to determine accurately—for example, the dollar value of the loss in market share if information on a new product is released prematurely and a company loses its competitive edge. A further complication is that some information assets acquire a value over time that is beyond the *intrinsic value* of the asset under consideration. The higher *acquired value* is the more appropriate value in most cases.

Asset valuation techniques are discussed in more detail earlier in this chapter. Once an organization has estimated the worth of various assets, it can begin to examine the potential loss that could occur from an exploited vulnerability or threat occurrence. This process results in the estimate of potential loss per risk. Several questions must be asked as part of this process:

- What damage could occur, and what financial impact would it have?
- What would it cost to recover from the attack, in addition to the financial impact of damage?
- What is the **single loss expectancy (SLE)** for each risk? Note that SLE = **exposure factor (EF)** × asset value (AV).

For example, if a Web site has an estimated value of $1 million, as determined by an asset valuation, and a hacker defacement scenario indicates that a deliberate act of sabotage or vandalism could damage 10 percent of the Web site, then the SLE for the Web site would be $1 million × 0.10 = $100,000. This estimate is then used to calculate another value called annualized loss expectancy, which will be discussed shortly.

As difficult as it is to estimate the value of information, estimating the probability of a threat occurrence or attack is even more difficult. Tables, books, or records are not always available to indicate the frequency or probability of a given attack, although sources are available for some asset-threat pairs. For instance, insurance underwriters know the likelihood that a tornado or thunderstorm will destroy a building of a specific type of construction within a specified region of the country. In most cases, however, an organization can rely only on its internal information to calculate the security of its information assets. Even if network, systems, and security administrators have been actively and accurately tracking occurrences, the organization's information is sketchy at best. As a result, this information is usually estimated.

In most cases, the probability of a threat occurring is shown in a loosely derived table that indicates the probability of an attack from each threat type within a given time frame (for example, once every 10 years). This value is commonly referred to as the **annualized rate of occurrence (ARO)**. As you learned earlier in this chapter, many attacks occur much more frequently than every year or two. For example, a successful deliberate act of sabotage or vandalism might occur once every two years, in which case the ARO would be 50 percent (0.50). Other kinds of network attacks can occur multiple times per second. To standardize calculations, you convert the rate to a yearly (annualized) value. This value is expressed as the probability of a threat occurrence.

Once each asset's worth is known, the next step is to ascertain how much loss is expected from a single expected attack and how often these attacks occur. When those values are established, an equation can be completed to determine the overall lost potential per risk. This value is usually determined through the **annualized loss expectancy (ALE)**, which is calculated from the ARO and SLE:

ALE = SLE × ARO

Using the previous example of a Web site that might suffer a deliberate act of sabotage or vandalism and that has an SLE of $100,000 and an ARO of 0.50, the ALE would be calculated as follows:

ALE = $100,000 × 0.50 = $50,000

Unless the organization increases the level of security on its Web site, it can expect to lose $50,000 every year. Armed with this figure, the organization's information security design team can justify expenditures for controls and safeguards and deliver a budgeted value for planning purposes. Note that noneconomic factors are sometimes considered in this process, so even in cases when ALE amounts are not huge, control budgets can be justified.

The Cost-Benefit Analysis (CBA) Formula

In its simplest definition, CBA (or economic feasibility) determines whether a particular control is worth its cost. CBAs may be calculated before a control or safeguard is implemented to determine if the control is worth implementing. CBAs can also be calculated after controls have been functioning for a while. Observation over time adds precision to evaluating the benefits of the safeguard and determining whether it is functioning as intended. While many techniques exist, the CBA is most easily calculated using the ALE from earlier assessments before implementation of the proposed control, which is known as ALE(prior). Subtract the revised ALE, which is estimated based on the control being in place; this revised value is known as ALE(post). Complete the calculation by subtracting the **annualized cost of a safeguard (ACS)**.

$$CBA = ALE(prior) - ALE(post) - ACS$$

For another perspective on cost-benefit analyses, read the SEI Report entitled "SQUARE Project: Cost-Benefit Analysis Framework for Information Security Improvement Projects in Small Companies." The report is available from www.sei.cmu.edu/reports/04tn045.pdf.

❯ Implementation, Monitoring, and Assessment of Risk Controls

The selection of a control strategy is not the end of a process. The strategy and its accompanying controls must be implemented and then monitored on an ongoing basis to determine their effectiveness and to accurately calculate the estimated residual risk. Figure 5-14 shows how this cyclical process is used to ensure that risks are controlled. Note that there is no exit from this cycle; it continues as long as the organization continues to function.

The implementation process follows the standard SDLC approach outlined in Chapter 1. The monitoring process involves the selection and adoption of effective performance measures (metrics), as discussed in greater detail in Chapter 12. As the organization conducts ongoing operations, information security staff must continuously observe the performance of all implemented controls, including those outsourced to external companies. Staff must also observe the adopted mitigation strategies to ensure that they keep the organization's residual risk at the determined level, below its risk appetite.

Once controls are implemented, it is crucial to continually examine their benefits to determine when they must be upgraded, supplemented, or replaced. As Frederick Avolio stated in his article "Best Practices in Network Security":

> *Security is an investment, not an expense. Investing in computer and network security measures that meet changing business requirements and risks makes it possible to satisfy changing business requirements without hurting the business' viability.*[23]

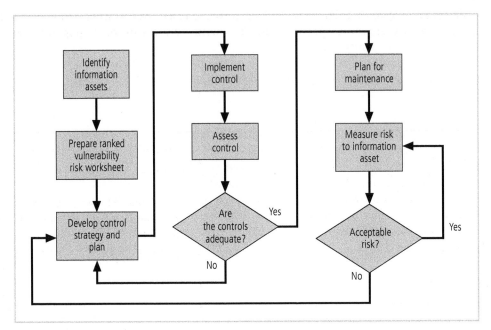

Figure 5-14 Risk control cycle

Quantitative Versus Qualitative Risk Management Practices

Key Terms

qualitative assessment An asset valuation approach that uses categorical or non-numeric values rather than absolute numerical measures.

quantitative assessment An asset valuation approach that attempts to assign absolute numerical measures.

The steps described in the previous section were performed using actual values or estimates. This approach is known as a **quantitative assessment**. However, an organization might decide that it cannot apply specific numbers to these values. Fortunately, it can perform these steps using an evaluation process called **qualitative assessment**, which does not use numerical measures. For example, instead of assigning a value of once every 10 years to the ARO, the organization could list all possible attacks on a particular set of information and rate each by the probability of occurrence, using scales rather than specific estimates. A sample scale could include a value of none to represent no chance of occurrence, then values of low, medium, high, and very high, with the final value representing almost certain occurrence. Of course, organizations may prefer other scales, such as A–Z, 0–10, 1–5, or 0–20. Using scales also relieves the organization of the difficulty of determining exact values. Many of these scales can be used in any situation that requires a value, even in asset valuation. For example, instead of estimating that a particular piece of information is worth $1 million, you can value it on a scale of 1–20, with 20 indicating extremely critical information, such as a soda manufacturer's secret recipe or those 11 herbs and spices of a popular fried chicken restaurant.

> ## Benchmarking and Best Practices

Key Terms

benchmarking An attempt to improve information security practices by comparing an organization's efforts against practices of a similar organization or an industry-developed standard to produce results it would like to duplicate. Sometimes referred to as external benchmarking.
best business practices Security efforts that are considered among the best in the industry.
metrics-based measures Performance measures or metrics based on observed numerical data.
performance gap The difference between an organization's observed and desired performance.
process-based measures Performance measures or metrics based on intangible activities.

Instead of determining the financial value of information and then implementing security as an acceptable percentage of that value, an organization could take a different approach to risk management and look to peer organizations for benchmarks. **Benchmarking** involves seeking out and studying practices used in other organizations that produce results you would like to duplicate in your organization. An organization typically benchmarks itself against other institutions by selecting a measure upon which to base the comparison. The organization then measures the difference between the way it conducts business and the way the other organizations do business. The industry Web site Best Practices Online put it this way:

> Benchmarking can yield great benefits in the education of executives and the realized performance improvements of operations. In addition, benchmarking can be used to determine strategic areas of opportunity. In general, it is the application of what is learned in benchmarking that delivers the marked and impressive results so often noted. The determination of benchmarks allows one to make a direct comparison. Any identified gaps are improvement areas.[24]

When benchmarking, an organization typically uses one of two types of measures to compare practices: **metrics-based measures** or process-based measures.

Metrics-based measures are based on numerical standards, such as:

- Numbers of successful attacks
- Staff-hours spent on systems protection
- Dollars spent on protection
- Numbers of security personnel
- Estimated value in dollars of the information lost in successful attacks
- Loss in productivity hours associated with successful attacks

An organization uses numerical standards like these to rank itself against competing organizations with a similar size or market and then determine how it measures up to the competitors. **Performance gaps** provide insight into areas that an organization should work on to improve its security postures and defenses.

The other measures commonly used in benchmarking are **process-based measures,** which are generally less focused on numbers and are more strategic than metrics-based measures. For each area the organization is interested in benchmarking, process-based measures enable it to examine the activities it performs in pursuit of its goal, rather than the specifics of how the goals are attained. The primary focus is the *method* the organization uses to accomplish a particular process, rather than the outcome. In information security, two categories of benchmarks are used: standards of due care and due diligence, and best practices.

For legal reasons, an organization may be forced to adopt a certain minimum level of security, as discussed in Chapter 3. When organizations adopt levels of security for a legal defense, they may need to show they did what any *prudent* organization would do in similar circumstances. This standard of due care makes it insufficient to implement standards and then ignore them. The application of controls at or above prescribed levels and the maintenance of those standards of due care show that the organization has performed due diligence.

The security an organization is expected to maintain is complex and broad in scope. It may therefore be impossible for an organization to rank as the "best in class" in any or all categories. Based on the budgets assigned to the protection of information, it may also be financially impossible to provide a level of security equal to that of organizations with greater revenues. Sometimes organizations want to implement the most technologically advanced and most secure levels of protection, but for financial reasons or other reasons they cannot. Such organizations should remember the adage, "Good security now is better than perfect security never."[25] It would also be counterproductive to establish costly, state-of-the-art security in one area, only to leave other areas exposed. Organizations must make sure they have met a reasonable level of security across the board, protecting all information, before beginning to improve individual areas to reach a higher standard.

Security efforts that seek to provide a superior level of performance in the protection of information are referred to as **best business practices,** or simply best practices or recommended practices. Even the standards promoted on the Internet as requests for comments (RFCs) have best practices (see *www.rfc-editor.org/categories/rfc-best.html*). Best security practices are security efforts that are among the finest in the industry, balancing the need for access to information with adequate protection. Best practices seek to provide as much security as possible for information and systems while maintaining a solid degree of fiscal responsibility. Companies that deploy best practices may not be the best in every area, but they may have established an extremely high standard or successful security effort in one or more areas. Benchmarking best practices is accomplished using the metrics-based or process-based measures described earlier.

While few commercial equivalents exist, many of the government's best security practices (BSPs) are applicable to security in both the public and private sectors. NIST, for example, has collected sample policies, strategies, and other practice-related documents for use as guidelines.

You can sometimes get advice for selecting control strategies from government sources. For organizations that operate in industries regulated by governmental agencies, their recommendations are effectively requirements. For other organizations, government regulations are excellent sources of information for controlling information security risks.

Applying Best Practices The preceding sections presented several sources to consider when applying standards to your organization. You can study documented best practice processes or procedures that have been shown to be effective or that have been recommended by a trusted person or organization, and then evaluate how they apply to your organization. When considering best practices for adoption, think about the following:

- Does your organization resemble the identified target organization that is considering the best practice? Is your organization in a similar industry as the target? A strategy that works well in manufacturing organizations often has little bearing in a nonprofit organization. Does your organization face similar challenges as the target? If your organization does not have a functioning information security program, a best-practice target that assumes you do is not useful. Is your organization's structure similar to the target's? Obviously, a best practice proposed for a home office setting is not appropriate for a multinational company.

- Can your organization expend resources similar to those identified with the best practice? If your approach is significantly limited by the organization's resources, it is not useful to submit a best-practice proposal that assumes unlimited funding.

- Is your organization in a similar threat environment as the one proposed in the best practice? A best practice from months or even weeks ago may not be appropriate for the current threat environment. Think of the best practices for Internet connectivity that were required for modern organizations in 2001 and compare them to today's best practices.

 A good source for best practices information is the CERT Web site (www.cert.org). Microsoft publishes its security practices on its Safety & Security Center Web site (www.microsoft.com/en-us/security/default.aspx).

Microsoft focuses on the following seven key areas for home users:

1. Use antivirus software.
2. Use strong passwords.
3. Verify your software security settings.
4. Update product security.
5. Build personal firewalls.
6. Back up early and often.
7. Protect against power surges and loss.

For small businesses, Microsoft recommends the following:

1. Protect desktops and laptops—Keep software up to date, protect against viruses, and set up a firewall.

2. Keep data safe—Implement a regular backup procedure to safeguard critical business data, set permissions, and use encryption.

3. Use the Internet safely—Unscrupulous Web sites, popups, and animations can be dangerous. Set rules about Internet usage.

4. Protect the network—Remote network access is a security risk you should closely monitor. Use strong passwords and be especially cautious about wireless networks.

5. Protect servers—Servers are the network's command center. Protect your servers.

6. Secure line-of-business applications—Make sure that critical business software is fully secure around the clock.

7. Manage computers from servers—Without stringent administrative procedures in place, security measures may be unintentionally jeopardized by users.[26]

In support of security efforts, Microsoft offers "The Ten Immutable Laws of Security" as follows:

Law #1: If a bad guy can persuade you to run his program on your computer, it's not solely your computer anymore.

Law #2: If a bad guy can alter the operating system on your computer, it's not your computer anymore.

Law #3: If a bad guy has unrestricted physical access to your computer, it's not your computer anymore.

Law #4: If you allow a bad guy to run active content in your Web site, it's not your Web site anymore.

Law #5: Weak passwords trump strong security.

Law #6: A computer or connected device is only as secure as the administrator is trustworthy.

Law #7: Encrypted data is only as secure as its decryption key.

Law #8: An out-of-date antimalware scanner is only marginally better than no scanner at all.

Law #9: Absolute anonymity isn't practically achievable, online or offline.

Law #10: Technology is not a panacea.[27]

Problems With the Application of Benchmarking and Best Practices

The biggest problem with benchmarking and best practices in information security is that organizations don't talk to each other. A successful attack is viewed as an organizational failure, not as a lesson. Because these valuable lessons are not recorded, disseminated, and evaluated, the entire industry suffers. However, more and more security administrators are joining professional associations and societies (such as the Information Systems Security Association), sharing stories, and publishing the lessons learned. Security administrators often submit sanitized accounts of attacks to security journals after removing details that could identify the targeted organization. Still, most organizations refuse to acknowledge, much less publicize, the occurrence of successful attacks.

Another problem with benchmarking is that no two organizations are identical. Even if two organizations are producing goods or services in the same market, their sizes, compositions, management philosophies, organizational cultures, technological infrastructures, and security budgets may differ dramatically. Thus, even if these organizations did exchange specific information, it may not apply in other contexts. What organizations seek most are lessons and examples rather than specific technologies they should adopt, because they know that security is a managerial problem, not a technical one. If security were a technical problem, implementing a certain technology could solve the problem regardless of industry or organizational composition. In fact, however, the number and types of variables that affect an organization's security can differ radically among businesses.

A third problem is that best practices are a moving target. What worked well two years ago may be completely worthless against today's threats. Security practices must keep abreast of new threats in addition to the methods, techniques, policies, guidelines, educational and training approaches, and technologies used to combat those threats.

A final issue to consider is that simply researching information security benchmarks doesn't necessarily prepare a practitioner for what to do next. It is said that those who cannot remember the past are condemned to repeat it. In security, those who do not prepare for common attacks see them occur again and again. However, preparing for past threats does not safeguard against new challenges to come.

Baselining

Key Terms

baseline An assessment of the performance of some action or process against which future performance is assessed; the first measurement (benchmark) in benchmarking.
baselining The process of conducting a baseline. See also *baseline*.

An activity related to benchmarking is **baselining**. For example, an organization could establish a **baseline** to measure the number of attacks against it per week. In the future, this baseline can serve as a reference point to determine if the average number of attacks is increasing or decreasing. In information security, baselining can provide the foundation for internal benchmarking. The information gathered for an organization's first risk assessment becomes the baseline for future comparisons. Therefore, it is important for the initial baseline to be accurate.

When baselining, it is useful to have a guide to the overall process. The National Institute of Standards and Technology has two publications specifically written to support these activities:

- Security SP 800-27, Rev. A, *Engineering Principles for Information Technology Security (A Baseline for Achieving Security)*, June 2004
- SP 800-53, Rev. 4, *Security and Privacy Controls for Federal Information Systems and Organizations*, April 2013, and NIST Special Publication 800-53A, Rev. 4: *Assessing*

Security and Privacy Controls in Federal Information Systems and Organizations: Building Effective Assessment Plans, December 2014.

 To read more about baselining, visit http://csrc.nist.gov/publications/PubsSPs.html.

Other Feasibility Studies

Key Terms

behavioral feasibility See *operational feasibility.*

operational feasibility An examination of how well a particular solution fits within the organization's culture and the extent to which users are expected to accept the solution. Also known as *behavioral feasibility.*

organizational feasibility An examination of how well a particular solution fits within the organization's strategic planning objectives and goals.

political feasibility An examination of how well a particular solution fits within the organization's political environment—for example, the working relationship within the organization's communities of interest or between the organization and its external environment.

technical feasibility An examination of how well a particular solution is supportable given the organization's current technological infrastructure and resources, which include hardware, software, networking, and personnel.

An organization's readiness for any proposed set of controls can be determined using several other qualitative approaches, including operational, technical, and political feasibility analyses. The methods for these feasibility evaluations are discussed in the following sections.

Organizational Feasibility Organizational feasibility analysis examines how the proposed control must contribute to the organization's strategic objectives. Above and beyond their impact on the bottom line, the organization must determine how the proposed alternatives contribute to its business objectives. Does the implementation align with the strategic planning for the information systems, or does it require deviation from the planned expansion and management of the current systems? An organization should not invest in technology that alters its fundamental ability to explore certain avenues and opportunities. For example, suppose that a university decides to implement a new firewall without considering its organizational feasibility. Consequently, the technology group requires a few months to learn enough about the firewall to completely configure it. Then, a few months after implementation begins, someone discovers that the firewall in its current configuration does not permit outgoing Web-streamed media. If one of the university's business goals is the pursuit of distance-learning opportunities and the firewall prevents the pursuit of that goal, the firewall has failed the organizational feasibility measure and should be modified or replaced.

Operational Feasibility Operational feasibility analysis addresses several key areas that are not covered by the other feasibility measures. **Operational feasibility**, also known as **behavioral feasibility**, measures employees' acceptance of proposed changes. A fundamental requirement of systems development is user buy-in. If users do not accept a new technology, policy, or program, it will fail. Users may not openly oppose a change, but if they do not support a control, they will find ways of disabling or circumventing it, thereby creating another vulnerability. One of the most common methods for obtaining user acceptance and support is to encourage user involvement. To promote user involvement, an organization can take three simple steps: communicate, educate, and involve.

Organizations should *communicate* with system users throughout the development of the security program to let them know that changes are coming. Users should be notified about implementation timetables and schedules as well as the dates, times, and locations of upcoming briefings and training. The organization should outline the purpose of proposed changes and explain how they will enable everyone to work more securely. In addition, organizations should design training to *educate* employees about how to work under the new constraints and avoid any negative impact on performance. Users are frustrated by new programs that prevent them from accomplishing their duties, especially if they receive only a promise of eventual training. The organization must also *involve* users by asking them what they want from the new systems and what they will tolerate from them, and by including selected representatives from various constituencies in the development process. These three basic undertakings—communication, education, and involvement—can reduce resistance to change and build resilience for change. Resilience is an ethereal quality that allows workers to tolerate change and accept it as a necessary part of their jobs.

Technical Feasibility In addition to the economic costs and benefits of proposed controls, the project team must also consider the **technical feasibility** of their design, implementation, and management. Some safeguards, especially technology-based safeguards, are extremely difficult to implement, configure, and manage. Does the organization have the hardware and software necessary to support a new firewall system? If not, can it be obtained? Technical feasibility also examines whether the organization has the expertise to manage the new technology. Does the organization have a staff that is qualified (and possibly certified) to install and manage a new firewall system? If not, can staff be spared from their current obligations to attend formal training and education programs that prepare them to administer the new systems? Or, must personnel be hired? In the current job environment, how difficult is it to find qualified personnel? These issues must be examined in detail before a new set of controls is acquired. Many organizations rush to acquire new safeguards without completely examining the associated requirements.

Political Feasibility For some organizations, the most important feasibility evaluated may be **political feasibility**. Politics has been defined as "the art of the possible."[28] The information security controls that limit an organization's actions or behaviors must fit within the realm of the possible before they can be effectively implemented, and that realm includes the availability of staff resources. In some cases, resources are provided directly to the information security community under a budget apportionment model. The management and professionals involved in information security then allocate resources to activities and projects using processes of their own design.

In other organizations, resources are first allocated to the IT community of interest, and the information security team must compete for these resources. In some cases, cost-benefit analysis and the other forms of justification discussed in this chapter are used in an allocation process to make rational decisions about the relative merit of various activities and projects. Unfortunately, these decisions are politically charged in some settings and are not made in accordance with the organization's greater goals.

Another methodology for budget allocation requires the information security team to propose and justify resource use for activities and projects in the context of the entire organization. This approach requires arguments for information security spending that articulate the benefit of the expense for the whole organization, so that members of all communities of interest can understand its value.

Recommended Risk Control Practices

If an organization seeks to implement a control strategy that requires a budget of $50,000, the planned expenditures must be justified and budget authorities must be convinced to spend up to *$50,000 to protect a particular asset from an identified threat*. Unfortunately, most budget authorities focus on trying to cut a percentage from the total figure to save the organization money. This underlines the importance of developing strong justifications for specific action plans and providing concrete estimates in those plans.

Another factor to consider is that each control or safeguard affects more than one asset-threat pair. If a new $50,000 firewall is installed to protect the Internet connection infrastructure from the threat posed by hackers launching port-scanning attacks, the same firewall may protect the Internet connection infrastructure from other threats and attacks. In addition, the firewall may protect other information assets from other threats and attacks. In the end, the chosen controls may be a balanced mixture that provides the greatest value to as many asset-threat pairs as possible. This reveals another facet of the risk management problem: information security professionals manage a dynamic matrix covering a broad range of threats, information assets, controls, and identified vulnerabilities. Each time a control is added to the matrix, it undoubtedly changes the loss expectancy of the information asset vulnerability for which it has been designed, and it may alter the loss expectancy for other information asset vulnerabilities. To put it more simply, if you add one safeguard, you decrease the risk associated with all subsequent control evaluations. To make matters even more complex, the action of implementing a control may change the values assigned or calculated in a prior estimate.

Between the challenging task of valuating information assets and the dynamic nature of loss expectancy calculations, it's no wonder organizations would like a way to implement controls that don't involve such complex, inexact, and dynamic calculations. There is an ongoing search for ways to design security architectures in which safeguards can be applied to several vulnerabilities at once instead of applying specific controls to each identified information asset vulnerability.

› Documenting Results

The results of risk management activities can be delivered via a report on a systematic approach to risk management, a project-based risk assessment, or a topic-specific risk assessment.

When the organization is pursuing an overall risk management program, it requires a systematic report that enumerates the opportunities for controlling risk. This report documents a series of proposed controls, each of which has been justified by one or more feasibility or rationalization approaches. At a minimum, each information asset-threat pair should have a documented control strategy that clearly identifies any residual risk after the proposed strategy has been executed. Furthermore, each control strategy should articulate which of the five fundamental risk-reducing approaches will be used or how they might be combined, and how they should justify the findings by referencing the feasibility studies. Additional preparatory work for project management should be included where available.

Another option is to create an action plan to document the outcome of the control strategy for each information asset-threat pair. This action plan includes concrete tasks, each with accountability assigned to an organizational unit or employee. The plan may also include hardware and software requirements, budget estimates, and detailed timelines to activate the project management activities needed to implement the control.

Sometimes a risk assessment report is prepared for a specific IT project at the request of the project manager, either because it is required by organizational policy or because it is good project management practice. On some occasions, the project risk assessment may be requested by auditors or senior management if they perceive that an IT project has sidestepped the organization's information security objectives. The project risk assessment should identify the sources of risk in the finished IT system, with suggestions for remedial controls, as well as risks that might impede the completion of the project. For example, a new application usually requires a project risk assessment with the system design and then periodically as the project evolves toward completion.

Finally, when management requires details about a specific risk to the organization, risk assessment may be documented in a topic-specific report. These reports are usually prepared at the direction of senior management to focus on a narrow area of operational risk to an information system. For example, an emergent vulnerability might be reported to management, which then asks for a specific risk assessment. For a more complete treatment of documenting the results of risk management activities, see Chapter 12.

❭ The NIST Risk Management Framework

In 2009, the U.S. government, through NIST, changed the fundamental approach to certifying and accrediting (C&A) federal information systems, bringing the government into alignment with industry. The focus moved from formal C&A activities to a risk management life cycle model with the publication of NIST SP 800-37 Rev. 1, *Guide for Applying the Risk Management Framework to Federal Information Systems: A Security Life Cycle Approach*.

This document, most recently updated in June 2014, established a common approach to using a Risk Management Framework (RMF) for information security practice and made it the standard for the U.S. government. According to Special Publication 800-39: *Managing Information Security Risk: Organization, Mission, and Information System View*:

> *Risk management is a comprehensive process that requires organizations to: (i) frame risk (i.e., establish the context for risk-based decisions); (ii) assess risk; (iii) respond to risk once determined; and (iv) monitor risk on an ongoing basis using effective organizational communications and a feedback loop for continuous improvement in the risk-related activities of organizations. Risk management is carried out as a holistic, organization-wide activity that addresses risk from the strategic level to the tactical level, ensuring that risk-based decision making is integrated into every aspect of the organization.*
>
> *The first component of risk management addresses how organizations frame risk or establish a risk context—that is, describing the environment in which*

risk-based decisions are made. The purpose of the risk framing component is to produce a risk management strategy that addresses how organizations intend to assess risk, respond to risk, and monitor risk—making explicit and transparent the risk perceptions that organizations routinely use in making both investment and operational decisions. The risk frame establishes a foundation for managing risk and delineates the boundaries for risk-based decisions within organizations. Establishing a realistic and credible risk frame requires that organizations identify: (i) risk assumptions (e.g., assumptions about the threats, vulnerabilities, consequences/ impact, and likelihood of occurrence that affect how risk is assessed, responded to, and monitored over time); (ii) risk constraints (e.g., constraints on the risk assessment, response, and monitoring alternatives under consideration); (iii) risk tolerance (e.g., levels of risk, types of risk, and degree of risk uncertainty that are acceptable); and (iv) priorities and trade-offs (e.g., the relative importance of missions/business functions, trade-offs among different types of risk that organizations face, time frames in which organizations must address risk, and any factors of uncertainty that organizations consider in risk responses). The risk framing component and the associated risk management strategy also include any strategic-level decisions on how risk to organizational operations and assets, individuals, other organizations, and the nation, is to be managed by senior leaders/executives. Integrated, enterprise-wide risk management includes, for example, consideration of: (i) the strategic goals/objectives of organizations; (ii) organizational missions/business functions prioritized as needed; (iii) mission/business processes; (iv) enterprise and InfoSec architectures; and (v) system development life cycle processes.

The second component of risk management addresses how organizations assess risk within the context of the organizational risk frame. The purpose of the risk assessment component is to identify: (i) threats to organizations (i.e., operations, assets, or individuals) or threats directed through organizations against other organizations or the nation; (ii) vulnerabilities internal and external to organizations; (iii) the harm (i.e., consequences/impact) to organizations that may occur given the potential for threats exploiting vulnerabilities; and (iv) the likelihood that harm will occur. The end result is a determination of risk (i.e., the degree of harm and likelihood of harm occurring). To support the risk assessment component, organizations identify: (i) the tools, techniques, and methodologies that are used to assess risk; (ii) the assumptions related to risk assessments; (iii) the constraints that may affect risk assessments; (iv) roles and responsibilities; (v) how risk assessment information is collected, processed, and communicated throughout organizations; (vi) how risk assessments are conducted within organizations; (vii) the frequency of risk assessments; and (viii) how threat information is obtained (i.e., sources and methods).

The third component of risk management addresses how organizations respond to risk once that risk is determined based on the results of risk assessments. The purpose of the risk response component is to provide a consistent, organization-wide, response to risk in accordance with the organizational risk frame by: (i) developing alternative courses of action for responding to risk; (ii) evaluating the alternative courses of action; (iii) determining appropriate courses of action consistent with organizational risk tolerance; and (iv) implementing risk responses based on selected courses of action. To support the risk response component, organizations describe the types of risk responses that can be implemented (i.e., accepting, avoiding, mitigating, sharing, or transferring risk). Organizations also identify the tools, techniques, and methodologies used to develop courses of action for responding to risk, how courses of action are evaluated, and how risk responses are communicated across organizations and as appropriate, to external entities (e.g., external service providers, supply chain partners).

The fourth component of risk management addresses how organizations monitor risk over time. The purpose of the risk monitoring component is to: (i) verify that planned risk response measures are implemented and InfoSec requirements derived from/traceable to organizational missions/business functions, federal legislation, directives, regulations, policies, standards, and guidelines are satisfied; (ii) determine the ongoing effectiveness of risk response measures following implementation; and (iii) identify risk-impacting changes to organizational information systems and the environments in which the systems operate.

To support the risk monitoring component, organizations describe how compliance is verified and how the ongoing effectiveness of risk responses is determined (e.g., the types of tools, techniques, and methodologies used to determine the sufficiency/correctness of risk responses and if risk mitigation measures are implemented correctly, operating as intended, and producing the desired effect with regard to reducing risk). In addition, organizations describe how changes that may impact the ongoing effectiveness of risk responses are monitored.[29]

This approach is illustrated in Figure 5-15.

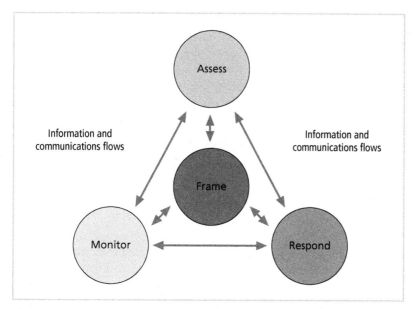

Figure 5-15 NIST risk management process

Source: NIST.[30]

Selected Readings

- *Against the Gods: The Remarkable Story of Risk*, by Peter L. Bernstein. 1998. John Wiley and Sons.
- *Information Security Risk Analysis*, Second Edition, by Thomas R. Peltier. 2005. Auerbach.
- *The Security Risk Assessment Handbook: A Complete Guide for Performing Security Risk Assessments*, by Douglas J. Landoll. 2005. CRC Press.
- *Guide for Conducting Risk Assessments*, NIST SP 800-30, Rev. 1, September 2012 (*http://csrc.nist.gov/publications/PubsSPs.html*)
- *Guide for Applying the Risk Management Framework to Federal Information Systems: A Security Life Cycle Approach*, NIST SP 800-37 Rev. 1, February 2010 (*http://csrc.nist.gov/publications/PubsSPs.html*)
- *Managing Information Security Risk: Organization, Mission, and Information System View*, NIST SP 800-39, March 2011 (*http://csrc.nist.gov/publications/PubsSPs.html*)

Chapter Summary

- Risk management examines and documents the information technology security being used in an organization. Risk management helps an organization identify vulnerabilities in its information systems and take carefully reasoned steps to assure the confidentiality, integrity, and availability of all components in those systems.

- A key component of a risk management strategy is the identification, classification, and prioritization of the organization's information assets.

- The human resources, documentation, and data information assets of an organization are more difficult to identify and document than tangible assets, such as hardware and software.

- After performing a preliminary classification of information assets, the organization should examine the threats it faces. There are 12 categories of threats to information security.

- To fully understand each threat and the impact it can have on the organization, each identified threat must be examined through a threat assessment process.

- The goal of risk assessment is to assign a risk rating or score that represents the relative risk for a specific vulnerability of an information asset.

- After vulnerabilities are identified and ranked, the organization must choose a strategy to control the risks from them. The five control strategies are defense, transference, mitigation, acceptance, and termination.

- The economic feasibility study determines the costs associated with protecting an asset. The formal documentation process of feasibility is called a cost-benefit analysis.

- Benchmarking is an alternative method to economic feasibility analysis that seeks out and studies practices used in other organizations to produce desired results in one's own organization.

- The primary goal of information security is to achieve an acceptably reduced level of residual risk—the amount of risk unaccounted for after the application of controls and other risk management strategies in line with the organization's risk appetite, also known as risk tolerance.

Review Questions

1. What is risk management? Why is the identification of risks and vulnerabilities to assets so important in risk management?

2. According to Sun Tzu, what two key understandings must you achieve to be successful in battle?

3. Who is responsible for risk management in an organization? Which community of interest usually takes the lead in information security risk management?

4. In risk management strategies, why must periodic review be part of the process?

5. Why do networking components need more examination from an information security perspective than from a systems development perspective?

6. What value does an automated asset inventory system have during risk identification?

7. What information attribute is often of great value for local networks that use static addressing?

8. When devising a classification scheme for systems components, is it more important that the asset identification list be comprehensive or mutually exclusive?

9. What's the difference between an asset's ability to generate revenue and its ability to generate profit?

10. What are vulnerabilities? How do you identify them?

11. What is competitive disadvantage? Why has it emerged as a factor?

12. What five strategies for controlling risk are described in this chapter?

13. Describe the defense strategy for controlling risk. List and describe the three common methods.

14. Describe the transference strategy for controlling risk. Describe how outsourcing can be used for this purpose.

15. Describe the mitigation strategy for controlling risk. What three planning approaches are discussed in the text as opportunities to mitigate risk?

16. How is an incident response plan different from a disaster recovery plan?

17. What is risk appetite? Explain why it varies among organizations.

18. What is a cost-benefit analysis?

19. What is single loss expectancy? What is annualized loss expectancy?

20. What is residual risk?

Exercises

1. If an organization must evaluate the following three information assets for risk management, which vulnerability should be evaluated first for additional controls? Which should be evaluated last?

   - Switch L47 connects a network to the Internet. It has two vulnerabilities: it is susceptible to hardware failure at a likelihood of 0.2, and it is subject to an SNMP buffer overflow attack at a likelihood of 0.1. This switch has an impact rating of 90 and has no current controls in place. You are 75 percent certain of the assumptions and data.

   - Server WebSrv6 hosts a company Web site and performs e-commerce transactions. It has a Web server version that can be attacked by sending it invalid Unicode values. The likelihood of that attack is estimated at 0.1. The server has been assigned an impact value of 100, and a control has been implanted that reduces the impact of the vulnerability by 75 percent. You are 80 percent certain of the assumptions and data.

   - Operators use an MGMT45 control console to monitor operations in the server room. It has no passwords and is susceptible to unlogged misuse by the operators. Estimates show the likelihood of misuse is 0.1. There are no controls in place on this asset; it has an impact rating of 5. You are 90 percent certain of the assumptions and data.

2. Using the data classification scheme in this chapter, identify and classify the information in your personal computer or personal digital assistant. Based on the potential for misuse or embarrassment, what information would be confidential, sensitive but unclassified, or for public release?

3. Suppose XYZ Software Company has a new application development project with projected revenues of $1.2 million. Using the following table, calculate the ARO and ALE for each threat category the company faces for this project.

Threat Category	Cost per Incident (SLE)	Frequency of Occurrence
Programmer mistakes	$5,000	1 per week
Loss of intellectual property	$75,000	1 per year
Software piracy	$500	1 per week
Theft of information (hacker)	$2,500	1 per quarter
Theft of information (employee)	$5,000	1 per 6 months
Web defacement	$500	1 per month
Theft of equipment	$5,000	1 per year
Viruses, worms, Trojan horses	$1,500	1 per week
Denial-of-service attacks	$2,500	1 per quarter
Earthquake	$250,000	1 per 20 years
Flood	$250,000	1 per 10 years
Fire	$500,000	1 per 10 years

4. How might XYZ Software Company arrive at the values in the table shown in Exercise 3? For each entry, describe the process of determining the cost per incident and frequency of occurrence.

5. Assume that a year has passed and XYZ has improved security by applying several controls. Using the information from Exercise 3 and the following table, calculate the post-control ARO and ALE for each threat category listed.

Why have some values changed in the Cost per Incident and Frequency of Occurrence columns? How could a control affect one but not the other? Assume that the values in the Cost of Control column are unique costs directly associated with protecting against the threat. In other words, don't consider overlapping costs between controls. Calculate the CBA for the planned risk control approach in each threat category. For each threat category, determine whether the proposed control is worth the costs.

Threat Category	Cost per Incident	Frequency of Occurrence	Cost of Control	Type of Control
Programmer mistakes	$5,000	1 per month	$20,000	Training
Loss of intellectual property	$75,000	1 per 2 years	$15,000	Firewall/IDS
Software piracy	$500	1 per month	$30,000	Firewall/IDS
Theft of information (hacker)	$2,500	1 per 6 months	$15,000	Firewall/IDS
Theft of information (employee)	$5,000	1 per year	$15,000	Physical security
Web defacement	$500	1 per quarter	$10,000	Firewall
Theft of equipment	$5,000	1 per 2 years	$15,000	Physical security
Viruses, worms, Trojan horses	$1,500	1 per month	$15,000	Antivirus
Denial-of-service attacks	$2,500	1 per 6 months	$10,000	Firewall
Earthquake	$250,000	1 per 20 years	$5,000	Insurance/ backups
Flood	$50,000	1 per 10 years	$10,000	Insurance/ backups
Fire	$100,000	1 per 10 years	$10,000	Insurance/ backups

Case Exercises

As Charlie wrapped up the meeting, he ticked off a few key reminders for everyone involved in the asset identification project.

"Okay, everyone, before we finish, please remember that you should try to make your asset lists complete, but be sure to focus your attention on the more valuable assets first. Also, remember that we evaluate our assets based on business impact to profitability first, and then economic cost of replacement. Make sure you check with me about any questions that come up. We will schedule our next meeting in two weeks, so please have your draft inventories ready."

Discussion Questions

1. Did Charlie effectively organize the work before the meeting? Why or why not? Make a list of important issues you think should be covered by the work plan. For each issue, provide a short explanation.

2. Will the company get useful information from the team it has assembled? Why or why not?

3. Why might some attendees resist the goals of the meeting? Does it seem that each person invited was briefed on the importance of the event and the issues behind it?

Ethical Decision Making

Suppose Amy Windahl left the kickoff meeting with a list of over 200 assets that needed to be evaluated. When she looked at the amount of effort needed to finish assessing the asset values and their risk evaluations, she decided to "fudge" the numbers so that she could attend a concert and then spend the weekend with her friends. In the hour just before the meeting in which the data was due, she made up some values without much consideration beyond filling in the blanks. Is Amy's approach to her assignment ethical?

After the kickoff meeting, suppose Charlie had said, "Amy, the assets in your department are not that big of a deal for the company, but everyone on the team has to submit something. Just put anything on the forms so we can check you off the list, and then you will get the bonus being paid to all team members. You can buy me lunch for the favor."

Is Amy now ethically justified in falsifying her data? Has Charlie acted ethically by establishing an expected payback for this arrangement?

Endnotes

1. Sun Tzu. *The Art of War.* 1988. Translation by Griffith, Samuel B. Oxford: Oxford University Press, 84.

2. *The Art of War* photo from the University of California, Riverside Collection. Photo by vlasta2 from *http://flickr.com/photos/bluefootedbooby/370458424/.* Reprinted under file licensed under the Creative Commons Attribution 2.0 generic license. Accessed 17 October 2016.

3. Deleersnyder, Sebastien. OWASP AppSec Europe 2006. "Bootstrapping the Application Assurance Process." Accessed 17 October 2016 from *www.owasp.org/images/3/34/OWASPAppSecEU2006_Bootstrapping_the_Application_Assurance_Process.ppt.*

4. Godwin, Mike. "When Copying Isn't Theft." *Electronic Frontier Foundation Online.* Accessed 17 October 2016 from *https://w2.eff.org/legal/cases/SJG/?f=phrack_riggs_neidorf_godwin.article.*

5. White House Executive Order 13526. "Classified National Security Information." 29 December 2009. Accessed 17 October 2016 from *https://www.whitehouse.gov/the-press-office/executive-order-classified-national-security-information.*

6. National Institute of Standards and Technology. "Sensitivity of Information." *CSL Bulletin.* November 1992. Accessed 17 October 2016 from *http://csrc.nist.gov/publications/nistbul/csl92-11.txt.*

7. Bridis, Ted. "Microsoft Hacked! Code Stolen?" *ZDNet News Online.* 27 October 2000. Accessed 17 October 2016 from *www.zdnet.com/news/microsoft-hacked-codes tolen/111513.*

8. Whitman, Michael, and Mattord, Herb. "Threats to Information Security Revisited." *Journal of Information Systems Security*, 2012, 8(1).

9. Whitman, Michael. "Enemy at the Gates: Threats to Information Security." *Communications of the ACM*, August 2003, 46(8).

10. This table is compiled from data published by the Computer Security Institute and the FBI over the years.

11. Derigiotis, David. "Hacker insurance for businesses: Interview on CNBC." Accessed 11 July 2016 from *http://video.cnbc.com/gallery/?video=3000235457.*

12. FAIR Basic Risk Assessment Guide. Accessed 9 February 2014 from *www.riskmanage mentinsight.com/media/docs/FAIR_brag.pdf.*

13. Ibid.

14. Ibid.

15. Ibid.

16. Ibid.

17. Ibid.

18. Ibid.

19. Ibid.

20. Greenberg, Jack M. "McDonald's Issues First Worldwide Social Responsibility Report." *CSRwire.* 14 April 2002. Accessed 17 October 2016 from *www.csrwire .com/press_releases/25172-McDonald-s-Issues-First-Worldwide-Social-Responsibility -Report.*

21. Peters, Thomas J., and Waterman, Robert H. *In Search of Excellence: Lessons from America's Best Run Companies.* New York: Harper and Row, 1982.

22. Horowitz, Alan S. "Top 10 Security Mistakes." *Computerworld* 35, no. 28 (9 July 2001): 38.

23. Avolio, Frederick M. "Best Practices in Network Security." *Network Computing* 11, no. 5 (20 March 2000): 60–66.

24. Best Practices, LLC. "What is Benchmarking?" *Best Practices Online.* Accessed 17 October 2016 from *www.best-in-class.com/bestp/domrep.nsf/bb282ab5b9f8fa6d85256 dd6006b3e81/960c22c0f471200685256e150069728b!OpenDocument.*

25. Avolio, Frederick M. "Best Practices in Network Security." *Network Computing* 11, no. 5 (20 March 2000): 60–66.

26. Adapted from Microsoft's "Security Guide for Small Business." Accessed 9 February 2014 from *http://download.microsoft.com/download/3/a/2/3a208c3c-f355-43ce-bab4 -890db267899b/Security_Guide_for_Small_Business.pdf.*

27. The Microsoft Security Response Center. *The Ten Immutable Laws of Security (Version 2.0).* Accessed 11 July 2016 from *https://technet.microsoft.com/en-us/library/bb278941 .aspx.*

28. Mann, Thomas. "Politics Is Often Defined as the Art of the Possible." Speech in the Library of Congress, Washington, DC, 29 May 1945.

29. National Institute of Standards and Technology. *Managing Information Security Risk: Organization, Mission, and Information System View.* SP 800-39. March 2011. Accessed 17 October 2016 from *http://nvlpubs.nist.gov/nistpubs/Legacy/SP/nistspecial publication800-39.pdf.*

30. Ibid.

chapter 6

Security Technology: Access Controls, Firewalls, and VPNs

If you think technology can solve your security problems, then you don't understand the problems and you don't understand the technology.

BRUCE SCHNEIER, AMERICAN CRYPTOGRAPHER,
COMPUTER SECURITY SPECIALIST, AND WRITER

Kelvin Urich came into the meeting room a few minutes late. He took the empty chair at the head of the conference table, flipped open his notepad, and went straight to the point. "Okay, folks, I'm scheduled to present a plan to Charlie Moody and the IT planning staff in two weeks. I saw in the last project status report that you still don't have a consensus for the DMZ architecture. Without that, we can't specify the needed hardware or software, so we haven't even started costing the project and planning for deployment. We cannot make acquisition and operating budgets, and I will look very silly at the presentation. What seems to be the problem?"

Laverne Nguyen replied, "Well, we seem to have a difference of opinion among the members of the architecture team. Some of us want to set up bastion hosts, which are simpler and cheaper to implement, and others want to use a screened subnet with proxy servers—much more complex, more difficult to design but higher overall security. That decision will affect the way we implement application and Web servers."

Miller Harrison, a contractor brought in to help with the project, picked up where Laverne had left off. "We can't seem to move beyond this impasse, but we have done all the planning up to that point."

Kelvin asked, "Laverne, what does the consultant's report say?"

Laverne said, "Well, there is a little confusion about that. The consultant is from Costly & Firehouse, one of the big consulting firms. She proposed two alternative designs, one that seems like an adequate, if modest design and another that might be a little more than we need. The written report indicates we have to make the decision about which way to go, but when we talked, she really built up the expensive plan and kind of put down the more economical plan."

Miller looked sour.

Kelvin said, "Sounds like we need to make a decision, and soon. Get a conference room reserved for tomorrow, ask the consultant if she can come in for a few hours first thing, and let everyone on the architecture team know we will meet from 8 to 11 on this matter. Now, here is how I think we should prepare for the meeting."

LEARNING OBJECTIVES

Upon completion of this material, you should be able to:

- Discuss the role of access control in information systems, and identify and discuss the four fundamental functions of access control systems
- Define authentication and explain the three commonly used authentication factors
- Describe firewall technologies and the various categories of firewalls
- Discuss the various approaches to firewall implementation
- Identify the various approaches to control remote and dial-up access by authenticating and authorizing users
- Describe virtual private networks (VPNs) and discuss the technology that enables them

Introduction

Technical controls are essential to a well-planned information security program, particularly to enforce policy for the many IT functions that are not under direct human control. Network and computer systems make millions of decisions every second, and they operate in ways and at speeds that people cannot control in real time. Technical control solutions, when properly implemented, can improve an organization's ability to balance the often conflicting objectives of making information readily and widely available and of preserving the information's confidentiality and integrity. This chapter, along with Chapters 7 and 8, describes the function of many common technical controls and explains how they fit into the physical design of an information security program. Students who want to acquire expertise on the configuration and maintenance of technology-based control systems will require additional education and usually specialized training.

Access Control

Key Terms

access control The selective method by which systems specify who may use a particular resource and how they may use it.

access control list (ACL) Specifications of authorization that govern the rights and privileges of users to a particular information asset. ACLs include user access lists, matrices, and capabilities tables.

attribute A characteristic of a subject (user or system) that can be used to restrict access to an object. Also known as a *subject attribute*.

attribute-based access control (ABAC) An access control approach whereby the organization specifies the use of objects based on some attribute of the user or system.

capabilities table In a lattice-based access control, the row of attributes associated with a particular subject (such as a user).

discretionary access controls (DACs) Access controls that are implemented at the discretion or option of the data user.

lattice-based access control (LBAC) A variation on the MAC form of access control, which assigns users a matrix of authorizations for particular areas of access, incorporating the information assets of subjects such as users and objects.

mandatory access control (MAC) A required, structured data classification scheme that rates each collection of information as well as each user. These ratings are often referred to as sensitivity or classification levels.

nondiscretionary access controls (NDACs) Access controls that are implemented by a central authority.

role-based access control (RBAC) An example of a nondiscretionary control where privileges are tied to the role a user performs in an organization, and are inherited when a user is assigned to that role. Roles are considered more persistent than tasks. RBAC is an example of an LDAC.

subject attribute See *attribute*.

task-based access control (TBAC) An example of a nondiscretionary control where privileges are tied to a task a user performs in an organization and are inherited when a user is assigned to that task. Tasks are considered more temporary than roles. TBAC is an example of an LDAC.

6

Access control is the method by which systems determine whether and how to admit a user into a trusted area of the organization—that is, information systems, restricted areas such as computer rooms, and the entire physical location. Access control is achieved through a combination of policies, programs, and technologies. To understand access controls, you must first understand they are focused on the permissions or privileges that a subject (user or system) has on an object (resource), including *if, when,* and from *where* a subject may access an object and especially *how* the subject may use that object.

In the early days of access controls during the 1960s and 1970s, the government defined only mandatory access controls (MACs) and discretionary access controls. These definitions were later codified in the Trusted Computer System Evaluation Criteria (TCSEC) documents from the U.S. Department of Defense (DoD). As the definitions and applications evolved, MAC became further refined as a specific type of lattice-based, nondiscretionary access control, as described in the following sections.

In general, access controls can be discretionary or nondiscretionary (see Figure 6-1).

Discretionary access controls (DACs) provide the ability to share resources in a peer-to-peer configuration that allows users to control and possibly provide access to information or resources at their disposal. The users can allow general, unrestricted access, or they can allow specific people or groups of people to access these resources. For example, a user might have a hard drive that contains information to be shared with office coworkers. This user can elect to allow access to specific coworkers by providing access by name in the share control function.

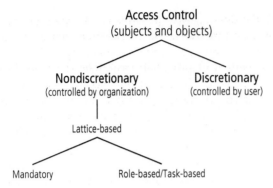

Figure 6-1 Access control approaches

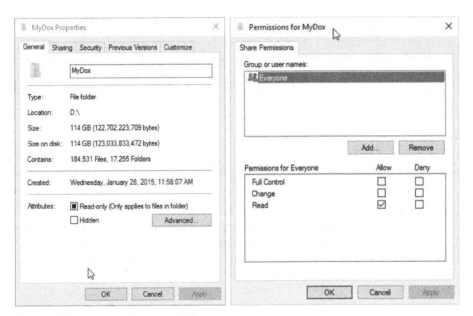

Figure 6-2 Example Windows 10 discretionary access control

Source: Microsoft Windows 10.

Figure 6-2 shows an example of a discretionary access control from Microsoft Windows 10.

Nondiscretionary access controls (NDACs) are managed by a central authority in the organization. A form of nondiscretionary access controls is called **lattice-based access control (LBAC)**, in which users are assigned a matrix of authorizations for particular areas of access. The authorization may vary between levels, depending on the classification of authorizations that users possess for each group of information or resources. The lattice structure contains subjects and objects, and the boundaries associated with each pair are demarcated. Lattice-based control specifies the level of access each subject has to each object, as implemented in **access control lists (ACLs)** and **capabilities tables** (see Chapter 4).

Some lattice-based controls are tied to a person's duties and responsibilities; such controls include **role-based access controls (RBACs)** and **task-based access controls (TBACs)**.

Role-based controls are associated with the duties a user performs in an organization, such as a position or temporary assignment like project manager, while task-based controls are tied to a particular chore or responsibility, such as a department's printer administrator. Some consider TBACs a sub-role access control and a method of providing more detailed control over the steps or stages associated with a role or project. These controls make it easier to maintain the restrictions associated with a particular role or task, especially if different people perform the role or task. Instead of constantly assigning and revoking the privileges of employees who come and go, the administrator simply assigns access rights to the role or task. Then, when users are associated with that role or task, they automatically receive the corresponding access. When their turns are over, they are removed from the role or task and access is revoked. Roles tend to last for a longer term and be related to a position, whereas tasks are much more granular and short-term. In some organizations the terms are used synonymously.

Mandatory access controls (MACs) are also a form of lattice-based, nondiscretionary access controls that use data classification schemes; they give users and data owners limited control over access to information resources. In a data classification scheme, each collection of information is rated, and all users are rated to specify the level of information they may access. These ratings are often referred to as sensitivity levels, and they indicate the level of confidentiality the information requires. These items were covered in greater detail in Chapter 5.

A newer approach to the lattice-based access controls promoted by NIST is **attribute-based access controls (ABACs)**.

> *"There are characteristics or **attributes** of a subject such as name, date of birth, home address, training record, and job function that may, either individually or when combined, comprise a unique identity that distinguishes that person from all others. These characteristics are often called **subject attributes.**"*[1]

An ABAC system simply uses one of these attributes to regulate access to a particular set of data. This system is similar in concept to looking up movie times on a Web site that requires you to enter your zip code to select a particular theatre, or a home supply or electronics store that asks for your zip code to determine if a particular discount is available at your nearest store. According to NIST, ABAC is actually the parent approach to lattice-based, MAC, and RBAC controls, as they all are based on attributes.

 For more information on ABAC and access controls in general, read NIST SP 800-162 at http:// csrc.nist.gov/publications/PubsSPs.html and NIST IR 7316 at http://csrc.nist.gov/publications/ PubsNISTIRs.html.

❯ Access Control Mechanisms

> ### Key Terms
>
> **access control matrix** An integration of access control lists (focusing on assets) and capabilities tables (focusing on users) that results in a matrix with organizational assets listed in the column headings and users listed in the row headings. The matrix contains ACLs in columns for a particular device or asset and capabilities tables in rows for a particular user.
>
> **accountability** The access control mechanism that ensures all actions on a system—authorized or unauthorized—can be attributed to an authenticated identity. Also known as *auditability*.

asynchronous token An authentication component in the form of a token—a card or key fob that contains a computer chip and a liquid crystal display and shows a computer-generated number used to support remote login authentication. This token does not require calibration of the central authentication server; instead, it uses a challenge/response system.

auditability See *accountability*.

authentication The access control mechanism that requires the validation and verification of an unauthenticated entity's purported identity.

authentication factors Three mechanisms that provide authentication based on something an unauthenticated entity knows, something an unauthenticated entity has, and something an unauthenticated entity is.

authorization The access control mechanism that represents the matching of an authenticated entity to a list of information assets and corresponding access levels.

dumb card An authentication card that contains digital user data, such as a personal identification number (PIN), against which user input is compared.

identification The access control mechanism whereby unverified or unauthenticated entities who seek access to a resource provide a label by which they are known to the system.

passphrase A plain-language phrase, typically longer than a password, from which a virtual password is derived.

password A secret word or combination of characters that only the user should know; a password is used to authenticate the user.

smart card An authentication component similar to a dumb card that contains a computer chip to verify and validate several pieces of information instead of just a PIN.

strong authentication In access control, the use of at least two different authentication mechanisms drawn from two different factors of authentication.

synchronous token An authentication component in the form of a token—a card or key fob that contains a computer chip and a liquid crystal display and shows a computer-generated number used to support remote login authentication. This token must be calibrated with the corresponding software on the central authentication server.

virtual password The derivative of a passphrase. See *passphrase*.

In general, all access control approaches rely on the following four mechanisms, which represent the four fundamental functions of access control systems:

- Identification: I am a user of the system.

- Authentication: I can prove I'm a user of the system.

- Authorization: Here's what I can do with the system.

- Accountability: You can track and monitor my use of the system.

Identification Identification is a mechanism whereby unverified or unauthenticated entities who seek access to a resource provide a label by which they are known to the system. This label is called an identifier (ID), and it must be mapped to one and only one entity within the security domain. Sometimes the unauthenticated entity supplies the label, and sometimes it is applied to the entity. Some organizations use composite identifiers by concatenating elements—department codes, random numbers, or special characters—to make unique identifiers within the security domain. Other organizations generate random IDs to protect resources from potential attackers. Most organizations use a single piece of unique information, such as a complete name or the user's first initial and surname.

Authentication Authentication is the process of validating an unauthenticated entity's purported identity. There are three widely used authentication mechanisms, or **authentication factors**:

- Something you know
- Something you have
- Something you are

Something You Know This factor of authentication relies on what the unverified user or system knows and can recall—for example, a password, passphrase, or other unique authentication code, such as a personal identification number (PIN). A **password** is a private word or combination of characters that only the user should know. One of the biggest debates in the information security industry concerns the complexity of passwords. On one hand, a password should be difficult to guess, which means it cannot be a series of letters or a word that is easily associated with the user, such as the name of the user's spouse, child, or pet. By the same token, a password should not be a series of numbers easily associated with the user, such as a phone number, Social Security number, or birth date. On the other hand, the password must be easy for the user to remember, which means it should be short or easily associated with something the user can remember.

A **passphrase** is a series of characters that is typically longer than a password and can be used to derive a **virtual password**. By using the words of the passphrase as cues to create a stream of unique characters, you can create a longer, stronger password that is easy to remember. For example, while a typical password might be "23skedoo," a typical passphrase might be "MayTheForceBeWithYouAlways," represented as the virtual password "MTFBWYA."

Users increasingly employ longer passwords or passphrases to provide effective security, as discussed in Chapter 2 and illustrated in Table 2-3. As a result, it is becoming increasingly difficult to track the multitude of system usernames and passwords needed to access information for a typical business or personal transaction. The credit reporting service Experian found that the average user has 26 online accounts, but uses only five different passwords. For users between the ages of 25 and 34, the average number of accounts jumps to 40.[2] A common method of keeping up with so many passwords is to write them down, which is a cardinal sin in information security. A better solution is automated password-tracking storage, like the application shown in Figure 6-3. This example shows a mobile application that can be synchronized across multiple platforms, including Apple IOS, Android, Windows, Macintosh, and Linux, to manage access control information in all its forms.

Something You Have This authentication factor relies on something an unverified user or system has and can produce when necessary. One example is **dumb cards**, such as ID cards or ATM cards with magnetic stripes that contain the digital (and often encrypted) user PIN, which is compared against the number the user enters. The **smart card** contains a computer chip that can verify and validate several pieces of information instead of just a PIN. Another common device is the token—a card or key fob with a computer chip and a liquid crystal display that shows a computer-generated number used to support remote login authentication.

Tokens are synchronous or asynchronous. Once **synchronous tokens** are synchronized with a server, both the server and token use the same time or a time-based database to generate a number that must be entered during the user login phase. **Asynchronous tokens** don't require that the server and tokens maintain the same time setting. Instead, they use a

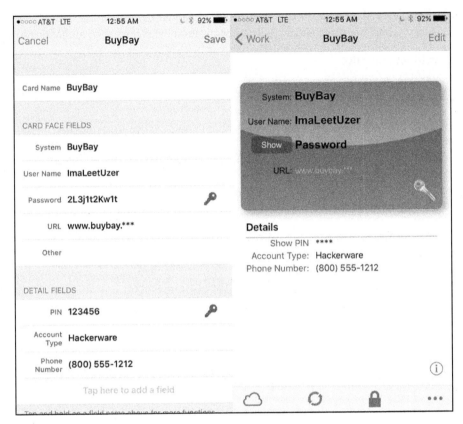

Figure 6-3 eWallet

Source: Ilium Software.

challenge/response system, in which the server challenges the unauthenticated entity during login with a numerical sequence. The unauthenticated entity places this sequence into the token and receives a response. The prospective user then enters the response into the system to gain access. Some examples of synchronous and asynchronous tokens are presented in Figure 6-4.

Something You Are or Can Produce This authentication factor relies on individual characteristics, such as fingerprints, palm prints, hand topography, hand geometry, or retina and iris scans, or something an unverified user can produce on demand, such as voice patterns, signatures, or keyboard kinetic measurements. Some of these characteristics are known collectively as biometrics, which is covered later in this chapter.

Note that certain critical logical or physical areas may require the use of **strong authentication**— at least two authentication mechanisms drawn from two different factors of authentication, most often something you have and something you know. For example, access to a bank's ATM services requires a banking card plus a PIN. Such systems are called two-factor authentication because two separate mechanisms are used. Strong authentication requires that at least one of the mechanisms be something other than what you know.

Figure 6-4 Access control tokens

Source: RSA.

Authorization Authorization is the matching of an authenticated entity to a list of information assets and corresponding access levels. This list is usually an ACL or **access control matrix**.

In general, authorization can be handled in one of three ways:

- Authorization for each authenticated user, in which the system performs an authentication process to verify each entity and then grants access to resources for only that entity. This process quickly becomes complex and resource-intensive in a computer system.
- Authorization for members of a group, in which the system matches authenticated entities to a list of group memberships and then grants access to resources based on the group's access rights. This is the most common authorization method.
- Authorization across multiple systems, in which a central authentication and authorization system verifies an entity's identity and grants it a set of credentials.

Authorization credentials, which are also called authorization tickets, are issued by an authenticator and are honored by many or all systems within the authentication domain. Sometimes called single sign-on (SSO) or reduced sign-on, authorization credentials are becoming more common and are frequently enabled using a shared directory structure such as the Lightweight Directory Access Protocol (LDAP).

Accountability Accountability, also known as **auditability**, ensures that all actions on a system—authorized or unauthorized—can be attributed to an authenticated identity. Accountability is most often accomplished by means of system logs, database journals, and the auditing of these records.

Systems logs record specific information, such as failed access attempts and systems modifications. Logs have many uses, such as intrusion detection, determining the root cause of a system failure, or simply tracking the use of a particular resource.

⟩ Biometrics

> ### Key Terms
>
> **biometric access control** The use of physiological characteristics to provide authentication for a provided identification. Biometric means "life measurement" in Greek. Sometimes referred to as *biometrics*.
>
> **crossover error rate (CER)** Also called the equal error rate, the point at which the rate of false rejections equals the rate of false acceptances.
>
> **false accept rate** The rate at which fraudulent users or nonusers are allowed access to systems or areas as a result of a failure in the biometric device. This failure is also known as a Type II error or a false positive.
>
> **false reject rate** The rate at which authentic users are denied or prevented access to authorized areas as a result of a failure in the biometric device. This failure is also known as a Type I error or a false negative.
>
> **minutiae** In biometric access controls, unique points of reference that are digitized and stored in an encrypted format when the user's system access credentials are created.

Biometric access control relies on recognition—the same thing you rely on to identify friends, family, and other people you know. The use of biometric-based authentication is expected to have a significant impact in the future as technical and ethical issues are resolved with the technology.

Biometric authentication technologies include the following:

- Fingerprint comparison of the unauthenticated person's actual fingerprint to a stored fingerprint
- Palm print comparison of the unauthenticated person's actual palm print to a stored palm print
- Hand geometry comparison of the unauthenticated person's actual hand to a stored measurement
- Facial recognition using a photographic ID card, in which a human security guard compares the unauthenticated person's face to a photo
- Facial recognition using a digital camera, in which an unauthenticated person's face is compared to a stored image
- Retinal print comparison of the unauthenticated person's actual retina to a stored image
- Iris pattern comparison of the unauthenticated person's actual iris to a stored image

Among all possible biometrics, only three human characteristics are usually considered truly unique:

- Fingerprints
- Retina of the eye (blood vessel pattern)

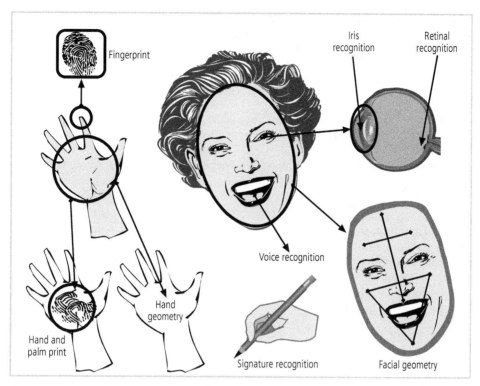

Figure 6-5 Biometric recognition characteristics

- Iris of the eye (random pattern of features found in the iris, including freckles, pits, striations, vasculature, coronas, and crypts)

Figure 6-5 depicts some of these human recognition characteristics.

Most of the technologies that scan human characteristics convert these images to some form of **minutiae**. Each subsequent access attempt results in a measurement that is compared with an encoded value to verify the user's identity. A problem with this method is that some human characteristics can change over time due to normal development, injury, or illness, which means that system designers must create fallback or failsafe authentication mechanisms.

Signature and voice recognition technologies are also considered to be biometric access control measures. Signature recognition has become commonplace; retail stores use it, or at least signature capture, for authentication during a purchase. The customer signs a digital pad with a special stylus that captures the signature. The signature is digitized and either saved for future reference or compared with a signature in a database for validation. Currently, the technology for signature capturing is much more widely accepted than that for signature comparison because signatures change due to several factors, including age, fatigue, and the speed with which the signature is written.

Voice recognition works in a similar fashion; the system captures and stores an initial voiceprint of the user reciting a phrase. Later, when the user attempts to access the system, the authentication process requires the user to speak the same phrase so that the technology can compare the current voiceprint against the stored value.

Effectiveness of Biometrics Biometric technologies are evaluated on three basic criteria: the false reject rate, which is the percentage of authorized users who are denied access; the false accept rate, which is the percentage of unauthorized users who are granted access; and the crossover error rate, the level at which the number of false rejections equals the false acceptances.

The **false reject rate** describes the number of legitimate users who are denied access because of a failure in the biometric device. This failure is known as a Type I error. While a nuisance to unauthenticated people who are authorized users, this error rate is probably of little concern to security professionals because rejection of an authorized user represents no threat to security. Therefore, the false reject rate is often ignored unless it reaches a level high enough to generate complaints from irritated unauthenticated people. For example, most people have experienced the frustration of having a credit card or ATM card fail to perform because of problems with the magnetic strip. In the field of biometrics, similar problems can occur when a system fails to pick up the various information points it uses to authenticate a prospective user properly.

The **false accept rate** conversely describes the number of unauthorized users who somehow are granted access to a restricted system or area, usually because of a failure in the biometric device. This failure is known as a Type II error and is unacceptable to security professionals.

The **crossover error rate (CER)**, the point at which false reject and false accept rates intersect, is possibly the most common and important overall measure of accuracy for a biometric system. Most biometric systems can be adjusted to compensate both for false positive and false negative errors. Adjustment to one extreme creates a system that requires perfect matches and results in a high rate of false rejects, but almost no false accepts. Adjustment to the other extreme produces a low rate of false rejects, but excessive false accepts. The trick is to find the balance between providing the requisite level of security and minimizing the frustrations of authentic users. Thus, the optimal setting is somewhere near the point at which the two error rates are equal—the CER. CERs are used to compare various biometrics and may vary by manufacturer. If a biometric device provides a CER of 1 percent, its failure rates for false rejections and false acceptance are both 1 percent. A device with a CER of 1 percent is considered superior to a device with a CER of 5 percent.

Acceptability of Biometrics As you've learned, a balance must be struck between a security system's acceptability to users and how effective it is in maintaining security. Many biometric systems that are highly reliable and effective are considered intrusive by users. As a result, many information security professionals don't implement these systems, in an effort to avoid confrontation and possible user boycott of the biometric controls. Table 6-1 shows how certain biometrics rank in terms of effectiveness and acceptance. Interestingly, the orders of effectiveness and acceptance are almost exactly opposite.

 For more information on using biometrics for identification and authentication, read NIST SP 800-76-1 and SP 800-76-2 at http://csrc.nist.gov/publications/PubsSPs.html.

Biometrics	Universality	Uniqueness	Permanence	Collectability	Performance	Acceptability	Circumvention
Face	H	L	M	H	L	H	L
Facial Thermogram	H	H	L	H	M	H	H
Fingerprint	M	H	H	M	H	M	H
Hand Geometry	M	M	M	H	M	M	M
Hand Vein	M	M	M	M	M	M	H
Eye: Iris	H	H	H	M	H	H	H
Eye: Retina	H	H	M	L	H	L	H
DNA	H	H	H	L	H	L	L
Odor & Scent	H	H	H	L	L	M	L
Voice	M	L	L	M	L	H	L
Signature	L	L	L	H	L	H	L
Keystroke	L	L	L	M	L	M	M
Gait	M	L	L	H	L	H	M

Table 6-1 **Ranking of Biometric Effectiveness and Acceptance**

Note: In the table, H = High, M = Medium, and L = Low.

From multiple sources.[3]

❯ Access Control Architecture Models

> ### Key Terms
>
> **covert channels** Unauthorized or unintended methods of communications hidden inside a computer system.
>
> **reference monitor** Within TCB, a conceptual piece of the system that manages access controls—in other words, it mediates all access to objects by subjects.
>
> **storage channels** TCSEC-defined covert channels that communicate by modifying a stored object, such as in steganography.
>
> **timing channels** TCSEC-defined covert channels that communicate by managing the relative timing of events.
>
> **trusted computing base (TCB)** Under the Trusted Computer System Evaluation Criteria (TCSEC), the combination of all hardware, firmware, and software responsible for enforcing the security policy.

Security access control architecture models, which are often referred to simply as architecture models, illustrate access control implementations and can help organizations quickly make improvements through adaptation. Formal models do not usually find their way directly into usable implementations; instead, they form the theoretical foundation that an implementation uses. These formal models are discussed here so you can become familiar with them and see how they are used in various access control approaches. When a specific implementation is put into place, noting that it is based on a formal model may lend credibility, improve its reliability, and lead to improved results. Some models are implemented into computer hardware and software, some are implemented as policies and practices, and some are implemented in both. Some models focus on the confidentiality of information, while others focus on the information's integrity as it is being processed.

The first models discussed here—specifically, the trusted computing base, the Information Technology System Evaluation Criteria, and the Common Criteria—are used as evaluation models and to demonstrate the evolution of trusted system assessment, which include evaluations of access controls. The later models—Bell-LaPadula, Biba, and others—demonstrate implementations in some computer security systems to ensure that the confidentiality, integrity, and availability of information is protected by controlling the access of one part of a system on another.

TCSEC's Trusted Computing Base   The Trusted Computer System Evaluation Criteria (TCSEC) is an older DoD standard that defines the criteria for assessing the access controls in a computer system. This standard is part of a larger series of standards collectively referred to as the Rainbow Series because of the color coding used to uniquely identify each document (see Figure 6-6). TCSEC is also known as the "Orange Book" and is considered the cornerstone of the series. As described later in this chapter, this series was replaced in 2005 with a set of standards known as the Common Criteria, but information security

Figure 6-6 The TCSEC Rainbow Series

Source: Wikimedia Commons.[4]

professionals should be familiar with the terminology and concepts of this legacy approach. For example, TCSEC uses the concept of the **trusted computing base (TCB)** to enforce security policy. In this context, "security policy" refers to the rules of configuration for a system rather than a managerial guidance document. TCB is only as effective as its internal control mechanisms and the administration of the systems being configured. TCB is made up of the hardware and software that has been implemented to provide security for a particular information system. This usually includes the operating system kernel and a specified set of security utilities, such as the user login subsystem.

The term "trusted" can be misleading—in this context, it means that a component is part of TCB's security system, but not that it is necessarily trustworthy. The frequent discovery of flaws and delivery of patches by software vendors to remedy security vulnerabilities attest to the relative level of trust you can place in current generations of software.

Within TCB is an object known as the **reference monitor,** which is the piece of the system that manages access controls. Systems administrators must be able to audit or periodically review the reference monitor to ensure it is functioning effectively, without unauthorized modification.

One of the biggest challenges in TCB is the existence of **covert channels.** Covert channels could be used by attackers who seek to exfiltrate sensitive data without being detected. Data loss prevention technologies monitor standard and covert channels to attempt to reduce an attacker's ability to accomplish exfiltration. For example, the cryptographic technique known as steganography allows the embedding of data bits in the digital version of graphical images, allowing a user to hide a message in a picture. TCSEC defines two kinds of covert channels:

- **Storage channels,** which are used in steganography, as described above, and in the embedding of data in TCP or IP header fields. For more details on steganography, see Chapter 10.

- **Timing channels,** which are used in a system that places a long pause between packets to signify a 1 and a short pause between packets to signify a 0.

For more information on the Rainbow Series, visit http://csrc.nist.gov/publications/secpubs /rainbow/ or www.fas.org/irp/nsa/rainbow.htm.

ITSEC The Information Technology System Evaluation Criteria (ITSEC), an international set of criteria for evaluating computer systems, is very similar to TCSEC. Under ITSEC, Targets of Evaluation (ToE) are compared to detailed security function specifications, resulting in an assessment of systems functionality and comprehensive penetration testing. Like TCSEC, ITSEC was functionally replaced for the most part by the Common Criteria, which are described in the following section. The ITSEC rates products on a scale of E1 to the highest level of E6, much like the ratings of TCSEC and the Common Criteria. E1 is roughly equivalent to the EAL2 evaluation of the Common Criteria, and E6 is roughly equivalent to EAL7.

The Common Criteria The Common Criteria for Information Technology Security Evaluation, often called the Common Criteria or just CC, is an international standard

(ISO/IEC 15408) for computer security certification. It is widely considered the successor to both TCSEC and ITSEC in that it reconciles some differences between the various other standards. Most governments have discontinued their use of the other standards. CC is a combined effort of contributors from Australia, New Zealand, Canada, France, Germany, Japan, the Netherlands, Spain, the United Kingdom, and the United States. In the United States, the National Security Agency (NSA) and NIST were the primary contributors. CC and its companion, the Common Methodology for Information Technology Security Evaluation (CEM), are the technical basis for an international agreement called the Common Criteria Recognition Agreement (CCRA), which ensures that products can be evaluated to determine their particular security properties. CC seeks the widest possible mutual recognition of secure IT products.[5] The CC process assures that the specification, implementation, and evaluation of computer security products are performed in a rigorous and standard manner.[6]

CC terminology includes:

- Target of Evaluation (ToE): The system being evaluated
- Protection Profile (PP): User-generated specification for security requirements
- Security Target (ST): Document describing the ToE's security properties
- Security Functional Requirements (SFRs): Catalog of a product's security functions
- Evaluation Assurance Levels (EALs): The rating or grading of a ToE after evaluation

EAL is typically rated on the following scale:

- EAL1: Functionally Tested: Confidence in operation against nonserious threats
- EAL2: Structurally Tested: More confidence required but comparable with good business practices
- EAL3: Methodically Tested and Checked: Moderate level of security assurance
- EAL4: Methodically Designed, Tested, and Reviewed: Rigorous level of security assurance but still economically feasible without specialized development
- EAL5: Semiformally Designed and Tested: Certification requires specialized development above standard commercial products
- EAL6: Semiformally Verified Design and Tested: Specifically designed security ToE
- EAL7: Formally Verified Design and Tested: Developed for extremely high-risk situations or for high-value systems.[7]

For more information on the Common Criteria, visit www.niap-ccevs.org or www.common criteriaportal.org.

Bell-LaPadula Confidentiality Model

The Bell-LaPadula (BLP) confidentiality model is a "state machine reference model"—in other words, a model of an automated system that is able to manipulate its state or status over time. BLP ensures the confidentiality of the modeled system by using MACs, data classification, and security clearances. The intent of any state machine model is to devise a conceptual approach in which the system being modeled can always be in a known secure condition; in other words, this kind of model is provably secure. A system that serves as a reference monitor compares the level of data classification with the clearance of the entity requesting access; it allows access only if the clearance is equal to or higher than the classification. BLP security rules prevent information from being moved from a level of higher security to a lower level. Access modes can be one of two types: simple security and the * (star) property.

Simple security (also called the read property) prohibits a subject of lower clearance from reading an object of higher clearance, but it allows a subject with a higher clearance level to read an object at a lower level (read down).

The * property (the write property), on the other hand, prohibits a high-level subject from sending messages to a lower-level object. In short, subjects can read down and objects can write or append up. BLP uses access permission matrices and a security lattice for access control.[8]

This model can be explained by imagining a fictional interaction between General Bell, whose thoughts and actions are classified at the highest possible level, and Private LaPadula, who has the lowest security clearance in the military. It is prohibited for Private LaPadula to read anything written by General Bell and for General Bell to write in any document that Private LaPadula could read. In short, the principle is "no read up, no write down."

Biba Integrity Model The Biba integrity model is similar to BLP. It is based on the premise that higher levels of integrity are more worthy of trust than lower ones. The intent is to provide access controls to ensure that objects or subjects cannot have less integrity as a result of read/write operations. The Biba model assigns integrity levels to subjects and objects using two properties: the simple integrity (read) property and the integrity * property (write).

The simple integrity property permits a subject to have read access to an object only if the subject's security level is lower than or equal to the level of the object. The integrity * property permits a subject to have write access to an object only if the subject's security level is equal to or higher than that of the object.

The Biba model ensures that no information from a subject can be passed on to an object in a higher security level. This prevents contaminating data of higher integrity with data of lower integrity.[9]

This model can be illustrated by imagining fictional interactions among some priests, a monk named Biba, and some parishioners in the Middle Ages. Priests are considered holier (of greater integrity) than monks, who are in turn holier than parishioners. A priest cannot read (or offer) Masses or prayers written by Biba the Monk, who in turn cannot read items written by his parishioners. Biba the Monk is also prohibited from writing in a priest's sermon books, just as parishioners are prohibited from writing in Biba's book. These properties prevent the lower integrity of the lower level from corrupting the "holiness" or higher integrity of the upper level. On the other hand, higher-level entities can share their writings with the lower levels without compromising the integrity of the information. This example illustrates the "no write up, no read down" principle behind the Biba model.

Clark-Wilson Integrity Model The Clark-Wilson integrity model, which is built upon principles of change control rather than integrity levels, was designed for the commercial environment. The model's change control principles are:

- No changes by unauthorized subjects
- No unauthorized changes by authorized subjects
- The maintenance of internal and external consistency

Internal consistency means that the system does what it is expected to do every time, without exception. External consistency means that the data in the system is consistent with similar data in the outside world.

This model establishes a system of subject-program-object relationships so that the subject has no direct access to the object. Instead, the subject is required to access the object using a well-formed transaction via a validated program. The intent is to provide an environment where security can be proven through the use of separated activities, each of which is provably secure. The following controls are part of the Clark-Wilson model:

- Subject authentication and identification
- Access to objects by means of well-formed transactions
- Execution by subjects on a restricted set of programs

The elements of the Clark-Wilson model are:

- Constrained data item (CDI): Data item with protected integrity
- Unconstrained data item: Data not controlled by Clark-Wilson; nonvalidated input or any output
- Integrity verification procedure (IVP): Procedure that scans data and confirms its integrity
- Transformation procedure (TP): Procedure that only allows changes to a constrained data item

All subjects and objects are labeled with TPs. The TPs operate as the intermediate layer between subjects and objects. Each data item has a set of access operations that can be performed on it. Each subject is assigned a set of access operations that it can perform. The system then compares these two parameters and either permits or denies access by the subject to the object.[10] As an example, consider a database management system (DBMS) that sits between a database user and the actual data. The DBMS requires the user to be authenticated before accessing the data, only accepts specific inputs (such as SQL queries), and only provides a restricted set of operations, in accordance with its design. This example illustrates the Clark-Wilson model controls.

Graham-Denning Access Control Model The Graham-Denning access control model has three parts: a set of objects, a set of subjects, and a set of rights. The subjects are composed of two things: a process and a domain. The domain is the set of constraints that control how subjects may access objects. The set of rights governs how subjects may manipulate the passive objects. This model describes eight primitive protection rights, called commands, which subjects can execute to have an effect on other subjects or objects. Note that these commands are similar to the rights a user can assign to an entity in modern operating systems.[11]

The eight primitive protection rights are:

1. Create object
2. Create subject
3. Delete object
4. Delete subject
5. Read access right
6. Grant access right
7. Delete access right
8. Transfer access right

Harrison-Ruzzo-Ullman Model The Harrison-Ruzzo-Ullman (HRU) model defines a method to allow changes to access rights and the addition and removal of subjects and objects, a process that the Bell-LaPadula model does not allow. Because systems change over time, their protective states need to change. HRU is built on an access control matrix and includes a set of generic rights and a specific set of commands. These include:

- Create subject/create object
- Enter right X into
- Delete right X from
- Destroy subject/destroy object

By implementing this set of rights and commands and restricting the commands to a single operation each, it is possible to determine if and when a specific subject can obtain a particular right to an object.[12]

Brewer-Nash Model (Chinese Wall) The Brewer-Nash model, commonly known as a Chinese Wall, is designed to prevent a conflict of interest between two parties. Imagine that a law firm represents two people who are involved in a car accident. One sues the other, and the firm has to represent both. To prevent a conflict of interest, the individual attorneys should not be able to access the private information of these two litigants. The Brewer-Nash model requires users to select one of two conflicting sets of data, after which they cannot access the conflicting data.[13]

Firewalls

dynamic packet-filtering firewall A firewall type that can react to network traffic and create or modify configuration rules to adapt.

firewall In information security, a combination of hardware and software that filters or prevents specific information from moving between the outside network and the inside network.

packet-filtering firewall A networking device that examines the header information of data packets that come into a network and determines whether to drop them (deny) or forward them to the next network connection (allow), based on its configuration rules.

state table A tabular record of the state and context of each packet in a conversation between an internal and external user or system. A state table is used to expedite traffic filtering.

stateful packet inspection (SPI) firewall A firewall type that keeps track of each network connection between internal and external systems using a state table and that expedites the filtering of those communications. Also known as a stateful inspection firewall.

static packet-filtering firewall A firewall type that requires the configuration rules to be manually created, sequenced, and modified within the firewall.

trusted network The system of networks inside the organization that contains its information assets and is under the organization's control.

untrusted network The system of networks outside the organization over which the organization has no control. The Internet is an example of an untrusted network.

In commercial and residential construction, firewalls are concrete or masonry walls that run from the basement through the roof to prevent a fire from spreading from one section of the building to another. In aircraft and automobiles, a firewall is an insulated metal barrier that keeps the hot and dangerous moving parts of the motor separate from the flammable interior where the passengers sit. A **firewall** in an information security program is similar to a building's firewall in that it prevents specific types of information from moving between two different levels of networks, such as an **untrusted network** like the Internet and a **trusted network** like the organization's internal network. Some organizations place firewalls that have different levels of trust between portions of their network environment, often to add extra security for the most important applications and data. The firewall may be a separate computer system, a software service running on an existing router or server, or a separate network that contains several supporting devices. Firewalls can be categorized by processing mode, development era, or structure.

❯ Firewall Processing Modes

Firewalls fall into several major categories of processing modes: packet-filtering firewalls, application layer proxy firewalls, media access control layer firewalls, and hybrids.[14] Hybrid firewalls use a combination of the other modes; in practice, most firewalls fall into this category because most implementations use multiple approaches.

Packet-Filtering Firewalls The **packet-filtering firewall** examines the header information of data packets that come into a network. A packet-filtering firewall installed on a TCP/IP-based network typically functions at the IP layer and determines whether to deny (drop) a packet or allow (forward) it to the next network connection, based on the rules programmed into the firewall. Packet-filtering firewalls examine every incoming packet header and can selectively filter packets based on header information such as destination address, source address, packet type, and other key information. Figure 6-7 shows the structure of an IPv4 packet.

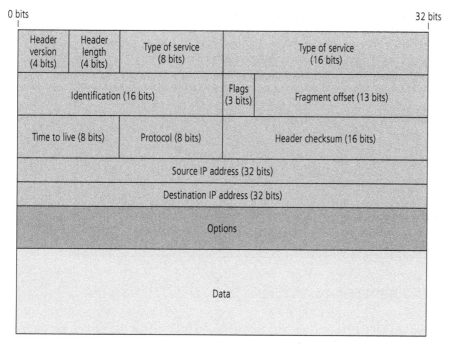

Figure 6-7 IP packet structure

Packet-filtering firewalls scan network data packets looking for compliance with the rules of the firewall's database or violations of those rules. Filtering firewalls inspect packets at the network layer, or Layer 3, of the Open Systems Interconnect (OSI) model, which represents the seven layers of networking processes. (The OSI model is illustrated later in this chapter in Figure 6-11.) If the device finds a packet that matches a restriction, it stops the packet from traveling from one network to another. The restrictions most commonly implemented in packet-filtering firewalls are based on a combination of the following:

- IP source and destination address
- Direction (inbound or outbound)
- Protocol, for firewalls capable of examining the IP protocol layer
- Transmission Control Protocol (TCP) or User Datagram Protocol (UDP) source and destination port requests, for firewalls capable of examining the TCP/UPD layer

Packet structure varies depending on the nature of the packet. The two primary service types are TCP and UDP, as noted above. Figures 6-8 and 6-9 show the structures of these two major elements of the combined protocol known as TCP/IP.

Simple firewall models examine two aspects of the packet header: the destination and source address. They enforce address restrictions through ACLs, which are created and modified by the firewall administrators. Figure 6-10 shows how a packet-filtering router can be used as a firewall to filter data packets from inbound connections and allow outbound connections

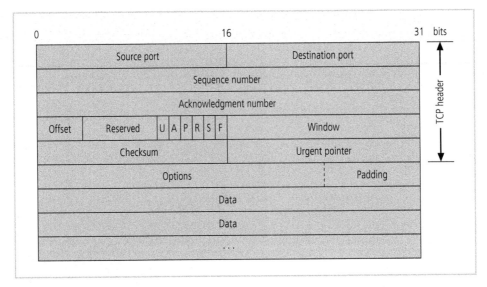

Figure 6-8 TCP packet structure

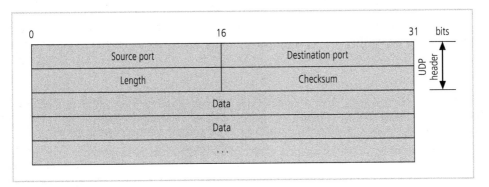

Figure 6-9 UDP datagram structure

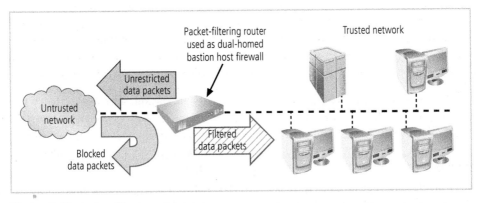

Figure 6-10 Packet-filtering router

Source Address	Destination Address	Service (e.g., HTTP, SMTP, FTP)	Action (Allow or Deny)
172.16.x.x	10.10.x.x	Any	Deny
192.168.x.x	10.10.10.25	HTTP	Allow
192.168.0.1	10.10.10.10	FTP	Allow

Table 6-2 Sample Firewall Rule and Format

unrestricted access to the public network. Dual-homed bastion host firewalls are discussed later in this chapter.

To better understand an address restriction scheme, consider an example. If an administrator configured a simple rule based on the content of Table 6-2, any connection attempt made by an external computer or network device in the 192.168.x.x address range (192.168.0.0–192.168.255.255) to the Web server at 10.10.10.25 would be allowed. The ability to restrict a specific service rather than just a range of IP addresses is available in a more advanced version of this first-generation firewall. Additional details on firewall rules and configuration are presented later in this chapter.

The ability to restrict a specific service is now considered standard in most routers and is invisible to the user. Unfortunately, such systems are unable to detect whether packet headers have been modified, which is an advanced technique used in IP spoofing attacks and other attacks.

The three subsets of packet-filtering firewalls are **static packet filtering, dynamic packet filtering,** and **stateful packet inspection (SPI)**. They enforce **address restrictions,** rules designed to prohibit packets with certain addresses or partial addresses from passing through the device. Static packet filtering requires that the filtering rules be developed and installed with the firewall. The rules are created and sequenced by a person who either directly edits the rule set or uses a programmable interface to specify the rules and the sequence. Any changes to the rules require human intervention. This type of filtering is common in network routers and gateways.

A dynamic packet-filtering firewall can react to an emergent event and update or create rules to deal with that event. This reaction could be positive, as in allowing an internal user to engage in a specific activity upon request, or negative, as in dropping all packets from a particular address when an increased presence of a particular type of malformed packet is detected. While static packet-filtering firewalls allow entire sets of one type of packet to enter in response to authorized requests, dynamic packet filtering allows only a particular packet with a particular source, destination, and port address to enter. This filtering works by opening and closing "doors" in the firewall based on the information contained in the packet header, which makes dynamic packet filters an intermediate form between traditional static packet filters and application proxies. (These proxies are described in the next section.)

SPI firewalls, also called stateful inspection firewalls, keep track of each network connection between internal and external systems using a **state table**. A state table tracks the state and context of each packet in the conversation by recording which station sent what packet and when. Like first-generation firewalls, stateful inspection firewalls perform packet filtering, but they take it a step further. Whereas simple packet-filtering firewalls only allow or deny certain packets based on their address, a stateful firewall can expedite incoming packets that are responses to internal requests. If the stateful firewall receives an incoming packet that it cannot match in its state table, it refers to its ACL to determine whether to allow the packet to pass.

The primary disadvantage of this type of firewall is the additional processing required to manage and verify packets against the state table. Without this processing, the system is vulnerable to a DoS or DDoS attack. In such an attack, the system receives a large number of external packets, which slows the firewall because it attempts to compare all of the incoming packets first to the state table and then to the ACL. On the positive side, these firewalls can track connectionless packet traffic, such as UDP and remote procedure calls (RPC) traffic. Dynamic SPI firewalls keep a dynamic state table to make changes to the filtering rules within predefined limits, based on events as they happen.

A state table looks like a firewall rule set but has additional information, as shown in Table 6-3. The state table contains the familiar columns for source IP, source port, destination IP, and destination port, but it adds information for the protocol used (UDP or TCP), total time in seconds, and time remaining in seconds. Many state table implementations allow a connection to remain in place for up to 60 minutes without any activity before the state entry is deleted. The example in Table 6-3 shows this value in the Total Time column. The Time Remaining column shows a countdown of the time left until the entry is deleted.

Source Address	Source Port	Destination Address	Destination Port	Time Remaining (in seconds)	Total Time (in seconds)	Protocol
192.168.2.5	1028	10.10.10.7	80	2,725	3,600	TCP

Table 6-3 State Table Entries

Application Layer Proxy Firewalls

Key Terms

application firewall See *application layer proxy firewall*.

application layer proxy firewall A device capable of functioning both as a firewall and an application layer proxy server.

demilitarized zone (DMZ) An intermediate area between two networks designed to provide servers and firewall filtering between a trusted internal network and the outside, untrusted network. Traffic on the outside network carries a higher level of risk.

proxy server A server that exists to intercept requests for information from external users and provide the requested information by retrieving it from an internal server, thus protecting and minimizing the demand on internal servers. Some proxy servers are also cache servers.

reverse proxy A proxy server that most commonly retrieves information from inside an organization and provides it to a requesting user or system outside the organization.

The **application layer proxy firewall**, also known as an **application firewall**, is frequently installed on a dedicated computer separate from the filtering router, but it is commonly used in conjunction with a filtering router. The application firewall is also known as a **proxy server** (or **reverse proxy**) because it can be configured to run special software that acts as a proxy for a service request. For example, an organization that runs a Web server can avoid exposing it to direct user traffic by installing a proxy server configured with the registered domain's URL. This proxy server receives requests for Web pages, accesses the Web server on behalf of the external client, and returns the requested pages to the users. These servers can store the most recently accessed pages in their internal cache, and are thus also called *cache servers*. The benefits from this type of implementation are significant. For one, the proxy server is placed in an unsecured area of the network or in the **demilitarized zone (DMZ)** so that it is exposed to the higher levels of risk from less trusted networks, rather than exposing the Web server to such risks. Additional filtering routers can be implemented behind the proxy server, limiting access to the more secure internal system and providing further protection.

The primary disadvantage of application layer proxy firewalls is that they are designed for one or a few specific protocols and cannot easily be reconfigured to protect against attacks on other protocols. Because these firewalls work at the application layer by definition, they are typically restricted to a single application, such as FTP, Telnet, HTTP, SMTP, or SNMP. The processing time and resources necessary to read each packet down to the application layer diminishes the ability of these firewalls to handle multiple types of applications.

Media Access Control Layer Firewalls

> **Key Term**
>
> **media access control layer firewall** A firewall designed to operate at the media access control sublayer of the network's data link layer (Layer 2).

While not as well known or widely referenced as the firewall approaches described in the previous sections, **media access control layer firewalls** make filtering decisions based on the specific host computer's identity, as represented by its media access control (MAC) or network interface card (NIC) address, which operates at the data link layer of the OSI model or the subnet layer of the TCP/IP model. Thus, media access control layer firewalls link the addresses of specific host computers to ACL entries that identify the specific types of packets that can be sent to each host, and block all other traffic. While media access control layer firewalls are also referred to as MAC layer firewalls, we don't do so here to avoid confusion with mandatory access controls (MACs).

Figure 6-11 shows where each of the firewall processing modes inspects data in the OSI model.

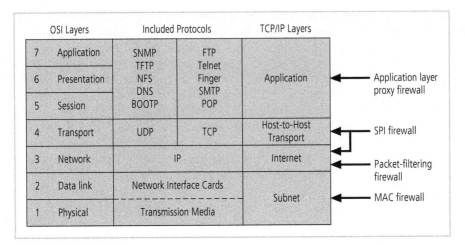

Figure 6-11 Firewall types and protocol models

Hybrid Firewalls

Hybrid firewalls combine the elements of other types of firewalls—that is, the elements of packet filtering, application layer proxy, and media access control layer firewalls. A hybrid firewall system may actually consist of two separate firewall devices; each is a separate firewall system, but they are connected so that they work in tandem. For example, a hybrid firewall system might include a packet-filtering firewall that is set up to screen all acceptable requests, then pass the requests to a proxy server, which in turn requests services from a Web server deep inside the organization's networks. An added advantage to the hybrid firewall approach is that it enables an organization to make a security improvement without completely replacing its existing firewalls.

The most recent generations of firewalls aren't really new; they are hybrids built from capabilities of modern networking equipment that can perform a variety of tasks according to the organization's needs. The first type of hybrid firewall is known as **Unified Threat Management (UTM)**. These devices are categorized by their ability to perform the work of an SPI firewall, network intrusion detection and prevention system, content filter, spam filter, and malware scanner and filter. UTM systems take advantage of increasing memory capacity and processor capability and can reduce the complexity associated with deploying, configuring, and integrating multiple networking devices. With the proper configuration, these devices are even able to "drill down" into the protocol layers and examine application-specific data, encrypted data, compressed data, and encoded data. The primary disadvantage of UTM systems is the creation of a single point of failure if the device has technical problems.

The second type of hybrid firewall is known as the **Next Generation Firewall** (**NextGen** or **NGFW**). Similar to UTM devices, NextGen firewalls combine traditional firewall functions with other network security functions, such as deep packet inspection, IDPSs, and the ability to decrypt encrypted traffic. The functions are so similar to those of UTM devices that the difference may lie only in the vendor's description. According to Kevin Beaver of Principle Logic, LLC, the only difference may be one of scope: "Unified Threat Management systems do a good job at a lot of things, while Next Generation Firewalls do an excellent job at just a handful of things."[15] Again, careful review of the solution's capabilities against the organization's needs will facilitate selection of the best equipment. Organizations with tight budgets may benefit from "all-in-one" devices, while larger organizations with more staff and funding may prefer separate devices that can be managed independently and function more efficiently on their own platforms.

OFFLINE

Residential Versus Commercial Firewalls

When selecting a firewall, size does matter. CPU size and capability, memory, and drive space are system factors that need to be scaled depending on the amount of traffic that will be processed by the firewall device. The most common categories of firewalls are commercial-grade and small office/home office (SOHO). SOHO devices are also known as residential-grade firewalls; they may consist of software on the user's computer or a stand-alone device that is often incorporated into the Internet connection appliance from the Internet service provider (ISP).

Most commercial-grade firewalls are dedicated *appliances*. Specifically, they are stand-alone units running on fully customized computing platforms that provide both the physical network connection and firmware programming necessary to perform their function, which might be static packet filtering, application proxy services, or some other task. Some firewall appliances use highly customized, sometimes proprietary hardware systems that are developed exclusively as firewall devices. Other commercial firewall systems are actually off-the-shelf, general-purpose computer systems that run custom application software on standard operating systems like Windows, Linux, UNIX, or specialized variants of these operating systems. Most SOHO firewalls are either simplified, dedicated appliances running on computing devices or application software installed directly on the user's computer.

Some vendors create significantly different hardware platforms that run virtually the same software. This allows both the commercial and SOHO appliances to use the same operating systems and/or management software, and thus simplify the

(continues)

implementations. Other vendors tend to specialize in a particular market, as commercial appliances usually need much more sophisticated software and SOHO appliances need more simplified approaches. Cisco's Adaptive Security Appliance (ASA) has versions ranging from the SOHO-level 5505 to much larger appliances, such as 5515, 5525, and 5535. All of these devices use the same Adaptive Security Device Manager, as shown in Figures 6-12 and 6-13.

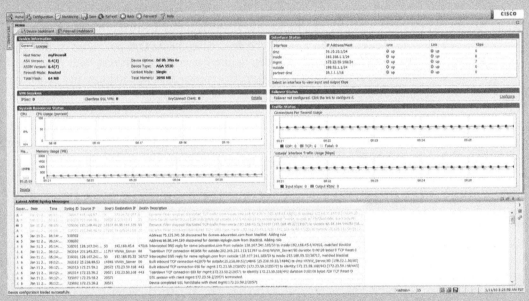

Figure 6-12 Cisco's Adaptive Security Device Manager device dashboard

Source: Cisco.

As more small businesses and residences obtain fast Internet connections with digital subscriber lines (DSL) or cable modem connections, they become increasingly vulnerable to attacks. What many small business and work-from-home users don't realize is that these high-speed services are always on; therefore, the computers connected to them are likely to be visible to the scans performed by attackers. One of the most effective methods of improving computing security in the residential setting is by using a SOHO-grade firewall that has the power and versatility of a commercial-grade appliance, but much simpler management software.

Many of these firewalls provide more than simple NAT services. As illustrated in Figures 6-14 and 6-15, some SOHO/residential firewalls include packet filtering, port filtering, and simple intrusion detection systems, and some can even restrict access to specific MAC addresses. Users may be able to configure port forwarding and enable outside users to access specific TCP or UDP ports on particular computers on the protected network.

Figure 6-13 Cisco's Adaptive Security Device Manager firewall dashboard

Source: Cisco.

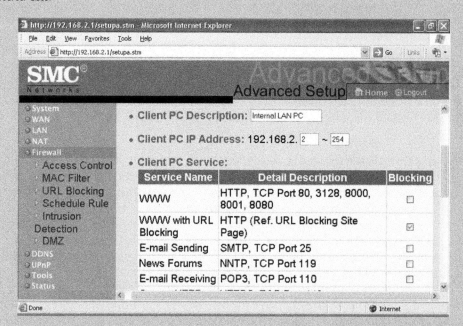

Figure 6-14 Barricade firewall screen

Source: SMC Barricade.

(continues)

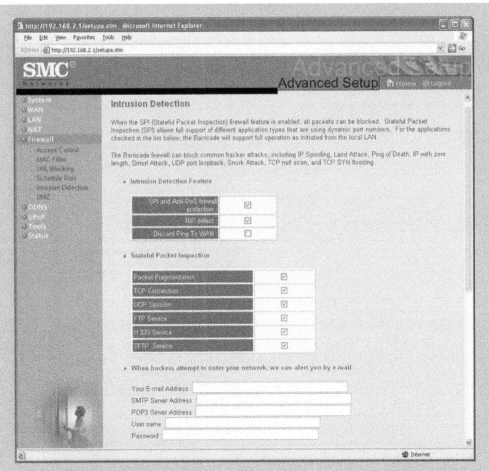

Figure 6-15 Barricade firewall/intrusion detection screen

Source: SMC Barricade.

Which type of firewall should the residential user implement? Many users swear by their software firewalls, and personal experience will produce a variety of opinionated perspectives. Ask yourself this question: *Where* would you rather defend against the attacker? The software option allows the hacker inside your computer to battle a piece of software that is often free and may not be correctly installed, configured, patched, upgraded, or designed. If the software happens to have a known vulnerability, the attacker could bypass it and then have unrestricted access to your system. With a hardware firewall, even if the attacker manages to crash the firewall system, your computer and information are still safe behind the now disabled connection. The hardware firewall's use of nonroutable addresses further extends the protection, making it virtually impossible for the attacker to reach your information. A former student of one of this book's authors responded to this debate by installing a hardware firewall and then visiting a hacker chat room. He challenged the group to penetrate his system. A few days later, he received an e-mail from a hacker who claimed to have accessed his system. The hacker included a graphic of a screen showing a C:\ prompt, which he claimed was from the student's system. After doing a bit of research, the student found out that the firewall had an image stored in firmware that was designed to distract attackers. The image displayed a command window with a DOS prompt. The hardware (NAT) solution had withstood the challenge.

 For reviews of firewall software, visit http://reviews.cnet.com. To download firewall software, visit http://download.cnet.com.

〉 Firewall Architectures

Key Terms

bastion host A device placed between an external, untrusted network and an internal, trusted network. Also known as a *sacrificial host*, a bastion host serves as the sole target for attack and should therefore be thoroughly secured.

extranet A segment of the DMZ where additional authentication and authorization controls are put into place to provide services that are not available to the general public.

Network Address Translation (NAT) A technology in which multiple real, routable external IP addresses are converted to special ranges of internal IP addresses, usually on a one-to-one basis; that is, one external valid address directly maps to one assigned internal address.

Port Address Translation (PAT) A technology in which multiple real, routable external IP addresses are converted to special ranges of internal IP addresses, usually on a one-to-many basis; that is, one external valid address is mapped dynamically to a range of internal addresses by adding a unique port number to the address when traffic leaves the private network and is placed on the public network.

sacrificial host See *bastion host*.

screened host architecture A firewall architectural model that combines the packet filtering router with a second, dedicated device such as a proxy server or proxy firewall.

screened subnet architecture A firewall architectural model that consists of one or more internal bastion hosts located behind a packet filtering router on a dedicated network segment, with each host performing a role in protecting the trusted network.

single bastion host See *bastion host*.

The value of a firewall comes from its ability to filter out unwanted or dangerous traffic as it enters the network perimeter of an organization. A challenge to the value proposition offered by firewalls is the changing nature of the way networks are used. As organizations implement cloud-based IT solutions, bring your own device (BYOD) options for employees, and other emerging network solutions, the network perimeter may be dissolving for them. One reaction is the use of a software-defined perimeter that uses secure VPN technology to deliver network connectivity only to verified devices, regardless of location. Regardless of the approach companies take to meet these challenges, they will often make use of expertise from other companies that offer managed security services (MSS). These companies assist their clients with highly available monitoring services from secure network operations centers (NOCs). Many companies still rely on the defined network perimeter as their first line of network security defense.

All firewall devices can be configured in several network connection architectures. These approaches are sometimes mutually exclusive, but sometimes they can be combined. The configuration that works best for a particular organization depends on three factors: the objectives of the network, the organization's ability to develop and implement the architectures, and the budget available for the function. Although hundreds of variations exist, three architectural implementations of firewalls are especially common: single bastion hosts, screened host firewalls, and screened subnet firewalls.

Single Bastion Hosts
The next option in firewall architecture is a single firewall that provides protection behind the organization's router. As you saw in Figure 6-10 earlier, the **single bastion host** architecture can be implemented as a packet filtering router, or it could be a firewall behind a router that is not configured for packet filtering. Any system, router, or firewall that is exposed to the untrusted network can be referred to as a **bastion host**. The bastion host is sometimes referred to as a **sacrificial host** because it stands alone on the network perimeter. This architecture is simply defined as the presence of a single protection device on the network perimeter. It is commonplace in residential SOHO environments. Larger organizations typically look to implement architectures with more defense in depth, with additional security devices designed to provide a more robust defense strategy.

The bastion host is usually implemented as a *dual-homed host* because it contains two network interfaces: one that is connected to the external network and one that is connected to the internal network. All traffic must go through the device to move between the internal and external networks. Such an architecture lacks defense in depth, and the complexity of the ACLs used to filter the packets can grow and degrade network performance. An attacker who infiltrates the bastion host can discover the configuration of internal networks and possibly provide external sources with internal information.

Implementation of the bastion host architecture often makes use of **Network Address Translation (NAT)**. RFC 2663 uses the term *network address and port translation (NAPT)* to describe both NAT and Port Address Translation (PAT), which is described later in this section. NAT is a method of mapping valid, external IP addresses to special ranges of nonroutable internal IP addresses, known as private IPv4 addresses, to create another barrier to intrusion from external attackers. In IPv6 addressing, these addresses are referred to as *Unique Local Addresses (ULA)*, as defined by RFC 4193. The internal addresses used by NAT consist of three different ranges. Organizations that need a large group of addresses for internal use will use the private IP address ranges reserved for nonpublic networks, as shown in Table 6-4. Messages sent with internal addresses within these three reserved ranges cannot be routed externally, so if a computer with one of these internal-use addresses is directly connected to the external network and avoids the NAT server, its traffic cannot be routed on the public network. Taking advantage of this, NAT prevents external attacks from reaching internal machines with addresses in specified ranges. If the NAT server is a multi-homed bastion host, it translates between the true, external IP addresses assigned to the organization by public network naming authorities and the internally assigned, nonroutable IP addresses. NAT translates by dynamically assigning addresses to internal

Classful Description	Usable Addresses	From	To	CIDR Mask	Decimal Mask
Class A or 24 Bit	~16.5 million	10.0.0.0	10.255.255.255	/8	255.0.0.0
Class B or 20 Bit	~1.05 million	172.16.0.0	172.31.255.255	/12 or /16	255.240.0.0 or 255.255.0.0
Class C or 16 Bit	~65,500	192.168.0.0	192.168.255.255	/16 or /24	255.255.0.0 or 255.255.255.0
IPv6 Space	~65,500 sets of 18.45 quintillion (18.45 × 10^18)	fc00::/7, where the first 7 digits are fixed (1111 110x), followed by a 10-digit organization ID, then 4 digits of subnet ID and 16 digits of host ID. ([F][C or D]xx:xxxx:xxxx:yyyy:zzzz:zzzz:zzzz:zzzz).			

Table 6-4   Reserved Nonroutable Address Ranges

Note that CIDR stands for classless inter-domain routing.

Source: Internet Engineering Task Force, RFC 1466 (http://tools.ietf.org/html/rfc1466).

6

communications and tracking the conversations with sessions to determine which incoming message is a response to which outgoing traffic.

A variation on NAT is **Port Address Translation (PAT)**. Where NAT performs a one-to-one mapping between assigned external IP addresses and internal private addresses, PAT performs a one-to-many assignment that allows the mapping of many internal hosts to a single assigned external IP address. The system is able to maintain the integrity of each communication by assigning a unique port number to the external IP address and mapping the address + port combination (known as a socket) to the internal IP address. Multiple communications from a single internal address would have a unique matching of the internal IP address + port to the external IP address + port, with unique port addresses for each communication. Figure 6-16 shows an example configuration of a dual-homed firewall that uses NAT to protect the internal network.

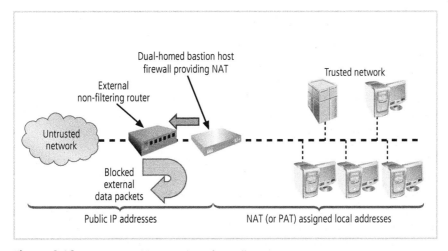

Figure 6-16   Dual-homed bastion host firewall

Screened Host Architecture A screened host architecture combines the packet-filtering router with a separate, dedicated firewall, such as an application proxy server, which retrieves information on behalf of other system users and often caches copies of Web pages and other needed information on its internal drives to speed up access. This approach allows the router to prescreen packets to minimize the network traffic and load on the internal proxy. The application proxy examines an application layer protocol, such as HTTP, and performs the proxy services. Because an application proxy may retain working copies of some Web documents to improve performance, unanticipated losses can result if it is compromised and the documents were not designed for general access. As such, the screened host firewall may present a promising target because compromise of the bastion host can lead to attacks on the proxy server that could disclose the configuration of internal networks and possibly provide attackers with internal information. To its advantage, this configuration requires the external attack to compromise two separate systems before the attack can access internal data. In this way, the bastion host protects the data more fully than the router alone. Figure 6-17 shows a typical configuration of a screened host architecture.

Screened Subnet Architecture (with DMZ) The dominant architecture today is the screened subnet used with a DMZ. The DMZ can be a dedicated port on the firewall device linking a single bastion host, or it can be connected to a screened subnet, as shown in Figure 6-18. Until recently, servers that provided services through an untrusted network were commonly placed in the DMZ. Examples include Web servers, file transfer protocol (FTP) servers, and certain database servers. More recent strategies using proxy servers have provided much more secure solutions.

A common arrangement is a subnet firewall that consists of two or more internal bastion hosts behind a packet-filtering router, with each host protecting the trusted network. There are many variants of the screened subnet architecture. The first general model consists of

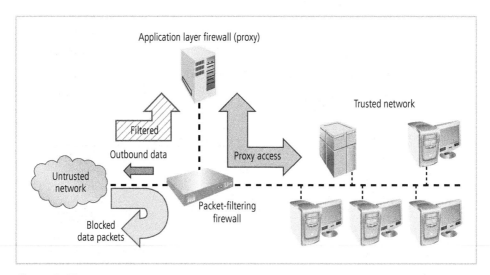

Figure 6-17 Screened host architecture

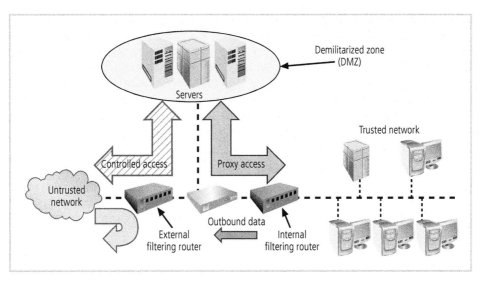

Figure 6-18 Screened subnet (DMZ)

two filtering routers, with one or more dual-homed bastion hosts between them. In the second general model, as illustrated in Figure 6-19, the connections are routed as follows:

- Connections from the outside or untrusted network are routed through an external filtering router.

- Connections from the outside or untrusted network are routed into—and then out of—a routing firewall to the separate network segment known as the DMZ.

- Connections into the trusted internal network are allowed only from the DMZ bastion host servers.

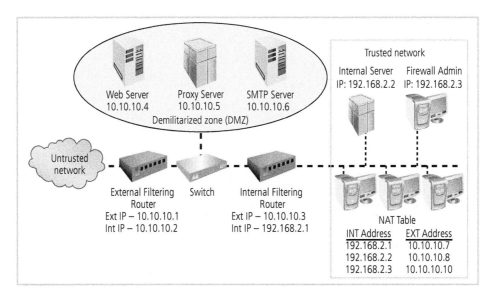

Figure 6-19 Example network configuration

The **screened subnet architecture** is an entire network segment that performs two functions. First, it protects the DMZ systems and information from outside threats by providing a level of intermediate security, which means the network is more secure than general public networks but less secure than the internal network. Second, the screened subnet protects the internal networks by limiting how external connections can gain access to them. Although extremely secure, the screened subnet can be expensive to implement and complex to configure and manage. The value of the information it protects must justify the cost.

Another facet of the DMZ is the creation of an area known as an extranet. An **extranet** is a segment of the DMZ where additional authentication and authorization controls are put into place to provide services that are not available to the general public. An example is an online retailer that allows anyone to browse the product catalog and place items into a shopping cart, but requires extra authentication and authorization when the customer is ready to check out and place an order.

❯ Selecting the Right Firewall

When trying to determine the best firewall for an organization, you should consider the following questions:

1. Which type of firewall technology offers the right balance between protection and cost for the needs of the organization?

2. What features are included in the base price? What features are available at extra cost? Are all cost factors known?

3. How easy is it to set up and configure the firewall? Does the organization have staff on hand that are trained to configure the firewall, or would the hiring of additional employees (or contractors or managed service providers) be required?

4. Can the firewall adapt to the growing network in the target organization?

The most important factor, of course, is the extent to which the firewall design provides the required protection. The next important factor is cost, which may keep a certain make, model, or type of firewall out of reach. As with all security decisions, certain compromises may be necessary to provide a viable solution under the budgetary constraints stipulated by management.

❯ Configuring and Managing Firewalls

Key Term

configuration rules The instructions a system administrator codes into a server, networking device, or security device to specify how it operates.

Once the firewall architecture and technology have been selected, the organization must provide for the initial configuration and ongoing management of the firewall(s). Good policy and practice dictates that each firewall device, whether a filtering router, bastion host, or other implementation, must have its own set of **configuration rules**. In theory, packet-filtering firewalls examine each incoming packet using a rule set to determine whether to allow or deny the packet. That set of rules is made up of simple statements that identify source and destination addresses and the type of requests a packet contains based on the ports specified in the packet. In fact, the configuration of firewall policies can be complex and difficult. IT professionals who are familiar with application programming can appreciate the difficulty of debugging both syntax errors and logic errors. Syntax errors in firewall policies are usually easy to identify, as the systems alert the administrator to incorrectly configured policies. However, logic errors, such as allowing instead of denying, specifying the wrong port or service type, and using the wrong switch, are another story. A myriad of simple mistakes can take a device designed to protect users' communications and turn it into one giant choke point. A choke point that restricts all communications or an incorrectly configured rule can cause other unexpected results. For example, novice firewall administrators often improperly configure a virus-screening e-mail gateway to operate as a type of e-mail firewall. Instead of screening e-mail for malicious code, it blocks all incoming e-mail and causes a great deal of frustration among users.

Configuring firewall policies is as much an art as it is a science. Each configuration rule must be carefully crafted, debugged, tested, and placed into the firewall's rule base in the proper sequence. Good, correctly sequenced firewall rules ensure that the actions taken comply with the organization's policy. In a well-designed, efficient firewall rule set, rules that can be evaluated quickly and govern broad access are performed before rules that may take longer to evaluate and affect fewer cases. The most important thing to remember when configuring firewalls is that when security rules conflict with the performance of business, security often loses. If users can't work because of a security restriction, the security administration is usually told in no uncertain terms to remove the safeguard. In other words, organizations are much more willing to live with potential risk than certain failure.

Best Practices for Firewalls This section outlines some of the best practices for firewall use.[16] Note that these rules are not presented in any particular sequence. For sequencing of rules, refer to the next section.

- All traffic from the trusted network is allowed out. This rule allows members of the organization to access the services they need. Filtering and logging of outbound traffic can be implemented when required by specific organizational policies.

- The firewall device is never directly accessible from the public network for configuration or management purposes. Almost all administrative access to the firewall device is denied to internal users as well. Only authorized firewall administrators access the device through secure authentication mechanisms, preferably via a method that is based on cryptographically strong authentication and uses two-factor access control techniques.

- Simple Mail Transfer Protocol (SMTP) data is allowed to enter through the firewall, but is routed to a well-configured SMTP gateway to filter and route messaging traffic securely.

- All Internet Control Message Protocol (ICMP) data should be denied, especially on external interfaces. Known as the ping service, ICMP is a common method for hacker reconnaissance and should be turned off to prevent snooping.

- Telnet (terminal emulation) access should be blocked to all internal servers from the public networks. At the very least, Telnet access to the organization's Domain Name System (DNS) server should be blocked to prevent illegal zone transfers and to prevent attackers from taking down the organization's entire network. If internal users need to access an organization's network from outside the firewall, the organization should enable them to use a virtual private network (VPN) client or other secure system that provides a reasonable level of authentication.

- When Web services are offered outside the firewall, HTTP traffic should be blocked from internal networks through the use of some form of proxy access or DMZ architecture. That way, if any employees are running Web servers for internal use on their desktops, the services are invisible to the outside Internet. If the Web server is behind the firewall, allow HTTP or HTTPS traffic (also known as Secure Sockets Layer or SSL) so users on the Internet at large can view it. The best solution is to place the Web servers that contain critical data inside the network and use proxy services from a DMZ (screened network segment), and to restrict Web traffic bound for internal network addresses to allow only those requests that originated from internal addresses. This restriction can be accomplished using NAT or other stateful inspection or proxy server firewalls. All other incoming HTTP traffic should be blocked. If the Web servers only contain advertising, they should be placed in the DMZ and rebuilt on a timed schedule or when—not *if*, but *when*—they are compromised.

- All data that is not verifiably authentic should be denied. When attempting to convince packet-filtering firewalls to permit malicious traffic, attackers frequently put an internal address in the *source* field. To avoid this problem, set rules so that the external firewall blocks all inbound traffic with an organizational source address.

Firewall Rules As you learned earlier in this chapter, firewalls operate by examining a data packet and performing a comparison with some predetermined logical rules. The logic is based on a set of guidelines programmed by a firewall administrator or created dynamically based on outgoing requests for information. This logical set is commonly referred to as firewall rules, a rule base, or firewall logic. Most firewalls use packet header information to determine whether a specific packet should be allowed to pass through or be dropped. Firewall rules operate on the principle of "that which is not permitted is prohibited," also known as expressly permitted rules. In other words, unless a rule explicitly permits an action, it is denied.

When your organization (or even your home network) uses certain cloud services, like backup providers or Application as a Service providers, or implements some types of device automation, such as the Internet of Things, you may have to make firewall rule adjustments. This may include allowing remote servers access to specific on-premise systems or requiring firewall controls to block undesirable outbound traffic. When these special circumstances occur, you will need to understand how firewall rules are implemented.

To better understand more complex rules, you must be able to create simple rules and understand how they interact. In the exercise that follows, many of the rules are based on the best practices outlined earlier. Note that some of the example rules may be implemented automatically by certain brands of firewalls. Therefore, it is imperative to become well trained on a particular brand of firewall before attempting to implement one in any setting outside of a lab. For the purposes of this discussion, assume a network configuration as illustrated in Figure 6-19, with an internal and external filtering firewall.

The exercise discusses the rules for both firewalls and provides a recap at the end that shows the complete rule sets for each filtering firewall. Note that separate access control lists are created for each interface on a firewall and are *bound* to that interface. This creates a set of unidirectional flow checks for dual-homed hosts, for example, which means that some of the rules shown here are designed for *inbound* traffic from the untrusted side of the firewall to the trusted side, and some rules are designed for *outbound* traffic from the trusted side to the untrusted side. It is important to ensure that the appropriate rule is used, as permitting certain traffic on the wrong side of the device can have unintended consequences. These examples assume that the firewall can process information beyond the IP level (TCP/UDP) and thus can access source and destination port addresses. If it could not, you could substitute the IP "Protocol" field for the source and destination port fields.

Some firewalls can filter packets by protocol name as opposed to protocol port number. For instance, Telnet protocol packets usually go to TCP port 23, but they can sometimes be redirected to another much higher port number in an attempt to conceal the activity. The system (or well-known) port numbers are 0 through 1023, user (or registered) port numbers are 1024 through 49151, and dynamic (or private) port numbers are 49152 through 65535. See *www.iana.org/assignments/port-numbers* for more information.

The example shown in Table 6-5 uses the port numbers associated with several well-known protocols to build a rule base.

Rule set 1: Responses to internal requests are allowed. In most firewall implementations, it is desirable to allow a response to an internal request for information. In stateful firewalls, this response is most easily accomplished by matching the incoming traffic to an outgoing request in a state table. In simple packet filtering, this response can be accomplished by setting the following rule for the external filtering router. (Note that the network address for the destination ends with .0; some firewalls use a notation of .x instead.) Use extreme

Port Number	Protocol
7	Echo
20	File Transfer [Default Data] (FTP)
21	File Transfer [Control] (FTP)
23	Telnet
25	Simple Mail Transfer Protocol (SMTP)
53	Domain Name System (DNS)
80	Hypertext Transfer Protocol (HTTP)
110	Post Office Protocol version 3 (POP3)
161	Simple Network Management Protocol (SNMP)

Table 6-5 Well-Known Port Numbers

Source Address	Source Port	Destination Address	Destination Port	Action
Any	Any	10.10.10.0	>1023	Allow

Table 6-6 Rule Set 1

caution in deploying this rule, as some attacks use port assignments above 1023. However, most modern firewalls use stateful inspection filtering and make this concern obsolete.

The rule is shown in Table 6-6. It states that *any* inbound packet destined for the internal network and for a destination port greater than 1023 is allowed to enter. The inbound packets can have any source address and be from any source port. The destination address of the internal network is 10.10.10.0, and the destination port is any port beyond the range of well-known ports. Why allow all such packets? While outbound communications request information from a specific port (for example, a port 80 request for a Web page), the response is assigned a number outside the well-known port range. If multiple browser windows are open at the same time, each window can request a packet from a Web site, and the response is directed to a specific destination port, allowing the browser and Web server to keep each conversation separate. While this rule is sufficient for the external firewall, it is dangerous to allow any traffic in just because it is destined to a high port range. A better solution is to have the internal firewall use state tables that track connections and thus prevent dangerous packets from entering this upper port range. Again, this practice is known as stateful packet inspection. This is one of the rules allowed by default by most modern firewall systems.

Rule set 2: The firewall device is never accessible directly from the public network. If attackers can directly access the firewall, they may be able to modify or delete rules and allow unwanted traffic through. For the same reason, the firewall itself should never be allowed to access other network devices directly. If hackers compromise the firewall and then use its permissions to access other servers or clients, they may cause additional damage or mischief. The rules shown in Table 6-7 prohibit anyone from directly accessing the firewall, and prohibit the firewall from directly accessing any other devices. Note that this example is for the external filtering router and firewall only. Similar rules should be crafted for the internal router. Why are there separate rules for each IP address? The 10.10.10.1 address regulates external access to and by the firewall, while the 10.10.10.2 address regulates internal access. Not all attackers are outside the firewall!

Source Address	Source Port	Destination Address	Destination Port	Action
Any	Any	10.10.10.1	Any	Deny
Any	Any	10.10.10.2	Any	Deny
10.10.10.1	Any	Any	Any	Deny
10.10.10.2	Any	Any	Any	Deny

Table 6-7 Rule Set 2

Source Address	Source Port	Destination Address	Destination Port	Action
10.10.10.0	Any	Any	Any	Allow

Table 6-8   Rule Set 3

Note that if the firewall administrator needs direct access to the firewall from inside or outside the network, a permission rule allowing access from his or her IP address should preface this rule. The interface can also be accessed on the opposite side of the device, as traffic would be routed through the box and "boomerang" back when it hits the first router on the far side. Thus, the rule protects the interfaces in both the inbound and outbound rule set.

Rule set 3: All traffic from the trusted network is allowed out. As a general rule, it is wise not to restrict outbound traffic unless separate routers and firewalls are configured to handle it, to avoid overloading the firewall. If an organization wants control over outbound traffic, it should use a separate filtering device. The rule shown in Table 6-8 allows internal communications out, so it would be used on the outbound interface.

Why should rule set 3 come after rule sets 1 and 2? It makes sense to allow rules that unambiguously affect the most traffic to be placed earlier in the list. The more rules a firewall must process to find one that applies to the current packet, the slower the firewall will run. Therefore, most widely applicable rules should come first because the firewall employs the first rule that applies to any given packet.

Rule set 4: The rule set for SMTP data is shown in Table 6-9. As shown, the packets governed by this rule are allowed to pass through the firewall, but are all routed to a well-configured SMTP gateway. It is important that e-mail traffic reach your e-mail server and *only* your e-mail server. Some attackers try to disguise dangerous packets as e-mail traffic to fool a firewall. If such packets can reach only the e-mail server and it has been properly configured, the rest of the network ought to be safe. Note that if the organization allows home access to an internal e-mail server, then it may want to implement a second, separate server to handle the POP3 protocol that retrieves mail for e-mail clients like Outlook and Thunderbird. This is usually a low-risk operation, especially if email encryption is in place. More challenging is the transmission of e-mail using the SMTP protocol, a service that is attractive to spammers who may seek to hijack an outbound mail server.

Rule set 5: All ICMP data should be denied. Pings, formally known as ICMP Echo requests, are used by internal systems administrators to ensure that clients and servers can communicate. There is virtually no legitimate use for ICMP outside the network, except to test the perimeter routers. ICMP may be the first indicator of a malicious attack. It's best to make

Source Address	Source Port	Destination Address	Destination Port	Action
Any	Any	10.10.10.6	25	Allow

Table 6-9   Rule Set 4

Source Address	Source Port	Destination Address	Destination Port	Action
10.10.10.0	Any	Any	7	Allow
Any	Any	10.10.10.0	7	Deny

Table 6-10 Rule Set 5

all directly connected networking devices "black holes" to external probes. A common networking diagnostic command in most operating systems is traceroute; it uses a variation of the ICMP Echo requests, so restricting this port provides protection against multiple types of probes. Allowing internal users to use ICMP requires configuring two rules, as shown in Table 6-10.

The first of these two rules allows internal administrators and users to use ping. Note that this rule is unnecessary if the firewall uses internal permissions rules like those in rule set 2. The second rule in Table 6-10 does not allow anyone else to use ping. Remember that rules are processed in order. If an internal user needs to ping an internal or external address, the firewall allows the packet and stops processing the rules. If the request does not come from an internal source, then it bypasses the first rule and moves to the second.

Rule set 6: Telnet (terminal emulation) access should be blocked to all internal servers from the public networks. Though it is not used much in Windows environments, Telnet is still useful to systems administrators on UNIX and Linux systems. However, the presence of external requests for Telnet services can indicate an attack. Allowing internal use of Telnet requires the same type of initial permission rule you use with ping. See Table 6-11. Again, this rule is unnecessary if the firewall uses internal permissions rules like those in rule set 2.

Rule set 7: When Web services are offered outside the firewall, HTTP and HTTPS traffic should be blocked from the internal networks via the use of some form of proxy access or DMZ architecture. With a Web server in the DMZ, you simply allow HTTP to access the Web server and then use the cleanup rule described later in rule set 8 to prevent any other access. To keep the Web server inside the internal network, direct all HTTP requests to the proxy server and configure the internal filtering router/firewall only to allow the proxy server to access the internal Web server. The rule shown in Table 6-12 illustrates the first example.

This rule accomplishes two things: it allows HTTP traffic to reach the Web server, and it uses the cleanup rule (Rule 8) to prevent non-HTTP traffic from reaching the Web server.

Source Address	Source Port	Destination Address	Destination Port	Action
10.10.10.0	Any	10.10.10.0	23	Allow
Any	Any	10.10.10.0	23	Deny

Table 6-11 Rule Set 6

Source Address	Source Port	Destination Address	Destination Port	Action
Any	Any	10.10.10.4	80	Allow

Table 6-12 Rule Set 7a

If someone tries to access the Web server with non-HTTP traffic (other than port 80), then the firewall skips this rule and goes to the next one.

Proxy server rules allow an organization to restrict all access to a device. The external firewall would be configured as shown in Table 6-13.

The effective use of a proxy server requires that the DNS entries be configured as if the proxy server were the Web server. The proxy server is then configured to repackage any HTTP request packets into a new packet and retransmit to the Web server inside the firewall. The retransmission of the repackaged request requires that the rule shown in Table 6-14 enables the proxy server at 10.10.10.5 to send to the internal router, assuming the IP address for the internal Web server is 10.10.10.8. Note that when an internal NAT server is used, the rule for the inbound interface uses the externally routable address because the device performs rule filtering *before* it performs address translation. For the outbound interface, however, the address is in the native 192.168.x.x format.

The restriction on the source address then prevents anyone else from accessing the Web server from outside the internal filtering router/firewall.

Rule set 8: The cleanup rule. As a general practice in firewall rule construction, if a request for a service is not explicitly allowed by policy, that request should be denied by a rule. The rule shown in Table 6-15 implements this practice and blocks any requests that aren't

Source Address	Source Port	Destination Address	Destination Port	Action
Any	Any	10.10.10.5	80	Allow

Table 6-13 Rule Set 7b

Source Address	Source Port	Destination Address	Destination Port	Action
10.10.10.5	Any	10.10.10.8	80	Allow

Table 6-14 Rule Set 7c

Source Address	Source Port	Destination Address	Destination Port	Action
Any	Any	Any	Any	Deny

Table 6-15 Rule Set 8

explicitly allowed by other rules. This is another rule that is usually allowed by default by most modern firewall devices. It is included here for discussion purposes.

Additional rules that restrict access to specific servers or devices can be added, but they must be sequenced before the cleanup rule. The specific sequence of the rules becomes crucial because once a rule is fired, that action is taken and the firewall stops processing the rest of the rules in the list. Misplacement of a particular rule can result in unintended consequences and unforeseen results. One organization installed an expensive new firewall only to discover that the security it provided was too perfect—nothing was allowed in and nothing was allowed out! Not until the firewall administrators realized that the rules were out of sequence was the problem resolved.

Tables 6-16 through 6-19 show the rule sets in their proper sequences for both the external and internal firewalls.

Note that the first rule prevents spoofing of internal IP addresses. The rule that allows responses to internal communications (rule 6 in Table 6-16) comes after the four rules prohibiting direct communications to or from the firewall (rules 2–5 in Table 6-16). In reality, rules 4 and 5 are redundant—rule 1 covers their actions. They are listed here for illustrative purposes. Next come the rules that govern access to the SMTP server, denial of ping and Telnet access, and access to the HTTP server. If heavy traffic to the HTTP server is expected, move the HTTP server rule closer to the top (for example, into the position of rule 2), which would expedite rule processing for external communications. Rules 8 and 9 are actually unnecessary because the cleanup rule would take care of their tasks. The final rule in Table 6-16 denies any other types of communications.

In the outbound rule set (see Table 6-17), the first rule allows the firewall, system, or network administrator to access any device, including the firewall. Because this rule is on the

Rule #	Source Address	Source Port	Destination Address	Destination Port	Action
1	10.10.10.0	Any	Any	Any	Deny
2	Any	Any	10.10.10.1	Any	Deny
3	Any	Any	10.10.10.2	Any	Deny
4	10.10.10.1	Any	Any	Any	Deny
5	10.10.10.2	Any	Any	Any	Deny
6	Any	Any	10.10.10.0	>1023	Allow
7	Any	Any	10.10.10.6	25	Allow
8	Any	Any	10.10.10.0	7	Deny
9	Any	Any	10.10.10.0	23	Deny
10	Any	Any	10.10.10.4	80	Allow
11	Any	Any	Any	Any	Deny

Table 6-16 External Filtering Firewall Inbound Interface Rule Set

Rule #	Source Address	Source Port	Destination Address	Destination Port	Action
1	10.10.10.12	Any	10.10.10.0	Any	Allow
2	Any	Any	10.10.10.1	Any	Deny
3	Any	Any	10.10.10.2	Any	Deny
4	10.10.10.1	Any	Any	Any	Deny
5	10.10.10.2	Any	Any	Any	Deny
6	10.10.10.0	Any	Any	Any	Allow
7	Any	Any	Any	Any	Deny

Table 6-17 External Filtering Firewall Outbound Interface Rule Set

outbound side, you do not need to worry about external attackers. The next four rules prohibit access to and by the firewall itself, and the remaining rules allow outbound communications and deny all else.

Note the similarities and differences in the two firewalls' rule sets. The rule sets for the internal filtering router/firewall, shown in Tables 6-18 and 6-19, must both protect against traffic to the internal network (192.168.2.0) and allow traffic from it. Most of the rules in Tables 6-18 and 6-19 are similar to those in Tables 6-16 and 6-17: they allow responses to internal communications, deny communications to and from the firewall itself, and allow all outbound internal traffic.

Because the 192.168.2.x network is an unroutable network, external communications are handled by the NAT server, which maps internal (192.168.2.0) addresses to external (10.10.10.0) addresses. This prevents an attacker from compromising one of the internal boxes and accessing the internal network with it. The exception is the proxy server, which is covered by rule 7 in Table 6-18 on the internal router's inbound interface. This proxy server should be very carefully configured. If the organization does not need it, as in cases where all externally accessible services are provided from machines in the DMZ, then rule

Rule #	Source Address	Source Port	Destination Address	Destination Port	Action
1	Any	Any	10.10.10.3	Any	Deny
2	Any	Any	10.10.10.7	Any	Deny
3	10.10.10.3	Any	Any	Any	Deny
4	10.10.10.7	Any	Any	Any	Deny
5	Any	Any	10.10.10.0	>1023	Allow
7	10.10.10.5	Any	10.10.10.8	Any	Allow
8	Any	Any	Any	Any	Deny

Table 6-18 Internal Filtering Firewall Inbound Interface Rule Set

6

Rule #	Source Address	Source Port	Destination Address	Destination Port	Action
1	Any	Any	10.10.10.3	Any	Deny
2	Any	Any	192.168.2.1	Any	Deny
3	10.10.10.3	Any	Any	Any	Deny
4	192.168.2.1	Any	Any	Any	Deny
5	Any	Any	192.168.2.0	>1023	Allow
6	192.168.2.0	Any	Any	Any	Allow
7	Any	Any	Any	Any	Deny

Table 6-19 Internal Filtering Firewall Outbound Interface Rule Set

7 is not needed. Note that Tables 6-18 and 6-19 have no ping and Telnet rules because the external firewall filters out these external requests. The last rule, rule 8, provides cleanup and may not be needed, depending on the firewall.

❯ Content Filters

Key Terms

content filter A software program or hardware/software appliance that allows administrators to restrict content that comes into or leaves a network—for example, restricting user access to Web sites from material that is not related to business, such as pornography or entertainment.

data loss prevention A strategy to gain assurance that the users of a network do not send high-value information or other critical information outside the network.

reverse firewall See *content filter*.

Besides firewalls, a **content filter** is another utility that can help protect an organization's systems from misuse and unintentional denial-of-service problems. A content filter is a software filter—technically not a firewall—that allows administrators to restrict access to content from within a network. It is essentially a set of scripts or programs that restricts user access to certain networking protocols and Internet locations, or that restricts users from receiving general types or specific examples of Internet content. Some content filters are combined with reverse proxy servers, which is why many are referred to as **reverse firewalls**, as their primary purpose is to restrict internal access to external material. In most common implementation models, the content filter has two components: rating and filtering. The rating is like a set of firewall rules for Web sites and is common in residential content filters. The rating can be complex, with multiple access control settings for different levels of the organization, or it can be simple, with a basic allow/deny scheme like that of a firewall. The filtering is a method used to restrict specific access requests to identified resources, which may be Web sites, servers, or other resources the content filter administrator configures. The result is like a reverse ACL (technically speaking, a capabilities table); an ACL normally records a set of users who have access to resources, but the control list records resources that the user cannot access.

The first content filters were systems designed to restrict access to specific Web sites, and were stand-alone software applications. These could be configured in either an exclusive or inclusive manner. In an exclusive mode, certain sites are specifically excluded, but the problem with this approach is that an organization might want to exclude thousands of Web sites, and more might be added every hour. The inclusive mode works from a list of sites that are specifically permitted. In order to have a site added to the list, the user must submit a request to the content filter manager, which could be time-consuming and restrict business operations. Newer models of content filters are protocol-based, examining content as it is dynamically displayed and restricting or permitting access based on a logical interpretation of content.

The most common content filters restrict users from accessing Web sites that are obviously not related to business, such as pornography sites, or they deny incoming spam e-mail. Content filters can be small add-on software programs for the home or office, such as the ones recommended by Tech Republic[17]: NetNanny, K9, Save Squid, DansGuardian, and OpenDNS. Content filters can also be built into corporate firewall applications, such as Microsoft's Forefront Threat Management Gateway (TMG), which was formerly known as the Microsoft Internet Security and Acceleration (ISA) Server. Microsoft's Forefront TMG is actually a UTM firewall that has content filtering capabilities. The benefit of implementing content filters is the assurance that employees are not distracted by nonbusiness material and cannot waste the organization's time and resources. The downside is that these systems require extensive configuration and ongoing maintenance to update the list of unacceptable destinations or the source addresses for incoming restricted e-mail. Some newer content filtering applications, like newer antivirus programs, come with a service of downloadable files that update the database of restrictions. These applications work by matching either a list of disapproved or approved Web sites and by matching key content words, such as "nude," "naked," and "sex." Of course, creators of restricted content have realized this and work to bypass the restrictions by suppressing such words, creating additional problems for networking and security professionals.

One use of content filtering technology is to implement **data loss prevention**. When implemented, network traffic is monitored and analyzed. If patterns of use and keyword analysis reveal that high-value information is being transferred, an alert may be invoked or the network connection may be interrupted.

 For a list of reviewed small business content filters, visit www.toptenreviews.com and search for "Small Business Content Filter Reviews."

Protecting Remote Connections

The networks that organizations create are seldom used only by people at one location. When connections are made between networks, the connections are arranged and managed carefully. Installing such network connections requires using leased lines or other data channels provided by common carriers; therefore, these connections are usually permanent and secured under the requirements of a formal service agreement. However, a more flexible option for network access must be provided for employees working in their homes, contract workers hired for specific assignments, or other workers who are traveling. In the past, organizations provided these remote connections exclusively through dial-up services like Remote Authentication Service (RAS). As high-speed Internet connections have become mainstream, other options such as virtual private networks (VPNs) have become more popular. However, a 2015 CNN Money report indicates that over 2.1 million subscribers still use dial-up services through America Online. Why? According to a 2009 report from the Pew Research Center, 32 percent of dial-up users report that they can't afford the upgrade.[18]

❯ Remote Access

> ### Key Terms
>
> **Kerberos** An authentication system that uses symmetric key encryption to validate an individual user's access to various network resources by keeping a database containing the private keys of clients and servers that are in the authentication domain it supervises.
>
> **Remote Authentication Dial-In User Service (RADIUS)** A computer connection system that centralizes the management of user authentication by placing the responsibility for authenticating each user on a central authentication server.
>
> **war dialer** An automatic phone-dialing program that dials every number in a configured range (for example, 555–1000 to 555–2000) and checks whether a person, answering machine, or modem picks up.

Before the Internet emerged, organizations created their own private networks and allowed individual users and other organizations to connect to them using dial-up or leased line connections. In the current networking environment, where high-speed Internet connections are commonplace, dial-up access and leased lines from customer networks are almost nonexistent. The connections between company networks and the Internet use firewalls to safeguard that interface. Although connections via dial-up and leased lines are becoming less popular, they are still quite common. Also, a widely held view is that these unsecured, dial-up connection points represent a substantial exposure to attack. An attacker who suspects that an organization has dial-up lines can use a device called a war dialer to locate the connection points. A **war dialer** dials every number in a configured range, such as 555–1000 to 555–2000, and checks to see if a person, answering machine, or modem picks up. If a modem answers, the war dialer program makes a note of the number and then moves to the next target number. The attacker then attempts to hack into the network via the identified modem connection using a variety of techniques. Dial-up network connectivity is usually less sophisticated than that deployed with Internet connections. For the most part, simple username and password schemes are the only means of authentication. However, some technologies, such as RADIUS systems, TACACS, and CHAP password systems, have improved the authentication process, and some systems now use strong encryption.

RADIUS, Diameter, and TACACS RADIUS and TACACS are systems that authenticate the credentials of users who are trying to access an organization's network via a

dial-up connection. Typical dial-up systems place the responsibility for user authentication on the system directly connected to the modems. If there are multiple points of entry into the dial-up system, this authentication system can become difficult to manage. The **Remote Authentication Dial-In User Service (RADIUS)** system centralizes the responsibility for authenticating each user on the RADIUS server. RADIUS was initially described in RFCs 2058 and 2059, and is currently described in RFCs 2865 and 2866, among others.

When a network access server (NAS) receives a request for a network connection from a dial-up client, it passes the request and the user's credentials to the RADIUS server. RADIUS then validates the credentials and passes the resulting decision (accept or deny) back to the accepting remote access server. Figure 6-20 shows the typical configuration of an NAS system.

An emerging alternative that is derived from RADIUS is the Diameter protocol. The *Diameter protocol* defines the minimum requirements for a system that provides authentication, authorization, and accounting (AAA) services and that can go beyond these basics and add commands and/or object attributes. Diameter security uses respected encryption standards such as Internet Protocol Security (IPSec) or Transport Layer Security (TLS); its cryptographic capabilities are extensible and will be able to use future encryption protocols as they are implemented. Diameter-capable devices are emerging into the marketplace, and this protocol is expected to become the dominant form of AAA services.

The *Terminal Access Controller Access Control System (TACACS)*, defined in RFC 1492, is another remote access authorization system that is based on a client/server configuration. Like RADIUS, it contains a centralized database, and it validates the user's credentials at this TACACS server. The three versions of TACACS are the original version, Extended TACACS, and TACACS+. Of these, only TACACS+ is still in use. The original version combines authentication and authorization services. The extended version separates the steps needed to authenticate individual user or system access attempts from the steps needed

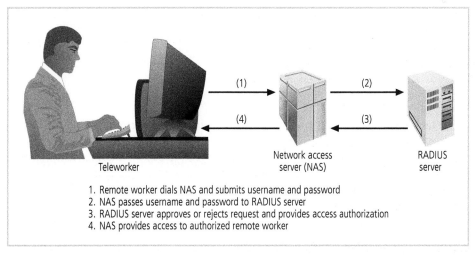

1. Remote worker dials NAS and submits username and password
2. NAS passes username and password to RADIUS server
3. RADIUS server approves or rejects request and provides access authorization
4. NAS provides access to authorized remote worker

Figure 6-20 RADIUS configuration

to verify that the authenticated individual or system is allowed to make a given type of connection. The extended version keeps records for accountability and to ensure that the access attempt is linked to a specific individual or system. The TACACS+ version uses dynamic passwords and incorporates two-factor authentication.

Kerberos Two authentication systems can provide secure third-party authentication: Kerberos and SESAME. **Kerberos**—named after the three-headed dog of Greek mythology that guards the gates to the underworld—uses symmetric key encryption to validate an individual user to various network resources. Kerberos, as described in RFC 4120, keeps a database containing the private keys of clients and servers—in the case of a client, this key is simply the client's encrypted password. Network services running on servers in the network register with Kerberos, as do the clients that use those services. The Kerberos system knows these private keys and can authenticate one network node (client or server) to another. For example, Kerberos can authenticate a user once—at the time the user logs in to a client computer—and then, later during that session, it can authorize the user to have access to a printer without requiring the user to take any additional action. Kerberos also generates temporary session keys, which are private keys given to the two parties in a conversation. The session key is used to encrypt all communications between these two parties. Typically a user logs into the network, is authenticated to the Kerberos system, and is then authenticated to other resources on the network by the Kerberos system itself.

Kerberos consists of three interacting services, all of which use a database library:

1. *Authentication server (AS), which is a Kerberos server that authenticates clients and servers.*

2. *Key Distribution Center (KDC), which generates and issues session keys.*

3. *Kerberos ticket granting service (TGS), which provides tickets to clients who request services. In Kerberos, a ticket is an identification card for a particular client that verifies to the server that the client is requesting services and that the client is a valid member of the Kerberos system and therefore authorized to receive services. The ticket consists of the client's name and network address, a ticket validation starting and ending time, and the session key, all encrypted in the private key of the server from which the client is requesting services.*

Kerberos is based on the following principles:

- *The KDC knows the secret keys of all clients and servers on the network.*

- *The KDC initially exchanges information with the client and server by using these secret keys.*

- *Kerberos authenticates a client to a requested service on a server through TGS and by issuing temporary session keys for communications between the client and KDC, the server and KDC, and the client and server.*

- *Communications then take place between the client and server using these temporary session keys.*[19]

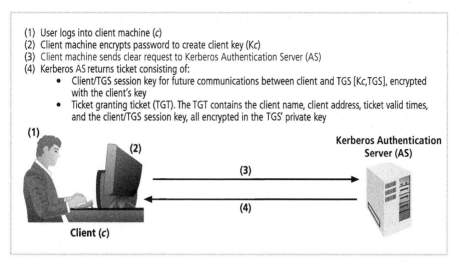

(1) User logs into client machine (c)
(2) Client machine encrypts password to create client key (Kc)
(3) Client machine sends clear request to Kerberos Authentication Server (AS)
(4) Kerberos AS returns ticket consisting of:
  • Client/TGS session key for future communications between client and TGS [Kc,TGS], encrypted with the client's key
  • Ticket granting ticket (TGT). The TGT contains the client name, client address, ticket valid times, and the client/TGS session key, all encrypted in the TGS' private key

(1)

(2)

Kerberos Authentication
Server (AS)

(3)

(4)

Client (c)

Figure 6-21 Kerberos login

Figures 6-21 and 6-22 illustrate this process.

If the Kerberos servers are subjected to denial-of-service attacks, no client can request services. If the Kerberos servers, service providers, or clients' machines are compromised, their private key information may also be compromised.

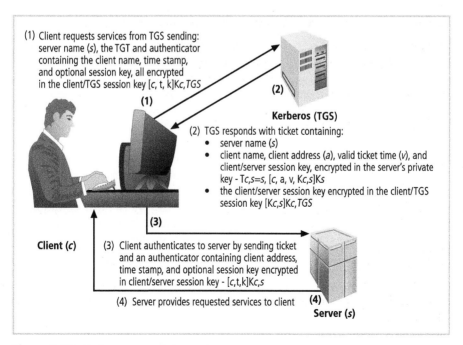

(1) Client requests services from TGS sending: server name (s), the TGT and authenticator containing the client name, time stamp, and optional session key, all encrypted in the client/TGS session key [c, t, k]Kc,TGS

(1)

(2)

Kerberos (TGS)

(2) TGS responds with ticket containing:
  • server name (s)
  • client name, client address (a), valid ticket time (v), and client/server session key, encrypted in the server's private key - Tc,s=s, [c, a, v, Kc,s]Ks
  • the client/server session key encrypted in the client/TGS session key [Kc,s]Kc,TGS

(3)

Client (c)

(3) Client authenticates to server by sending ticket and an authenticator containing client address, time stamp, and optional session key encrypted in client/server session key - [c,t,k]Kc,s

(4) Server provides requested services to client

(4)

Server (s)

Figure 6-22 Kerberos request for services

For more information on Kerberos, including available downloads, visit the MIT Kerberos page at http://web.mit.edu/Kerberos/.

SESAME The Secure European System for Applications in a Multivendor Environment (SESAME), defined in RFC 1510, is the result of a European research and development project partly funded by the European Commission. SESAME is similar to Kerberos in that the user is first authenticated to an authentication server and receives a token. The token is then presented to a privilege attribute server, instead of a ticket-granting service as in Kerberos, as proof of identity to gain a privilege attribute certificate (PAC). The PAC is like the ticket in Kerberos; however, a PAC conforms to the standards of the European Computer Manufacturers Association (ECMA) and the International Organization for Standardization/ International Telecommunications Union (ISO/ITU-T). The remaining differences lie in the security protocols and distribution methods. SESAME uses public key encryption to distribute secret keys. SESAME also builds on the Kerberos model by adding sophisticated access control features, more scalable encryption systems, improved manageability, auditing features, and the option to delegate responsibility for allowing access.

❭ Virtual Private Networks (VPNs)

Key Terms

hybrid VPN A combination of trusted and secure VPN implementations.

secure VPN A VPN implementation that uses security protocols to encrypt traffic transmitted across unsecured public networks.

trusted VPN Also known as a legacy VPN, a VPN implementation that uses leased circuits from a service provider who gives contractual assurance that no one else is allowed to use these circuits and that they are properly maintained and protected.

virtual private network (VPN) A private, secure network operated over a public and insecure network. A VPN keeps the contents of the network messages hidden from observers who may have access to public traffic.

Virtual private networks (VPNs) are implementations of cryptographic technology. (You will learn more about them in Chapter 8.) A VPN is a private data network that uses the public telecommunications infrastructure to create a means for private communication via a tunneling protocol coupled with security procedures.[20] VPNs are commonly used to securely extend an organization's internal network connections to remote locations. The VPNC defined three VPN technologies: trusted VPNs, secure VPNs, and hybrid VPNs. A **trusted VPN**, also known as a legacy VPN, uses leased circuits from a service provider and conducts packet switching over these leased circuits. The organization must trust the service provider, who gives contractual assurance that no one else is allowed to use these circuits and that the circuits are properly maintained and protected—hence the name *trusted* VPN.[21] **Secure VPNs** use security protocols like IPSec to encrypt traffic transmitted across unsecured public networks like the Internet. A **hybrid VPN** combines the two, providing encrypted transmissions (as in secure VPN) over some or all of a trusted VPN network.

A VPN that proposes to offer a secure and reliable capability while relying on public networks must accomplish the following, regardless of the specific technologies and protocols being used:

- *Encapsulation* of incoming and outgoing data, in which the native protocol of the client is embedded within the frames of a protocol that can be routed over the public network and be usable by the server network environment.

- *Encryption* of incoming and outgoing data to keep the data contents private while in transit over the public network, but usable by the client and server computers and/or the local networks on both ends of the VPN connection.

- *Authentication* of the remote computer and perhaps the remote user as well. Authentication and subsequent user authorization to perform specific actions are predicated on accurate and reliable identification of the remote system and user.

In the most common implementation, a VPN allows a user to turn the Internet into a private network. As you know, the Internet is anything but private. However, an individual user or organization can set up tunneling points across the Internet and send encrypted data back and forth, using the IP packet-within-an-IP packet method to transmit data safely and securely. VPNs are simple to set up and maintain, and usually require only that the tunneling points be dual-homed—that is, connecting a private network to the Internet or to another outside connection point. VPN support is built into most Microsoft server software, including 2012, and client support for VPN services is built into most Windows clients. While connections for true private network services can cost hundreds of thousands of dollars to lease, configure, and maintain, an Internet VPN can cost very little. A VPN can be implemented in several ways. IPSec, the dominant protocol used in VPNs, uses either transport mode or tunnel mode. IPSec can be used as a standalone protocol or coupled with the Layer Two Tunneling Protocol (L2TP).

Transport Mode In transport mode, the data within an IP packet is encrypted, but the header information is not. This allows the user to establish a secure link directly with the remote host, encrypting only the data contents of the packet. The downside of this implementation is that packet eavesdroppers can still identify the destination system. Once attackers know the destination, they may be able to compromise one of the end nodes and acquire the packet information from it. On the other hand, transport mode eliminates the need for special servers and tunneling software, and allows end users to transmit traffic from anywhere, which is especially useful for traveling or telecommuting employees. Figure 6-23 illustrates the transport mode methods of implementing VPNs.

Transport mode VPNs have two popular uses. The first is the end-to-end transport of encrypted data. In this model, two end users can communicate directly, encrypting and decrypting their communications as needed. Each machine acts as the end-node VPN server and client. In the second, a remote access worker or teleworker connects to an office network over the Internet by connecting to a VPN server on the perimeter. This allows the teleworker's system to work as if it were part of the local area network. The VPN server

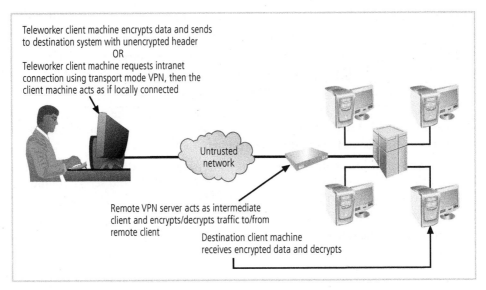

Teleworker client machine encrypts data and sends to destination system with unencrypted header

OR

Teleworker client machine requests intranet connection using transport mode VPN, then the client machine acts as if locally connected

Untrusted network

Remote VPN server acts as intermediate client and encrypts/decrypts traffic to/from remote client

Destination client machine receives encrypted data and decrypts

Figure 6-23   Transport mode VPN

in this example acts as an intermediate node, encrypting traffic from the secure intranet and transmitting it to the remote client, and decrypting traffic from the remote client and transmitting it to its final destination. This model frequently allows the remote system to act as its own VPN server, which is a weakness, because most work-at-home employees do not have the same level of physical and logical security they would have in an office.

Tunnel Mode   Tunnel mode establishes two perimeter tunnel servers to encrypt all traffic that will traverse an unsecured network. In tunnel mode, the entire client packet is encrypted and added as the data portion of a packet addressed from one tunneling server to another. The receiving server decrypts the packet and sends it to the final address. The primary benefit of this model is that an intercepted packet reveals nothing about the true destination system.

An example of a tunnel mode VPN is provided with Microsoft's Internet Security and Acceleration (ISA) Server. With ISA Server, an organization can establish a gateway-to-gateway tunnel, encapsulating data within the tunnel. ISA can use the Point-to-Point Tunneling Protocol (PPTP), L2TP, or IPSec technologies. Additional information about these protocols is provided in Chapter 8. Figure 6-24 shows an example of tunnel mode VPN implementation. On the client end, a Windows user can establish a VPN by configuring his or her system to connect to a VPN server. The process is straightforward. First, the user connects to the Internet through an ISP or direct network connection. Second, the user establishes the link with the remote VPN server. Figure 6-25 shows the connection screens used to configure the VPN link.

 For more information on VPNs, read the reviews of the best VPN services at PC Magazine's Web site (www.pcmag.com) and search for "Best VPN Services."

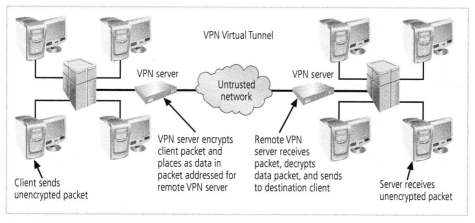

Figure 6-24 Tunnel mode VPN

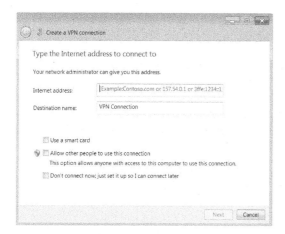

Figure 6-25 VPN client in Windows

Source: Microsoft.

Selected Readings

Many excellent sources of additional information are available in the area of information security. The following can add to your understanding of this chapter's content:

- *Guide to Firewalls and VPNs*, by Michael E. Whitman, Herbert J. Mattord, and Andrew Green. 2012. Cengage Learning.
- NIST SP 800-41, Rev. 1. *Guidelines on Firewalls and Firewall Policy*. September 2009.
- NIST SP 800-77. *Guide to IPSec VPNs*. December 2005.

Chapter Summary

- Access control is a process by which systems determine if and how to admit a user into a trusted area of the organization.

- Mandatory access controls offer users and data owners little or no control over access to information resources. MACs are often associated with a data classification scheme in which each collection of information is rated with a sensitivity level. This type of control is sometimes called lattice-based access control.

- Nondiscretionary controls are strictly enforced versions of MACs that are managed by a central authority, whereas discretionary access controls are implemented at the discretion or option of the data user.

- All access control approaches rely on identification, authentication, authorization, and accountability.

- Authentication is the process of validating an unauthenticated person's purported identity. The three widely used types of authentication factors are something a person knows, something a person has, and something a person is or can produce.

- Strong authentication requires a minimum of two authentication mechanisms drawn from two different authentication factors.

- A firewall is any device that prevents a specific type of information from moving between the outside network, known as the untrusted network, and the inside network, known as the trusted network.

- Firewalls can be categorized into four groups: packet filtering, MAC layers, application gateways, and hybrid firewalls.

- Packet-filtering firewalls can be implemented as static filtering, dynamic filtering, and stateful inspection firewalls.

- The three common architectural implementations of firewalls are single bastion hosts, screened hosts, and screened subnets.

- Firewalls operate by evaluating data packet contents against logical rules. This logical set is most commonly referred to as firewall rules, a rule base, or firewall logic.

- Content filtering can improve security and assist organizations in improving the manageability of their technology.

- Dial-up protection mechanisms help secure organizations that use modems for remote connectivity. Kerberos and SESAME are authentication systems that add security to this technology.

- Virtual private networks enable remote offices and users to connect to private networks securely over public networks.

Review Questions

1. What is the typical relationship among the untrusted network, the firewall, and the trusted network?

2. What is the relationship between a TCP packet and UDP packet? Will any specific transaction usually involve both types of packets?

3. How is an application layer proxy firewall different from a packet-filtering firewall?

4. How is static filtering different from dynamic filtering of packets? Which is perceived to offer improved security?

5. What is stateful inspection? How is state information maintained during a network connection or transaction?

6. Explain the conceptual approach that should guide the creation of firewall rule sets.

7. What special function does a cache server perform? Why is this useful for larger organizations?

8. Describe how the various types of firewalls interact with network traffic at various levels of the OSI model.

9. What is a hybrid firewall?

10. Describe Unified Threat Management. Why might it be a better approach than single-point solutions that perform the same functions? How does UTM differ from Next Generation Firewalls?

11. What is a Next Generation Firewall (NextGen or NGFW)?

12. What is the primary value of a firewall?

13. What is Port Address Translation (PAT) and how does it work?

14. How do screened host architectures for firewalls differ from screened subnet firewall architectures? Which offers more security for the information assets that remain on the trusted network?

15. What is a sacrificial host? What is a bastion host?

16. What is a DMZ? Is this really an appropriate name for the technology, considering the function this type of subnet performs?

17. What questions must be addressed when selecting a firewall for a specific organization?

18. What is RADIUS? What advantage does it have over TACACS?

19. What is a content filter? Where is it placed in the network to gain the best result for the organization?

20. What is a VPN? Why is it becoming more widely used?

Exercises

1. Using the Web, search for "software firewalls." Examine the various alternatives available and compare their functionality, cost, features, and type of protection. Create a weighted ranking according to your own evaluation of the features and specifications of each software package.

2. Using Figure 6-18, create one or more rules necessary for both the internal and external firewalls to allow a remote user to access an internal machine from the Internet using the Timbuktu software. Your answer requires researching the ports used by this software packet.

3. Suppose management wants to create a "server farm" for the configuration in Figure 6-18 that allows a proxy firewall in the DMZ to access an internal Web server (rather than a Web server in the DMZ). Do you foresee any technical difficulties in deploying this architecture? What are the advantages and disadvantages to this implementation?

4. Using the Internet, determine what applications are commercially available to enable secure remote access to a PC.

5. Using a Microsoft Windows system, open Internet Explorer. Click Internet Options on the Tools menu. Examine the contents of the Security and Privacy tabs. How can these tabs be configured to provide: (a) content filtering and (b) protection from unwanted items like cookies?

Case Exercises

The next morning at 8 a.m., Kelvin called the meeting to order. The first person to address the group was Susan Hamir, the network design consultant from Costly & Firehouse, LLC. She reviewed the critical points from the design report, going over its options and outlining the trade-offs in the design choices.

When she finished, she sat down and Kelvin addressed the group again: "We need to break the logjam on this design issue. We have all the right people in this room to make the right choice for the company. Now here are the questions I want us to consider over the next three hours." Kelvin pressed the key on his PC to show a slide with a list of discussion questions on the projector screen.

Discussion Questions

1. What questions do you think Kelvin should have included on his slide to start the discussion?

2. If the questions were broken down into two categories, they would be cost versus maintaining high security while keeping flexibility. Which is more important for SLS?

Ethical Decision Making

Suppose that Ms. Hamir stacked the deck with her design proposal. In other words, she purposefully under-designed the less expensive solution and produced a cost estimate for the higher-end version that she knew would come in over budget if it were chosen. She also knew that SLS had a tendency to hire design consultants to do build projects. Is it unethical to produce a consulting report that steers a client toward a specific outcome?

Suppose instead that Ms. Hamir had prepared a report that truthfully recommended the more expensive option as the better choice for SLS in her best professional opinion. Further suppose that SLS management decided on the less expensive option solely to reduce costs without regard to the project's security outcomes. Would she be ethically sound to urge reconsideration of such a decision?

Endnotes

1. Hu et al. National Institute of Standards and Technology. *Guide to Attribute Based Access Control (ABAC) Definition and Considerations.* SP 800-162. January 2014. Accessed 12 August 2016 from *nvlpubs.nist.gov/nistpubs/specialpublications/NIST .sp.800-162.pdf.*

2. Tagat, Anurag. "Online Fraud: Too Many Accounts, Too Few Passwords." 18 July 2012. Accessed 12 August 2016 from *www.techradar.com/us/news/internet/online -fraud-too-many-accounts-too-few-passwords-1089283.*

3. From multiple sources, including: Jain, A., Ross, A., and Prabhakar, S. "An Introduction to Biometric Recognition." *IEEE Transactions on Circuits and Systems for Video Technology* 14, no. 8. January 2004. Accessed 12 August 2016 from *www.cse.msu .edu/~rossarun/pubs/RossBioIntro_CSVT2004.pdf*; Yun, W. "The '123' of Biometric Technology." 2003. Accessed 12 August 2016 from *www.newworldencyclopedia.org /entry/Biometrics*; DJW, "Analysis of Biometric Technology and Its Effectiveness for Identification Security." *Yahoo Voices.* 5 May 2011. Accessed 12 August 2016 from *http://voices.yahoo.com/analysis-biometric-technology-its-effectiveness-7607914.html.*

4. The TCSEC Rainbow Series. Used under published permissions. Accessed 12 August 2016 from *http://commons.wikimedia.org/wiki/File:Rainbow_series_documents.jpg.*

5. "The Common Criteria." *Common Criteria.* Accessed 12 August 2016 from *www.com moncriteriaportal.org.*

6. Ibid.

7. Ibid.

8. McIntyre, G., and Krausem, M. "Security Architecture and Design." *Official (ISC)² Guide to the CISSP CBK, 2ⁿᵈ Ed.* Edited by Tipton, H., and Henry, K. Boca Raton, FL: Auerbach Publishers, 2010.

9. Ibid.

10. Ibid.

11. Ibid.

12. Ibid.

13. Ibid.

14. Avolio, Frederic. "Firewalls and Internet Security, the Second Hundred (Internet) Years." Accessed 17 October 2016 from *www.cisco.com/c/en/us/about/press/internet -protocol-journal/back-issues/table-contents-1/ipj-archive/article09186a00800c85ae .html*.

15. Beaver, Kevin. "Finding clarity: Unified threat management systems vs. next-gen fire-walls." Accessed 29 July 2015 from *http://searchsecurity.techtarget.com/tip/Finding-clarity -Unified-threat-management-systems-vs-next-gen-firewalls*.

16. Taylor, Laura. "Guidelines for Configuring your Firewall Rule-Set." Tech *Update Online*. 12 April 2001. Accessed 12 August 2016 from *www.zdnet.com/news/guidelines -for-configuring-your-firewall-rule-set/298790*.

17. Wallen, Jack. "Five Content Filters Suitable for Both Home and Business." 24 Septem-ber 2012. Accessed 12 August 2016 from *www.techrepublic.com/blog/five-apps/five -content-filters-suitable-for-both-home-and-business/*.

18. Pagliery, J. "OMG: 2.1 million people still use AOL dial-up." CNN Money Online. 8 May 2015. Accessed 11 August 2016 from *http://money.cnn.com/2015/05/08 /technology/aol-dial-up/*.

19. Krutz, Ronald L., and Vines, Russell Dean. 2001. *The CISSP Prep Guide: Mastering the Ten Domains of Computer Security*. New York: John Wiley and Sons Inc., 40.

20. VPN Consortium. "VPN Technologies: Definitions and Requirements." March 2006. Accessed 12 August 2016 from *www.vpnc.org/vpn-technologies.html*.

21. Ibid.

Security Technology: Intrusion Detection and Prevention Systems, and Other Security Tools

Do not wait; the time will never be just right. Start where you stand, and work with whatever tools you may have at your command, and better tools will be found as you go along.

NAPOLEON HILL (1883–1970),
FOUNDER OF *THE SCIENCE OF SUCCESS*

Miller Harrison was going to make them sorry and make them pay. Earlier today, his contract with SLS had been terminated and he'd been sent home. Oh sure, the big-shot manager, Charlie Moody, had said Miller would still get paid for the two weeks remaining in his contract, and that the decision was based on "changes in the project and evolving needs as project work continued," but Miller knew better. He knew he'd been let go because of that know-nothing Kelvin and his simpering lapdog Laverne Nguyen. And now he was going to show them and everyone else at SLS who knew more about security.

Miller knew that the secret to hacking into a network successfully was to apply the same patience, attention to detail, and dogged determination that defending a network required. He also knew that the first step in a typical hacking protocol was footprinting—that is, getting a fully annotated diagram of the network. Miller already had one—in a violation of company policy, he had brought a copy home last week when Laverne first started trying to tell him how to do his job.

When they terminated his contract today, Miller's supervisors made him turn in his company laptop and then actually had the nerve to search his briefcase. By then, however, Miller had already stashed all the files and access codes he needed to attack SLS's systems.

To begin, he thought about activating his VPN client to connect to the SLS network from his free Wi-Fi connection at his favorite coffee shop. But then he remembered that Charlie Moody had confiscated the crypto-token that enabled him to use the VPN for remote access, and it would also be obvious who had attacked the system. No problem, Miller thought. Let's see how good SLS is at protecting its antiquated dial-up lines. He connected his laptop to its wireless cellular modem and entered the number for SLS's legacy modem bank; he had gotten the number from the network administrator's desk. "Silly man," he thought, "writing passwords on sticky notes." After the connection was established, Miller positioned his hands on the keyboard and then read the prompt on his screen:

SLS Inc. Company Use Only. Unauthorized use is prohibited and subject to prosecution.

Enter Passphrase:

Miller muttered under his breath. Apparently the SLS security team had rerouted all dial-up connections to the same RADIUS authentication server that the VPN used. So, he was locked out of the back door, but no worries. Miller moved on to his next option, which was to use a back door of his very own. It consisted of a zombie program he'd installed on the company's extranet quality assurance server. No one at SLS worried about securing the QA server because it did not store any production data. In fact, the server wasn't even subject to the change control procedures that were applied to other systems on the extranet.

Miller's action was risky, as there was a slight chance that SLS had added the server to the host intrusion detection and prevention system it deployed last quarter. If so, Miller would be detected before he got too far. He activated the program he used to remotely control the zombie program and typed in the IP address of the computer running the zombie. No response. He opened a command window and pinged the zombie. The computer at that address answered each ping promptly, which meant it was alive and well. Miller checked the zombie's UDP port number and ran an Nmap scan against the port on that system. No response. He cursed the firewall, the policy that controlled it, and the technicians who kept it up to date.

With all of his planned payback cut off at the edge of SLS's network, he decided to continue his hack by going back to the first step—specifically, to perform a detailed fingerprinting of all SLS Internet addresses. Because the front door and both back doors were locked, it was time to get a new floor plan. He launched a simple network port scanner from his Linux laptop and configured it to scan the entire IP address range for SLS's extranet. With a single keystroke, he unleashed the port scanner on the SLS network.

LEARNING OBJECTIVES

Upon completion of this material, you should be able to:

- Identify and describe the categories and models of intrusion detection and prevention systems
- Describe the detection approaches employed by modern intrusion detection and prevention systems
- Define and describe honeypots, honeynets, and padded cell systems
- List and define the major categories of scanning and analysis tools, and describe the specific tools used within each category

Introduction

The protection of an organization's information assets relies at least as much on managerial controls as on technical safeguards, but properly implemented technical solutions guided by policy are an essential component of an information security program. Chapter 6 introduced the subject of security technology and covered some specific technologies, including firewalls, dial-up protection mechanisms, content filtering, and VPNs. This chapter builds on that discussion by describing additional, more advanced technologies that organizations can use to enhance the security of their information assets. These technologies include intrusion detection and prevention systems, honeypots, honeynets, padded cell systems, and scanning and analysis tools.

Intrusion Detection and Prevention Systems

Key Terms

intrusion An adverse event in which an attacker attempts to gain entry into an information system or disrupt its normal operations, almost always with the intent to do harm.

intrusion detection and prevention system (IDPS) The general term for a system that can both detect and modify its configuration and environment to prevent intrusions. An IDPS encompasses the functions of both intrusion detection systems and intrusion prevention technology.

intrusion detection system (IDS) A system capable of automatically detecting an intrusion into an organization's networks or host systems and notifying a designated authority.

An **intrusion** occurs when an attacker attempts to gain entry into an organization's information systems or disrupt their normal operations. Even when such attacks are self-propagating, as with viruses and distributed denial-of-service attacks, they are almost always instigated by someone whose purpose is to harm an organization. Often, the differences among intrusion types lie with the attacker—some intruders don't care which organizations they harm and prefer to remain anonymous, while others crave notoriety. While every intrusion is an incident, not every incident is an intrusion; examples include service outages and natural disasters.

As you learned in Chapter 4, "Planning for Security," intrusion *prevention* consists of activities that deter an intrusion. Some important intrusion prevention activities are writing and implementing good enterprise information security policy; planning and executing effective information security programs; installing and testing technology-based information security countermeasures, such as firewalls and intrusion detection and prevention systems; and conducting and measuring the effectiveness of employee training and awareness activities.

Intrusion *detection* consists of procedures and systems that identify system intrusions. Intrusion *reaction* encompasses the actions an organization takes when an intrusion is detected. These actions seek to limit the loss from an intrusion and return operations to a normal state as rapidly as possible. Intrusion *correction* activities complete the restoration of operations to a normal state and seek to identify the source and method of the intrusion to ensure that the same type of attack cannot occur again—thus reinitiating intrusion prevention.

Information security **intrusion detection systems (IDSs)** became commercially available in the late 1990s. An IDS works like a burglar alarm in that it detects a violation and activates an alarm. This alarm can be a sound, a light or other visual signal, or a silent warning, such as an e-mail message or pager alert. With almost all IDSs, system administrators can choose the configuration of various alerts and the alarm levels associated with each type of alert. Many IDSs enable administrators to configure the systems to notify them directly of trouble via e-mail or pagers. The systems can also be configured—again like a burglar alarm—to notify an external security service of a "break-in." The configurations that enable IDSs to provide customized levels of detection and response are quite complex. A current extension of IDS technology is the incorporation of *intrusion prevention* technology, which can prevent an intrusion from successfully attacking the organization by means of an active response. Because you seldom find such technology that does not also have detection capabilities, the term **intrusion detection and prevention system (IDPS)** is commonly used.

According to NIST SP 800-94, Rev. 1, IDPSs use several response techniques, which can be divided into the following groups:

- An IDPS is capable of interdicting the attack by itself, without human intervention. This could be accomplished by:
  - Terminating the user session or network connection over which the attack is being conducted
  - Blocking access to the target system or systems from the source of the attack, such as a compromised user account, inbound IP address, or other attack characteristic
  - Blocking all access to the targeted information asset

- The IDPS can modify its environment by changing the configuration of other security controls to disrupt an attack. This could include modifying a firewall's rule set or configuring another network device to shut down the communications channel to filter the offending packets.

- Some IDPSs are capable of changing an attack's components by replacing malicious content with benign material or by quarantining a network packet's contents.[1]

❯ IDPS Terminology

To understand how an IDPS works, you must first become familiar with some IDPS terminology.

- **Alarm clustering and compaction**: A process of grouping almost identical alarms that occur nearly at the same time into a single higher-level alarm. This consolidation reduces the number of alarms, which reduces administrative overhead and identifies a relationship among multiple alarms. Clustering may be based on combinations of frequency, similarity in attack signature, similarity in attack target, or other criteria that are defined by system administrators.

- **Alarm filtering**: The process of classifying IDPS alerts so they can be more effectively managed. An IDPS administrator can set up alarm filtering by running the system for a while to track the types of false positives it generates and then adjusting the alarm classifications. For example, the administrator may set the IDPS to discard alarms produced by false attack stimuli or normal network operations. Alarm filters are similar to packet filters in that they can filter items by their source or destination IP addresses, but they can also filter by operating systems, confidence values, alarm type, or alarm severity.

- **Alert** or **alarm**: An indication or notification that a system has just been attacked or is under attack. IDPS alerts and alarms take the form of audible signals, e-mail messages, pager notifications, or pop-up windows.

- **Confidence value**: The measure of an IDPS's ability to correctly detect and identify certain types of attacks. The confidence value an organization places in the IDPS is based on experience and past performance measurements. The confidence value, which is based on *fuzzy logic*, helps an administrator determine the likelihood that an IDPS alert or alarm indicates an actual attack in progress. For example, if a system deemed 90 percent capable of accurately reporting a denial-of-service (DoS) attack sends a DoS alert, there is a high probability that an actual attack is occurring.

- **Evasion**: The process by which attackers change the format and/or timing of their activities to avoid being detected by an IDPS.

- **False attack stimulus**: An event that triggers an alarm when no actual attack is in progress. Scenarios that test the configuration of IDPSs may use false attack stimuli to determine if the IDPSs can distinguish between these stimuli and real attacks.

- **False negative**: The failure of an IDPS to react to an actual attack event. This is the most grievous IDPS failure, given that its purpose is to detect and respond to attacks.

- **False positive**: An alert or alarm that occurs in the absence of an actual attack. A false positive can sometimes be produced when an IDPS mistakes normal system activity for an attack. False positives tend to make users insensitive to alarms and thus reduce their reactions to actual intrusion events.

- **Noise**: Alarm events that are accurate and noteworthy but do not pose significant threats to information security. Unsuccessful attacks are the most common source of IDPS noise, although some noise might be triggered by scanning and enumeration tools run by network users without harmful intent.

- **Site policy**: The rules and configuration guidelines governing the implementation and operation of IDPSs within the organization.

- **Site policy awareness**: An IDPS's ability to dynamically modify its configuration in response to environmental activity. A so-called dynamic IDPS can adapt its reactions in response to administrator guidance over time and the local environment. A dynamic IDPS logs events that fit a specific profile instead of minor events, such as file modifications or failed user logins. A smart IDPS knows when it does *not* need to alert the administrator—for example, when an attack is using a known and documented exploit from which the system is protected.

- **True attack stimulus**: An event that triggers an alarm and causes an IDPS to react as if a real attack is in progress. The event may be an actual attack, in which an attacker is attempting a system compromise, or it may be a drill, in which security personnel are using hacker tools to test a network segment.

- **Tuning**: The process of adjusting an IDPS to maximize its efficiency in detecting true positives while minimizing false positives and false negatives.

❯ Why Use an IDPS?

Key Terms

known vulnerability A published weakness or fault in an information asset or its protective systems that may be exploited and result in loss.

zero day vulnerability An unknown or undisclosed vulnerability in an information asset or its protection systems that may be exploited and result in loss. This vulnerability is also referred to as *zero day* (or *zero hour*) because once it is discovered, the technology owners have zero days to identify, mitigate, and resolve the vulnerability.

There are several compelling reasons to acquire and use an IDPS, beginning with its primary function of intrusion detection. These reasons include documentation, deterrence, and other benefits, as described in the following sections.[2]

Intrusion Detection The primary purpose of an IDPS is to identify and report an intrusion. By detecting the early signs of an intrusion, the organization can quickly contain the attack and prevent or at least substantially mitigate loss or damage to information assets. The notification process is critical; if the organization is not notified that an intrusion is under way, the IDPS serves no real purpose. Once notified, the organization's IR team can activate the IR plan and contain the intrusion. Notification is described later in this chapter.

IDPSs can also help administrators detect the preambles to attacks, which are known as *attack reconnaissance*. Most attacks begin with an organized and thorough probing of the organization's network environment and its defenses. This initial probing is called *doorknob rattling* and is accomplished through two general activities. *Footprinting* refers to activities that gather information about the organization and its network activities and assets, while *fingerprinting* refers to activities that scan network locales for active systems and then identify the network services offered by the host systems. A system that can detect the early warning signs of footprinting and fingerprinting functions like a neighborhood watch that spots would-be burglars as they case the community. This early detection enables administrators to prepare for a potential attack or to minimize potential losses from an attack.

IDPSs can also help the organization protect its assets when its networks and systems are still exposed to **known vulnerabilities** or are unable to respond to a rapidly changing threat environment. Many factors can delay or undermine an organization's ability to secure its systems from attack and subsequent loss. For example, even though popular information security technologies such as scanning tools allow security administrators to evaluate the readiness of their systems, they may still fail to detect or correct a known deficiency or check for vulnerabilities too infrequently. In addition, even when a vulnerability is detected in a timely manner, it cannot always be corrected quickly. Also, because such corrective measures usually require that the administrator install patches and upgrades, they are subject to fluctuations in the administrator's workload.

Note that vulnerabilities might be known to vulnerability-tracking groups without being known to the organization. The number and complexity of reported vulnerabilities continue to increase, so it is extremely difficult to stay on top of them. Instead, organizations rely on developers to identify problems and patch systems, yet there is inevitably a delay between detection and distribution of a patch or update to resolve the vulnerability. Similarly, substantial delays are common between the detection of a new virus or worm and the distribution of a signature that allows antimalware applications to detect and contain the threat.

To further complicate the matter, services that are known to be vulnerable sometimes cannot be disabled or otherwise protected because they are essential to ongoing operations. When a system has a known vulnerability or deficiency, an IDPS can be set up to detect attacks or attempts to exploit existing weaknesses, an important part of the strategy of defense in depth.

While a diligent organization may be well prepared against known vulnerabilities, it's the unknown that still causes the organization concern. **Zero day vulnerabilities** (or zero day attacks) are unknown or undisclosed vulnerabilities that can't be predicted or prepared for. They are called *zero day* (or *zero hour*) because once they are discovered, the technology owners have zero days to identify, mitigate, and resolve the vulnerability. Unfortunately, most of these vulnerabilities become "known" only when they are used in an attack. Therefore, it is critical for the organization to diligently monitor online trade press and industry user groups to stay abreast of such issues.

Organizations continue to expand the number of items on networks they manage and where those items are operated. The Internet of Things finds more and different devices being connected and used, while cloud service use results in valuable assets housed in places where defenses are established with software-defined perimeters in place of the old-school hardware-enforced perimeter. These changes in how networks are used and what can be found on them make the need for IDPS technologies even more pronounced.

Data Collection In the process of analyzing data and network activity, IDPSs can be configured to log data for later analysis. This logging function allows the organization to examine *what* happened after an intrusion occurred and *why*. As an accountability function, logging may even provide the *who* if the individual responsible for the intrusion works within the organization. Even when intruders are not internal, some information may be available, such as where they are connecting from (IP address) and how they connected (browser details). Logging also allows improvement in incident response; evaluation by specialized log monitors, as described later in this chapter; and assessment of the effectiveness of the IDPS itself.

Even if an IDPS fails to prevent an intrusion, it can still contribute to the after-attack review by assisting investigators in determining how the attack occurred, what the intruder accomplished, and which methods the attacker employed. This information can be used to remedy deficiencies and to prepare the organization's network environment for future attacks. The IDPS can also provide forensic information that may be useful if the attacker is caught and then prosecuted or sued.

Examining this information to understand attack frequencies and attributes can help identify insufficient, inappropriate, or compromised security measures. This process can also provide insight for management into threats the organization faces and can help justify current and future expenditures to support and improve incident detection controls. When asked for funding to implement additional security technology, upper management usually requires documentation of the threat from which the organization must be protected.

Attack Deterrence Another reason to install an IDPS is that it serves as a deterrent by increasing the fear of detection among would-be attackers. If internal and external users know that an organization has an IDPS, they are less likely to probe the system or attempt to compromise it, just as criminals are much less likely to break into a house that appears to have a burglar alarm.

Other Reasons to Deploy an IDPS Data collected by an IDPS can also help management with quality assurance and continuous improvement; IDPSs consistently pick up information about attacks that have successfully compromised the outer layers of information security controls, such as a firewall. This information can be used to identify and repair flaws in the security and network architectures, which helps the organization expedite its incident response and make other continuous improvements.

An IDPS can provide a level of quality control for security policy implementation. This can be accomplished when the IDPS is used to detect incomplete firewall configuration when inappropriate network traffic is allowed that should have been filtered at the firewall. This detection could alert administrators to a poorly configured or compromised firewall. IDPSs may also be used to identify security policy violations.

Certain IDPSs can monitor network traffic and systems data in an effort to flag suspicious data transfers and detect unusual activities that could indicate data theft. If the organization's employees have no reason to copy data files over a certain size, an IDPS may be able to detect large file transfers, either from a host-based or network-based IDPS. Similarly, certain protected files may be specified to flag or notify administrators if they are accessed, copied, or modified. This is one of the primary functions of a host-based IDPS, which is described later in this chapter.

Another use of the intrusion awareness that an IDPS provides, even when alerts are given after the actual intrusion, is part of the process known as the *kill chain*. This concept, an

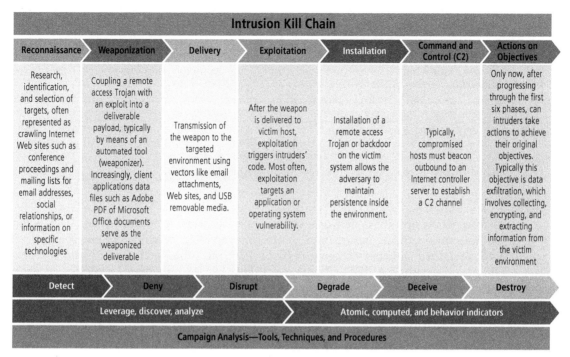

Figure 7-1 The cyberattack and kill chain

Source: https://countuponsecurity.com/tag/kill-chain/.

adaptation of combat tactics brought to the world of information security by Lockheed Martin, is that the success of an attack can be disrupted at several points in the sequence. By disrupting the attack at any point up to the final exfiltration of its proceeds, potential losses can be stopped. Figure 7-1 shows the various steps in the attack sequence and the associated opportunities to interrupt using the kill chain.

❯ Types of IDPSs

Key Terms

agent See *sensor*.

application protocol verification The process of examining and verifying the higher-order protocols (HTTP, FTP, and Telnet) in network traffic for unexpected packet behavior or improper use.

host-based IDPS (HIDPS) An IDPS that resides on a particular computer or server, known as the host, and monitors activity only on that system. Also known as a system integrity verifier.

inline sensor An IDPS sensor intended for network perimeter use and deployed in close proximity to a perimeter firewall to detect incoming attacks that could overwhelm the firewall.

mirror port See *monitoring port*.

monitoring port Also known as a switched port analysis (SPAN) port or mirror port, a specially configured connection on a network device that can view all the traffic that moves through the device.

network-based IDPS (NIDPS) An IDPS that resides on a computer or appliance connected to a segment of an organization's network and monitors traffic on that segment, looking for indications of ongoing or successful attacks.

passive mode An IDPS sensor setting in which the device simply monitors and analyzes observed network or system traffic.

protocol stack verification The process of examining and verifying network traffic for invalid data packets—that is, packets that are malformed under the rules of the TCP/IP protocol.

sensor A hardware and/or software component deployed on a remote computer or network segment and designed to monitor network or system traffic for suspicious activities and report back to the host application. For example, IDPS sensors report to an IDPS application.

switched port analysis (SPAN) port See *monitoring port*.

IDPSs generally operate as network- or host-based systems. A network-based IDPS is focused on protecting network information assets by examining network communications traffic. Two specialized subtypes of network-based IDPSs are the wireless IDPS and the network behavior analysis (NBA) IDPS. The wireless IDPS focuses on wireless networks, as the name indicates, while the NBA IDPS examines traffic flow on a network in an attempt to recognize abnormal patterns like DDoS, malware, and policy violations.

A host-based IDPS protects the server or host's information assets, usually by monitoring the files stored on the system and sometimes by monitoring the actions of connected users; the example shown in Figure 7-2 monitors both network connection activity and current information states on host servers. The application-based model works on one or more host systems that support a single application and defends that application from special forms of attack.

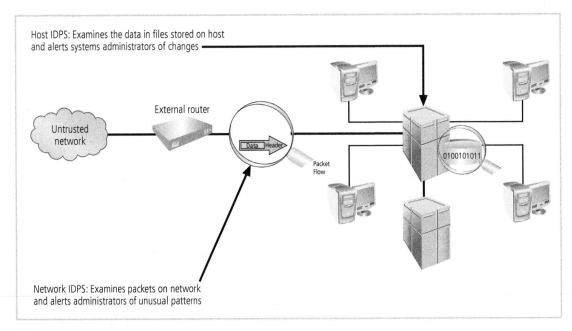

Figure 7-2 Intrusion detection and prevention systems

Network-Based IDPS A network-based IDPS (NIDPS) consists of a specialized hardware appliance and/or software designed to monitor network traffic. The NIDPS may include separate management software, referred to as a console, and a number of specialized hardware and/or software components referred to as **agents** or **sensors**. These agents can be installed on other network segments and/or network technologies to remotely monitor network traffic at multiple locations for a potential intrusion, reporting back to the central NIDPS application. When the NIDPS identifies activity that it is programmed to recognize as an attack, it responds by sending notifications to administrators. When examining incoming packets, an NIDPS looks for patterns within network traffic such as large collections of related items of a certain type, which could indicate that a DoS attack is under way. An NIDPS also examines the exchange of a series of related packets in a certain pattern, which could indicate that a port scan is in progress. An NIDPS can detect many more types of attacks than a host-based IDPS, but it requires a much more complex configuration and maintenance program.

An NIDPS or an NIDPS sensor is installed at a specific place in the network, such as inside an edge router, where it is possible to monitor traffic into and out of a particular network segment. The NIDPS can be deployed to monitor a specific grouping of host computers on a specific network segment, or it may be installed to monitor all traffic between the systems that make up an entire network. When placed next to a hub, switch, or other key networking device, the NIDPS may use that device's monitoring port. A **monitoring port**, also known as a **switched port analysis (SPAN) port** or **mirror port**, is capable of viewing all traffic that moves through the entire device. In the early 1990s, before switches became standard for connecting networks in a shared-collision domain, hubs were used. Hubs receive traffic from one node and retransmit it to all other nodes. This configuration allows any device connected to the hub to monitor all traffic passing through the hub. Unfortunately, it also represents a security risk because anyone connected to the hub can monitor all the traffic that moves through the network segment. Switches, on the other hand, create dedicated point-to-point links between their ports. These links create a higher level of transmission security and privacy to effectively prevent anyone from capturing and thus eavesdropping on the traffic passing through the switch. Unfortunately, the ability to capture the traffic is necessary for the use of an IDPS. Thus, monitoring ports are required. These connections enable network administrators to collect traffic from across the network for analysis by the IDPS, as well as for occasional use in diagnosing network faults and measuring network performance.

Figure 7-3 shows data from the Snort Network IDPS Engine. In this case, the display is a sample screen from Snorby, a client that can manage Snort as well as display generated alerts.

To determine whether an attack has occurred or is under way, NIDPSs compare measured activity to known signatures in their knowledge base. The comparisons are made through a special implementation of the TCP/IP stack that reassembles the packets and applies protocol stack verification, application protocol verification, or other verification and comparison techniques.

In the process of **protocol stack verification**, NIDPSs look for invalid data packets—that is, packets that are malformed under the rules of the TCP/IP protocol. A data packet is verified

Figure 7-3 Snorby demo

Source: github.com/snorby.

when its configuration matches one that is defined by the various Internet protocols. The elements of these protocols (IP, TCP, UDP, and application layers such as HTTP) are combined in a complete set called the *protocol stack* when the software is implemented in an operating system or application. Many types of intrusions, especially DoS and DDoS attacks, rely on the creation of improperly formed packets to take advantage of weaknesses in the protocol stack in certain operating systems or applications.

 For more information on the Snort Network IDPS Engine, visit www.snort.org. For more information on the Snorby front end for Snort and other IDPSs, visit github.com/snorby.

In **application protocol verification**, the higher-order protocols (HTTP, SMTP, and FTP) are examined for unexpected packet behavior or improper use. Sometimes an attack uses valid protocol packets but in excessive quantities; in the case of the tiny fragment attack, the packets are also excessively fragmented. While protocol stack verification looks for violations in the protocol packet *structure*, application protocol verification looks for violations in the protocol packet's *use*. One example of this kind of attack is DNS cache poisoning, in which valid packets exploit poorly configured DNS servers to inject false information and corrupt the servers' answers to routine DNS queries from other systems on the network. Unfortunately, this higher-order examination of traffic can have the same effect on an IDPS as it can on a firewall—that is, it slows the throughput of the system. It may be necessary to have more than one NIDPS installed, with one of them performing protocol stack verification and one performing application protocol verification.

The advantages of NIDPSs include the following:

- Good network design and placement of NIDPS devices can enable an organization to monitor a large network using only a few devices.

- NIDPSs are usually passive devices and can be deployed into existing networks with little or no disruption to normal network operations.

- NIDPSs are not usually susceptible to direct attack and may not be detectable by attackers.[3]

The disadvantages of NIDPSs include the following:

- An NIDPS can become overwhelmed by network volume and fail to recognize attacks it might otherwise have detected. Some IDPS vendors are accommodating the need for ever faster network performance by improving the processing of detection algorithms in dedicated hardware circuits. Additional efforts to optimize rule set processing may also reduce the overall effectiveness of detecting attacks.

- NIDPSs require access to all traffic to be monitored. The broad use of switched Ethernet networks has replaced the ubiquity of shared-collision domain hubs. Because many switches have limited or no monitoring port capability, some networks are not capable of providing aggregate data for analysis by an NIDPS. Even when switches do provide monitoring ports, they may not be able to mirror all activity with a consistent and reliable time sequence.

- NIDPSs cannot analyze encrypted packets, making some network traffic invisible to the process. The increasing use of encryption that hides the contents of some or all packets by some network services (such as SSL, SSH, and VPN) limits the effectiveness of NIDPSs.

- NIDPSs cannot reliably ascertain whether an attack was successful, which requires ongoing effort by the network administrator to evaluate logs of suspicious network activity.

- Some forms of attack are not easily discerned by NIDPSs, specifically those involving fragmented packets. In fact, some NIDPSs are so vulnerable to malformed packets that they may become unstable and stop functioning.[4]

Wireless NIDPS A wireless IDPS monitors and analyzes wireless network traffic, looking for potential problems with the wireless protocols (Layers 2 and 3 of the OSI model). Unfortunately, wireless IDPSs cannot evaluate and diagnose issues with higher-layer protocols like TCP and UDP. Wireless IDPS capability can be built into a device that provides a wireless access point (AP).

Sensors for wireless networks can be located at the access points, on specialized sensor components, or incorporated into selected mobile stations. Centralized management stations collect information from these sensors, much as other network-based IDPSs do, and aggregate the information into a comprehensive assessment of wireless network intrusions. The implementation of wireless IDPSs includes the following issues:

- Physical security: Unlike wired network sensors, which can be physically secured, many wireless sensors are located in public areas like conference rooms, assembly areas, and hallways to obtain the widest possible network range. Some of these locations may even be outdoors; more and more organizations are deploying networks in external locations. Thus, the physical security of these devices may require additional configuration and monitoring.

- Sensor range: A wireless device's range can be affected by atmospheric conditions, building construction, and the quality of the wireless network card and access point. Some IDPS tools allow an organization to identify the optimal location for sensors by modeling the wireless footprint based on signal strength. Sensors are most effective when their footprints overlap.

- Access point and wireless switch locations: Wireless components with bundled IDPS capabilities must be carefully deployed to optimize the IDPS sensor detection grid. The minimum range is just that; you must guard against the possibility of an attacker connecting to a wireless access point from a range far beyond the minimum.

- Wired network connections: Wireless network components work independently of the wired network when sending and receiving traffic between stations and access points. However, a network connection eventually integrates wireless traffic with the organization's wired network. In places where no wired network connection is available, it may be impossible to deploy a sensor.

- Cost: The more sensors you deploy, the more expensive the configuration. Wireless components typically cost more than their wired counterparts, so the total cost of ownership of IDPSs for both wired and wireless varieties should be carefully considered.

- AP and wireless switch locations: The locations of APs and wireless switches are important for organizations buying bundled solutions (APs with preinstalled IDPS applications).[5]

In addition to the traditional types of intrusions detected by other IDPSs, the wireless IDPS can also detect existing WLANs and WLAN devices for inventory purposes as well as detect the following types of events:

- Unauthorized WLANs and WLAN devices
- Poorly secured WLAN devices
- Unusual usage patterns
- The use of wireless network scanners
- DoS attacks and conditions
- Impersonation and man-in-the-middle attacks[6]

Wireless IDPSs are generally more accurate than other types of IDPSs, mainly because of the reduced set of protocols and packets they have to examine. However, they are unable to detect certain passive wireless protocol attacks, in which the attacker monitors network traffic without active scanning and probing. They are also susceptible to evasion techniques, which are described earlier in this chapter. By simply looking at wireless devices, which are often visible in public areas, attackers can design customized evasion methods to exploit the system's channel scanning scheme. Wireless IDPSs can protect their associated WLANs, but they may be susceptible to logical and physical attacks on the wireless access point or the IDPS devices themselves.

The best-configured security technology in the world cannot withstand an attack using a well-placed brick.[7]

7

Network Behavior Analysis System NBA systems identify problems related to the flow of network traffic. They use a version of the anomaly detection method described later in this section to identify excessive packet flows that might occur in the case of equipment malfunction, DoS attacks, virus and worm attacks, and some forms of network policy violations. NBA IDPSs typically monitor internal networks but occasionally monitor connections between internal and external networks. Intrusion detection and prevention typically includes the following relevant flow data:

- Source and destination IP addresses
- Source and destination TCP or UDP ports or ICMP types and codes
- Number of packets and bytes transmitted in the session
- Starting and ending timestamps for the session[8]

  *Most NBA sensors can be deployed in **passive mode** only, using the same connection methods (e.g., network tap, switch spanning port) as network-based IDPSs. Passive sensors that are performing direct network monitoring should be placed so that they can monitor key network locations, such as the divisions between networks, and key network segments, such as demilitarized zone (DMZ) subnets. **Inline sensors** are typically intended for network perimeter use, so they would be deployed in close proximity to the perimeter firewalls, often between the firewall and the Internet border router to limit incoming attacks that could overwhelm the firewall.*[9]

NBA sensors can most commonly detect:

- DoS attacks (including DDoS attacks)
- Scanning
- Worms

- Unexpected application services, such as tunneled protocols, back doors, and use of forbidden application protocols

- Policy violations

NBA sensors offer the following intrusion prevention capabilities, which are grouped by sensor type:

- Passive only: Ending the current TCP session. A passive NBA sensor can attempt to end an existing TCP session by sending TCP reset packets to both endpoints.

- Inline only: Performing inline firewalling. Most inline NBA sensors offer firewall capabilities that can be used to drop or reject suspicious network activity.

- Both passive and inline:

  - Reconfiguring other network security devices. Many NBA sensors can instruct network security devices such as firewalls and routers to reconfigure themselves to block certain types of activity or route it elsewhere, such as to a quarantined virtual local area network (VLAN).

  - Running a third-party program or script. Some NBA sensors can run an administrator-specified script or program when certain malicious activity is detected.[10]

Host-Based IDPS While a network-based IDPS resides on a network segment and monitors activities across that segment, a **host-based IDPS (HIDPS)** or an HIDPS sensor resides on a particular computer or server, known as the host, and monitors activity only on that system. HIDPSs are also known as system integrity verifiers because they benchmark and monitor the status of key system files and detect when an intruder creates, modifies, or deletes monitored files. An HIDPS has an advantage over an NIDPS in that it can access encrypted information traveling over the network and use it to make decisions about potential or actual attacks. Also, because the HIDPS works on only one computer system, all the traffic it examines traverses that system. The packet delivery mode, whether switched or in a shared-collision domain, is not a factor.

An HIDPS is also capable of monitoring system configuration databases, such as Windows registries, in addition to stored configuration files like .ini, .cfg, and .dat files. Most HIDPSs work on the principle of configuration or change management, which means that they record the sizes, locations, and other attributes of system files. The HIDPS triggers an alert when file attributes change, new files are created, or existing files are deleted. An HIDPS can also monitor systems logs for predefined events. The HIDPS examines these files and logs to determine if an attack is under way or has occurred; it also examines whether the attack is succeeding or was successful. The HIDPS maintains its own log file so that an audit trail is available even when hackers modify files on the target system to cover their tracks. Once properly configured, an HIDPS is very reliable. The only time an HIDPS produces a false positive alert is when an authorized change occurs for a monitored file. This action can be quickly reviewed by an administrator, who may choose to disregard subsequent changes to the same set of files. If properly configured, an HIDPS can also detect when users attempt to modify or exceed their access authorization level.

An HIDPS classifies files into various categories and then sends notifications when changes occur. Most HIDPSs provide only a few general levels of alert notification. For example, an administrator can configure an HIDPS to report changes in a system folder, such as C:\Windows, and configure changes to a security-related application, such as C:\TripWire. The configuration rules may classify changes to a specific application folder (for example, C:\Program Files\Microsoft Office) as normal and hence unreportable. Administrators can configure the system to log all activity but to send them a page or e-mail only if a reportable security event occurs. Because frequent modifications occur to data files and to internal application files such as dictionaries and configuration files, a poorly configured HIDPS can generate a large volume of false alarms.

Managed HIDPSs can monitor multiple computers simultaneously by creating a configuration file on each monitored host and by making each HIDPS report back to a master console system, which is usually located on the system administrator's computer. This master console monitors the information provided by the managed hosts and notifies the administrator when it senses recognizable attack conditions. Figure 7-4 shows a sample screen from Tripwire, a popular HIDPS.

One of the most common methods of categorizing folders and files is by color coding. Critical systems components are coded red and usually include the system registry, any folders

7

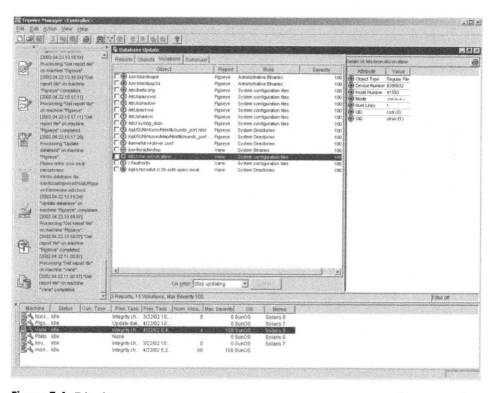

Figure 7-4 Tripwire

Source: Tripwire.

containing the OS kernel, and application software. Critically important data should also be included in the red category. Support components, such as device drivers and other relatively important files, are generally coded yellow. User data is usually coded green, not because it is unimportant, but because monitoring changes to user data is practically difficult and strategically less urgent. User data files are frequently modified, but systems kernel files, for example, should only be modified during upgrades or installations. If the preceding three-tier system is too simplistic, an organization can use a scale of 0–100, as long as the scale doesn't become excessively granular. For example, an organization could easily create confusion for itself by classifying level 67 and 68 intrusions. Sometimes simpler is better.

The advantages of HIDPSs include:

- An HIDPS or one of its sensors can detect local events on host systems and detect attacks that may elude a network-based IDPS.
- An HIDPS functions on the host system, where encrypted traffic will have been decrypted and is available for processing.
- The use of switched network protocols does not affect an HIDPS.
- An HIDPS can detect inconsistencies in how applications and systems programs were used by examining the records stored in audit logs. This can enable the HIDPS to detect some types of attacks, including Trojan horse programs.[11]

The disadvantages of HIDPSs include:

- HIDPSs pose more management issues because they are configured and managed on each monitored host. An HIDPS requires more management effort to install, configure, and operate than a comparably sized NIDPS solution.
- An HIDPS is vulnerable both to direct attacks and to attacks against the host operating system. Either attack can result in the compromise or loss of HIDPS functionality.
- An HIDPS is not optimized to detect multihost scanning, nor is it able to detect scanning from network devices that are not hosts, such as routers or switches. Unless complex correlation analysis is provided, the HIDPS will not be aware of attacks that span multiple devices in the network.
- An HIDPS is susceptible to some DoS attacks.
- An HIDPS can use large amounts of disk space to retain the host OS audit logs; for the HIDPS to function properly, it may be necessary to add disk capacity to the system.
- An HIDPS can inflict a performance overhead on its host systems, and in some cases may reduce system performance below acceptable levels.[12]

❯ IDPS Detection Methods

Key Terms

anomaly-based detection Also known as *behavior-based detection*, an IDPS detection method that compares current data and traffic patterns to an established baseline of normalcy.
behavior-based detection See *anomaly-based detection*.

clipping level A predefined assessment level that triggers a predetermined response when surpassed. Typically, the response is to write the event to a log file and/or notify an administrator.

knowledge-based detection See *signature-based detection.*

misuse detection See *signature-based detection.*

signature-based detection Also known as *knowledge-based detection* or *misuse detection*, the examination of system or network data in search of patterns that match known attack signatures.

signatures Patterns that correspond to a known attack.

stateful protocol analysis (SPA) The comparison of vendor-supplied profiles of protocol use and behavior against observed data and network patterns in an effort to detect misuse and attacks.

IDPSs use a variety of detection methods to monitor and evaluate network traffic. Three methods dominate: signature-based detection, anomaly-based detection, and stateful protocol analysis.

Signature-Based Detection An IDPS that uses **signature-based detection** (sometimes called **knowledge-based detection** or **misuse detection**) examines network traffic in search of patterns that match known **signatures**—that is, preconfigured, predetermined attack patterns. Signature-based technology is widely used because many attacks have clear and distinct signatures:

- Footprinting and fingerprinting activities use ICMP, DNS querying, and e-mail routing analysis.

- Exploits use a specific attack sequence designed to take advantage of a vulnerability to gain access to a system.

- DoS and DDoS attacks, during which the attacker tries to prevent the normal usage of a system, overload the system with requests so that its ability to process them efficiently is compromised or disrupted.[13]

A potential problem with the signature-based approach is that new attack patterns must continually be added to the IDPS's database of signatures; otherwise, attacks that use new strategies will not be recognized and might succeed. Another weakness of the signature-based method is that a slow, methodical attack involving multiple events might escape detection. The only way signature-based detection can resolve this vulnerability is to collect and analyze data over longer periods of time, a process that requires substantially greater data storage capability and additional processing capacity. However, detection in real time becomes extremely unlikely.

Similarly, using signature-based detection to compare observed events with known patterns is relatively simplistic; the technologies that deploy it typically cannot analyze some application or network protocols, nor can they understand complex communications.

Anomaly-Based Detection Anomaly-based detection (or **behavior-based detection**) collects statistical summaries by observing traffic that is known to be normal. This normal period of evaluation establishes a performance baseline over a period of time known as the *training period.* Once the baseline is established, the IDPS periodically samples network activity and uses statistical methods to compare the sampled activity to the baseline. When the measured activity is outside the baseline parameters—exceeding the **clipping level**—the IDPS sends an alert to the administrator. The baseline data can include variables such as host memory or CPU usage, network packet types, and packet quantities.

The profiles compiled by an anomaly-based detection IDPS are generally either static or dynamic. Static profiles do not change until modified or recalibrated by an administrator. Dynamic profiles periodically collect additional observations on data and traffic patterns and then use that information to update their baselines. This can prove to be a vulnerability if the attacker uses a very slow attack, because the system using the dynamic detection method interprets attack activity as normal traffic and updates its profile accordingly.

The advantage of anomaly-based detection is that the IDPS can detect new types of attacks because it looks for abnormal activity of any type. Unfortunately, these systems require much more overhead and processing capacity than signature-based IDPSs because they must constantly compare patterns of activity against the baseline. Another drawback is that these systems may not detect minor changes to system variables and may generate many false positives. If the actions of network users or systems vary widely, with periods of low activity interspersed with periods of heavy packet traffic, this type of IDPS may not be suitable because the dramatic swings will almost certainly generate false alarms. Because of the complexity of anomaly-based detection, its impact on the overhead computing load of the host computer, and the number of false positives it can generate, this type of IDPS is less commonly used than the signature-based type.

Stateful Protocol Analysis As you learned in Chapter 6, stateful inspection firewalls track each network connection between internal and external systems using a state table to record which station sent which packet and when. An IDPS extension of this concept is **stateful protocol analysis (SPA)**. SPA uses the opposite of a signature approach. Instead of comparing known attack patterns against observed traffic or data, the system compares known normal or benign protocol profiles against observed traffic. These profiles are developed and provided by the protocol vendors. Essentially, the IDPS knows how a protocol such as FTP is supposed to work, and therefore can detect anomalous behavior. By storing relevant data detected in a session and then using it to identify intrusions that involve multiple requests and responses, the IDPS can better detect specialized, multisession attacks. This process is sometimes called *deep packet inspection* because SPA closely examines packets at the application layer for information that indicates a possible intrusion.[14]

SPA can examine authentication sessions for suspicious activity as well as for attacks that incorporate unusual commands, such as commands that are out of sequence or submitted repeatedly. SPA can also detect intentionally malformed commands or commands that are outside the expected length parameters.[15]

The models used for SPA are similar to signatures in that they are provided by vendors. These models are based on industry protocol standards established by such entities as the Internet Engineering Task Force, but they vary along with the protocol implementations in such documents. Also, proprietary protocols are not published in sufficient detail to enable an IDPS to provide accurate and comprehensive assessments.

Unfortunately, the analytical complexity of session-based assessments is the principal drawback to this type of IDPS method. It also requires heavy processing overhead to track multiple simultaneous connections. Additionally, unless a protocol violates its fundamental behavior, this IDPS method may completely fail to detect an intrusion. One final concern is that the IDPS may actually interfere with the normal operations of the protocol it is examining.[16]

Log File Monitors

> ### Key Terms
>
> **log file monitor (LFM)** An attack detection method that reviews the log files generated by computer systems, looking for patterns and signatures that may indicate an attack or intrusion is in process or has already occurred.
>
> **security information and event management (SIEM)** A software-enabled approach to aggregating, filtering, and managing the reaction to events, many of which are collected by logging activities of IDPSs and network management devices.

A **log file monitor (LFM)** IDPS is similar to an NIDPS. Using an LFM, the system reviews the log files generated by servers, network devices, and even other IDPSs, looking for patterns and signatures that may indicate an attack or intrusion is in process or has already occurred. This attack detection is enhanced by the fact that the LFM can look at multiple log files from different systems. The patterns that signify an attack can be subtle and difficult to distinguish when one system is examined in isolation, but they may be more identifiable when the events recorded for the entire network and each of its component systems can be viewed as a whole. Of course, this holistic approach requires considerable resources because it involves the collection, movement, storage, and analysis of very large quantities of log data.

Log file monitoring is often implemented in organizations with the use of a **security information and event management (SIEM)** software-enabled system. Coined in 2005 by Mark Nicolett and Amrit Williams of The Gartner Group, SIEM is a combination of software and procedures implemented across an organization that collects, analyzes, reports, and sometimes can react to events determined by patterns of events found in the aggregated data. Data sources for SIEM systems can include IDPS products, identity and access management systems, network communication devices, and specific host systems. SIEM systems often are tasked to provide alerts and intelligence to manage the reaction to many forms of adverse events that might affect the organization. SIEM implementation may be a requirement for some compliance programs that organizations must follow. SIEM systems are often used to manage the incident reaction process once incident response protocols are invoked.

⟩ IDPS Response Behavior

Each IDPS responds to external stimulation in a different way, depending on its configuration and function. Some respond in active ways, collecting additional information about the intrusion, modifying the network environment, or even taking action against the intrusion. Others respond in passive ways—for example, by setting off alarms or notifications or collecting passive data through SNMP traps.

IDPS Response Options When an IDPS detects a possible intrusion, it has several response options, depending on the organization's policy, objectives, and system capabilities. When configuring an IDPS's responses, the system administrator must ensure that a response to an attack or potential attack does not inadvertently exacerbate the situation. For example, if an NIDPS reacts to suspected DoS attacks by severing the network connection, the attack is a success. Similar attacks repeated at intervals will thoroughly disrupt an organization's business operations.

An analogy to this approach is a car thief who spots a desirable target early in the morning, strikes the car with a rolled-up newspaper to trigger the alarm, and then ducks into the bushes. The car owner wakes up, checks the car, determines there is no danger, resets the alarm, and goes back to bed. The thief repeats the triggering action every half-hour or so until the owner disables the alarm, leaving the thief free to steal the car without worrying about the alarm.

IDPS responses can be classified as active or passive. An active response is a definitive action that is automatically initiated when certain types of alerts are triggered. These responses can include collecting additional information, changing or modifying the environment, and taking action against the intruders. Passive-response IDPSs simply report the information they have collected and wait for the administrator to act. Generally, the administrator chooses a course of action after analyzing the collected data. A passive IDPS is the more common implementation, although most systems include some active options that are disabled by default.

The following list describes some of the responses an IDPS can be configured to produce. Note that some of these responses apply only to a network-based or host-based IDPS, while others are applicable to both.[17]

- Audible/visual alarm: The IDPS can trigger a sound file, beep, whistle, siren, or other audible or visual notification to alert the administrator of an attack. The most common type of notification is the computer pop-up, which can be configured with color indicators and specific messages. The pop-up can also contain specifics about the suspected attack, the tools used in the attack, the system's level of confidence in its own determination, and the addresses and locations of the systems involved.

- SNMP traps and plug-ins: The Simple Network Management Protocol contains trap functions, which allow a device to send a message to the SNMP management console indicating that a certain threshold has been crossed, either positively or negatively. The IDPS can execute this trap to inform the SNMP console an event has occurred. Some advantages of this operation include the relatively standard implementation of SNMP in networking devices; the ability to configure the network system to use SNMP traps in this manner; the ability to use systems specifically to handle SNMP traffic, including IDPS traps; and the ability to use standard communications networks.

- E-mail message: The IDPS can send e-mail to notify network administrators of an event. Many administrators use smartphones and other e-mail devices to check for alerts and other notifications frequently. Organizations should use caution in relying on e-mail systems as the primary means of communication from an IDPS because attacks or even routine performance issues can disrupt, delay, or block such messages.

- Phone, pager, or SMS message: The IDPS can be configured to dial a phone number and send a preconfigured pager or SMS text message.

- Log entry: The IDPS can enter information about the event into an IDPS system log file or operating system log file. This information includes addresses, times, involved systems, and protocol information. The log files can be stored on separate servers to prevent skilled attackers from deleting entries about their intrusions.

- Evidentiary packet dump: Organizations that require an audit trail of IDPS data may choose to record all log data in a special way. This method allows the organization to perform further analysis on the data and to submit the data as evidence in a civil or criminal case. Once the data has been written using a cryptographic hashing algorithm (see Chapter 8), it becomes evidentiary documentation—that is, suitable for criminal or civil court use. However, this packet logging can be resource-intensive, especially in DoS attacks.

- Take action against the intruder: Although it is not advisable, organizations can take action against an intruder using trap-and-trace, back-hacking, or trace-back methods. Such responses involve configuring intrusion detection systems to trace the data from the target system back to the attacking system to initiate a counterattack. While this response may sound tempting, it may not be legal. An organization only owns a network to its perimeter, so conducting traces or back-hacking to systems beyond that point may make the organization just as criminally liable as the original attackers. Also, the "attacking system" is sometimes a compromised intermediary system; in other cases, attackers use address spoofing. In either situation, a counterattack would actually harm an innocent third party. Any organization that plans to configure retaliation efforts into an automated IDPS is strongly encouraged to seek legal counsel.

- Launch program: An IDPS can be configured to execute a specific program when it detects specific types of attacks. Several vendors have specialized tracking, tracing, and response software that can be part of an organization's intrusion response strategy.

- Reconfigure firewall: An IDPS can send a command to the firewall to filter out suspected packets by IP address, port, or protocol. (Unfortunately, it is still possible for a skilled attacker to break into a network simply by spoofing a different address, shifting to a different port, or changing the protocols used in the attack.) While it may not be easy, an IDPS can block or deter intrusions via one of the following methods:

  - Establishing a block for all traffic from the suspected attacker's IP address or even from the entire source network the attacker appears to be using. This blocking can be set for a specific period of time and reset to normal rules after that period has expired.

  - Establishing a block for specific TCP or UDP port traffic from the suspected attacker's address or source network. Only services that seem to be under attack are blocked.

  - Blocking all traffic to or from the organization's Internet connection or other network interface if the severity of the suspected attack warrants such a response.[18]

  - Terminating the session: Terminating the session by using the TCP/IP protocol specified packet *TCP close* is a simple process. Some attacks would be deterred or blocked by session termination, but others would simply continue when the attacker issues a new session request.

- Terminating the connection: The last resort for an IDPS under attack is to terminate the organization's internal or external connections. Smart switches can cut traffic to or from a specific port if the connection is linked to a system that is malfunctioning or otherwise interfering with efficient network operations. As indicated earlier, this response should be the last attempt to protect information, as termination may actually be the goal of the attacker.

Note: The following sections have been adapted from NIST SP 800-94 and SP 800-94, Rev. 1, "Guide to Intrusion Detection and Prevention Systems," and their predecessor, NIST SP 800-31, "Intrusion Detection Systems."

Reporting and Archiving Capabilities Many, if not all, commercial IDPSs can generate routine reports and other detailed documents, such as reports of system events and intrusions detected over a particular reporting period. Some systems provide statistics or logs in formats that are suitable for inclusion in database systems or for use in report generating packages.

Failsafe Considerations for IDPS Responses Failsafe features protect an IDPS from being circumvented or defeated by an attacker. Several functions require failsafe measures; for instance, IDPSs need to provide silent, reliable monitoring of attackers. If the response function of an IDPS breaks this silence by broadcasting alarms and alerts in plaintext over the monitored network, attackers can detect the IDPS and directly target it in the attack. Encrypted tunnels or other cryptographic measures that hide and authenticate communications are excellent ways to ensure the reliability of the IDPS.

❯ Selecting IDPS Approaches and Products

The wide array of available intrusion detection products addresses a broad range of security goals and considerations; selecting products that represent the best fit for a particular organization is challenging. The following considerations and questions can help you prepare a specification for acquiring and deploying an intrusion detection product.

Technical and Policy Considerations To determine which IDPS best meets an organization's needs, first consider its environment in technical, physical, and political terms.

What Is Your Systems Environment? The first requirement for a potential IDPS is that it function in your systems environment. This is important; if an IDPS is not designed to accommodate the information sources on your systems, it will not be able to see anything— neither normal activity nor an attack—on those systems.

- What are the technical specifications of your systems environment?

  First, specify the technical attributes of your systems environment, including network diagrams and maps that specify the number and locations of hosts; operating systems for each host; the number and types of network devices, such as routers, bridges, and switches; the number and types of terminal servers and dial-up connections; and descriptions of any network servers, including their types, configurations, and the application software and versions running on each. If you run an enterprise network management system, specify it here.

- What are the technical specifications of your current security protections?

    Describe the security protections you already have in place. Specify numbers, types, and locations of network firewalls, identification and authentication servers, data and link encryptors, antivirus packages, access control products, specialized security hardware (such as crypto accelerators for Web servers), virtual private networks, and any other security mechanisms on your systems.

- What are the goals of your enterprise?

    Some IDPSs are designed to accommodate the special needs of certain industries or market niches, such as electronic commerce, health care, or financial services.

    Define the functional goals of your enterprise that are supported by your systems. Several goals can be associated with a single organization.

- How formal is the system environment and management culture in your organization?

    Organizational styles vary depending on their function and traditional culture. For instance, the military and other organizations that deal with national security tend to operate with a high degree of formality, especially when contrasted with universities or other academic environments. Some IDPSs support enforcement of formal use policies, with built-in configuration options that can enforce common issue-specific or system-specific security policies, as well as provide a library of reports for typical policy violations or routine matters.

What Are Your Security Goals and Objectives? The next step is to articulate the goals and objectives you want to attain by using an IDPS.

- Is your organization primarily concerned with protecting itself from outside threats?

    Perhaps the easiest way to identify security goals is by categorizing your organization's threat concerns. Identify its concerns regarding external threats.

- Is your organization concerned about insider attacks?

    Address concerns about threats that originate within your organization. For example, a shipping clerk might attempt to access and alter the payroll system, or an authorized user might exceed his privileges and violate your organization's security policy or laws. As another example, a customer service agent might be driven by curiosity to access earnings and payroll records for company executives.

- Does your organization want to use the output of your IDPS to determine new needs?

    System usage monitoring is sometimes a generic system management tool used to determine when system assets require upgrading or replacement.

- Does your organization want to use an IDPS to maintain managerial control over network usage rather than security controls?

Some organizations implement system use policies that may be classified as personnel management rather than system security. For example, they might prohibit access to pornographic Web sites or other sites, or prohibit the use of organizational systems to send harassing e-mail or other messages. Some IDPSs provide features that detect such violations of management controls.

What Is Your Existing Security Policy? You should review your existing organization security policy because it is the template against which your IDPS will be configured. You may find that you need to augment the policy or derive the following items from it.

- How is it structured?

  It is helpful to articulate the goals outlined in the security policy. These goals include standard security goals, such as integrity, confidentiality, and availability, as well as more generic management goals, such as privacy, protection from liability, and manageability.

- What are the general job descriptions of your system users?

  List the general job functions of system users as well as the data and network access that each function requires. Several functions are often applied to a single user.

- Does the policy include reasonable use policies or other management provisions?

  As mentioned above, the security policies of many organizations include system use policies.

- Has your organization defined processes for dealing with specific policy violations?

  It is helpful to know what the organization plans to do when the IDPS detects that a policy has been violated. If the organization doesn't intend to react to such violations, it may not make sense to configure the IDPS to detect them. On the other hand, if the organization wants to respond to such violations, the IDPS's staff should be informed so it can deal with alarms in an appropriate manner.

Organizational Requirements and Constraints
Your organization's operational goals, constraints, and culture will affect the selection of the IDPS and other security tools and technologies to protect your systems. Consider the following requirements and limitations.

What Requirements Are Levied from Outside the Organization?

- Is your organization subject to oversight or review by another organization?
- If so, does that oversight authority require IDPSs or other specific system security resources?
- Are there requirements for public access to information on your organization's systems? Do regulations or statutes require that information to be accessible by the public during certain hours of the day or during certain intervals?
- Are any other security-specific requirements levied by law? Are there legal requirements for protection of personal information stored on your systems? Such information can include earnings or medical records. Are there legal requirements for investigating security violations that divulge or endanger personal information?

- Are there internal audit requirements for security best practices or due diligence?

  Do any of these audit requirements specify functions that the IDPSs must provide or support?

- Is the system subject to accreditation?

  If so, what is the accreditation authority's requirement for IDPSs or other security protection?

- Are there requirements for law enforcement investigation and resolution of security incidents?

  Do they require any IDPS functions, especially those that involve collection and protection of IDPS logs as evidence?

What Are Your Organization's Resource Constraints? IDPSs can protect the systems of an organization, but at a price. It makes little sense to incur additional expenses for IDPS features if your organization does not have sufficient systems or personnel to handle the alerts they will generate.

- What is the budget for acquisition and life cycle support of intrusion detection hardware, software, and infrastructure?

  Remember that the IDPS software is not the only element of the total cost of ownership; you may also have to acquire a system for running the software, obtain specialized assistance to install and configure the system, and train your personnel. Ongoing operations may also require additional staff or outside contractors.

- Is there sufficient staff to monitor an intrusion detection system full time?

  Some IDPSs require around-the-clock attendance by systems personnel. If your organization cannot meet this requirement, you may want to explore systems that accommodate part-time attendance or unattended use.

- Does your organization have authority to instigate changes based on the findings of an intrusion detection system?

  You and your organization must be clear about how to address problems uncovered by an IDPS. If you are not empowered to handle incidents that arise as a result of monitoring, you should coordinate your selection and configuration of the IDPS with the person who is empowered.

IDPS Product Features and Quality

It's important to evaluate any IDPS product by carefully considering the following questions:

Is the Product Sufficiently Scalable for Your Environment? Many IDPSs cannot function within large or widely distributed enterprise network environments.

How Has the Product Been Tested? Simply asserting that an IDPS has certain capabilities does not demonstrate they are real. You should request demonstrations of an IDPS to evaluate its suitability for your environment and goals.

- Has the product been tested against functional requirements?

  Ask the vendor about any assumptions made for the goals and constraints of customer environments.

- Has the product been tested for performance against anticipated load?

  Ask vendors for details about their products' ability to perform critical functions with high reliability under load conditions similar to those expected in the production environment.

- Has the product been tested to reliably detect attacks?

  Ask vendors for details about their products' ability to respond to attacks reliably.

- Has the product been tested against attack?

  Ask vendors for details about their products' security testing. If the product includes network-based vulnerability assessment, ask whether test routines that produce system crashes or other denials of service have been identified and flagged in system documentation and interfaces.

What User Level of Expertise Is Targeted by the Product?
Different IDPS vendors target users with different levels of technical and security expertise. Ask vendors to describe their assumptions about users of their products.

Is the Product Designed to Evolve as the Organization Grows?
An important goal of product design is the ability to adapt to your needs over time.

- Can the product adapt to growth in user expertise?

  Ask here whether the IDPS's interface can be configured on the fly to accommodate shortcut keys, customizable alarm features, and custom signatures. Ask also whether these features are documented and supported.

- Can the product adapt to growth and change of the organization's systems infrastructure?

  This question addresses the ability of the IDPS to scale to an expanding and increasingly diverse network. Most vendors have experience in adapting their products as target networks grow. Ask also about commitments to support new protocol standards and platform types.

- Can the product adapt to growth and change in the security threat environment?

  This question is especially critical given the current Internet threat environment, in which 30 to 40 new attacks are posted to the Web every month.

What Are the Support Provisions for the Product?
Like other systems, IDPSs require maintenance and support over time. These needs should be identified in a written report.

- What are the commitments for product installation and configuration support?

  Many vendors provide expert assistance to customers when installing and configuring IDPSs. Other vendors expect your own staff to handle such functions, and provide only telephone or e-mail support.

- What are the commitments for ongoing product support?

  Ask about the vendor's commitment to supporting your use of its IDPS product.

- Are subscriptions to signature updates included?

  Most IDPSs are misuse detectors, so their value is only as good as the signature database against which events are analyzed. Most vendors provide subscriptions to signature updates for a year or other specified period of time.

- How often are subscriptions updated?

  In today's threat environment, in which 30 to 40 new attacks are published every month, this is a critical question.

- After a new attack is made public, how quickly will the vendor ship a new signature?

  If you are using IDPSs to protect highly visible or heavily traveled Internet sites, it is critical that you receive the signatures for new attacks as soon as possible.

- Are software updates included?

  Most IDPSs are software products and therefore subject to bugs and revisions. Ask the vendor about its support for software updates and bug patches, especially for the product you purchase.

- How quickly will software updates and patches be issued after a problem is reported to the vendor?

  Software bugs in IDPSs can allow attackers to nullify their protective effect, so any problems must be fixed reliably and quickly.

- Are technical support services included? What is the cost?

  In this category, technical support services mean vendor assistance in tuning or adapting your IDPS to accommodate special needs. These needs might include monitoring a custom or legacy system within your enterprise or reporting IDPS results in a custom protocol or format.

- What are the provisions for contacting technical support via e-mail, telephone, online chats, or Web-based reporting?

  The contact provisions will probably tell you whether technical support services are accessible enough to support incident handling or other time-sensitive needs.

- Are any guarantees associated with the IDPS?

  As with other software products, IDPSs traditionally come with few guarantees; however, in an attempt to gain market share, some vendors are initiating guarantee programs.

- What training resources does the vendor provide?

  Once an IDPS is selected, installed, and configured, your personnel can operate it, but they need to be trained in its use. Some vendors provide this training as part of the product package.

- What additional training resources are available from the vendor and at what cost?

  If the vendor does not provide training as part of the IDPS package, you should budget appropriately to train your personnel.

7

❯ Strengths and Limitations of IDPSs

Although intrusion detection systems are a valuable addition to an organization's security infrastructure, they have strengths and weaknesses, like any technology. As you plan the security strategy for your organization's systems, you need to understand what IDPSs can be trusted to do and what goals might be better served by other security mechanisms.

Strengths of Intrusion Detection and Prevention Systems   Intrusion detection and prevention systems perform the following functions well:

- Monitoring and analysis of system events and user behaviors
- Testing the security states of system configurations
- Baselining the security state of a system, then tracking any changes to that baseline
- Recognizing patterns of system events that correspond to known attacks
- Recognizing patterns of activity that statistically vary from normal activity
- Managing operating system audit and logging mechanisms and the data they generate
- Alerting appropriate staff by appropriate means when attacks are detected
- Measuring enforcement of security policies encoded in the analysis engine
- Providing default information security policies
- Allowing people who are not security experts to perform important security monitoring functions

Limitations of Intrusion Detection and Prevention Systems   Intrusion detection systems cannot perform the following functions:

- Compensating for weak or missing security mechanisms in the protection infrastructure, such as firewalls, identification and authentication systems, link encryption systems, access control mechanisms, and virus detection and eradication software
- Instantaneously detecting, reporting, and responding to an attack when there is a heavy network or processing load
- Detecting newly published attacks or variants of existing attacks
- Effectively responding to attacks launched by sophisticated attackers
- Automatically investigating attacks without human intervention
- Resisting all attacks that are intended to defeat or circumvent them
- Compensating for problems with the fidelity of information sources
- Dealing effectively with switched networks

There is also the considerable challenge of configuring an IDPS to respond accurately to a perceived threat. Once a device is empowered to react to an intrusion by filtering or even severing a communication session or by severing a communication circuit, the impact from a false positive becomes significant. It's one thing to fill an administrator's e-mail box or compile a large log file with suspected attacks; it's quite another to shut down critical communications. Some forms of attacks, conducted by attackers called *IDPS terrorists*, are designed to trip the organization's IDPS, essentially causing the organization to conduct its own DoS attack by overreacting to an actual but insignificant attack.

Note: The preceding sections were drawn and adapted from NIST SP 800-94 and SP 800-94, Rev. 1, "Guide to Intrusion Detection and Prevention Systems," and their predecessor, NIST SP 800-31, "Intrusion Detection Systems."

> Deployment and Implementation of an IDPS

Key Terms

blacklist A list of systems, users, files, or addresses that have been associated with malicious activity; it is commonly used to block those entities from systems or network access.

centralized IDPS control strategy An IDPS implementation approach in which all control functions are implemented and managed in a central location.

fully distributed IDPS control strategy An IDPS implementation approach in which all control functions are applied at the physical location of each IDPS component.

partially distributed IDPS control strategy An IDPS implementation approach that combines the best aspects of the centralized and fully distributed strategies.

threshold A value that sets the limit between normal and abnormal behavior. See also *clipping level*.

whitelist A list of systems, users, files, or addresses that are known to be benign; it is commonly used to expedite those entities' access to systems or networks.

Deploying and implementing an IDPS is not always a straightforward task. The strategy for deploying an IDPS should account for several factors, the foremost being how the IDPS will be managed and where it should be placed. These factors determine the number of administrators needed to install, configure, and monitor the IDPS, as well as the number of management workstations, the size of the storage needed for data generated by the systems, and the ability of the organization to detect and respond to remote threats.

NIST SP 800-94, Rev. 1 provides the following recommendations for implementation:

- Organizations should ensure that all IDPS components are secured appropriately; IDPSs are a prime target for attackers. If they can compromise the IDPS, they are then free to conduct unobserved attacks on other systems.

- Organizations should consider using multiple types of IDPS technologies to achieve more comprehensive and accurate detection and prevention of malicious activity. Defense in depth, even within IDPS technologies, is key to detecting the wide and varied attack strategies the organization faces.

- Organizations that plan to use multiple types of IDPS technologies or multiple products of the same IDPS technology type should consider whether the IDPSs should be integrated. Using integrated technologies provides much easier configuration and administration. Using a common management platform provides multidevice cross-assessments and reporting.

- Before evaluating IDPS products, organizations should define the requirements that the products should meet. Knowing what you need in an IDPS can prevent purchasing a product that does not solve the organization's problems, and can save time and money in the long haul.

- When evaluating IDPS products, organizations should consider using a combination of data sources to evaluate the products' characteristics and capabilities. Vendors have been known to "influence" reviews by using friendly reviewers or just writing their own and posting them to review sites. Finding multiple reviews from different sources should provide more accurate insight into the strengths and weaknesses of any technology.[19]

IDPS Control Strategies A control strategy determines how an organization supervises and maintains the configuration of an IDPS. It also determines how the input and output of the IDPS are managed. The three common control strategies for an IDPS are centralized, partially distributed, and fully distributed. The IT industry has been exploring technologies and practices to enable the distribution of computer processing cycles and data storage for many years. These explorations have long considered the advantages and disadvantages of the centralized strategy versus strategies with varying degrees of distribution. In the early days of computing, all systems were fully centralized, resulting in a control strategy that provided high levels of security and control as well as efficiencies in resource allocation and management. During the 1980s and 1990s, with the rapid growth in networking and computing capabilities, the trend was to implement a fully distributed strategy. In the mid-1990s, however, the high costs of a fully distributed architecture became apparent, and the IT industry shifted toward a mixed strategy of partially distributed control. A strategy of partial distribution, in which some features and components are distributed and others are centrally controlled, has emerged as the recommended practice for IT systems in general and for IDPS control systems in particular.

Centralized Control Strategy In a centralized IDPS control strategy, all IDPS control functions are implemented and managed in a central location, as represented in Figure 7-5 by the large square symbol labeled "IDS Console." The IDPS console includes the management software, which collects information from the remote sensors (the triangular symbols in the figure), analyzes the systems or networks, and determines whether the current situation has deviated from the preconfigured baseline. All reporting features are implemented and managed from this central location.

The primary advantages of this strategy are cost and control. With one central implementation, there is one management system, one place to monitor the status of the systems or networks, one location for reports, and one staff to perform needed administrative tasks. This centralization of IDPS management supports task specialization because all managers are either located near the IDPS management console or can acquire an authenticated remote connection to it, and technicians are located near the remote sensors. This means that each person can focus on an assigned task. In addition, the central control group can evaluate the systems and networks as a whole, and because it can compare pieces of information from all sensors, the group is better positioned to recognize a large-scale attack.

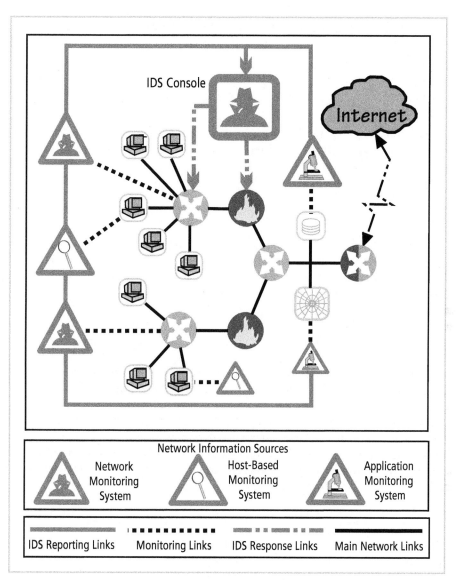

Figure 7-5 Centralized IDPS control[20]

Source: Adapted from Scarfone and Mell, NIST SP 800-94.

Fully Distributed Control Strategy A fully distributed IDPS control strategy, illustrated in Figure 7-6, is the opposite of the centralized strategy. All control functions are applied at the physical location of each IDPS component; in the figure, these functions are represented as small square symbols enclosing a computer icon. Each monitoring site uses its own paired sensors to perform its own control functions and achieve the necessary detection, reaction, and response. Thus, each sensor/agent is best configured to deal with its own

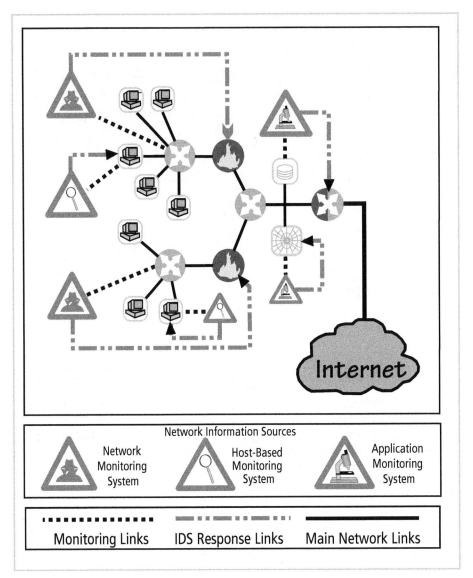

Network Information Sources

Network Monitoring System

Host-Based Monitoring System

Application Monitoring System

Monitoring Links   IDS Response Links   Main Network Links

Figure 7-6   Fully distributed IDPS control[21]

Source: Adapted from Scarfone and Mell, NIST SP 800-94.

environment. Because the IDPSs do not have to wait for a response from a centralized control facility, their response time to individual attacks is greatly enhanced.

Partially Distributed Control Strategy A **partially distributed IDPS control strategy**, depicted in Figure 7-7, combines the best aspects of the other two strategies. While the individual agents can still analyze and respond to local threats, their reporting to a hierarchical central facility enables the organization to detect widespread attacks. This blended approach

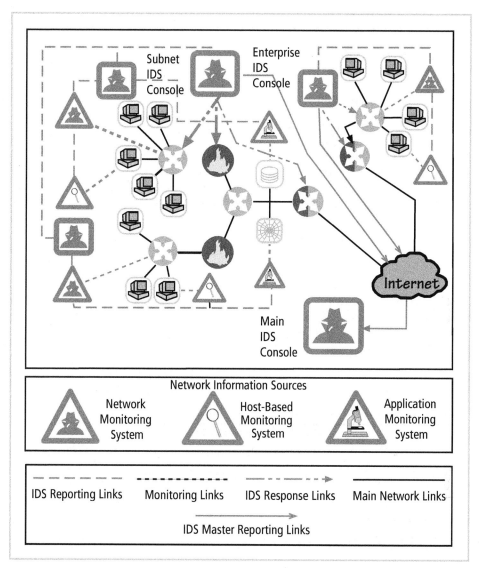

Figure 7-7   Partially distributed IDPS control[22]

Source: Adapted from Scarfone and Mell, NIST SP 800-94.

to reporting is one of the more effective methods of detecting intelligent attackers, especially those who probe an organization at multiple points of entry, trying to identify the systems' configurations and weaknesses before launching a concerted attack. The partially distributed control strategy also allows the organization to optimize for economy of scale in the implementation of key management software and personnel, especially in the reporting areas. When the organization can create a pool of security managers to evaluate reports from multiple distributed IDPS systems, it becomes more capable of detecting distributed attacks before they become unmanageable.

IDPS Deployment   Given the highly technical skills required to implement and configure IDPSs and the imperfection of the technology, great care must be taken when deciding where to locate the components, both in their physical connection to the network and host devices and in how they are logically connected to each other. Because IDPSs are designed to detect, report, and even react to anomalous stimuli, placing IDPSs in an area where such traffic is common can result in excessive reporting. Moreover, locating the administrators' monitoring systems in such areas can desensitize them to the information flow and cause them to miss actual attacks in progress.

As an organization selects an IDPS and prepares for implementation, planners must select a deployment strategy that is based on a careful analysis of the organization's information security requirements and that integrates with the existing IT infrastructure while causing minimal impact. After all, the purpose of the IDPS is to detect anomalous situations, not create them. One consideration is the skill level of the personnel who install, configure, and maintain the systems. An IDPS is a complex system in that it involves numerous remote monitoring agents, both on individual systems and networks, which require proper configuration to gain the proper authentication and authorization. As the IDPS is deployed, each component should be installed, configured, fine-tuned, tested, and monitored. A mistake in any step of the deployment process may produce a range of problems—from a minor inconvenience to a network-wide disaster. Thus, the people who install the IDPS and the people who use and manage the system require proper training.

NIDPSs and HIDPSs can be used in tandem to cover the individual systems that connect to an organization's networks and the networks themselves. It is important to use a phased implementation strategy so the entire organization isn't affected at once. A phased implementation strategy also allows security technicians to resolve problems that do arise without compromising the very information security the IDPS is installed to protect. When sequencing the implementation, the organization should first implement the NIDPSs, as they are easier to configure than their host-based counterparts. After the NIDPSs are configured and running without problems, the HIDPSs can be installed to protect the critical systems on the host server. Once the NIDPSs and HIDPSs are working, administrators should scan the network with a vulnerability scanner like Nmap or Nessus to determine if it picks up anything new or unusual and if the IDPS can detect the scans.

Deploying Network-Based IDPSs   The placement of the sensor agents is critical to the operation of all IDPSs, but especially for NIDPSs. NIST recommends the following four locations for NIDPS sensors, as illustrated in Figure 7-8.

Location 1: Behind each external firewall, in the network DMZ. This location has the following characteristics:

- The IDPS sees attacks that originate from the outside and may penetrate the network's perimeter defenses.

- The IDPS can identify problems with the network firewall policy or performance.

- The IDPS sees attacks that might target the Web server or FTP server, both of which commonly reside in this DMZ.

- Even if the incoming attack is not detected, the IDPS can sometimes recognize patterns in the outgoing traffic that suggest the server has been compromised.

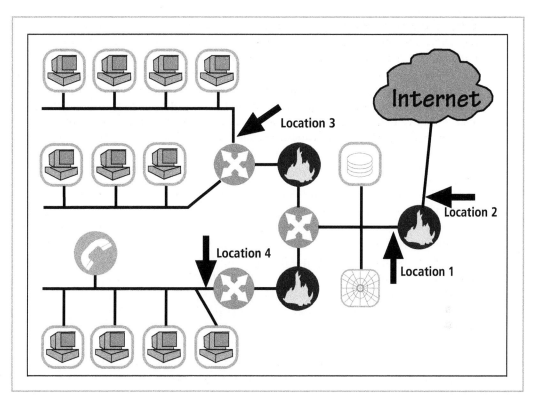

Figure 7-8 Network IDPS sensor locations[23]

Source: Adapted from Scarfone and Mell, NIST SP 800-94.

Location 2: Outside an external firewall. This location has the following characteristics:

- The IDPS documents the number of attacks originating on the Internet that target the network.
- The IDPS documents the types of attacks originating on the Internet that target the network.

Location 3: On major network backbones. This location has the following characteristics:

- The IDPS monitors a large amount of a network's traffic, thus increasing its chances of spotting attacks.
- The IDPS detects unauthorized activity by authorized users within the organization's security perimeter.

Location 4: On critical subnets. This location has the following characteristics:

- The IDPS detects attacks that target critical systems and resources.
- This location allows organizations with limited resources to focus on the most valuable network assets.[24]

Deploying Host-Based IDPSs The proper implementation of HIDPSs can be a painstaking and time-consuming task, as each HIDPS must be customized to its host systems. Deployment begins with implementing the most critical systems first. This poses a dilemma for the deployment team because the first systems to be implemented are mission-critical, and any problems in the installation could be catastrophic to the organization. Thus, it may be beneficial to practice an implementation on one or more test servers configured on a network segment that resembles the mission-critical systems. Practice helps the installation team gain experience and helps determine if the installation might trigger any unusual events. Gaining an edge on the learning curve by training on nonproduction systems benefits the overall deployment process by reducing the risk of unforeseen complications.

Installation continues until all systems are installed or the organization reaches the planned degree of coverage it will accept, in terms of the number of systems or percentage of network traffic. To provide ease of management, control, and reporting, each HIDPS should be configured to interact with a central management console.

Just as technicians can install the HIDPS in offline systems to develop expertise and identify potential problems, users and managers can learn about the operation of the HIDPS by using a test facility. This facility could use the offline systems configured by technicians and be connected to the organization's backbone to allow the HIDPS to process actual network traffic. This setup will also enable technicians to create a baseline of normal traffic for the organization. During system testing, training scenarios can be developed that enable users to recognize and respond to common attacks. To ensure effective and efficient operation, the management team can establish policy for the operation and monitoring of the HIDPS.

❯ Measuring the Effectiveness of IDPSs

When selecting an IDPS, an organization typically examines the following four measures of comparative effectiveness:

- *Thresholds: A **threshold** is a value that usually specifies a maximum acceptable level, such as x failed connection attempts in 60 seconds, or x characters for a filename length. Thresholds are most often used for anomaly-based detection and stateful protocol analysis.*

- *Blacklists and whitelists: A **blacklist** is used to document hosts, TCP or UDP port numbers, ICMP types and codes, applications, usernames, URLs, filenames, or file extensions, that have been associated with malicious activity. Blacklists, also known as hot lists, typically allow IDPSs to block activity that is highly likely to be malicious, and may also be used to assign a higher priority to alerts that match blacklist entries. Some IDPSs generate dynamic blacklists that are used to temporarily block recently detected threats (e.g., activity from an attacker's IP address). A **whitelist** is a list of discrete entities that are known to be benign. Whitelists are typically used on a granular basis, such as protocol by protocol, to reduce or ignore false positives involving known benign activity from trusted hosts. Whitelists and blacklists are most commonly used in signature-based detection and stateful protocol analysis.*

- *Alert settings: Most IDPS technologies allow administrators to customize each alert type. Examples of actions that can be performed on an alert type include:*
  - *Toggling it on or off*

- *Setting a default priority or severity level*
- *Specifying what information should be recorded and what notification methods (e.g., e-mail, pager) should be used*
- *Specifying which prevention capabilities should be used*

Some products also suppress alerts if an attacker generates many alerts in a short period of time and may also temporarily ignore all future traffic from the attacker. This is to prevent the IDPS from being overwhelmed by alerts.

- *Code viewing and editing: Some IDPS technologies permit administrators to see some or all of the detection-related code. This is usually limited to signatures, but some technologies allow administrators to see additional code, such as programs used to perform stateful protocol analysis.*[25]

Once implemented, IDPSs are evaluated using two dominant metrics. First, administrators evaluate the number of attacks detected in a known collection of probes. Second, the administrators examine the level of use at which the IDPSs fail; this level is commonly measured in megabits per second of network traffic. An evaluation of an IDPS might read something like this: *At 100 Mb/s, the IDPS was able to detect 97 percent of directed attacks.* This is a dramatic change from the previous method used for assessing IDPS effectiveness, which was based on the total number of signatures the system was currently running—somewhat of a "more is better" approach. This evaluation method was flawed for several reasons. Not all IDPSs use simple signature-based detection, and some systems use the almost infinite combination of network performance characteristics in anomaly-based detection to identify a potential attack. Also, some sophisticated signature-based systems actually use *fewer* signatures or rules than older, simpler versions—in direct contrast to traditional signature-based assessments, these systems suggest that less may actually be more. Recognizing that the size of the signature base is an insufficient measure of an IDPS's effectiveness led to the development of stress test measurements for evaluating its performance. These measurements only work, however, if the administrator has a collection of known negative and positive actions that can be proven to elicit a desired response. Because developing this collection can be tedious, most IDPS vendors provide testing mechanisms to verify that their systems are performing as expected. Some of these testing processes enable the administrator to do the following:

- Record and retransmit packets from a real virus or worm scan.
- Record and retransmit packets from a real virus or worm scan with incomplete TCP/IP session connections (missing SYN packets).
- Conduct a real virus or worm attack against a hardened or sacrificial system.

This last measure is important because future IDPSs will probably include much more detailed information about the overall site configuration. According to an expert in the field, "It may be necessary for the IDPSs to be able to actively probe a potentially vulnerable machine, in order to either preload its configuration with correct information or perform a retroactive assessment. An IDPS that performed some kind of actual system assessment would be a complete failure in today's generic testing labs, which focus on replaying attacks and scans against nonexistent machines."[26]

With the rapid growth in technology, each new generation of IDPSs will require new testing methodologies. However, the measured values that continue to hold interest for IDPS administrators and managers will most certainly include some assessment of how much traffic the IDPS can handle, the numbers of false positives and false negatives it generates, and a measure of the IDPS's ability to detect actual attacks. Vendors of IDPS systems could also include a report of alarms sent and the relative accuracy of the system in correctly matching the alarm level to the true seriousness of the threat. Some planned metrics for IDPSs include the flexibility of signatures and detection policy customization.

IDPS administrators may soon be able to purchase tools that test IDPS effectiveness. Until these tools are available from a neutral third party, however, the diagnostics from IDPS vendors will always be suspect. No vendor, no matter how reliable, would provide a test that its system would fail.

One note of caution: There is a strong tendency among IDPS administrators to use common vulnerability assessment tools, such as Nmap or Nessus, to evaluate the capabilities of an IDPS. While this may seem like a good idea, the tools will not work as expected because most IDPS systems are equipped to recognize the differences between a locally implemented vulnerability assessment tool and a true attack.

To accurately assess the effectiveness of IDPS systems, the testing process should be as realistic as possible in its simulation of an actual event. This means coupling realistic traffic loads with realistic levels of attacks. You cannot expect an IDPS to respond to a few packet probes as if they represent a DoS attack. In one reported example, a program was used to create a synthetic load of network traffic made up of many TCP sessions, with each session consisting of a SYN (synchronization) packet, a series of data, and ACK (acknowledgment) packets, but no FIN or connection termination packets. Of the several IDPS systems tested, one of them crashed due to lack of resources while it waited for the sessions to be closed. Another IDPS passed the test with flying colors because it did not perform state tracking on the connections. Neither of the tested IDPS systems worked as expected, but the one that didn't perform state tracking was able to remain working and therefore received a better score on the test.[27]

Honeypots, Honeynets, and Padded Cell Systems

Key Terms

honeynet A monitored network or network segment that contains multiple honeypot systems.
honeypot An application that entices people who are illegally perusing the internal areas of a network by providing simulated rich content while the software notifies the administrator of the intrusion.
padded cell system A protected honeypot that cannot be easily compromised.

A class of powerful security tools that go beyond routine intrusion detection are known variously as honeypots, honeynets, or padded cell systems. To understand why these tools are not yet widely used, you must first understand how they differ from a traditional IDPS.

Honeypots are decoy systems designed to lure potential attackers away from critical systems. In the industry, they are also known as decoys, lures, and flytraps. When several honeypot systems are connected together on a network segment, it may be called a **honeynet**. A honeypot system or honeynet subnetwork contains pseudo-services that emulate well-known services, but it is configured in ways that make it look vulnerable to attacks. This combination is meant to lure attackers into revealing themselves—the idea is that once organizations have detected these attackers, they can better defend their networks against future attacks that target real assets. In sum, honeypots are designed to do the following:

- Divert an attacker from critical systems.

- Collect information about the attacker's activity.

- Encourage the attacker to stay on the system long enough for administrators to document the event and perhaps respond.

Because the information in a honeypot appears to be valuable, any unauthorized access to it constitutes suspicious activity. Honeypots are outfitted with sensitive monitors and event loggers that detect attempts to access the system and collect information about the potential attacker's activities. A simple IDPS that specializes in honeypot techniques is called Deception Toolkit; Figure 7-9 shows the configuration of this honeypot as it waits for an attack.

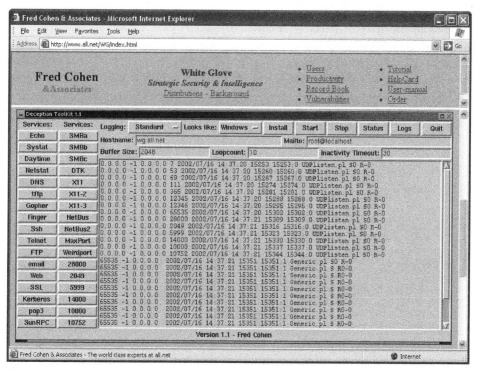

Figure 7-9 Deception Toolkit

Source: Fred Cohen & Associates, used with permission.

A hardened honeypot, or **padded cell system**, operates in tandem with a traditional IDPS. After attracting attackers with tempting data, the IDPS detects the attackers, and then the padded cell system seamlessly transfers them to a special simulated environment where they can cause no harm—hence the name *padded cell*. As in honeypots, this environment can be filled with interesting data, which can convince an attacker that the attack is going according to plan. Like honeypots, padded cells are well-instrumented and offer unique opportunities for a target organization to monitor the actions of an attacker.

IDPS researchers have used padded cell and honeypot systems since the late 1980s, but until recently no commercial versions of these products were available. It is important to seek guidance from legal counsel before using either of these systems in your operating environment, because using an attractant and then launching a back hack or counterstrike might be illegal in some areas, and could make the organization vulnerable to a lawsuit or criminal complaint.

The advantages and disadvantages of using the honeypot or padded cell approach are summarized in the following lists.

Advantages:

- Attackers can be diverted to targets that they cannot damage.
- Administrators have time to decide how to respond to an attacker.
- Attackers' actions can be easily and more extensively monitored, and the records can be used to refine threat models and improve system protections.
- Honeypots may be effective at catching insiders who are snooping around a network.

Disadvantages:

- The legal implications of using such devices are not well understood.
- Honeypots and padded cells have not yet been shown to be generally useful security technologies.
- An expert attacker, once diverted into a decoy system, may become angry and launch a more aggressive attack against an organization's systems.
- Administrators and security managers need a high level of expertise to use these systems.[28]

❯ Trap-and-Trace Systems

> ### Key Terms
>
> **back hack** The process of illegally attempting to determine the source of an intrusion by tracing it and trying to gain access to the originating system.
>
> **enticement** The act of attracting attention to a system by placing tantalizing information in key locations.
>
> **entrapment** The act of luring a person into committing a crime in order to get a conviction.
>
> **pen register** An application that records information about outbound communications.
>
> **trap-and-trace application** An application that combines the function of honeypots or honeynets with the capability to track the attacker back through the network.

Trap-and-trace applications, which are an extension of the attractant technologies discussed in the previous section, are still in use. These systems use a combination of techniques to detect an intrusion and then trace it back to its source. The trap usually consists of a honeypot or padded cell and an alarm. While the intruders are distracted (or trapped) by what they perceive to be successful intrusions, the system notifies the administrator of their presence. The trace feature is an extension of the honeypot or padded cell approach. The trace— which is similar to caller ID—is a process by which the organization attempts to identify an entity discovered in unauthorized areas of the network or systems. If the intruder is someone inside the organization, administrators are completely within their power to track the person and turn the case over to internal or external authorities. If the intruder is outside the organization's security perimeter, then numerous legal issues arise. One popular professional trap-and-trace software suite, Symantec's ManHunt, and companion honeypot application, ManTrap, were discontinued in 2006. No similar products have taken their place due to the drawbacks and complications of using these technologies.

Trap-and-trace systems are similar to **pen registers**, earlier versions of which recorded numbers that were dialed in voice communications. Older pen registers were much like key loggers for phones, but more current models and trap-and-trace systems are used in data networks as well as voice communications networks. According to the Electronic Frontier Foundation, trap-and-trace systems record inbound communications attributes such as phone numbers or IP addresses, while pen registers are used frequently in law enforcement and antiterrorism operations to record outbound communications attributes.[29]

On the surface, trap-and-trace systems seem like an ideal solution. Security is no longer limited to defense; security administrators can now go on the offensive to track down perpetrators and turn them over to the appropriate authorities. Under the guise of justice, less scrupulous administrators may even be tempted to **back hack**, or break into a hacker's system to find out as much as possible about the hacker. Vigilante justice would be an appropriate term for these activities, which are deemed unethical by most codes of professional conduct. In tracking the hacker, administrators may end up wandering through other organizations' systems, especially if a more wily hacker has used IP spoofing, compromised systems, or other techniques to throw trackers off the trail. In other words, the back-hacking administrator becomes the hacker.

Trap-and-trace systems and pen registers are covered under Title 18, U.S. Code Chapter 206, §3121, which essentially states that you can't use one unless you're a service provider attempting to prevent misuse and (1) it is used for systems maintenance and testing, (2) it is used to track connections, or (3) you have permission from the user of the service:

> *Except as provided in this section, no person may install or use a pen register or a trap and trace device without first obtaining a court order under section 3123 of this title or under the Foreign Intelligence Surveillance Act of 1978 (50 U.S.C. 1801 et seq.).*
>
> *(b) Exception—The prohibition of subsection (a) does not apply with respect to the use of a pen register or a trap and trace device by a provider of electronic or wire communication service—*
>
> *1. relating to the operation, maintenance, and testing of a wire or electronic communication service or to the protection of the rights or property of such*

provider, or to the protection of users of that service from abuse of service or unlawful use of service; or

2. *to record the fact that a wire or electronic communication was initiated or completed in order to protect such provider, another provider furnishing service toward the completion of the wire communication, or a user of that service, from fraudulent, unlawful or abusive use of service; or*

3. *where the consent of the user of that service has been obtained.*[30]

There are more legal drawbacks to trap and trace. The trap portion frequently involves honeypots or honeynets; when using them, administrators should be careful not to cross the line between **enticement** and **entrapment**. Enticement is legal and ethical, but entrapment is not. It is difficult to gauge the effect of such systems on average users, especially if they have been nudged into looking at the information. Administrators should also be wary of the *wasp trap syndrome*, which describes a concerned homeowner who installs a wasp trap in his back yard to trap the few insects he sees flying about. Because these traps use scented bait, however, they wind up attracting far more wasps than were originally present. Security administrators should keep the wasp trap syndrome in mind before implementing honeypots, honeynets, padded cells, or trap-and-trace systems.

❯ Active Intrusion Prevention

Some organizations want to do more than simply wait for the next attack, so they implement active countermeasures. One tool that provides active intrusion prevention is known as LaBrea. This "sticky" honeypot and IDPS works by taking up the unused IP address space within a network. When LaBrea notes an ARP request, it checks to see if the requested IP address is valid on the network. If the address is not being used by a real computer or network device, LaBrea pretends to be a computer at that IP address and allows the attacker to complete the TCP/IP connection request, known as the three-way handshake. Once the handshake is complete, LaBrea changes the TCP sliding window size to a low number to hold open the attacker's TCP connection for many hours, days, or even months. Holding the connection open but inactive greatly slows down network-based worms and other attacks. It also gives LaBrea time to notify system and network administrators about anomalous behavior on the network.

 For more information on LaBrea, visit its Web page at http://labrea.sourceforge.net/labrea-info .html.

Scanning and Analysis Tools

> ### Key Terms
>
> **attack protocol** A logical sequence of steps or processes used by an attacker to launch an attack against a target system or network.
> **fingerprinting** The systematic survey of a targeted organization's Internet addresses collected during the footprinting phase to identify the network services offered by the hosts in that range.
> **footprinting** The organized research and investigation of Internet addresses owned or controlled by a target organization.

To secure a network, someone in the organization must know exactly where the network needs to be secured. Although this step may sound simple and obvious, many companies skip it. They install a perimeter firewall and then relax, lulled into a sense of security by this single layer of defense. To truly assess the risks within a computing environment, you must deploy technical controls using a strategy of defense in depth, which is likely to include IDPSs, active vulnerability scanners, passive vulnerability scanners, automated log analyzers, and protocol analyzers (commonly referred to as sniffers). As you've learned, an IDPS helps to secure networks by detecting intrusions; the remaining items in the preceding list help administrators identify where the network needs securing. More specifically, scanner and analysis tools can find vulnerabilities in systems, holes in security components, and unsecured aspects of the network.

Although some information security experts may not perceive them as defensive tools, scanners, sniffers, and other vulnerability analysis applications can be invaluable because they enable administrators to see what the attacker sees. Some of these tools are extremely complex and others are rather simple. Some tools are expensive commercial products, but many of the best scanning and analysis tools are developed by the hacker community or open-source project teams and are available for free on the Web. Good administrators should have several hacking Web sites bookmarked and should try to keep up with chat room discussions on new vulnerabilities, recent conquests, and favorite assault techniques. Security administrators are well within their rights to use tools that potential attackers use in order to examine network defenses and find areas that require additional attention.

In the military, there is a long and distinguished history of generals inspecting the troops under their command before battle. In a similar way, security administrators can use vulnerability analysis tools to inspect the host computers and network devices under their supervision. A word of caution, though: many of these scanning and analysis tools have distinct signatures, and some Internet service providers (ISPs) scan for these signatures. If the ISP discovers someone using hacker tools, it can revoke that user's access privileges. Therefore, administrators are advised to establish a working relationship with their ISPs and notify them of any plans that could lead to misunderstandings.

For example, Figures 7-10 and 7-11 show that running a perfectly legal home version of Nessus causes the host computer's Norton Security Suite to interpret the Nessus scans as malware.

Scanning tools are typically used as part of an **attack protocol** to collect information that an attacker needs to launch a successful attack. The process of collecting publicly available information about a potential target is known as **footprinting**. The attacker uses public Internet data sources to perform keyword searches and identify the network addresses of an organization. This research is augmented by browsing the organization's Web pages. Web pages usually contain information about internal systems, the people who develop the Web pages, and other tidbits that can be used for social engineering attacks. For example, the *view source* option on most popular Web browsers allows users to see the source code behind the graphics. Details in the source code of the Web page can provide clues to potential attackers and give them insight into the configuration of an internal network, such as the locations and directories for Common Gateway Interface (CGI) script bins and the names or addresses of computers and servers.

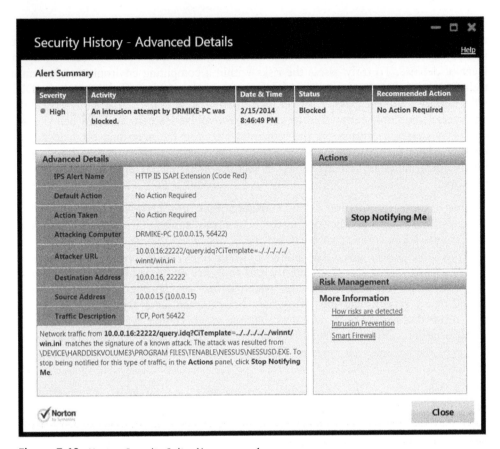

Figure 7-10 Norton Security Suite: Nessus scan 1

Source: Norton by Symantec.

In addition, public business Web sites such as Forbes or Yahoo Business often reveal information about their company structure, commonly used company names, and other details that attackers find useful. Furthermore, common search engines allow attackers to query for any site that links to their proposed target. By doing a bit of initial Internet research, an attacker can often find additional Internet locations that are not commonly associated with the company—that is, business-to-business (B2B) partners and subsidiaries. Armed with this information, the attacker can find the "weakest link" into the target network.

For example, consider a company that has a large data center in Atlanta. The data center has been secured, so an attacker will have a difficult time breaking into it via the Internet. However, the attacker has run a "link" query on a search engine and found a small Web server that links to the company's main Web server. After further investigation, the attacker learns that the server was set up by an administrator at a remote facility that has an unrestricted internal link into the company's corporate data center. The attacker can attack the weaker site at the remote facility and use the compromised internal network to attack the true target. While it may seem trite or clichéd, the old saying that "a chain is only as strong as its weakest link" is very relevant to network and computer security. If a company has a trusted network

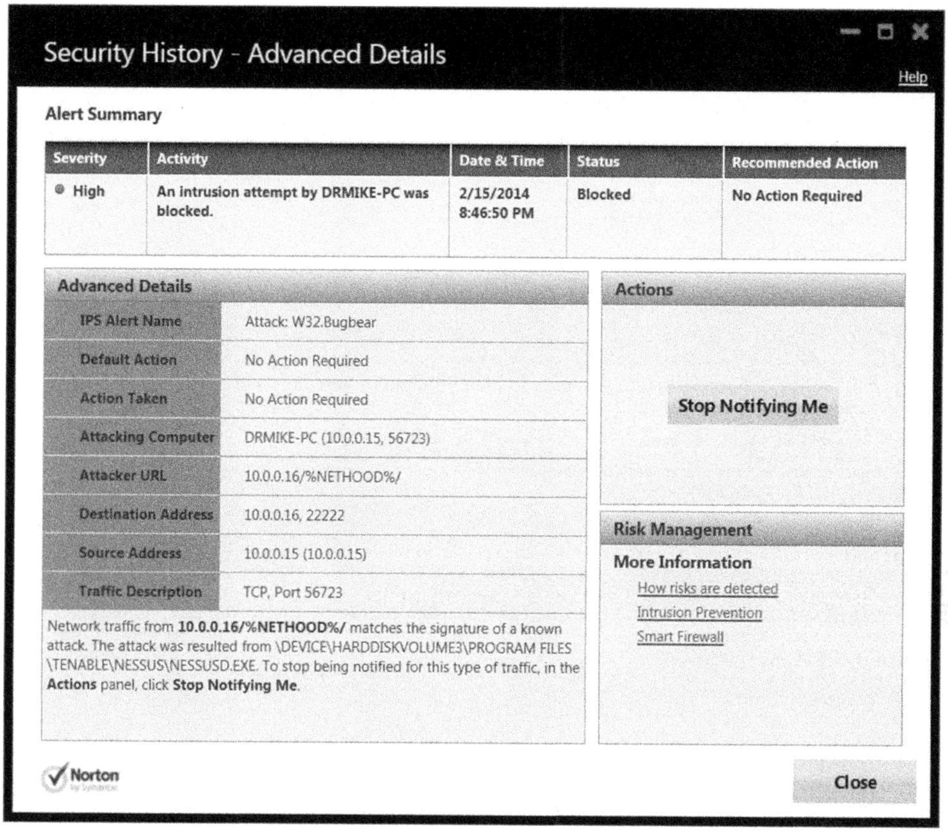

Figure 7-11 Norton Security Suite: Nessus scan 2

Source: Norton by Symantec.

connection with 15 business partners, one weak business partner can compromise all 16 networks.

To assist in footprint intelligence collection, you can use an enhanced Web scanner that examines entire Web sites for valuable pieces of information, such as server names and e-mail addresses. One such scanner is called Sam Spade (see Figure 7-12), which you can obtain by searching the Web for a copy of the last version (1.14). Sam Spade can perform a host of scans and probes, such as sending multiple ICMP information requests (pings), attempting to retrieve multiple and cross-zoned DNS queries, and performing network analysis queries known as traceroutes from the commonly used UNIX command. All of these scans are powerful diagnostic and hacking activities, but Sam Spade is not considered hackerware (hacker-oriented software). Rather, it is a utility that is useful to network administrators and miscreants alike.

For Linux or BSD systems, a tool called GNU Wget allows a remote user to "mirror" entire Web sites. With this tool, attackers can copy an entire Web site and then go through the source HTML, JavaScript, and Web-based forms at their leisure, collecting and collating all of the data from the source code that will help them mount an attack.

Figure 7-12 Sam Spade

Source: Sam Spade.

The next phase of the attack protocol is a data-gathering process called **fingerprinting**. Finger-printing deploys various tools that are described in the following sections to reveal useful information about the internal structure and nature of the target system or network to be attacked. These tools were created to find vulnerabilities in systems and networks quickly and with a minimum of effort. They are valuable to the network defender because they can quickly pinpoint parts of the systems or network that need prompt repair to close vulnerabilities.

❯ Port Scanners

Key Terms

attack surface The functions and features that a system exposes to unauthenticated users.
port scanners Tools used both by attackers and defenders to identify or fingerprint active computers on a network, the active ports and services on those computers, the functions and roles of the machines, and other useful information.

Port scanning utilities, or **port scanners**, are tools that can either perform generic scans or those for specific types of computers, protocols, or resources. You need to understand the network environment and the scanning tools at your disposal so you can use the one best suited to the data collection task at hand. For instance, if you are trying to identify a Windows computer in a typical network, a built-in feature of the operating system, *nbtstat*, may provide your answer very quickly without the use of a scanner. This tool does not work on some networks, however.

The more specific the scanner is, the more useful its information is to attackers and defenders. However, you should keep a generic, broad-based scanner in your toolbox to help locate and identify unknown rogue nodes on the network. Probably the most popular port scanner is Nmap, which runs both on UNIX and Windows systems.

 For more information on Nmap, visit its Web site at http://nmap.org.

A port is a network channel or connection point in a data communications system. Within the TCP/IP networking protocol, TCP and User Datagram Protocol (UDP) port numbers differentiate the multiple communication channels that connect to the network services offered on a network device. Each application within TCP/IP has a unique port number. Some have default ports but can also use other ports. Some of the well-known port numbers are shown in Table 7-1. In all, 65,536 port numbers are in use for TCP and another 65,536 port numbers are used for UDP. Services that use the TCP/IP protocol can run on any port; however, services with reserved ports generally run on ports 1–1023. Port 0 is not used. Port numbers greater than 1023 are typically referred to as ephemeral ports and may be randomly allocated to server and client processes.

Why secure open ports? Simply put, an attacker can use an open port to send commands to a computer, potentially gain access to a server, and possibly exert control over a networking device. As a rule of thumb, any port that is not absolutely necessary for conducting business should be secured or removed from service. For example, if a business doesn't host Web services, there is no need for port 80 to be available on its servers.

The number and nature of the open ports on a system are an important part of its **attack surface**. As a general design goal, security practitioners seek to reduce the attack surface of each system to minimize the potential for latent defects and unintended consequences to cause losses.

Port Number	Protocol
7	Echo
20	File Transfer [Default Data] (FTP)
21	File Transfer [Control] (FTP)
23	Telnet
25	Simple Mail Transfer Protocol (SMTP)
53	Domain Name System (DNS)
80	Hypertext Transfer Protocol (HTTP)
110	Post Office Protocol version 3 (POP3)
161	Simple Network Management Protocol (SNMP)

Table 7-1 Commonly Used Port Numbers

❯ Firewall Analysis Tools

Understanding exactly where an organization's firewall is located and the functions of its existing rule sets are very important steps for any security administrator. Several tools automate the remote discovery of firewall rules and assist the administrator (or attacker) in analyzing the rules to determine what they allow and reject.

The Nmap tool mentioned earlier has some advanced options that are useful for firewall analysis. For example, the option called *idle scanning*, which is run with the –I switch, allows the Nmap user to bounce a scan across a firewall by using one of the idle DMZ hosts as the initiator of the scan. More specifically, most operating systems do not use truly random IP packet identification numbers (IP IDs), so if the DMZ has multiple hosts and one of them uses non-random IP IDs, the attacker can query the server and obtain the currently used IP ID as well as the known algorithm for incrementing IP IDs. The attacker can then spoof a packet that is allegedly from the queried server and destined for an internal IP address behind the firewall. If the port is open on the internal machine, the machine replies to the server with a SYN-ACK packet, which forces the server to respond with a TCP RESET packet. In its response, the server increments its IP ID number. The attacker can now query the server again to see if the IP ID has incremented. If it has, the attacker knows that the internal machine is alive and has the queried service port open. In a nutshell, running the Nmap idle scan allows attackers to scan an internal network as if they were on a trusted machine inside the DMZ.

Firewalk is another tool that can be used to analyze firewalls. Written by noted network security experts Mike Schiffman and David Goldsmith, Firewalk uses incrementing Time-To-Live (TTL) packets to determine the path into a network as well as the default firewall policy. Running Firewalk against a target machine reveals where routers and firewalls are filtering traffic to the target host.

 For more information on Firewalk, read Goldsmith and Schiffman's article at http://packetfactory .openwall.net/projects/firewalk/firewalk-final.pdf. Firewalk can be obtained from http://packet stormsecurity.com/UNIX/audit/firewalk/.

A final firewall analysis tool worth consideration is HPING, which is a modified ping client. It supports multiple protocols and has a command-line method of specifying nearly any ping parameter. For instance, you can use HPING with modified TTL values to determine the infrastructure of a DMZ. You can use HPING with specific ICMP flags to bypass poorly configured firewalls that allow all ICMP traffic to pass through and find internal systems. For more information about HPING, go to *www.hping.org*.

Administrators who are wary of using the same tools that attackers use should remember two important points. Regardless of the tool that is used to validate or analyze a firewall's configuration, user intent dictates how the gathered information is used. To defend a computer or network well, administrators must understand the ways it can be attacked. Thus, a tool that can help close an open or poorly configured firewall will help the network defender minimize the risk from attack.

❯ Operating System Detection Tools

The ability to detect a target computer's operating system is very valuable to an attacker. Once the OS is known, the attacker can easily determine all of the vulnerabilities to which it is susceptible. Many tools use networking protocols to determine a remote computer's OS.

One such tool is XProbe, which uses ICMP to determine the remote OS. When run, XProbe sends many different ICMP queries to the target host. As reply packets are received, XProbe matches these responses from the target's TCP/IP stack with its own internal database of known responses. Because most OSs have a unique way of responding to ICMP requests, XProbe is very reliable in finding matches and thus detecting the operating systems of remote computers. Therefore, system and network administrators should restrict the use of ICMP through their organization's firewalls and, when possible, within their internal networks.

 For more information on XProbe, visit its Web site at www.sourceforge.net/projects/xprobe.

> Vulnerability Scanners

Key Terms

active vulnerability scanner An application that scans networks to identify exposed usernames and groups, open network shares, configuration problems, and other vulnerabilities in servers.
passive vulnerability scanner A scanner that listens in on a network and identifies vulnerable versions of both server and client software.

Active vulnerability scanners examine networks for highly detailed information. An active scanner is one that initiates traffic on the network to determine security holes. An example of a vulnerability scanner is Nessus, a professional freeware utility that uses IP packets to identify hosts available on the network, the services (ports) they offer, their operating system and OS version, the type of packet filters and firewalls in use, and dozens of other network characteristics. Figures 7-13 and 7-14 show sample screens from Nessus.

Figure 7-13 Tenable Nessus: summary

Source: Nessus.

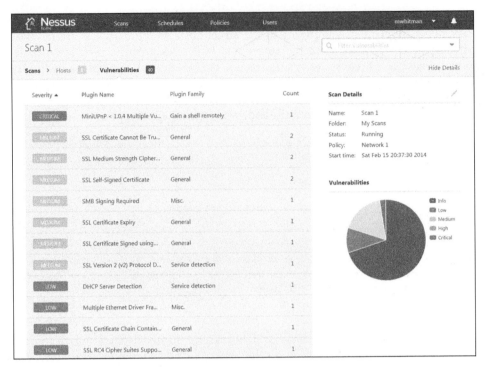

Figure 7-14 Tenable Nessus: detail

Source: Nessus.

Vulnerability scanners should be proficient at finding known, documented holes. But what happens if a Web server is from a new vendor or a new application was created by an internal development team? In such cases, you should consider using a class of vulnerability scanners called black-box scanners, or fuzzers. Fuzz testing is a straightforward technique that looks for vulnerabilities in a program or protocol by feeding random input to the program or a network running the protocol. Vulnerabilities can be detected by measuring the outcome of the random inputs. One example of a fuzz scanner is SPIKE, which has two primary components. The first is the SPIKE Proxy, which is a full-blown proxy server. As Web site visitors use the proxy, SPIKE builds a database of each traversed page, form, and other Web-specific information. When the Web site owner determines that enough history has been collected to fully characterize the Web sites, SPIKE can be used to check them for bugs. In other words, administrators can use the usage history collected by SPIKE to traverse all known pages, forms, and active programs such as asp and cgibin, and then can test the system by attempting overflows, SQL injection, cross-site scripting, and many other classes of Web attacks.

A list of the top commercial and residential vulnerability scanners includes the following products:[31]

- Core Impact
- GFI LanGuard

- Microsoft Baseline Security Analyzer (MBSA)
- Nessus
- Nexpose
- Nipper
- OpenVAS
- QualysGuard
- Retina
- Secunia PSI
- Security Administrator's Integrated Network Tool (SAINT)

The Nessus scanner features a class of attacks called *destructive*. If enabled, Nessus attempts common overflow techniques against a target host. Fuzzers or black-box scanners and Nessus in destructive mode can be very dangerous tools, so they should be used only in a lab environment. In fact, these tools are so powerful that even experienced system defenders are not likely to use them in the most aggressive modes on their production networks. At the time of this writing, the most popular scanners seem to be Nessus, OpenVAS, and Nexpose. The Nessus scanner was originally open source, but is now strictly commercial. OpenVAS was created as a variant from the last free version of Nessus, and is therefore a good open-source alternative. Nexpose offers free limited and commercial versions.

Often, some members of an organization require proof that a system is vulnerable to a certain attack. They may require such proof to avoid having system administrators attempt to repair systems that are actually not broken, or because they have not yet built a satisfactory relationship with the vulnerability assessment team. In these instances, a class of scanners are available that actually exploit the remote machine and allow the vulnerability analyst (sometimes called a penetration tester) to create an account, modify a Web page, or view data. These tools can be very dangerous and should be used only when absolutely necessary. Three such tools are Core Impact, Immunity's CANVAS, and the Metasploit Framework.

Of these three tools, only the Metasploit Framework is available without a license fee. The Metasploit Framework is a collection of exploits coupled with an interface that allows penetration testers to automate the custom exploitation of vulnerable systems. For instance, if you wanted to exploit a Microsoft Exchange server and run a single command (perhaps add the user "security" into the administrators group), the tool allows you to customize the overflow in this manner. Figure 7-15 shows the Metasploit Framework in action.

 For more information on Metasploit, visit www.metasploit.com.

A **passive vulnerability scanner** listens in on the network and identifies vulnerable versions of both server and client software. At the time of this writing, two primary vendors offer this type of scanning solution: Tenable Network Security, with its Passive Vulnerability Scanner (PVS); and Watcher Web Security Scanner from Casaba (see Figure 7-16). The advantage of using passive scanners is that they do not require vulnerability analysts to obtain approval prior to testing. These tools simply monitor the network connections to and from a server to obtain a list of vulnerable applications. Furthermore, passive vulnerability scanners can find client-side vulnerabilities that are typically not found by active scanners. For instance, an

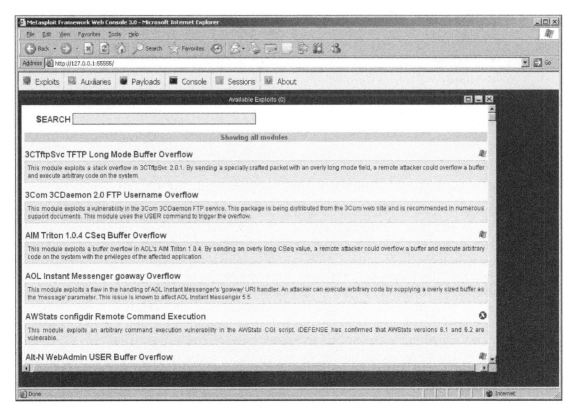

Figure 7-15 Metasploit

Source: Metasploit Framework.

active scanner operating without domain Admin rights would be unable to determine the version of Internet Explorer running on a desktop machine, but a passive scanner could make that determination by observing traffic to and from the client.

Figures 7-17 and 7-18 show Tenable's PVS.

❭ Packet Sniffers

> **Key Term**
>
> **packet sniffer** A software program or hardware appliance that can intercept, copy, and interpret network traffic.

A **packet sniffer** or network protocol analyzer can provide a network administrator with valuable information for diagnosing and resolving networking issues. In the wrong hands, however, a sniffer can be used to eavesdrop on network traffic. Commercial and open-source sniffers are both available—for example, Sniffer is a commercial product and Snort is open-source software. An excellent network protocol analyzer is Wireshark (*www.wireshark*

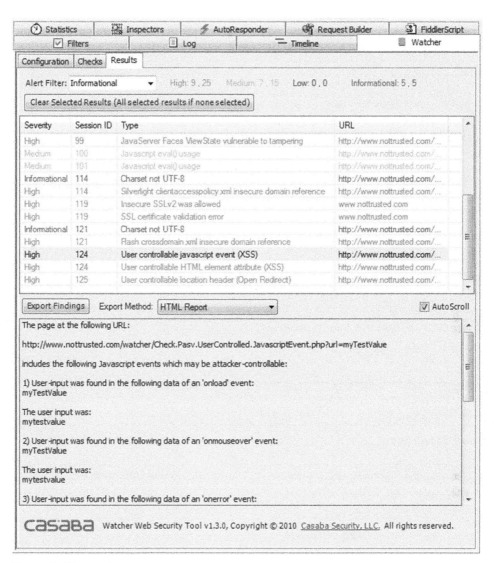

Figure 7-16 Watcher Web Security Scanner

Source: Casaba Security LLC.

.org), formerly known as Ethereal, which is available in open-source and commercial versions. Wireshark allows the administrator to examine data both from live network traffic and captured traffic. Wireshark's features include a language filter and TCP session reconstruction utility. Figure 7-19 shows a sample screen from Wireshark. To use these types of programs most effectively, the user must be connected to a network from a central location. Simply tapping into an Internet connection floods you with more data than you can readily process, and technically the action constitutes a violation of the U.S. Wiretap Act.

To use a packet sniffer legally, the administrator must (1) be on a network that the organization owns, (2) be under direct authorization of the network's owners, and (3) have knowledge

Figure 7-17 Tenable PVS: host summary

Source: Tenable Network Security®.

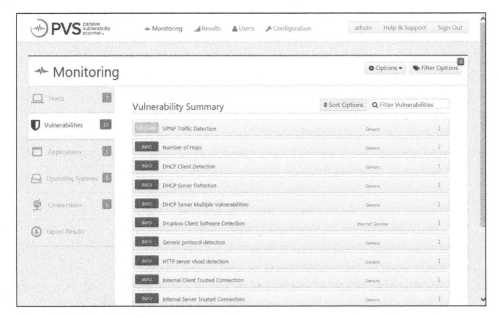

Figure 7-18 Tenable PVS: vulnerability summary

Source: Tenable Network Security®.

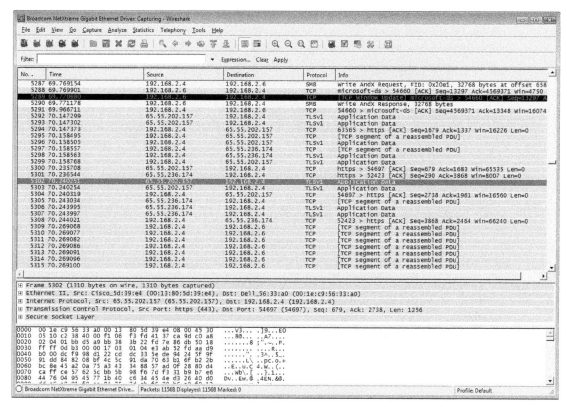

Figure 7-19 Wireshark

Source: Wireshark.

and consent of the content's creators. If all three conditions are met, the administrator can selectively collect and analyze packets to identify and diagnose problems on the network. Consent is usually obtained by having all system users sign a release when they are issued a user ID and passwords. These three conditions are the same requirements for employee monitoring in general; therefore, packet sniffing should be construed as a form of employee monitoring.

Many administrators feel safe from sniffer attacks when their computing environment is primarily a switched network, but they couldn't be more wrong. Several open-source sniffers support alternate networking approaches and can enable packet sniffing in a switched network environment. Two of these approaches are ARP-spoofing and session hijacking, which uses tools like Ettercap. To secure data in transit across any network, organizations must use a carefully designed and implemented encryption solution to assure uncompromised content privacy.

❯ Wireless Security Tools

802.11 wireless networks have sprung up as subnets on nearly all large networks. A wireless connection is convenient, but it has many potential security holes. An organization that spends all of its time securing the wired network while ignoring wireless networks is exposing itself to a security breach. As a security professional, you must assess the risk of wireless networks. A wireless security toolkit should include the ability to sniff wireless traffic, scan wireless hosts, and assess the level of privacy or confidentiality afforded on the wireless network. Sectools.org identified the top wireless tools:

- Aircrack, a wireless network protocol cracking tool
- Kismet, a powerful wireless network protocol sniffer, network detector, and IDPS, which works by passively sniffing the networks
- NetStumbler, a freeware Windows file parser available at *www.netstumbler.org*
- inSSIDer, an enhanced scanner for Windows, OS X, and Android
- KisMac, a GUI passive wireless stumbler for Mac OS X (a variation of Kismet)

NetStumbler is offered as freeware and can be found at *www.netstumbler.org*. Figure 7-20 shows NetStumbler being run from a Windows client. Another wireless tool, AirSnare, is freeware that can be run on a low-end wireless workstation. AirSnare monitors the airwaves for any new devices or access points. When it finds one, AirSnare sounds an alarm to alert administrators that a new and potentially dangerous wireless apparatus is attempting access on a closed wireless network. Figure 7-21 shows AirSnare in action.

The tools discussed in this chapter help the attacker and the defender prepare themselves to complete the next steps in the attack protocol: attack, compromise, and exploit. These steps are beyond the scope of this text, and are usually covered in more advanced classes on computer and network attack and defense.

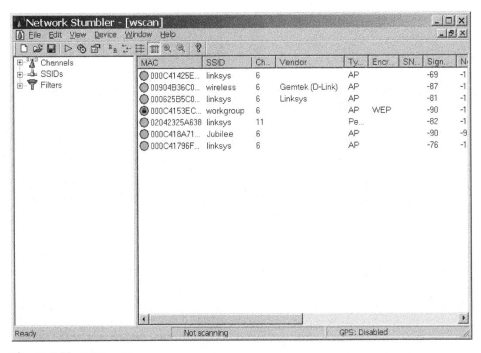

Figure 7-20 NetStumbler

Source: NetStumbler.

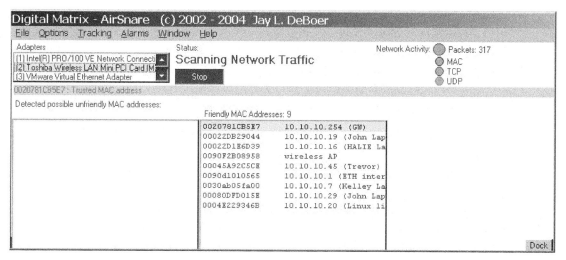

Figure 7-21 AirSnare

Source: AirSnare.

 For more information on these and other security tools, visit Insecure.org's security Web site at sectools.org. For more information on the site's owner and the author of the NMap tool, visit Fyodor's page at insecure.org/fyodor/.

Selected Readings

- *Intrusion Detection and Prevention*, by Carl Endorf, Gene Schultz, and Jim Mellander. 2003. McGraw-Hill Osborne Media.

- *Intrusion Detection Systems*, by Rebecca Bace and Peter Mell. National Institute of Standards and Technology (NIST) Special Publication 800-31. Available from the archive section of the NIST Computer Security Resource Center at *http://csrc.nist.gov*.

- *Guide to Intrusion Detection and Prevention Systems*, by Karen Scarfone and Peter Mell. NIST Special Publication 800-94. Available from the NIST Computer Security Resource Center at *http://csrc.nist.gov*.

Chapter Summary

- Intrusion detection systems (IDSs) identify potential intrusions and sound an alarm. The more recently developed intrusion detection and prevention systems (IDPSs) also detect intrusions and can take action to defend the network.

- An IDPS works like a burglar alarm by detecting network traffic that violates the system's configured rules and activating an alarm.

- A network-based IDPS (NIDPS) monitors network traffic and then notifies the appropriate administrator when a predefined event occurs. A host-based IDPS (HIDPS) resides on a particular computer or server and monitors activity on that system.

- Signature-based IDPSs, also known as knowledge-based IDPSs, examine data traffic for patterns that match signatures—preconfigured, predetermined attack patterns. Statistical anomaly-based IDPSs, also known as behavior-based IDPSs, collect data from normal traffic and establish a baseline. When an activity is found to be outside the baseline parameters (or clipping level), these IDPSs activate an alarm to notify the administrator.

- Selecting IDPS products that best fit an organization's needs is a challenging and complex process. A wide array of products and vendors are available, each with its own approach and capabilities.

- Deploying and implementing IDPS technology is a complex undertaking that requires knowledge and experience. After deployment, each organization should measure the effectiveness of its IDPS and then continue with periodic assessments over time.

- Honeypots are decoy systems designed to lure potential attackers away from critical systems. In the security industry, these systems are also known as decoys, lures, or flytraps. Two variations on this technology are known as honeynets and padded cell systems.

- Trap-and-trace applications are designed to react to an intrusion event by tracing it back to its source. This process is fraught with professional and ethical issues—some people in the security field believe that the back hack in the trace process is as significant a violation as the initial attack.

- Active intrusion prevention seeks to limit the damage that attackers can perpetrate by making the local network resistant to inappropriate use.

- Scanning and analysis tools are used to pinpoint vulnerabilities in systems, holes in security components, and unsecured aspects of the network. Although these tools are used by attackers, they can also be used by administrators to learn more about their own systems and to identify and repair system weaknesses before they result in losses.

Review Questions

1. What common security system is an IDPS most like? In what ways are these systems similar?

2. How does a false positive alarm differ from a false negative alarm? From a security perspective, which is less desirable?

3. How does a network-based IDPS differ from a host-based IDPS?

4. How does a signature-based IDPS differ from a behavior-based IDPS?

5. What is a monitoring (or SPAN) port? What is it used for?

6. List and describe the three control strategies proposed for IDPSs.

7. What is a honeypot? How is it different from a honeynet?

8. How does a padded cell system differ from a honeypot?

9. What is network footprinting?

10. What is network fingerprinting?

11. How are network footprinting and network fingerprinting related?

12. Why do many organizations ban port scanning activities on their internal networks?

13. Why would ISPs ban outbound port scanning by their customers?

14. What is an open port? Why is it important to limit the number of open ports to those that are absolutely essential?

15. What is a system's attack surface? Why should it be minimized when possible?

16. What is a vulnerability scanner? How is it used to improve security?

17. What is the difference between active and passive vulnerability scanners?

18. What is Metasploit Framework? Why is it considered riskier to use than other vulnerability scanning tools?

19. What kind of data and information can be found using a packet sniffer?

20. What capabilities should a wireless security toolkit include?

Exercises

1. A key feature of hybrid IDPS systems is event correlation. After researching event correlation online, define the following terms as they are used in this process: compression, suppression, and generalization.

2. ZoneAlarm is a PC-based firewall and IDPS tool. Visit the product manufacturer at *www.zonelabs.com* and find the product specification for the IDPS features of ZoneAlarm. Which ZoneAlarm products offer these features?

3. Using the Internet, search for commercial IDPS systems. What classification systems and descriptions are used, and how can they be used to compare the features and components of each IDPS? Create a comparison spreadsheet to identify the classification systems you find.

4. Use the Internet to search for "live DVD security toolkit." Read a few Web sites to learn about this class of tools and their capabilities. Write a brief description of a live DVD security toolkit.

5. Several online passphrase generators are available. Locate at least two on the Internet and try them. What did you observe?

Case Exercises

Miller Harrison was still working his way through his attack protocol.

Nmap started out as it usually did, by giving the program identification and version number. Then it started reporting back on the first host in the SLS network. It reported all of the open ports on this server. The program moved on to a second host and began reporting back the open ports on that system, too. Once it reached the third host, however, it suddenly stopped.

Miller restarted Nmap, using the last host IP as the starting point for the next scan. No response. He opened another command window and tried to ping the first host he had just port-scanned. No luck. He tried to ping the SLS firewall. Nothing. He happened to know the IP address for the SLS edge router. He pinged that and got the same result. He had been blackholed, meaning his IP address had been put on a list of addresses from which the SLS edge router would no longer accept packets. Ironically, the list was his own doing. The IDPS he had been helping SLS configure seemed to be working just fine at the moment. His attempt to hack the SLS network was shut down cold.

Discussion Questions

1. Do you think Miller is out of options as he pursues his vendetta? If you think he could take additional actions in his effort to damage the SLS network, what are they?

2. Suppose a system administrator at SLS read the details of this case. What steps should he or she take to improve the company's information security program?

3. Consider Miller's hacking attempt in light of the intrusion kill chain described earlier and shown in Figure 7-1. At which phase in the kill chain has SLS countered his vendetta?

Ethical Decision Making

It seems obvious that Miller is breaking at least a few laws in his attempt at revenge. Suppose that when his scanning efforts had been detected, SLS not only added his IP address to the list of sites banned from connecting to the SLS network, the system also triggered a response to seek out his computer and delete key files on it to disable his operating system.

Would such an action by SLS be ethical? Do you think that action would be legal?

Suppose instead that Miller had written a routine to constantly change his assigned IP address to other addresses used by his ISP. If the SLS intrusion system determined what Miller was doing and then added the entire range of ISP addresses to the banned list, thus stopping any user of the ISP from connecting to the SLS network, would SLS's action be ethical?

What if SLS were part of an industry consortium that shared IP addresses flagged by its IDPS, and all companies in the group blocked all of the ISP's users for 10 minutes? These users would be blocked from accessing perhaps hundreds of company networks. Would that be an ethical response by members of the consortium? What if these users were blocked for 24 hours?

Endnotes

1. Scarfone, K., and Mell, P. National Institute of Standards and Technology. *Guide to Intrusion Detection and Prevention Systems (IDPS)*. SP 800-94, Rev. 1. (DRAFT) 2012. Accessed 20 August 2016 from *http://csrc.nist.gov/publications/PubsSPs.html*.

2. Ibid.

3. Scarfone, K., and Mell, P. National Institute of Standards and Technology. *Guide to Intrusion Detection and Prevention Systems (IDPS)*. SP 800-94. 2007. Accessed 20 August 2016 from *http://csrc.nist.gov/publications/PubsSPs.html*.

4. Ibid.

5. Scarfone, K., and Mell, P. National Institute of Standards and Technology. *Guide to Intrusion Detection and Prevention Systems (IDPS)*. SP 800-94, Rev. 1. (DRAFT) 2012. Accessed 20 August 2016 from *http://csrc.nist.gov/publications/PubsSPs.html*.

6. Ibid.

7. Ibid.

8. Ibid.

9. Ibid.

10. Ibid.

11. Scarfone, K., and Mell, P. National Institute of Standards and Technology. *Guide to Intrusion Detection and Prevention Systems (IDPS)*. SP 800-94. 2007. Accessed 20 August 2016 from *http://csrc.nist.gov/publications/PubsSPs.html*.

12. Ibid.

13. Scarfone, K., and Mell, P. National Institute of Standards and Technology. *Guide to Intrusion Detection and Prevention Systems (IDPS)*. SP 800-94, Rev. 1. (DRAFT) 2012. Accessed 20 August 2016 from *http://csrc.nist.gov/publications/PubsSPs.html*.

14. Ibid.

15. Ibid.

16. Ibid.

17. Ibid.

18. Ranum, Marcus J. "False Positives: A User's Guide to Making Sense of IDS Alarms." ICSA Labs IDSC. February 2003. Accessed 16 August 2016 from *http://manualzz .com/doc/19760767/false-positives—a-user%E2%80%99s-guide-to-participating-v -endors*.

19. Scarfone, K., and Mell, P. National Institute of Standards and Technology. *Guide to Intrusion Detection and Prevention Systems (IDPS)*. SP 800-94, Rev. 1. (DRAFT) 2012. Accessed 20 August 2016 from *http://csrc.nist.gov/publications/PubsSPs.html*.

20. Scarfone, K., and Mell, P. National Institute of Standards and Technology. *Guide to Intrusion Detection and Prevention Systems (IDPS)*. SP 800-94. 2007. Accessed 20 August 2016 from *http://csrc.nist.gov/publications/PubsSPs.html*.

21. Ibid.

22. Ibid.

23. Ibid.

24. Scarfone, K., and Mell, P. National Institute of Standards and Technology. *Guide to Intrusion Detection and Prevention Systems (IDPS)*. SP 800-94, Rev. 1. (DRAFT) 2012. Accessed 20 August 2016 from *http://csrc.nist.gov/publications/PubsSPs.html*.

7

25. Ibid.

26. Scarfone, K., and Mell, P. National Institute of Standards and Technology. *Guide to Intrusion Detection and Prevention Systems (IDPS)*. SP 800-94. 2007. Accessed 20 August 2016 from *http://csrc.nist.gov/publications/PubsSPs.html*.

27. Scarfone, K., and Mell, P. National Institute of Standards and Technology. *Guide to Intrusion Detection and Prevention Systems (IDPS)*. SP 800-94, Rev. 1. (DRAFT) 2012. Accessed 20 August 2016 from *http://csrc.nist.gov/publications/PubsSPs.html*.

28. "Acquiring and Deploying Intrusion Detection Systems." National Institute of Standards and Technology. Accessed 20 August 2016 from *http://csrc.nist.gov/publications/nistbul /11-99.pdf*.

29. "Pen Registers" and "Trap-and-Trace Devices." Accessed 20 August 2016 from *https:// web.archive.org/web/20090724111137/https://ssd.eff.org/wire/govt/pen-registers*.

30. 18 U.S. Code Chapter 206. "Pen Registers and Trap-and-Trace Devices." Accessed 20 August 2016 from *https://www.law.cornell.edu/uscode/text/18/part-II/chapter-206*.

31. SecTools.Org: Top 125 Network Security Tools. Accessed 20 August 2016 from *http:// sectools.org/tag/vuln-scanners/*.

chapter 8

Cryptography

Yet it may roundly be asserted that human ingenuity cannot concoct a cipher which human ingenuity cannot resolve.

EDGAR ALLAN POE, *THE GOLD BUG*

Peter Hayes, CFO of Sequential Label and Supply, was working late. He opened an e-mail from the manager of the accounting department. The e-mail had an attachment—probably a spreadsheet or a report of some kind—and from the file icon he could tell it was encrypted. He saved the file to his computer's hard drive and then double-clicked the icon to open it.

His computer operating system recognized that the file was encrypted and started the decryption program, which prompted Peter for his passphrase. Peter's mind went blank. He couldn't remember the passphrase. "Oh, good grief!" he said to himself, reaching for his phone.

"Charlie, good, you're still here. I'm having trouble with a file in my e-mail program. My computer is prompting me for my passphrase, and I think I forgot it."

"Uh-oh," said Charlie.

"What do you mean 'Uh-oh'?"

"I mean you're S.O.L." Charlie replied. "Simply outta luck."

"Out of luck?" said Peter. "Why? Can't you do something? I have quite a few files that are encrypted with this PGP program. I need my files."

Charlie let him finish, then said, "Peter, remember how I told you it was important to remember your passphrase?" Charlie heard a sigh on the other end of the line, but decided to ignore it. "And do you remember I said that PGP is only free for individuals and that you weren't to use it for company files since we didn't buy a license for the company? I only set that program up on your personal laptop for your home e-mail—for when your sister wanted to send you some financial records. When did you start using it on SLS systems for company business?"

"Well," Peter answered, "the manager of my accounting department had some financials that were going to be ready a few weeks ago while I was traveling. I sort of told him that you set me up on this PGP crypto thing and he googled it and set up his own account. Then, I swapped public keys with him before I left, and he sent the files to me securely by e-mail while I was in Dubai. It worked out great. So the next week I encrypted quite a few files. Now I can't get to any of them because I can't seem to remember my passphrase." There was a long pause, and then he asked, "Can you hack it for me?"

Charlie chuckled and then said, "Sure, Peter, no problem. Send me the files and I'll put the biggest server we have to work on it. Since we set you up in PGP with 256-bit AES, I should be able to apply a little brute force and crack the key to get the plaintext in a hundred trillion years or so."

LEARNING OBJECTIVES

Upon completion of this material, you should be able to:

- Chronicle the most significant events and discoveries in the history of cryptology
- Explain the basic principles of cryptography
- Describe the operating principles of the most popular cryptographic tools
- List and explain the major protocols used for secure communications

Introduction

Key Terms

cryptanalysis The process of obtaining the plaintext message from a ciphertext message without knowing the keys used to perform the encryption.
cryptography The process of making and using codes to secure information.
cryptology The field of science that encompasses cryptography and cryptanalysis.

The science of cryptology is not as enigmatic as you might think. A variety of cryptographic techniques are used regularly in everyday life. For example, open your newspaper to the entertainment section and you'll find the daily cryptogram, a word puzzle that involves unscrambling letters to find a hidden message. Also, although it is a dying art, many secretaries still use shorthand, or stenography, an abbreviated, symbolic writing method, to take rapid dictation. A form of cryptography is used even in knitting patterns, where directions are written in a coded form in patterns such as K1P1 (knit 1, purl 1) that only an initiate can understand.

These examples illustrate one important application of cryptography—the efficient and rapid transmittal of information—but cryptography also protects and verifies data transmitted via information systems.

The science of encryption, known as **cryptology**, encompasses cryptography and cryptanalysis. **Cryptography** comes from the Greek words *kryptos*, meaning "hidden," and *graphein*, meaning "to write," and involves making and using codes to secure messages. **Cryptanalysis** involves cracking or breaking encrypted messages back into their unencrypted origins. Cryptography uses mathematical algorithms that are usually known to all. After all, it's not the knowledge of the algorithm that protects the encrypted message, it's the knowledge of the key—a series of characters or bits injected into the algorithm along with the original message to create the encrypted message. An individual or system usually encrypts a plaintext message into ciphertext, making it unreadable to unauthorized people—those without the key needed to decrypt the message back into plaintext, where it can be read and understood.

The field of cryptology is so vast that it can fill many volumes. This textbook provides only a general overview of cryptology and some specific information about a few cryptographic tools. In the early sections of this chapter, you will learn the background of cryptology as well as key concepts in cryptography and common cryptographic tools. In later sections, you will learn about common cryptographic protocols and some of the attack methods used against cryptosystems.

Foundations of Cryptology

Cryptology has an extensive, multicultural history. People have been making, using, and breaking codes for thousands of years, and they will not stop any time soon. Table 8-1 provides a brief overview of the history of cryptosystems.

Date	Event
1900 B.C.	Egyptian scribes used nonstandard hieroglyphs while inscribing clay tablets; this is the first documented use of written cryptography.
1500 B.C.	Mesopotamian cryptography surpassed that of the Egyptians, as demonstrated by a tablet that was discovered to contain an encrypted formula for pottery glazes; the tablet used symbols that have different meanings depending on the context.
500 B.C.	Hebrew scribes writing the book of Jeremiah used a reversed alphabet substitution cipher known as ATBASH.
487 B.C.	The Spartans of Greece developed the *skytale*, a system consisting of a strip of papyrus wrapped around a wooden staff. Messages were written down the length of the staff, and the papyrus was unwrapped. The decryption process involved wrapping the papyrus around a shaft of similar diameter.
50 B.C.	Julius Caesar used a simple substitution cipher to secure military and government communications. To form an encrypted text, Caesar shifted the letters of the alphabet three places. In addition to this monoalphabetic substitution cipher, Caesar strengthened his encryption by substituting Greek letters for Latin letters.

Table 8-1 History of Cryptology (*continues*)

Date	Event
Fourth to sixth centuries	*The Kama Sutra of Vatsayana* listed cryptography as the 44th and 45th of the 64 arts (yogas) that men and women should practice: *(44) The art of understanding writing in cipher, and the writing of words in a peculiar way; (45) The art of speaking by changing the forms of the word.*
725	Abu 'Abd al-Rahman al-Khalil ibn Ahmad ibn 'Amr ibn Tammam al Farahidi al-Zadi al Yahmadi wrote a book (now lost) on cryptography; he also solved a Greek cryptogram by guessing the plaintext introduction.
855	Abu Wahshiyyaan-Nabati, a scholar, published several cipher alphabets that were used to encrypt magic formulas.
1250	Roger Bacon, an English monk, wrote *Epistle of Roger Bacon on the Secret Works of Art and of Nature and Also on the Nullity of Magic*, in which he described several simple ciphers.
1392	*The Equatorie of the Planetis*, an early text possibly written by Geoffrey Chaucer, contained a passage in a simple substitution cipher.
1412	*Subhalasha*, a 14-volume Arabic encyclopedia, contained a section on cryptography, including both substitution and transposition ciphers, as well as ciphers with multiple substitutions, a technique that had never been used before.
1466	Leon Battista Alberti, the father of Western cryptography, worked with polyalphabetic substitution and designed a cipher disk.
1518	Johannes Trithemius wrote the first printed book on cryptography and invented a steganographic cipher, in which each letter was represented as a word taken from a succession of columns. He also described a polyalphabetic encryption method using a rectangular substitution format that is now commonly used. He is credited with introducing the method of changing substitution alphabets with each letter as it is deciphered.
1553	Giovan Batista Bellaso introduced the idea of the passphrase (password) as a key for encryption. His polyalphabetic encryption method is misnamed for another person who later used the technique; it is called the Vigenère Cipher today.
1563	Giovanni Battista Porta wrote a classification text on encryption methods, categorizing them as transposition, substitution, and symbol substitution.
1623	Sir Francis Bacon described an encryption method that employed one of the first uses of steganography; he encrypted his messages by slightly changing the typeface of a random text so that each letter of the cipher was hidden within the text.
1790s	Thomas Jefferson created a 26-letter wheel cipher, which he used for official communications while ambassador to France; the concept of the wheel cipher would be reinvented in 1854 and again in 1913.
1854	Charles Babbage reinvented Thomas Jefferson's wheel cipher.
1861–5	During the U.S. Civil War, Union forces used a substitution encryption method based on specific words, and the Confederacy used a polyalphabetic cipher whose solution had been published before the start of the war.
1914–17	Throughout World War I, the Germans, British, and French used a series of transposition and substitution ciphers in radio communications. All sides expended considerable effort to try to intercept and decode communications, and thereby created the science of cryptanalysis. British cryptographers broke the Zimmerman Telegram, in which the Germans offered Mexico U.S. territory in return for Mexico's support. This decryption helped to bring the United States into the war.
1917	William Frederick Friedman, the father of U.S. cryptanalysis, and his wife, Elizabeth, were employed as civilian cryptanalysts by the U.S. government. Friedman later founded a school for cryptanalysis in Riverbank, Illinois.
1917	Gilbert S. Vernam, an AT&T employee, invented a polyalphabetic cipher machine that used a nonrepeating random key.

Table 8-1   History of Cryptology

Date	Event
1919	Hugo Alexander Koch filed a patent in the Netherlands for a rotor-based cipher machine; in 1927, Koch assigned the patent rights to Arthur Scherbius, the inventor of the Enigma machine.
1927–33	During Prohibition, criminals in the United States began using cryptography to protect the privacy of messages used in illegal activities.
1937	The Japanese developed the Purple machine, which was based on principles similar to those of Enigma, and used mechanical relays from telephone systems to encrypt diplomatic messages. By 1940, a team headed by William Friedman had broken the code generated by this machine and constructed a machine that could quickly decode Purple's ciphers.
1939–42	The Allies secretly broke the Enigma cipher, undoubtedly shortening World War II.
1942	Navajo code talkers entered World War II; in addition to speaking a language that was unknown outside a relatively small group within the United States, the Navajos developed code words for subjects and ideas that did not exist in their native tongue.
1948	Claude Shannon suggested using frequency and statistical analysis in the solution of substitution ciphers.
1970	Dr. Horst Feistel led an IBM research team in the development of the Lucifer cipher.
1976	A design based on Lucifer was chosen by the U.S. National Security Agency as the Data Encryption Standard, which found worldwide acceptance.
1976	Whitfield Diffie and Martin Hellman introduced the idea of public-key cryptography.
1977	Ronald Rivest, Adi Shamir, and Leonard Adleman developed a practical public-key cipher both for confidentiality and digital signatures; the RSA family of computer encryption algorithms was born.
1978	The initial RSA algorithm was published in *Communications of the ACM*.
1991	Phil Zimmermann released the first version of PGP (Pretty Good Privacy); PGP was released as freeware and became the worldwide standard for public cryptosystems.
2000	Rijndael's cipher was selected as the Advanced Encryption Standard.

Table 8-1 History of Cryptology (*continued*)

Today, many common IT tools use embedded encryption technologies to protect sensitive information within applications. For example, all the popular Web browsers use built-in encryption features to enable secure e-commerce, such as online banking and Web shopping.

Since World War II, there have been restrictions on the export of cryptosystems, and they continue today, as you saw in Figure 3-4. In 1992, encryption tools were officially listed as Auxiliary Military Technology under the Code of Federal Regulations: International Traffic in Arms Regulations.[1] These restrictions are due in part to the role cryptography played in World War II, and the belief of the American and British governments that the cryptographic tools they developed were far superior to those in lesser developed countries. As a result, both governments believe such countries should be prevented from using cryptosystems to communicate potential terroristic activities or gain an economic advantage.

 For more information on the history of cryptology, visit the National Security Agency's National Cryptologic Museum (see www.nsa.gov/about/cryptologic_heritage/museum) or visit the online Crypto Museum at www.cryptomuseum.com.

❯ Terminology

To understand the fundamentals of cryptography, you must know the meanings of the following terms:

- **Algorithm:** The mathematical formula or method used to convert an unencrypted message into an encrypted message. This sometimes refers to the programs that enable the cryptographic processes.

- **Bit stream cipher:** An encryption method that involves converting plaintext to ciphertext one bit at a time.

- **Block cipher:** An encryption method that involves dividing the plaintext into blocks or sets of bits and then converting the plaintext to ciphertext one block at a time.

- **Cipher:** When used as a verb, the transformation of the individual components (characters, bytes, or bits) of an unencrypted message into encrypted components or vice versa (see *decipher* and *encipher*); when used as a noun, the process of encryption or the algorithm used in encryption, and a term synonymous with *cryptosystem*.

- **Ciphertext** or **cryptogram:** The unintelligible encrypted or encoded message resulting from an encryption.

- **Code:** The process of converting components (words or phrases) of an unencrypted message into encrypted components.

- **Decipher:** See *Decryption*.

- **Decryption:** The process of converting an encoded or enciphered message (ciphertext) back to its original readable form (plaintext). Also referred to as *deciphering*.

- **Encipher:** See *Encryption*.

- **Encryption:** The process of converting an original message (plaintext) into a form that cannot be used by unauthorized individuals (ciphertext). Also referred to as *enciphering*.

- **Key** or **cryptovariable:** The information used in conjunction with the algorithm to create the ciphertext from the plaintext; it can be a series of bits used in a mathematical algorithm or the knowledge of how to manipulate the plaintext. Sometimes called a cryptovariable.

- **Keyspace:** The entire range of values that can be used to construct an individual key.

- **Link encryption:** A series of encryptions and decryptions between a number of systems, wherein each system in a network decrypts the message sent to it and then reencrypts the message using different keys and sends it to the next neighbor. This process continues until the message reaches the final destination.

- **Plaintext** or **cleartext:** The original unencrypted message that is encrypted and is the result of successful decryption.

- **Steganography:** The process of hiding messages; for example, hiding a message within the digital encoding of a picture or graphic so that it is almost impossible to detect that the hidden message even exists.

- **Work factor:** The amount of effort (usually expressed in units of time) required to perform cryptanalysis on an encoded message.

Cipher Methods

There are two methods of encrypting plaintext: the *bit stream* method or the *block cipher* method, as defined in the previous section. In the bit stream method, each bit in the plaintext is transformed into a cipher bit one bit at a time. In the block cipher method, the message is divided into blocks—for example, sets of 8-, 16-, 32-, or 64-bit blocks—and then each block of plaintext bits is transformed into an encrypted block of cipher bits using an algorithm and a key. Bit stream methods commonly use algorithm functions like the exclusive OR operation (XOR), whereas block methods can use substitution, transposition, XOR, or some combination of these operations, as described in the following sections. Note that most computer-based encryption methods operate on data at the level of its binary digits (bits), while others operate at the byte or character level.

You may wonder if you need to know all of the technical details about cipher methods that follow in this section. Although most security professionals will not get involved in designing cryptographic algorithms (or cipher methods) or even wind up using them directly, you have probably used many of them indirectly when you browse the Web, and it is certainly helpful to understand how the tools work. At some point you may need to know these fundamental building blocks of cryptography so you can understand your options when evaluating commercial or open-source cipher methods.

❯ Substitution Cipher

Key Terms

monoalphabetic substitution A substitution cipher that only incorporates a single alphabet in the encryption process.

polyalphabetic substitution A substitution cipher that incorporates two or more alphabets in the encryption process.

substitution cipher An encryption method in which one value is substituted for another.

Vigenère cipher An advanced type of substitution cipher that uses a simple polyalphabetic code.

A **substitution cipher** exchanges one value for another—for example, it might exchange a letter in the alphabet with the letter three values to the right, or it might substitute one bit for another bit four places to its left. A three-character substitution to the right results in the following transformation of the standard English alphabet.

Initial alphabet:	ABCDEFGHIJKLMNOPQRSTUVWXYZ	yields
Encryption alphabet:	DEFGHIJKLMNOPQRSTUVWXYZABC	

Within this substitution scheme, the plaintext MOM would be encrypted into the ciphertext PRP.

This is a simple enough method by itself, but it becomes very powerful if combined with other operations. The previous example of substitution is based on a single alphabet and thus is known as a **monoalphabetic substitution**. More advanced substitution ciphers use two or more alphabets, and are referred to as **polyalphabetic substitutions**.

To extend the previous example, consider the following block of text:

Plaintext:	ABCDEFGHIJKLMNOPQRSTUVWXYZ
Substitution cipher 1:	DEFGHIJKLMNOPQRSTUVWXYZABC
Substitution cipher 2:	GHIJKLMNOPQRSTUVWXYZABCDEF
Substitution cipher 3:	JKLMNOPQRSTUVWXYZABCDEFGHI
Substitution cipher 4:	MNOPQRSTUVWXYZABCDEFGHIJKL

The first row here is the plaintext, and the next four rows are four sets of substitution ciphers, which taken together constitute a single polyalphabetic substitution cipher. To encode the word TEXT with this cipher, you substitute a letter from the second row for the first letter in TEXT, a letter from the third row for the second letter, and so on—a process that yields the ciphertext WKGF. Note how the plaintext letter T is transformed into a W or an F, depending on its order of appearance in the plaintext. Complexities like these make this type of encryption substantially more difficult to decipher when one doesn't have the algorithm (in this case, the rows of ciphers) and the key, which is the substitution method. A logical extension to this process is to randomize the cipher rows completely in order to create a more complex operation.

One example of a monoalphabetic substitution cipher is the cryptogram in the daily newspaper (see Figure 8-1). Another example is the once famous Radio Orphan Annie decoder pin (shown in Figure 8-2), which consisted of two alphabetic rings that could be rotated to a predetermined pairing to form a simple substitution cipher. The device was made to be worn as a pin so one could always be at the ready. As mentioned in Table 8-1, Julius Caesar reportedly used a three-position shift to the right to encrypt his messages (A became D, B became E, and so on), so this substitution cipher was given his name—the *Caesar Cipher.*

An advanced type of substitution cipher that uses a simple polyalphabetic code is the **Vigenère cipher.** The cipher is implemented using the Vigenère square (or table), also known as a *tabula recta*—a term invented by Johannes Trithemius in the 1500s. Table 8-2 illustrates the setup of the Vigenère square, which is made up of 26 distinct cipher alphabets. In the

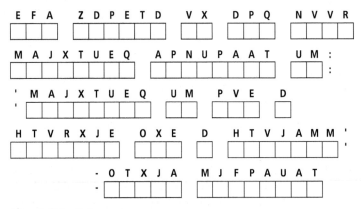

Figure 8-1 Daily cryptogram

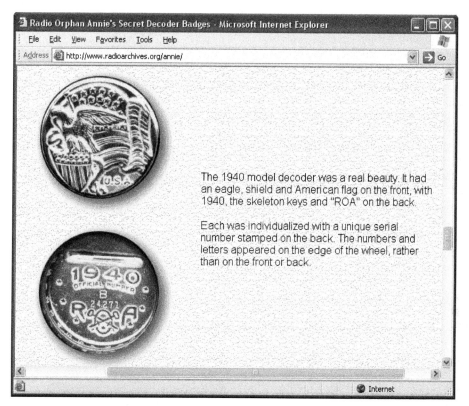

Figure 8-2 Radio Orphan Annie's decoder pin

Source: www.RadioArchives.com.

header row and column, the alphabet is written in its normal order. In each subsequent row, the alphabet is shifted one letter to the right until a 26 × 26 block of letters is formed.

You can use the Vigenère square in several ways. For example, you could perform an encryption by simply starting in the first row, finding a substitute for the first letter of plaintext, and then moving down the rows for each subsequent letter of plaintext. With this method, the word SECURITY in plaintext becomes TGFYWOAG in ciphertext.

A much more sophisticated way to use the Vigenère square is to use a keyword to represent the shift. To accomplish this, you begin by writing a keyword above the plaintext message. For example, suppose the plaintext message is "SACK GAUL SPARE NO ONE" and the keyword is ITALY. We thus end up with the following:

```
ITALYITALYITALYITA
SACKGAULSPARENOONE
```

Now you use the keyword letter and the message (plaintext) letter below it in combination. Returning to the Vigenère square, notice how the first column of text, like the first row, forms the normal alphabet. To perform the substitution, start with the first combination of keyword and message letters, IS. Use the keyword letter to locate the column and the

	A	B	C	D	E	F	G	H	I	J	K	L	M	N	O	P	Q	R	S	T	U	V	W	X	Y	Z
A	A	B	C	D	E	F	G	H	I	J	K	L	M	N	O	P	Q	R	S	T	U	V	W	X	Y	Z
B	B	C	D	E	F	G	H	I	J	K	L	M	N	O	P	Q	R	S	T	U	V	W	X	Y	Z	A
C	C	D	E	F	G	H	I	J	K	L	M	N	O	P	Q	R	S	T	U	V	W	X	Y	Z	A	B
D	D	E	F	G	H	I	J	K	L	M	N	O	P	Q	R	S	T	U	V	W	X	Y	Z	A	B	C
E	E	F	G	H	I	J	K	L	M	N	O	P	Q	R	S	T	U	V	W	X	Y	Z	A	B	C	D
F	F	G	H	I	J	K	L	M	N	O	P	Q	R	S	T	U	V	W	X	Y	Z	A	B	C	D	E
G	G	H	I	J	K	L	M	N	O	P	Q	R	S	T	U	V	W	X	Y	Z	A	B	C	D	E	F
H	H	I	J	K	L	M	N	O	P	Q	R	S	T	U	V	W	X	Y	Z	A	B	C	D	E	F	G
I	I	J	K	L	M	N	O	P	Q	R	S	T	U	V	W	X	Y	Z	A	B	C	D	E	F	G	H
J	J	K	L	M	N	O	P	Q	R	S	T	U	V	W	X	Y	Z	A	B	C	D	E	F	G	H	I
K	K	L	M	N	O	P	Q	R	S	T	U	V	W	X	Y	Z	A	B	C	D	E	F	G	H	I	J
L	L	M	N	O	P	Q	R	S	T	U	V	W	X	Y	Z	A	B	C	D	E	F	G	H	I	J	K
M	M	N	O	P	Q	R	S	T	U	V	W	X	Y	Z	A	B	C	D	E	F	G	H	I	J	K	L
N	N	O	P	Q	R	S	T	U	V	W	X	Y	Z	A	B	C	D	E	F	G	H	I	J	K	L	M
O	O	P	Q	R	S	T	U	V	W	X	Y	Z	A	B	C	D	E	F	G	H	I	J	K	L	M	N
P	P	Q	R	S	T	U	V	W	X	Y	Z	A	B	C	D	E	F	G	H	I	J	K	L	M	N	O
Q	Q	R	S	T	U	V	W	X	Y	Z	A	B	C	D	E	F	G	H	I	J	K	L	M	N	O	P
R	R	S	T	U	V	W	X	Y	Z	A	B	C	D	E	F	G	H	I	J	K	L	M	N	O	P	Q
S	S	T	U	V	W	X	Y	Z	A	B	C	D	E	F	G	H	I	J	K	L	M	N	O	P	Q	R
T	T	U	V	W	X	Y	Z	A	B	C	D	E	F	G	H	I	J	K	L	M	N	O	P	Q	R	S
U	U	V	W	X	Y	Z	A	B	C	D	E	F	G	H	I	J	K	L	M	N	O	P	Q	R	S	T
V	V	W	X	Y	Z	A	B	C	D	E	F	G	H	I	J	K	L	M	N	O	P	Q	R	S	T	U
W	W	X	Y	Z	A	B	C	D	E	F	G	H	I	J	K	L	M	N	O	P	Q	R	S	T	U	V
X	X	Y	Z	A	B	C	D	E	F	G	H	I	J	K	L	M	N	O	P	Q	R	S	T	U	V	W
Y	Y	Z	A	B	C	D	E	F	G	H	I	J	K	L	M	N	O	P	Q	R	S	T	U	V	W	X
Z	Z	A	B	C	D	E	F	G	H	I	J	K	L	M	N	O	P	Q	R	S	T	U	V	W	X	Y

Table 8-2 The Vigenère Square

message letter to find the row, and then look for the letter at their intersection. Thus, for column "I" and row "S," you will find the ciphertext letter "A." After you follow this procedure for each letter in the message, you will produce the encrypted ciphertext ATCVEINLDNIKEYMWGE. One weakness of this method is that any keyword-message letter combination containing an "A" row or column reproduces the plaintext message letter. For example, the third letter in the plaintext message, the C (of SACK), has a combination of AC, and thus is unchanged in the ciphertext. To minimize the effects of this weakness, you should avoid choosing a keyword that contains the letter "A."

❭ Transposition Cipher

Like the substitution operation, the transposition cipher is simple to understand, but if properly used, it can produce ciphertext that is difficult to decipher. In contrast to the substitution cipher, however, the **transposition cipher** or **permutation cipher** simply rearranges the bits or bytes (characters) within a block to create the ciphertext. For an example, consider the following transposition key pattern.

Key pattern: $8 \rightarrow 3, 7 \rightarrow 6, 6 \rightarrow 2, 5 \rightarrow 7, 4 \rightarrow 5, 3 \rightarrow 1, 2 \rightarrow 8, 1 \rightarrow 4$

In this key, the bit or byte (character) in position 1 moves to position 4. When operating on binary data, position 1 is at the far right of the data string, and counting proceeds from right to left. Next, the bit or byte in position 2 moves to position 8, and so on. This cipher is similar to another newspaper puzzle favorite: the word jumble, as illustrated in Figure 8-3. In the jumble, words are scrambled, albeit with no defined pattern. Upon unscrambling, the words provide key characters used to decode a separate message.

8

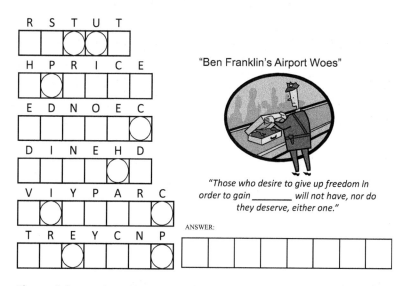

Figure 8-3 Word jumble

The following rows show the numbering of bit locations for this key; the plaintext message 00100101011010111001010101010100, which is broken into 8-bit blocks for clarity; and the ciphertext that is produced when the transposition key depicted above is applied to the plaintext.

Bit locations:	87654321 87654321 87654321 87654321
Plaintext 8-bit blocks:	00100101|01101011|10010101|01010100
Ciphertext:	00001011|10111010|01001101|01100001

Reading from right to left in this example, the first bit of plaintext (position 1 of the first byte) becomes the fourth bit (in position 4) of the first byte of the ciphertext. Similarly, the second bit of the plaintext (position 2) becomes the eighth bit (position 8) of the ciphertext, and so on.

To examine further how this transposition key works, look at its effects on a plaintext message comprised of letters instead of bits. Replacing the 8-bit block of plaintext with the example plaintext message presented earlier, "SACK GAUL SPARE NO ONE," yields the following.

Letter locations:	87654321|87654321|87654321
Plaintext:	__ENO_ON|_ERAPS_L|UAG_KCAS
Key:	Same key as above, but characters transposed, not bits.
Ciphertext:	ON_ON_E_|_AEPL_RS|A_AKSUGC

Here, you read from right to left to match the order in which characters would be transmitted from a sender on the left to a receiver on the right. The letter in position 1 of the first block of plaintext, "S," moves to position 4 in the ciphertext. The process is continued until the letter "U," the eighth letter of the first block of plaintext, moves to the third position of the ciphertext. This process continues with subsequent blocks using the same specified pattern. Obviously, the use of different-sized blocks or multiple transposition patterns would enhance the strength of the cipher.

In addition to being credited with inventing a substitution cipher, Julius Caesar was associated with an early version of the transposition cipher. In the Caesar block cipher, the recipient of the coded message knows to fit the text to a prime number square. In practice, this means that if there are fewer than 25 characters, the recipient uses a 5 × 5 square. For example, if you received the Caesar ciphertext shown below, you would make a square of five columns and five rows, and then write the letters of the message into the square, filling the slots from left to right and top to bottom. Then you would read the message from the opposite direction—that is, from top to bottom, left to right.

Ciphertext:	SGS_NAAPNECUAO_KLR _ _ _ EO
	S G S _ N
	A A P N E
	C U A O _
	K L R _ _
	_ _ E O _

Reading from top to bottom, left to right reveals the plaintext "SACK GAUL SPARE NO ONE."

When mechanical and electronic cryptosystems became more widely used, transposition ciphers and substitution ciphers were combined to produce highly secure encryption processes. To make the encryption even stronger and more difficult to cryptanalyze, the keys and block sizes can be increased to 128 bits or more, which produces substantially more complex substitutions or transpositions. These systems use a *block padding method* to fill the last block of the plaintext with random characters to facilitate the algorithm.

❯ Exclusive OR

Key Term

exclusive OR operation (XOR) A function within Boolean algebra used as an encryption function in which two bits are compared. If the two bits are identical, the result is a binary 0; otherwise, the result is a binary 1.

The **exclusive OR operation (XOR)** is a function of Boolean algebra in which two bits are compared and a binary result is generated. XOR encryption is a very simple symmetric cipher that is used in many applications where security is not a defined requirement. Table 8-3 shows an XOR table with the results of all possible combinations of two bits.

To see how XOR works, consider an example in which the plaintext is the word "CAT." The ASCII binary representation of the plaintext is 01000011 01000001 01010100.

In order to encrypt the plaintext, a key value should be selected. In this case, the bit pattern for the letter "V" (01010110) is used, and is repeated for each character to be encrypted, written from left to right. Performing the XOR operation on the two bit streams (the plaintext and the key) produces the result shown in Table 8-4.

The bottom row of Table 8-4, "Cipher," is read from left to right and contains the bit stream that will be transmitted. When this cipher is received, it can be decrypted using the key value

First Bit	Second Bit	Result
0	0	0
0	1	1
1	0	1
1	1	0

Table 8-3 XOR Table

Text Value	Binary Value
CAT as bits	0 1 0 0 0 0 1 1 0 1 0 0 0 0 0 1 0 1 0 1 0 1 0 0
VVV as key	0 1 0 1 0 1 1 0 0 1 0 1 0 1 1 0 0 1 0 1 0 1 1 0
Cipher	0 0 0 1 0 1 0 1 0 0 0 1 0 1 1 1 0 0 0 0 0 0 1 0

Table 8-4 Example XOR Encryption

"V." Note that the XOR encryption method is very simple to implement and equally simple to break. The XOR encryption method should not be used by itself when an organization is transmitting or storing sensitive data. Actual encryption algorithms used to protect data typically use the XOR operator as part of a more complex encryption process.

You can combine XOR with a block cipher to produce a simple but powerful operation. In the example that follows (again read from left to right), the first row shows a character message "5E5+•" requiring encryption. The second row shows this message in binary notation. In order to apply an 8-bit block cipher method, the binary message is broken into 8-bit blocks in the row labeled "Message blocks." The fourth row shows the 8-bit key (01010101) chosen for the encryption. To encrypt the message, you must perform the XOR operation on each 8-bit block by using the XOR function on the message bit and the key bit to determine the bits of the ciphertext. The result is shown in the row labeled "Ciphertext." This ciphertext can now be sent to a receiver, who will be able to decipher the message simply by knowing the algorithm (XOR) and the key (01010101).

Message (text):	"5E5+•"				
Message (binary):	00110101	01000101	00110101	00101011	10010101
Message blocks:	00110101	01000101	00110101	00101011	10010101
Key:	01010101	01010101	01010101	01010101	01010101
Ciphertext:	01100000	00010000	01100000	01111110	11000000

If the receiver cannot apply the key to the ciphertext and derive the original message, either the cipher was applied with an incorrect key or the cryptosystem was not used correctly.

❯ Vernam Cipher

> **Key Term**
>
> **Vernam cipher** A cryptographic technique developed at AT&T and known as the "one-time pad," this cipher uses a set of characters for encryption operations only one time and then discards it.

Also known as the one-time pad, the **Vernam cipher**, developed by Gilbert Vernam in 1917 while working at AT&T Bell Labs, uses a set of characters only one time for each encryption process (hence the name *one-time pad*). The pad in the name comes from the days of manual encryption and decryption when the key values for each ciphering session were prepared by hand and bound into an easy-to-use form—a pad of paper. To perform the Vernam cipher encryption, the pad values are added to numeric values representing the plaintext that needs to be encrypted. Each character of the plaintext is turned into a number and a pad value for that position is added to it. The resulting sum for that character is then converted back to a ciphertext letter for transmission. If the sum of the two values exceeds 26, then 26 is subtracted from the total. The process of keeping a computed number within a specific range is called a *modulo*; thus, requiring that all numbers be in the range of 1–26 is referred to as *modulo 26*. In this process, a number larger than 26 has 26 sequentially subtracted from it until the number is in the proper range.

To examine the Vernam cipher and its use of modulo, consider the following example, which uses "SACK GAUL SPARE NO ONE" as plaintext. In the first step of this encryption process, the letter "S" is converted into the number 19 because it is the nineteenth letter of the alphabet. The same conversion is applied to the rest of the letters of the plaintext message, as shown below.

Plaintext:	S	A	C	K	G	A	U	L	S	P	A	R	E	N	O	O	N	E
Plaintext value:	19	01	03	11	07	01	21	12	19	16	01	18	05	14	15	15	14	05
One-time pad text:	F	P	Q	R	N	S	B	I	E	H	T	Z	L	A	C	D	G	J
One-time pad value:	06	16	17	18	14	19	02	09	05	08	20	26	12	01	03	04	07	10
Sum of plaintext & pad:	25	17	20	29	21	20	23	21	24	24	21	44	17	15	18	19	21	15
After modulo subtraction:				03								18						
Ciphertext:	Y	Q	T	C	U	T	W	U	X	X	U	R	Q	O	R	S	U	O

Rows three and four in this example show the one-time pad text that was chosen for this encryption and the one-time pad value, respectively. As you can see, the pad value, like the plaintext value, is derived from the position of each pad text letter in the alphabet. Thus, the pad text letter "F" is assigned the position number 06. This conversion process is repeated for the entire one-time pad text. Next, the plaintext value and the one-time pad value are added together—the first sum is 25. Because 25 is in the range of 1 to 26, no modulo 26 subtraction is required. The sum remains 25, and yields the ciphertext "Y," as shown above. Skipping ahead to the fourth character of the plaintext, "K," you find that its plaintext value is 11. The pad text is "R" and the pad value is 18. The sum of 11 and 18 is 29. Because 29 is larger than 26, 26 is subtracted from it, which yields the value 3. The ciphertext for this plaintext character is then the third letter of the alphabet, "C."

Decryption of any ciphertext generated from a one-time pad requires either knowledge of the pad values or the use of elaborate and very difficult cryptanalysis (or so the encrypting party hopes). Using the pad values and the ciphertext, the decryption process works as follows: "Y" becomes the number 25, from which you subtract the pad value for the first letter of the message, 06. This yields a value of 19, or the letter "S." This pattern continues until the fourth letter of the ciphertext, where the ciphertext letter is "C" and the pad value is 18. Subtracting 18 from 3 yields negative 15. Because of modulo 26, which requires that all numbers are in the range of 1–26, you must *add* 26 to the negative 15. This operation yields a sum of 11, which means the fourth letter of the message is "K."

 For more information about Gilbert Vernam and his cryptography work, view the video "Encryption, Episode 2: The Vernam Cipher" by visiting http://techchannel.att.com/ and using the search box.

❯ Book-Based Ciphers

Two related encryption methods made popular by spy movies involve using the text in a book as the key to decrypt a message. These methods are the book cipher and the running key cipher. A third method, the template cipher, is not really a cipher but is related to this discussion.

Book Cipher In a book cipher, the ciphertext consists of a list of codes representing the page number, line number, and word number of the plaintext word. The algorithm is the mechanical process of looking up the references from the ciphertext and converting each reference to a word by using the ciphertext's value and the key (the book). For example, from a copy of a particular popular novel, one may send the message 259,19,8; 22,3,8; 375,7,4; 394,17,2. Although almost any book can be used, dictionaries and thesauruses are typically the most popular sources, as they are likely to contain almost any word that might be needed. The recipient of a running key cipher must first know which book is used—in this case, suppose it is the science fiction novel *A Fire Upon the Deep*, the 1992 TOR edition. To decrypt the ciphertext, the receiver acquires the book, turns to page 259, finds line 19, and selects the eighth word in that line (which is "sack"). Then the receiver turns to page 22, line 3, selects the eighth word again, and so forth. In this example, the resulting message is "SACK ISLAND SHARP PATH." If a dictionary is used, the message consists only of the page number and the number of the word on the page. An even more sophisticated version might use multiple books, perhaps even in a particular sequence for each word or phrase.

Running Key Cipher Similar in concept to the book cipher is the running key cipher, which uses a book for passing the key to a cipher that is similar to the Vigenère cipher. The sender provides an encrypted message with a short sequence of numbers that indicate the page, line, and word number from a predetermined book to be used as the key or *indicator block*. Unlike the Vigenère cipher, if the key needs to be extended in a running key cipher, you don't repeat the key. Instead, you continue the text from the indicator block. From this point, you follow the same basic method as the Vigenère cipher, using the tabula recta to find the column based on the plaintext, and the row based on the key-indicator block letter.

Reversing the processes deciphers the ciphertext, using the ciphertext letter and key. You simply use the row or column corresponding to the key letter, find the ciphertext in the row or column of text, and then identify the letter on the opposing axis. The mirrored layout of the table simplifies the selection of rows or columns during encryption and decryption.

Template Cipher The template cipher or perforated page cipher is not strictly an encryption cipher, but more of an example of steganography. The template cipher involves the use of a hidden message in a book, letter, or other message. The receiver must use a page with a specific number of holes cut into it and place it over the book page or letter to extract the hidden message. Commonly shown in movies where an inmate sends coded messages from prison, this cipher is both difficult to execute and easy to detect, provided either party is physically searched. The presence of the perforated page is a clear indicator that some form of hidden message communication is occurring. A much simpler method would be to employ a variation of *acrostics*, where the first letter of each line of a message (or every nth letter) would spell out a hidden message.

❯ Hash Functions

> **Key Terms**
>
> **hash algorithms** Public functions that create a hash value, also known as a message digest, by converting variable-length messages into a single fixed-length value.

> **hash functions** Mathematical algorithms that generate a message summary or digest (sometimes called a fingerprint) to confirm message identity and integrity.
>
> **hash value** See *message digest*.
>
> **message authentication code (MAC)** A key-dependent, one-way hash function that allows only specific recipients (symmetric key holders) to access the message digest.
>
> **message digest** A value representing the application of a hash algorithm on a message that is transmitted with the message so it can be compared with the recipient's locally calculated hash of the same message. If both hashes are identical after transmission, the message has arrived without modification. Also known as a *hash value*.
>
> **Secure Hash Standard (SHS)** A standard issued by the National Institute of Standards and Technology (NIST) that specifies secure algorithms, such as SHA-1, for computing a condensed representation of a message or data file.

In addition to ciphers, another important encryption technique that is often incorporated into cryptosystems is the hash function. **Hash functions** are mathematical algorithms used to confirm the identity of a specific message and confirm that the content has not been changed. While they do not create ciphertext, hash functions confirm message identity and integrity, both of which are critical functions in e-commerce.

Hash algorithms are used to create a **hash value**, also known as a message digest, by converting variable-length messages into a single fixed-length value. The **message digest** is a fingerprint of the author's message that is compared with the recipient's locally calculated hash of the same message. If both hashes are identical after transmission, the message has arrived without modification. Hash functions are considered one-way operations in that the same message always provides the same hash value, but the hash value itself cannot be used to determine the contents of the message.

Hashing functions do not require the use of keys, but it is possible to attach a **message authentication code (MAC)** to allow only specific recipients to access the message digest. Because hash functions are one-way, they are used in password verification systems to confirm the identity of the user. In such systems, the hash value, or message digest, is calculated based on the originally issued password, and this message digest is stored for later comparison. When the user logs on for the next session, the system calculates a hash value based on the user's password input, and this value is compared against the stored value to confirm identity.

The **Secure Hash Standard (SHS)** is issued by the National Institute of Standards and Technology (NIST). Standard document FIPS 180-4 specifies SHA-1 (Secure Hash Algorithm 1) as a secure algorithm for computing a condensed representation of a message or data file. SHA-1 produces a 160-bit message digest, which can be used as an input to a digital signature algorithm. SHA-1 is based on principles modeled after MD4, which is part of the MDx family of hash algorithms created by Ronald Rivest. New hash algorithms, SHA-256, SHA-384, and SHA-512, have been proposed by NIST as standards for 128, 192, and 256 bits, respectively. The number of bits used in the hash algorithm is a measurement of the algorithm's strength against collision attacks. SHA-256 is essentially a 256-bit block cipher algorithm that creates a key by encrypting the intermediate hash value, with the message block functioning as the key. The compression function operates on each 512-bit message block and a 256-bit intermediate message digest.[2] As shown in Figure 8-4, free tools are available that can calculate hash values using a number of popular algorithms.

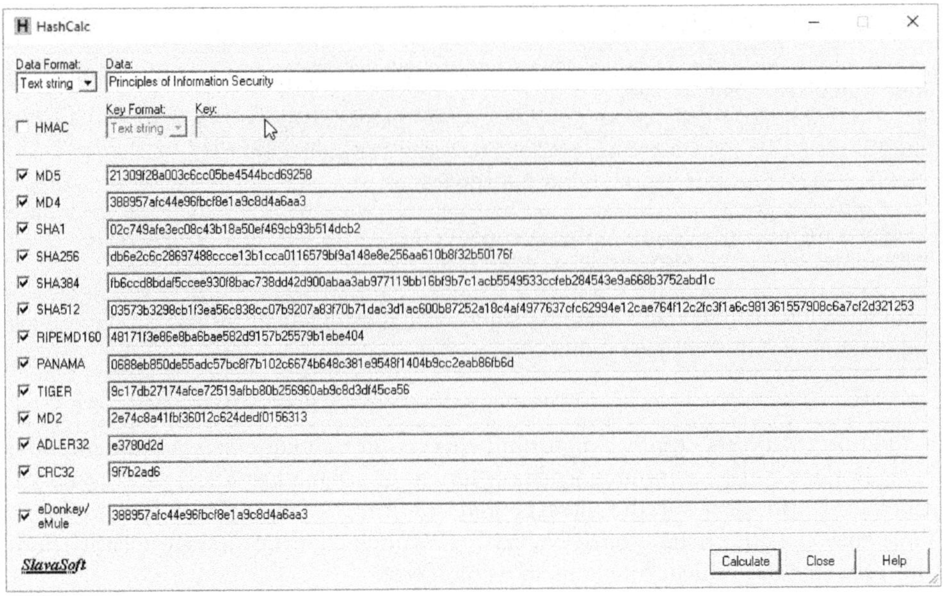

Figure 8-4 Various hash values

Source: SlavaSoft HashCalc.

> *For more information on the Secure Hash Standard, read FIPS 180-4 at http://csrc.nist.gov /publications/PubsFIPS.html.*

An attack method called rainbow cracking has generated concern about the strength of the processes used for password hashing. In general, if attackers gain access to a file of hashed passwords, they can use the application RainbowCrack and its combination of brute force and dictionary attacks to reveal user passwords. Passwords that are dictionary words or poorly constructed can be easily cracked. Well-constructed passwords that are of sufficient length can take a long time to crack even using the fastest computers, but by using a rainbow table—a database of precomputed hashes from sequentially calculated passwords—the rainbow cracker simply looks up the hashed password and reads out the text version. No brute force is required. This type of attack is more properly classified as a *time-memory trade-off attack.*

To defend against such an attack, you must first protect the file of hashed passwords and implement strict limits on the number of attempts allowed per login session. You can also use an approach called *password hash salting.* Salting is the process of providing a random piece of data to the hashing function when the hash is first calculated. The use of the salt value creates a different hash; when a large set of salt values are used, rainbow cracking fails because the time-memory trade-off is no longer in the attacker's favor. The salt value is not kept a secret: It is stored along with the account identifier so that the hash value can be re-created during authentication.[3] Additional techniques include *key stretching* and *key strengthening.* Key stretching involves repeating the hashing algorithm up to several thousand times to continuously inject the password, salt value, and interim hash results back into the process. Key strengthening extends the key with the salt value, but then deletes the salt value.

Cryptographic Algorithms

In general, cryptographic algorithms are often grouped into two broad categories—symmetric and asymmetric—but in practice, today's popular cryptosystems use a combination of both algorithms. Symmetric and asymmetric algorithms are distinguished by the types of keys they use for encryption and decryption operations.

❯ Symmetric Encryption

Key Terms

Advanced Encryption Standard (AES) The current federal standard for the encryption of data, as specified by NIST. AES is based on the Rijndael algorithm, which was developed by Vincent Rijmen and Joan Daemen.

private-key encryption See *symmetric encryption*.

secret key A key that can be used in symmetric encryption both to encipher and decipher the message.

symmetric encryption A cryptographic method in which the same algorithm and secret key are used both to encipher and decipher the message.

TECHNICAL DETAILS

Cryptographic Notation

The notation used to represent the encryption process varies, depending on its source. The notation in this text uses the letter M to represent the original message, C to represent the ending ciphertext, E to represent the enciphering or encryption process, D to represent the decryption or deciphering process, and K to represent the key. This notation can be used as follows:

- $E(M) = C$: encryption (E) is applied to a message (M) to create ciphertext (C).
- $D[C] = D[E(M)] = M$: by decrypting (D) an encrypted message [E(M)], you get the original message (M).
- $E(M,K) = C$: encrypting (E) the message (M) with the key (K) results in the ciphertext (C). If more than one key (K) is used in a multiple-round encryption, the keys are numbered K1, K2, and so on.
- $D(C,K) = D[E(M,K),K] = M$; that is, decrypting the ciphertext with key K results in the original plaintext message.

To encrypt a plaintext set of data, you can use one of two methods: bit stream and block cipher. In the bit stream method, each bit is transformed into a cipher bit, one after the other. In the block cipher method, the message is divided into

(continues)

> blocks—for example, 8-, 16-, 32-, or 64-bit blocks—and then each is transformed using the algorithm and key. Bit stream methods most commonly use algorithm functions like XOR, whereas block methods can use XOR, transposition, or substitution.

Encryption methodologies that require the same **secret key** to encipher and decipher the message are performing **private-key encryption** or **symmetric encryption**. Symmetric encryption methods use mathematical operations that can be programmed into extremely fast computing algorithms so that encryption and decryption are executed quickly, even by small computers. As you can see in Figure 8-5, one of the challenges is that both the sender and the recipient must have the secret key. Also, if either copy of the key falls into the wrong hands, messages can be decrypted by others and the sender and intended receiver may not know a message was intercepted. The primary challenge of symmetric key encryption is getting the key to the receiver, a process that must be conducted *out of band* to avoid interception. In other words, the process must use a channel or band other than the one carrying the ciphertext.

There are a number of popular symmetric encryption cryptosystems. One of the most widely known is the *Data Encryption Standard (DES)*; it was developed by IBM and is based on the company's Lucifer algorithm, which uses a key length of 128 bits. As implemented, DES uses a 64-bit block size and a 56-bit key. DES was adopted by NIST in 1976 as a federal standard for encryption of nonclassified information, after which it became widely employed in commercial applications. DES enjoyed increasing popularity for almost 20 years until 1997, when users realized that a 56-bit key size did not provide acceptable levels of security. In 1998, a group called the Electronic Frontier Foundation (*www.eff.org*) used a specially designed computer to break a DES key in just over 56 hours. Since then, it has been

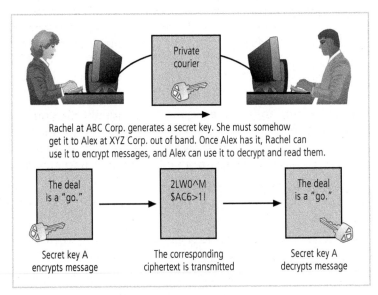

Figure 8-5 Example of symmetric encryption

theorized that a dedicated attack supported by the proper hardware (not necessarily a specialized computer) could break a DES key in less than a day.

Triple DES (3DES) was created to provide a level of security far beyond that of DES. 3DES was an advanced application of DES, and while it did deliver on its promise of encryption strength beyond DES, it soon proved too weak to survive indefinitely—especially as computing power continued to double every 18 months. Within just a few years, 3DES needed to be replaced.

The successor to 3DES is the **Advanced Encryption Standard (AES)**. AES is a federal information processing standard (FIPS) that specifies a cryptographic algorithm used within the U.S. government to protect information in federal agencies that are not part of the national defense infrastructure. (Agencies that are considered a part of national defense use more secure methods of encryption, which are provided by the National Security Agency.) The requirements for AES stipulate that the algorithm should be unclassified, publicly disclosed, and available royalty-free worldwide. AES was developed to replace both DES and 3DES.

TECHNICAL DETAILS

8

Triple DES (3DES)

3DES was designed to surpass the security provided by standard DES. (In between, there was a 2DES; however, it was statistically shown not to provide significantly stronger security than DES.) 3DES uses three 64-bit keys for an overall key length of 192 bits. 3DES encryption is the same as that of standard DES, repeated three times. 3DES can be employed using two or three keys and a combination of encryption or decryption for additional security. The most common implementations involve encrypting and/or decrypting with two or three different keys, as described in the following steps. 3DES employs 48 rounds in its encryption computation, generating ciphers that are approximately 256 times stronger than standard DES ciphers but that require only three times longer to process. One example of 3DES encryption is as follows:

1. In the first operation, 3DES encrypts the message with key 1, decrypts it with key 2, and then encrypts it again with key 1. In cryptographic notation, this is [E{D[E(M,K1)],K2},K1]. Decrypting with a different key is essentially another encryption, but it reverses the application of the traditional encryption operations.

2. In the second operation, 3DES encrypts the message with key 1, encrypts it again with key 2, and then encrypts it a third time with key 1 again, or [E{E[E(M,K1)], K2},K1].

3. In the third operation, 3DES encrypts the message three times with three different keys: [E{E[E(M,K1)],K2},K3]. This is the most secure level of encryption possible with 3DES.

While 3DES remains an approved algorithm for some uses, its expected useful life is limited. Historically, cryptographic standards approved by FIPS have been adopted on a voluntary basis by organizations outside government entities. The AES selection process involved cooperation between the U.S. government, private industry, and academia from around the world. AES was approved by the Secretary of Commerce as the official federal governmental standard on May 26, 2002.

AES implements a block cipher called the Rijndael Block Cipher with a variable block length and a key length of 128, 192, or 256 bits. Experts estimate that the special computer used by the Electronic Frontier Foundation to crack DES within a couple of days would require approximately 4,698,864 quintillion years (4,698,864,000,000,000,000,000) to crack AES. To learn more about AES, see the nearby Technical Details feature.

 For more information on the Advanced Encryption Standard, read FIPS 197 at http://csrc.nist.gov /publications/PubsFIPS.html.

⟩ Asymmetric Encryption

Key Terms

asymmetric encryption A cryptographic method that incorporates mathematical operations involving both a public key and a private key to encipher or decipher a message. Either key can be used to encrypt a message, but then the other key is required to decrypt it.
public-key encryption See *asymmetric encryption.*

While symmetric encryption systems use a single key both to encrypt and decrypt a message, **asymmetric encryption** uses two different but related keys. Either key can be used to encrypt or decrypt the message. However, if key A is used to encrypt the message, only key B can decrypt it; if key B is used to encrypt a message, only key A can decrypt it. Asymmetric encryption can be used to provide elegant solutions to problems of secrecy and verification. This technique has its greatest value when one key is used as a private key, which means it is kept secret (much like the key in symmetric encryption) and is known only to the owner of the key pair. The other key serves as a public key, which means it is stored in a public location where anyone can use it. For this reason, the more common name for asymmetric encryption is **public-key encryption.**

Consider the following example, as illustrated in Figure 8-6. Alex at XYZ Corporation wants to send an encrypted message to Rachel at ABC Corporation. Alex goes to a public-key registry and obtains Rachel's public key. Remember that the foundation of asymmetric encryption is that the same key cannot be used both to encrypt and decrypt the same message. So, when Rachel's public key is used to encrypt the message, only her private key can be used to decrypt the message; that private key is held by Rachel alone. Similarly, if Rachel wants to respond to Alex's message, she goes to the registry where Alex's public key is held and uses it to encrypt her message, which of course can only be read by Alex's private key. This approach, which keeps private keys secret and encourages the sharing of public keys in reliable directories, is an elegant solution to the key management problems of symmetric key applications.

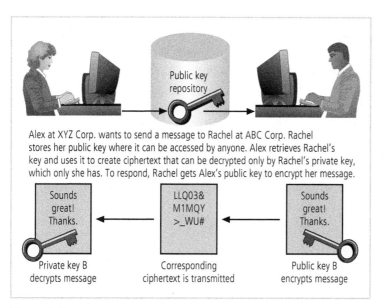

Alex at XYZ Corp. wants to send a message to Rachel at ABC Corp. Rachel stores her public key where it can be accessed by anyone. Alex retrieves Rachel's key and uses it to create ciphertext that can be decrypted only by Rachel's private key, which only she has. To respond, Rachel gets Alex's public key to encrypt her message.

| Sounds great! Thanks. | LLQ03& M1MQY >_WU# | Sounds great! Thanks. |
| Private key B decrypts message | Corresponding ciphertext is transmitted | Public key B encrypts message |

Figure 8-6 Example of asymmetric encryption

TECHNICAL DETAILS

Advanced Encryption Standard (AES)

Of the many ciphers that were submitted from around the world for consideration in the AES selection process, five finalists were chosen: MARS, RC6, Rijndael, Serpent, and Twofish. On October 2, 2000, NIST announced the selection of Rijndael; it was approved as the official U.S. standard 18 months later. The AES version of Rijndael can use a multiple round-based system. Depending on the key size, the number of rounds varies from 9 to 13: for a 128-bit key, nine rounds plus one end round are used; for a 192-bit key, 11 rounds plus one end round are used; and for a 256-bit key, 13 rounds plus one end round are used. Once Rijndael was adopted for the AES, the ability to use variable-sized blocks was standardized to a single 128-bit block for simplicity. The four steps within each Rijndael round are described as follows:

1. "The Byte Sub step. Each byte of the block is replaced by its substitute in an S-box (substitution box). [*Author's note: The calculation of the S-box values is beyond the scope of this text.*]

(continues)

2. The Shift Row step. Considering the block to be made up of bytes 1 to 16, these bytes are arranged in a rectangle and shifted as follows:

from					to			
1	5	9	13		1	5	9	13
2	6	10	14		6	10	14	2
3	7	11	15		11	15	3	7
4	8	12	16		16	4	8	12

Other shift tables are used for larger blocks.

3. The Mix Column step. Matrix multiplication is performed; each column is multiplied by the matrix:

2	3	1	1
1	2	3	1
1	1	2	3
3	1	1	2

4. The Add Round Key step. This simply XORs in the subkey for the current round.

The extra final round omits the Mix Column step, but is otherwise the same as a regular round."[4]

Asymmetric algorithms are one-way functions, meaning they are simple to compute in one direction, but complex to compute in the opposite direction. This is the foundation of public-key encryption. It is based on a hash value, which is calculated from an input number using a hashing algorithm, as you learned earlier in this chapter. This hash value is essentially a summary of the original input values. It is virtually impossible to derive the original values without knowing how they were used to create the hash value. For example, if you multiply 45 by 235, you get 10,575. This is simple enough. But if you are simply given the number 10,575, can you determine which two numbers were multiplied to produce it?

Now assume that each multiplier is 200 digits long and prime. The resulting multiplicative product could be up to 400 digits long. Imagine the time you'd need to factor out those numbers. There is a shortcut, however. In mathematics, it is known as a trapdoor (which is different from the software trapdoor). A mathematical trapdoor is a "secret mechanism that enables you to easily accomplish the reverse function in a one-way function."[5] With a trapdoor, you can use a key to encrypt or decrypt the ciphertext, but not both, thus requiring two keys. The public key becomes the true key, and the private key is derived from the public key using the trapdoor.

One of the most popular public-key cryptosystems is RSA, whose name is derived from Rivest-Shamir-Adleman, the algorithm's developers. The *RSA algorithm* was the first public-key encryption algorithm developed (in 1977) and published for commercial use. It is very popular and has been embedded in essentially all widely available Web browsers to provide security for e-commerce applications. The patented RSA algorithm has become the de facto standard for public-use encryption applications.

For more information on how the RSA algorithm works, read RFC 3447, "Public-Key Cryptography Standards (PKCS) #1: RSA Cryptography Specifications," Version 2.1, which is available from www.rfc-editor.org/rfc/rfc3447.txt.

The problem with asymmetric encryption, as shown earlier in Figure 8-6, is that holding a single conversation between two parties requires four keys. Moreover, if four organizations want to exchange communications, each party must manage its private key and four public keys. In such scenarios, determining which public key is needed to encrypt a particular message can become a rather confusing problem, and with more organizations in the loop, the problem expands. This is why asymmetric encryption is sometimes regarded by experts as inefficient. Compared with symmetric encryption, asymmetric encryption is also not as efficient in terms of CPU computations. Consequently, hybrid systems, such as those described later in this chapter in the "public key infrastructure (PKI)" section, are more commonly used than pure asymmetric systems.

 The RSA organization is now a division of EMC Corporation. For information about the annual RSA security conference, see www.rsaconference.com. You can also visit the home pages of RSA's developers. For example, Ronald L. Rivest's home page is at http://people.csail.mit.edu/rivest/. Adi Shamir's home page is at www.wisdom.weizmann.ac.il/math/profile/scientists/shamir-profile.html. Len Adleman's home page is at www.usc.edu/dept/molecular-science/fm-adleman.htm.

❯ Encryption Key Size

When deploying ciphers, it is important for users to decide on the size of the cryptovariable or key, because the strength of many encryption applications and cryptosystems is measured by key size. How exactly does key size affect the strength of an algorithm? Typically, the length of the key increases the number of random guesses that have to be made in order to break the code. Creating a larger universe of possibilities increases the time required to make guesses, and thus a longer key directly influences the strength of the encryption.

It may surprise you to learn that when it comes to cryptosystems, the security of encrypted data is *not* dependent on keeping the encrypting algorithm secret. In fact, algorithms should be published and often are, to enable research to uncover their weaknesses. The security of any cryptosystem depends on keeping some or all elements of the cryptovariable(s) or key(s) secret, and effective security is maintained by manipulating the size (bit length) of the keys and following proper procedures and policies for key management.

For a simple example of how key size is related to encryption strength, suppose you have an algorithm that uses a three-bit key. You may recall from earlier in the chapter that keyspace is the range from which the key can be drawn. Also, you may recall that in binary notation, three bits can be used to represent values from 000 to 111, which correspond to the numbers 0 to 7 in decimal notation and thus provide a keyspace of eight keys. This means an algorithm that uses a three-bit key has eight possible keys; the numbers 0 to 7 in binary are 000, 001, 010, 011, 100, 101, 110, and 111. If you know how many keys you have to choose from, you can program a computer to try all the keys in an attempt to crack the encrypted message.

The preceding statement makes a few assumptions: (1) you know the algorithm, (2) you have the encrypted message, and (3) you have time on your hands. It is easy to satisfy the first criterion. The encryption tools that use DES can be purchased over the counter. Many of these tools are based on encryption algorithms that are standards, as is DES itself, and therefore it is relatively easy to get a cryptosystem based on DES that enables you to decrypt an encrypted message if you possess the key. The second criterion requires the interception of an encrypted message, which is illegal but not impossible. As for the third criterion, the task required is a brute force attack, in which a computer randomly or sequentially selects possible keys of the known size and applies them to the encrypted text or a piece of the encrypted text. If the result is plaintext—bingo! But, as indicated earlier in this chapter, it can take quite a long time to exert brute force on more advanced cryptosystems. In fact, the strength of an algorithm is determined by how long it takes to guess the key.

When it comes to keys, how big is big? At the beginning of this section, you learned that a three-bit system has eight possible keys. An eight-bit system has 256 possible keys. If you use a 24-bit key, which is puny by modern standards, you have almost 16.8 million possible keys. Even so, a modern PC, such as the one described in Table 8-5, could discover this key in mere seconds. But, as the table shows, the amount of time needed to crack a cipher by guessing its key grows exponentially with each additional bit.

One thing to keep in mind is that even though the estimated time to crack grows rapidly with respect to the number of bits in the encryption key and the odds of cracking seem insurmountable at first glance, Table 8-5 doesn't account for the fact that high-end computing power has increased and continues to be more accessible. Making this even more challenging is the use of graphics processing units (GPUs) found in video cards. These powerful processors can be programmed to perform cryptanalysis calculations, usually at a faster rate than the computer's primary CPU. Therefore, even the once-standard 56-bit encryption can't stand up anymore to brute force attacks by personal computers, especially if multiple computers are used together to crack these keys. Each additional computer reduces the amount of time needed. Two computers can divide the keyspace—the entire set of possible combinations of bits that can be the cryptovariable or key—and crack the key in approximately half the time, and so on. Thus, 43 computers can crack a 64-bit key in just under one year; 12 times as many computers would do it in just under a month. This means people who have access to multiple systems or grid computing environments can radically speed up brute force key-breaking efforts. However, an even greater concern is the ease with which you can read messages encrypted by what appear to be uncrackable algorithms if you have the key. Key management (and password management) is the most critical aspect of any cryptosystem in protecting encrypted information, and is even more important in many cases than key strength.

Why, then, do encryption systems such as DES incorporate multiple elements or operations? Consider this: If a cryptosystem uses the same operation (XOR, substitution, or transposition) multiple consecutive times, it gains no additional benefit. For example, using a substitution cipher and substituting B for A, then R for B, and then Q for R, has the same effect as substituting Q for A. Similarly, by transposing a character in position 1, then position 4, then position 3, a cryptosystem could more easily have transposed the character from position 1 to position 3. There is no net advantage for sequential operations unless each subsequent operation is different. Therefore, to substitute, then transpose, then XOR, then substitute again, the cryptosystem will have dramatically scrambled, substituted, and recoded the original plaintext with ciphertext, which the cryptosystem hopes is unbreakable without the key.

It is estimated that to crack an encryption key using a brute force attack, a computer needs to perform a maximum of 2^k operations (2^k guesses), where k is the number of bits in the key. In reality, the average estimated time to crack is half that time.

The estimated average time to crack is based on a 2015-era PC with an Intel i7-6700K Quad Core CPU performing 207.23 Dhrystone GIPS (billion instructions per second) at 4.0 GHz**

Key Length (Bits)	Maximum Number of Operations (Guesses)	Maximum Time to Crack	Estimated Average Time to Crack
16	65,536	0.0000003 seconds	0.00000016 seconds
24	16,777,216	0.00008 seconds	0.00004 seconds
32	4,294,967,296	0.02 seconds	0.01 seconds
56	7.E+16	4.02 days	2.01 days
64	2.E+19	42.93 years	21.47 years
128	3.E+38	19,005,227,625,557,100,000,000 years	9,502,613,812,778,540,000,000 years
256	1.E+77	6,467,143,840,295,770,000,000,000,000,000,000,000,000,000,000,000,000,000 years	3,233,571,920,147,890,000,000,000,000,000,000,000,000,000,000,000,000 years
512	1.E+154	748,844,096,666,088,000,000,000,000,000,000,000,000,000,000,000,000,000,000,000,000,000,000,000,000,000,000,000,000,000,000,000,000,000,000,000,000 years	374,422,048,333,044,000,000,000,000,000,000,000,000,000,000,000,000,000,000,000,000,000,000,000,000,000,000,000,000,000,000,000,000,000,000,000 years

Table 8-5 Encryption Key Power

**Note: The authors acknowledge that this benchmark is based on a very specific application test and that the results are not generalizable. However, these calculations are shown to illustrate the relative difference between key length strength rather than to accurately depict time to crack. Even using the much more conservative TechSpot 7-zip benchmark, which clocked this CPU at 25,120 MIPS (or 25.12 GIPS), the estimated average time to crack would only be approximately 8.25 times slower than the numbers shown, resulting in an average time to crack of 16.6 days, as opposed to the 2.01 days shown above for a 56-bit key length.

Some new 2016-era CPUs are approximately twice as fast as the version shown here on the 7-zip benchmarks, but they do not include Dhrystone benchmarks (such as the Intel Core i7-6950X with 10 cores/20 threads).

Source: www.techspot.com/review/1187-intel-core-i7-6950x-broadwell-e/page4.html.

Cryptographic Tools

The ability to conceal the contents of sensitive messages and verify the contents of messages and the identities of their senders can be important in all areas of business. To be useful, these cryptographic capabilities must be embodied in tools that allow IT and information security practitioners to apply the elements of cryptography in the everyday world of computing. This section covers some of the widely used tools that bring the functions of cryptography to the world of information systems.

❯ Public Key Infrastructure (PKI)

Public key infrastructure (PKI) systems are based on public-key cryptosystems and include digital certificates and certificate authorities (CAs). **Digital certificates** allow the PKI components and their users to validate keys and identify key owners. (Digital certificates are explained in more detail later in this chapter.) PKI systems and their digital certificate registries enable the protection of information assets by making verifiable digital certificates readily available to business applications. This, in turn, allows the applications to implement several key characteristics of information security and integrate these characteristics into the following business processes across an organization:

- Authentication: Individuals, organizations, and Web servers can validate the identity of each party in an Internet transaction.

- Integrity: Content signed by the certificate is known not to have been altered while in transit from host to host or server to client.

- Privacy: Information is protected from being intercepted during transmission.

- Authorization: The validated identity of users and programs can enable authorization rules that remain in place for the duration of a transaction; this reduces overhead and allows for more control of access privileges for specific transactions.

- Nonrepudiation: Customers or partners can be held accountable for transactions, such as online purchases, which they cannot later dispute.

A typical PKI solution protects the transmission and reception of secure information by integrating the following components:

- A **certificate authority (CA)**, which issues, manages, authenticates, signs, and revokes users' digital certificates. These certificates typically contain the user name, public key, and other identifying information.

- A **registration authority (RA)**, which handles certification functions such as verifying registration information, generating end-user keys, revoking certificates, and validating user certificates, in collaboration with the CA.

- Certificate directories, which are central locations for certificate storage that provide a single access point for administration and distribution.

- Management protocols, which organize and manage communications among CAs, RAs, and end users. This includes the functions and procedures for setting up new users, issuing keys, recovering keys, updating keys, revoking keys, and enabling the transfer of certificates and status information among the parties involved in the PKI's area of authority.

- Policies and procedures, which assist an organization in the application and management of certificates, in the formalization of legal liabilities and limitations, and in actual business use.

Common implementations of PKI include systems that issue digital certificates to users and servers, directory enrollment, key issuing systems, tools for managing key issuance, and verification and return of certificates. These systems enable organizations to apply an enterprise-wide solution that allows users within the PKI's area of authority to engage in authenticated and secure communications and transactions.

The CA performs many housekeeping activities regarding the use of keys and certificates that are issued and used in its zone of authority. Each user authenticates himself or herself with the CA. The CA can issue new or replacement keys, track issued keys, provide a directory of public-key values for all known users, and perform other management activities. When a private key is compromised or the user loses the privilege of using keys in the area of authority, the CA can revoke the user's keys. The CA periodically distributes a **certificate revocation list (CRL)** to all users. When important events occur, specific applications can make a real-time request to the CA to verify any user against the current CRL.

The issuance of certificates and their keys by the CA enables secure, encrypted, nonrepudiable e-business transactions. Some applications allow users to generate their own certificates and keys, but a key pair generated by the end user can only provide nonrepudiation, not reliable encryption. A central system operated by a CA or RA can generate cryptographically strong keys that are considered independently trustworthy by all users, and can provide services for users such as private-key backup, key recovery, and key revocation.

The strength of a cryptosystem relies on both the raw strength of its key's complexity and the overall quality of its key management security. PKI solutions can provide several mechanisms for limiting access and possible exposure of the private keys. These mechanisms include password protection, smart cards, hardware tokens, and other hardware-based key storage devices that are memory-capable, like flash memory or PC memory cards. PKI users should select the key security mechanisms that provide an appropriate level of key protection for their needs. Managing the security and integrity of the private keys used for nonrepudiation or the encryption of data files is critical to successfully using the encryption and nonrepudiation services within the PKI's area of trust.[6]

 For more information on public-key cryptography, read FIPS 191: "Entity Authentication Using Public Key Cryptography" at http://csrc.nist.gov/publications/PubsFIPS.html.

❯ Digital Signatures

Key Terms

Digital Signature Standard (DSS) The NIST standard for digital signature algorithm usage by federal information systems. DSS is based on a variant of the ElGamal signature scheme.

> **digital signatures** Encrypted message components that can be mathematically proven as authentic.
> **nonrepudiation** The process of reversing public-key encryption to verify that a message was sent by the sender and thus cannot be refuted.

Digital signatures were created in response to the rising need to verify information transferred via electronic systems. Asymmetric encryption processes are used to create digital signatures. When an asymmetric cryptographic process uses the sender's private key to encrypt a message, the sender's public key must be used to decrypt the message. When the decryption is successful, the process verifies that the message was sent by the sender and thus cannot be refuted. This process is known as **nonrepudiation,** and is the principle of cryptography that underpins the authentication mechanism collectively known as a digital signature. **Digital signatures,** therefore, are encrypted messages that can be mathematically proven as authentic.

The management of digital signatures is built into most Web browsers. For example, the digital signature management screen in Internet Explorer is shown in Figure 8-7. In general, digital signatures should be created using processes and products that are based on the **Digital Signature Standard (DSS).** When processes and products are certified as DSS compliant, they have been approved and endorsed by U.S. federal and state governments, as well as by many foreign governments, as a means of authenticating the author of an electronic document.

DSS algorithms can be used in conjunction with the sender's public and private keys, the receiver's public key, and the Secure Hash Standard to quickly create messages that are both encrypted and nonrepudiable. This process first creates a message digest using the hash algorithm, which is then input into the digital signature algorithm along with a random number to generate the digital signature. The digital signature function also depends on the sender's private key and other information provided by the CA. The resulting encrypted message contains the digital signature, which can be verified by the recipient using the sender's public key.

 For more information on the Digital Signature Standard, read FIPS 186-4 at http://csrc.nist.gov /publications/PubsFIPS.html.

❭ Digital Certificates

As you learned earlier in this chapter, a digital certificate is an electronic document or container file that contains a key value and identifying information about the entity that controls the key. The certificate is often issued and certified by a third party, usually a certificate authority. A digital signature attached to the certificate's container file certifies the file's origin and integrity. This verification process often occurs when you download or update software via the Internet. For example, the window in Figure 8-8 shows that the downloaded files do come from the purported originating agency, Amazon.com, and thus can be trusted.

Unlike digital signatures, which help authenticate the origin of a message, digital certificates authenticate the cryptographic key that is embedded in the certificate. When used properly, these certificates enable diligent users to verify the authenticity of any organization's certificates. This process is much like what happens when the Federal Deposit Insurance Corporation (FDIC) issues its logo to assure customers that a bank is authentic. Different client-server

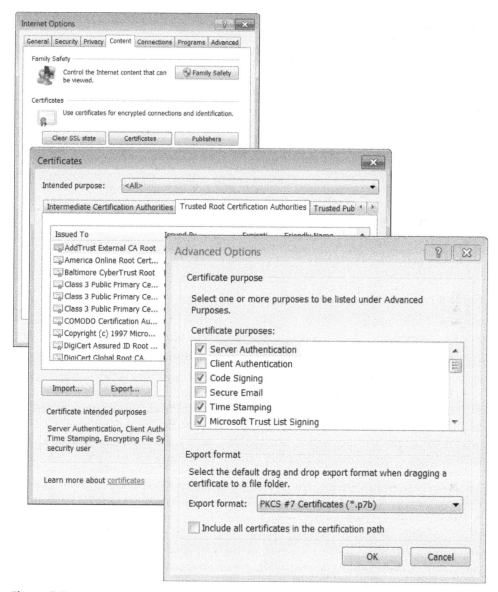

Figure 8-7 Digital signature in Windows Internet Explorer

Source: Windows Internet Explorer.

applications use different types of digital certificates to accomplish their assigned functions, as follows:

- The CA application suite issues and uses certificates (keys) that identify and establish a trust relationship with a CA to determine what additional certificates can be authenticated.

- Mail applications use Secure/Multipurpose Internet Mail Extension (S/MIME) certificates for signing and encrypting e-mail as well as for signing forms.

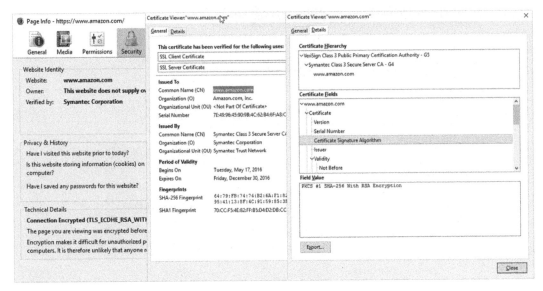

Figure 8-8 Example digital certificate

Source: Amazon.com.

- Development applications use object-signing certificates to identify signers of object-oriented code and scripts.

- Web servers and Web application servers use Secure Sockets Layer (SSL) certificates to authenticate servers via the SSL protocol in order to establish an encrypted SSL session. The SSL protocol is explained later in this chapter.

- Web clients use client SSL certificates to authenticate users, sign forms, and participate in single sign-on solutions via SSL.

Two popular certificate types are created using Pretty Good Privacy (PGP) and applications that conform to International Telecommunication Union's (ITU-T) X.509 version 3. The X.509 v3 certificate, whose structure is outlined in Table 8-6, is an ITU-T recommendation that essentially defines a directory service that maintains a database of information (also known as a repository) about a group of users holding X.509 v3 certificates. These certificates bind a *distinguished name (DN)*, which uniquely identifies a certificate entity, to a user's public key. The certificate is signed and placed in the directory by the CA for retrieval and verification by the user's associated public key. The X.509 v3 standard's recommendation does not specify an encryption algorithm, although RSA, with its hashed digital signature, is typically used.

❯ Hybrid Cryptography Systems

Key Terms

Diffie-Hellman key exchange A hybrid cryptosystem that facilitates exchanging private keys using public-key encryption.

session keys Limited-use symmetric keys for temporary communications during an online session.

X.509 v3 Certificate Structure
Version
Certificate Serial Number
• Algorithm ID • Algorithm ID • Parameters
Issuer Name
• Validity • Not Before • Not After
Subject Name
Subject Public-Key Information • Public-Key Algorithm • Parameters • Subject Public Key
Issuer Unique Identifier (Optional)
Subject Unique Identifier (Optional)
Extensions (Optional) • Type • Criticality • Value
Certificate Signature Algorithm
Certificate Signature

Table 8-6 X.509 v3 Certificate Structure[7]

Source: Stallings, W. Cryptography and Network Security, Principles and Practice.

Except in digital certificates, asymmetric key encryption in its pure form is not widely used. However, it is often used in conjunction with symmetric key encryption—in other words, as part of a hybrid encryption system. The most common hybrid system is based on the **Diffie-Hellman key exchange**, which uses asymmetric encryption to exchange **session keys**. These are limited-use symmetric keys that allow two entities to conduct quick, efficient, secure communications based on symmetric encryption, which is more efficient than asymmetric encryption for sending messages. Diffie-Hellman provides the foundation for subsequent developments in public-key encryption. It protects data from exposure to third parties, which is sometimes a problem when keys are exchanged out of band.

A hybrid encryption approach is illustrated in Figure 8-9, and it works as follows: Alex at XYZ Corp. wants to communicate with Rachel at ABC Corp., so Alex first creates a session key. Alex encrypts a message with this session key, and then gets Rachel's public key. Alex uses Rachel's public key to encrypt both the session key and the message, which is already encrypted. Alex transmits the entire package to Rachel, who uses her private key to decrypt

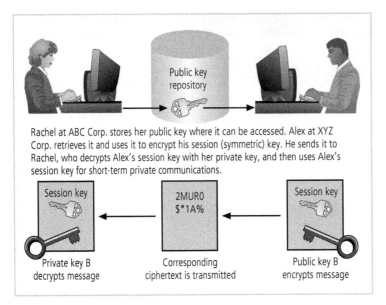

Rachel at ABC Corp. stores her public key where it can be accessed. Alex at XYZ Corp. retrieves it and uses it to encrypt his session (symmetric) key. He sends it to Rachel, who decrypts Alex's session key with her private key, and then uses Alex's session key for short-term private communications.

Figure 8-9 Example of hybrid encryption

the package containing the session key and the encrypted message, and then uses the session key to decrypt the message. Rachel can then continue to use only this session key for electronic communications until the session key expires. The asymmetric session key is used in the much more efficient processes of symmetric encryption and decryption. After the session key expires, usually in a few minutes, a new session key is chosen and shared using the same process.

 For more information on Diffie and Hellman, see Whitfield Diffie's home page at http://cisac.fsi .stanford.edu/people/whitfield_diffie and Martin Hellman's home page at www-ee.stanford.edu /~hellman/.

> Steganography

Key Term

steganography The process of hiding messages; for example, hiding a message within the digital encoding of a picture or graphic so that it is almost impossible to detect that the hidden message even exists.

The word **steganography**—the art of secret writing—is derived from the Greek words *steganos*, meaning "covered," and *graphein*, meaning "to write." The Greek historian Herodotus described one of the first steganographers, a fellow Greek who warned of an imminent invasion by writing a message on the wood beneath a wax writing tablet.[8] While steganography is technically not a form of cryptography, it is another way of protecting the confidentiality of information in transit. The most popular modern version of steganography involves hiding information within files that contain digital pictures or other images.

To understand how this form of steganography works, you must first know a little about how images are stored. Most computer graphics standards use a combination of three color values—red, blue, and green (RGB)—to represent a picture element, or pixel. Each of the three color values usually requires an 8-bit code for that color's intensity; for example, 00000000 is the code for no red and 11111111 is maximum red. Each color image pixel requires 3 colors × 8 bits = 24 bits to represent the color mix and intensity. Some image encoding standards use more or fewer bits per pixel. When a picture is created by a digital camera or a computer program, the number of horizontal and vertical pixels captured and recorded is known as the image's *resolution*. Thus, for example, if 1024 horizontal pixels are recorded and 768 vertical pixels are captured, the image has 1024 × 768 resolution and is said to have 786,432 pixels, or three-quarters of a megapixel. An image that is 1024 × 768 pixels contains 786,432 groups of 24 bits to represent the red, green, and blue data. The raw image size can be calculated as 1024 × 768 × 24, or 5.66 megabytes. There are plenty of bits in this picture data file in which to hide a secret message.

To the naked eye, there is no discernible difference between a pixel with a red intensity of 00101001 and a slightly different pixel with a red intensity level of 00101000. Using this approach provides a steganographer with one bit of payload per color (or three bits per pixel) to be used to encode data into an image file. If a steganographic process uses three bits per pixel for all 786,432 pixels, it will be able to store 236 kilobytes of hidden data within the uncompressed image.

Some steganographic tools can calculate the largest image that can be stored before being detectable. Messages can also be hidden in computer files that do not hold images; if such files do not use all of their available bits, data can be placed where software ignores it and people almost never look. Some applications can hide messages in .bmp, .wav, .mp3, and .au files, as well as in otherwise unused storage space on CDs and DVDs. Another approach is to hide a message in a text or document file and store the payload in what appears to be unused whitespace.

Even before the attacks of September 11, 2001, U.S. federal agencies came to believe that terrorist organizations were "hiding maps and photographs of terrorist targets and posting instructions for terrorist activities in sports chat rooms, pornographic bulletin boards, and other Web sites" using steganographic methods. No documented proof of this activity has been made public.[9] However, the Electronic Frontier Foundation (*www.eff.org*) established that the U.S. Secret Service worked with several manufacturers of color laser printers to use steganography to encode printer serial numbers in printed documents.

 For more information on steganography, read Kristy Westphal's article on Symantec's Community Web site at www.symantec.com/connect/articles/steganography-revealed, or visit the Steganography Analysis and Research Center at www.sarc-wv.com/.

Protocols for Secure Communications

Most of the software applications currently used to protect the confidentiality of information are not true cryptosystems. Instead, they are applications to which cryptographic protocols have been added. This is perhaps particularly true of Internet protocols; some experts claim that the Internet and its corresponding protocols were designed without any consideration for security, which was added later as an afterthought. Whether or not this is true, the lack of threats in the environment in which the Internet was launched allowed it to grow rapidly. But, as the number of threats grew, so did the need for additional security measures.

❯ Securing Internet Communication with S-HTTP and SSL

Key Terms
_____

Secure HTTP (S-HTTP) An extended version of Hypertext Transfer Protocol that provides for the encryption of protected Web pages transmitted via the Internet between a client and server.
Secure Sockets Layer (SSL) A security protocol developed by Netscape to use public-key encryption to secure a channel over the Internet.

S-HTTP (Secure Hypertext Transfer Protocol) and SSL are two protocols designed to enable secure network communications across the Internet. S-HTTP and SSL ensure Internet security via different mechanisms and can be used independently or together.

Netscape developed the **Secure Sockets Layer (SSL)** protocol to use public-key encryption to secure a channel over the Internet, thus enabling secure communications. Most popular browsers, including Internet Explorer, use SSL. In addition to providing data encryption, integrity, and server authentication, SSL can provide client authentication when properly configured.

 For more information on the SSL protocol, read RFC 6101 at www.rfc-editor.org/info/rfc6101.

In April 2014, a vulnerability was revealed in a widely used implementation of the SSL protocol. Web servers with the Heartbleed bug allow an attacker to bypass some of the controls that protect sensitive information. Web servers that use an unpatched version of the popular OpenSSL tool to implement Secure Sockets Layer/Transport Layer Security (SSL/TLS) can be tricked by an attacker to reveal the memory areas of the server. Those areas may contain critical information such as encryption keys, passwords, or account numbers. The Heartbleed bug is classified as a buffer overread error. The OpenSSL tool is widely used for Internet sites around the world.

After the bug was made widely known, a patched version of the OpenSSL toolset was soon released, and most server administrators and Web hosting providers were able to make their platforms secure again. Unless the toolset is updated and the Web sites purge the keys that have been issued, they remain vulnerable to data loss.

The name of the bug comes from a feature implemented in OpenSSL that maintains the connection between host and client while data is not being transmitted between them. The so-called heartbeat packets were intended to maintain session awareness between the server and the client. The bug was that the heartbeat message included a feature to allow the transmission of a selectable quantity of data. In normal use, no data was requested by the client. If the server allowed the client to request data from the heartbeat packet, significant quantities of current server memory would be sent to the client system, including data the server administrator would not want released. The patch corrected this unintended data from being sent.

The SSL protocol works as follows: during a normal client/server HTTP session, the client requests access to a portion of the Web site that requires secure communications, and the server sends a message to the client indicating that a secure connection must be established. The client sends its public key and security parameters. This handshaking phase is complete when the server finds a public key match and sends a digital certificate to the client to authenticate itself. Once the client verifies that the certificate is valid and trustworthy, the SSL session is established. Until the client or the server terminates the session, any amount of data can be transmitted securely.

SSL provides two protocol layers within the TCP framework: SSL Record Protocol and Standard HTTP. The *SSL Record Protocol* is responsible for the fragmentation, compression, encryption, and attachment of an SSL header to the plaintext prior to transmission. Received encrypted messages are decrypted and reassembled for presentation to the higher levels of the protocol. The SSL Record Protocol provides basic security and communication services to the top levels of the SSL protocol stack. *Standard HTTP* provides the Internet communication services between client and host without consideration for encryption of the data that is transmitted between client and server.

Secure HTTP (S-HTTP) is an extended version of Hypertext Transfer Protocol that provides for the encryption of individual messages transmitted via the Internet between a client and server. S-HTTP is the application of SSL over HTTP, which allows the encryption of all information passing between two computers through a protected and secure virtual connection. Unlike SSL, in which a secure channel is established for the duration of a session, S-HTTP is designed for sending individual messages over the Internet; therefore, a session must be established for each individual exchange of data. To establish a session, the client and server must have compatible cryptosystems and agree on the configuration. The S-HTTP client then must send the server its public key so that the server can generate a session key. The session key from the server is then encrypted with the client's public key and returned to the client. After the client decrypts the key using its private key, the client and server possess identical session keys, which they can use to encrypt the messages sent between them.

S-HTTP can provide confidentiality, authentication, and data integrity through a variety of trust models and cryptographic algorithms. In addition, this protocol is designed for easy integration with existing HTTP applications and for implementation in conjunction with HTTP.

❯ Securing E-mail with S/MIME, PEM, and PGP

> **Key Terms**
>
> **Privacy-Enhanced Mail (PEM)** A standard proposed by the Internet Engineering Task Force (IETF) that uses 3DES symmetric key encryption and RSA for key exchanges and digital signatures.
>
> **Secure Multipurpose Internet Mail Extensions (S/MIME)** A security protocol that builds on the encoding format of the Multipurpose Internet Mail Extensions (MIME) protocol and uses digital signatures based on public-key cryptosystems to secure e-mail.

A number of cryptosystems have been adapted to work with the dominant e-mail protocols in an attempt to incorporate some degree of security into this notoriously insecure communication medium. Some popular adaptations are described in this section.

Secure Multipurpose Internet Mail Extensions (S/MIME) builds on the encoding format of the Multipurpose Internet Mail Extensions (MIME) protocol and uses digital signatures based on public-key cryptosystems to secure e-mail. In 1993, the Internet Engineering Task Force (IETF) proposed the **Privacy-Enhanced Mail (PEM)** standard to use 3DES symmetric key encryption and RSA for key exchanges and digital signatures; however, it was never widely deployed. *Pretty Good Privacy (PGP)* was developed by Phil Zimmermann, and uses the IDEA cipher for message encoding. PGP also uses RSA for symmetric key exchange and digital signatures. PGP is discussed in more detail later in this chapter.

The first commonly used Internet e-mail standard was SMTP/RFC 822, also called SMTP, but this standard has problems and limitations, such as an inability to transmit executable files or binary objects and an inability to handle character sets other than 7-bit ASCII. These limitations make SMTP unwieldy for organizations that need greater security and support for international character sets. MIME, whose message header fields are shown in Table 8-7, was developed to address the problems associated with SMTP. In the table, you can see that MIME's message header fields were designed to identify and describe the e-mail message and to handle a variety of e-mail content. In addition to the message header fields, the MIME specification includes predefined content types and conversion transfer encodings, such as 7-bit, 8-bit, binary, and radix-64, which it uses to deliver e-mail messages reliably across a wide range of systems.

Header Field	Function
MIME-version	States conformity to RFCs 2045 and 2046
Content-ID	Identifies MIME entities
Content-type	Describes data in body of message
Content-description	Describes body object
Content-transfer-encoding	Identifies type of conversion used in message body

Table 8-7 MIME Message Header Fields[10]

Source: Stallings, W. Cryptography and Network Security, Principles and Practice.

S/MIME, an extension to MIME, is the second generation of enhancements to the SMTP standard. MIME and S/MIME have the same message header fields, except for those added to support new functionality. Like MIME, S/MIME uses a canonical form format, which allows it to standardize message content type among systems, but it has the additional ability to sign, encrypt, and decrypt messages. Table 8-8 summarizes the functions and algorithms used by S/MIME. It should be mentioned that PGP is functionally similar to S/MIME, incorporates some of the same algorithms, and can interoperate with S/MIME to some degree.

 For more information on securing MIME, visit www.rfc-editor.org and search on S/MIME and MIME to see the numerous standards on the subject.

Function	Algorithm
Hash code for digital signatures	Secure Hash Algorithm 1 (SHA-1)
Digital signatures	DSS
Encryption session keys	ElGamal (variant of Diffie-Hellman)
Digital signatures and session keys	RSA
Message encryption	3DES, RC2

Table 8-8 **S/MIME Functions and Algorithms**

❯ Securing Web Transactions with SET, SSL, and S-HTTP

Key Term

Secure Electronic Transactions (SET) A protocol developed by credit card companies to protect against electronic payment fraud.

Just as PGP, PEM, and S/MIME work to secure e-mail operations, a number of related protocols work to secure Web browsers, especially at e-commerce sites. Among these protocols are SET, SSL, S-HTTP, Secure Shell (SSH-2), and IP Security (IPSec). You learned about SSL and S-HTTP earlier in this chapter.

Secure Electronic Transactions (SET) was developed by MasterCard and Visa in 1997 to protect against electronic payment fraud. SET uses DES to encrypt credit card information transfers and RSA for key exchange. SET provides security both for Internet-based credit card transactions and credit card swipe systems in retail stores. SSL, as you learned earlier in this chapter, also provides secure online e-commerce transactions. SSL uses a number of algorithms, but mainly relies on RSA for key transfer and uses IDEA, DES, or 3DES for encrypted symmetric key-based data transfer. Figure 8-8, shown earlier, illustrates the kind of certificate and SSL information that appears when you check out of an e-commerce site. If your Web connection does not automatically display such certificates, you can right-click in your browser's window and select *Properties* to view the connection encryption and certificate properties.

❯ Securing Wireless Networks with WEP and WPA

Wireless local area networks (also known by the brand name Wi-Fi, or wireless fidelity networks) are thought by many in the IT industry to be inherently insecure. The communication channel between the wireless network interface of any computing device and the access point that provides its services uses radio transmissions. Without some form of protection, these radio signals can be intercepted by anyone with a wireless packet sniffer. To prevent interception of these communications, wireless networks must use some form of cryptographic security control. Two sets of protocols are widely used to help secure wireless transmissions: Wired Equivalent Privacy and Wi-Fi Protected Access. Both are designed for use with the IEEE 802.11 wireless networks.

Wired Equivalent Privacy (WEP) WEP was an early attempt to provide security with the 802.11 network protocol. It is now considered too cryptographically weak to provide any meaningful protection from eavesdropping, but for a time it did provide some measure of security for low-sensitivity networks. WEP uses the RC4 cipher stream to encrypt each packet using a 64-bit key. This key is created using a 24-bit initialization vector and a 40-bit key value. The packets are formed with an XOR function to use the RC4 key value stream to encrypt the data packet. A 4-byte integrity check value (ICV) is calculated for each packet and then appended.[11] According to many experts, WEP is too weak for use in most network settings for the following reasons:[12]

- Key management is not effective because most networks use a single shared secret key value for each node. Synchronizing key changes is a tedious process, and no key management is defined in the protocol, so keys are seldom changed.
- The initialization vector (IV) is too small, resulting in the recycling of IVs. An attacker can reverse-engineer the RC4 cipher stream and decrypt subsequent packets, or can forge future packets. In 2007, a brute force decryption was accomplished in less than one minute.[13]

In summary, an intruder who collects enough data can threaten a WEP network in just a few minutes by decrypting or altering the data being transmitted, or by forging the WEP key to gain unauthorized access to the network. WEP also lacks a means of validating user credentials to ensure that only authorized network users are allowed to access it.[14]

Wi-Fi Protected Access (WPA and WPA2) WPA was created to resolve the issues with WEP. WPA has a key size of 128 bits; instead of static, seldom-changed keys, it uses dynamic keys created and shared by an authentication server. WPA accomplishes this through the use of the Temporal Key Integrity Protocol (TKIP). TKIP is a suite of algorithms that attempts to deliver the best security possible given the constraints of the wireless network environment. The algorithms are designed to work with legacy networking devices. TKIP adds four new algorithms in addition to those that were used in WEP:

- A cryptographic message integrity code, or MIC, called Michael, to defeat forgeries
- A new IV sequencing discipline to remove replay attacks from the attacker's arsenal
- A per-packet key mixing function to decorrelate the public IVs from weak keys
- A rekeying mechanism to provide fresh encryption and integrity keys, undoing the threat of attacks stemming from key reuse.[15]

While it offered dramatically improved security over WEP, WPA was not the most secure wireless protocol design. Some compromises were made in the security design to allow compatibility with existing wireless network components. Protocols to replace TKIP are currently under development. Table 8-9 provides a summary of the differences between WEP and WPA.

In 2004, WPA2 was made available as a replacement for WPA. WPA2 provided many of the elements missing from WPA, most notably AES-based encryption. Beginning in 2006, WPA2 became mandatory for all new Wi-Fi devices. WPA2 is backward-compatible with WPA, although some older network cards have difficulty using it.

	WEP	WPA
Encryption	Broken by scientists and hackers	Overcomes all WEP shortcomings
	40-bit key	128-bit key
	Static key—the same value is used by everyone on the network	Dynamic keys—each user is assigned a key per session with additional keys calculated for each packet
	Manual key distribution—each key is typed by hand into each device	Automatic key distribution
Authentication	Broken; used WEP key itself for authentication	Improved user authentication, using stronger 802.1X and EAP

Table 8-9 WEP Versus WPA

Source: www.wi-fi.org/files/wp_8_WPA%20Security_4-29-03.pdf.

 For more information on the WPA2 standard, read the IEEE 802.11i-2004 standard available from http://standards.ieee.org/getieee802/download/802.11i-2004.pdf.

Next Generation Wireless Protocols Robust Secure Network (RSN) is a protocol for establishing secure communications over an 802.11 wireless network. It is a part of the 802.11i standard. RSN uses AES along with 802.1x and EAP. RSN extends AES with the Counter Mode CBC MAC Protocol (CCMP). AES supports key lengths of up to 256 bits, but it is not compatible with older hardware. However, a specification called Transitional Security Network (TSN) allows RSN and WEP to coexist on the same wireless local area network (WLAN). Note, however, that a WLAN on which devices still use WEP is not optimally secured.

The RSN protocol functions as follows:

1. The wireless network interface card (NIC) sends a probe request.
2. The wireless access point sends a probe response with an RSN Information Exchange (IE) frame.
3. The wireless NIC requests authentication via one of the approved methods.
4. The wireless access point provides authentication for the wireless NIC.
5. The wireless NIC sends an association request with an RSN IE frame.
6. The wireless access point sends an association response.[16]

Bluetooth Bluetooth is a de facto industry standard for short-range wireless communications between devices. It is used to establish communications links between wireless telephones and headsets, between PDAs and desktop computers, and between laptops. It was established by Ericsson scientists, and soon involved Intel, Nokia, IBM, and Toshiba. Microsoft, Lucent Technologies, and 3Com joined the industry group shortly after its inception. Almost a billion Bluetooth-enabled devices could be in use by the end of the decade.

The Bluetooth wireless communications link can be exploited by anyone within a range of approximately 30 feet, unless suitable security controls are implemented. In discoverable mode—which allows other Bluetooth systems to detect and connect—devices can easily be accessed, much like a shared folder on a networked computer. Even in nondiscoverable mode, the device is susceptible to access by other devices that have connected with it in the past.[17] By default, Bluetooth does not authenticate connections; however, Bluetooth does implement some degree of security when devices access certain services, such as dial-up accounts and local-area file transfers. Paired devices—usually a computer or a phone and a peripheral that a user plans to connect to it—require that the same passkey be entered on both devices. This key is used to generate a session key, which is used for all future communications. Unfortunately, some attacks can get around this key. If attackers use a device to simulate a Bluetooth access point, they can trick the device into connecting with it. The fake access point can capture and store all communications, including the passkey submission.

In August 2005, one of the first attacks on Bluetooth-enabled smartphones occurred. At the World Championships in Athletics in Helsinki, a virus called Cabir infected dozens of phones. It spread quickly via a prompt that many users accepted without thinking, thus downloading the virus. Cabir only drained the phones' batteries, but it demonstrated that such devices are not immune to this type of attack. A Finnish security firm, F-Secure, deployed staff to the event to assist in removing the virus.[18]

The only way to secure Bluetooth-enabled devices is to incorporate a twofold approach: Turn off Bluetooth when you do not intend to use it and do not accept an incoming communications pairing request unless you know the identity of the requestor.

❯ Securing TCP/IP with IPSec and PGP

> **Key Terms**
>
> **application header (AH) protocol** In IPSec, a protocol that provides system-to-system authentication and data integrity verification, but does not provide secrecy for the content of a network communication.
>
> **encapsulating security payload (ESP) protocol** In IPSec, a protocol that provides secrecy for the contents of network communications as well as system-to-system authentication and data integrity verification.
>
> **IP Security (IPSec)** The primary and now dominant cryptographic authentication and encryption product of the IETF's IP Protocol Security Working Group. A framework for security development within the TCP/IP family of protocol standards, IPSec provides application support for all uses within TCP/IP, including virtual private networks.
>
> **transport mode** In IPSec, an encryption method in which only a packet's IP data is encrypted, not the IP headers themselves; this method allows intermediate nodes to read the source and destination addresses.
>
> **tunnel mode** In IPSec, an encryption method in which the entire IP packet is encrypted and inserted as the payload in another IP packet. This requires other systems at the beginning and end of the tunnel to act as proxies to send and receive the encrypted packets and then transmit the packets to their ultimate destination.

IP Security (IPSec) is an open-source protocol framework for security development within the TCP/IP family of protocol standards. It is used to secure communications across IP-based networks such as LANs, WANs, and the Internet. The protocol is designed to protect data integrity, user confidentiality, and authenticity at the IP packet level. IPSec is the crypto-graphic authentication and encryption product of the IETF's IP Protocol Security Working Group. It is often described as the security system from IP version 6, the future version of the TCP/IP protocol, retrofitted for use with IP version 4 (the current version). IPSec is defined in Request for Comments (RFC) 1825, 1826, and 1827, and is widely used to create virtual private networks (VPNs), which were described in Chapter 6. IPSec itself is actually an open framework.

IPSec includes the IP Security protocol itself, which specifies the information to be added to an IP packet as well as how to encrypt packet data; and the Internet Key Exchange, which uses an asymmetric-based key exchange and negotiates the security associations. IPSec operates in two modes: transport and tunnel. In **transport mode**, only the IP data is encrypted, not the IP headers. This allows intermediate nodes to read the source and destination addresses. In **tunnel mode**, the entire IP packet is encrypted and then placed into the content portion of another IP packet. This requires other systems at the beginning and end of the tunnel to act as proxies and to send and receive the encrypted packets. These systems then transmit the decrypted packets to their true destinations.

IPSec uses several different cryptosystems:

- Diffie-Hellman key exchange for deriving key material between peers on a public network
- Public-key cryptography for signing the Diffie-Hellman exchanges to guarantee the identity of the two parties
- Bulk encryption algorithms, such as DES, for encrypting the data
- Digital certificates signed by a certificate authority to act as digital ID cards[19]

Within IPSec, IP layer security is achieved by means of an application header protocol or an encapsulating security payload protocol. The **application header (AH) protocol** provides system-to-system authentication and data integrity verification, but does not provide secrecy for the content of a network communication. The **encapsulating security payload (ESP) protocol** provides secrecy for the contents of network communications as well as system-to-system authentication and data integrity verification. When two networked systems form an association that uses encryption and authentication keys, algorithms, and key lifetimes, they can implement either the AH or the ESP protocol, but not both. If the security functions of both protocols are required, multiple security associations must be bundled to provide the correct sequence through which the IP traffic must be processed to deliver the desired security features.

The AH protocol is designed to provide data integrity and IP packet authentication. Although AH does not provide confidentiality protection, IP packets are protected from replay attacks and address spoofing as well as other types of cyberattacks against open networks. Figure 8-10 shows the packet format of the IPSec authentication header protocol. As shown in this diagram, the security parameters index (SPI) references the session key and algorithm used to protect the data being transported. Sequence numbers allow packets to arrive out of sequence for reassembly. The integrity check value (ICV) of the authentication data serves as a checksum to verify that the packet itself is unaltered. Whether used in IPv4 or IPv6, authentication secures the entire packet, excluding mutable fields in the new IP

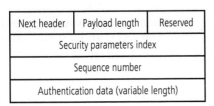

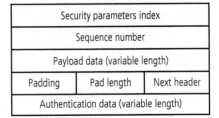

Next header: Identifies the next higher level protocol, such as TCP or ESP.

Payload length: Specifies the AH content's length.

Reserved: For future use.

Security parameters index: Identifies the security association for this IP packet.

Sequence number: Provides a monotonically increasing counter number for each packet sent. Allows the recipient to order the packet and provides protection against replay attacks.

Authentication data: Variable-length data (multiple of 32 bits) containing the ICV (integrity check value) for this packet.

Security parameters index: Identifies the security association for this IP packet.

Sequence number: Provides a monotonically increasing counter number for each packet sent. Allows the recipient to order the packets and provides protection against replay attacks.

Payload data: Contains the encrypted data of the IP packet.

Padding: Space for adding bytes if required by encryption algorithm; also helps conceal the actual payload size.

Pad length: Specifies how much of the payload is padding.

Next header: Identifies the next higher level protocol, such as TCP.

Authentication data: Variable-length data (multiple of 32 bits) containing the ICV (integrity check value) for this packet.

Figure 8-10 IPSec headers

header. In tunnel mode, however, the entire inner IP packet is secured by the authentication header protocol.

The ESP protocol provides confidentiality services for IP packets across insecure networks. ESP can also provide the authentication services of AH. Figure 8-10 shows information about the ESP packet header. ESP in tunnel mode can be used to establish a virtual private network, assuring encryption and authentication between networks communicating via the Internet. In tunnel mode, the entire IP packet is encrypted with the attached ESP header. A new IP header is attached to the encrypted payload, providing the required routing information.

An ESP header is inserted into the IP packet prior to the TCP header, and an ESP trailer is placed after the IPv4 packet. If authentication is desired, an ESP authentication data field is appended after the ESP trailer. The complete transport segment, in addition to the ESP trailer, is encrypted. In an IPv6 transmission, the ESP header is placed after the hop-by-hop and routing headers. Encryption under IPv6 covers the transport segment and the ESP trailer. Authentication in both IPv4 and IPv6 covers the ciphertext data plus the ESP header. IPSec ESP-compliant systems must support the implementation of the DES algorithm using the

CBC (cipher block chaining) mode, which incorporates the following encryption algorithms: Triple DES, IDEA, RC5, CAST, and Blowfish.

 For more information on IPSec, read RFC 4301, "Security Architecture for the Internet Protocol" at www.rfc-editor.org/info/rfc4301. Other related RFCs include RFC 4302, "IP Authentication Header," and RFC 4303, "IP Encapsulating Security Payload," plus a host of related RFCs. Search on IPSec at www.rfc-editor.org/ for more information.

PGP Pretty Good Privacy (PGP) is a hybrid cryptosystem that combines some of the best available cryptographic algorithms. It has become the open-source de facto standard for encryption and authentication of e-mail and file storage applications. Both freeware and low-cost commercial versions of PGP are available for a wide variety of platforms. Table 8-10 lists the PGP functions.

The PGP security solution provides six services: authentication by digital signatures, message encryption, compression, e-mail compatibility, segmentation, and key management.

As shown in Table 8-10, one of the algorithms used in PGP public-key encryption is Secure Hash Algorithm 1 (SHA-1), which computes hash values for calculating a 160-bit hash code based on the plaintext message. The hash code is then encrypted with DSS or RSA and appended to the original message. The recipient uses the sender's public key to decrypt and recover the hash code. Using the same encryption algorithm, the recipient then generates a new hash code from the same message. If the two hash codes are identical, then the message and the sender are authentic. A sender may also want the entire contents of the message protected from unauthorized view. 3DES, IDEA, or CAST, which are all standard algorithms, may be used to encrypt the message contents with a unique, randomly generated 128-bit session key. The session key is encrypted by RSA, using the recipient's public key, and then appended to the message. The recipient uses his or her private key with RSA to decrypt and recover the session key. The recovered session key is used to decrypt the message. Authentication and message encryption can be used together by first digitally signing the message with a private key, encrypting the message with a unique session key, and then encrypting the session key with the intended recipient's public key.

PGP uses the freeware ZIP algorithm to compress the message after it has been digitally signed but before it is encrypted. This saves space and generates a more secure encrypted document because a smaller file offers an attacker fewer chances to look for patterns in the data and fewer characters with which to perform frequency analysis. PGP also uses a

Function	Algorithm	Application
Public-key encryption	RSA/SHA-1 or DSS/SHA-1	Digital signatures
Conventional encryption	3DES, RSA, IDEA, or CAST	Message encryption
File management	ZIP	Compression

Table 8-10 PGP Functions[20]

Source: The International PGP Home Page.

process known as Radix-64, which encodes nontextual data and assures that encrypted data can be transferred using e-mail systems by maintaining the required 8-bit blocks of ASCII text. The format maps three octets of binary data into four ASCII characters and appends a cyclic redundancy check (CRC) to detect transmission errors.

Because many Internet facilities impose restrictions on message size, PGP can automatically subdivide messages into a manageable stream size. This segmentation is performed after all other encryption and conversion functions have been processed. At the recipient end, PGP reassembles the segment's message blocks prior to decompression and decryption.

PGP does not impose a rigid structure for public-key management, but it can assign a level of trust within the confines of PGP, though it does not specify the actual degree of trust the user should place in any specific key. Trust can be addressed and assured by using the public-key ring structure. In this structure, each specific set of public-key credentials is associated with a key legitimacy field, a signature trust field, and an owner trust field. Each of these fields contains a trust-flag byte that identifies whether the credential is trusted in that field. If the trust of a given credential is broken, as when a key is compromised, the owner can issue a digitally signed key revocation certificate that updates the credential trust bytes when the credential is next verified.

Selected Readings

- *Applied Cryptography*, Second Edition, by Bruce Schneier. 1996. John Wiley & Sons.
- Public Key Infrastructure: Building Trusted Applications and Web Services, by John R. Vacca. 2004. Auerbach.

Chapter Summary

- Encryption is the process of converting a message into a form that is unreadable to unauthorized people.
- The science of encryption, known as cryptology, encompasses cryptography (making and using encryption codes) and cryptanalysis (breaking encryption codes).
- Cryptology has a long history and continues to change and improve.
- Two basic processing methods are used to convert plaintext data into encrypted data—bit stream and block ciphering. The other major methods used for scrambling data include substitution ciphers, transposition ciphers, the XOR function, the Vigenère cipher, and the Vernam cipher.
- The strength of many encryption applications and cryptosystems is determined by key size. All other things being equal, the length of the key directly affects the strength of the encryption.

- Hash functions are mathematical algorithms that generate a message summary, or digest, that can be used to confirm the identity of a specific message and confirm that the message has not been altered.

- Most cryptographic algorithms can be grouped into two broad categories: symmetric and asymmetric. In practice, most popular cryptosystems are hybrids that combine symmetric and asymmetric algorithms.

- Public key infrastructure (PKI) is an integrated system of software, encryption methodologies, protocols, legal agreements, and third-party services that enables users to communicate securely. PKI includes digital certificates and certificate authorities.

- Digital signatures are encrypted messages that are independently verified by a central facility, and which provide nonrepudiation. A digital certificate is an electronic document, similar to a digital signature, which is attached to a file to certify it came from the organization that claims to have sent it and was not modified from its original format.

- Steganography is the hiding of information. It is not properly a form of cryptography, but is similar in that it is used to protect confidential information while in transit.

- S-HTTP (Secure Hypertext Transfer Protocol), Secure Electronic Transactions (SET), and SSL (Secure Sockets Layer) are protocols designed to enable secure communications across the Internet. IPSec is the protocol used to secure communications across any IP-based network, such as LANs, WANs, and the Internet. Secure Multipurpose Internet Mail Extensions (S/MIME), Privacy Enhanced Mail (PEM), and Pretty Good Privacy (PGP) are protocols that are used to secure electronic mail. PGP is a hybrid cryptosystem that combines some of the best available cryptographic algorithms; it has become the open-source de facto standard for encryption and authentication of e-mail and file storage applications.

- Wireless networks require their own cryptographic protection. Originally protected with WEP and WPA, most modern Wi-Fi networks are now protected with WPA2. Bluetooth—a short-range wireless protocol used predominantly for wireless phones and PDAs—can be exploited by anyone within its 30-foot range.

- Most well-known encryption methods are released to the information security and computer security communities for testing, which leads to the development of more secure algorithms.

Review Questions

1. What are cryptography and cryptanalysis?

2. What was the earliest reason for the use of cryptography?

3. What is a cryptographic key, and what is it used for? What is a more formal name for a cryptographic key?

4. What are the three basic operations in cryptography?

5. What is a hash function, and what can it be used for?

6. What does it mean to be "out of band"? Why is it important to exchange keys out of band in symmetric encryption?

7. What is the fundamental difference between symmetric and asymmetric encryption?

8. How does public key infrastructure add value to an organization seeking to use cryptography to protect information assets?

9. What are the components of PKI?

10. What is the difference between a digital signature and a digital certificate?

11. What critical issue in symmetric and asymmetric encryption is resolved by using a hybrid method like Diffie-Hellman?

12. What is steganography, and what can it be used for?

13. Which security protocols are predominantly used in Web-based e-commerce?

14. Which security protocols are used to protect e-mail?

15. IPSec can be implemented using two modes of operation. What are they?

16. Which kind of attack on cryptosystems involves using a collection of pre-identified terms? Which kind of attack involves sequential guessing of all possible key combinations?

17. If you were setting up an encryption-based network, what key size would you choose and why?

18. What is the typical key size of a strong encryption system used on the Web today?

19. What encryption standard is currently recommended by NIST?

20. What are the most popular encryption systems used over the Web?

Exercises

1. Go to a popular online e-commerce site like Amazon.com. Place several items in your shopping cart, and then go to check out. When you reach the screen that asks for your credit card number, right-click on the Web browser and select "Properties." What can you find out about the cryptosystems and protocols in use to protect this transaction?

2. Repeat Exercise 1 on a different Web site. Does this site use the same or different protocols? Describe them.

3. Perform a Web search for "Symantec Desktop Email Encryption (powered by PGP Technology)." Download and install the trial version. Using the tool and your favorite e-mail program, send a PGP-signed e-mail to your instructor. What looks different in this e-mail compared with your other e-mails?

4. Perform a Web search for "Announcing the Advanced Encryption Standard (AES)." Read this document, which is a FIPS 197 standard. Write a short overview of the development and implementation of this cryptosystem.

5. Search the Web for "steganographic tools." What do you find? Download and install a trial version of one of the tools. Embed a short text file within an image. In a side-by-side comparison, can you tell the difference between the original image and the image with the embedded file?

Case Exercises

Charlie was getting ready to head home when the phone rang. Caller ID showed it was Peter.

"Hi, Peter," Charlie said into the receiver. "Want me to start the file cracker on your spreadsheet?"

"No, thanks," Peter answered, taking the joke well. "I remembered my passphrase. But I want to get your advice on what we need to do to make the use of encryption more effective and to get it properly licensed for the whole company. I see the value in using it for certain kinds of information, but I'm worried about forgetting a passphrase again, or even worse, that someone else forgets a passphrase or leaves the company. How would we get their files back?"

"We need to use a feature called key recovery, which is usually part of PKI software," said Charlie. "Actually, if we invest in PKI software, we could solve that problem as well as several others."

"OK," said Peter. "Can you see me tomorrow at 10 o'clock to talk about this PKI solution and how we can make better use of encryption?"

Discussion Questions

1. Was Charlie exaggerating when he gave Peter an estimate for the time required to crack the encryption key using a brute force attack?

2. Are there any tools that someone like Peter could use safely, other than a PKI-based system that implements key recovery, to avoid losing his passphrase?

Ethical Decision Making

Suppose Charlie had installed key logger software on all company computer systems and had made a copy of Peter's encryption key. Suppose that Charlie had this done without policy authority and without anyone's knowledge, including Peter's.

1. Would the use of such a tool be an ethical violation on Charlie's part? Is it illegal?

2. Suppose that Charlie had implemented the key logger with the knowledge and approval of senior company executives, and that every employee had signed a release that acknowledged the company can record all information entered on company systems. Two days after Peter's call, Charlie calls back to give Peter his key: "We got lucky and cracked it early." Charlie says this to preserve Peter's illusion of privacy. Is such a "little white lie" an ethical action on Charlie's part?

Endnotes

1. Epic.org. "International Traffic in Arms Regulations: Code of Federal Regulations [EXCERPTS]." Title 22—Foreign Relations; Chapter I—Department of State; Subchapter M. 1 April 1992. Accessed 28 August 2016 from *http://epic.org/crypto/export_controls /itar.html.*

2. Andersson, T. "Polyalphabetic Substitution." *Le Canard Volant Non Identifie Online.* 30 January 1999. Accessed 28 August 2016 from *http://cvni.net/radio/nsnl/nsnl010 /nsnl10poly.html.*

3. Paladion Networks. "Rainbow Cracking and Password Security." *Paladion Networks Online.* 15 February 2006. Accessed 28 August 2016 from *http://paladion.net/rain bow-cracking-and-password-security/.*

4. Daemen, J., and Rijmen, V. "AES Proposal: Rijndael." Accessed 28 August 2016 from *http://csrc.nist.gov/archive/aes/rijndael/Rijndael-ammended.pdf.*

5. National Institute of Standards and Technology. *Data Encryption Standards (DES).* FIPS PUB 46-3. 25 October 1999.

6. Kuhn, D., Hu, V., Polk, W., and Chang, S. "Introduction to Public Key Technology and the Federal PKI Infrastructure." February 2001. Accessed 28 August 2016 from *http://csrc.nist.gov/publications/PubsSPs.html.*

7. Stallings, W. *Cryptography and Network Security, Principles and Practice.* 1999. New Jersey: Prentice Hall.

8. Conway, M. "Code Wars: Steganography, Signals Intelligence, and Terrorism." Accessed 28 August 2016 from *http://doras.dcu.ie/494/1/know_tech_pol_16_2_2003 .pdf.*

9. McCullagh, D. "Bin Laden: Steganography Master?" Accessed 28 August 2016 from *http://archive.wired.com/politics/law/news/2001/02/41658?currentPage=all.*

10. Stallings, W. *Cryptography and Network Security, Principles and Practice.* 1999. New Jersey: Prentice Hall.

11. Scarfone, K., Dicio, D., Sexton, M., and Tibbs, C. National Institute of Standards and Technology. *Guide to Securing Legacy IEEE 802.11 Wireless Networks.* SP 800-48, Rev. 1. July 2008. Accessed 28 August 2016 from *http://csrc.nist.gov/publications /PubsSPs.html.*

12. Interop Net Labs. "What's Wrong with WEP?" 9 September 2002. Accessed 28 August 2016 from *www.opus1.com/www/whitepapers/whatswrongwithwep.pdf.*

13. Leyden, J. "WEP Key Wireless Cracking Made Easy." *The Register.* 4 April 2007. Accessed 28 August 2016 from *www.theregister.co.uk/2007/04/04/wireless_code_cracking.*

14. Wi-Fi Alliance. "Wi-Fi Protected Access: Strong, Standards-Based, Interoperable Security for Today's Wi-Fi Networks." 2003. Accessed 28 August 2016 from *www.ans -vb.com/Docs/Whitepaper_Wi-Fi_Security4-29-03.pdf.*

15. CISCO. "Security: Encryption Manager." Accessed 28 August 2016 from *www.cisco .com/web/techdoc/wireless/access_points/online_help/eag/123-02.JA/1400BR/h_ap_sec_ap -key-security.html.*

16. "What Is RSN (Robust Secure Network)?" *Tech FAQ Online.* Accessed 28 August 2016 from *www.tech-faq.com/rsn-robust-secure-network.shtml.*

17. Bialoglowy, M. "Bluetooth Security Review, Part I: Introduction to Bluetooth." Created 24 April 2005 and updated 2 November 2010. Accessed 28 August 2016 from *www.symantec.com/connect/articles/bluetooth-security-review-part-1.*

18. Leyden, J. "Cabir Mobile Worm Gives Track Fans the Run Around." 12 August 2005. Accessed 28 August 2016 from *www.theregister.co.uk/2005/08/12/cabir_stadium_out break/.*

19. National Institute of Standards and Technology. *ITL Bulletin.* March 2001. Accessed 28 August 2016 from *http://csrc.nist.gov/publications/nistbul/03-01.pdf.*

20. The International PGP Home Page. *PGPI Online.* Accessed 28 August 2016 from *www.pgpi.org.*

8

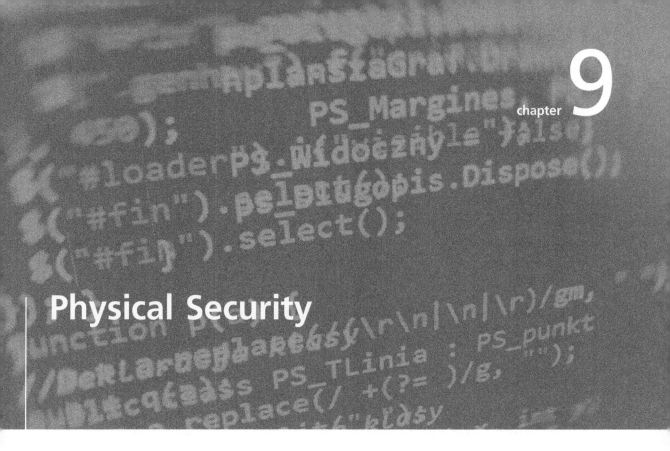

chapter 9

Physical Security

If someone really wants to get at the information, it is not difficult if they can gain physical access to the computer or hard drive.
MICROSOFT WHITE PAPER, JULY 1999

Amy Windahl was back early from lunch. As she was walking toward the SLS building from the parking lot, she saw one of the accounting department employees enter through the building's double glass doors. Behind him followed someone she didn't recognize, a tall, blond man in nondescript, business-casual clothes. The two of them walked past the lobby security guard and headed for the elevators. Amy got on the next elevator and pressed the button for her floor.

When the elevator doors opened, she saw the blond man in the second-floor elevator lobby looking at the company's phone list. She walked over to the secure doors that led to the offices and cocked her right hip, where her badge was clipped, toward the sensor for the locks. When she heard the electric lock release, Amy went through. As the door began to shut, the stranger grabbed it and came through behind her.

Amy knew now that he was a *tailgater*, a person who follows authorized people after they have used their badges to open locked doors. Just last week, a security bulletin had emphasized that tailgaters should be reported. Everyone in the staff meeting had joked about turning each other in the next time any two of them came through a door together. But now Amy understood the seriousness of the bulletin.

501

Amy went back to the second-floor lobby and used the phone there to call building security and report the tailgater.

"Do you guys want to check it out?" she asked the security officer on duty.

"Yes, ma'am. We have someone nearby. I'll have him meet you in the lobby," said the security dispatcher.

When the security officer arrived, Amy described the man and said, "He went down the hall, toward the programming offices."

The guard said, "Wait here. If he comes through here again, call Dispatch at extension 3333. I'll be right back."

A few minutes later, Amy saw the blond man walking briskly toward the doors; the guard was right behind him. As the stranger opened the door, the guard called out, "Sir, please stop. I need to speak with you. What's your name?" Before the blond man could answer, the elevator opened, and two more guards came into the lobby.

The stranger said, "Alan Gaskin."

The guard asked, "What's your business here?"

"Just visiting a friend," said the man.

"And who would that be?" the guard asked.

The stranger looked a bit surprised and then said, "Uh, William Walters, in the accounting department, I think."

The guard reached for his PDA and punched a few buttons. Then he said, "Mr. Gaskin, there are no employees with that name working here, in accounting or any other department. Do you want to try another answer?"

The intruder took a few steps toward the stairwell, but the other two guards cut him off. As they held the man's arms to keep him from escaping, a brown paper bag dropped from under his jacket, its contents spilling on the carpet. Amy saw two smartphones, a watch, and a wallet.

The first guard radioed Dispatch. "Contact the local police and advise them we've caught a thief and we plan to press charges." The other guards led the man toward the elevators while the first guard told Amy: "Ma'am, please call your supervisor and tell her you'll be delayed. We will need a statement from you."

LEARNING OBJECTIVES

Upon completion of this material, you should be able to:

- Discuss the relationship between information security and physical security
- Describe key physical security considerations, including fire control and surveillance systems
- Identify critical physical environment considerations for computing facilities, including uninterruptible power supplies

Introduction

As you learned in Chapter 1, information security requires the protection of both data and physical assets. You have already learned about many of the mechanisms used to protect data, including firewalls, intrusion detection systems, and monitoring software. Most technology-based controls can be circumvented if an attacker gains physical access to the devices being controlled. In other words, if it is easy to steal the hard drives from a computer system, then the information on those hard drives is not secure. Therefore, **physical security** is just as important as logical security to an information security program.

In earlier chapters, you encountered a number of threats to information security that could be classified as threats to physical security. For example, an employee accidentally spilling coffee on a laptop threatens the physical security of its information—in this case, the threat is an act of human error or failure. A compromise to intellectual property can include an employee installing computer software beyond the number of licenses purchased by the organization. An act of espionage or trespass could be committed by a competitor sneaking into a facility with a camera. Sabotage or vandalism can be physical attacks on individuals or property. Theft includes employees stealing computer equipment, credentials, passwords, and laptops. Quality-of-service deviations from service providers, especially power and water utilities, also represent physical security threats, as do various environmental anomalies. In his book *Fighting Computer Crime*, Donn B. Parker lists the following "Seven Major Sources of Physical Loss":

1. Extreme temperature: heat, cold
2. Gases: war gases, commercial vapors, humid or dry air, suspended particles
3. Liquids: water, chemicals
4. Living organisms: viruses, bacteria, people, animals, insects
5. Projectiles: tangible objects in motion, powered objects
6. Movement: collapse, shearing, shaking, vibration, liquefaction, flow waves, separation, slide
7. Energy anomalies: electrical surge or failure, magnetism, static electricity, aging circuitry; radiation: sound, light, radio, microwave, electromagnetic, atomic[1]

As with all other areas of security, the implementation of physical security measures requires sound organizational policy. Physical security policies guide users in the appropriate use of computing resources and information assets, as well as in protecting their own safety in day-to-day operations. Physical security is designed and implemented in several layers. Each of the organization's communities of interest is responsible for components within these layers, as follows:

- General management is responsible for the security of the facility and the policies and standards for secure operation. This includes exterior security, fire protection, and building access, as well as other controls such as guards, guard dogs, and door locks.

- IT management and professionals are responsible for environmental and access security in technology equipment locations, and for the policies and standards that govern secure equipment operation. This includes access to server rooms, power conditioning, server room temperature and humidity controls, and more specialized controls like static and dust contamination equipment.
- Information security management and professionals are responsible for risk assessments and for reviewing the physical security controls implemented by the other two groups.

Physical Access Controls

A number of physical access controls are uniquely suited to governing the movement of people within an organization's facilities—specifically, controlling their physical access to company resources. While logical access to systems in the Internet age is a very important subject, the control of physical access to an organization's assets is also of critical importance. Some of the technology used to control physical access is also used to control logical access, including biometrics, smart cards, and wireless-enabled keycards.

Before learning more about physical access controls, you need to understand what makes a facility secure. An organization's general management oversees its physical security. Commonly, a building's access controls are operated by a group called **facilities management**. Larger organizations may have an entire staff dedicated to facilities management, while smaller organizations often outsource these duties.

In facilities management, the term **secure facility** might bring to mind military bases, maximum-security prisons, and nuclear power plants. While securing a facility does require adherence to rules and procedures, the environment does not necessarily have to be that constrained. A facility does not have to resemble a fortress to minimize risk from physical attacks. In fact, a secure facility can sometimes use its natural terrain, local traffic flow, and surrounding development to enhance its physical security, along with protection mechanisms such as fences, gates, walls, guards, and alarms.

A secure facility includes the same defense-in-depth strategy as logical network security. Any intrusion attempt, whether natural or man-made, should be confronted with multiple layers of defense, including those for the facility's location, the drive to and onto the facility grounds, and multiple layers of physical access controls needed to gain access to information. This could start with a facility guard at the employee parking lot, continue through a keycard mantrap (explained later in this chapter), and end in the lock-and-key process necessary to access the employee's individual office. While every business will not need such an extensive or expensive strategy, this chapter describes many affordable, feasible, and secure methods of protecting an organization's physical presence.

> Physical Security Controls

Key Terms

badge An identification card typically worn in a visible location to quickly verify an authorized member. The badge may or may not show the wearer's name.

biometric lock A lock that reads a unique biological attribute such as a fingerprint, iris, retina, or palm and then uses that input as a key.

closed-circuit television (CCT) A video capture and recording system used to monitor a facility.

contact and weight sensor An alarm sensor designed to detect increased pressure or contact at a specific location, such as a floor pad or a window.

electromechanical lock A lock that can accept a variety of inputs as keys, including magnetic strips on ID cards, radio signals from badges, personal identification numbers (PINs) typed into a keypad, or some combination of these to activate an electrically powered locking mechanism.

fail-safe lock An electromechanical device that automatically releases the lock protecting a control point if a power outage occurs. This type of lock is used for fire safety locations.

fail-secure lock An electromechanical device that stays locked and maintains the security of the control point if a power outage occurs.

identification (ID) card A document used to verify the identity of a member of an organization, group, or domain.

mantrap A small room or enclosure with separate entry and exit points, designed to restrain a person who fails an access authorization attempt.

mechanical lock A physical lock that may rely on either a key or numerical combination to rotate tumblers and release the hasp. Also known as a manual lock.

motion detector An alarm sensor designed to detect movement within a defined space.

plenum A space between the ceiling in one level of a commercial building and the floor of the level above. The plenum is used for air return.

proximity reader An electronic signal receiver used with an electromechanical lock that allows users to place their cards within the reader's range and release the locking mechanism.

tailgating The process of gaining unauthorized entry into a facility by closely following another person through an entrance and using the credentials of the authorized person to bypass a control point.

thermal detector An alarm sensor designed to detect a defined rate of change in the ambient temperature within a defined space.

vibration sensor An alarm sensor designed to detect movement of the sensor rather than movement in the environment.

An organization's communities of interest should consider several physical security controls when implementing physical security inside and outside the facility. Some of the major controls are:

- Walls, fencing, and gates
- Guards
- Dogs
- ID cards and badges
- Locks and keys
- Mantraps
- Electronic monitoring

- Alarms and alarm systems
- Computer rooms and wiring closets
- Interior walls and doors

Walls, Fencing, and Gates Some of the oldest and most reliable elements of physical security are walls, fencing, and gates. While not every organization needs to implement external perimeter controls, walls and fences with suitable gates are an essential starting point when employees require access to physical locations the organization owns or controls. These types of controls vary widely in appearance and function; they range from chain-link or privacy fences that control parking or walking areas to imposing concrete or masonry barriers designed to withstand the blast of a car bomb. Each exterior perimeter control requires expert planning to ensure that it fulfills security goals and presents an image appropriate to the organization.

Guards Controls like fences and walls with gates are static, and are therefore unresponsive to actions unless they are programmed to react to specific stimuli, such as opening for

OFFLINE

Guard Duty

"General Orders:
 I will guard everything within the limits of my post and quit my post only when properly relieved.
 I will obey my special orders and perform all of my duties in a military manner.
 I will report violations of my special orders, emergencies, and anything not covered in my instructions to the commander of the relief."[2]

How do guards meet these responsibilities? They apply the force necessary to accomplish their missions, including deadly force in approved situations. Deadly force is the application of coercive control that may result in death or severe bodily harm. It is applied only to the extent necessary to make an apprehension.
 "Deadly force can only be used for [the following situations]:

1. Self-defense in the event of imminent danger of death or serious bodily harm;

2. To prevent the actual theft or destruction of property designated for protection; and

3. As directed by the Standard Operating Procedures of his individual guard post."[3]

In the military, guard duty is a serious responsibility. Guards must memorize, understand, and comply with their general orders and the orders particular to their assignments.

someone who has the correct key. Guards, on the other hand, can evaluate each situation as it arises and make reasoned responses. Most guards have clear *standard operating procedures (SOPs)* that help them act decisively in unfamiliar situations. An issue with human guards, beyond the high cost, is the human tendency to boredom and distraction, making supervision and oversight of guards a management concern. In the military, guards are given general orders as well as special orders that are particular to their posts. For more details, see the nearby Offline feature, "Guard Duty."

Dogs For an organization that is protecting valuable resources, dogs can be an important part of physical security if they are integrated into the plan and managed properly. Guard dogs are useful because their keen sense of smell and hearing can detect intrusions that human guards cannot, and they can be placed in harm's way when necessary to avoid risking the life of a person.

ID Cards and Badges An **identification (ID) card** is typically carried concealed, whereas a **badge** is worn and visible. Both devices can serve a number of purposes. First, they serve as simple forms of biometrics in that they use the cardholder's picture to authenticate access to the facility. Some organizations choose names or badges that display the wearer's name and/or organization unit data; others show nothing except the wearer's photograph. The cards may be visibly coded to specify which buildings or areas may be accessed. Second, ID cards that have a magnetic strip or radio chip can be read by automated control devices and allow an organization to restrict access to sensitive areas within the facility. ID cards and badges are not foolproof, however; even the cards designed to communicate with locks can be duplicated, stolen, or modified. Because of this inherent weakness, such devices should not be an organization's only means of controlling access to restricted areas.

Another inherent weakness of cards and badges is the human factor. As depicted in this chapter's opening vignette, **tailgating** occurs when an authorized person opens a door and other people also enter (see Figure 9-1). The problem becomes especially dangerous when the tailgater is not authorized to enter. Making employees aware of tailgating through a security awareness program is one way to combat this problem. There are also technological means of discouraging tailgating, such as turnstiles or mantraps, which are discussed in a following section. These extra levels of control are usually expensive because they require floor space and construction, and they are inconvenient for the people who are required to use them. Consequently, anti-tailgating controls are used only where there is a significant security risk from unauthorized entry.

Locks and Keys There are two types of lock mechanisms: mechanical and electromechanical. The **mechanical lock** may rely on a key—a carefully shaped piece of metal rotated to turn tumblers that release secured loops of steel, aluminum, or brass. Alternatively, a mechanical lock may have a dial that rotates slotted discs until the slots on each of the multiple discs are aligned and then retracts a securing bolt, as in combination and safe locks. Although mechanical locks are conceptually simple, some of the technologies they use are quite complex. Some of these modern enhancements have led to the creation of the

Figure 9-1 Tailgating

electromechanical lock. **Electromechanical locks** can accept a variety of inputs as keys, including magnetic strips on ID cards, radio signals from badges, personal identification numbers (PINs) typed into a keypad, or some combination of these to activate an electrically powered locking mechanism.

Locks can also be divided into four categories based on the triggering process: manual, programmable, electronic, and biometric. Manual locks, such as padlocks and combination locks, are commonplace and well understood. If you have the key or combination, you can open the lock. These locks are often preset by the manufacturer and therefore are unchangeable. In other words, once manual locks are installed into doors, they can only be changed by trained locksmiths. Programmable locks can be changed after they are put in service, allowing for combination or key changes without a locksmith and even allowing the owner to change to another access method to upgrade security. Many examples of these types of locks are shown in Figure 9-2. Mechanical push-button locks, shown on the left in the figure, are popular for securing computer rooms and wiring closets because they have a code that can be reset and they don't require electricity to operate.

 For more information on electromechanical locks, visit www.maglocks.com/access-guide.

Electromechanical locks can be integrated into alarm systems and combined with other building management systems. These locks can also be integrated with sensors to create various combinations of locking behavior. One combination is a system that coordinates the use of fire alarms and locks to improve safety during fires and other alarm conditions. Such a system changes a location's required level of access authorization when the location is in an alarm condition. Another example is a combination system in which a lock is fitted with a sensor that notifies guard stations when the lock is activated. Another common form of electronic locks are electric strike locks, which usually require people to announce

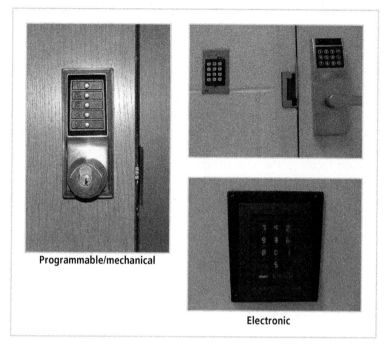

Programmable/mechanical

Electronic

Figure 9-2 Locks

themselves before being "buzzed" through a locked door. In general, electronic locks lend themselves to situations in which they can be activated or deactivated by a switch controlled by a secretary, guard, or other agent. Electronic push-button locks, like their mechanical cousins, have a numerical keypad over the knob; the user must enter a personal code to open the door. These locks typically use batteries to power the keypad.

As described previously, some locks use smart cards—keys that contain computer chips. These smart cards can carry critical information, provide strong authentication, and offer a number of other features. Keycard readers based on smart cards are often used to secure computer rooms, communications closets, and other restricted areas. The card reader can track entry and provide accountability. In a locking system that uses smart cards, employees' access levels can be adjusted according to their status, so personnel changes do not require replacement of the lock. A specialized type of keycard reader is the **proximity reader**, which allows people simply to place their cards within the reader's range instead of inserting them. Some of these readers can recognize the card even when it is inside a pocket or bag.

The most sophisticated locks are **biometric locks**. Finger, palm, and hand readers, iris and retina scanners, and voice and signature readers fall into this category. The technology that underlies biometric devices was discussed in Chapter 6.

The management of keys and locks is fundamental to fulfilling general management's responsibility to secure an organization's physical environment. As you will learn in Chapter 11, when people are hired, fired, laid off, or transferred, their physical or logical access controls must be appropriately adjusted. Otherwise, employees can clean out their offices and take more than their personal effects. Also, locksmiths should be carefully screened and monitored before they are hired, as they might have complete access to the facility.

Sometimes locks fail, so facilities need to have alternative procedures in place for controlling access. These procedures must take into account that locks fail in one of two ways. A door lock that fails and causes the door to become unlocked is called a **fail-safe lock**; a door lock that fails and causes the door to remain locked is called a **fail-secure lock**. In practice, the most common reason that technically sophisticated locks fail is loss of power and activation through fire control systems. A fail-safe lock is normally used to secure an exit when a door must be unlocked in case of fire or another event. A fail-secure lock is used when human safety is not the dominant factor in the area being controlled. For example, in a situation in which the security of nuclear or biological weapons is vital, preventing a loss of control of the facility or the weapons is more critical to security than protecting the personnel guarding the weapons.

Locks are often implemented within organizations in a systematic fashion, whether mechanical locks are used in a pattern approach with specific and master keys or electromechanical locks are used with complex access control lists and a centrally managed authorization model. Some high-security situations may require a stronger approach, with more complexity that requires multiple keys, multiple locks, and even dissimilar, separate locking systems, such as one requiring both a keycard and a biometric scanner. Understanding lock mechanisms is important because locks can be exploited by an intruder to gain access to the secured location. If an electronic lock is short-circuited, it may become fail-safe and allow the intruder to bypass the control and enter the room.

Mantraps A common enhancement for locks in very high-security areas is the **mantrap**. To gain access to a facility, area, or room, a person enters the mantrap, requests access via some form of electronic or biometric lock and key, and then exits the mantrap into the facility if confirmed. Otherwise, the person cannot leave the mantrap until a security official overrides the enclosure's automatic locks. Figure 9-3 provides an example of a typical mantrap layout.

Electronic Monitoring Monitoring equipment can record events that guards and dogs might miss, and is useful in areas where other types of physical controls are not practical. Although you may not know it, many of you are already subject to video monitoring cameras, which are concealed in the silver globes attached to the ceilings of many retail stores. Attached to these cameras are video cassette recorders (VCRs) and related machinery that capture the video feed. Electronic monitoring includes **closed-circuit television (CCT)** systems. Some CCT systems collect constant video feeds, while others rotate input from a number of cameras, sampling each area in turn.

These video monitoring systems have drawbacks; for the most part they are passive and do not prevent access or prohibited activity. Another drawback is that people must view the video output because there are few intelligent systems capable of reliably evaluating a video feed, and those are prohibitively expensive. To determine if unauthorized activities have occurred, a security staff member must constantly review the information in real time or review the information collected in video recordings. For this reason, CCT is more often

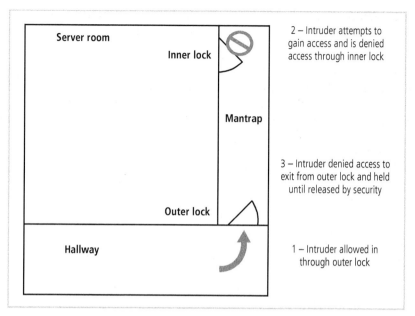

Server room

Inner lock

Mantrap

Outer lock

Hallway

2 – Intruder attempts to gain access and is denied access through inner lock

3 – Intruder denied access to exit from outer lock and held until released by security

1 – Intruder allowed in through outer lock

Figure 9-3 Mantraps

used for evidence collection after a break-in than as a detection instrument. In high-security areas such as banks, casinos, and shopping centers, however, security personnel monitor CCT systems constantly, looking for suspicious activity.

Alarms and Alarm Systems Closely related to monitoring systems are the alarms that notify people or systems when a predetermined event or activity occurs. Alarms, which are similar to the IDPSs you learned about in Chapter 7, can detect a *physical* intrusion or other untoward event. This could be a fire, a break-in, an environmental disturbance such as flooding, or an interruption in services, such as a loss of power. One example of an alarm system is the burglar alarm commonly found in residential and commercial environments. Burglar alarms detect intrusions into unauthorized areas and notify either a local or remote security agency to react. To detect intrusions, these systems rely on different types of sensors, including motion detectors, thermal detectors, glass breakage detectors, weight sensors, and contact sensors.

Motion detectors are either active or passive. Some motion sensors emit energy beams, usually in the form of infrared or laser light, ultrasonic sound or sound waves, or some form of electromagnetic radiation. If the energy from the beam projected into the monitored area is disrupted, the alarm is activated. Other types of motion sensors are passive in that they constantly measure the infrared or ultrasonic energy from the monitored space and detect rapid changes in this energy. The passive measurement of these energies can be blocked or disguised and is therefore fallible. For example, **thermal detectors** can detect when a person with a normal body temperature of 98.6 degrees Fahrenheit enters a room with a temperature of 65 degrees Fahrenheit, because the person's presence changes the room's ambient temperature. Thermal detectors are also used in fire detection, as you will learn in later sections. **Contact**

9

and weight sensors, for example, work when a foot steps on a pressure-sensitive pad under a rug or when a window is opened. **Vibration sensors** also fall into this category, except that they detect movement of the sensor rather than movement in the environment.

Computer Rooms and Wiring Closets

Computer Rooms and Wiring Closets Computer rooms and wiring and communications closets require special attention to ensure the confidentiality, integrity, and availability of information. For an outline of the physical and environmental controls needed for computer rooms, read the following Technical Details feature.

For more information on considerations for designing high-performance data centers, visit http://hightech.lbl.gov/ and read the Pacific Gas and Electric Data Center Best Practices Guide at www.pge.com/includes/docs/pdfs/mybusiness/energysavingsrebates/incentivesbyindustry/DataCenters_BestPractices.pdf.

Logical access controls are easily defeated if an attacker gains physical access to the computing equipment. Custodial staff members are often the least scrutinized people who have access to an organization's offices, yet custodians are given the greatest degree of unsupervised access. They are often handed the master keys to the entire building and then ignored, even though they collect paper from every office, dust many desks, and move large containers from every area. Therefore, it is not difficult for a custodian to gather critical information and computer media or copy proprietary and classified information. An organization's custodians should not be under constant suspicion of espionage, but their wide-reaching access can be a vulnerability that attackers exploit to gain unauthorized information. Factual accounts exist of technically trained agents working as custodians in the offices of their competition. Thus, custodial staff should be carefully supervised not only by the organization's general management but by information security management.

Interior Walls and Doors

Interior Walls and Doors The security of information assets can sometimes be compromised by improper construction of a facility's walls and doors. The walls in a facility typically consist of two types: standard interior and firewall. Building codes require that each floor have a number of firewalls—walls that limit the spread of damage should a fire break out in an office. While the network firewalls discussed in an earlier chapter isolate the logical subnetworks of the organization, physical firewalls isolate the physical spaces of the organization's offices. Between the firewalls, standard interior walls compartmentalize the individual offices. Unlike firewalls, these interior walls reach only partially to the next floor, which leaves a space between the ceiling and the floor of the next level. This space is called a **plenum**, and is usually one to three feet wide to allow for ventilation systems that can inexpensively collect returned air from the offices on the floor. For security, however, this design is not ideal, because a person can climb over the wall from one office to the next. As a result, all computer rooms, wiring closets, and other high-security areas must be surrounded by firewall-grade walls to provide physical security against potential intruders and fires. A quick online search of *business, burglary, interior walls* will reveal hundreds, perhaps thousands, of examples of perpetrators exploiting interior walls in a much more straightforward manner. It is a fairly common practice to break into a low-security business in a mini-mall, use a sledgehammer to break through the drywall walls that separate the businesses, and then rob each in turn.

TECHNICAL DETAILS

Physical and Environmental Controls for Computer Rooms

The following list of physical and environmental controls for computer rooms is intended to be representative, not comprehensive.

- Card keys for building and entrances to work area
- Guards at all entrances and exits, 24 hours a day
- Cipher lock on computer room door
- Raised floor in computer room
- Dedicated cooling system
- Humidifier in tape library
- Emergency lighting in computer room
- Four fire extinguishers rated for electrical fires
- One fire extinguisher with a combined class B and class C fire control rating (these ratings are discussed later in this chapter)
- Smoke, water, and heat detectors
- Emergency power shutoff switch by exit door
- Surge suppressor
- Emergency replacement server
- Zoned dry-pipe sprinkler system
- Uninterruptible power supply for LAN (large area network) servers
- Power strips and suppressors for peripherals
- Power strips and suppressors for computers
- Controlled access to file server room
- Plastic sheets for water protection
- Closed-circuit television monitors[4]

The doors that allow access into high-security rooms should also be evaluated, because standard office doors often provide little or no security. For example, an author of this textbook once was locked out of his office when his key broke off in the lock. When the locksmith arrived, he carried a curious contraption. Instead of disassembling the lock, he produced a long piece of heavy-duty wire bent into the shape of a bow, with a string tied to each end. He slid one end of the bow through the one-inch gap under the door, stood it on end, and yanked the string. The wire bow slid over the door handle and the string looped over it. When the locksmith yanked the string, the door swung open.

To see the door-unlocking "bow" in action, visit http://gizmodo.com/5477600/hotel-locks-defeated-by-piece-of-wire-secured-by-towel, or search on the term "hotel locks defeated by piece of wire."

This information is not meant to teach you how to access interior offices, but to warn you that no office is completely secure. How can you avoid this problem? In most interior offices, you can't. Instead, information security professionals must educate the organization's employees about how to secure the information and systems within their offices.

To secure doors, install push or crash bars on computer rooms and closets. These bars are much more difficult to open from the outside than standard pull handles and thus provide much higher levels of security, but they also allow for a safe exit in the event of an emergency. Rooms that contain high-value items like computer servers should be constructed with floor-to-ceiling, solid walls that prevent crawling over or punching through.

Fire Security and Safety

The most important security concern is the safety of the people in an organization's physical space—workers, customers, clients, and others. The most serious threat to that safety is fire. Fires account for more property damage, personal injury, and death than any other threat to physical security. It is imperative that physical security plans implement strong measures to detect and respond to fires and fire hazards.

 For more information on fire safety, including discussions of detection and response systems, visit the National Fire Protection Association's Web site at www.nfpa.org.

〉 Fire Detection and Response

Key Terms

air-aspirating detector A fire detection sensor used in high-sensitivity areas that works by taking in air, filtering it, and passing it through a chamber that contains a laser beam. The alarm triggers if the beam is broken.

clean agent A fire suppression agent that does not leave any residue after use or interfere with the operation of electrical or electronic equipment.

deluge system A fire suppression sprinkler system that keeps all individual sprinkler heads open and applies water to all areas when activated.

dry-pipe system A fire suppression sprinkler system that has pressurized air in all pipes. The air is released in the event of a fire, allowing water to flow from a central area.

fire suppression systems Devices that are installed and maintained to detect and respond to a fire, potential fire, or combustion danger.

fixed-temperature sensor A fire detection sensor that works by detecting the point at which the ambient temperature in an area reaches a predetermined level.

flame detector A fire detection system that works by detecting the infrared or ultraviolet light produced by an open flame.

gaseous (or chemical gas) emission systems Fire suppression systems that operate through the delivery of gases rather than water.

ionization sensor A fire detection sensor that works by exposing the ambient air to a small amount of a harmless radioactive material within a detection chamber; an alarm is triggered when the level of electrical conductivity changes within the chamber.

photoelectric sensor A fire detection sensor that works by projecting an infrared beam across an area. If the beam is interrupted, presumably by smoke, the alarm or suppression system is activated.

pre-action system A fire suppression sprinkler system that employs a two-phase response to a fire. When a fire is detected anywhere in the facility, the system will first flood all pipes, then activate only the sprinkler heads in the area of the fire.

rate-of-rise sensor A fire detection sensor that works by detecting an unusually rapid increase in the area temperature within a relatively short period of time.

smoke detection system A category of fire detection systems that focuses on detecting the smoke from a fire.

sprinkler system A fire suppression system designed to apply a liquid, usually water, to all areas in which a fire has been detected.

thermal detection system A category of fire detection systems that focuses on detecting the heat from a fire.

water mist sprinkler A fire suppression sprinkler system that relies on ultra-fine mists to reduce the ambient temperature below that needed to sustain a flame.

wet-pipe system A fire suppression sprinkler system that contains pressurized water in all pipes and has some form of valve in each protected area.

Fire suppression systems typically work by denying an environment one of the three requirements for a fire to burn: temperature (an ignition source), fuel, and oxygen. While the temperature of ignition, or *flame point*, depends on the material, it can be as low as a few hundred degrees. Paper, the most common combustible in an office, has a flame point of 451 degrees Fahrenheit, a fact used to dramatic effect in Ray Bradbury's novel *Fahrenheit 451*. Paper can reach its flame point when exposed to a carelessly dropped cigarette, malfunctioning electrical equipment, or other accidental or purposeful acts.

Water and water mist systems, which are described later in this section, work to reduce the temperature of the flame in order to extinguish it and to saturate some types of fuels (such as paper) to prevent ignition. Carbon dioxide (CO_2) systems rob fire of its oxygen. Soda acid systems deny fire its fuel, preventing the fire from spreading. Gas-based systems, such as Halon and its approved replacements by the Environmental Protection Agency (EPA), disrupt the fire's chemical reaction but leave enough oxygen for people to survive for a short time. Before a fire can be suppressed, however, it must be detected.

Fire Detection Fire detection systems fall into two general categories: manual and automatic. Manual fire detection systems include human responses, such as calling the fire department, and manually activated alarms, such as sprinklers and gaseous systems. Organizations must use care when manually triggered alarms are tied directly to suppression systems because false alarms are not uncommon. Organizations should also ensure that proper security remains in place until all employees and visitors have been cleared from the building and their evacuation has been verified. During the chaos of a fire evacuation, an attacker can easily slip into offices and obtain sensitive information. To help prevent such intrusions, fire safety programs often designate a person from each office area to serve as a floor monitor.

There are three basic types of fire detection systems: thermal detection, smoke detection, and flame detection. **Thermal detection systems** contain a sophisticated heat sensor that operates in one of two ways. **Fixed-temperature sensors** detect when the ambient temperature in an area reaches a predetermined level—usually 135 to 165 degrees Fahrenheit, or 57 to 74 degrees Celsius.[5] **Rate-of-rise sensors** detect an unusually rapid increase in the area temperature within a relatively short period of time. In either case, the alarm and suppression systems are activated if the criteria are met. Thermal detection systems are inexpensive and easy to maintain. Unfortunately, they usually don't catch a problem until it is already in progress, as in a full-blown fire. As a result, thermal detection systems are not a sufficient means of fire protection in areas where human safety could be at risk. They are also not recommended for areas that contain high-value items or items that could be easily damaged by high temperatures.

Smoke detection systems are perhaps the most common means of detecting a potentially dangerous fire, and they are required by building codes in most residential dwellings and commercial buildings. Smoke detectors operate in one of three ways. **Photoelectric sensors** use infrared beams that activate the alarm when interrupted, presumably by smoke. **Ionization sensors** contain a small amount of a harmless radioactive material within a detection chamber. When certain by-products of combustion enter the chamber, they change the level of electrical conductivity within the chamber and activate the detector. Ionization sensors are much more sophisticated than photoelectric sensors and can detect fires much earlier, because invisible by-products can be detected long before enough visible material enters a photoelectric sensor to trigger a reaction. **Air-aspirating detectors** are sophisticated systems that are used in high-sensitivity areas. They work by taking in air, filtering it, and moving it through a chamber that contains a laser beam. If the laser beam is diverted or refracted by smoke particles, the system is activated. These types of systems are typically much more expensive than systems that use photoelectric or ionization sensors; however, they are much better at early detection and are commonly used in areas where extremely valuable materials are stored.

The third major category of fire detection systems is the **flame detector**, which detects the infrared or ultraviolet light produced by an open flame. These systems compare a scanned area's light signature to a database of known flame light signatures to determine whether to activate the alarm and suppression systems. While highly sensitive, flame detection systems are expensive and must be installed where they can scan all areas of the protected space. They are not typically used in areas where human lives are at stake; however, they are quite suitable for chemical storage areas where normal chemical emissions might activate smoke detectors.

Fire Suppression Fire suppression systems can consist of portable, manual, or automatic apparatus. Portable extinguishers are used in a variety of situations where direct application of suppression is preferred or a fixed apparatus is impractical. Portable extinguishers are much more efficient for smaller fires because triggering an entire building's sprinkler systems can cause extensive damage. Portable extinguishers are rated by the type of fire they can combat, as follows:

- Class A fires: These fires involve ordinary combustible fuels such as wood, paper, textiles, rubber, cloth, and trash. Class A fires are extinguished by agents that interrupt the ability of the fuel to be ignited. Water and multipurpose dry chemical fire extinguishers are ideal for these types of fires.

- Class B fires: These fires are fueled by combustible liquids or gases, such as solvents, gasoline, paint, lacquer, and oil. Class B fires are extinguished by agents that remove oxygen from the fire. Carbon dioxide, multipurpose dry chemical, and Halon fire extinguishers are ideal for these types of fires.

- Class C fires: These fires are caused by energized electrical equipment or appliances. Class C fires are extinguished with nonconducting agents only. Carbon dioxide, multipurpose dry chemical, and Halon fire extinguishers are ideal for these types of fires. Never use a water fire extinguisher on a Class C fire.

- Class D fires: These fires are fueled by combustible metals, such as magnesium, lithium, and sodium. Class D fires require special extinguishing agents and techniques.

- Class K fires: These fires are fueled by combustible cooking oil and fats in commercial kitchens. These fires are classified as Class F in Europe and Australasian environments. These fires require special water mist, dry powder, or CO_2 agents to extinguish.

Manual and automatic fire response systems include those designed to apply suppressive agents. They are usually either sprinkler or gaseous systems. All **sprinkler systems** are designed to apply a liquid, usually water, to all areas in which a fire has been detected, but an organization can choose from one of three implementations: wet-pipe, dry-pipe, or pre-action systems. A **wet-pipe system** contains pressurized water in all pipes and has some form of valve in each protected area. When the system is activated, the valves open, sprinkling the area. This system is best for areas where a fire represents a serious risk to people, but damage to property is not a major concern. The most obvious drawback to this type of system is water damage to office equipment and materials. A wet-pipe system is not usually appropriate in computer rooms, wiring closets, or anywhere electrical equipment is used or stored. There is also the risk of accidental or unauthorized activation. Figure 9-4 shows a wet-pipe water sprinkler system that is activated when the ambient temperature reaches 140 to 150 degrees Fahrenheit, bringing the special liquid in the glass tube to a boil and causing the tube to shatter and open the valve. Once the valve is open, water flows through the diffuser and over the area.

A **dry-pipe system** is designed to work in areas where electrical equipment is used. Instead of holding water in the distribution pipes as a standard wet-pipe system does, this type of system contains pressurized air. The air holds valves closed, keeping the water away from the target areas until the system is triggered. When a fire is detected, the sprinkler heads are activated, the pressurized air escapes, and water fills the pipes and exits through the sprinkler heads. This reduces the risk of accidental leakage from the system. **Deluge systems** keep the pipes empty and all of the individual sprinkler heads open; as soon as the system is activated, water is immediately applied to all areas. This is not the optimal solution for computing environments, as other more sophisticated systems can suppress the fire without damaging computer equipment.

A variation of the dry-pipe system is the **pre-action system**. This approach has a two-phase response to a fire. Under normal conditions, the system has nothing in the delivery pipes. When a fire is detected, the first phase is initiated, and valves allow water to enter the system. At that point, the system resembles a wet-pipe system. The pre-action system does not

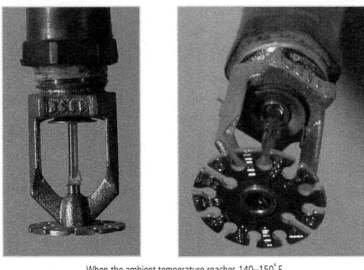

When the ambient temperature reaches 140–150° F,
the liquid-filled glass tube trigger breaks, releasing the stopper and
allowing water to hit the diffuser, spraying water throughout the area

Figure 9-4 Water sprinkler system

deliver water into the protected space until the individual sprinkler heads are triggered, at which time water flows only into the area of the activated sprinkler heads.

Water mist sprinklers, the newest form of sprinkler systems, rely on ultra-fine mists instead of traditional shower-type systems. The water mist systems work like a traditional water system by reducing the ambient temperature around the flame, minimizing its ability to sustain the necessary temperature needed to maintain combustion. Unlike traditional water sprinkler systems, however, these systems produce a fog-like mist that stays buoyant (airborne) much longer because the droplets are much less susceptible to gravity. As a result, a much smaller quantity of water is required; also, the fire is extinguished more quickly, which causes less collateral damage. Compared with gaseous systems, which are discussed next, water-based systems are inexpensive, nontoxic, and can often be created by using an existing sprinkler system that may have been present in earlier construction.

Gaseous Emission Systems Gaseous (or chemical gas) emission systems can be used in the suppression of fires. They are often used to protect chemical and electrical processing areas, as well as facilities that house computing systems. A typical configuration of such systems is shown in Figure 9-5.

Gaseous fire suppression systems are either self-pressurizing or must be pressurized with an additional agent. Until recently, the only two major types of gaseous systems were carbon dioxide and Halon. Carbon dioxide extinguishes a fire by removing its supply of oxygen. Unfortunately, any living organisms that also rely on oxygen are similarly extinguished. As a result, carbon dioxide systems are not commonly used in residential or office

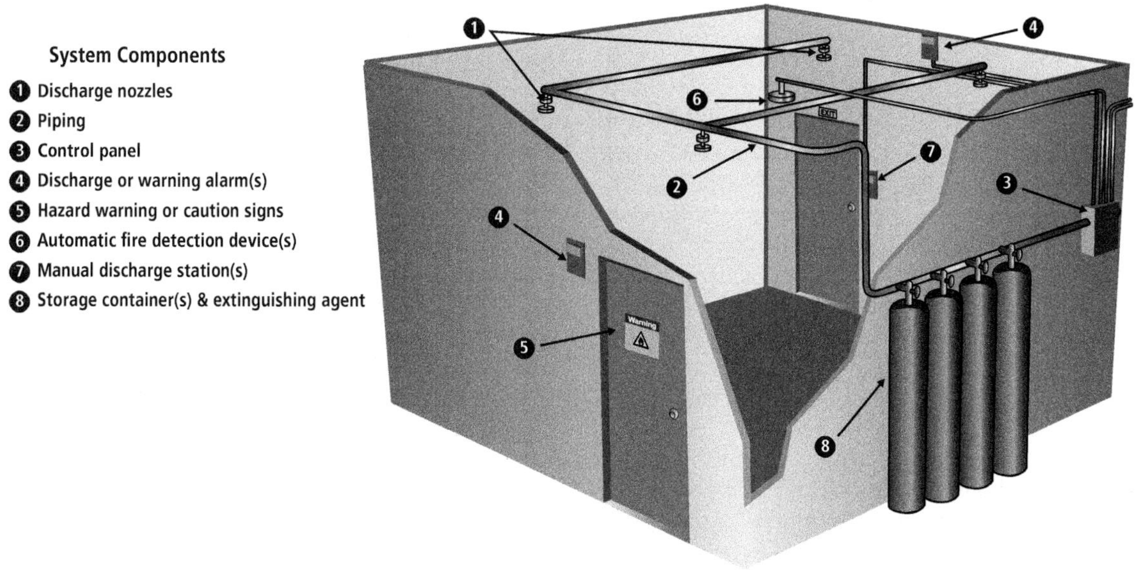

System Components

1 Discharge nozzles
2 Piping
3 Control panel
4 Discharge or warning alarm(s)
5 Hazard warning or caution signs
6 Automatic fire detection device(s)
7 Manual discharge station(s)
8 Storage container(s) & extinguishing agent

Figure 9-5 Gaseous fire suppression system

environments, where people or animals are likely to be present. The alternative is Halon. Halon is one of a few chemicals designated as a **clean agent**, which means that it does not leave any residue after use, nor does it interfere with the operation of electrical or electronic equipment. As a result, Halon gas-based systems are the preferred solution for computer rooms and communications closets. Unlike carbon dioxide, Halon does not rob the fire of its oxygen, but instead relies on a chemical reaction with the flame to extinguish it. Therefore, Halon is much safer than carbon dioxide when people or animals are present. Although Halon can cause suffocation like a carbon dioxide system, the dosage levels required are much higher, so Halon-based systems provide additional time for people to exit areas. Because the EPA has classified Halon as an ozone-depleting substance, new installations of the controlled types of Halon are prohibited in commercial and residential locations. The alternatives are less effective, but safer than Halon.

A physical security plan requires that every building have clearly marked fire exits and maps posted throughout the facility. It is important to have drills to rehearse fire alarm responses and designate people to be in charge of escorting everyone from the location and ensuring that no one is left behind. It is also important to have fire suppression systems that are both manual and automatic, and that are inspected and tested regularly.

Failure of Supporting Utilities and Structural Collapse

Supporting utilities, such as heating, ventilation, and air conditioning, power, and water, have a significant impact on a facility's safe operation. Extreme temperatures and humidity levels, electrical fluctuations, and the interruption of water, sewage, and garbage services can create conditions that inject vulnerabilities in systems designed to protect information. Thus, each of these utilities must be properly managed to prevent damage to information and information systems.

❯ Heating, Ventilation, and Air Conditioning

Key Terms

electrostatic discharge (ESD) The release of ambient static electricity into a ground.
humidity The amount of moisture in the air.
static electricity An imbalance of electrical charges in the atmosphere or on the surface of a material, caused by triboelectrification.
triboelectrification The exchange of electrons between two materials when they make contact, resulting in one object becoming more positively charged and the other more negatively charged.

Although traditionally a responsibility of facilities management, the operation of the heating, ventilation, and air-conditioning (HVAC) system can have a dramatic impact on information, information systems, and their protection. Specifically, the temperature, filtration, humidity, and static electricity controls must be monitored and adjusted to reduce risks to information systems.

Temperature and Filtration Computer systems are electronic, and therefore are subject to damage from extreme temperatures and particulate contamination. Temperatures as low as 100 degrees Fahrenheit can damage computer media, and at 175 degrees Fahrenheit, computer hardware can be damaged or destroyed. When the temperature approaches 32 degrees Fahrenheit, media are susceptible to cracking and computer components can actually freeze together. Rapid changes in temperature from hot to cold or vice versa can produce condensation, which can create short circuits or otherwise damage systems and components. The optimal temperature for a computing environment and for people is between 70 and 74 degrees Fahrenheit. Properly installed and maintained systems keep the environment within the manufacturer-recommended temperature range. In the past, people thought it was necessary to fully filter all particles from the air flow of the HVAC system. Modern computing equipment is designed to work better in typical office environments, so the need to provide extensive filtration for air conditioning is now limited to particularly sensitive environments such as chip fabrication and component assembly areas. In other words, filtration is no longer as significant as it once was for most commercial data processing facilities.

Humidity and Static Electricity High **humidity** levels create condensation problems, and low humidity levels can increase the amount of static electricity in the environment. With condensation comes the short-circuiting of electrical equipment and the potential for mold and rot in paper-based information storage. **Static electricity** is caused by **triboelectrification**, which occurs when two materials make contact and exchange electrons. As a result, one object becomes more positively charged and the other more negatively charged. When a third object with an opposite charge or ground is encountered, electrons flow again, and a spark is produced. One of the leading causes of damage to sensitive circuitry is **electrostatic discharge (ESD)**. Integrated circuits in a computer are designed to use between two and five

Voltage	Possible Damage
40	High probability of damage to sensitive circuits and transistors
1,000	Scrambles monitor display
1,500	Can cause disk drive data loss
2,000	High probability of system shutdown
4,000	May jam printers
17,000	Causes certain and permanent damage to almost all microcircuitry

Table 9-1 Static Charge Damage in Computers[6]

volts of electricity; any voltage level above this range introduces a risk of microchip damage. Static electricity is not noticeable to human beings until levels approach 1,500 volts, and the spark can't be seen until the level approaches 4,000 volts before being discharged. Moreover, a person can generate a discharge of up to 12,000 volts merely by walking across a carpet. Table 9-1 shows some static charge voltages and the damage they can cause to systems.

In general, ESD damage to chips produces two types of failures. Immediate failures, also known as catastrophic failures, occur right away, are often totally destructive, and require chip replacement. Latent failures or delayed failures can occur weeks or even months after the damage occurs. The chip may suffer intermittent problems, although given the overall poor quality of some popular operating systems, this type of damage may be hard to notice. As a result, it is imperative to maintain an optimal level of humidity between 40 percent and 60 percent in the computing environment. Humidity levels below this range create static, and levels above it create condensation. Humidification or dehumidification systems can regulate humidity levels.

Ventilation Shafts While the ductwork in residential buildings is quite small, it may be large enough for a person to climb through in large commercial buildings. This is one of Hollywood's favorite methods for having villains or heroes enter buildings, but ventilation shafts aren't quite as negotiable as the movies would have you believe. In fact, with moderate security precautions, these shafts can be completely eliminated as a security vulnerability. In most new buildings, the ducts to individual rooms are no larger than 12 inches in diameter and are composed of flexible, insulated tubes. The size and nature of the ducts precludes most people from using them, but access may be possible via the plenum. If the ducts are much larger, the security team can install wire mesh grids at various points to compartmentalize the runs.

❯ Power Management and Conditioning

Key Terms

delta conversion online UPS An uninterruptible power supply (UPS) that is similar to a double conversion online UPS except that it incorporates a delta transformer, which assists in powering the inverter while outside power is available.

double conversion online UPS A UPS in which the protected device draws power from an output inverter. The inverter is powered by the UPS battery, which is constantly recharged from the outside power.

ground fault circuit interruption A special circuit device designed to immediately disconnect a power supply when a sudden discharge (ground fault) is detected.

line-interactive UPS A UPS in which a pair of inverters and converters draw power from the outside source both to charge the battery and provide power to the internal protected device.

noise The presence of additional and disruptive signals in network communications or electrical power delivery.

standby ferroresonant UPS A UPS in which the outside power source directly feeds the internal protected device. The UPS serves as a battery backup, incorporating a ferroresonant transformer instead of a converter switch, providing line filtering and reducing the effect of some power problems, and reducing noise that may be present in the power as it is delivered.

standby (or offline) UPS An offline battery backup that detects the interruption of power to equipment and activates a transfer switch that provides power from batteries through a DC to AC converter until normal power is restored or the computer is shut down.

Electrical power is another aspect of the organization's physical environment that is usually considered within the realm of physical security. Power systems used by information-processing equipment must be properly installed and correctly grounded. Because computers sometimes use the normal 60-Hertz cycle of electricity in alternating current to synchronize their clocks, **noise** that interferes with this cycle can result in inaccurate time clocks or, even worse, unreliable internal clocks inside the CPU.

Grounding and Amperage Grounding ensures that the returning flow of current is properly discharged to the ground. If the grounding elements of the electrical system are not properly installed, anyone who touches a computer or other electrical device could become a ground source, which can cause damage to the equipment and injury or death to the person. In areas where water can accumulate, computing and other electrical equipment must be uniquely grounded using **ground fault circuit interruption** (GFCI) equipment. GFCI is capable of quickly identifying and interrupting a ground fault—for example, a situation in which a person comes into contact with water and becomes a better ground than the electrical circuit's current source.

Power should also be provided in sufficient amperage to support needed operations. Nothing is more frustrating than plugging in a number of computers only to have a circuit breaker trip. Consult a qualified electrician when designing or remodeling computer rooms to make sure sufficiently high-amperage circuits are available to provide the needed power. Overloading a circuit not only trips circuit breakers, it can create a load on an electrical cable that exceeds the amount the cable is rated to handle, increasing its risk of overheating and starting a fire.

 For more information on GFCI, visit the OSHA site at www.osha.gov/SLTC/etools/construction/electrical_incidents/gfci.html.

Uninterruptible Power Supply The primary power source for an organization's computing equipment is most often the electric utility that serves the area where the buildings are located. This source of power can experience interruptions. Therefore, organizations should identify the computing systems that are critical to their operations and that must continue to operate during interruptions, and then make sure those systems are connected to a device that assures the delivery of electric power without interruption. This device is called an uninterruptible power supply (UPS).

The capacity of UPS devices is measured using the volt-ampere (or VA) power output rating. UPS devices typically run up to 1,000 VA and can be engineered to exceed 10,000 VA. A typical PC might use 200 VA, and a server in a computer room may need 2,000 to 5,000 VA, depending on how much running time is required. Figure 9-6 shows several types of UPSs. This section describes the following basic configurations: the standby, line-interactive, standby online hybrid, standby ferroresonant, double conversion online, and delta conversion online.

A **standby** or **offline UPS** is an offline battery backup that detects the interruption of power to equipment and activates a transfer switch that provides power from batteries through a DC to AC converter until normal power is restored or the computer is shut down. Because this type of UPS is not truly uninterruptible, it is often referred to as a standby power supply (SPS). The advantage of an SPS is that it is the most cost-effective type of UPS. However, the savings may be outweighed by the system's significant drawbacks, such as its limited run time and the amount of time it takes to switch from standby to active. Switching time may also become an issue because very sensitive computing equipment may not be able to handle the transfer delay, causing it to reset and suffer data loss or damage. Also, SPS systems do

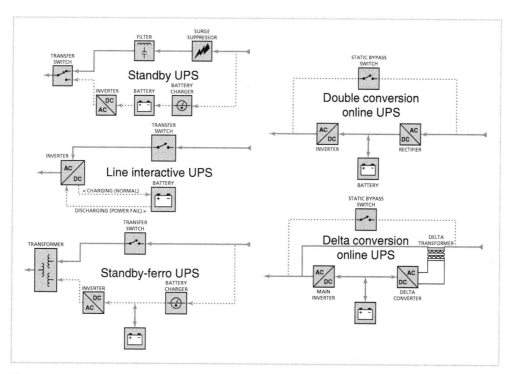

Figure 9-6 Types of uninterruptible power supplies[7]

not provide power conditioning, a feature of more sophisticated UPSs. As a result, an SPS is seldom used in critical computing applications and is best suited for home and light office use.

A **standby ferroresonant UPS** improves upon the standby UPS design. It is still an offline UPS, with the electrical service providing the primary source of power and the UPS serving as a battery backup. The primary difference is that a ferroresonant transformer replaces the UPS transfer switch. The transformer provides line filtering to the primary power source, reducing the effect of some power problems and reducing noise that may be present in the power as it is delivered. This transformer also stores energy in its coils, thereby providing a buffer to fill in the gap between the interruption of service and the activation of an alternate source of power (usually a battery backup). This greatly reduces the probability of system reset and data loss. Standby ferroresonant UPS systems are better suited to settings that require a large capacity of conditioned and reliable power because they are available for uses up to 14,000 VA. With the improvement in other UPS designs, however, many manufacturers have abandoned this design in favor of other configurations.

The **line-interactive UPS** has a substantially different design than the previously mentioned UPS models. In line-interactive UPSs, the internal components of the standby models are replaced with a pair of inverters and converters. The primary power source, as with both the SPS and the ferroresonant UPS, remains the power utility, with a battery serving as backup. However, the inverters and converters both charge the battery and provide power when needed. When utility power is interrupted, the converter begins supplying power to the systems. Because this device is always connected to the output as opposed to relying on a switch, this model has a much faster response time and incorporates power conditioning and line filtering.

In a **double conversion online UPS**, the primary power source is the inverter, and the power feed from the utility is constantly recharging the battery, which in turn powers the output inverter. This model allows constant use of the system while completely eliminating power fluctuation. This model of UPS can deliver a constant, smooth, conditioned power stream to the computing systems. If the utility-provided power fails, the computer systems are unaffected as long as the batteries hold out. The online UPS is considered the top-of-the-line option and is the most expensive. The only major drawback, other than cost, is that the system generates a lot of heat: the process constantly converts power from the utility's AC feed to the DC used by the battery storage and then converts it back to AC for use by the systems. An improved model, the **delta conversion online UPS**, resolves this issue by incorporating a device known as a delta-conversion unit, which allows some of the incoming power to be fed directly to the destination computers, thus reducing the amount of energy wasted and heat generated. Should the power fail, the delta unit shuts off and the batteries automatically compensate for the increased power draw.

Selecting the best UPS can be a lesson in electrical engineering because you must calculate the load that the protected systems require from the UPS. This calculation can be quite complex and challenging. Fortunately, many UPS vendors provide sample scenarios that can help you select the optimal device. Because high-quality, commercial-grade UPSs may cost hundreds of thousands of dollars, you should select the smallest UPS necessary to provide the desired effect. To manually calculate the rating needed in a UPS, you should begin by reviewing the computer systems and all connected support equipment to be protected. For example, the back panel of a monitor may indicate that it is rated at 110 volts and 2 amps. Because volts multiplied by amps yields the power needs of a device, you can calculate the power needed to run the device using the equation $110 \times 2 = 220$. In other words, the rating of the monitor is 220 VA. Now suppose the computer draws 3 amps at 110 volts, and therefore has a rating of 330 VA. Together the total is 550 VA. Once you have this information, you can select a UPS capable of supporting this power level. Generally, UPS systems provide information for how long they run at specific VA levels. Some smaller-scale UPSs can run for approximately six minutes at 600 VA at full voltage. You should look for a UPS that provides enough time for the computing equipment to ride out minor power fluctuations, and for the user to shut down the computer safely if necessary.

Emergency Shutoff One important aspect of power management in any environment is the ability to stop power immediately if the current represents a safety risk to people or machines. Most computer rooms and wiring closets are equipped with an emergency power shutoff, which is usually a large red button that is prominently placed to facilitate access and that has a cover to prevent unintentional use. These devices are the last line of defense against personal injury and machine damage in the event of flooding or sprinkler activation. The last person out of the computer room hits the switch to stop the flow of electricity to the room, preventing water from short-circuiting the computers. While it is never advisable to allow water to come into contact with a computer, there is a much higher probability of recovering the systems if the power was off when they got wet. At a minimum, hard drives and other sealed devices may be recoverable. Some disaster recovery companies specialize in water damage recovery.

〉 Water Problems

Another critical utility is water service. On the one hand, lack of water poses problems to systems, including fire suppression and air-conditioning systems. On the other hand, a surplus of water or water pressure poses a real threat. Flooding and leaks can be catastrophic to paper and electronic storage of information. Water damage can result in complete failure of computer systems and the structures that house them. Therefore, it is important to integrate water detection systems into the alarm systems that regulate overall operations of the facility.

〉 Structural Collapse

Unavoidable environmental factors or forces of nature can cause failures in the structures that house the organization. Structures are designed and constructed with specific load limits, and overloading these design limits inevitably results in structural failure, which could cause personal injury and even loss of life. Scheduling periodic inspections by qualified civil engineers enables managers to identify potentially dangerous structural conditions before a structure fails.

〉 Maintenance of Facility Systems

As with any phase of the security process, the implementation of physical security must be constantly documented, evaluated, and tested. Once the physical security of a facility is established, it must be diligently maintained. Ongoing maintenance of systems is required as part of the systems' operations. Documentation of the facility's configuration, operation, and function should be integrated into disaster recovery plans and standard operating procedures. Testing provides information necessary to improve physical security in the facility and identifies weak points.

Interception of Data

Key Terms

electromagnetic radiation (EMR) The transmission of radiant energy through space, commonly referred to as radio waves.

TEMPEST A U.S. government program designed to protect computers from electronic remote eavesdropping by reducing EMR emissions.

There are three methods of data interception: direct observation, interception of data transmission, and electromagnetic interception. The first method, *direct observation*, requires that a person be close enough to the information to breach confidentiality. The physical security mechanisms described in the previous sections limit the possibility of a person accessing unauthorized areas and directly observing information. However, there is a risk when the information is removed from a protected facility. If an employee is browsing company documents over lunch in a restaurant or takes work home, the risk of direct observation rises substantially. A competitor can more easily intercept vital information at a typical employee's home than at a secure office. Incidences of interception, such as shoulder surfing, can be avoided if employees are prohibited from removing sensitive information from the office or are required to implement strong security at their homes.

The second method, *interception of data transmissions*, has become easier in the age of the Internet. If attackers can access the media transmitting the data, they needn't be anywhere near the source of the information. In some cases, the attacker can use sniffer software to collect data, as you learned in previous chapters. Other means of interception, such as tapping into a LAN, require some proximity to the organization's computers or networks. It is important for network administrators to conduct periodic physical inspections of all data ports to ensure that no unauthorized taps have occurred. If direct wiretaps are a concern, the organization should consider using fiber-optic cable; it is difficult to splice and therefore much more resistant to tapping. If wireless LANs are used, the organization should be concerned about eavesdropping because an attacker can snoop from a location that might be hundreds of feet from the organization's building, depending on the strength of the wireless access points (WAPs). Because wireless LANs are uniquely susceptible to eavesdropping and current wireless sniffers are very potent tools, all wireless communications should be secured via encryption. Incidentally, U.S. laws that deal with wiretapping do not cover wireless communications, except for commercial cellular phone calls; courts have ruled that users have no expectation of privacy with radio-based communications media.

The third method of data interception, *electromagnetic interception*, sounds like it could be from a *Star Trek* episode. For decades, scientists have known that electricity moving through cables emits electromagnetic signals (EM). It is possible to eavesdrop on these signals and therefore determine the data carried on the cables without actually tapping into them. In 1985, scientists proved that computer monitors also emitted radio waves, and that images on the screens could be reconstructed from these signals.[8] More recently, scientists have determined that certain devices with light-emitting diode (LED) displays actually emit information encoded in the light that pulses in these LEDs.[9]

Whether data in devices that emit **electromagnetic radiation** (**EMR**) can actually be monitored, processed, and reconstructed has been a subject of debate and rumor for many years. James Atkinson, an electronics engineer certified by the National Security Agency (NSA), says that practical monitoring of electronic emanations does not exist and claims that stories about such monitoring are just urban legends. He goes on to say that most modern computers are shielded to prevent interference with other household and office equipment—not to prevent eavesdropping. Atkinson does concede that receiving emanations from a computer monitor is theoretically possible, but notes that it would be extremely difficult, expensive, and impractical.[10]

Legend or not, a good deal of money is being spent by the U.S. government and military to protect computers from electronic remote eavesdropping. In fact, the government has developed a program named **TEMPEST** to reduce the risk of EMR monitoring. (In keeping with the speculative fancy surrounding this topic, some people believe that the acronym TEMPEST was originally a code word created by the U.S. government in the 1960s, but was later defined as Transient Electromagnetic Pulse Emanation Surveillance Technology or Telecommunications Electronics Material Protected from Emanating Spurious Transmissions.) In general, TEMPEST involves the following procedures: ensuring that computers are placed as far as possible from outside perimeters, installing special shielding inside the CPU case, and implementing a host of other restrictions, including maintaining distances from plumbing and other infrastructure components that carry radio waves. Additional information about TEMPEST and its associated controls is available at *www.fas.org/irp/program/security/tempest .htm*. Regardless of whether the threat from eavesdropping on electromagnetic emanations is real, many procedures that protect against emanations also protect against threats to physical security.

 For more information on TEMPEST and additional insights into many aspects of security, read the 1994 report to the U.S. Secretary of Defense and the Director of Central Intelligence. This report, "Redefining Security," is available at www.fas.org/sgp/library/jsc/.

Securing Mobile and Portable Systems

Mobile computing requires even more security than typical computing infrastructures on the organization's premises. Most mobile computing systems—laptops, tablets, and smartphones—have valuable corporate information stored within them, and some are configured to facilitate user access into the organization's secure computing facilities. Many users may be keeping clues about the organization's computing and network environment in their portable devices. Many users like the convenience of allowing the portable device to remember their usernames and passwords because it provides faster and easier access and because they frequently have multiple accounts with different usernames and passwords. While it is tempting to allow devices to store authentication credentials and enable easier access to frequently used accounts, the downside of setting up these arrangements on a portable device is obvious: loss of the device means loss of the access control mechanisms.

Many devices, including desktop and laptop computers, smartphones, and tablets, can now be configured to send their location if reported lost or stolen, wipe themselves of all user data, or even disable themselves completely. For example, Absolute Software's CompuTrace is computer software that is installed on a laptop, as illustrated in Figure 9-7. Periodically, when the computer is connected to the Internet, the software reports itself and the computer's electronic serial number to a central monitoring center. If the laptop is reported stolen, this software can trace the computer to its current location for possible recovery. The software is undetectable on the system, even if the thief knows the software is installed. Moreover, CompuTrace remains installed even if the laptop's hard drive is reformatted and the operating system is reinstalled.

Also available for laptops are burglar alarms made up of a device that contains a motion detector, GPS transceiver, and/or RFID tag. If the device is armed and the laptop is moved more than expected, the alarm triggers a loud buzzer or horn. The security system may also disable the computer or use an encryption option to render its stored information unusable. These devices often allow active tracking to recover a device if necessary.

For maximum security, laptops should be secured at all times. If you are traveling with a laptop, you should always have it in your possession. Special care should be exercised when flying, as laptop thefts are common in airports. The following list from the Metropolitan Police of the District of Columbia explains how to prevent your laptop from being stolen or damaged:

- "Don't leave your devices in an unlocked vehicle, even if the vehicle is in your driveway or garage, and *never* leave it in plain sight, even if the vehicle is locked—that's just inviting trouble. If you must leave your devices in a vehicle, the best place is in the trunk. If you don't have a trunk, try to conceal them or fit them under a seat and lock the doors.

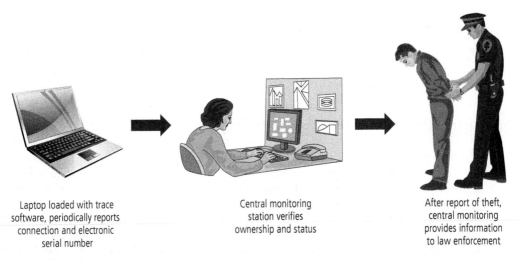

| Laptop loaded with trace software, periodically reports connection and electronic serial number | Central monitoring station verifies ownership and status | After report of theft, central monitoring provides information to law enforcement |

Figure 9-7 Laptop recovery

- Carry your devices in a nondescript carrying case, briefcase, or bag when moving about. Placing these items in a case designed for computers is an immediate alert to thieves that you have these valuable devices.

- *Do not* leave a meeting or conference room without your laptop or personal electronics. Take them with you.

- Lock your device in a safe place when not in use or use a cable lock that wraps around a desk or chair leg.

- Apply distinctive paint markings (such as indelible markers) to make your laptop unique and easily identifiable.

- Consider purchasing a theft alarm system specially made for laptops and other electronics.

- Be aware that if your computer is stolen, automatic log-ins can make it easy for a thief to send inappropriate messages with your account. Use password protection and require a person to log in every time the computer goes to sleep or powers down.

- Back up your information using cloud-based storage or on portable media such as a CD, DVD, flash drive, or other backup media. Store the discs someplace safe."[11]

⟩ Remote Computing Security

Key Terms

telecommuting A work arrangement in which employees work from an off-site location and connect to an organization's equipment electronically. Also known as *telework*.
telework See *telecommuting*.
virtual organization A group of people brought together for a specific task, usually from different organizations, divisions, or departments.

Remote site computing, which is becoming increasingly popular, involves a wide variety of computing sites outside the organization's main facility and includes all forms of telecommuting. **Telecommuting** (or **telework**) involves off-site computing that uses Internet connections, dial-up connections, connections over leased point-to-point links between offices, and other mechanisms.

Telecommuting from users' homes deserves special attention. One of the appeals of telecommuting is that employees can avoid physical commuting and have more time to focus on their work. But, as more people become telecommuters, the risk to information traveling via their often unsecured connections is substantial. The problem is that not enough organizations provide secure connections to their office networks, and even fewer provide secure systems if the employee's home computer is compromised. To secure the entire network, the organization must dedicate security resources to protecting these home connections. Although the installation of a virtual private network (VPN) may go a long way toward protecting the data in transmission, telecommuters frequently store office data on their home systems, in home filing cabinets, and on off-site media. To ensure a secure process, the computers that telecommuters use must be made *more* secure than the organization's systems, because they are outside the security perimeter. An attacker who breaks into someone's home would probably find a much lower level of security than at an office. Most office systems require users to log in, but the telecommuter's home computer is probably a personal machine. Thus, it has a much less secure operating system or may not require a password. Telecommuters must use a securable device with a client operating system that can be configured to require password authentication. They must store all loose data in locking filing cabinets and loose media in locking fire safes. They must handle data at home more carefully than they would at the office, because the general level of security for the average home is less than that of a commercial building.

The same principles apply to workers using portable computing devices on the road. Employees who use tablets, smartphones, and notebook computers in hotel rooms should presume that their unencrypted transmissions are being monitored, and that any unsecured notebook computer can be stolen. The off-site worker using leased facilities does not know who else is attached to the network and who might be listening to his or her data conversations. VPNs are a must in all off-site to on-site communications, and the use of associated advanced authentication systems is strongly recommended.

Although it is possible to secure remote sites, organizations cannot assume that employees will invest their own funds for security. Many organizations barely tolerate telecommuting for a number of reasons, foremost among them that such employees generally require two sets of computing equipment, one for the office and one for the home. This extra expense is difficult to justify, especially when the employee is the only one gaining the benefit from telecommuting. In rare cases in which allowing employees or consultants to telecommute is the only way for them to gain extremely valuable skills, the organization is usually willing to do what is necessary to secure its systems. Only when additional research into telecommuting clearly displays a bottom-line advantage do organizations begin to invest sufficient resources into securing telecommuting equipment.

However, some organizations do support telecommuting, and they typically fall into one of three groups. The first is the mature and fiscally sound organization with a sufficient budget to support telecommuting and thus enhance its standing with employees and its own image. In recent years, the option to telecommute has become more important in organizational rankings developed by various magazines. Some organizations seek to improve employee work conditions and improve their position in best-workplace rankings by adding telecommuting as an option for employees. The second group consists of new high-technology companies with large numbers of geographically diverse employees who telecommute almost exclusively. These companies use technology extensively and are determined to make it the cornerstone of their organizations. The third group overlaps with the second, and is called a virtual organization. A **virtual organization** is a group of people from different organizations who form a virtual company, either in leased facilities or through 100-percent telecommuting arrangements. When the job is done, the organization is either redirected or dissolved. These organizations rely almost exclusively on remote computing and telecommuting, but they are rare and therefore are not well documented or studied.

 For more information on telework, including the Telework Enhancement Act of 2010, visit www .telework.gov.

Special Considerations for Physical Security

An organization must account for several special considerations when developing a physical security program. The first is the question of whether to handle physical security in-house or to outsource it. As with any aspect of information security, the make-or-buy decision should not be made lightly. Many qualified and professional agencies can provide physical security consulting and services. The benefits of outsourcing physical security include gaining the experience and knowledge of these agencies, many of which have been in the field for decades. Outsourcing unfamiliar operations always frees an organization to focus on its primary objectives rather than support operations. The disadvantages include the expense, the loss of control over individual components of physical security, and the need to trust another company to perform an essential business function. An organization must trust the processes used by the contracted company and its ability to hire and retain trustworthy employees who respect the security of the contracting company, even though they have no allegiance to it. This level of trust is often the most difficult aspect of the decision to outsource, because the reality of outsourcing physical security is that an outside agency will be providing a safeguard that the organization administers only marginally.

Another physical security consideration is social engineering. As you learned in previous chapters, social engineering involves using people skills to obtain confidential information from employees. While most social engineers prefer to use the telephone or computer to solicit information, some attempt to access the information more directly. Technically proficient agents can be placed in janitorial positions at a competitor's office, and an outsider can gain access to an organization's resources in other ways. For example, most organizations do not have thorough procedures for authenticating and controlling visitors who access their facility. When no procedure is in place, no one gives the wandering repairman, service worker, or city official a second look. It is not difficult to get a clipboard, dress like a repairman or building inspector, and move freely throughout a building. If you look like you have a mission and appear competent, most people will leave you alone. Organizations can combat this type of attack by requiring all people who enter the facility to display appropriate visitor badges and be escorted in restricted areas.

Selected Readings

- *Effective Physical Security, Third Edition*, by Lawrence Fennelly. 2004. Butterworth Heinemann.
- *Build the Best Data Center Facility for Your Business*, by Douglas Alger. 2005. Cisco Press.
- *Guard Force Management, Updated Edition*, by Lucien Canton. 2003. Butterworth Heinemann.

Chapter Summary

- Physical security requires the design, implementation, and maintenance of countermeasures that protect the physical resources of an organization.

- Many threats to information security can also be classified as threats to physical security. An organization's policy should guide the planning for physical security throughout the development life cycle.

- In facilities management, a secure facility is a physical location that has controls to minimize the risk of attacks from physical threats. A secure facility can use natural terrain, traffic flow, and urban development, and can complement these environmental elements with protection mechanisms, such as fences, gates, walls, guards, and alarms.

- The management of keys and locks is a fundamental part of general management's responsibility for the organization's physical environment.

- A fail-safe lock is typically used on an exit door when human safety in a fire or other emergency is the essential consideration. A fail-secure lock is used when human safety is not a factor.

- Monitoring equipment can record events that guards and dogs might miss, and can be used in areas where other types of physical controls are not practical.

- As with any phase of the security process, the implementation of physical security must be constantly documented, evaluated, and tested. Once the physical security of a facility is established, it must be diligently maintained.

- Fire detection systems are devices that detect and respond to a fire or potential fire. Fire suppression systems stop the progress of a fire once activated.

- The three basic types of fire detection systems are thermal detection, smoke detection, and flame detection.

- Four environmental variables controlled by HVAC systems can cause damage to information systems: temperature, filtration, humidity, and static electricity.

- Computer systems depend on stable power supplies to function; when power levels are too high, too low, or too erratic, computer circuitry can be damaged or destroyed. The power provided to computing and networking equipment should contain no unwanted fluctuations and no embedded signaling.

- Water problems and the weakening and subsequent failure of a building's physical structure represent potential threats to personal safety and to the integrity and availability of information assets.

- Data can be intercepted electronically and manually. The three routes of data interception are direct observation, interception of data transmission, and interception of electromagnetic radiation.

- TEMPEST is a technology that prevents the possible loss of data from the emission of electromagnetic radiation (EMR).

- With the increased use of laptops, handhelds, and PDAs, organizations should be aware that mobile computing requires even more security than the average in-house system.

- Remote site computing requires a secure extension of the organization's internal networks and special attention to security for any connected home or off-site computing technology.

■ Like computing equipment, classified information should be inventoried and managed. If multiple copies are made of a classified document, they should be numbered and tracked.

Review Questions

1. What is physical security? What are the primary threats to physical security? How are they manifested in attacks against the organization?

2. What are the roles of an organization's IT, security, and general management with regard to physical security?

3. How does physical access control differ from logical access control, which is described in earlier chapters? How are they similar?

4. Define a secure facility. What is the primary objective of designing such a facility? What are some secondary objectives of designing a secure facility?

5. Why are guards considered the most effective form of control for situations that require decisive action in the face of unfamiliar stimuli? Why are they usually the most expensive controls to deploy? What is another issue with human guards, beyond the high cost? When should dogs be used for physical security?

6. List and describe the four categories of locks. In which situation is each type of lock preferred?

7. What are the two possible modes of locks when they fail? What implications do these modes have for human safety? In which situation is each preferred?

8. What is a mantrap? When should it be used?

9. What is the most common form of alarm? What does it detect? What types of sensors are commonly used in this type of alarm system?

10. Describe a physical firewall that is used in buildings. List reasons that an organization might need a firewall for physical security controls.

11. What is considered the most serious threat within the realm of physical security? Why is it valid to consider this threat the most serious?

12. What three elements must be present for a fire to ignite and continue to burn? How do fire suppression systems manipulate the three elements to quell fires?

13. List and describe the three fire detection technologies covered in the chapter. Which is the most commonly used?

14. List and describe the four classes of fire described in the text. Does the class of the fire dictate how to control it?

15. What is Halon and why is its use restricted?

16. What is the relationship between HVAC and physical security? What four physical characteristics of the indoor environment are controlled by a properly designed HVAC system? What are the optimal temperature and humidity ranges for computing systems?

17. List and describe the four primary types of UPS systems. Which is the most effective and the most expensive, and why?

18. What two critical factors are affected when water is not available in a facility? Why are they important to the operation of the organization's information assets?

19. List and describe the three fundamental ways that data can be intercepted. How does a physical security program protect against each of these data interception methods?

20. What can you do to reduce the risk of theft of portable computing devices, such as smartphones, tablets, and notebooks?

Exercises

1. Assume that your organization is planning to have an automated server room that functions without human assistance. Such a room is often called a lights-out server room. Describe the fire control system(s) you would install in that room.

2. Assume you have converted an area of general office space into a server room. Describe the factors you would consider for each of the following components:

   a. Walls and doors

   b. Access control

   c. Fire detection

   d. Fire suppression

   e. Heating, ventilating, and air conditioning

   f. Power quality and distribution

3. Assume you have been asked to review the power needs of a stand-alone computer system that processes important but noncritical data. Although the system does not have to be online at all times, it stores valuable data that could be corrupted if the power system were suddenly interrupted. Which UPS features are most important to such a system? Which type of UPS do you recommend for it?

4. Using a floor plan from a building you are familiar with, design an electronic monitoring plan that includes closed-circuit television, burglar alarms with appropriate sensors, fire detectors, and suppression and access controls for key entrances.

5. Define the required wattage for a UPS to be used with the following systems:

   a. Monitor: 2 amps; CPU: 3 amps; printer: 3 amps

   b. Monitor: 3 amps; CPU: 4 amps; printer: 3 amps

   c. Monitor: 3 amps; CPU: 4 amps; printer: 4 amps

6. Search the Web for a UPS that provides the wattage necessary to run the systems described in Exercise 5 for at least 15 minutes during a power outage.

Case Exercises

Amy walked into her office cubicle and sat down. The entire episode with the blond man had taken well over two hours of her day. Plus, the police officers had told her the district attorney would also want to speak with her, which meant she would have to spend even more time dealing with this incident. She hoped her manager would understand.

Discussion Questions

1. Based on this case study, what security awareness measures, training documents, and posters had an impact on this event?

2. Do you think that Amy should have done anything differently? What would you have done in her situation?

Ethical Decision Making

Suppose that the blond man in the scenario was someone Amy knew socially. Suppose she also knew he had no relationship to the company and no business being in the building. If Amy chose not to make a report about the event, would she be violating her ethical position?

Endnotes

1. Parker, Donn B. *Fighting Computer Crime*. 1998. New York: John Wiley and Sons Inc., 250–251.

2. Army Study Guide. "Guard Duty." Accessed 26 October 2016 from *www.armystudy guide.com/content/army_board_study_guide_topics/guard_duty/guard-duty-study-guide .shtml*.

3. Ibid.

4. Swanson, Marianne. National Institute of Standards and Technology. *Guide for Developing Security Plans for Federal Information Systems*. SP 800-18, Rev. 1. February 2006. Accessed 30 August 2016 from *http://csrc.nist.gov/publications/PubsSPs.html*.

5. Artim, Nick. *An Introduction to Fire Detection, Alarm, and Automatic Fire Sprinklers*. Emergency Management, Technical Leaflet 2, Sec. 3. Middlebury: Fire Safety Network.

6. Webopedia. "Static Electricity and Computers." *Webopedia Online*. May 2003. Accessed 30 August 2016 from *www.webopedia.com/DidYouKnow/Compu ter_Science/static.asp*.

7. Rasmussen, N. "The Different Types of UPS Systems." *White Paper 1 Revision 7*. 2011. Accessed 30 August 2016 from *www.apcmedia.com/salestools/SADE-5TNM3Y /SADE-5TNM3Y_R7_EN.pdf*.

8. Van Eck, Wim. "Electromagnetic Radiation from Video Display Units: An Eavesdropping Risk?" *Computers & Security* 4 (1985): 269–286.

9. Loughry, Joe, and Umphress, David A. "Information Leakage from Optical Emanations." *ACM Transactions on Information and System Security* 7, no. 7 (March 2002).

10. PC Privacy. "Is Tempest a Threat or Hoax?" *PC Privacy* 8, no. 4 (April 2000).

11. Metropolitan Police of the District of Columbia. "Tips for Preventing Theft of Laptops and Personal Electronics." *Government of the District of Columbia Online*. Accessed 30 August 2016 from *http://mpdc.dc.gov/page/tips-preventing-theft-laptops-and -personal-electronics*.

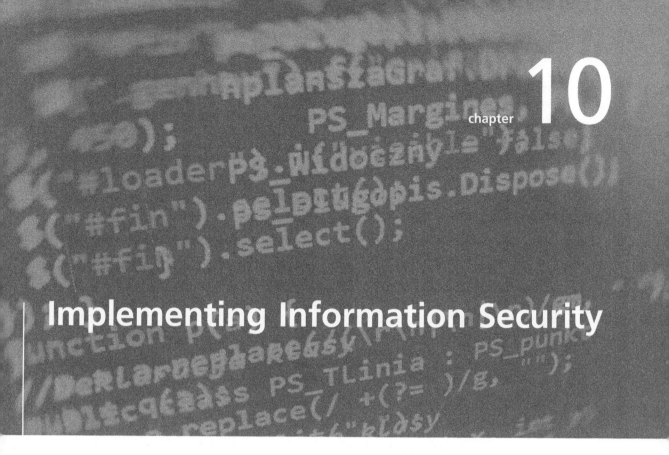

chapter 10

Implementing Information Security

Change is good. You go first!

DILBERT (BY SCOTT ADAMS)

Kelvin Urich arrived early for the change control meeting. In the large, empty conference room, he reviewed his notes and then flipped through the handouts one final time. During the meeting last week, the technical review committee had approved his ideas, and now he was confident that the project plan he'd developed was complete, tight, and well-ordered.

The series of change requests resulting from this project would keep the company's technical analysts busy for months to come, but he hoped that the scope and scale of the project, and the vast improvements it was sure to bring to the SLS information security program, would inspire his colleagues. To help the project proceed smoothly, he had loaded his handouts with columns of tasks, subtasks, and action items, and had assigned dates to every action step and personnel to each required task. He checked that the handouts were organized properly and that he had plenty of copies. Everything was under control.

Naomi Jackson, the change control supervisor, also arrived a few minutes early. She nodded to Kelvin as she placed a stack of revised agendas in the middle of the conference table. Everyone attending had received the detailed report of planned changes the previous day. Charlie Moody came in, also nodding to Kelvin, and took his usual seat.

Once the room filled, Naomi said, "Time to get started." She picked up her copy of the planned change report and announced the first change control item for discussion, Item 742.

One of the members of the UNIX support team responded, "As planned," meaning that the item, a routine maintenance procedure for the corporate servers, would occur as scheduled.

Naomi continued down the list in numeric order. Most items received the response "As planned" from the sponsoring team member. Occasionally, someone answered "Cancelled" or "Will be rescheduled," but for the most part, the review of the change items proceeded as usual until it came to Kelvin's information security change requests.

Naomi said, "Items 761 through 767. Kelvin Urich from the security team is here to discuss these items with the change control group."

Kelvin distributed his handouts around the table. He waited, a little nervously, until everyone had a copy, and then began speaking: "I'm sure most of you are already aware of the information security upgrades we've been working on for the past few months. We've created an overall strategy based on the revised policies that were published last month and a detailed analysis of the threats to our systems. As the project manager, I've created what I think is a very workable plan. The seven change requests on the list today are all network changes and are each a top priority. In the coming weeks, I'll be sending each department head a complete list of all planned changes and the expected dates. Of course, detailed change requests will be filed in advance for change control meetings, but each department can find out when any item is planned by checking the master list. As I said, there are more changes coming, and I hope we can all work together to make this a success."

"Comments or questions?" asked Naomi.

Instantly six hands shot into the air. All of them belonged to senior technical analysts. Kelvin realized belatedly that none of these analysts were on the technical review committee that had approved his plan. He also noticed that half the people in the room, like Amy Windahl from the user group and training committee, were busy pulling calendars and PDAs out of briefcases and bags, and that Davey Martinez from Accounting was engaged in a private but heated discussion with Charlie Moody, Kelvin's boss. Charlie did not look pleased.

Above the noise, Kelvin heard someone say, "I should have been warned if we are going to have all this work dumped on us all at once." Someone else said, "We can't make this happen on this schedule."

Amid the sudden chaos that had broken out during an otherwise orderly meeting, it occurred to Kelvin that his plan might not be as simple as he'd thought. He braced himself—it was going to be a very long afternoon.

LEARNING OBJECTIVES

Upon completion of this material, you should be able to:

- Explain how an organization's information security blueprint becomes a project plan
- Discuss the many organizational considerations that a project plan must address
- Explain the significance of the project manager's role in the success of an information security project
- Describe the need for professional project management for complex projects
- Discuss technical strategies and models for implementing a project plan
- List and discuss the nontechnical problems that organizations face in times of rapid change

Introduction

First and foremost, an information security project manager must realize that implementing an information security project takes time, effort, and a great deal of communication and coordination. This chapter and the next discuss how to successfully execute the information security blueprint. In general, the implementation phase is accomplished by changing the configuration and operation of the organization's information systems to make them more secure. It includes changes to the following:

- Procedures (for example, through policy)
- People (for example, through training)
- Hardware (for example, through firewalls)
- Software (for example, through encryption)
- Data (for example, through classification)

As you may recall from earlier chapters, effective planning for information security involves collecting information about an organization's objectives, its technical architecture, and its information security environment. These elements are used to form the information security blueprint, which is the foundation for protecting the confidentiality, integrity, and availability of the organization's information. The realization of these objectives will require an organization to define and execute a project. Successful projects require the application of a management specialty known as **project management.**

During the implementation phase, the organization translates its blueprint for information security into a **project plan**. The project plan instructs the people who are executing the implementation phase. These instructions focus on the security control changes needed to improve the security of the hardware, software, procedures, data, and people that make up the organization's information systems. The project plan as a whole must describe how to acquire and implement the needed security controls and create a setting in which those controls achieve the desired outcomes.

Information Security Project Management

As the opening vignette of this chapter illustrates, organizational change is not easily accomplished. The following sections discuss the issues a project plan must address, including project leadership; managerial, technical, and budgetary considerations; and organizational resistance to the change.

The major steps in executing the project plan are as follows:

- Planning the project
- Supervising tasks and action steps
- Wrapping up

The project plan can be developed in any number of ways. Each organization has to determine its own project management methodology for IT and information security projects. Whenever possible, information security projects should follow the organization's project management practices. Many organizations now make use of a *project office*—a centralized resource to maximize the benefits of a standardized approach to project management. One such benefit is the leveraging of common project management practices across the organization to enable reallocation of resources without confusion or delays.

❯ Developing the Project Plan

Key Terms

deliverable A completed document or program module that can either serve as the beginning point for a later task or become an element in the finished project.

milestone A specific point in the project plan when a task that has a noticeable impact on the plan's progress is complete.

predecessors Tasks or action steps that come before the specific task at hand.

projectitis A situation in project planning in which the project manager spends more time documenting project tasks, collecting performance measurements, recording project task information, and updating project completion forecasts in the project management software than accomplishing meaningful project work.

request for proposal (RFP) A document specifying the requirements of a project, provided to solicit bids from internal or external contractors.

resources Components required for the completion of a project, which could include skills, personnel, time, money, and material.

successors Tasks or action steps that come after the specific task at hand.

work breakdown structure (WBS) A list of the tasks to be accomplished in the project, the skill sets or individual employees needed to perform the tasks, the start and end dates for tasks, the estimated resources required, and the dependencies among tasks.

Planning for the implementation phase requires the creation of a detailed project plan, which is often assigned either to a project manager or the project champion. This person manages the project and delegates parts of it to other decision makers. Often the project manager is from the IT community of interest because most other employees lack the requisite information security background, management authority, and technical knowledge.

The project plan can be created using a simple planning tool such as the **work breakdown structure (WBS)**. An example is shown in Table 10-1. To use the WBS approach, you first break down the project plan into its major tasks. The major project tasks are placed into the WBS, along with the following attributes for each:

- Work to be accomplished (activities and deliverables)
- The people or skill sets assigned to perform the task

Task or Subtask	Resources	Start (S) & End (E) Dates	Estimated Effort in Hours	Estimated Capital Expense	Estimated Noncapital Expense	Depend-encies
1 Contact field office and confirm network assumptions	Network architect	S: 9/22 E: 9/22	2	$0	$200	
2 Purchase standard firewall hardware						
2.1 Order firewall through purchasing group	Network architect	S: 9/23 E: 9/23	1	$0	$100	1
2.2 Order firewall from manufacturer	Purchasing group	S: 9/24 E: 9/24	2	$4,500	$100	2.1
2.3 Firewall delivered	Purchasing group	E: 10/3	1	$0	$50	2.2
3 Configure firewall	Network architect	S: 10/3 E: 10/5	8	$0	$800	2.3
4 Package and ship firewall to field office	Student intern	S: 10/6 E: 10/15	2	$0	$85	3
5 Work with local technical resource to install and test	Network architect	S: 10/22 E: 10/31	6	$0	$600	4
6 Penetration test						
6.1 Request penetration test	Network architect	S: 11/1 E: 11/1	1	$0	$100	5
6.2 Perform penetration test	Penetration test team	S: 11/2 E: 11/12	9	$0	$900	6.1
6.3 Verify that results of penetration test were passing	Network architect	S: 11/13 E: 11/15	2	$0	$200	6.2
7 Get remote office sign-off and update all network drawings and documentation	Network architect	S: 11/16 E: 11/30	8	$0	$800	6.2

Table 10-1 Example Project Plan Work Breakdown Structure

10

- Start and end dates for the task, when known
- Amount of effort required for completion, in hours or work days
- Estimated capital expenses for the task
- Estimated noncapital expenses for the task
- Identification of dependencies between and among tasks

Each major task in the WBS is then further divided into either smaller tasks (subtasks) or specific action steps. For the sake of simplicity, the sample project plan outlined in the table and described later in this chapter divides each major task into action steps. In an actual project plan, major tasks are often much more complex and must be divided into subtasks before action steps can be identified and assigned to a specific person or skill set. Given the variety of possible projects, there are few formal guidelines for determining the appropriate level of detail—that is, the level at which a task or subtask should become an action step. However, one hard-and-fast rule can help you make this determination: a task or subtask becomes an action step when it can be completed by one person or skill set and has a single deliverable.

The WBS can be prepared with a simple spreadsheet program. The use of more complex project management software often leads to **projectitis**, in which the project manager spends more time working with the project management software than accomplishing meaningful project work. Recall Kelvin's handouts from the opening vignette, which were loaded with dates and details. His case of projectitis led him to develop an elegant, detailed plan before gaining consensus for the required changes. Because he was new to project management, he did not realize that simpler software tools could help him focus on organizing and coordinating with the project team.

Work to Be Accomplished
The work to be accomplished encompasses both activities and **deliverables**. Ideally, the project planner provides a label and a thorough description for the task. The description should be complete enough to avoid ambiguity during the tracking process later, yet should not be so detailed as to make the WBS unwieldy. For instance, if the task is to write firewall specifications for the preparation of a **request for proposal (RFP)**, the planner should note that the deliverable is a specification document suitable for distribution to vendors.

Assignees
The project planner should describe the skills or personnel, often referred to as **resources**, needed to accomplish the task. The naming of individual employees should be avoided in early planning efforts, a rule Kelvin ignored when he named employees for every task in the first draft of his project plan. Instead of making individual assignments, the project plan should focus on organizational roles or known skill sets. For example, if any of the engineers in the networks group can write the specifications for a router, the assigned resource would be noted as "network engineer" in the WBS. As planning progresses, however, specific tasks and action steps should be assigned to individual employees. For example, when *only* the manager of the networks group can evaluate responses to the RFP and make an award for a contract, the project planner should assign the network manager as the resource for this task.

Start and End Dates
In the early stages of planning, the project planner should attempt to specify completion dates only for major project **milestones**. For example, the date for sending the final RFP to vendors is a milestone because it signals that all RFP preparation work is complete. Assigning too many dates to too many tasks early in the planning process exacerbates projectitis. This is another mistake Kelvin made, and was a significant cause of the resistance he faced from his coworkers. Planners can avoid this pitfall by assigning only key or milestone start and end dates early in the process. Later, planners may add start and end dates as needed.

Amount of Effort Planners need to estimate the effort required to complete each task, subtask, or action step. Estimating effort hours for technical work is a complex process. Even when an organization has formal governance, technical review processes, and change control procedures, it is always good practice to ask the people who are most familiar with the tasks to make these estimates. After these estimates are made, the people assigned to action steps should review the estimated effort hours, understand the tasks, and agree with the estimates. Had Kelvin collaborated with his peers more effectively and adopted a more flexible planning approach, much of the resistance he encountered in the meeting would not have emerged.

Estimated Capital Expenses Planners need to estimate the capital expenses required for the completion of each task, subtask, or action item. While each organization budgets and expends capital according to its own established procedures, most differentiate between capital outlays for durable assets and expenses for other purposes. For example, a firewall device that costs $5,000 may be a capital outlay for an organization, but it might not consider a $5,000 software package to be a capital outlay because its accounting rules classify all software as expense items, regardless of cost.

Estimated Noncapital Expenses Planners need to estimate the noncapital expenses for the completion of each task, subtask, or action item. In business, capital expenses are those for revenue-producing projects that are expected to yield a return on investment, usually more than a year in the future. Noncapital expenses do not meet the criteria for capital expenditures. Some organizations require that current expenses for a project include a recovery charge for staff time, while others exclude employee time and consider only contract or consulting time used by the project as a noncapital expense. As mentioned earlier, it is important to determine the cost accounting practices of the organization for which the plan is to be used. For example, at some companies, a project to implement a firewall may charge only the costs of the firewall hardware as capital and consider all costs for labor and software as expense, regarding the hardware element as a durable good that has a lifespan of many years. Another organization might use the aggregate of all cash outflows associated with the implementation as the capital charge and make no charges to the expense category for everything needed to complete the project. The justification behind using this aggregate of all costs, which might include charges for items like hardware, labor, and freight, is that the newly implemented capability is expected to last for many years and is an improvement to the organization's infrastructure. A third company may charge the whole project as expense if the aggregate amount falls below a certain threshold, under the theory that small projects are a cost of ongoing operations.

Task Dependencies Whenever possible, planners should note the dependencies of other tasks or action steps on the one at hand, including task **predecessors** and **successors**. Multiple types of dependencies can exist, but such details are typically covered in courses on project management and are beyond the scope of this text.

A process for developing a simple WBS-style project plan is provided in the following steps. In this example, a small information security project has been assigned to Jane Smith for planning. The project is to design and implement a firewall for a small office. The hardware is a standard organizational product and will be installed at a location that already has a network connection.

Jane's first step is to list the major tasks:

1. Contact field office and confirm network assumptions.

2. Purchase standard firewall hardware.

3. Configure firewall.

4. Package and ship firewall to field office.

5. Work with local technical resource to install and test firewall.

6. Coordinate vulnerability assessment by penetration test team.

7. Get remote office sign-off and update all network drawings and documentation.

After all the people involved review and refine Jane's plan, she revises it to add more dates to the tasks listed, as shown in Table 10-1.

 For more information on project management certifications in the federal sector, visit www.fai .gov/drupal/certification/program-and-project-managers-fac-ppm.

❯ Project Planning Considerations

Key Term

project scope A description of a project's features, capabilities, functions, and quality level, used as the basis of a project plan.

As the project plan is developed, adding detail is not always straightforward. The following sections discuss factors that project planners must consider as they decide what to include in the work plan, how to break tasks into subtasks and action steps, and how to accomplish the objectives of the project.

Financial Considerations Regardless of an organization's information security needs, the amount of effort that can be expended depends on the available funds. A cost-benefit analysis (CBA), as described in Chapter 5, is typically prepared and must be reviewed and verified prior to the development of the project plan. The CBA determines the impact that a specific technology or approach can have on the organization's information assets and what it may cost.

Each organization has its own approach to the creation and management of budgets and expenses. In many organizations, the information security budget is a subsection of the overall IT budget. In others, information security is a separate budget category that may have the same degree of visibility and priority as the IT budget. Regardless of where information security items are located in the budget, monetary constraints determine what can and cannot be accomplished.

Public organizations tend to be more predictable in their budget processes than private organizations because the budgets of public organizations are usually the product of legislation or public meetings. This makes it difficult to obtain additional funds once the budget is determined. Also, some public organizations rely on temporary or renewable grants for their budgets and must stipulate their planned expenditures when the grant applications are written. If new expenses arise, funds must be requested via new grant applications. Also, grant expenditures are usually audited and cannot be misspent. However, many public organizations must spend all budgeted funds within the fiscal year—otherwise, the subsequent year's budget is reduced by the unspent amount. As a result, these organizations often conduct end-of-fiscal-year spend-a-thons. This is often the best time to acquire, for example, that remaining piece of technology needed to complete the information security architecture.

Private (for-profit) organizations have budgetary constraints that are determined by the marketplace. When a for-profit organization initiates a project to improve security, the funding comes from the company's capital and expense budgets. Each for-profit organization determines its capital budget and the rules for managing capital spending and expenses differently. In almost all cases, however, budgetary constraints affect the planning and actual expenditures for information security. For example, a preferred technology or solution may be sacrificed for a less desirable but more affordable solution. The budget ultimately guides the information security implementation.

To justify the amount budgeted for a security project at either a public or for-profit organization, it may be useful to benchmark expenses of similar organizations. Most for-profit organizations publish the components of their expense reports. Similarly, public organizations must document how funds are spent. A savvy information security project manager might find a number of similarly sized organizations with larger expenditures for security to justify planned spending. While such tactics may not improve this year's budget, they could improve future budgets. Ironically, attackers can also help information security project planners justify the information security budget. If attacks successfully compromise secured information systems, management may be more willing to support the information security budget.

Priority Considerations In general, the most important information security controls in the project plan should be scheduled first. Budgetary constraints may have an effect on the assignment of a project's priorities. As you learned in Chapter 5, the implementation of controls is guided by the prioritization of threats and the value of the threatened information assets. A less important control may be prioritized if it addresses a group of specific vulnerabilities and improves the organization's security posture to a greater degree than other high-priority controls.

Time and Scheduling Considerations Time and scheduling can affect a project plan at dozens of points, including the time between ordering and receiving a security control, which may not be immediately available; the time it takes to install and configure the control; the time it takes to train the users; and the time it takes to realize the control's return on investment. For example, if a control must be in place before an organization can implement its electronic commerce product, the selection process is likely to be influenced by the speed of acquisition and implementation of the various alternatives.

Staffing Considerations The need for qualified, trained, and available personnel also constrains the project plan. An experienced staff is often needed to implement technologies and to develop and implement policies and training programs. If no staff members are trained to configure a new firewall, the appropriate personnel must be trained or hired.

Procurement Considerations There are often constraints on the selection of equipment and services—for example, some organizations require the use of particular service vendors or manufacturers and suppliers. These constraints may limit which technologies can be acquired. For example, in a recent budget cycle, the authors' lab administrator was considering selecting an automated risk analysis software package. The leading candidate promised to integrate everything, including vulnerability scanning, risk weighting, and control selection. Upon receipt of the RFP, the vendor issued a bid to meet the desired requirements for a heart-stopping $75,000, plus a 10 percent annual maintenance fee. If an organization has an annual information security budget of $30,000, it must eliminate a package like this from consideration. Also, consider the chilling effect on innovation when an organization requires elaborate supporting documentation and complex bidding for even small-scale purchases. Such procurement constraints, which are designed to control losses from occasional abuses, may actually increase costs when the lack of operating agility is taken into consideration.

Organizational Feasibility Considerations Whenever possible, security-related technological changes should be transparent to system users, but sometimes such changes require new procedures—for example, additional authentication or validation. A successful project requires that an organization be able to assimilate the proposed changes. New technologies sometimes require new policies, employee training, and education. Scheduling training after the new processes are in place—after the users have had to deal with the changes without preparation—can create tension and resistance, and might undermine security operations. Untrained users may develop ways to work around unfamiliar security procedures, and their bypassing of controls may create additional vulnerabilities. Conversely, users should not be prepared so far in advance that they forget the new training techniques and requirements. The optimal time frame for training is usually one to three weeks before the new policies and technologies come online.

Training and Indoctrination Considerations The size of the organization and the normal conduct of business may preclude a large training program for new security procedures or technologies. If so, the organization should conduct a phased-in or pilot implementation, such as roll-out training for one department at a time. See the section titled "Conversion Strategies" later in the chapter for details about various implementation approaches. When a project involves a change in policies, it may be sufficient to brief supervisors on the new policy and assign them the task of updating end users in regularly scheduled meetings. Project planners must ensure that compliance documents are also distributed and that all employees are required to read, understand, and agree to the new policies.

Scope Considerations The project scope of any given project plan should be carefully reviewed and kept as small as possible given the project's objectives. To control project scope, organizations should implement large information security projects in stages, as in the bull's-eye approach discussed later in this chapter.

For several reasons, the scope of information security projects must be evaluated and adjusted with care. First, in addition to the challenge of handling many complex tasks at one time, the installation of information security controls can disrupt the ongoing operations of an organization, and may also conflict with existing controls in unpredictable ways. For example, if you install a new packet filtering router and a new application proxy firewall at the same time and users are blocked from accessing the Web as a result, which technology caused the conflict? Was it the router, the firewall, or an interaction between the two? Limiting the project scope to a set of manageable tasks does not mean that the project should only allow change to one component at a time, but a good plan carefully considers the number of tasks that are planned for the same time in a single department.

Recall from the opening vignette that all of Kelvin's change requests are in the area of networking, where the dependencies are particularly complex. If the changes in Kelvin's project plan are not deployed exactly as planned, or if unanticipated complexities arise, there could be extensive disruption to Sequential Label and Supply's daily operations. For instance, an error in the deployment of the primary firewall rules could interrupt all Internet connectivity, which might make detection and recovery from the error more difficult.

❯ The Need for Project Management

> **Key Terms**
>
> **gap analysis** The process of comparing measured results against expected results, then using the resulting "gap" as a measure of project success and as feedback for project management.
> **project wrap-up** A process of bringing a project to a conclusion, addressing any pending issues and the overall project effort, and identifying ways to improve the process in the future.

10

Project management requires a unique set of skills and a thorough understanding of a broad body of specialized knowledge. In the opening vignette, Kelvin's inexperience as a project manager makes this all too clear. Realistically, most information security projects require a trained project manager—a CISO or a skilled IT manager who is trained in project management techniques. Even experienced project managers are advised to seek expert assistance when engaging in a formal bidding process to select advanced or integrated technologies or outsourced services.

Supervised Implementation   Although it is not an optimal solution, some organizations designate a champion from the general management community of interest to supervise the implementation of an information security project plan. In this case, groups of tasks are delegated to individuals or teams from the IT and information security communities of interest. An alternative is to designate a senior IT manager or the CIO of the organization to lead the implementation. In this case, the detailed work is delegated to cross-functional teams.

The best solution is to designate a suitable person from the information security community of interest. In the final analysis, each organization must find the project leadership that best suits its specific needs and the personalities and politics of the organizational culture.

Executing the Plan Once a project is under way, it is managed using a process known as **gap analysis** (also known as a negative feedback loop or cybernetic loop), which ensures that progress is measured periodically. When significant deviation occurs, corrective action is taken to bring the deviating task back into compliance with the project plan; otherwise, the project is revised in light of new information. See Figure 10-1 for an overview of this process.

Corrective action is taken in two basic situations: either the estimate is flawed or performance has lagged. When an estimate is flawed, as when the number of effort hours required is underestimated, the plan should be corrected and downstream tasks updated to reflect the change. When performance has lagged—for example, due to high turnover of skilled employees—corrective action may take the form of adding resources, making longer schedules, or reducing the quality or quantity of the deliverable. Corrective action decisions are

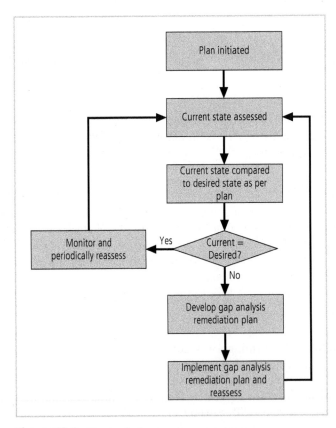

Figure 10-1 Gap analysis

usually expressed in terms of trade-offs. Often a project manager can adjust one of the three following planning parameters for the task being corrected:

- Effort and money allocated
- Elapsed time or scheduling impact
- Quality or quantity of the deliverable

When too much effort and money are being spent, you may decide to take more time to complete the project tasks or to lower the deliverable quality or quantity. If the task is taking too long to complete, you should probably add more resources in staff time or money or decrease the deliverable quality or quantity. If the quality of the deliverable is inadequate, you must usually add more resources in staff time or money or take longer to complete the task. Of course, there are complex dynamics among these variables, and these simplistic solutions do not serve in all cases, but this simple trade-off model can help the project manager to analyze available options.

Project Wrap-up Project wrap-up is usually handled as a procedural task and assigned to a mid-level IT or information security manager. These managers collect documentation, finalize status reports, and deliver a final report and a presentation at a wrap-up meeting. The goal of the wrap-up is to resolve any pending issues, critique the overall project effort, and draw conclusions about how to improve the process for the future.

 For more information on project management, visit the Project Management Institute's Web site at www.pmi.org.

❯ Security Project Management Certifications

For information security professionals who seek additional credentials and recognition for their project management experience, some certifications are available.

GIAC Certified Project Manager The SANS Institute offers a program that focuses on security professionals and managers with project management responsibilities who seek to demonstrate their mastery of project management methods and strategies.[1] Candidates for the certification may either study on their own or enroll in the SANS IT Project Management course. The program focuses on the following topic areas:

- Earned value technique (EVT)
- Leadership and management strategy
- Project communication management
- Project cost management
- Project human resource management
- Project integration management
- Project management framework and approach

- Project procurement management
- Project quality management
- Project risk management
- Project scope management
- Project stakeholder management
- Project time management[2]

IT Security Project Management The EC-Council offers the Project Management in Information Technology Security (PMITS) certification as a milestone in its Certified E-Business Professional program. This program focuses on the following topics:

- Components of project management in IT security
- Organizing the IT security project
- Developing the IT security project team
- Planning the IT security project
- Managing the IT project management
- Building quality into IT security projects
- Closing out the IT project management
- Defining a corporate IT project plan
- General IT security plan
- IT operational security plan[3]

Certified Security Project Manager The Security Industry Association (SIA) is a consortium focused predominantly on physical security, but it also incorporates information security into its programs. It has a certification program called the Certified Security Project Manager, which signifies completion of its project manager course, a body of self-study, and the completion of a final examination.

 For more information on the SANS GIAC Certified Project Manager certification, visit www.giac .org/certification/certified-project-manager-gcpm. For more information on the EC-Council's PMITS certification, visit www.eccouncil.org. For more information on the SIA certification, visit www.siaonline.org.

Technical Aspects of Implementation

Some aspects of the implementation process are technical and deal with the application of technology, while others deal with the human interface to technical systems. The following sections discuss conversion strategies, prioritization among multiple components, outsourcing, and technology governance.

〉 Conversion Strategies

As the components of the new security system are planned, provisions must be made for the changeover from the previous method of performing a task to the new method. Just like IT systems, information security projects require careful conversion planning. This section discusses the four basic approaches for changing from an old system or process to a new one. The approaches are illustrated in Figure 10-2.

Direct Changeover Also known as going "cold turkey," a **direct changeover** involves stopping the old method and beginning the new one. This approach could be as simple as having employees follow the existing procedure one week and then use a new procedure the next. Some cases of direct changeover are simple, such as requiring employees to begin using a new password with a stronger degree of authentication on an announced date. Some may be more complex, such as requiring the entire company to change procedures when the network team disables an old firewall and activates a new one. The primary drawback to the direct changeover approach is that if the new system fails or needs modification, users may be without services while the system's bugs are worked out. Complete testing of the new system in advance of the direct changeover reduces the probability of such problems.

10

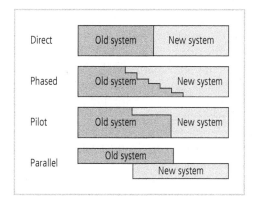

Figure 10-2 Conversion strategies

Phased Implementation A phased implementation is the most common conversion strategy and involves a measured rollout of the planned system, with only part of the system being brought out and disseminated across an organization before the next piece is implemented. This could mean that the security group implements only a small portion of the new security profile, giving users a chance to get used to it and resolving issues as they arise. This is usually the best approach to security project implementation. For example, if an organization seeks to update both its VPN and IDPS systems, it may first introduce the new VPN solution that employees can use to connect to the organization's network while they're traveling. Each week another department will be allowed to use the new VPN, with this process continuing until all departments are using the new approach. Once the new VPN has been phased into operation, revisions to the organization's IDPS can begin.

Pilot Implementation In a pilot implementation, the entire security system is put in place in a single office, department, or division before expanding to the rest of the organization. The pilot implementation works well when an isolated group can serve as the "guinea pig," which prevents any problems with the new system from dramatically interfering with the performance of the organization as a whole. The operation of a research and development group, for example, may not affect the real-time operations of the organization and could assist security in resolving issues that emerge.

Parallel Operations The parallel operations strategy involves running two systems concurrently; in terms of information systems, it might involve running two firewalls concurrently, for example. Although this approach is complex, it can reinforce an organization's information security by allowing the old system(s) to serve as backup for the new systems if they fail or are compromised. Drawbacks usually include the need to deal with both systems and maintain both sets of procedures.

❯ The Bull's-Eye Model

Key Term

bull's-eye model A method for prioritizing a program of complex change; it requires that issues be addressed from the general to the specific and focuses on systematic solutions instead of individual problems.

A proven method for prioritizing a program of complex change is the **bull's-eye model**. This methodology, which goes by many different names and has been used by many organizations, requires that issues be addressed from the general to the specific and that the focus be on systematic solutions instead of individual problems. The increased capabilities—that is, increased expenditures—are used to improve the information security program in a systematic and measured way. As presented here and illustrated in Figure 10-3, the approach relies on a process of project plan evaluation in four layers:

1. Policies: This is the outer, or first, ring in the bull's-eye diagram. The critical importance of policies has been emphasized throughout this textbook, particularly in Chapter 4.

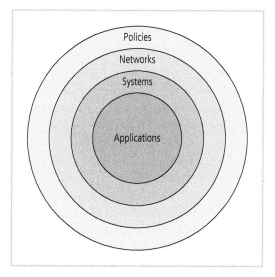

Figure 10-3 The bull's-eye model

The foundation of all effective information security programs is sound information security policy and information technology policy. Because policy establishes the ground rules for the use of all systems and describes what is appropriate and inappropriate, it enables all other information security components to function correctly. When deciding how to implement complex changes and choose from conflicting options, you can use policy to clarify what the organization is trying to accomplish with its efforts.

2. Networks: In the past, most information security efforts focused on this layer, so until recently information security was often considered synonymous with network security. In today's computing environment, implementing information security is more complex because networking infrastructure often comes into contact with threats from the public network. If an organization is new to the Internet and examines its policy environment to define how the new company networks should be defended, it will soon find that designing and implementing an effective DMZ is the primary way to secure those networks. Secondary efforts in this layer include providing the necessary authentication and authorization when allowing users to connect over public networks to the organization's systems.

3. Systems: Many organizations find that the problems of configuring and operating information systems in a secure fashion become more difficult as the number and complexity of these systems grow. This layer includes computers used as servers, desktop computers, and systems used for process control and manufacturing systems.

4. Applications: The layer that receives attention last deals with the application software systems used by the organization to accomplish its work. This includes packaged applications, such as office automation and e-mail programs, as well as high-end enterprise resource planning (ERP) packages than span the organization. Custom application software developed by the organization for its own needs is also included.

By reviewing the information security blueprint and the current state of the organization's information security efforts in terms of these four layers, project planners can determine which areas require expanded capabilities. The bull's-eye model can also be used to evaluate the sequence of steps taken to integrate parts of the information security blueprint into a project plan. As suggested by its bull's-eye shape, this model dictates the following:

- Until sound and usable IT and information security policies are developed, communicated, and enforced, no additional resources should be spent on other controls.

- Until effective network controls are designed and deployed, all resources should go toward achieving that goal, unless resources are needed to revisit the policy needs of the organization.

- After policies and network controls are established, implementation should focus on the information, process, and manufacturing systems of the organization. Until there is well-informed assurance that all critical systems are being configured and operated in a secure fashion, all resources should be spent on reaching that goal.

- Once there is assurance that policies are in place, networks are secure, and systems are safe, attention should move to assessing and remediating the security of the organization's applications. This is a complicated and vast area of concern for many organizations, and most neglect to analyze the impact of information security on existing systems and their own proprietary systems. As in all planning efforts, attention should be paid to the most critical applications first.

› To Outsource or Not

Not every organization needs to develop an information security department or program of its own. Just as some organizations outsource part or all of their IT operations, so too can organizations outsource their information security programs. The expense and time required to develop an effective information security program may be beyond the means of some organizations, so it may be in their best interest to hire professional services to help their IT departments implement such a program.

When an organization outsources most or all of its IT services, information security should be part of the contract arrangement with the supplier. Organizations that handle most of their own IT operations may choose to outsource the more specialized information security functions. Small and medium-sized organizations often hire outside consultants for penetration testing and information security program audits. Organizations of all sizes frequently outsource network monitoring functions to make certain that their systems are adequately secured and to gain assistance in watching for attempted or successful attacks.

 For an interesting article on outsourcing security, visit renowned security consultant and author Bruce Schneier's Web page at www.schneier.com/essay-084.html.

› Technology Governance and Change Control

> **Key Terms**
>
> **change control** A method of regulating the modification of systems within the organization by requiring formal review and approval for each change.
>
> **technology governance** A process organizations use to manage the effects and costs of technology implementation, innovation, and obsolescence.

Other factors that determine the success of an organization's IT and information security programs are technology governance and change control. Governance was covered in detail in Chapter 4.

Technology governance guides how frequently technical systems are updated and how technical updates are approved and funded. Technology governance also facilitates communication about technical advances and issues across the organization.

Medium-sized and large organizations deal with the impact of technical change on their operations through a **change control** process. By managing the process of change, the organization can do the following:

- Improve communication about change across the organization.

- Enhance coordination between groups within the organization as change is scheduled and completed.

- Reduce unintended consequences by having a process to resolve conflict and disruption that change can introduce.

- Improve quality of service as potential failures are eliminated and groups work together.

- Assure management that all groups are complying with the organization's policies for technology governance, procurement, accounting, and information security.

Effective change control is an essential part of the IT operation in all but the smallest organizations. The information security group can also use the change control process to ensure that the organization follows essential process steps that assure confidentiality, integrity, and availability when systems are upgraded across the organization.

› The Center for Internet Security's Critical Security Controls

To provide guidance for the implementation of security controls in the organization, the Center for Internet Security operates the Multi-state Information Sharing & Analysis Center (MS-ISAC), which serves as a sponsor and host of a concise, prioritized list of the most critical and widespread cyberattacks and a library of methods that can be used to control them. The MS-ISAC was created in response to industry practices that have seen security standards and requirement frameworks come and go; it makes an effort to address the risks that organizations face when using enterprise systems. These efforts often seem to devolve into a set of rote compliance reports, resulting in a diversion of resources that may have been better spent making actual improvements in the security posture to meet evolving threats rather than writing reports to address threats from the past. This state of affairs was noted in 2008 by the U.S. National Security Agency (NSA), which undertook an "offense must inform defense" approach that sought to enable the selection and implementation of controls based on a prioritization model with an intention to block actual threats instead of generating compliance documentation. The result was the emergence of a global consortium drawn from industry and government that became known as the Critical Security Controls (the Controls). MS-ISAC was charged with a coordinating role in this process.

The Controls sought to deliver functionality that focused on emerging advanced targeted threats, placing an emphasis on practical control approaches. The Controls were offered in a framework that emphasized standardization of approach and the use of automated techniques where possible, seeking to deliver a high degree of effectiveness and an essential efficiency to operations. The Controls are recognized as a subset of the controls enumerated in the National Institute of Standards and Technology (NIST) SP 800-53 (currently in Draft Rev. 5), and are not intended to supplant the NIST directives, including the Cybersecurity Framework developed in response to Executive Order 13636. Rather, this effort is a means of implementing a smaller number of actionable controls that deliver maximum results from a modest set of resource inputs using a structured list of priorities.

> *Since the Controls were derived from the most common attack patterns and were vetted across a very broad community of government and industry, with very strong consensus on the resulting set of controls, they serve as the basis for immediate high-value action.*[4]

A partial list of the 2016 critical controls (Version 6.0) follows:

1. *Inventory of Authorized and Unauthorized Devices—Actively manage (inventory, track, and correct) all hardware devices on the network [...].*

2. *Inventory of Authorized and Unauthorized Software—Actively manage [...] all software on the network [...].*

3. *Secure Configurations for Hardware and Software on Mobile Devices, Laptops, Workstations, and Servers—Establish, implement, and actively manage [...] the security configuration of laptops, servers, and workstations [...].*

4. *Continuous Vulnerability Assessment and Remediation—Continuously acquire, assess, and take action on new information in order to identify vulnerabilities, remediate, and minimize the window of opportunity for attackers.*

5. *Malware Defenses—Control the installation, spread, and execution of malicious code [...].*

6. *Application Software Security—Manage the security life cycle of all [...] software [...].*

7. *Wireless Access Control—Manage the processes and tools used to track, control, prevent, and correct the security use of wireless local area networks [...].*

8. *Data Recovery Capability—The processes and tools used to properly back up critical information with a proven methodology for timely recovery of it.*

9. *Security Skills Assessment and Appropriate Training to Fill Gaps—For all functional roles in the organization [...], identify the specific knowledge, skills, and abilities needed to support defense of the enterprise; develop and execute an integrated plan to assess, identify gaps, and remediate through policy, organizational planning, training, and awareness programs.*

10. *Secure Configurations for Network Devices such as Firewalls, Routers, and Switches— Establish, implement, and actively manage [...] the security configuration of network infrastructure [...].*

11. *Limitation and Control of Network Ports, Protocols, and Services—Manage (track/control/correct) the ongoing operational use of ports, protocols, and services on networked devices [...].*

12. *Controlled Use of Administrative Privileges—The processes and tools used to track, control, prevent, and correct the use, assignment, and configuration of administrative privileges on computers, networks, and applications.*

13. *Boundary Defense—Detect, prevent, and correct the flow of information transferring networks of different trust levels with a focus on security-damaging data.*

14. *Maintenance, Monitoring, and Analysis of Audit Logs—Collect, manage, and analyze audit logs of events that could help detect, understand, or recover from an attack.*

15. *Controlled Access Based on the Need to Know—Control the processes and tools used to track, control, prevent, and correct secure access to critical assets (e.g., information, resources, systems) according to the formal determination of which persons, computers, and applications have a need and right to access these critical assets based on an approved classification.*

16. *Account Monitoring and Control [...].*

17. *Data Protection [...].*

18. *Incident Response and Management [...].*

19. *Secure Network Engineering [...].*

20. *Penetration Tests and Red Team Exercises [...].*[5]

Nontechnical Aspects of Implementation

Some aspects of information security implementation are not technical in nature, but deal instead with the human interface to technical systems. The sections that follow discuss the topic of creating a culture of change management and considerations for organizations facing change.

❯ The Culture of Change Management

The prospect of change, the familiar shifting to the unfamiliar, can cause employees to resist the change, either unconsciously or consciously. Regardless of whether the changes are perceived as good or bad, employees tend to prefer the old way of doing things. Even when employees embrace changes, the stress of actually making the changes and adjusting to new procedures can increase the probability of mistakes or create vulnerabilities in systems. By understanding and applying some basic tenets of change management, project managers can lower employee resistance to change and can even build resilience for it, thereby making ongoing change more palatable to the entire organization.

The basic foundation of change management requires people who are making the changes to understand that organizations typically have cultures that represent their mood and philosophy. Disruptions to this culture must be properly addressed and their effects minimized. One of the oldest models of change is the Lewin change model,[6] which consists of three simplistic stages:

- Unfreezing: Thawing hard-and-fast habits and established procedures. Preparing the organization for upcoming changes facilitates the implementation of new processes, systems, and procedures. Training and awareness programs assist in this preparation.

- Moving: Transitioning between the old way and the new. The physical implementation of new methods, using the strategies outlined earlier in this chapter, requires the organization to recognize the cessation of old ways of work and reinforces the need to use the new methods.

- Refreezing: The integration of the new methods into the organizational culture, which is accomplished by creating an atmosphere in which the changes are accepted as the preferred way of accomplishing the necessary tasks.

❯ Considerations for Organizational Change

An organization can take steps to make its employees more amenable to change. These steps reduce resistance to change at the beginning of the planning process and encourage members of the organization to be more flexible as changes occur.

Reducing Resistance to Change from the Start The level of resistance to change affects the ease with which an organization can implement procedural and managerial changes. The more ingrained the existing methods and behaviors are, the more difficult it will probably be to make the change. It's best, therefore, to improve interactions between the affected members of the organization and project planners in the early phases of an information security improvement project. These interactions can be improved through a three-step process in which project managers communicate, educate, and involve.

Communication is the first and most critical step. Project managers must communicate with employees so they know a new security process is being considered and that their feedback is essential to making it work. You must also constantly update employees on the progress of the project's changes and provide information on the expected completion dates. This ongoing series of updates keeps the process from being a last-minute surprise and primes people to accept the change more readily when it finally arrives.

At the same time, you must update and educate employees about exactly how the proposed changes will affect them individually and within the organization. While detailed information may not be available in earlier stages of a project plan, details that can be shared with employees may emerge as the project progresses. Education also involves teaching employees to use the new systems once they are in place. As discussed earlier, this means delivering high-quality training programs at the appropriate times.

Finally, project managers can reduce resistance to change by involving employees in the project plan. This means getting key representatives from user groups to serve as members of the project development process. In systems development, this process is referred to as *joint application development*, or JAD. Identifying a liaison between IT and information security implementers and the organization's general population can serve the project team well in early planning stages, when unforeseen problems with acceptance of the project may need to be addressed.

Developing a Culture That Supports Change An ideal organization fosters resilience to change. This means the organization understands that change is a necessary part of the culture, and that embracing change is more productive than fighting it. To develop such a culture, the organization must successfully accomplish many projects that require change. A resilient culture can be either cultivated or undermined by management's approach. Strong management support for change, with a clear executive-level champion, enables the organization to recognize the necessity for change and its strategic importance. Weak management support, with overly delegated responsibility and no champion, sentences the project to almost certain failure. In such a case, employees sense the low priority assigned to the project and do not communicate with the development team because the effort seems useless.

 For a sample change management and control policy template, visit the ISO27001security.com Web page at www.iso27001security.com/ISO27k_Model_policy_on_change_management _and_control.docx.

Information Systems Security Certification and Accreditation

> ## Key Terms
>
> **accreditation** The process that authorizes an IT system to process, store, or transmit information.
> **certification** In information security, the comprehensive evaluation of an IT system's technical and nontechnical security controls that establishes the extent to which a particular design and implementation meets a set of predefined security requirements, usually in support of an accreditation process.

At first glance, it may seem that only systems for handling secret government data require security certification or accreditation. However, organizations are increasingly finding that their systems need to have formal mechanisms for verification and validation in order to comply with recent federal regulations that protect personal privacy.

10

> Certification Versus Accreditation

In security management, **accreditation** is what authorizes an IT system to process, store, or transmit information. It is issued by a management official and is a means of assuring that systems are of adequate quality. It also challenges managers and technical staff to find the best methods to assure security, given technical constraints, operational constraints, and mission requirements. In the same vein, **certification** is the evaluation of an IT system's security controls to support the accreditation process. Organizations pursue accreditation or certification to gain a competitive advantage or to provide assurance to their customers. Federal systems require accreditation under OMB Circular A-130 and the Computer Security Act of 1987. Accreditation demonstrates that management has identified an acceptable risk level and provided resources to control unacceptable risk levels.

Certification and accreditation (C&A) are not permanent. Just as standards of due diligence and due care require ongoing maintenance, most C&A processes typically require reaccreditation or recertification every three to five years.

❯ The NIST Security Life Cycle Approach

Two documents provide guidance for the certification and accreditation of U.S. information systems: SP 800-37, Rev. 1, *Guide for Applying the Risk Management Framework to Federal Information Systems: A Security Life Cycle Approach*; and CNSS Instruction-1000: *National Information Assurance Certification and Accreditation Process (NIACAP)*.

Information processed by the U.S. government is grouped into one of three categories: national security information (NSI), non-NSI, and the intelligence community. National security information is processed on national security systems (NSSs), which are managed and operated by the Committee on National Security Systems (CNSS). Non-NSSs are managed and operated by the National Institute of Standards and Technology (NIST). Intelligence community information is a separate category and is handled according to guidance from the office of the Director of National Intelligence.

An NSS is defined as any information system, including any telecommunications system, used or operated by an agency, a contractor of any agency, or other organization on behalf of an agency, that has the following characteristics:

- Involves intelligence activities
- Involves cryptologic activities related to national security
- Involves command and control of military forces
- Involves equipment that is an integral part of a weapon or weapon system
- Is subject to subparagraph (B) of the Federal Information Security Management Act of 2002, is critical to the direct fulfillment of military or intelligence missions, or is protected at all times by procedures for information that have been specifically authorized under criteria established by an executive order or an act of Congress to be kept classified in the interest of national defense or foreign policy.

Subparagraph (B) states that this criterion "does not include a system that is to be used for routine administration and business applications (including payroll, finance, logistics, and personnel management applications)."[7]

National security information must be processed on NSSs, which have more stringent requirements. NSSs process a mix of NSI and non-NSI and are accredited using CNSS guidance. Non-NSS systems follow NIST guidance. More than 20 major government agencies store, process, or transmit NSI, and many of them have both NSSs and systems that are not rated as NSSs. You can learn more about the CNSS community and how NSSs are managed and operated at *www.cnss.gov*.

In recent years, the Joint Task Force Transformation Initiative Working Group of the U.S. government and NIST have worked to overhaul the formal C&A program for non-NSI systems. The program has been modified from a separate C&A process into an integrated Risk Management Framework (RMF), which can be used for normal operations and still provide assurance that the systems are capable of reliably housing confidential information. NIST SP 800-37, Rev. 1, provides a detailed description of the new RMF process. The following section is adapted from this document.

> *The revised process emphasizes: (i) building information security capabilities into federal information systems through the application of state-of-the-practice*

management, operational, and technical security controls; (ii) maintaining aware-
ness of the security state of information systems on an ongoing basis through
enhanced monitoring processes; and (iii) providing essential information to senior
leaders to facilitate decisions regarding the acceptance of risk to organizational
operations and assets, individuals, other organizations, and the nation arising
from the operation and use of information systems.

... The risk management process described in this publication changes the tradi-
tional focus of C&A as a static, procedural activity to a more dynamic approach
that provides the capability to more effectively manage information system-related
security risks in highly diverse environments of complex and sophisticated cyber
threats, ever-increasing system vulnerabilities, and rapidly changing missions.

... The guidelines in SP 800-37, Rev. 1 are applicable to all federal information
systems other than those systems designated as national security systems as
defined in 44 U.S.C., Section 3542.[8]

Risk management is the subject of Chapter 5, but because the U.S. government is replacing
the old C&A process with a formal RMF, that framework is briefly described here. As the
reference for its RMF, SP 800-37, Rev. 1 specifically refers to NIST SP 800-39, a new publication titled *Integrated Enterprise-Wide Risk Management: Organization, Mission and Infor-*
mation Systems View. The NIST RMF builds on a three-tiered approach to risk management
that addresses risk-related concerns at the organization level, the mission and business process level, and the information system level, as illustrated in Figure 10-4.

Tier 1 addresses risk from an organizational perspective with the development of
a comprehensive governance structure and organization-wide risk management
strategy ...

Tier 2 addresses risk from a mission and business process perspective and is
guided by the risk decisions at Tier 1. Tier 2 activities are closely associated
with enterprise architecture ...

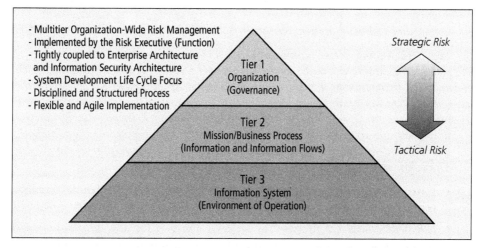

Figure 10-4 Tiered Risk Management Framework

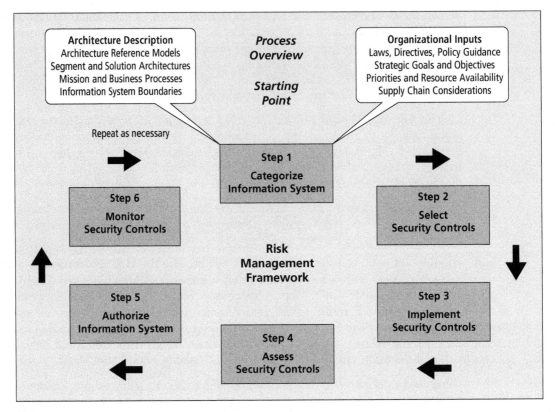

Figure 10-5 Risk Management Framework

Tier 3 addresses risk from an information system perspective and is guided by the risk decisions at Tiers 1 and 2. Risk decisions at Tiers 1 and 2 impact the ultimate selection and deployment of needed safeguards and countermeasures (i.e., security controls) at the information system level. Information security requirements are satisfied by the selection of appropriate management, operational, and technical security controls from NIST Special Publication 800-53.

The Risk Management Framework (RMF), which is illustrated in Figure 10-5, provides a disciplined and structured process that integrates information security and risk management activities into the system development life cycle. The RMF operates primarily at Tier 3 in the risk management hierarchy but can also have interactions at Tiers 1 and 2 (e.g., providing feedback from ongoing authorization decisions to the risk executive [function], dissemination of updated threat and risk information to authorizing officials and information system owners). The RMF steps include:

- *Categorize the information system and the information processed, stored, and transmitted by that system based on an impact analysis.*

- *Select an initial set of baseline security controls for the information system based on the security categorization; tailoring and supplementing the security control baseline as needed based on an organizational assessment of risk and local conditions.*

- *Implement the security controls and describe how the controls are employed within the information system and its environment of operation.*

- *Assess the security controls using appropriate assessment procedures to determine the extent to which the controls are implemented correctly, operating as intended, and producing the desired outcome with respect to meeting the security requirements for the system.*

- *Authorize information system operation based on a determination of the risk to organizational operations and assets, individuals, other organizations, and the nation resulting from the operation of the information system and the decision that this risk is acceptable.*

- *Monitor the security controls in the information system on an ongoing basis, including assessing control effectiveness, documenting changes to the system or its environment of operation, conducting security impact analyses of the associated changes, and reporting the security state of the system to designated organizational officials.*[9]

With regard to using the RMF:

The organization has significant flexibility in deciding which families of security controls or specific controls from selected families in NIST Special Publication 800-53 are appropriate for the different types of allocations. Since the security control allocation process involves the assignment and provision of security capabilities derived from security controls, the organization ensures that there is effective communication among all entities either receiving or providing such capabilities. This communication includes, for example, ensuring that common control authorization results and continuous monitoring information are readily available to those organizational entities inheriting common controls, and that any changes to common controls are effectively communicated to those affected by such changes. [Figure 10-6] illustrates security control allocation within an organization and using the RMF to produce information for senior leaders (including authorizing officials) on the ongoing security state of organizational information systems and the missions and business processes supported by those systems.[10]

Chapter 3 of SP 800-37, Rev. 1, provides detailed guidance for implementing the RMF, including information on primary responsibility, supporting roles, the system development life cycle phase, supplemental guidance, and references. An overview of the tasks involved is shown in Table 10-2.

Why is it important that you know this information? Your organization may someday want to become a government contractor, if it isn't already. These guidelines apply to all systems that connect to U.S. government entities not identified as national security systems or as containing national security information.

 For more information on these and related NIST Special Publications, visit the CSRC Web Site at http://csrc.nist.gov/publications/PubsSPs.html.

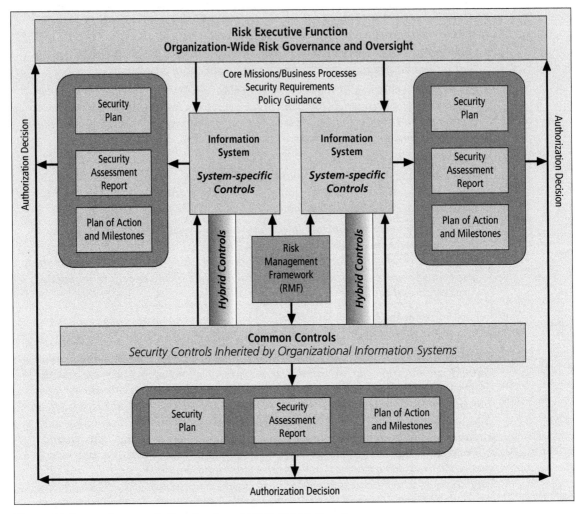

Figure 10-6 Security control allocation from NIST SP 800-37, Rev. 1

› NSTISS Certification and Accreditation

National security interest systems have their own security C&A standards, which also follow the guidance of OMB Circular A-130. CNSS, formerly known as the National Security Telecommunications and Information Systems Security Committee (NSTISSC), has a C&A document titled *NSTISS Instruction 1000: National Information Assurance Certification and Accreditation Process (NIACAP)*. The following section contains excerpts from this document and provides an overview of the purpose and process of this C&A program.

RMF Step 1—Categorize Information System

1-1 (Security Categorization): Categorize the information system and document the results of the security categorization in the security plan.

1-2 (Information System Description): Describe the information system, including the system boundary, and document the description in the security plan.

1-3 (Information System Registration): Register the information system with appropriate organizational program/management offices.

Milestone Checkpoint for RMF Step 1:

- Has the organization completed a security categorization of the information system, including the information to be processed, stored, and transmitted by the system?
- Are the results of the security categorization process for the information system consistent with the organization's enterprise architecture and commitment to protecting organizational mission/business processes?
- Do the results of the security categorization process reflect the organization's risk management strategy? Has the organization adequately described the characteristics of the information system?
- Has the organization registered the information system for purposes of management, accountability, coordination, and oversight?

RMF Step 2—Select Security Controls

2-1 (Common Control Identification): Identify the security controls provided by the organization as common controls for organizational information systems and document the controls in a security plan or equivalent document.

2-2 (Security Control Selection): Select the security controls for the information system and document the controls in the security plan.

2-3 (Monitoring Strategy): Develop a strategy for the continuous monitoring of security control effectiveness and any proposed or actual changes to the information system and its environment of operation.

2-4 (Security Plan Approval): Review and approve the security plan.

Milestone Checkpoint for RMF Step 2:

- Has the organization allocated all security controls to the information system as system-specific, hybrid, or common controls?
- Has the organization used its formal or informal risk assessment to inform and guide the security control selection process?
- Has the organization identified authorizing officials for the information system and all common controls inherited by the system?
- Has the organization tailored and supplemented the baseline security controls to ensure that the controls, if implemented, adequately mitigate risks to the organization's operations and assets, individual employees, other organizations, and the nation?
- Has the organization addressed minimum assurance requirements for the security controls employed within the information system and inherited by it?
- Has the organization consulted information system owners when identifying common controls to ensure that the security capability provided by the inherited controls is sufficient to deliver adequate protection?
- Has the organization supplemented the common controls with system-specific or hybrid controls when the security baselines of the common controls are less than those of the information system inheriting the controls?
- Has the organization documented the common controls inherited from external providers?
- Has the organization developed a continuous monitoring strategy for the information system, including monitoring of security control effectiveness for system-specific, hybrid, and common controls, that reflects the organization's risk management strategy and commitment to protecting critical missions and business functions?
- Have appropriate organizational officials approved security plans containing system-specific, hybrid, and common controls?

RMF Step 3—Implement Security Controls

3-1 (Security Control Implementation): Implement the security controls specified in the security plan.

3-2 (Security Control Documentation): Document the security control implementation as appropriate in the security plan; provide a functional description of the control implementation, including planned inputs, expected behavior, and expected outputs.

Table 10-2 Executing the Risk Management Framework Tasks *(continues)*

Milestone Checkpoint for RMF Step 3:

- Has the organization allocated security controls as system-specific, hybrid, or common controls consistent with the enterprise architecture and information security architecture?
- Has the organization demonstrated the use of sound information system and security engineering methodologies in integrating information technology products into the information system and in implementing the security controls contained in the security plan?
- Has the organization documented how common controls inherited by organizational information systems have been implemented?
- Has the organization documented how system-specific and hybrid security controls have been implemented within the information system, taking into account specific technologies and platform dependencies?
- Has the organization taken into account the minimum assurance requirements when implementing security controls?

RMF Step 4—Assess Security Controls

4-1 (Assessment Preparation): Develop, review, and approve a plan to assess the security controls.

4-2 (Security Control Assessment): Assess the security controls in accordance with the assessment procedures defined in the security assessment plan.

4-3 (Security Assessment Report): Prepare the security assessment report, which documents the issues, findings, and recommendations from the security control assessment.

4-4 (Remediation Actions): Conduct initial remediation actions on security controls based on the findings and recommendations of the security assessment report and reassess remediated control(s), as appropriate.

Milestone Checkpoint for RMF Step 4:

- Has the organization developed a comprehensive plan to assess the security controls employed within the information system or inherited by it?
- Was the assessment plan reviewed and approved by appropriate organizational officials?
- Has the organization considered the appropriate level of assessor independence for the security control assessment?
- Has the organization provided all of the essential supporting materials needed by the assessor(s) to conduct an effective security control assessment?
- Has the organization examined opportunities for reusing assessment results from previous assessments or from other sources?
- Did the assessor(s) complete the security control assessment in accordance with the stated assessment plan? Did the organization receive the completed security assessment report with appropriate findings and recommendations from the assessor(s)?
- Did the organization take the necessary remediation actions to address the most important weaknesses and deficiencies in the information system and its environment of operation, based on the findings and recommendations in the security assessment report?
- Did the organization update appropriate security plans based on the findings and recommendations in the security assessment report and any subsequent changes to the information system and its environment of operation?

RMF Step 5—Authorize Information System

5-1 (Plan of Action and Milestones): Prepare the plan of action and milestones based on the findings and recommendations of the security assessment report, excluding any remediation actions taken.

5-2 (Security Authorization Package): Assemble the security authorization package and submit it to the authorizing official for adjudication.

5-3 (Risk Determination): Determine the risk to the organization's operations (including mission, functions, image, or reputation), organizational assets, individual employees, other organizations, or the nation.

5-4 (Risk Acceptance): Determine if the risk to the organization's operations, organizational assets, individual employees, other organizations, or the nation is acceptable.

Table 10-2   Executing the Risk Management Framework Tasks (*continued*)

Source: NIST SP 800-37, Rev. 1.

1. The document establishes the minimum national standards for certifying and accrediting national security systems. This process provides a standard set of activities, general tasks, and a management structure to certify and accredit systems that will maintain the information assurance (IA) and security posture of a system or site. This process focuses on an enterprise-wide view of the information system (IS) in relation to the organization's mission and the IS business case.

2. The NIACAP is designed to certify that the IS meets documented accreditation requirements and will continue to maintain the accredited security posture throughout the system life cycle.

The key to the NIACAP is the agreement between the IS program manager, designated approving authority (DAA), certification agent (certifier), and user representative. These parties resolve critical schedule, budget, security, functionality, and performance issues.

The NIACAP agreements are documented in the system security authorization agreement (SSAA), which is used to guide and document the results of the C&A process. The objective is to use the SSAA to establish an evolving yet binding agreement on the level of security required before system development begins or changes are made to a system. After accreditation, the SSAA becomes the baseline security configuration document.

The minimum NIACAP roles include the program manager, DAA, certifier, and user representative. Additional roles may be added to increase the integrity and objectivity of C&A decisions. For example, the information systems security officer (ISSO) usually performs a key role in maintaining the security posture after accreditation and may also play a key role in the system C&A.

The SSAA:

- Describes the operating environment and threat
- Describes the system security architecture
- Establishes the C&A boundary of the system to be accredited
- Documents the formal agreement among the DAA(s), certifier, program manager, and user representative
- Documents all requirements necessary for accreditation
- Minimizes documentation requirements by consolidating applicable information into the SSAA; this information includes the security policy, concept of operations, architecture description, and test procedures
- Documents the NIACAP plan
- Documents test plans and procedures, certification results, and residual risk
- Forms the baseline security configuration document

The NIACAP is composed of four phases, as shown from several perspectives in Figures 10-7 to 10-11. These phases are definition, verification, validation, and post accreditation.

Phase 1, definition, determines the necessary security measures and effort level to achieve certification and accreditation. The objective of Phase 1 is to agree on the security requirements, C&A boundary, schedule, level of effort, and resources required.

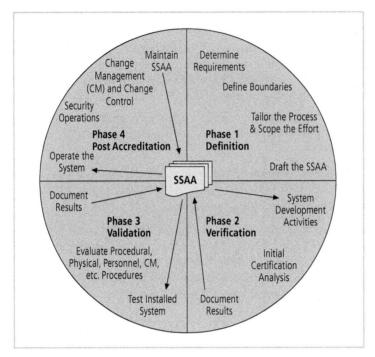

Figure 10-7 Overview of the NIACAP process

Source: NSTISSI-1000.

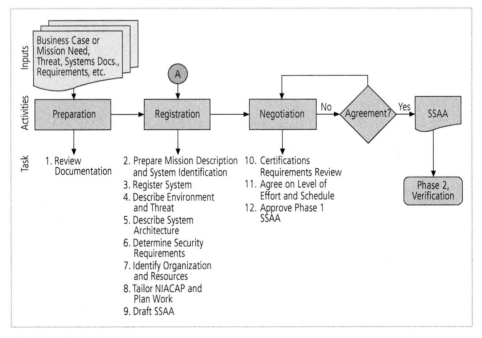

Figure 10-8 NIACAP Phase 1, Definition

Source: NSTISSI-1000.

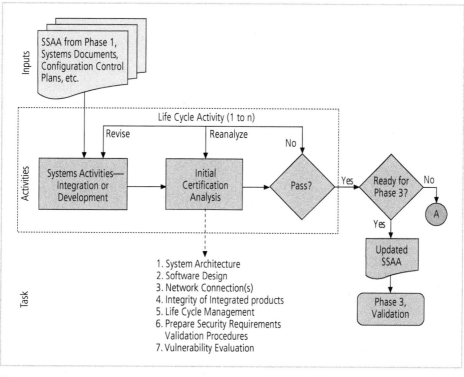

Figure 10-9 NIACAP Phase 2, Verification

Source: NSTISSI-1000.

10

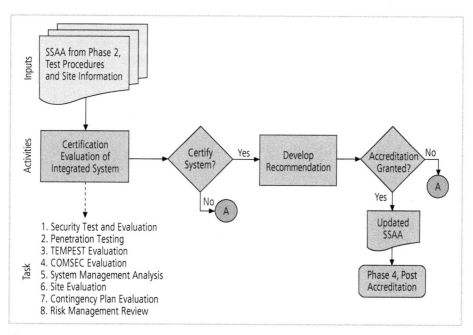

Figure 10-10 NIACAP Phase 3, Validation

Source: NSTISSI-1000.

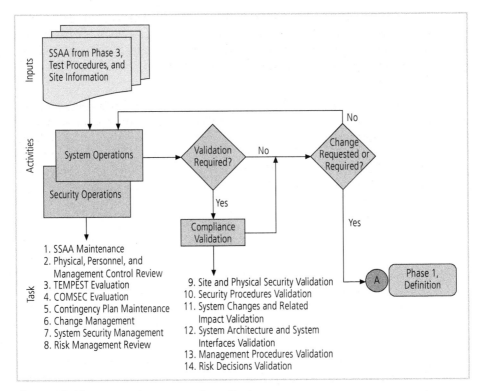

Figure 10-11 NIACAP Phase 4, Post Accreditation

Source: NSTISSI-1000.

Phase 2, verification, verifies the evolving or modified system's compliance with the information in the SSAA. The objective of Phase 2 is to ensure that the fully integrated system is ready for certification testing.

Phase 3, validation, validates compliance of the fully integrated system with the security policy and requirements stated in the SSAA. The objective of Phase 3 is to produce the required evidence to support the DAA in making an informed decision to grant approval to operate the system. This approval is either accreditation or an interim approval to operate (IATO).

 For more information on the NIACAP process, visit the FISMA Web site at www.fismacenter.com /nstissi_1000.pdf.

Phase 4, post accreditation, starts after the system has been certified and accredited for operations. Phase 4 includes activities necessary for the continuing operation of the accredited IS and manages the changing threats and small-scale changes a system faces through its life cycle. The objective of Phase 4 is to ensure that secure system management, operation, and maintenance sustain an acceptable level of residual risk.

The accreditation process itself is so complex that professional certifiers must be trained. The CNSS has a set of training standards for federal information technology workers who deal with information security. One of these documents, NSTISSI-4015, provides a national training standard for systems certifiers (see *www.ecs.csus.edu/csc /iac/nstissi_4015.pdf*).

A qualified systems certifier must be formally trained in the fundamentals of information security and have field experience. Systems certifiers should have system administrator and/ or basic ISSO experience, and be familiar with the knowledge, skills, and abilities required of the DAA, as illustrated in NSTISSI-4015. Once professionals complete training based on NSTISSI-4015, which includes material from NSTISSI-1000, they are eligible to be a federal agency systems certifier. Note that NSTISSI-1000 is currently under revision; an updated version could be available within the next few years.

> ISO 27001/27002 Systems Certification and Accreditation

Many larger organizations outside the United States apply the standards provided under the International Standards Organization, standards ISO 27001 and 27002, as discussed in Chapter 4. Recall that the standards were originally created to provide a foundation for British certification of information security management systems (ISMSs). Organizations that want to demonstrate their systems have met this international standard must follow the certification process, which includes the following phases:

> *The first phase of the process involves your company preparing and getting ready for the certification of your ISMS: developing and implementing your ISMS, using and integrating your ISMS into your day-to-day business processes, training your staff, and establishing an ongoing program of ISMS maintenance.*

> *The second phase involves employing one of the accredited certification bodies to carry out an audit of your ISMS.*

> *The certificate that is awarded will last for three years, after which the ISMS needs to be recertified. Therefore, there is a third phase of the process (assuming the certification has been successful and a certificate has been issued), which involves the certification body visiting your ISMS site on a regular basis (e.g., every 6–9 months) to carry out a surveillance audit.*[11]

Figure 10-12 shows the process flow of ISMS certification and accreditation.

10

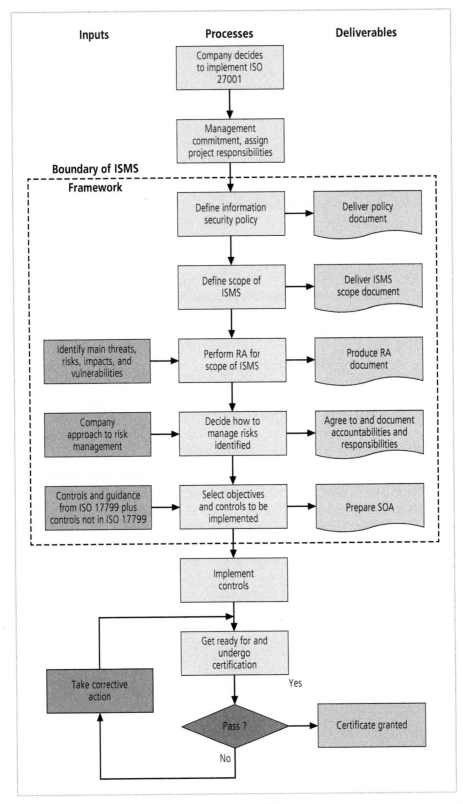

Figure 10-12 ISMS certification and accreditation[12]

Selected Readings

- *Information Technology Project Management*, Fifth Edition, by Kathy Schwalbe. Course Technology. 2007. Boston.
- *The PMI Project Management Fact Book*, Second Edition, by the Project Management Institute. 2001. Newtown Square, PA.
- NIST SP 800-37, Rev. 1, *Guide for Applying the Risk Management Framework to Federal Information Systems: A Security Life Cycle Approach*.
- NIST DRAFT SP 800-39, *Managing Risk from Information Systems: An Organizational Perspective*.

Chapter Summary

- The implementation phase of the security systems development life cycle involves modifying the configuration and operation of the organization's information systems to make them more secure. Such changes include those to procedures, people, hardware, software, and data.

- During the implementation phase, the organization translates its blueprint for information security into a concrete project plan.

- Before developing a project plan, management should articulate and coordinate the organization's information security vision and objectives with the involved communities of interest.

- The major steps in executing the project plan are planning the project, supervising tasks and action steps within the plan, and wrapping up the plan.

- Each organization determines its own project management methodology for IT and information security projects. Whenever possible, an organization's information security projects should be in line with its project management practices.

- Planning for the implementation phase involves the creation of a detailed project plan. The project plan can be created by using a simple planning tool such as the work breakdown structure (WBS). The plan can be prepared with a simple desktop PC spreadsheet program or with more complex project management software. The WBS involves addressing major project tasks and their related attributes, including the following:

  - Work to be accomplished (activities and deliverables)
  - Individual employees or skill sets assigned to perform the task
  - Start and end dates for the task, when known
  - Amount of effort required for completion, in hours or days
  - Estimated capital expenses for the task
  - Estimated noncapital expenses for the task
  - Identification of task interdependencies

10

- Constraints and considerations should be addressed when developing the project plan, including financial, procurement, priority, time and scheduling, staffing, scope, organizational feasibility, training and indoctrination, change control, and technology governance considerations.

- Organizations usually designate a professional project manager to lead a security information project. Alternatively, some organizations designate a champion from a senior level of general management or a senior IT manager, such as the CIO.

- Once a project is under way, it can be managed to completion using a process known as a negative feedback loop or cybernetic loop. This process involves measuring variances from the project plan and then taking corrective action when needed.

- As the components of the new security system are planned, provisions must be made for the changeover from the previous method of performing a task to the new method(s). The four common conversion strategies for performing this changeover are:

  - Direct changeover

  - Phased implementation

  - Pilot implementation

  - Parallel operations

- The bull's-eye model is a proven method for prioritizing a program of complex change. Using this method, the project manager can address issues from the general to the specific and focus on systematic solutions instead of individual problems.

- When the expense and time required to develop an effective information security program is beyond the reach of an organization, it should outsource the program to competent professional services.

- Technology governance is a complex process that an organization uses to manage the impacts and costs of technology implementation, innovation, and obsolescence.

- The change control process is a method that medium-sized and large organizations use to deal with the impact of technical change on their operations.

- As with any project, certain aspects of change must be addressed. In any major project, the prospect of moving from the familiar to the unfamiliar can cause employees to resist change, consciously or unconsciously.

- Implementing and securing information systems often requires external certification or accreditation.

- Accreditation is the authorization of an IT system to process, store, or transmit information. This authorization is issued by a management official to assure that systems are of adequate quality.

- Certification is a comprehensive evaluation of an IT system's technical and nontechnical security controls to validate an accreditation process.

- A variety of accreditation and certification processes are used globally, including the U.S. federal agency system and the ISO 27001 and 27002 standards.

Review Questions

1. What is a project plan? List what a project plan can accomplish.

2. What is the value of a statement of vision and objectives? Why is it needed before a project plan is developed?

3. What categories of constraints to project plan implementation are noted in the chapter? Explain each of them.

4. List and describe the three major steps in executing the project plan.

5. What is a work breakdown structure (WBS)? Is it the only way to organize a project plan?

6. What is projectitis? How is it cured or its impact minimized?

7. List and define the common attributes of tasks within a WBS.

8. How does a planner know when a task has been subdivided to an adequate degree and can be classified as an action step?

9. What is a deliverable? Name two uses for deliverables.

10. What is a resource? What are the two types?

11. Why is it a good practice to delay naming specific people as resources early in the planning process?

12. What is a milestone, and why is it significant to project planning?

13. Why is it good practice to assign start and end dates sparingly in the early stages of project planning?

14. Who is the best judge of effort estimates for project tasks and action steps? Why?

15. Within project management, what is a dependency? What is a predecessor? What is a successor?

16. What is a negative feedback loop? How is it used to keep a project in control?

17. When a task is not being completed according to the plan, what two circumstances are likely to be involved?

18. List and describe the four basic conversion strategies that are used when converting to a new system. Under which circumstances is each strategy the best approach?

19. What is technology governance? What is change control? How are they related?

20. What are certification and accreditation when applied to information systems security management? List and describe at least two certification or accreditation processes.

10

Exercises

1. Create a first draft of a WBS from the following scenario. Make assumptions as needed based on the section about project planning considerations and constraints in this chapter. In your WBS, describe the skill sets required for the tasks you have planned.

    Sequential Label and Supply has a problem with employees surfing the Web to access material the company deems inappropriate for a professional environment. Therefore, SLS wants to insert a filtering device in the company Internet connection that blocks certain Web locations and content. According to the vendor, the filter is a hardware appliance that costs $18,000 and requires 150 hours to install and configure. Technical support for the filter costs 18 percent of the purchase price and includes a training allowance for the year. A software component that runs on the administrator's desktop computer is needed to administer the filter; this component costs $550. A monthly subscription provides the list of sites to be blocked and costs $250 per month. An estimated four hours per week are required for administrative functions.

2. If you have access to commercial project management software, such as Microsoft Project, use it to complete a project plan based on the data shown in Table 10-2. Prepare a simple WBS report or Gantt chart that shows your work.

3. Write a job description for Kelvin Urich, the project manager described in the opening vignette of this chapter. Be sure to identify key characteristics of the ideal candidate, as well as work experience and educational background. Also, justify why your job description is suitable for potential candidates of this position.

4. Search the Web for job descriptions of project managers. You can use any number of Web sites, including *www.monster.com* or *www.dice.com*, to find at least 10 IT-related job descriptions. What common elements do you find among the job descriptions? What is the most unusual characteristic among them?

Case Exercises

Charlie looked across his desk at Kelvin, who was absorbed in the sheaf of handwritten notes from the meeting. Charlie had asked Kelvin to come to his office and discuss the change control meeting from earlier that day.

"So what do you think?" Charlie asked.

"I think I was blindsided by a bus!" Kelvin replied. "I thought I had considered all the possible effects of the change in my project plan. I tried to explain this, but everyone acted as if I had threatened their lives."

"In a way you did, or rather you threatened their jobs," Charlie stated. "Some people believe that change is the enemy."

"But these changes are important."

"I agree," Charlie said. "But successful change usually occurs in small steps. What's your top priority?"

"All the items on this list are top priorities," Kelvin said. "I haven't even gotten to the second tier."

"So what should you do to accomplish these top priorities?" Charlie asked.

"I guess I should reprioritize within my top tier, but what then?"

"The next step is to build support before the meeting, not during it," Charlie said, smiling. "Never go into a meeting where you haven't done your homework, especially when other people in the meeting can reduce your chance of success."

Discussion Questions

1. What project management tasks should Kelvin perform before his next meeting?

2. What change management tasks should Kelvin perform before his next meeting, and how do these tasks fit within the project management process?

3. Had you been in Kelvin's place, what would you have done differently to prepare for this meeting?

Ethical Decision Making

Suppose Kelvin has seven controls listed as the top tier of project initiatives. At his next meeting with Charlie, he provides a rank-ordered list of these controls with projected losses over the next 10 years for each if it is not completed. Also, he has estimated the 10-year cost for developing, implementing, and operating each control. Kelvin has identified three controls as being the most advantageous for the organization *in his opinion*. As he prepared the slides for the meeting, he "adjusted" most projected losses upward to the top end of the range estimate given by the consultant who prepared the data. For the projected costs of his preferred controls, he chose to use the lowest end of the range provided by the consultant.

Do you think Kelvin has had an ethical lapse by cherry-picking the data for his presentation?

Suppose that instead of choosing data from the range provided by the consultant, Kelvin simply made up better numbers for his favorite initiatives. Is this an ethical lapse?

Suppose Kelvin has a close friend who works for a firm that makes and sells software for a specific control objective on the list. When Kelvin prioritized the list of his preferences, he made sure that specific control was at the top of the list. Kelvin planned to provide his friend with internal design specifications and the assessment criteria to be used for vendor selection for the initiative. Has Kelvin committed an ethical lapse?

Endnotes

1. The SANS Institute. "GIAC Certified Project Manager (GCPM)." Accessed 30 August 2016 from *www.giac.org/certification/certified-project-manager-gcpm*.

2. Ibid.

3. EC-Council. Project Management in IT Security Exam Information. Accessed 30 August 2016 from *www.ecccoe.com/images/download/brochure/PM-2015.pdf*.

4. "CIS Controls for Effective Cyber Defense Download." Version 6.0. Accessed 30 August 2016 from *www.cisecurity.org/critical-controls*.

5. Ibid.

6. Schein, Edgar H. "Kurt Lewin's Change Theory in the Field and in the Classroom: Notes Toward a Model of Managed Learning." Working paper, MIT Sloan School of Management. Accessed 30 August 2016 from *http://link.springer.com/article/10.1007/BF02173417*.

7. Federal Information Security Management Act of 2002. Title 44, U.S. Code Section 3542.

8. National Institute of Standards and Technology. Joint Task Force Transformation Initiative. *Guide for Applying the Risk Management Framework to Federal Information Systems: A Security Life Cycle Approach*. SP 800-37, Rev. 1. February 2010. Accessed 30 August 2016 from *http://csrc.nist.gov/publications/PubsSPs.html*.

9. Ibid.

10. Ibid.

11. Ibid.

12. The ISO 27000 Directory ISO 27001 Certification Process. Accessed 30 August 2016 from *www.iso27001certificates.com/certification_directory.htm*.

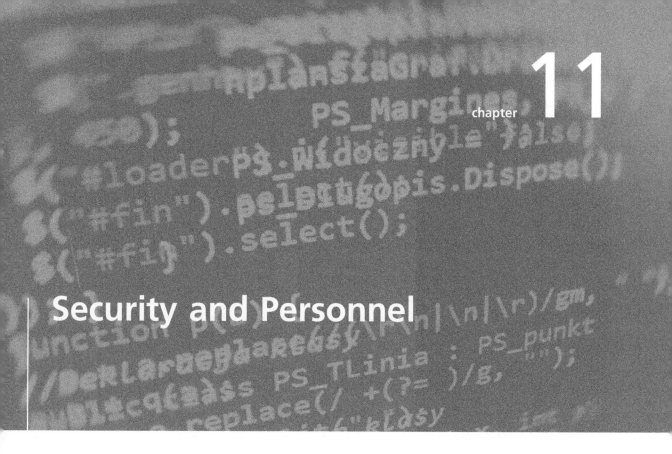

chapter 11

Security and Personnel

I think we need to be paranoid optimists.

ROBERT J. EATON, CHAIRMAN OF THE BOARD OF
MANAGEMENT, DAIMLERCHRYSLER AG (RETIRED)

Among Iris Majwubu's morning e-mails was a message from Charlie Moody, with the subject line "I need to see you." As she opened the message, Iris wondered why on earth the company CISO needed to see her. The e-mail read:

From: Charles Moody [cmoody@slsco.com]

To: Iris Majwubu [imajwubu@slsco.com]

Subject: I need to see you

Iris,

Since you were a material witness in the investigation, I wanted to advise you of the status of the Magruder case. We completed all of the personnel actions on this matter yesterday, and it is now behind us.

I wanted to thank you for the key role you played in helping the Corporate Security Department resolve this security matter in its early stages, so no company assets were compromised.

Please set up an appointment with me in the next few days to discuss a few things.

—Charlie

Two days later, Iris entered Charlie Moody's office. He rose from his desk as she entered.

"Come in, Iris," Charlie said. "Have a seat."

Nervously, she chose a chair closest to the door, not anticipating that Charlie would come around his desk and sit down next to her. As he took his seat, Iris noticed that the folder in his hand looked like her personnel file. She took a deep breath, unsure exactly why Charlie had her file.

"I'm sure you're wondering why I asked you to meet with me," said Charlie. "The company really appreciates your efforts in the Magruder case. Because you followed policy and acted so quickly, we avoided a significant loss. You were right to bring that issue to your manager's attention rather than confronting Magruder directly. You not only made the right choice, but you acted quickly and showed a positive attitude throughout the whole situation—basically, I think you demonstrated an information security mindset. And that's why I'd like to offer you a transfer to Kelvin Urich's security projects team. I think they would really benefit from having someone like you on board."

"I'm glad I was able to help," Iris said, "but I'm not sure what to say. I've been a DBA for three years here. I really don't know much about information security other than what I learned from the company training and awareness sessions."

"That's not a problem," Charlie said. "What you don't know you can learn." He smiled.

"So how about it, are you interested in the job?"

Iris said, "It does sound interesting, but to be honest I hadn't been considering a career change." She paused for a moment, then added, "I am willing to think about it, though. But I have a few questions...."

LEARNING OBJECTIVES

Upon completion of this material, you should be able to:

- Describe where and how the information security function should be positioned within organizations
- Explain the issues and concerns related to staffing the information security function
- List and describe the credentials that information security professionals can earn to gain recognition in the field
- Discuss how an organization's employment policies and practices can support the information security effort
- Identify the special security precautions that must be taken when using contract workers
- Explain the need for the separation of duties
- Describe the special requirements needed to ensure the privacy of personnel data

Introduction

When implementing information security, an organization must first address how to position and label the security function. Second, the information security community of interest must plan for the function's proper staffing or for adjustments to the staffing plan. Third, the IT community of interest must assess the impact of information security on every IT function and adjust job descriptions and documented practices accordingly. Finally, the general management community of interest must work with information security professionals to integrate solid information security concepts into the organization's personnel management practices.

To assess the effect that the changes will have on the organization's personnel management practices, the organization should conduct a behavioral feasibility study *before* the program is implemented—that is, during the planning phase. The study should include an investigation into the levels of employee acceptance of change and resistance to it. Employees often feel threatened when an organization is creating or enhancing an information security program. They may perceive the program to be a manifestation of a Big Brother attitude, and might have questions such as:

- Will management be monitoring my work or my e-mail?
- Will information security staff go through my hard drive looking for evidence to fire me?
- Will the information security changes affect how efficient and effective I am in my job?

As you learned in Chapter 10, resolving these sorts of doubts and reassuring employees about the role of information security programs are fundamental objectives of implementation. Thus, it is important to gather employee feedback early and respond to it quickly. This chapter explores the issues involved in positioning the information security unit within the organization and in staffing the information security function. The chapter also discusses how to manage the many personnel challenges that arise across the organization and demonstrates why these challenges should be considered part of the organization's overall information security program.

Positioning and Staffing the Security Function

There are several valid choices for positioning the Information Security department within an organization. The model commonly used by large organizations places the information security department within the Information Technology department and usually designates a CISO (chief information security officer) or CSO (chief security officer) to lead the function. The CISO most commonly reports directly to the company's top computing executive, the CIO or vice president for IT. Such a structure implies that the goals and objectives of the CISO and CIO are aligned, but this is not always the case. By its very nature, an information security program can sometimes work at odds with the goals and objectives of the Information Technology department as a whole. The CIO, as the executive in charge of the organization's technology, strives for *efficiency* in the availability, processing, and accessing of company information. Thus, anything that limits access or slows information processing can impede the CIO's mission.

The CISO's function is more like that of an internal auditor in that the CISO must direct the Information Security department to examine data in transmission and storage to detect suspicious traffic, and examine systems to discover information security faults and flaws in technology, software, and employees' activities and processes. These examinations can affect the speed at which the organization's information is processed and accessed. Because the addition of multiple layers of security inevitably slows users' access to information, information security may be viewed by some employees as a hindrance to the organization's operations. A good information security program maintains a careful balance between access and security, and works to educate all employees about the need for necessary delays to ensure the protection of critical information.

Because the goals and objectives of CIOs and CISOs tend to contradict each other, the trend among many organizations has been to separate the information security function from the IT division. An article in the IT industry magazine *Information Week* summarized the reasoning behind this trend quite succinctly: "The people who do and the people who watch shouldn't report to a common manager."[1] This sentiment was echoed in an ISO 27001 posting: "One of the most important things in information security is to avoid conflict of interest; that is, to separate the operations from control and audit."[2]

A survey conducted by the consulting firm Meta Group found that while only 3 percent of its clients position the Information Security department outside IT, these clients regarded such positioning as the mark of a forward-thinking organization. Another group, Forrester Research, concludes that the traditional structure of the CISO or CSO reporting to the CIO will be prevalent for years to come, but that it will begin to involve numerous variations in which different IT sections report information to the CSO, and thereby provide IS departments the critical input and control they need to protect the organization's IT assets.[3] In general, the data seems to suggest that while many organizations believe the CISO or CSO should function as an independent, executive-level decision maker, information security and IT are currently too closely aligned to separate into two departments.

In his book *Information Security Roles and Responsibilities Made Easy*, Charles Cresson Wood compiles the best practices from many industry groups regarding the positioning of information security programs. According to Wood, information security can be placed within any of the following organizational functions:

- IT, as a peer of other subfunctions such as networks, applications development, and the help desk
- Physical security, as a peer of physical security or protective services
- Administrative services, as a peer of human resources or purchasing
- Insurance and risk management
- The legal department

According to the 2015 SEC/CISE Threats to Information Protection Report, which included a current snapshot of the state of the industry, "Of those reporting they were the senior-most executive/manager responsible for security, exactly half (50.0 percent) indicated they reported to a top IT executive (CIO, CTO, VP-IT, etc.), 9.7 percent reported to a senior finance or accounting executive, and 5.6 percent reported to a senior operations executive (COO, CBO, etc.). Interestingly, 5.6 percent reported to some form of legal or regulatory executive (general counsel, VP of regulatory compliance, etc.) and 20.8 percent reported to an undisclosed general executive (VP, director). Of particular note were the 6.9 percent who indicated they reported to a specialized risk management executive (chief risk officer or executive director for risk management)." Only 15.5 percent of survey respondents reported directly to their company's top executive. Also, 45.1 percent had one executive between themselves and the top executive, while approximately 40 percent reported through three or more levels. The distance between these individuals and strategic decision makers is unsettling.[4]

Once the proper position of information security has been determined, the challenge is to design a reporting structure that balances the competing needs of each community of interest. The placement of information security in the reporting structure often reflects the fact that no one actually wants to manage it; thus, the unit is moved from place to place within the organization without regard for the impact on its effectiveness. Organizations should find a rational compromise by placing information security where it can best balance its duty to monitor compliance with its ability to provide the education, training, awareness, and customer service needed to make information security an integral part of the organization's culture. Also, the need to have the top security officer report directly to the executive management group instead of just the CIO becomes critical, especially if the security department is positioned in the IT function.

❭ Staffing the Information Security Function

The selection of information security personnel is based on several criteria, some of which are not within the control of the organization. Consider the fundamental concept of supply and demand. When the demand for any commodity—for example, a critical technical skill—increases too quickly, supply initially fails to meet demand. Many future IS professionals seek to enter the security market by gaining the skills, experience, and credentials they need to meet this demand. In other words, they enter high-demand markets by changing jobs, going to school, or becoming trained. Until the new supply reaches the demand level, organizations must pay the higher costs associated with limited supply. Once the supply meets or exceeds the demand, organizations can become more selective, and the amount they are willing to pay drops. Hiring trends swing back and forth like a pendulum, from high demand and low supply to the other extreme of low demand and high supply, because the economy is seldom in a state of equilibrium. In 2002, the information security industry enjoyed a period of high demand, with relatively few qualified and experienced applicants available for organizations seeking their services. The economic realities of 2003 through 2006—a climate of lower demand for all IT professionals—led to more limited job growth for information security practitioners. From 2008 to 2014, the lackluster performance of the U.S. economy stifled jobs across IT, not just in information security. In the last few years, the demand has begun to increase again.

The latest forecasts for IT hiring in general and information security in particular project more openings than in many previous years. According to the Bureau of Labor Statistics (BLS):

> *Employment of information security analysts is projected to grow 18 percent from 2014 to 2024, much faster than the average for all occupations. Demand for information security analysts is expected to be very high, as these analysts will be needed to create innovative solutions to prevent hackers from stealing critical information or causing problems for computer networks.*[5]

This information is illustrated with additional job outlook data in Figure 11-1.

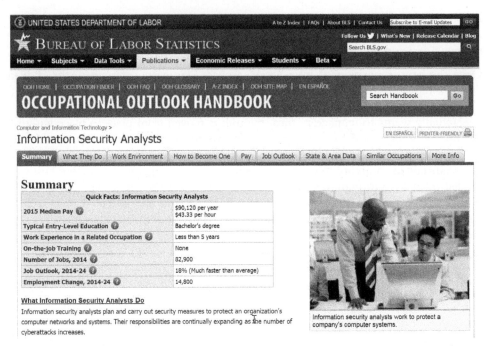

Figure 11-1 BLS job summary for information security analysts

Source: U.S. Bureau of Labor Statistics.

 For more information on job forecasts in information security, visit the Bureau of Labor Statistics at www.bls.gov and search on "information security."

The BLS data in Figure 11-1 only examines specific positions for an information security analyst. It does not consider the positions of a network and computer systems administrator or a computer and information systems manager with information security responsibilities. The BLS summaries for these two positions are provided in Figure 11-2. There are well over 800,000 positions in the IT arena that could potentially have information security responsibilities, with an estimated 120,000 more to be filled in the next decade.

Perhaps more meaningful to this discussion is the (ISC)^2 Global Information Security Workforce Study, which found that 46 percent of all respondents felt their information security analyst positions were understaffed. More importantly, this percentage included two-thirds of all responding C-level executives, those with the greatest influence over hiring and budget decisions. Respondents attributed the shortage to "three factors: business conditions; executives not fully understanding the need; and an inability to locate appropriate information security professionals."[6] The good news is that the study predicts an increase in information security personnel; more than 30 percent of respondents indicated that information security spending on personnel will increase.

 For more information on the (ISC)^2 Global Information Security Workforce Study, visit www .isc2cares.org/uploadedFiles/wwwisc2caresorg/Content/GISWS/FrostSullivan-(ISC)%C2%B2 -Global-Information-Security-Workforce-Study-2015.pdf.

Summary

Quick Facts: Network and Computer Systems Administrators	
2015 Median Pay ?	$77,810 per year $37.41 per hour
Typical Entry-Level Education ?	Bachelor's degree
Work Experience in a Related Occupation ?	None
On-the-job Training ?	None
Number of Jobs, 2014 ?	382,600
Job Outlook, 2014-24 ?	8% (As fast as average)
Employment Change, 2014-24 ?	30,200

Summary

Quick Facts: Computer and Information Systems Managers	
2015 Median Pay ?	$131,600 per year $63.27 per hour
Typical Entry-Level Education ?	Bachelor's degree
Work Experience in a Related Occupation ?	5 years or more
On-the-job Training ?	None
Number of Jobs, 2014 ?	348,500
Job Outlook, 2014-24 ?	15% (Much faster than average)
Employment Change, 2014-24 ?	53,700

Figure 11-2 BLS summaries for computer administrators and managers

Source: *www.bls.gov.*

11

Qualifications and Requirements A number of factors influence an organization's hiring decisions. Because information security has only recently emerged as a separate discipline, hiring in this field is complicated by a lack of understanding among organizations about what qualifications an information security professional should possess. In many organizations, information security teams currently lack established roles and responsibilities. Establishing better hiring practices in an organization requires the following:

- The general management community of interest should learn more about the skills and qualifications for information security positions and IT positions that affect information security.

- Upper management should learn more about the budgetary needs of information security and its positions. This knowledge will enable management to make sound fiscal decisions for information security and the IT functions that carry out many information security initiatives.

- The IT and general management communities should grant appropriate levels of influence and prestige to information security, especially to the role of CISO.

In most cases, organizations look for a technically qualified information security generalist who has a solid understanding of how an organization operates. In many fields, the more specialized professionals are more marketable. In information security, however, overspecialization can be risky. It is important, therefore, to balance technical skills with general knowledge about information security.

When hiring information security professionals, organizations frequently look for candidates who understand the following:

- How an organization operates at all levels
- That information security is usually a management problem and is seldom an exclusively technical problem
- How to work with people and collaborate with end users, and the importance of strong communications and writing skills
- The role of policy in guiding security efforts, and the role of education and training in making employees and other authorized users part of the solution rather than part of the problem
- Most mainstream IT technologies at a general level, not necessarily as an expert
- The terminology of IT and information security
- The threats facing an organization and how they can become attacks
- How to protect an organization's assets from information security attacks
- How business solutions, including technology-based solutions, can be applied to solve specific information security problems

Entry into the Information Security Profession

Many information security professionals enter the field through one of two career paths. Some come from law enforcement or the military, where they were involved in national security or cybersecurity. Others are technical professionals—networking experts, programmers, database administrators, and systems administrators—who find themselves working on information security applications and processes more often than traditional IT assignments. In recent years, a third, perhaps more traditional career path has developed: college students who select and tailor their degree programs to prepare for work in the field of information security. Figure 11-3 illustrates these career paths.

Many hiring managers in information security prefer to recruit security professionals who have proven IT skills and professional experience in another IT field. IT professionals who move into information security, however, tend to focus on technology, sometimes in place of general information security issues. Organizations can foster greater professionalism in the discipline by expanding beyond the hiring of proven IT professionals and instead filling positions by matching qualified candidates to clearly defined roles in information security.

According to the technical report "Hacking the Skills Shortage: A study of the international shortage in cybersecurity skills," written by the Center for Strategic and International Studies and sponsored by McAfee and Intel Security, "82% of survey respondents report a shortage of information security/cybersecurity skills; 71% of these respondents said the shortage of these skills is directly impacting the capabilities and function of their organization, including making them more vulnerable to attack, damaging their reputation, and leading to data breaches. About half indicated that a bachelor's degree is the minimum credential required for entry into the field, and 68% indicated that security competitions (like Capture the Flag and the Collegiate Cyber Defense Competition) played a role in developing critical security skills for new hires."[7]

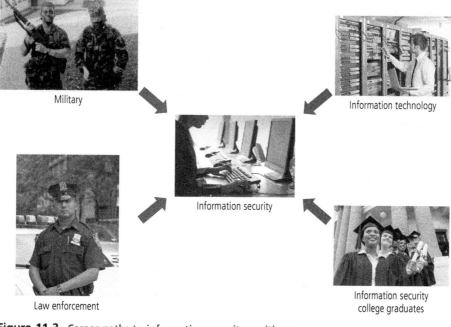

Military

Information technology

Law enforcement

Information security

Information security
college graduates

Figure 11-3 Career paths to information security positions

Bottom left: © pio3/Shutterstock.com. Bottom right: © michaeljung/Shutterstock.com.
Top right: © dotshock/Shutterstock.com. Center: © IM_photo/Shutterstock.com

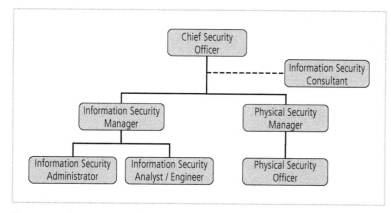

Figure 11-4 Positions in information security

Information Security Positions

The use of standard job descriptions can increase the degree of professionalism in the information security field and improve the consistency of roles and responsibilities among organizations. Organizations that expect to revise these roles and responsibilities can consult Charles Cresson Wood's book, *Information Security Roles and Responsibilities Made Easy*, which offers a set of model job descriptions for information security positions. The book also identifies the responsibilities and duties of IT staff members whose work involves information security.[8] Figure 11-4 illustrates a standard reporting structure for information security positions.

A study of information security positions by Schwartz, Erwin, Weafer, and Briney found that the positions can be classified into one of three areas: those that *define* information security programs, those that *build* the systems and create the programs to implement information security controls, and those that *administer* information security control systems and programs that have been created. The definers are managers who provide policy and planning and manage risk assessments. They are typically senior information security managers—they have extensive and broad knowledge, but not a lot of technical depth. The builders are techies who create security technical solutions to protect software, systems, and networks. The administrators apply the techies' tools in accordance with the decisions and guidance of the definers; they provide day-to-day systems monitoring and use to support an organization's goals and objectives. By clearly identifying which type of role it is seeking and then classifying all applicants into these three types and matching them, the organization can recruit more effectively.[9] Some examples of job titles shown in Figure 11-4 are discussed in the following sections.

Chief Information Security Officer (CISO) Although the exact title may vary, the CISO is typically the top information security officer in the organization. As indicated earlier in the chapter, the CISO is usually not an executive-level position, and frequently the person in this role reports to the chief information officer. Though CISOs are business managers first and technologists second, they must be conversant in all areas of information security, including the technical, planning, and policy areas. In many cases, the CISO is the major definer or architect of the information security program. The CISO performs the following functions:

- Manages the overall information security program for the organization
- Drafts or approves information security policies
- Works with the CIO on strategic plans, develops tactical plans, and works with security managers on operational plans
- Develops information security budgets based on available funding
- Sets priorities for the purchase and implementation of information security projects and technology
- Makes decisions or recommendations for the recruiting, hiring, and firing of security staff
- Acts as the spokesperson for the information security team

The most common certification for this type of position is the Certified Information Security Manager (CISM), which is described later in this chapter. A bachelor's degree is almost always required and in some cases a graduate degree is also preferred, although it may be from a number of possible disciplines, including information systems, computer science, another information technology field, criminal justice, military science, business, or other fields related to the broader topic of security.

A typical example of a CISO's job description is shown below. The example has been edited for length and is from a state government job posting, but it is very similar to postings in general industry.

Position: *Chief Information Security Officer*

Job duties: *The Chief Information Security Officer reports to the State's Deputy Division Administrator, DET and is responsible for the statewide security program. The CISO's role is to provide vision and leadership for developing and supporting security initiatives. The CISO directs the planning and implementation of enterprise IT system, business operation, and facility defenses against security breaches and vulnerability issues. This individual is also responsible for auditing existing systems, while directing the administration of security policies, activities, and standards.*

The CISO is responsible for providing regulatory oversight for information security. This oversight includes the development of enterprise-wide policy, procedures, and guidance for compliance with federal laws, regulations, and guidelines, and sound security and privacy practices. Additionally, the CISO is responsible for reviewing security program documentation developed to ensure compliance and further enhance security practices across all component agencies.

The CISO is responsible for deployed security across the enterprise, including platforms, network, and security tools. The CISO is also responsible for identifying and assessing internal and external threats, vulnerabilities and risks as well as ensuring that robust monitoring, timely detection, containment, and incident response necessary to mitigate the exposure caused by the breach is in place. The CISO provides leadership, guidance, direction, and authority for technology security across all corporate technology departments, including measurements applicable to services provided.

The CISO is responsible for ensuring that workflow within the division runs smoothly so that new technology projects are appropriately monitored for security risks and appropriate risk mitigation requirements are efficiently set forth and appropriately designed and delivered with the newly developed production system. Policies, procedures and technical standards and architecture will need to be regularly reviewed and updated to prevent unauthorized access of State of Wisconsin technology systems.

Special notes:

Due to the nature of the position, DOA will conduct a thorough background check on applicant prior to selection.

Job knowledge, skills, and abilities:

General:

- *Strong oral and written communication skills, including the ability to communicate business and technical concepts and information effectively to a wide range of audiences, including the public*

- *Strong interpersonal skills, including the ability to work independently with high-level government officials, business and IS managers and staff in federal, state and local agencies, and with division and department managers in a decentralized environment*

- *Strong project management skills*

- *Demonstrated ability to effectively interface with technical staff, senior management, and external parties*

- *Proven ability to plan and organize work, requiring an in-depth understanding of security issues and ability to integrate into the work of others*

11

- *Ability to defend and explain difficult issues with respect to key decisions and positions to staff and senior officials*
- *Experience in analyzing enterprise business and technology issues in a large corporation or government organization*
- *Ability to establish credibility so decisions and recommendations are adopted*
- *Ability to identify appropriate members and develop effective teams with specific knowledge and skills needed to develop solutions and make recommendations*
- *Resourceful in identifying and obtaining information sources needed to perform responsibilities effectively*

Technological/specific:

- *Must be an intelligent, articulate, and persuasive leader who can serve as an effective member of the senior management team and who is able to communicate security-related concepts to a broad range of technical and nontechnical staff*
- *Security background, experience in business management, and professional expertise in security and law*
- *Possess a strong technical background in information technology security*
- *Knowledge of secure software development*
- *Computer/network investigation skills and forensics knowledge*
- *Extensive knowledge of networks, system, database and applications security*
- *Demonstrated ability to work with management and staff at various levels of the organization to implement sound security practices*
- *Ability to provide technical direction to security architects and project consultants to ensure appropriate security requirements are set forth on new development efforts*
- *Knowledge of standards-based architectures, with an understanding of how to get there, including compliance monitoring and enforceability*
- *Experience with business continuity planning, auditing, and risk management, as well as contract and vendor negotiation*
- *Strong working knowledge of security principles (such as authentication, vulnerability testing, penetration testing, auditing, crime scene preservation and risk management) and security elements (such as locking systems, evacuation methods, perimeter controls, VPNs, and firewalls)*
- *Certifications such as Certified Protection Professional (CPP), Certified Information Systems Manager (CISM), or Certification for the Information Systems Security Professional (CISSP) preferred*[10]

Chief Security Officer (CSO) In some organizations, the CISO's position may be combined with physical security responsibilities or may even report to a security manager who is responsible for both logical (information) security and physical security. Such a position is generally referred to as a CSO. The CSO must be capable and knowledgeable in both information security requirements and the "guards, gates, and guns" approach to protecting the physical infrastructure, buildings, and grounds of a place of business.

To qualify for this position, the candidate must demonstrate experience as a security manager and with planning, policy, and budgets. As mentioned earlier, some organizations prefer to hire people with law enforcement experience. The following is a typical example of a CSO's job description:

Position: *Director of Security*

Responsibilities: *Reporting to the Senior Vice President of Administration, the Director of Corporate Security will be responsible for all issues related to the security and protection of the company's employees, executives, facilities, proprietary data and information. Accountable for the planning and design of the company's security programs and procedures, this individual will facilitate protection from and resolution of theft, threats, and other situations that may endanger the well-being of the organization. Working through a small staff, the Director will be responsible for executive protection, travel advisories, employee background checks, and a myriad of other activities throughout the corporation on a case-by-case basis. The Director will serve as the company's chief liaison with law enforcement agencies and, most importantly, will serve as a security consultant to all of the company's autonomously run divisions. Travel requirements will be extensive.*

Qualifications: *The ideal candidate will have a successful background with a federal law enforcement agency, or other applicable experience, that will afford this individual an established network of contacts throughout the country. Additional private industry experience with a sizeable corporation—or as a consultant to same—is preferable. A proactive attitude with regard to security and protection is a must. The successful candidate must be capable of strategically assessing ... client security needs and have a track record in areas such as crisis management, investigation, facility security, and executive protection. Finally, the candidate should have a basic understanding of the access and use of electronic information services as they apply to security issues. We seek candidates who are flexible enough to deal with varied business cultures and who possess the superior interpersonal skills to perform well in a consulting role where recommendations and advice are sought and valued, but perhaps not always acted upon. A college degree is required.*[11]

Security Manager Security managers are accountable for the day-to-day operation of the information security program. They accomplish objectives identified by the CISO and resolve issues identified by technicians. Management of technology requires a general understanding of that technology, but it does not necessarily require proficiency in the technology's configuration, operation, and fault resolution. Note that several positions have titles that contain the word *manager* or suggest management responsibilities, but only people who are responsible for management functions, such as scheduling, setting relative priorities, or administering budgetary control, should be considered true managers.

A candidate for this position often has a bachelor's degree in technology, business, or a security-related field, as well as a CISSP certification. Traditionally, managers earn the

CISSP or CISM, and technical professionals earn the Global Information Assurance Certification (GIAC). You will learn more about these certifications later in the chapter.

Security managers must have the ability to draft middle- and lower-level policies as well as standards and guidelines. They must have experience in traditional business matters, such as budgeting, project management, and personnel management. They must also be able to manage technicians, both in the assignment of tasks and in the monitoring of activities. Experience with business continuity planning is usually a plus.

The following is a typical example of a security manager's job description. Note that there are several types of security managers, as the position is much more specialized than that of CISO. Thus, when applying for a job as a security manager, you should read the job description carefully to determine exactly what the employer wants.

Position: *Information Security Manager*

Job description: *This management position reports to the Chief Information Security Officer. The successful candidate will manage the development of the information security programs and control systems in conformance with organizational policy and standards across the organization. This is a high-visibility role that involves the day-to-day management of IT Security staff and their career development. The principal accountabilities for this role are as follows:*

- *Develop and manage information security programs and control systems under the supervision of the CISO in conjunction with the evolving information security architecture of the organization.*

- *Monitor performance of information security programs and control systems to maintain alignment with organizational policy and common industry practices for emerging threats and technologies.*

- *Prepare and communicate risk assessments for business risk in software developments as well as ongoing systems events (to include merger, acquisition, and divestiture) and ensure effective risk management across the organization's IT systems.*

- *Represent the information security organization in the organization's change management process.*

- *Perform assigned duties in the area of incident response management and disaster recovery response.*

- *Supervise assigned staff and perform other general management tasks as assigned, including budgeting, staffing, and employee performance reviews.*

Compare the preceding general job description with the following more specific job description found in a recent advertisement:

Position: *IT Security Compliance Manager*

Job description: *A job has arisen for an IT Security Compliance Manager reporting to the IT Security Manager. In this role you will manage the development of the client's IT Security standards and operate a compliance program to ensure conformance at all stages of the systems life cycle. This is a key, hands-on role with the job holder taking an active part in the delivery of the compliance pro-gram. The role will also involve the day-to-day management of IT Security staff and their career development. The principal accountabilities for this role are as follows:*

- *Develop and manage an IT security compliance program.*

- *Develop the client's security standards in line with industry standards and emerging threats and technologies.*

- *Identify IT-related business risk in new software and game developments and ensure that effective risk management solutions are identified and complied with.*

- *Manage and conduct IT security compliance reviews in conjunction with oper-ational and IT Audit staff.*

- *Conduct investigations into security breaches or vulnerabilities.*

Candidate profile: *The ideal candidate should have five years' experience of man-aging the implementation of technical security controls and related operational procedures and must have sound business risk management skills. You must have a flexible approach to working and must be able and willing to work unso-ciable hours to meet the demands of the role.*[12]

The second example illustrates the confusion in the information security field regarding job titles and reporting relationships. The first job description identifies responsibilities for the position and describes points where information security interacts with other business func-tions, but the second spreads responsibilities among several business functions and does not seem to reflect a clearly defined role for the position or the information security unit within the organization. Until some similarity in job titles and expected roles and responsibilities emerges, information security job candidates should carefully research open positions instead of relying solely on the job title.

Security Analyst Security analysts, also commonly referred to as security technicians, security architects, or security engineers, are technically qualified employees who are tasked to configure firewalls, deploy IDPSs, implement security software, diagnose and trouble-shoot problems, and coordinate with systems and network administrators to ensure that an organization's security technology is properly implemented. A security analyst is often an entry-level position, but to be hired for this role, candidates must possess some technical skills. This often poses a dilemma for applicants, as many find it difficult to get a job in a new field without experience—they can only attain such experience by getting a job. As in the networking arena, security analysts tend to specialize in one major security technology group (firewalls, IDPSs, servers, routers, or software) and in one particular software or hardware package, such as Check Point firewalls, Nokia firewalls, or Tripwire IDPSs. These areas are sufficiently complex to warrant a high level of specialization, but to move up in the corporate hierarchy, security analysts must expand their knowledge horizontally—that is, gain an understanding of general organizational issues related to infor-mation security and its technical areas.

The technical qualifications and position requirements vary for a security analyst. Organiza-tions prefer an expert, certified, proficient technician. Regardless of the area of needed expertise, the job description covers some level of experience with a particular hardware and software package. Sometimes, familiarity with a technology secures an applicant an interview; however, actual experience in using the technology is usually required. The following is a typical job announcement for a security analyst:

> Position: *Firewall Engineering Consultant*
>
> Job Description: *Working for an exciting customer-focused security group within one of the largest managed network providers in the country. You will have the opportunity to expand your experience and gain all the technical and professional support to achieve within the group. Must have experience to third-line technical support of firewall technologies. Check Point certified. Experienced in Nokia systems.*
>
> Package: *Possible company car, discretionary bonus, private health care, on-call pay, and overtime pay.*[13]

Because overtime and on-call pay are listed, this job is probably an hourly position rather than a salaried one, which is common for security analysts.

Credentials for Information Security Professionals

As mentioned earlier, many organizations seek industry-recognized certifications to screen candidates for the required level of technical proficiency. Unfortunately, however, most existing certifications are relatively new and not fully understood by hiring organizations. The certifying bodies are working hard to educate employers and professionals on the value and qualifications of their certificate programs. In the meantime, employers are trying to understand the match between certifications and position requirements, and hopeful professionals are trying to gain meaningful employment based on their new certifications.

❯ (ISC)^2 Certifications

The International Information Systems Security Certification Consortium, known as (ISC)^2, offers security certifications such as the Certified Information Systems Security Professional (CISSP), the Systems Security Certified Practitioner (SSCP), and the Certified Secure Software Lifecycle Professional (CSSLP). You can visit the Web site at *www.isc2.org*.

CISSP The CISSP certification is considered the most prestigious for security managers and CISOs. It recognizes mastery of an internationally identified Common Body of Knowledge (CBK) in information security. To sit for the CISSP exam, the candidate must have at least five years of direct, full-time experience as a security professional working in at least two of the eight domains of information security knowledge, or four years of direct security work experience in two or more domains. The candidate must also have a four-year college degree.

The CISSP exam consists of 250 multiple-choice questions and must be completed within six hours. It tests candidates on their knowledge of the following eight domains:

- Security and risk management
- Asset security
- Security engineering
- Communications and network security
- Identity and access management
- Security assessment and testing
- Security operations
- Software development security

CISSP certification requires successful completion of the exam and an endorsement. Once candidates successfully complete the exam, they have nine months to submit an endorsement by an actively credentialed CISSP or by their employer as validation of their professional experience. After earning the certification, the CISSP holder must earn 120 hours of continuing professional education (CPE) every three years, with a minimum of 20 hours per year. The breadth and depth of each of the eight domains makes CISSP certification one of the most challenging to obtain in information security.[14]

CISSP Concentrations In addition to the major certifications that (ISC)^2 offers, a number of concentrations are available for CISSPs to demonstrate advanced knowledge beyond the CISSP CBK. Each concentration requires that the applicant be a CISSP in good standing, pass a separate examination, and maintain the certification through continuing professional education. These concentrations and their respective areas of knowledge are shown in the following list and presented on the (ISC)^2 Web site:

ISSAP®: Information Systems Security Architecture Professional

- *Access control systems and methodology*
- *Communications and network security*
- *Cryptography*
- *Security architecture analysis*
- *Technology-related business continuity planning and disaster recovery planning*
- *Physical security considerations*

ISSEP: Information Systems Security Engineering Professional

- *Systems security engineering*
- *Certification and accreditation/risk management framework*
- *Technical management*
- *U.S. government information assurance-related policies and issuances*

ISSMP: Information Systems Security Management Professional

- *Enterprise security management practices*
- *Business continuity planning and disaster recovery planning*

11

- *Security management practices*
- *System development security*
- *Law, investigations, forensics, and ethics*
- *Security compliance management*[15]

SSCP Because it is difficult to master the broad array of knowledge encompassed in the eight domains covered by the flagship CISSP exam, many security professionals seek less rigorous certifications, such as (ISC)^2's SSCP certification. The SSCP also has lower professional experience requirements than the CISSP. The SSCP focuses on practices, roles, and responsibilities as defined by experts from major information security industries.[16] Like the CISSP, the SSCP certification is more applicable to the security manager than to the technician, as the bulk of its questions focus on the operational nature of information security. Nevertheless, an information security analyst who seeks advancement can benefit from this certification.

The SSCP exam consists of 125 multiple-choice questions and must be completed within three hours. It covers seven domains:

- Access controls
- Security operations and administration
- Risk identification, monitoring, and analysis
- Incident response and recovery
- Cryptography
- Network and communications security
- Systems and application security

Many consider the SSCP to be a scaled-down version of the CISSP. The seven domains are not a subset of the CISSP domains; they contain slightly more technical content. As with the CISSP, SSCP holders must either earn continuing education credits to retain the certification or retake the exam.

CSSLP The Certified Secure Software Lifecycle Professional (CSSLP)[17] is another (ISC)^2 certification focused on the development of secure applications. To qualify for the CSSLP, you must have at least four years of recent experience in one or more of the following eight domains:

- Secure software concepts: Security implications in software development
- Secure software requirements: Capturing security requirements in the requirements-gathering phase
- Secure software design: Translating security requirements into application design elements
- Secure software implementation/coding: Unit testing for security functionality and resiliency to attack, and developing secure code and exploit mitigation

- Secure software testing: Integrated QA testing for security functionality and resiliency to attack
- Software acceptance: Security implications in the software acceptance phase
- Software deployment, operations, maintenance, and disposal: Security issues for steady-state operations and management of software
- Supply chain and software acquisition: Establishing relationships with suppliers and interacting with them on security-related issues such as service-level agreements and vulnerability management throughout the software development life cycle[18]

You must compose an essay in each of your four areas of expertise and submit it as your exam. This test is radically different from the multiple-choice exams (ISC)^2 normally administers. Once your experience has been verified and you successfully complete the essay exam, you can be certified. If necessary, you can qualify as an (ISC)^2 Associate until you obtain the requisite experience to qualify for the CSSLP.

CCFP The Certified Cyber Forensics Professional is one of the newest certifications from (ISC)^2. It encompasses six domains:

- Legal and ethical principles
- Investigations
- Forensic science
- Digital forensics
- Application forensics
- Hybrid and emerging technologies

Candidates must have a bachelor's degree plus three years of forensics or security experience in three of the six domains. As with other (ISC)^2 certifications, individuals who pass the certification test but do not meet the experience requirement may be designated as Associates of (ISC)^2 while completing their requirements.[19]

HCISPP Another new and relevant certification for information security professionals working in the healthcare field is the HealthCare Information Security and Privacy Practitioner (HCISPP). Similar to the CISSP but focused on security management topics and healthcare, this certification requires the candidate to demonstrate knowledge in six specialty domains on its 125-question multiple-choice exam:

- Healthcare industry
- Regulatory environment
- Privacy and security in healthcare
- Information governance and risk management
- Information risk assessment
- Third-party risk management

Candidates must have two or more years of experience in at least one of these domains and at least one year of experience in the top three domains (Healthcare industry, regulatory environment, or privacy and security in healthcare). The other year can be in any of the other domains and does not have to be experience in the healthcare field.[20]

CCSP   Completing the list of new $(ISC)^2$ certifications is the Certified Cloud Security Professional. This certification, co-sponsored by the Cloud Security Alliance, is aimed at professionals who are primarily responsible for specifying, acquiring, securing, and managing cloud-based services for their organization. The CCSP covers six domains on its 125-question multiple-choice exam:

- Architectural concepts and design requirements
- Cloud data security
- Cloud platform and infrastructure security
- Cloud application security
- Operations
- Legal and compliance

There are endorsement, experience, and continuing education requirements for this certification, as with all previously mentioned $(ISC)^2$ certifications.[21]

Associate of $(ISC)^2$ $(ISC)^2$ has an innovative approach to the experience requirement in its certification program. Its Associate of $(ISC)^2$ program is geared toward people who want to take the CISSP or SSCP exam before obtaining the requisite experience for certification.

Candidates who pass any of the described $(ISC)^2$ exams and agree to subscribe to the $(ISC)^2$ Code of Ethics as well as maintain Continuing Professional Education (CPE) credits and pay the appropriate fees can maintain their status as an Associate until they have logged the required years of experience.

❯ ISACA Certifications

ISACA (*www.isaca.org*) also offers several reputable security certifications, including the Certified Information Security Manager (CISM), Certified Information Systems Auditor (CISA), and the Certified in the Governance of Enterprise IT (CGEIT).

CISM   The CISM credential is geared toward experienced information security managers and others who may have similar management responsibilities. The CISM can assure executive management that a candidate has the required background knowledge needed for effective security management and consulting. This exam is offered annually. The CISM examination covers the following practice domains described in the ISACA 2016 Exam Candidate Information Guide:

1. Information Security Governance (24 percent): Establish and maintain an information security governance framework and supporting processes to ensure that the information

security strategy is aligned with organizational goals and objectives, information risk is managed appropriately and program resources are managed responsibly.

2. Information Risk Management and Compliance (33 percent): Manage information risk to an acceptable level to meet the business and compliance requirements of the organization.

3. Information Security Program Development and Management (25 percent): Establish and manage the information security program in alignment with the information security strategy.

4. Information Security Incident Management (18 percent): Plan, establish, and manage the capability to detect, investigate, respond to, and recover from information security incidents to minimize business impact.[22]

To be certified, the applicant must:

- Pass the examination.
- Adhere to a code of ethics promulgated by ISACA.
- Pursue continuing education as specified.
- Document five years of information security work experience with at least three years in information security management in three of the four defined areas of practice.

CISA The CISA credential is not specifically a security certification, but it does include many information security components. ISACA touts the certification as being appropriate for auditing, networking, and security professionals. CISA requirements are as follows:

- Successful completion of the CISA examination
- Experience as an information security auditor, with a minimum of five years' professional experience in information systems auditing, control, or security
- Agreement to the Code of Professional Ethics
- Payment of maintenance fees, a minimum of 20 contact hours of continuing education annually, and a minimum of 120 contact hours during a fixed three-year period
- Adherence to the Information Systems Auditing Standards

The exam covers the following areas of information systems auditing, as described in the ISACA 2016 Exam Candidate Information Guide:

1. The Process of Auditing Information Systems (21 percent): Provide audit services in accordance with IT audit standards to assist the organization with protecting and controlling information systems.

2. Governance and Management of IT (16 percent): Provide assurance that the necessary leadership and organizational structures and processes are in place to achieve objectives and to support the organization's strategy.

3. Information Systems Acquisition, Development and Implementation (18 percent): Provide assurance that the practices for the acquisition, development, testing, and implementation of information systems meet the organization's strategies and objectives.

11

4. Information Systems Operations, Maintenance and Support (20 percent): Provide assurance that the processes for information systems operations, maintenance and support meet the organization's strategies and objectives.

5. Protection of Information Assets (25 percent): Provide assurance that the organization's security policies, standards, procedures and controls ensure the confidentiality, integrity, and availability of information assets.[23]

The CISA exam is offered only a few times each year, so planning is a must.

CGEIT Also available from ISACA is the Certified in the Governance of Enterprise IT (CGEIT) certification. The exam is targeted at upper-level executives, including CISOs and CIOs, directors, and consultants with knowledge and experience in IT governance. The CGEIT areas of knowledge include risk management components, which make it an interesting certification for upper-level information security managers. The exam covers the following areas, as described in the ISACA 2016 Exam Candidate Information Guide:

1. Framework for the Governance of Enterprise IT (25 percent): Ensure the definition, establishment, and management of a framework for the governance of enterprise IT in alignment with the mission, vision, and values of the enterprise.

2. Strategic Management (20 percent): Ensure that IT enables and supports the achievement of enterprise objectives through the integration and alignment of IT strategic plans with enterprise strategic plans.

3. Benefits Realization (16 percent): Ensure that IT-enabled investments are managed to deliver optimized business benefits and that benefit realization outcome and performance measures are established, evaluated and progress is reported to key stakeholders.

4. Risk Optimization (24 percent): Ensure that an IT risk management framework exists to identify, analyze, mitigate, manage, monitor, and communicate IT-related business risk, and that the framework for IT risk management is in alignment with the enterprise risk management (ERM) framework.

5. Resource Optimization (15 percent): Ensure the optimization of IT resources, including information, services, infrastructure and applications, and people, to support the achievement of enterprise objectives.[24]

The certification requirements are similar to those for other ISACA certifications. Candidates must have at least one year of experience in IT governance and additional experience in at least two of the domains listed.

CRISC The newest ISACA certification is the Certified in Risk and Information Systems Control (CRISC). The certification is targeted at managers and employees with knowledge and experience in risk management. The CRISC areas of knowledge include risk management components, which make it an interesting certification for upper-level information security managers. The exam covers the following areas, as described in the ISACA 2016 Exam Candidate Information Guide:

1. IT Risk Identification (27 percent): Understand the identification of risk in the organization's environment, in support of its risk management strategy and business objectives.

2. IT Risk Assessment (28 percent): Analyze and assess likelihood and impact of risk on the organization's operations and objectives.

3. Risk Response and Mitigation (23 percent): Specify the organization's risk response and mitigation strategies.

4. Risk and Control Monitoring and Reporting (22 percent): Conduct ongoing monitoring and provide reporting of overall risk management activities in support of the organization's risk management strategies and business objectives.[25]

The certification requires the candidate to have a minimum of three years' experience in risk management and information systems control in at least two of the stated domains, and at least one year of that experience must be in one of the first two domains, although the candidate may elect to take the exam before fulfilling the experience requirement. This practice is accepted and encouraged by ISACA, but the candidate will not receive the certification until the experience requirement is met.

❯ SANS Certifications

In 1999, the SANS Institute, formerly known as the System Administration, Networking, and Security Institute (*www.sans.org*), developed a series of technical cybersecurity certifications known as the Global Information Assurance Certification (GIAC; *www.giac.org*). GIAC certifications not only test for knowledge, they require candidates to demonstrate application of that knowledge. With the introduction of the GIAC Information Security Professional (GISP), the GIAC Security Leadership Certification (GSLC), and several new managerial certifications, SANS now offers more than just technical certifications. The GIAC family of certifications covers 20 certifications in seven general areas: security administration, management, forensics, software security, audit, legal, and the capstone certification, the GIAC Security Expert (GSE). Unlike other certifications, some GIAC certifications require applicants to complete a written practical assignment that tests their ability to apply skills and knowledge. These assignments are submitted to the SANS Information Security Reading Room for review by security practitioners, potential certificate applicants, and others with an interest in information security. Only when the practical assignment is complete is the candidate allowed to take the online exam.

The GIAC certifications as of 2016 are shown in Table 11-1.

Most GIAC certifications are offered in conjunction with SANS training. For more information on the GIAC security-related certification requirements, visit *www.giac.org/certifications*.

❯ EC-Council Certifications

Another competitor in certifications for security management, EC-Council (*www.eccouncil .org*), now offers a Certified CISO (C|CISO) certification, which is designed to be a unique recognition for those at the peak of their professional careers. The C|CISO tests not only security domain knowledge, but knowledge of executive business management. The C|CISO includes the following domains:

- Domain 1: Governance (Policy, Legal, and Compliance): This domain focuses on the external regulatory and legal issues a CISO faces, as well as the strategic information security governance programs promoted in forward-thinking organizations. It also

Introductory	Security Administration	GIAC Information Security Fundamentals (GISF)
Intermediate	Security Administration	GIAC Security Essentials Certification (GSEC)
		Global Industrial Cyber Security Professional (GICSP)
	Management	GIAC Information Security Professional (GISP)
	Forensics	GIAC Certified Forensic Examiner (GCFE)
Advanced	Security Administration	GIAC Certified Perimeter Protection Analyst (GPPA)
		GIAC Certified Intrusion Analyst (GCIA)
		GIAC Certified Incident Handler (GCIH)
		GIAC Certified UNIX Security Administrator (GCUX)
		GIAC Certified Windows Security Administrator (GCWN)
		GIAC Certified Enterprise Defender (GCED)
		GIAC Certified Penetration Tester (GPEN)
		GIAC Web Application Penetration Tester (GWAPT)
	Management	GIAC Security Leadership Certification (GSLC)
		GIAC Certified Project Manager (GCPM)
	Software Security	GIAC Secure Software Programmer—.NET (GSSP-NET)
		GIAC Secure Software Programmer—Java (GSSP-JAVA)
	Audit	GIAC Systems and Network Auditor (GSNA)
	Forensics	GIAC Certified Forensic Analyst (GCFA)
	Legal	GIAC Law of Data Security & Investigations (GLEG)
	Security Administration	GIAC Assessing Wireless Networks (GAWN)
		GIAC Exploit Researcher and Advanced Penetration Tester (GXPN)
	Forensics	GIAC Reverse Engineering Malware (GREM)
Expert	GSE	GIAC Security Expert (GSE)

Table 11-1 Roadmap of GIAC Certifications[26]

contains areas related to security compliance to ensure that the organization conforms to applicable laws and regulations. Finally, it includes areas of information security standards, such as Federal Information Processing Standards and ISO 27000, and it incorporates areas in risk management.[27]

- Domain 2: IS Management Controls and Auditing Management (Projects, Technology, and Operations): This domain includes knowledge areas associated with information systems controls and auditing, similar to those found in ISACA certifications. These areas include developing, implementing, and monitoring IS controls as well as reporting the findings to executive management. Auditing areas include planning, conducting, and evaluating audits in the organization.[28]

- Domain 3: Management—Projects and Operations (Projects, Technology and Operations): This domain contains basic managerial roles and responsibilities any security manager would be expected to have mastered. It includes the fundamentals of management covered in earlier chapters, including planning, organizing, staffing, directing, and controlling security resources.[29]

- Domain 4: Information Security Core Competencies: This domain covers the common body of information security knowledge that any CISO would be expected to possess. The domain includes subdomains in the following areas:

  - Access control
  - Social engineering, phishing attacks, identity theft
  - Physical security
  - Risk management
  - Disaster recovery and business continuity planning
  - Firewalls, intrusion detection systems, intrusion prevention systems, and network defense systems
  - Wireless security
  - Viruses, Trojans, and malware threats
  - Secure coding best practices and securing Web applications
  - Hardening operating systems
  - Encryption technologies
  - Vulnerability assessment and penetration testing
  - Computer forensics and incident response[30]

- Domain 5: Strategic Planning and Finance: This domain addresses CISO tasks associated with conducting strategic planning and financial management of the security department. The domain includes performance measures, IT investments, internal and external analyses, and developing and implementing enterprise security architectures.[31]

EC-Council also offers a number of certifications that focus on the technical side of security:

- Certified network defender
- Certified ethical hacker
- Security analyst
- Forensic investigator
- Network defense architect
- Encryption specialist
- Advanced penetration testing
- Licensed penetration tester
- Advanced security Windows infrastructure
- Advanced mobile hacking & forensics
- Advanced hacking hardening corporate Web apps
- Advanced network defense

11

- Secure computer user
- Incident handler
- Secure programmer—Java
- Secure programmer—.NET
- Security specialist
- Disaster recovery professional

❯ CompTIA Certifications

CompTIA (*www.comptia.com*)—the organization that offered the first vendor-neutral professional IT certifications, the A+ series—now offers a program called the Security+ certification.

The CompTIA Security+ certification tests for entry-level security knowledge. Candidates must have two years of on-the-job networking experience. The exam covers industry-wide topics, including communication security, infrastructure security, cryptography, access control, authentication, external attack, and operational and organization security. CompTIA Security+ curricula are taught at colleges, universities, and commercial training centers around the globe. CompTIA Security+ is used as an elective or prerequisite to advanced vendor-specific and vendor-neutral security certifications.[33]

The exam covers the domains shown in Table 11-2.

❯ ISFCE Certifications

The International Society of Forensic Computer Examiners (ISFCE) offers two levels of certification.

Certified Computer Examiner (CCE) Certified Computer Examiner (CCE)® is a computer forensics certification provided by the ISFCE (*www.isfce.com*). To complete the CCE certification process, the applicant must:

- Have no criminal record
- Meet minimum experience, training, or self-training requirements

Domain	Percentage of Examination
1.0 Network Security	20%
2.0 Compliance and Operational Security	18%
3.0 Threats and Vulnerabilities	20%
4.0 Application, Data, and Host Security	15%
5.0 Access Control and Identity Management	15%
6.0 Cryptography	12%

Table 11-2 Domains Covered in the CompTIA Security+ Exam

Source: CompTIA.[32]

- Abide by the certification's code of ethical standards
- Pass an online examination
- Successfully perform actual forensic examinations on three test media

The CCE certification process covers the following areas:

- Ethics in practice
- Key legislation in, and its impact on, digital forensics
- Software licensing and validation
- General computer hardware used in data collection
- Networking and its involvement in forensics and data collection
- Common computer operating system and file systems organization and architecture
- Forensics data seizure procedures
- Casework and other forensics examination procedures
- Common computer media, as used as evidence, in physical and logical storage media operations, and procedures for sterilization and use
- Use of forensic boot disks
- Forensic examination skills and procedures[34]

> Certification Costs

Certifications cost money, and the more preferred certifications can be expensive. Individual certification exams can cost as much as $750, and certifications that require multiple exams can cost thousands of dollars. In addition, the cost of formal training to prepare for the exams can be significant. While you should not rely completely on certification preparation courses as groundwork for a real-world position, they can help you round out your knowledge and fill in gaps. Some certification exams, such as the CISSP, are very broad; others, such as components of the GIAC, are very technical. Given the nature of the knowledge needed to pass the examinations, most experienced professionals find the tests difficult without at least some review. Many prospective certificate holders engage in individual or group study sessions and purchase one of the many excellent exam review books on the subject.

Certifications are designed to recognize experts in their respective fields, but the cost of certification deters those who might take the exam just to see if they can pass. Most examinations require between two and three years of work experience, and they are often structured to reward candidates who have significant hands-on experience. Some certification programs require that candidates document certain minimum experience requirements before they are permitted to sit for the exams. Before attempting a certification exam, do your homework. Look into the exam's stated body of knowledge as well as its purpose and requirements to ensure that the time and energy spent pursuing the certification are worthwhile. Figure 11-5 shows several approaches to preparing for security certification.

11

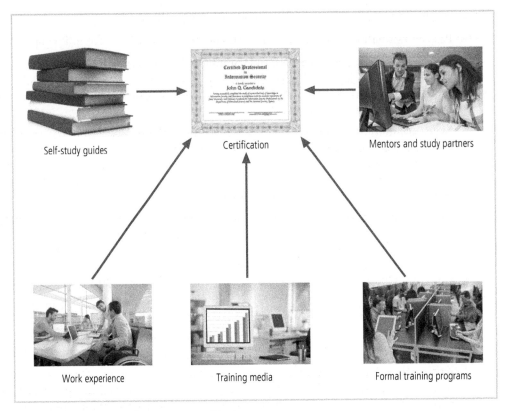

Self-study guides

Certification

Mentors and study partners

Work experience

Training media

Formal training programs

Figure 11-5 Preparing for security certification

Top left: © Hong Vo/Shutterstock.com. Bottom left: © Phovoir/Shutterstock.com. Bottom center: © Petinov Sergey Mihilovich /Shutterstock.com. Bottom right: © ESB Professional/Shutterstock.com. Top right: © Goodluz/Shutterstock.com.

On the topic of professional certification for information security practitioners, Charles Cresson Wood reports the following:

> With résumé fraud on the rise, one of the sure-fire methods for employers to be sure that the people they hire are indeed familiar with the essentials of the field is to insist that they have certain certifications. The certifications can then be checked with the issuing organizations to make sure that they have indeed been conferred on the applicant for employment. [...] The key is to insist that they have certain certifications. The [...] professional certifications are relevant primarily to centralized information security positions. They are not generally relevant to staff working in decentralized information security positions, unless these individuals intend to become information security specialists. You may also look for these certifications on the résumés of consultants and contractors working in the information security field. You may wish to list these designations in help-wanted advertisements, look for them on résumés, and ask about them during interviews. Automatic résumé scanning software can also be set up to search for these strings of characters.[35]

❯ Advice for Information Security Professionals

As a future information security professional, you may benefit from the following suggestions:

- Always remember: business before technology. Technology solutions are tools for solving business problems. Information security professionals are sometimes guilty of looking for ways to apply the newest technology to problems that do not require technology-based solutions.

- When evaluating a problem, look at the source of the problem first, determine what factors affect the problem, and see where organizational policy can lead you in designing a solution that is independent of technology. Then use technology to deploy the controls necessary for implementing the solution. Technology can provide elegant solutions to some problems, but it only exacerbates others.

- Your job is to protect the organization's information and information systems resources. Never lose sight of the goal: protecting the organization's information assets from losses. Some people get so wrapped up in the technology or implementation details that they lose track of the primary mission.

- Be heard and not seen. Information security should be transparent to users. With minor exceptions, the actions taken to protect information should not interfere with users' actions. Information security supports the work of end users, not the other way around. The only routine communications from the security team to users should be periodic awareness messages, training announcements, newsletters, and e-mails.

- Know more than you say, and be more skillful than you let on. Don't try to impress users, managers, and other nontechnical people with your level of knowledge and experience. One day you just might run into a Jedi master of information security who puts you in your place.

- Speak to users, not at them. Use their language, not yours. Users aren't impressed with technobabble and jargon. They may not comprehend all the TLAs (three-letter acronyms), technical components, software, and hardware necessary to protect their systems, but they do know how to short-circuit your next budget request or pick out the flaws in your business report.

- Your education is never complete. As sensitive as you are to the fact that information technology is ever evolving, you must be equally sensitive to the fact that information security education is never complete. Just when you think you have mastered the latest skills, you will encounter changes in threats, protection technology, your business environment, or the regulatory environment. As a security professional, you must expect to continue with the learning process throughout your entire career. This is best accomplished by seeking out periodic seminars, training programs, and formal education. Even if the organization or your pocketbook cannot afford the more extensive and expensive training programs and conferences, you can keep abreast of the market by reading trade magazines, textbooks, and news articles about security. You can also subscribe to the many mailing lists for information security professionals. Several are listed in the nearby Offline feature entitled "What's in a Name?" Join at least one professional information security association, such as the Information Systems Security Association (*www.issa.org*). Whatever approach you take, keep on top of the reading,

11

never stop learning, and make yourself the best-informed security professional possible. It can only enhance your worth to the organization and your career.

Employment Policies and Practices

To create an environment in which information security is taken seriously, an organization should make it a documented part of every employee's job description. In other words, the general management community of interest should integrate solid concepts for information security into the organization's employment policies and practices. This section examines important information security issues associated with recruiting, hiring, firing, and managing human resources in an organization.

From an information security perspective, the hiring of employees is a responsibility laden with potential security pitfalls. Therefore, the CISO and information security manager should work with the Human Resources department to incorporate information security into the guidelines used for hiring all personnel. Figure 11-6 highlights some of the hiring issues.

❭ Job Descriptions

The process of integrating information security into the hiring process begins with reviewing and updating all job descriptions. To prevent people from applying for positions based solely on access to sensitive information, the organization should avoid revealing access privileges to prospective employees when it advertises open positions.

❭ Interviews

Some interviews with job candidates are conducted with members of the Human Resources (HR) staff, while others include members of the department for which the position is being

Figure 11-6 Hiring issues

Top left: The Federal Bureau of Investigation. Bottom center: © Andrey_Popov/Shutterstock.com.

OFFLINE

What's in a Name?

Here are some job titles listed in job search databases that the authors reviewed to prepare this section. See if you can guess the position level based on the title.

- Senior security analyst
- SAP security analyst
- Security supervisor
- Direct loss prevention manager
- Security officer (not a guard job)
- Loss prevention consultant
- Site supervisor—security
- Safeguards and security specialist

   To perform your own job title search or search for an actual job in the field of information security, you can begin by reviewing the job search databases at the following Web sites:

- Commercial job listing sites such as *www.itsecurityjobs.com* and *securityjobs.net*
- U.S. federal agency position listings such as *www.usajobs.gov*
- General career Web sites have started to include more security-related opportunities, so be sure to use *monster.com* and *careerbuilder.com* in your search.

   For advice on looking for and obtaining jobs in information security and cybersecurity, visit *www.cyberdegrees.org/jobs*.

offered. An opening within the Information Security department creates a unique opportunity for the security manager to educate HR on the various certifications and specific experience each certification requires, as well as the qualifications of a good candidate. In all other areas of the organization, Information Security should advise HR to limit information provided to the candidate about responsibilities and access rights of the new hire. For organizations that include onsite visits as part of their initial or follow-up interviews, it is important to exercise caution when showing a candidate around the facility. Avoid tours through secure and restricted sites. Candidates who receive tours may be able to retain enough information about operations or information security functions to become a threat.

❯ Background Checks

A background check should be conducted before an organization extends an offer to a job candidate. A background check is an investigation into the candidate's past that looks for criminal behavior or other types of behavior that could indicate potential for future misconduct. Several government regulations specify what the organization can investigate and how much of the information uncovered can be allowed to influence the hiring decision. The security manager and HR manager should discuss these matters with legal counsel to determine what state, federal, and perhaps international regulations affect the hiring process.

Background checks differ in the level of detail and depth with which they examine a candidate. In the military, background checks determine the candidate's level of security classification, a requirement for many positions. In the business world, a background check can determine the level of trust the business places in the candidate. People being considered for security positions should expect to be subjected to a moderately high-level background check. Those considering careers in law enforcement or high-security positions may even be required to submit to polygraph tests. The following list summarizes various types of background checks and the information checked for each:

- Identity checks: Validation of identity and Social Security number
- Education and credential checks: Validation of institutions attended, degrees and certifications earned, and certification status
- Previous employment verification: Validation of where candidates worked, why they left, what they did, and for how long
- Reference checks: Validation of references and integrity of reference sources
- Social media review: Companies may review your social media activity for evidence of inappropriate or unprofessional actions.
- Worker's compensation history: Investigation of claims from worker's compensation
- Motor vehicle records: Investigation of driving records, suspensions, and DUIs
- Drug history: Screening for drugs and drug usage, past and present
- Credit history: Investigation of credit problems, financial problems, and bankruptcy
- Civil court history: Investigation of the candidate's involvement as a plaintiff or defendant in civil suits
- Criminal court history: Investigation of criminal background, arrests, convictions, and time served

As mentioned, there are federal regulations for the use of personal information in employment practices, including the Fair Credit Reporting Act (FCRA), which governs the activities of consumer credit reporting agencies and the uses of information procured from them.[36] These credit reports generally contain information about a job candidate's credit history, employment history, and other personal data.

Among other things, the FCRA prohibits employers from obtaining these reports unless the candidate is informed in writing that such a report will be requested as part of the employment process. The FCRA also allows the candidate to request information about the nature and type of reporting used in making the employment decision and subsequently enables the candidate to learn the content of these reports. The FCRA also restricts the periods of time these reports can address. If the candidate earns less than $75,000 per year, the report can contain only seven years of negative credit information. If the candidate earns $75,000 or more per year, there is no time limitation. Note that "any person who knowingly and willfully obtains information on a consumer from a consumer reporting agency under false pretenses shall be fined under title 18, United States Code, imprisoned for not more than two years, or both."[37]

> Employment Contracts

Once a candidate has accepted a job offer, the employment contract becomes an important security instrument. Many of the policies discussed in Chapter 4—specifically, the fair and responsible use policies—require an employee to agree in writing to monitoring and nondisclosure agreements. If existing employees refuse to sign these agreements, security personnel are placed in a difficult situation. They may not be able to force employees to sign or to deny employees access to the systems necessary to perform their duties. With new employees, however, security personnel are in a different situation because the procedural step of policy acknowledgment can be made a requirement of employment. Policies that govern employee behavior and are applied to all employees may be classified as "employment contingent upon agreement." This classification means the potential employee must agree in a written affidavit to conform with binding organizational policies before being hired. Some organizations choose to execute the remainder of the employment contract *after* the candidate has signed the security agreements. Although this may seem harsh, it is a necessary component of the security process. Employment contracts may also contain restrictive clauses regarding the creation and ownership of intellectual property while the candidate is employed by the organization. These provisions may require the employee to actively protect the organization's information assets—especially assets that are critical to security.

> New Hire Orientation

When new employees are introduced into the organization's culture and workflow, they should receive an extensive information security briefing as part of their employee orientation. All major policies should be explained, along with procedures for performing necessary security operations and the new position's other information security requirements. In addition, the levels of authorized access should be outlined for new employees, and training should be provided regarding the secure use of information systems. By the time new employees are ready to report to their positions, they should be thoroughly briefed on the security components of their particular jobs and on the rights and responsibilities of all personnel in the organization.

> On-the-Job Security Training

The organization should integrate the security awareness education described in Chapter 4 into a new hire's job orientation and make it a part of every employee's on-the-job security training. Keeping security at the forefront of employees' minds helps minimize their mistakes and is therefore an important part of the information security team's mission. Formal external and informal internal seminars should also be used to increase the security awareness of employees, especially that of security employees. An example of the importance of proper security training awareness for employees can be found in *The 9/11 Commission Report*, a U.S. congressional examination published three years after the terrorist attacks of September 11, 2001. As the following excerpt shows, security investigators reviewed the videotapes from security checkpoints in airports as the terrorists were passing through, and found the security process inadequate not from a technological standpoint but from human shortcomings:

> When the local civil aviation security office of the Federal Aviation Administration (FAA) later investigated these security screening operations, the screeners recalled nothing out of the ordinary. They could not recall that any of the passengers they screened were CAPPS [computer-assisted passenger prescreening system] selectees. We asked a screening expert to review the videotape of the hand-wanding, and he found the quality of the screener's work to have been "marginal at best." The screener should have "resolved" what set off the alarm; and in the case of both Moqed and Hazmi, it was clear that he did not.[38]

This excerpt illustrates how physical security depends on the human element. The maintenance of information security also depends heavily on the consistent vigilance of people. In many information security breaches, the hardware and software usually accomplished what they were designed to do, but people failed to make the correct decisions and follow-up choices. Education and regular training of employees and authorized users are important elements of information security, and therefore cannot be ignored.

❯ Evaluating Performance

To heighten information security awareness and minimize risky workplace behavior, organizations should incorporate information security into employee performance evaluations. For example, if employees have been observed keeping system passwords on notes stuck to their monitors, they should be warned. If such behavior continues, they should be reminded of their failure to comply with the organization's information security regulations during their annual performance review. In general, employees pay close attention to job performance evaluations and are more likely to take information security seriously if violations are documented in them.

❯ Termination

Key Term

exit interview A meeting with an employee who is leaving the organization to remind the employee of contractual obligations, such as nondisclosure agreements, and to obtain feedback about the employee's tenure.

Leaving the organization may or may not be a decision made by the employee. Organizations may downsize, be bought out or taken over, shut down, run out of business, or may be forced to lay off, fire, or relocate their work force. In any event, when an employee leaves an organization, several security issues arise. Key among these is the continuity of protection of all information to which the employee had access. Therefore, when an employee prepares to leave an organization, the following tasks must be performed:

- Access to the organization's systems must be disabled.
- Removable media must be returned.

- Hard drives must be secured.
- File cabinet locks must be changed.
- Office door locks must be changed.
- Keycard access must be revoked.
- Personal effects must be removed from the organization's premises.

After the employee has delivered keys, keycards, and other business property, he or she should be escorted from the premises.

In addition to the tasks just listed, many organizations use an **exit interview** to remind the employee of contractual obligations, such as nondisclosure agreements, and to obtain feedback about the employee's tenure in the organization. At this time, the employee should be reminded that failure to comply with contractual obligations could lead to civil or criminal action.

In reality, most employees are allowed to clean out their own offices and collect their personal belongings, and are simply asked to return their keys. From a security standpoint, these procedures are risky and lax because they expose the organization's information to disclosure and theft. To minimize such risks, an organization should have security-minded termination procedures that are followed consistently. In other words, the procedures should be followed regardless of the level of trust the organization had for the employee. However, a universally consistent approach is difficult and sometimes awkward to implement, which is why it's not often applied. Given the realities of workplaces, the simplest and best method for handling a departing employee may be to select one of the following scenarios, based on the employee's reasons for leaving.

Hostile Departures Hostile departures include termination for cause, permanent downsizing, temporary layoffs, and quitting in some instances. While the employee may not seem overly hostile, the unexpected termination of employment can prompt the person to lash out against the organization.

Before the employee knows he (or she) is leaving, or as soon as the hostile resignation is tendered, the security staff should terminate all logical and keycard access. In the case of involuntary terminations, the employee should be escorted into the supervisor's office for the bad news. Upon receiving the termination notice or tendering a hostile resignation, the employee should be escorted to his office or cubicle and allowed to collect personal effects. No organizational property can be taken from the premises, including pens, papers, and books, as well as portable digital media like CDs, DVDs, and memory devices. Regardless of the claim the employee makes on organizational property, he should not be allowed to take it from the premises. If the employee has property he strongly wants to retain, he should be informed that he can submit a written list of the items and the reasons he should be allowed to retain them. After the employee's personal property has been gathered, he should be asked to surrender all company property, such as keys, keycards, other organizational identification, physical access devices, PDAs, pagers, cell phones, and portable computers. The employee should then be escorted out of the building.

Friendly Departures Friendly departures include resignation, retirement, promotion, or relocation. In such cases, the employee may have tendered notice well in advance of the actual departure date. This scenario actually makes it more difficult for the security team to maintain positive control over the employee's access and information usage. Employee accounts are usually allowed to continue to exist, though an expiration date can be set for the employee's declared date of departure. Another complication associated with friendly departures is that the employees can come and go at will until their departure date, which means they will probably collect their own belongings and leave under their own recognizance. As with hostile departures, employees should be asked to drop off all organizational property on their way out for the final time.

For either type of departure, hostile or friendly, the offices and information used by the employee must be inventoried, files must be stored or destroyed, and all property must be returned to organizational stores. In either scenario, employees might foresee their departure well in advance and start taking home organizational information such as files, reports, and data from databases, perhaps thinking such items could be valuable in their future employment. This may be impossible to prevent. Only by scrutinizing systems logs after the employee has departed and sorting out authorized actions from systems misuse or information theft can the organization determine if a breach of policy or loss of information has occurred. If information is illegally copied or stolen, the action should be declared an incident and the appropriate policy followed.

Security Considerations for Temporary Employees, Consultants, and Other Workers

Temporary employees, contract employees, and other types of workers are not subject to rigorous screening, contractual obligations, and eventual secured termination, but they often have access to sensitive organizational information. As outlined in the sections that follow, relationships with workers in these categories should be carefully managed to prevent a possible information leak or theft.

❯ Temporary Employees

Some employees are hired by the organization to serve in a temporary position or to supplement the existing workforce. These employees do not work for the organization where they perform their duties, but instead are usually paid employees of a temp agency or organization that provides qualified workers at the paid request of another company. Temps typically provide secretarial or administrative support, and thus may be exposed to a wide range of information. Because they are not employed by the host organization, they are often not subject to the contractual obligations or general policies that govern other employees. If temps violate a policy or cause a problem, the strongest action the host organization can take is to terminate the relationships and request that the temps be censured. The employing agency is under no contractual obligation to comply, although it may censure the employee to appease an important client.

From a security standpoint, temporary employees' access to information should be limited to that necessary for them to perform their duties. The organization can attempt to have temporary employees sign nondisclosure agreements and fair use policies, but the temp agency may refuse, forcing the host organization to choose among finding a new temp agency, going without the assistance of the temp worker, or allowing the temp to work without the agreement. This can create a potentially awkward and dangerous situation, as temporary workers may inadvertently gain access to information that does not directly relate to their responsibilities. The only way to combat this threat is to ensure that the supervisor restricts the information to which the temp has access and makes sure all employees follow good security practices, especially clean desk policies and the security of classified data. Temps can provide great benefits to the host organization, but they should not be employed at the cost of sacrificing information security.

> Contract Employees

Contract employees are typically hired to perform specific services for the organization. In such cases, the host company often makes a contract with a parent organization rather than with an individual employee for a particular task. Typical contract employees include groundskeepers, maintenance workers, electrical contractors, mechanical service contractors, and other service and repair workers. Although some contract workers may require access to virtually all areas of the organization to do their jobs, they seldom need access to information or information resources, except when the organization has leased computing equipment or contracted with a disaster recovery service. Contract employees may also need access to various facilities, but this does not mean they should be allowed to wander freely in and out of buildings. For the organization to maintain a secure facility, all contract employees should be escorted from room to room, as well as into and out of the facility. When contract employees report for maintenance or repair services, security personnel should first verify that these services are actually scheduled or approved. As indicated in earlier chapters, attackers have been known to dress up as telephone repairmen, maintenance technicians, or janitors to gain physical access to a building. Therefore, direct supervision of contract employees is a necessity.

Another necessary aspect of hiring contract employees is making certain that restrictions or requirements are negotiated into the contract agreements when they are activated. The following regulations should be negotiated well in advance: The facility requires 24 to 48 hours' notice of a maintenance visit; the facility requires all onsite personnel to undergo background checks; and the facility requires advance notice for cancellation or rescheduling of a maintenance visit.

> Consultants

Sometimes, onsite contracted workers are self-employed or are employees of an organization hired for a specific, one-time purpose. These workers are typically referred to as consultants, and they have their own security requirements and contractual obligations. Contracts for consultants should specify all requirements for information or facility access before the consultants are allowed into the workplace. Security and technology consultants especially must be prescreened, escorted through work areas, and subjected to nondisclosure agreements to protect the organization from possible breaches of confidentiality. It is human nature (and a trait often found among consultants) to brag about the complexity of a particular job or an outstanding service provided to another client. If the organization does not want the consultant to mention their working relationship or to disclose any details about a particular system configuration, the organization must write these restrictions into the contract. Consultants typically request permission to present work samples to other companies as part of their résumés, but a client organization is not obligated to grant this permission and can even explicitly deny permission in writing. Organizations should also remember that just because they are paying an information security consultant, the protection of their information doesn't become the consultant's top priority.

〉 Business Partners

On occasion, businesses create strategic alliances with other organizations that want to exchange information, integrate systems, or simply discuss operations for mutual advantage. In these situations, a prior business agreement is needed to specify the level of exposure both organizations are willing to tolerate. Sometimes, one division of a company enters a strategic partnership with an organization that directly competes with another of the company's own divisions. If the strategic partnership evolves into an integration of both companies' systems, competing groups might exchange information that neither parent organization expected to share. As a result, both organizations must make a meticulous, deliberate determination of what information is to be exchanged, in what format, and with whom. Nondisclosure agreements must be in place. Also, as discussed in Chapter 2, the security levels of both systems must be examined before any physical integration takes place—once systems are connected, the vulnerability of one system becomes the vulnerability of all.

Internal Control Strategies

Key Terms

job rotation The requirement that every employee be able to perform the work of another employee.

least privilege The data access principle that ensures no unnecessary access to data exists by regulating members so they can perform only the minimum data manipulation needed. Least privilege implies a need to know.

need to know The principle of limiting users' access privileges to the specific information required to perform their assigned tasks.

separation of duties The information security principle that requires significant tasks to be split up so that more than one individual is required to complete them.

task rotation The requirement that all critical tasks can be performed by multiple individuals.

two-person control The organization of a task or process so that at least two individuals must work together to complete it. Also known as dual control.

Among internal control strategies, separation of duties is a cornerstone in the protection of information assets and the prevention of financial loss. **Separation of duties** is used to reduce the chance that an employee will violate information security and breach the confidentiality, integrity, or availability of information. The control stipulates that the completion of a significant task involving sensitive information requires at least two people. The idea behind this separation is that if only one person has authorization to access a particular set of information, there may be nothing the organization can do to prevent the person from copying the information and removing it from the premises. Separation of duties is especially important, and thus commonly implemented, when financial information must be protected. For example, consider that two people are required to issue a cashier's check at a bank. The first is authorized to prepare the check, acquire the numbered financial document, and ready the check for signature. The process then requires a second person, usually a supervisor, to sign the check. Only then can the check be issued. If one person had the authority to perform both functions, he could write a number of checks, sign them, and steal large sums from the bank.

The same level of control should be applied to critical data. One programmer updates the system and a supervisor or coworker accesses the file location in which the updates are stored. Or, one employee can be authorized to run backups to the system and another can install and remove the physical media.

A similar concept is known as **two-person control,** in which two employees review and approve each other's work. This concept is distinct from separation of duties, in which the two people work in sequence. In two-person control, each person completely finishes the necessary work and then submits it to the other coworker. Each coworker then examines the work performed, double-checking to make sure no errors or inconsistencies exist. Figure 11-7 illustrates these operations.

Another control used to prevent personnel from misusing information assets is **job rotation** (or **task rotation**). If one employee cannot feasibly learn the entire job of another, the organization should at least try to ensure that multiple employees on staff can perform each critical task. Such job or task rotations can greatly increase the chance that an employee's misuse of the system or abuse of information will be detected by another. They also ensure that no one employee performs actions that cannot be physically audited by another employee. In general, this method makes good business sense. One threat to information is the organization's inability to have multiple employees who can perform the same task in case one is unable to perform his or her normal duties. If everyone knows at least part of another worker's job, the organization can survive the loss of any one employee.

This leads to a control measure that may seem surprising: mandatory vacations. Why should a company *require* its employees to take vacations? A mandatory vacation of at least one week gives the organization the ability to audit the work of an employee. People who are stealing from the organization or otherwise misusing information or systems are generally

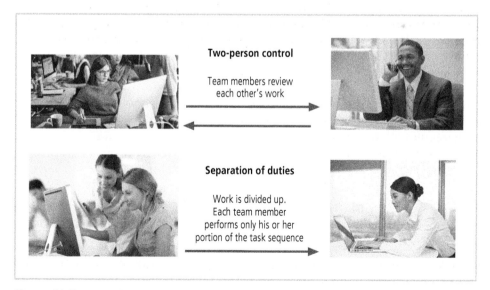

Figure 11-7 Internal control strategies

reluctant to take vacations, for fear that their actions will be detected. Therefore, all employees should be required to take a vacation so their jobs can be audited. This is not meant to imply that employees are untrustworthy, but to show how organizations must be creative with the control measures they apply, and even consider the security situation as a potential attacker would. The mandatory vacation policy is effective because it makes employees consider that they might be caught if they abuse the system. Information security professionals who think this practice impugns the character of their coworkers should note that some bonding authorities, auditing agencies, and oversight boards require mandatory vacations for all employees.

A related concept, *garden leave*, is used by some companies to restrict the flow of proprietary information when an employee leaves to join a competitor. When this procedure is invoked, an employee is paid salary and benefits for a period of time, often 15 or 30 days; is not allowed access to the former place of employment; and is not allowed to report to the new employer. The intent is to have employees lose the immediate value of any current knowledge about tactical intelligence at the former firm and ensure that the employee's recollections of specific details fade. Technically, such employees remain on the payroll of the former company, but they cannot go to work at their new company yet. The term *garden leave* comes from the fact that the employee can do little more than stay home and tend a garden for a while. In some organizations, employees are required to sign a covenant not to compete (CNC) or non-compete clause (NCC), which prevents them from working for a direct competitor within a specified time frame—usually a few months to several years. This clause is designed to minimize the loss of intellectual property when employees change jobs.

One final control measure is that employees should have access to the minimum amount of information necessary for them to perform their duties, and only as long as needed. In other words, there is no need for everyone in the organization to have access to all information. This principle is called **need to know**. A similar concept is **least privilege**, in which employees are restricted in their access and use of information based on their need to know. For example, an HR employee may have the need to know to access all employees' HR files, but may have the least privilege of only being allowed to edit (update) the employees' retirement benefits sections of their HR files. The whole purpose of information security is to allow people who need to use systems information to do so without being concerned about its confidentiality, integrity, and availability. Organizations should keep in mind that everyone who can access data probably will, with potentially devastating consequences for the organization's information security.

❯ Privacy and the Security of Personnel Data

Organizations are required by law to protect employee information that is sensitive or personal, as you learned in Chapter 3. This information includes employee addresses, phone numbers, Social Security numbers, medical conditions, and even names and addresses of family members.

In principle, personnel data is no different from other data that an organization's information security group must protect, but a great deal more regulation covers its protection. As a result, information security groups should ensure that this data receives at least the same level of protection as other important data in the organization, including intellectual property, strategic planning, and other business-critical information.

Selected Readings

There are many excellent sources of additional information in the area of information security. A few that can add to your understanding of this chapter are listed here:

- *Information Security Roles and Responsibilities Made Easy, Version 3*, by Charles Cresson Wood. 2012. Information Shield.

- *Management of Information Security, Fifth Edition*, by Michael E. Whitman and Herbert J. Mattord. 2017. Cengage Learning.

Chapter Summary

- Where to place the information security function within the organization is a key decision. The most popular options involve placing information security within IT or the physical security function. Organizations searching for a rational compromise should place the information security function where it can balance its need to enforce company policy with its need to deliver service to the entire organization.

- The selection of information security personnel is based on several criteria, not all of which are within the control of the organization.

- In most cases, organizations look for a technically qualified information security generalist with a solid understanding of how an organization operates. The following attributes are also desirable:

  - An attitude that information security is usually a management problem, not an exclusively technical problem

  - Good people skills, communication skills, writing skills, and a tolerance for users

  - An understanding of the role of policy in guiding security efforts

  - An understanding of the role of education and training in making users part of the solution

  - An understanding of the threats facing an organization, how they can become attacks, and how to protect the organization from information security attacks

  - A working knowledge of many common technologies and a general familiarity with most mainstream IT technologies

- Many information security professionals enter the field through one of two career paths: via law enforcement or military personnel, or from other professions related to technical information systems. In recent years, college students have been able to take courses that prepare them to enter the information security workforce directly.

- During the hiring process for an information security position, an organization should use standard job descriptions to increase the degree of professionalism among applicants and to make sure the position's roles and responsibilities are consistent with those of similar positions in other organizations. Studies of information security positions have found that they can be classified into one of three areas: those that define, those that build, and those that administer.

- When filling information security positions, many organizations indicate the level of proficiency required for the job by specifying that the candidate have recognizable certifications. Some of the more popular are:

  - The (ISC)^2 family of certifications, including the Certified Information Systems Security Professional (CISSP), a number of CISSP specialization certifications, the Systems Security Certified Practitioner (SSCP), the Associate of (ISC)^2, and several other specialized certifications

  - The ISACA family of certifications, including the Certified Information Security Manager (CISM), the Certified Information Systems Auditor (CISA), and several other specialized certifications

  - The Global Information Assurance Certification (GIAC) family of certifications, including the GIAC Information Security Professional and the GIAC Security Leadership Certification

  - CompTIA's Security+

  - ISFCE's Certified Computer Examiner

  - EC-Council's C|CISO

- The general management community of interest should integrate information security concepts into the organization's employment policies and practices. Areas in which information security should be a consideration include:

  - Hiring, including job descriptions, interviews, and background checks

  - Employment contracts

  - New hire orientation

  - Performance evaluation

  - Termination

- Organizations may need the special services of temporary employees, contract employees, consultants, and business partners, but these relationships should be carefully managed to prevent information leaks or theft.

- Separation of duties is a control used to reduce the chance of any person violating information security and breaching the confidentiality, integrity, or availability of information. According to the principle behind this control, any major task that involves sensitive information should require two people to complete.

Review Questions

1. What member of an organization should decide where the information security function belongs within the organizational structure? Why?

2. List and describe the options for placing the information security function within the organization. Discuss the advantages and disadvantages of each option.

3. For each major information security job title covered in the chapter, list and describe the key qualifications and requirements for the position.

4. What factors influence an organization's decisions to hire information security professionals?

5. Prioritize the list of general attributes that organizations seek when hiring information security professionals. In other words, list the most important attributes first. Use the list you developed to answer the previous review question.

6. What are critical considerations when dismissing an employee? Do they change according to whether the departure is friendly or hostile, or according to which position the employee is leaving?

7. How do security considerations for temporary or contract employees differ from those for regular full-time employees?

8. What career paths do most experienced professionals take when moving into information security? Are other pathways available? If so, describe them.

9. Why is it important to use specific and clearly defined job descriptions for hiring information security professionals?

10. What functions does the CISO perform?

11. What functions does the security manager perform?

12. What functions does the security analyst perform?

13. What rationale should an aspiring information security professional use in acquiring professional credentials?

14. List and describe the credentials of the information security certifications mentioned in this chapter.

15. Who should pay for the expenses of certification? Why?

16. List and describe the standard personnel practices that are part of the information security function. What happens to these practices when they are integrated with information security concepts?

17. Why shouldn't an organization give a job candidate a tour of secure areas during an interview?

18. List and describe the typical relationships that organizations have with temporary employees, contract employees, and consultants. What special security precautions must an organization consider for such workers, and why are they significant?

19. What is separation of duties? How can it be used to improve an organization's information security practices?

20. What is job rotation, and what benefits does it offer an organization?

Exercises

1. Search your library's database and the Web for an article about people who violate their organization's policy and are terminated. Did you find many? Why or why not?

2. Go to the (ISC)^2 Web site at *www.isc2.org*. Research the knowledge areas included in the tests for the CISSP and SSCP certifications. What areas must you study that are *not* included in this text?

3. Using the Web, identify some certifications with an information security component that were not discussed in this chapter.

4. Search the Web for at least five job postings for a security analyst. What qualifications do the listings have in common?

5. Search the Web for three different employee hiring and termination policies. Review each and look carefully for inconsistencies. Do each of the policies have sections that address information security requirements? What clauses should a termination policy contain to prevent disclosure of an organization's information? Create your own version of either a hiring policy or a termination policy.

Case Exercises

After her meeting with Charlie, Iris returned to her office. When she had completed her daily assignments, she began to make some notes about the information security position Charlie had offered her.

Discussion Questions

1. What questions should Iris ask Charlie about the new job, Kelvin's team, and the future of the company?

2. What questions should Iris ask Kelvin about the new job?

Ethical Decision Making

Suppose that Iris and Kelvin were involved in a romantic relationship, unknown to anyone else in the company. Such a relationship is not against company policy, but married employees are specifically prohibited from being in a direct reporting relationship with each other.

Should Iris inform Charlie about her relationship with Kelvin if she does not plan to apply for the transfer?

If she does apply for the job, but has no current plans for marriage, should she inform Charlie of her relationship?

Endnotes

1. Hayes, M. "Where the Chief Security Officer Belongs." *Information Week*. 22 February 2002. Accessed 10 October 2016 from *www.informationweek.com/where-the-chief-securityofficer-belongs/d/d-id/1013832?*.

2. Kosutic, D. "Chief Information Security Officer (CISO)—Where Does He Belong in an Org Chart?" Accessed 10 October 2016 from *http://blog.iso27001standard.com/2012/09/11/chief-information-security-officer-ciso-where-does-he-belong-in-an-org-chart/*.

3. Hunt, Steve. "The CISO in 2010 Still Touches Technology." *CSO Magazine*. July 2004.

4. Kennesaw State University Center for Information Security Education (CISE) and Security Executive Council (SEC). 2015 SEC/CISE Threats to Information Protection Report. Accessed 22 September 2016 from *www.securityexecutivecouncil.com/spotlight/?sid=29185*.

5. Bureau of Labor Statistics. *BLS Occupational Outlook Handbook*. Accessed 3 October 2016 from *www.bls.gov/ooh/computer-and-information-technology/information-security tyanalysts.htm*.

6. Frost and Sullivan. The 2015 (ISC)^2 Global Information Security Workforce Study. Accessed 21 September 2016 from *www.isc2cares.org/uploadedFiles/wwwisc2caresorg/Content/GISWS/FrostSullivan-(ISC)%C2%B2-Global-Information-Security-Workforce-Study-2015.pdf*.

7. Center for Strategic and International Studies. "Hacking the Skills Shortage: A study of the international shortage in cybersecurity skills." Accessed 22 September 2016 from *www.mcafee.com/us/resources/reports/rp-hacking-skills-shortage.pdf*.

8. Wood, Charles Cresson. *Information Security Roles and Responsibilities Made Easy*. 2012. Houston, TX: Information Shield Corporation, 55–94.

9. Schwartz, Eddie, Erwin, Dan, Weafer, Vincent, and Briney, Andy. "Roundtable: InfoSec Staffing Help Wanted!" *Information Security Magazine*. April 2001.

10. Wisconsin Jobs: Chief Information Security Officer. Accessed 10 October 2016 from *http://wiscjobs.state.wi.us/PUBLIC/print_view.asp?jobid=64037&annoid=64522*. Note that this link was disabled after the job was filled.

11. Security Jobs Network, Inc. "Sample Job Descriptions: Director of Security." *Security Jobs Network, Inc. Online*. Accessed 10 October 2016 from *securityjobs.net/documents/Director%20of%20Security%20Position,%20Cox.html*. Note that this link was disabled after the job was filled.

12. IT Security Jobs. "IT Security Vacancies." *SSR Personnel Online*. 22 July 2002. Accessed 5 July 2007 from *www.ssr-personnel.com/ucs/vacancies/IT%20Security.htm*. Note that this link was disabled after the job was filled.

13. IT Security Jobs. "623873—Firewall Engineering Consultant." *SSR Personnel Online*. 16 July 2002. Accessed 5 July 2007 from *www.itsecurityjobs.com/vacancies.htm*. Note that this link was disabled after the job was filled.

11

14. CISSP information brochure. (ISC)². Accessed 23 September 2016 from *www.isc2 .org/uploadedfiles/credentials_and_certifcation/cissp/cissp-information.pdf*.

15. "ISC² Concentrations." (ISC)². Accessed 10 October 2016 from *www.isc2.org /concentrations/default.aspx*.

16. "About SSCP Certification." (ISC)². Accessed 10 October 2016 from *www.isc2.org /sscp/default.aspx*.

17. "CSSLP." (ISC)². Accessed 10 October 2016 from *www.isc2.org/uploadedFiles/(ISC) 2_Public_Content/Certification_Programs/CSSLP/CSSLP-Brochure.pdf*.

18. "CSSLP Domains." (ISC)². Accessed 23 September 2016 from *www.isc2.org/csslpdo mains/default.aspx*.

19. "CCFP–Certified Cyber Forensics Professional." (ISC)². Accessed 3 October 2016 from *www.isc2.org/ccfp/default.aspx*.

20. "HCISPP–HealthCare Information Security and Privacy Practitioner." (ISC)². Accessed 3 October 2016 from *www.isc2.org/hcispp/default.aspx*.

21. "CCSP–Certified Cloud Security Professional." (ISC)². Accessed 3 October 2016 from *www.isc2.org/ccsp/default.aspx*.

22. "ISACA Exam Candidate Information Guide, 2016." ISACA. Accessed 10 October 2016 from *www.isaca.org/Certification/Documents/Candidates-Guide-2016_exp_Eng_1115.pdf*. If this link has been disabled, you can search for the information at *www.isaca.org*.

23. Ibid.

24. Ibid.

25. "CRISC Certification Job Practice." ISACA. Accessed 10 October 2016 from *www .isaca.org/Certification/CRISC-Certified-in-Risk-and-Information-Systems-Control/Pages /Job-Practice-Areas-2015.aspx*.

26. "Get Certified: Roadmap." GIAC. Accessed 10 October 2016 from *www.giac.org /certifications/get-certified/roadmap*.

27. "Domain 1: Governance (Policy, Legal & Compliance)." EC-Council. Accessed 10 October 2016 from *https://ciso.eccouncil.org/cciso-certification/cciso-domain-details/*.

28. "Domain 2: IS Management Controls and Auditing Management." EC-Council. Accessed 10 October 2016 from *https://ciso.eccouncil.org/cciso-certification/cciso-domain -details/*.

29. "Domain 3: Management – Projects and Operations (Projects, Technology & Operations)." EC-Council. Accessed 10 October 2016 from *https://ciso.eccouncil.org/cciso-certification /cciso-domain-details/*.

30. "Domain 4: Information Security Core Competencies." EC-Council. Accessed 10 October 2016 from *https://ciso.eccouncil.org/cciso-certification/cciso-domain-details/*.

31. "Domain 5: Strategic Planning & Finance." EC-Council. Accessed 10 October 2016 from *https://ciso.eccouncil.org/cciso-certification/cciso-domain-details/*.

32. "CompTIA Security+ (2011 Release) Certification Exam Objectives." Accessed 10 October 2016 from *https://certification.comptia.org/docs/default-source/exam-objectives /comptia-security-sy0-401.pdf*.

33. "CompTIA Security+." CompTIA. Accessed 10 October 2016 from *http://certification
    .comptia.org/getCertified/certifications/security.aspx*.

34. "CCE Certification Competencies." ISFCE. Accessed 10 October 2016 from *www
    .isfce.com/policies/CCE%20Certification%20Competencies.pdf*.

35. Wood, Charles Cresson. *Information Security Roles and Responsibilities Made Easy.*
    2012. Houston, TX: Information Shield Corporation, 577.

36. Background Check International, LLC. *"BCI." BCI Online.* Accessed 3 October 2016
    from *www.bcint.com*.

37. Federal Trade Commission. Fair Credit Reporting Act. 2002. 15 U.S.C., S. 1681 et seq.
    Accessed 3 October 2016 from *www.ftc.gov/enforcement/rules/rulemaking-regulatory
    -reform-proceedings/fair-credit-reporting-act*.

38. U.S. Congress. September 11th Commission Final Report. July 2004.

11

chapter 12

Information Security Maintenance

To improve is to change; to be perfect is to change often.
WINSTON CHURCHILL

Charlie Moody leaned back in his chair. It was Monday morning, the first workday after the biggest conversion weekend in the implementation of Sequential Label and Supply's information security project. Charlie had just reviewed the results. So far, everything had gone according to plan. The initial penetration tests run on Sunday afternoon were clean, and every change request processed in the past three months had gone through without any issues. Charlie was eager to return to the routine he had enjoyed before the attack on the company's network triggered the changes of the past few months.

Kelvin Urich tapped on the open door of Charlie's office. "Hey, Charlie," he said, "Have you seen the e-mail I just sent? There's an urgent vulnerability report on Bugtraq about the version of OpenSSL we use. Something called the Heartbleed bug. The open-source community just released a critical patch to be applied right away. Should I get the system programming team started on it?"

"Absolutely! Get them to pull the download from the distribution site as soon as they can," said Charlie. "But remember we need to follow our quality assurance steps carefully. Before they install it on a single production system, I want you to review the test results and QA report yourself. If you sign off, have them patch the servers for the HQ development team. Oh, and don't forget you need to get change orders into change control ASAP if we go forward on the patch and you plan to hit tonight's critical systems change window."

"I'll get right on it," Kelvin said.

After Kelvin left, Charlie pulled up Bugtraq on his PC. He was reading about the new vulnerability when he heard another knock on the door. It was Iris Majwubu.

"Hi, Charlie," Iris said. "Got a second?"

"Sure, Iris. How have you been? Settling in with Kelvin's team okay?"

She smiled and nodded. "Yeah, they're a good group. They have me studying the documentation trail from the time before the security program was implemented. I came to see you about the reassessment of the information asset inventory and the threat-vulnerability update that you asked for."

Charlie was confused for a second, but then he remembered the task he had assigned to Iris. "Oh, right," he said, with a slight grimace. "Sorry—I had put the quarterly asset and threat review out of my mind while we were busy implementing the blueprint. I suppose it's time to start planning for the regular reviews, isn't it?"

Iris handed him a folder and said, "Here's the first draft of the plan for the review project. Kelvin has already seen it, and he suggested I review it with you. Could you take a look and let me know when you would like to go over it?"

LEARNING OBJECTIVES

Upon completion of this material, you should be able to:

- Discuss the need for ongoing maintenance of the information security program
- List the recommended security management models
- Define a model for a full maintenance program
- Identify the key factors involved in monitoring the external and internal environment
- Describe how planning, risk assessment, vulnerability assessment, and remediation tie into information security maintenance
- Explain how to build readiness and review procedures into information security maintenance
- Discuss digital forensics and describe how to manage it
- Describe the process of acquiring, analyzing, and maintaining potential evidentiary material

Introduction

After successfully implementing and testing a new and improved information security profile, an organization may feel more confident about the level of protection it provides for its information assets. But it shouldn't, really. In all likelihood, a good deal of time has passed since the organization began implementing changes to the information security program. In that time, the dynamic aspects of the organization's environment will have changed. Almost all aspects of a company's environment are dynamic, meaning threats that were originally assessed in the early stages of the organization's risk management program have probably changed and new priorities have emerged. New types of attacks such as viruses, worms, and denial-of-service attacks have been developed, and new variants of existing attacks have probably emerged as well. In addition, a host of other variables outside and inside the organization have most likely changed.

Developing a comprehensive list of dynamic factors in an organization's environment is beyond the scope of this text. However, the following changes may affect an organization's information security environment:

- The acquisition of new assets and the divestiture of old assets
- The emergence of vulnerabilities associated with new or existing assets
- Shifting business priorities
- The formation of new partnerships
- The dissolution of old partnerships
- The departure of personnel who are trained, educated, and aware of policies, procedures, and technologies
- The hiring of personnel

As this list shows, by the time a cycle of the risk management program is completed, the environment of an organization has probably changed considerably. An information security team needs to be able to assure management periodically that the information security program is accommodating these changes. If the program is not adjusting adequately to change, it may be necessary to begin the cycle again. If an organization deals successfully with change and has created procedures and systems that can be adjusted to the environment, the existing security improvement program can continue to work well. Deciding whether to continue with the current improvement program or to renew the investigation, analysis, and design phases depends on how much change has occurred and how well the organization and its program for information security maintenance is adapting to its evolving environment.

Before learning about the maintenance model that the authors recommend, you need some background on the management and operation of an information security program. In this chapter, you will learn about the methods organizations use to monitor the three primary aspects of information security risk management, which are sometimes called the security triple: threats, assets, and vulnerabilities. You will also learn about digital forensics, a specialized area in information security that can become a valuable skill in some circumstances. Digital forensic techniques may be used when investigating events like network and system attacks or to support Human Resources or corporate security investigations into employee activities. In Chapter 4, you learned how incident response planning helps organizations anticipate, detect, react to, and recover from external and internal incidents. Digital forensics helps the organization understand what happened and how.

Security Management Maintenance Models

To manage and operate the ongoing security program, the information security community must adopt a management maintenance model. In general, management models are frameworks that structure the tasks of managing a particular set of activities or business functions.

❯ NIST SP 800-100, Information Security Handbook: A Guide for Managers

Key Terms

auditing The review of a system's use to determine if misuse or malfeasance has occurred.

build A snapshot of a particular version of software assembled or linked from its component modules.

build list A list of the versions of components that make up a build.

configuration A collection of components that make up a configuration item.

configuration and change management (CCM) An approach to implementing system change that uses policies, procedures, techniques, and tools to manage and evaluate proposed changes, track changes through completion, and maintain systems inventory and supporting documentation.[1]

configuration item A hardware or software item that will be modified and revised throughout its life cycle.

configuration management (CM) See *configuration and change management (CCM)*.

major release A significant revision of a version from its previous state.

minor release (update or patch) A minor revision of a version from its previous state.

revision date The date associated with a particular version or build.

software library A collection of configuration items that is usually controlled and that developers use to construct revisions and issue new configuration items.

version The recorded state of a particular revision of a software or hardware configuration item. The version number is often noted in a specific format, such as "M.N.b." In this notation, "M" is the major release number and "N.b" can represent various minor releases or builds within the major release.

NIST Special Publication (SP) 800-100, *Information Security Handbook: A Guide for Managers*,[2] provides managerial guidance for the establishment and implementation of an information security program. In particular, the handbook addresses the ongoing tasks expected of an information security manager once the program is working and day-to-day operations are established.

For each of the 13 areas of information security management presented in SP 800-100, there are specific monitoring activities—tasks that security managers should perform on an ongoing basis to monitor the function of the security program and take corrective actions when issues arise. Not all issues are negative, as in the opening scenario. Some are normal changes in the business environment, while others are changes in the technology environment—for example, the emergence of new technologies that could improve security or new security standards and regulations to which the organization should subscribe.

The following sections describe monitoring actions for the 13 information security areas. These sections were adapted from SP 800-100.

 For more information on NIST SP 800-100 and other NIST special publications, visit csrc.nist.gov/publications/PubsSPs.html.

1. Information Security Governance An effective information security governance program requires constant review. Agencies should monitor the status of their programs to ensure that:

- Ongoing information security activities are providing appropriate support to the agency's mission.

- Policies and procedures are current and aligned with evolving technologies, if appropriate.

- Controls are accomplishing their intended purpose.

Over time, policies and procedures may become inadequate because of changes in the agency's mission and operational requirements, threats, or the environment; deterioration in the degree of compliance; or changes in technology, infrastructure, or business processes. Periodic assessments and reports on activities can identify areas of noncompliance, remind users of their responsibilities, and demonstrate management's commitment to the security program. While an organization's mission does not frequently change, the agency may expand its mission to secure its programs and assets and require modification to its information security requirements and practices.

Table 12-1 provides a broad overview of key ongoing activities that can assist in monitoring and improving an agency's information governance activities.

2. Systems Development Life Cycle

As you learned in Chapter 1, the systems development life cycle (SDLC) is the overall process of developing, implementing, and retiring information systems through a multistep approach—initiation, analysis, design, implementation, and maintenance to disposal. Each phase of the SDLC includes a minimum set of information security activities required to effectively incorporate security into a system.

Activities	Description of Activities
Plans of Action and Milestones (POA&Ms)	POA&Ms assist in identifying, assessing, prioritizing, and monitoring the progress of corrective efforts for security weaknesses found in programs and systems. The POA&M tracks the measures implemented to correct deficiencies and to reduce or eliminate known vulnerabilities. POA&Ms can also assist in identifying performance gaps, evaluating an agency's security performance and efficiency, and conducting oversight.
Measurement and Metrics	Metrics are tools designed to improve performance and accountability through the collection, analysis, and reporting (measurement) of relevant performance data. Information security metrics monitor the accomplishment of goals and objectives by quantifying the implementation level of security controls and their efficiency and effectiveness, by analyzing the adequacy of security activities, and by identifying possible improvements. The terms *metric* and *measurement* seem to have some overlap in their meanings. A metric is usually meant to be a more abstract, higher-level, or subjective value, while measures tend to be more objective and concrete.
Continuous Assessment (CA)	The CA process monitors the initial security accreditation of an information system to track changes to it, analyzes the security impact of those changes, makes appropriate adjustments to the security controls and the system's security plan, and reports the system's security status to appropriate agency officials.
Configuration Management (CM)	CM is an essential component of monitoring the status of security controls and identifying potential security problems in information systems. This information can help security managers understand and monitor the evolving nature of vulnerabilities that appear in a system under their responsibility, thus enabling managers to direct appropriate changes as required.
Network Monitoring	Information about network performance and user behavior on the network helps security program managers identify areas in need of improvement and point out potential performance improvements. This information can be correlated with other sources of information, such as the POA&M and CM, to create a comprehensive picture of the security program.
Incident and Event Statistics	Incident statistics are valuable in determining the effectiveness of implemented security policies and procedures. Incident statistics provide security program managers with further insights into the status of security programs under their purview, help them observe performance trends in program activities, and inform them about the need to change policies and procedures.

Table 12-1 Ongoing Monitoring Activities of Information Security Governance[3]

Source: NIST SP 800-100.

SP 800-64 Rev. 2, *Security Considerations in the Information System Development Life Cycle*, presents a framework for incorporating security into all phases of the SDLC to ensure the selection, acquisition, and use of appropriate and cost-effective security controls. These considerations are summarized in Table 12-2.

A. Initiation Phase	
Needs Determination	• Define a problem that might be solved through product acquisition. • Establish and document the need and purpose of the system.
Security Categorization	• Identify information that will be transmitted, processed, or stored by the system and define applicable levels of categorizing information, especially the handling and safeguarding of personally identifiable information.
Preliminary Risk Assessment	• Establish an initial description of the system's basic security needs. A preliminary risk assessment should define the threat environment in which the system or product will operate.
B. Development/Acquisition Phase	
Requirements Analysis/ Development	• Conduct a more in-depth study of the need that draws on and further develops the work performed during the initiation phase. • Develop and incorporate security requirements into specifications. • Analyze functional requirements that may include the system security environment (such as enterprise information security policy and enterprise security architecture) and security functional requirements. • Analyze assurance requirements for acquisition and product integration activities and evidence that the product will provide required information security correctly and effectively.
Risk Assessment	• Conduct a formal risk assessment to identify system protection requirements. This analysis builds on the initial risk assessment performed during the initiation phase, but it is more in-depth and specific.
Cost Considerations and Reporting	• Determine how much of the product's acquisition and integration cost can be attributed to information security over the life cycle of the system. These costs include hardware, software, personnel, and training.
Security Planning	• Fully document agreed-upon security controls, whether they are planned or in place. • Develop the system security plan. • Develop documents that support the agency's information security program, such as the CM plan, contingency plan, incident response plan, security awareness and training plan, rules of behavior, risk assessment, security test and evaluation results, system interconnection agreements, security authorizations and accreditations, and plans of action and milestones. • Develop awareness and training requirements, including user manuals, operating manuals, and administrative manuals.
Security Control Development	• Develop, design, and implement security controls described in the respective security plans. For information systems that are currently in operation, their security plans may call for developing additional security controls to supplement existing controls or for modifying ineffective controls.
Developmental Security Test and Evaluation	• Test security controls developed for a new information system or product to ensure its proper and effective operation. • Develop the test plan, script, and scenarios.

Table 12-2 Ongoing Information Security Activities in the SDLC

Other Planning Components	• Ensure that all necessary components of product acquisition and integration are considered when incorporating security into the life cycle.
C. Implementation Phase	
Security Test and Evaluation	• Develop test data. • Test the unit, subsystem, and entire system. • Ensure that the system undergoes technical evaluation according to applicable laws, regulations, policies, guidelines, and standards.
Inspection and Acceptance	• Verify and validate that the functionality described in the specification is included in the deliverables.
System Integration/ Installation	• Integrate the system at the site where it will be deployed for operation. Enable security control settings and switches in accordance with vendor instructions and proper guidance for security implementation.
Security Certification	• Ensure that the controls are effectively implemented through established verification techniques and procedures, which gives the organization confidence that appropriate safeguards and countermeasures are in place to protect its information.
Security Accreditation	• Provide the necessary security authorization for an information system to process, store, or transmit information.
D. Operations/Maintenance Phase	

Configuration Management and Control	• Ensure adequate consideration of potential security impacts due to changes in an information system or its surrounding environment.
	• Develop CM plan
	  ○ Establish baselines
	  ○ Identify configuration
	  ○ Describe configuration control process
	  ○ Identify schedule for configuration audits

Continuous Monitoring	• Monitor security controls to ensure that they continue to be effective in their application through periodic testing and evaluation. • Perform self-administered audits, independent security audits, or other assessments periodically. Use automated tools, internal control audits, security checklists, and penetration testing. • Monitor the system and/or users by reviewing system logs and reports, using automated tools, reviewing change management, monitoring trade publications and other external sources, and performing periodic reaccreditation.
E. Disposal Phase	
Information Preservation	• Retain information as necessary to conform to current legal requirements and to accommodate future technology changes that may render the retrieval method obsolete. • Consult with the agency office for information on retaining and archiving federal records. Ensure the long-term storage of cryptographic keys for encrypted data. • Determine whether to archive, discard, or destroy information.
Media Sanitization	• Determine the sanitization level (overwrite, degauss, or destroy). • Delete, erase, and overwrite data as necessary.
Hardware and Software Disposal	• Dispose of hardware and software as directed by the governing agency's policy.

12

Table 12-2 Ongoing Information Security Activities in the SDLC[4] *(continued)*

Source: NIST SP 800-64, Rev. 2.

During this phase, the organization should continuously monitor system performance to ensure that it is consistent with established user and security requirements and that needed system modifications are incorporated.

For **configuration and change management (CCM)**, also known as **configuration management (CM)**, it is important to document proposed or actual changes in the system security plan. Information systems are typically in a constant state of evolution with upgrades to hardware, software, and firmware and possible modifications to the system's surrounding environment. Documenting information system changes and assessing their potential impact on system security is an essential part of continuous monitoring and key to avoiding a lapse in system security accreditation. Monitoring security controls helps to identify potential security problems in the information system that are not identified during the security impact analysis. This analysis is conducted as part of the CM and control process.

3. Awareness and Training

As you learned in Chapter 4, once the program has been implemented, processes must be put in place to monitor compliance and effectiveness. An automated tracking system should be designed to capture key information about program activity, such as courses, dates, audience, costs, and sources. The tracking system should capture this data at an agency level so it can be used to provide enterprise-wide analysis and reporting about awareness, training, and education initiatives.

Tracking compliance involves assessing the status of the program as indicated by the database information and mapping it to standards established by the agency. Reports can be generated and used to identify gaps or problems. Corrective action and necessary follow-up can then be taken. This follow-up may take the form of formal reminders to management; additional awareness, training, or education offerings; and the establishment of a corrective plan with scheduled completion dates. As the organization's environment changes, the security policies must evolve, and all awareness and training material should reflect these changes.

4. Capital Planning and Investment Control

Increased competition for limited resources requires that departments allocate available funding toward their highest-priority information security investments to afford the organization the appropriate degree of security for its needs. This goal can be achieved through a formal enterprise capital planning and investment control (CPIC) process designed to facilitate the expenditure of agency funds.

NIST SP 800-65, Rev. 1 DRAFT, *Recommendations for Integrating IT Security into the Capital Planning and Investment Control Process*, provides a seven-step process for prioritizing security activities and corrective actions for funding purposes:

1. Identify the baseline: Use information security measurements or other available data to baseline the current security posture.

2. Identify prioritization requirements: Evaluate the security posture against legislative requirements, other requirements from the chief information officer (CIO), and the agency's mission.

3. Conduct enterprise-level prioritization: Prioritize potential information security investments at the enterprise level against the agency's mission and prioritize the financial impact of implementing appropriate security controls.

4. Conduct system-level prioritization: Prioritize potential system-level corrective actions against the system category and corrective action impact.

5. Develop supporting materials: For enterprise-level investments, develop an initial conceptual business plan, business case analysis, and Exhibit 300. For system-level investments, adjust Exhibit 300 to request additional funding that mitigates prioritized weaknesses.

6. Implement an investment review board (IRB) and portfolio management: Prioritize agency-wide business cases against requirements and CIO priorities and determine the investment portfolio.

7. Submit any required budget approval paperwork.[5]

5. Interconnecting Systems

A system interconnection is defined as the direct connection of two or more information systems for sharing data and other information resources. Organizations choose to interconnect their information systems for a variety of reasons based on their needs. For example, they may interconnect information systems to exchange data, collaborate on joint projects, or securely store data and backup files.

Interconnecting information systems can expose the participating organizations to risk. For instance, if the interconnection is not properly designed, security failures could compromise the connected systems and their data. Similarly, if one of the connected systems is compromised, the interconnection could be used as a conduit to compromise the other system and its data.

NIST SP 800-47 details a four-phase life cycle management approach for interconnecting information systems that emphasizes information security:

- Phase 1: Planning the interconnection
- Phase 2: Establishing the interconnection
- Phase 3: Maintaining the interconnection
- Phase 4: Disconnecting the interconnection

Table 12-3 provides a checklist for organizations that are considering interconnecting multiple systems when developing an interconnection security agreement (ISA). While many parts of this agreement are specified for a federal government agency, referring to associated Special Publications and Federal Information Processing Standards (FIPS) can assist organizations in identifying issues to be resolved.

12

6. Performance Measurement

As described in Chapter 5, a program of performance measurement provides numerous financial and administrative benefits to organizations. Organizations can develop information security metrics that measure the effectiveness of their security program, and can provide data to be analyzed and used by program managers and system owners to isolate problems, justify investment requests, and target funds to the areas in need of improvement. By using specific measurements to target security investments, agencies can get the best value from available resources. The typical information performance management program consists of four interdependent components: senior management support, security policies and procedures, quantifiable performance measures, and analyses.

		YES	NO
1	**ISA Requirements:**		
A	Is there a formal requirement and justification for connecting two systems?		
B	Are there two systems being interconnected? If YES, have the systems been specified? If NO, the two systems need to be specified.		
C	Is there a list of benefits of required interconnection(s)?		
D	Is the agency name or organization that initiated the requirement listed?		
2	**System Security Considerations:**		
A	Has a security certification and accreditation of the system been completed?		
B	Has the security certification and accreditation status been verified?		
C	Are there security features in place to protect the confidentiality, integrity, and availability of the data and the systems being interconnected?		
D	Has each system's security categorization been identified per FIPS 199?		
E	Have minimum controls been identified for each system in accordance with NIST SP 800-53?		
F	Have both parties answered each subject item regardless of whether the subjected item only affects one party? If NO, both parties must go back and answer each item.		
G	Is there a general description of the information/data being made available, exchanged, or passed?		
H	Is there a description of the information services offered over the interconnected system by each participating organization? Such services include e-mail, file transfer protocols, database queries, file queries, and general computational services.		
I	Have system users been identified and has an approval been put in place?		
J	Is there a description of all system security technical services pertinent to the secure exchange of information and data among the systems in question?		
K	Are there documented rules of behavior for users of each system in the interconnection?		
L	Are there titles of the formal security policy or policies that govern each system?		
M	Are there procedures for incidents related to the interconnection?		
N	Are there audit requirements?		
3	**Topological Drawing:**		
A	A Is there a descriptive technical specification for the connections?		
4	**Signatory Authority:** The ISA is valid for one year after the last date on either signature below. At that time, it will be reviewed, updated if necessary, and revalidated. This agreement may be terminated upon 30 days of advance notice by either party or in the event of a security exception that would necessitate an immediate response.		

Table 12-3 ISA Checklist for Interconnecting Systems[6]

Source: NIST SP 800-47.

Information security measurements should be used for monitoring the performance of information security controls and initiating performance improvements. This iterative process consists of six phases, as depicted in greatly simplified form in Figure 12-1. In reality, a process like this does not often proceed in such a direct fashion; instead, give and take is common as control objectives are balanced against the availability of resources.

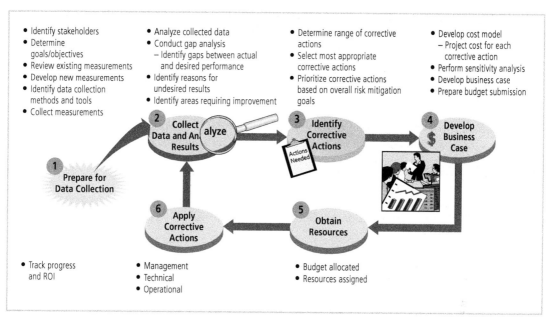

Figure 12-1 Information security measurement program implementation

Source: NIST SP 800-55 Rev. 1.[7]

Control Performance Baselines and Measurements

Control Performance Baselines and Measurements Because many technical controls for information security are implemented on common IT processors, they are affected by the same factors as most computer-based technologies. Therefore, it is important to monitor the performance of security systems and their underlying IT infrastructure to determine if they are working effectively. This type of performance monitoring is especially important for network appliances such as firewalls and content filters that look for inappropriate use of Internet resources and operate as pass-by devices. When these types of appliances are not sized correctly or are not properly tuned for sufficient performance, they do not stop the actions they are designed to block. Some common system and network measurements used in performance management are also applicable in security, especially when the components being managed involve the ebb and flow of network traffic. The following list—based on what is known as the 60% rule—offers a few guidelines that security personnel can use when exploring the issues of system and network performance.

- When the memory usage associated with a particular CPU-based system averages or exceeds 60 percent over prolonged periods, consider adding more memory.

- When the CPU usage associated with a particular CPU-based system averages or exceeds 60 percent over prolonged periods, consider an upgrade for the CPU or an increase in the number of CPUs dedicated to the function.

- When the network traffic on a particular link averages or exceeds 60 percent over prolonged periods, consider an upgrade to the link, which can be accomplished either by increasing the available bandwidth or segmenting the traffic.

- When the amount of data stored on a particular hard drive exceeds 60 percent of available capacity over a prolonged period, consider an upgrade, which can be accomplished either by replacing the hard drive with a larger-capacity drive or adding more drives.

To evaluate the performance of a security system, administrators must establish system performance baselines. Organizations should establish baselines for different criteria and for various periods of time, such as days of the week, weeks of the year, months of the year, and times of day, among others. Previous chapters of this text covered procedures for establishing baselines across industries and within organizations. In this context, a performance baseline is an expected level of performance against which all subsequent levels of performance are compared. For example, network traffic levels are deemed to be high when traffic reaches or surpasses the level of the performance baseline. To put it another way, the planning of capacity upgrades should begin before users complain about issues such as slow-loading Web pages.

While the details of developing and implementing security performance measurements is beyond the scope of this text, SP 800-55 Rev. 1, Performance Measurement Guide for Information Security, provides specific guidance and is a strongly recommended read. It is available from csrc.nist.gov/publications/nistpubs/800-55-Rev1/SP800-55-rev1.pdf.

7. Security Planning Planning for information security was discussed in detail in Chapter 4. Planning is one of the most crucial ongoing responsibilities in security management. Strategic, tactical, and operating plans must be developed that align with and support organizational and IT plans, goals, and objectives.

This section of SP 800-100 focuses on the controls available to address shortfalls identified in the planning process. FIPS 200: *Minimum Security Requirements for Federal Information and Information Systems*, specifies federal security requirements in 17 areas. In addition to reviewing the minimum security requirements in FIPS 200, private organizations would benefit from studying the controls in SP 800-53, *Recommended Security Controls for Federal Information Systems*. NIST SP 800-18 Rev. 1, *Guide for Developing Security Plans for Federal Information Systems*, provides a template for a systems security plan in Appendix A of the document.

8. Information Technology Contingency Planning Contingency planning, covered in Chapter 4, consists of a process for recovery and documentation of procedures for conducting recovery. The ongoing responsibilities of security management involve the maintenance of the contingency plan. The contingency plan must always be in a ready state for use immediately upon notification. Periodic reviews of the plan must be conducted to ensure currency of key personnel and vendor information, system components and dependencies, the recovery strategy, vital records, and operating requirements. While some changes may be obvious, such as personnel turnover or vendor changes, others require analysis. The business impact analysis should be reviewed periodically and updated with new information to identify new contingency requirements and priorities. Changes to the plan are noted in a record of changes, dated, and signed or initialed by the person making the change. The revised plan or plan sections are circulated to those with plan responsibilities. Because of the impact that plan changes may have on interdependent business processes or information systems, the changes must be clearly communicated and properly annotated at the beginning of the document.

9. Risk Management Risk management, covered in Chapter 5, is an ongoing effort as well. Risk identification, analysis, and management are a cyclic and fundamental part of continuous improvement in information security. The principal goal of risk management is to protect the organization and its ability to perform its mission, not just protect its information assets. Risk management is an essential management function of the organization that is tightly woven into the SDLC. Because risk cannot be eliminated entirely, the risk management process allows information security program managers to balance operating and economic costs of protective measures and achieve gains in mission capability. By employing practices and procedures designed to foster informed decision making, agencies help protect their information systems and the data that support their own mission.

Many risk management activities are conducted during a snapshot in time—a static representation of a dynamic environment. All the changes that occur to systems during normal, daily operations have the potential to adversely affect system security in some fashion. The goal of the evaluation and assessment process in risk management is to ensure that the system continues to operate safely and securely. This goal can be partially reached by implementing a strong configuration management program. In addition to monitoring the security of an information system on a continuous basis, agencies must track findings from the security control assessment to ensure they are addressed appropriately and do not pose risks to the system or introduce new ones.

The process of managing risk permeates the SDLC, from the early stages of project inception through the retirement of the system and its data. From inception forward, agencies should consider possible threats, vulnerabilities, and risks to the system so they can better prepare it to operate securely and effectively in its intended environment. During the security certification and accreditation process, a senior agency official determines whether the system is operating within an acceptable risk threshold.

10. Certification, Accreditation, and Security Assessments As described in Chapter 10, certification and accreditation for federal systems is radically changing for systems not designated as national security information systems. Some organizations need to review their own systems for certification and accreditation to be in compliance with banking, healthcare, international, or other regulations. Others may want the recognition offered by certifications like the ISO 27000 series. The security certification and accreditation process is designed to ensure that an information system operates with the appropriate management review, that there is ongoing monitoring of security controls, and that reaccreditation occurs periodically.

The continuous monitoring of a security assessment program, as a function of certification and accreditation, is an essential component of any security program. During this phase, the status of security controls in the information system is checked on an ongoing basis. An effective continuous monitoring program can be used to support the annual requirement specified in the Federal Information Security Management Act (FISMA) for assessing security controls in information systems. At a minimum, an effective monitoring program requires:

- Configuration management and configuration control processes for the information system
- Security impact analyses on changes to the information system
- Assessment of selected security controls in the information system and reporting of the system's security status to appropriate agency officials

12

To determine which security controls to select for review, agencies should first prioritize testing on "plan of action" items and milestone items that become closed. These newly implemented controls should be validated. Organizations should test against system-related security control changes that did not constitute a major change or require new certification and accreditation. Organizations should identify all security controls that are continuously monitored as annual testing and evaluation activities. Once this is complete, organizations should look at remaining controls that have not been tested that year and make a decision about further annual testing based on risk, the importance of the control, and the date of the last test. The results of continuous monitoring should be reviewed regularly by senior management and any necessary updates should be made to the system security plan. An example form for continuously monitoring reporting is provided in NIST SP 800-53A.

Part of the ongoing security assessment is **auditing**. Most computer-based systems used in information security can create logs of their activity. These logs are a vital part of the detective functions associated with determining what happened, when it happened, and how. Managing systems logs in large organizations is a complex process and is sometimes considered an art in itself. Unless security or systems administrators are vigilant, the logs can pile up quickly because systems are constantly writing the activity that occurs on them. Fortunately, automated tools known as log analyzers can consolidate systems logs, perform comparative analysis, and detect common occurrences or behavior of interest. Behavior of interest may include port scanning and other anomalous network activity, malware signatures, hacking attempts, and illicit use of controlled network resources or computer systems. Log analyzers, a component of some intrusion detection and prevention systems (IDPSs), can detect activities in real time. Each type of IDPS, whether host-, network-, or application-based, also creates logs. These logs are invaluable records of events and should be archived and stored for future review as needed. System intruders have been known to attempt to cover their tracks by erasing entries in logs, so wise administrators configure their systems to create duplicate copies of the logs and store the copies on sources that cannot be easily modified, like optical disk technologies such as CD-R and DVD-R. Many vendors offer log consolidation and analysis features that allow for integration of log files from multiple products, such as firewalls, network equipment, and even products from other vendors.

To assist organizations in meeting their reporting requirements, the information security assessment survey shown in Table 12-4 covers many of the areas typically required for inclusion in reports. The questionnaire can be customized for an organization or program and can be completed by the CIO, the CISO, or an independent assessor of the agency's information security program.

Each question should be answered for each level of IT security maturity.

- To answer "Yes" at the Policy maturity level, the topic should be documented in the organization's policy.
- To answer "Yes" at the Procedures maturity level, the topic should be documented in detailed procedures.
- To answer "Yes" at the Implemented maturity level, the implementation is verified by examining the procedures and program area documentation and interviewing key personnel.
- To answer "Yes" at the Tested maturity level, documents should be examined and interviews should be conducted to verify that the policies and procedures covered by

Program Questions	Policy	Proce-dures	Imple-mented	Tested	Integrated
1. Security Control Review Process Does management ensure that corrective information security actions are tracked using the plan of action and milestones (POA&M) process?					
2. Capital Planning and Investment Control Does the agency require the use of a business case, Exhibit 300, and Exhibit 53 to record the resources required for security at an acceptable level of risk for all programs and systems in the agency?					
3. Investment Review Board Is there an investment review board or similar group designated and empowered to ensure that all investment requests include the security resources needed or that all exceptions to this requirement are documented?					
4. Integrating Information Security into Capital Planning and Investment Control (CPIC) Is there integration of information security into the CPIC process?					
5. Budget and Resources Are information security resources, including personnel and funding, allocated to protect information and information systems in accordance with assessed risks?					
6. Systems and Projects Inventory Are IT projects and systems identified in an inventory and is the information about the IT projects and systems relevant to the investment management process? Is there a detailed inventory of systems?					
7. IT Security Measurements Are IT security measurements collected agency-wide and reported?					
8. Enterprise Architecture and the Enterprise Architecture Security and Privacy Profile Are system- and enterprise-level information security and privacy requirements and capabilities documented within the agency's enterprise architecture? Is that information used to understand the current risks to the agency's mission? Is that information used to help program and agency executives select the best security and privacy solutions to enable the mission?					
9. Critical Infrastructure Protection Plan If required in your agency, is there a documented critical infrastructure and key resources protection plan?					
10. Life Cycle Management (LCM) Is there a system life cycle management process that requires each system to be certified and accredited? Is each system officially approved to operate? Is the system LCM process communicated to appropriate people?					

Table 12-4 Information Security Program Questions[8]

Source: NIST SP 800-100.

the question are implemented, operating as intended, and providing the desired level of security.

- To answer "Yes" at the Integrated maturity level, policies, procedures, implementation, and testing are continually monitored and improvements are made as a normal business process of the organization.

11. Security Services and Products Acquisition
Information security services and products are essential elements of an organization's information security program. Such products are widely available in the marketplace and are frequently used by federal agencies. Security products and services should be selected and used to support the organization's overall program to manage the design, development, and maintenance of its information security infrastructure and to protect its mission-critical information. Agencies should apply risk management principles to help identify and mitigate risks associated with product acquisition.

When acquiring information security products, organizations are encouraged to conduct a cost-benefit analysis—one that also includes the costs associated with risk mitigation. This analysis should include a life cycle cost estimate for current products and one for each identified alternative while highlighting the benefits associated with each alternative. NIST SP 800-36, *Guide to Selecting Information Technology Security Products*, defines broad security product categories and then specifies product types, product characteristics, and environment considerations within those categories. The guide also provides a list of pertinent questions that agencies should ask when selecting products.

The process of selecting information security products and services involves numerous people throughout an organization. Each person or group involved in the process should understand the importance of security in the organization's information infrastructure and the security impacts of their decisions. Personnel might be included from across the organization to provide relevant perspective on information security needs that must be integrated into the solution.

Just as the SDLC supports the development of products, the security services life cycle (SSLC) provides a framework to help decision makers organize and coordinate their security efforts from initiation to completion. Figure 12-2 depicts the SSLC for obtaining security services at a high level. Table 12-5 provides a brief summary of each phase.

Vulnerabilities in IT products surface nearly every day, and many ready-to-use exploits are available on the Internet. Because IT products are often intended for a wide variety of audiences, restrictive security controls are usually not enabled by default, so many IT products are immediately vulnerable out of the box. Security program managers should review NIST SP 800-70, Rev. 3, *National Checklist Program for IT Products: Guidelines for Checklist Users and Developers*, which helps them develop and disseminate security checklists so that organizations and individual users can better secure their IT products. In its simplest form, a security configuration checklist is a series of instructions for configuring a product to a particular operating environment. This checklist is sometimes called a lockdown or hardening guide or benchmark.

12. Incident Response
As illustrated throughout this text, attacks on information systems and networks have become more numerous, sophisticated, and severe in recent years. While preventing such attacks would be the ideal course of action, not all security incidents

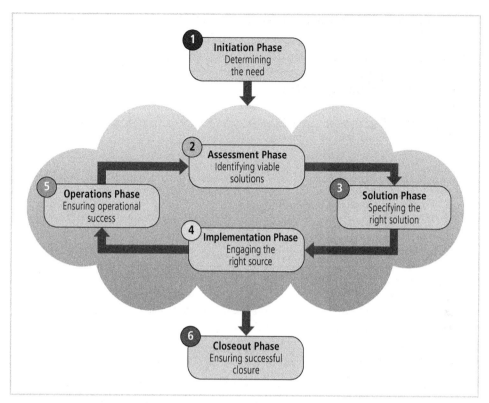

Figure 12-2 The information security services life cycle

Source: NIST SP 800-35.[9]

can be prevented. Every organization that depends on information systems and networks should identify and assess the risks to its systems and reduce those risks to an acceptable level. An important component of this risk management process is the trending analysis of past computer security incidents and the identification of effective ways to deal with them. A well-defined incident response capability helps the organization detect incidents rapidly, minimize loss and destruction, identify weaknesses, and restore IT operations rapidly.

As you learned in earlier chapters, the first clue that an attack is under way often comes from reports by observant users. Similarly, the first clue that a security system has a fault or error may also come from user feedback. In many organizations, help desks handle these user reports as well as other system problems. If an organization does not have a help desk, it should probably consider establishing one, or at least make other provisions to allow users to report suspicious system behavior. The nearby Offline feature discusses the function and organization of help desks.

Help desk personnel must be trained to distinguish a security problem from other system problems. As help desk personnel screen problems, they must also track the activities involved in resolving each complaint in a help desk information system. The tracking process is commonly implemented using a trouble ticket. A trouble ticket is opened when a user calls about an issue and is closed when help desk or technical support personnel resolve

Phase	Activity
Phase 1—Initiation	• Begins when the need to initiate the services life cycle is recognized • Consists of needs determination, security categorization, and the preliminary risk assessment
Phase 2—Assessment	• Involves developing an accurate portrait of the current environment before decision makers can implement a service and a service provider • Baselines the existing environment; metrics creation, gathering, and analysis; and total cost of ownership • Analyzes opportunities and barriers • Identifies options and risks
Phase 3—Solution	• Decision makers choose the appropriate solution from the viable options identified during the assessment phase • Develops the business case • Develops the service arrangement • Develops the implementation plan
Phase 4—Implementation	• Service providers are implemented during this phase • Identifies the service provider and develops the service agreement • Finalizes and executes the implementation plan • Manages expectations
Phase 5—Operations	• The service's life cycle becomes iterative; the service is working, the service provided is fully installed, and a constant assessment must be made of the service level and source performance • Monitors and measures organization performance • Evaluates current operations and directs actions for continuous improvement
Phase 6—Closeout	• Because of the iterative nature of the life cycle, the service and service provider could continue indefinitely, but this is unlikely • If the environment changes, information security program managers will identify triggers that initiate new and replacement services for information security • Selects the appropriate exit strategy • Implements the selected exit strategy

Table 12-5 The Information Security Services Life Cycle[10]

Source: NIST SP 800-36, Guide to Selecting Information Technology Security Products.

the issue. One key advantage to having formal help desk software is the ability to create and develop a knowledge base of common problems and solutions. This knowledge base can be searched when a user problem comes up; if it is similar to a problem that was already reported and resolved, complaints can be resolved more quickly. This knowledge base can also generate statistics about the frequency of problems by type, by user, or by application, and thus can detect trends and patterns in the data. Incidentally, some user problems may actually be created or influenced by a security program because modifications to firewalls, implementations of IDPS rules, or new systems policies in the network can directly affect how users interact with the systems. A significant number of help desk trouble tickets are the result of user access issues involving passwords and other mechanisms of authentication, authorization, and accountability. Proper user training and ongoing awareness campaigns can reduce these problems but not completely eliminate them.

OFFLINE

The Help Desk

With a relatively small investment in an IT help desk, an organization can improve the quality of its IT support and information security function. A small help desk with only a few call agents can provide service for an organization of several hundred users. Large organizations can also improve customer service through the use of a help desk, as long as it receives adequate funding and effective management.

Although it may function differently depending on the organization, a help desk commonly provides the following services:

- A single point of contact for service requests from users
- Initial screening of requests, answering common questions, solving common problems, and dispatching other types of calls to other units
- Entering all calls into a tracking system
- Dispatching service providers to respond to calls
- Reporting and analysis of call volumes, patterns, and process improvement
- Early detection of adverse events, which could escalate to incidents or foreshadow disasters

Other services that may be integrated into the help desk include:

- Desk-side support for common IT applications such as Windows, end-user computing tools, and common applications
- Managing new users
- Timely removal of users who no longer need system access
- Password management
- Smart card management
- Knowledge management for service requests and optimum resolutions
- Server configuration
- Network monitoring
- Server capacity monitoring
- Virus activity monitoring and virus pattern management

While each organization has its own approach to creating and developing a help desk solution, many help desks evolve and alter their mix of services over time.[11]

12

Figure 12-3 shows a system called Free Help Desk that is configured to support incident response reporting, change management reporting, and standard help desk requests.

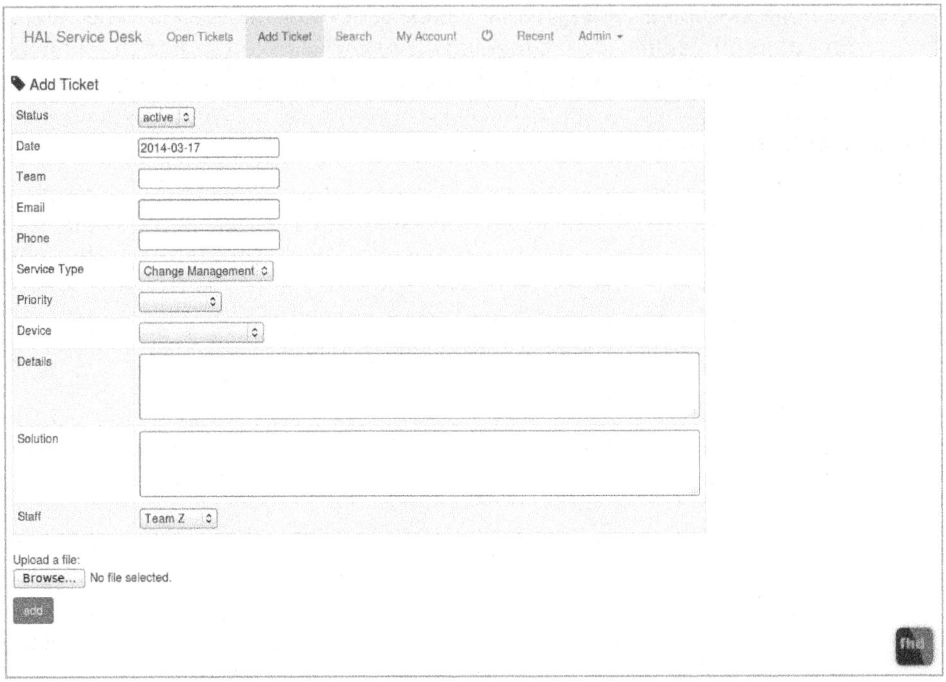

Figure 12-3 Free Help Desk

Source: www.freehelpdesk.org.

 The Free Help Desk application is available from www.freehelpdesk.org.

To resolve a problem, a support technician may need to visit a user's office to examine equipment or observe the user's procedures, or interact with other departments or workgroups. The help desk team sometimes includes a dedicated security technician. In any case, the person working to resolve the trouble ticket must document both the diagnosis and the resolution, as they are invaluable components of the knowledge base. Once the problem has been resolved and the results are documented, the ticket is closed.

13. Configuration and Change Management The purpose of configuration and change management is to manage the effects of changes or differences in configurations in an information system or network. In some organizations, configuration management is the identification, inventory, and documentation of the current information systems—hardware, software, and networking configurations. Change management is sometimes described as a separate function that only addresses modifications to this base configuration. Here, the two concepts are combined to address the current and proposed states of the information systems and the management of any needed modifications.

 To see an example framework for software product line practice—a best practice configuration management approach—visit the Software Engineering Institute's Web site at www.sei.cmu .edu/productlines/frame_report/config.man.htm.

Just as documents should have version numbers, revision dates, and other features designated to monitor and administer changes made to them, so too should the technical components of systems, such as software, hardware, and firmware. Several key terms are used in the management of configuration and change in technical components, as shown in the following hypothetical example.

Let's assume that XYZ Security Solutions Corporation has developed a new software application called Panacea, the Ultimate Security Solution. Panacea is the **configuration item**. Panacea's **configuration** consists of three major software components: See-all, Know-all, and Cure-all. Thus, Panacea is **version** 1.0, and it is built from its three components. The **build list** is See-all 1.0, Know-all 1.0, and Cure-all 1.0, as this is the first **major release** of the complete application and its components. The **revision date** is the date associated with the first **build**. To create Panacea, the programmers at XYZ Security Solutions pulled information from their **software library**. Suppose that while the application is being used in the field, the programmers discover a minor flaw in a subroutine. When they correct this flaw, they issue a **minor release**, Panacea 1.1. If at some point they need to make a major revision to the software to meet changing market needs or fix more substantial problems with the subcomponents, they would issue a major release, Panacea 2.0. In addition to the challenge of keeping applications at the current version level, administrators face the release of newer versions of operating systems and ongoing rollouts of newer hardware versions. The combination of updated hardware, operating systems, and applications is further complicated by the constant need for bug fixes and security updates to these elements.

CCM assists in streamlining change management processes and prevents changes that could adversely affect the security posture of a system. In its entirety, the CCM process reduces the risk that any changes to a system will compromise the system or data's confidentiality, integrity, or availability, because the process provides a repeatable mechanism for effecting system modifications in a controlled environment. In accordance with the CCM process, system changes must be tested prior to implementation to observe the effects of the change and minimize the risk of adverse results.

NIST SP 800-64, Rev. 2, *Security Considerations in the System Development Life Cycle*, states:

> *Configuration management and control procedures are critical to establishing an initial baseline of hardware, software, and firmware components for the information system and subsequently to controlling and maintaining an accurate inventory of any changes to the system. Changes to the hardware, software, or firmware of a system can have a significant impact on the security of the system … changes should be documented, and their potential impact on security should be assessed regularly.*[12]

NIST SP 800-53, Rev. 4, *Security and Privacy Controls for Federal Information Systems and Organizations*, defines seven CM controls that organizations are required to implement based on an information system's security categorization. The required CM controls are defined in Table 12-6.

The CM process identifies the steps required to ensure that all changes are properly requested, evaluated, and authorized. The CM process also provides a detailed, step-by-step procedure for identifying, processing, tracking, and documenting changes. An example CM process is described in the following sections.

Identifier	Title	Control
CM-1	Configuration Management Policy and Procedures	The organization: a. Develops, documents, and disseminates a CM policy that addresses purpose, scope, roles, responsibilities, management commitment, coordination among organizational entities, and compliance; and develops, documents, and disseminates procedures to facilitate the implementation of the CM policy and associated CM controls b. Reviews and updates the current CM policy and CM procedures
CM-2	Baseline Configuration	Under configuration control, the organization develops, documents, and maintains a current baseline configuration of the information system.
CM-3	Configuration Change Control	The organization: a. Determines the types of changes to the information system that are configuration-controlled b. Reviews proposed configuration-controlled changes to the information system and approves or disapproves such changes with explicit consideration for security impact analyses c. Documents configuration change decisions associated with the information system d. Implements approved configuration-controlled changes to the information system e. Retains records of configuration-controlled changes to the information system for a specified time period f. Audits and reviews activities associated with configuration-controlled changes to the information system g. Coordinates and provides oversight for configuration change control activities through the organization's configuration change control committee or board
CM-4	Security Impact Analysis	The organization analyzes changes to the information system to determine potential security impacts prior to change implementation.
CM-5	Access Restrictions for Change	The organization defines, documents, approves, and enforces physical and logical access restrictions associated with changes to the information system.
CM-6	Configuration Settings	The organization establishes and documents configuration settings for information technology products employed within the information system, using security configuration checklists that reflect the most restrictive mode consistent with operating requirements; implements the configuration settings; identifies, documents, and approves any deviations from established configuration settings for the organization's information system components based on operating requirements; and monitors and controls changes to the configuration settings in accordance with the organization's policies and procedures.
CM-7	Least Functionality	The organization configures the information system to provide only essential capabilities, and prohibits or restricts the use of certain functions, ports, protocols, and services.

Table 12-6   NIST SP 800-53, Rev. 4, Configuration Management Control Family[13]

Source: NIST SP 800-53, Rev. 4.

Step 1: Identify Change The first step of the CM process begins when a person or process associated with the information system identifies the need for a change. The change can be initiated by numerous people, such as users or system owners, or it may be identified by audit findings or other reviews. A change may consist of updating the fields or records of a database or upgrading the operating system with the latest security patches. Once the need for a change has been identified, a change request should be submitted to the appropriate decision-making body.

Step 2: Evaluate Change Request After initiating a change request, the organization must evaluate possible effects that the change may have on the system or other interrelated systems. An impact analysis of the change should be conducted using the following guidelines:

- Whether the change is viable and improves the performance or security of the system
- Whether the change is technically correct, necessary, and feasible within the system constraints
- Whether system security will be affected by the change
- Whether associated costs for implementing the change were considered
- Whether security components are affected by the change

Step 3: Implementation Decision Once the change has been evaluated and tested, one of the following actions should be taken:

- Approve: Implementation is authorized and may occur at any time after the appropriate authorization signature has been documented.
- Deny: The request is immediately denied regardless of circumstances and the information provided.
- Defer: The immediate decision is postponed until further notice. In this situation, additional testing or analysis may be needed before a final decision can be made.

Step 4: Implement Approved Change Request Once the decision has been made to implement the change, it should be moved from the test environment into production. If required, the personnel who update the production environment are not the same people who developed the change. This requirement provides greater assurance that unapproved changes are not implemented into production.

Step 5: Continuous Monitoring The CCM process calls for continuous system monitoring to ensure that it is operating as intended and that implemented changes do not adversely affect the system's performance or security posture. Agencies can achieve the goals of continuous system monitoring by performing configuration verification tests to ensure that the selected configuration for a given system has not been altered outside the established CCM process. In addition to configuration verification tests, agencies can also perform system audits. Both require an examination of system characteristics and supporting documentation to verify that the configuration meets user needs and ensure that the current configuration is the approved system configuration baseline.

As part of the overall CCM process, agencies should also perform patch management during this step. Patch management helps lower the potential risk to a network by "patching" or repairing known vulnerabilities in any of the network or system environments. Increasingly, vendors are proactive in developing fixes or antidotes to known vulnerabilities and releasing them to the public. Agencies must remain vigilant to ensure that they capture all relevant

12

fixes as they are released, test their implementation for adverse effects, and implement them after testing is concluded. Patching is associated with phases 2, 3, and 4 of the life cycle. In phase 2, patch management relates to risk management to prevent any vulnerability from being exploited and compromised. Phase 3 contains the testing to ensure that patching and any other changes do not negatively affect the system.

In general, configuration and change management should not interfere with use of the technology. One person on the security team should be appointed as the configuration manager or change manager and made responsible for maintaining appropriate data elements in the organization's cataloging mechanism, such as the specific version, revision date, and build associated with each piece of implemented hardware and software. In some cases, someone outside the implementation process might be better suited to this role because he might not be distracted by the installation, configuration, and troubleshooting of the new implementation. In the case of minor revisions, it may be simpler to have a procedure that requires documenting the machines on which a revision is installed, the date and time of the installation, and the name of the installer. While the documentation procedures required for configuration and change management may seem onerous, they enable security teams to quickly and accurately determine exactly which systems are affected when a new vulnerability arises. When stored in a comprehensive database with risk, threat, and attack information, configuration information enables organizations to respond quickly to new and rapidly changing threats and attacks.

❯ The Security Maintenance Model

While management models such as the ISO 27000 series and NIST SP 800-100, *Information Security Handbook: A Guide for Managers*, deal with methods to *manage* and *operate* systems, a maintenance model is designed to focus the organization's effort on *maintaining* systems. Figure 12-4 illustrates an approach recommended for dealing with change caused by information security maintenance. The figure diagrams a full maintenance program and serves as a framework for the discussion that follows.

The recommended maintenance model is based on five subject areas or domains:

- External monitoring
- Internal monitoring
- Planning and risk assessment
- Vulnerability assessment and remediation
- Readiness and review

The following sections explore each of these domains and their interactions.

Monitoring the External Environment

Key Term

external monitoring domain The component of the maintenance model that focuses on evaluating external threats to the organization's information assets.

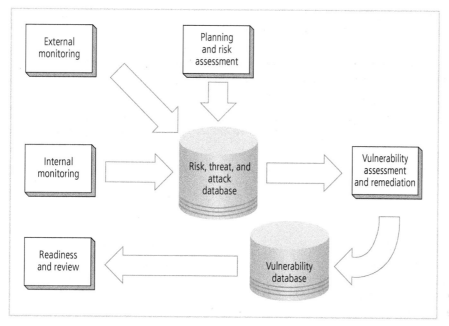

Figure 12-4 The maintenance model

During the Cold War, the Western alliance, led by the United States and Britain, confronted the Soviet Union and its allies. A key component of the Western alliance's defense was maintaining the ability to detect early warnings of attacks. The image of an ever-vigilant team of radar operators scanning the sky for incoming attacks could also represent the current world of information security, where teams of information security personnel must guard their organizations against dangerous and debilitating threats. While the stakes for modern organizations are not as critical as preventing nuclear war, they are nevertheless very high, especially at organizations that depend on information.

The objective of the **external monitoring domain** within the maintenance model is to provide early awareness of new and emerging threats, threat agents, vulnerabilities, and attacks so the organization can mount an effective and timely defense. Figure 12-5 shows the primary components of the external monitoring process.

External monitoring entails collecting intelligence from various data sources and then giving the intelligence context and meaning for use by decision makers within the organization.

Data Sources Acquiring data about threats, threat agents, vulnerabilities, and attacks is not difficult. There are many sources of raw intelligence and relatively few costs associated with gathering it. The challenge is turning this flood of good and timely data into information that decision makers can use. For this reason, many organizations outsource this component of the maintenance model. Service providers can provide a tailored supply of processed intelligence to organizations that can afford their subscription fees.

12

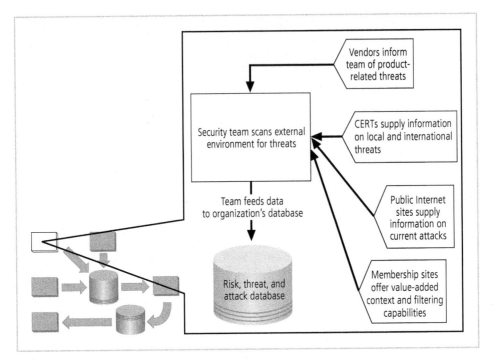

Figure 12-5 External monitoring

As shown in Figure 12-5, external intelligence can come from these classes of sources:

- Vendors: When an organization uses specific hardware and software as part of its information security program, the vendor often provides either direct support or indirect tools that allow user communities to support each other. This support often includes intelligence on emerging threats.

- CERT organizations: Computer emergency response teams (CERTs) exist in varying forms around the world. Often, US-CERT (*www.us-cert.gov*) is viewed as the definitive authority. Many states have CERT agencies, and many countries have CERT organizations to deal with national issues and threats. Your local, state, or national government may have a CERT outreach program to provide notification services at no direct cost. The U.S. Department of Homeland Security (DHS) works with the CERT/CC program at Carnegie Mellon University to provide the services at US-CERT.

- Public network sources: Many publicly accessible information sources, including mailing lists and Web sites, are freely available to organizations and people who have the time and expertise to use them. Table 12-7 lists some of these information security intelligence sources.

- Membership sites: Various groups and organizations provide value to subscribers by adding contextual detail to publicly reported events and offering filtering capabilities that allow subscribers to quickly pinpoint the possible impact to their own organizations.

Source Name	Type	Comments
US-CERT	Web site, mailing list, news	The CERT Coordination Center (CERT/CC), in conjunction with the U.S. Department of Homeland Security (DHS), provides the National Cyber Awareness System, which can send e-mail advisories and supporting information to registered organizations and individuals. You can select the type of notifications you need and register for the desired advisory list at *www.us-cert.gov/ncas*. Links to other resources are provided at *www.us-cert.gov/related-resources*.
National Vulnerability Database	Web site, news, data feeds	The U.S. government repository, hosted by NIST and sponsored by DHS, US-CERT, and the NCCIC, is an online repository for vulnerability management data. The content of the site can be used to support automation of vulnerability detection. NVD includes several databases of security-related software flaws, information on misconfigurations, checklists for assessment of vulnerabilities, and other related content like impact metrics. The contents of this database are synchronized with the *cve.mitre.org* database. Available at *nvd.nist.gov*.
CERT/CC	Web site, blogs, news	CERT/CC is a center of Internet security expertise at the Software Engineering Institute, a federally funded research and development center operated by Carnegie Mellon University. CERT/CC and DHS support the Web site, which is usually considered the definitive authority to be consulted when emerging threats become demonstrated vulnerabilities. See CERT/CC's home page at *www.cert.org*.
IBM's X-Force	Web site, news	A commercial site with a focus on the vendor's own commercial IDPS and other security products. The site also provides breaking news about emerging threats, and allows individuals to subscribe to alerts. See *www-03.ibm.com/security/xforce/resources.html*, formerly IBM's Internet Security Systems (ISS) at *www.iss.net*.
Insecure.org	Web site, mailing lists, blog	*Insecure.org* is the creation of the well-known hacker Fyodor. He and his associates operate the site and provide the Internet community with software (Nmap is the best known of the *insecure.org* tools) and information about vulnerabilities. Many topics are covered in the available lists at *seclists.org*.
Mitre	Web site, news	The dictionary of Common Vulnerabilities and Exploits (see *cve.mitre.org*) is an online database managed by the Mitre Corporation. Available from the site is information and news on current vulnerabilities and related exploitation methods.
Packet Storm	News	A commercial site providing news and discussion focusing on current security events and tools (see *packetstormsecurity.com*).
SecurityFocus	Web site, mailing lists	A commercial site providing general coverage and commentary on information security (see *www.securityfocus.com*). The site includes multiple information sources: • Bugtraq mailing list—The industry standard repository of detailed, full-disclosure discussions and announcements about computer security vulnerabilities. There are also multiple mailing lists of specialized categories under Bugtraq, like Focus on Microsoft, Focus on Apple, Focus on Virus, and Forensics. • The SecurityFocus Vulnerability Database • 31 SecurityFocus Mailing Lists

12

Table 12-7 External Intelligence Sources (*continues*)

Source Name	Type	Comments
Snort	Mailing list	Includes announcements and discussion of Snort, an open-source IDPS. The list includes discussions and information about the program and its rule sets and signatures. It can be a useful source for information about detecting emerging threats. Individuals can register for this mailing list at *lists.sourceforge.net/lists/listinfo/snort-sigs*.
SourceForge	Blogs	*SourceForge.net* maintains a large number of blogs and downloadable products for open-source software with integral comments, like Snort. To search for a particular topic, visit *https://sourceforge.net*.
Tenable	Web blog	Tenable's Web site dedicated to the Nessus vulnerability scanner. The Nessus Web site has information about emerging threats and how to test for them. The blog is at *www.tenable.com/taxonomy/term/349*. For product information, see *www.tenable.com/products/nessus-vulnerability-scanner*.
Bugtraq	Mailing list, Web resource	A set of moderated mailing lists, provided by SecurityFocus, full of detailed, full-disclosure discussions and announcements about computer security vulnerabilities (see descriptions of the individual mailing lists in the table entries that follow). The primary mailing list, called Bugtraq, provides time-sensitive coverage of emerging vulnerabilities, documenting how they are exploited and reporting on how to remediate them. Individuals can register for the flagship mailing list or any one of the entire family of Bugtraq mailing lists at *www.securityfocus.com/archive*.
Bugtraq Focus-IDS	Mailing list	Contains information about intrusion detection and prevention system vulnerabilities, and discusses both how to exploit them and how to use them in defending networks.
Bugtraq Focus-MS	Mailing list	Discusses the inner workings and underlying software weaknesses of Microsoft software products. It includes detailed discussions on the various security mechanisms available to help assess, secure, and remediate Microsoft software products.
Bugtraq Forensics	Mailing list	A discussion of technical and process methodologies for the application of computer forensics. The discussion is centered around technical methodology, audit trail analysis (technical procedures), general postmortem analysis (technical procedures), products and tools for use in this field (technical discussion), process methodology for evidence handling (technical discussion), search and seizure (nontechnical procedures and discussion), and evidence handling policies (nontechnical procedures and discussion).
Bugtraq Incidents	Mailing list	A lightly moderated mailing list that facilitates the quick exchange of security incident information. Topics include information about rootkits and back doors; new Trojan horses, viruses, and worms; sources of attacks; and telltale signs of intrusions.
Bugtraq Pen-test	Mailing list	Allows people to converse about professional penetration testing. The list is not OS-specific and has discussions on many varieties of networks and devices.
Bugtraq Vuln-dev	Mailing list	Contains reports of potential or undeveloped vulnerabilities. This is a full-disclosure list and can include exploit code.
Bugtraq Focus-virus	Mailing list	Discusses the inner workings and underlying issues of the various products, tools, and techniques available that may help secure systems from virus threats.

Table 12-7 External Intelligence Sources (*continued*)

For more information about the joint US-CERT program sponsored by DHS and CERT-CC, visit the Web site at www.us-cert.gov/about-us.

Regardless of where or how external monitoring data is collected, it is not useful unless it is analyzed in the context of the organization's security environment. To perform this evaluation and take appropriate actions in a timely fashion, the CISO must:

- Staff the function with people who understand the technical aspects of information security, have a comprehensive understanding of the organization's complete IT infrastructure, and have a thorough grounding in the organization's business operations.
- Provide documented and repeatable procedures.
- Train the primary and backup staff assigned to perform the monitoring tasks.
- Equip assigned staff with proper access and tools to perform the monitoring function.
- Cultivate expertise among monitoring analysts so they can cull meaningful summaries and actionable alerts from the vast flow of raw intelligence.
- Develop suitable communications methods for moving processed intelligence to designated internal decision makers in all three communities of interest—IT, information security, and general management.
- Integrate the incident response plan with the results of the external monitoring process to produce appropriate, timely responses.

Monitoring, Escalation, and Incident Response The basic function of the external monitoring process is to monitor activity, report results, and escalate warnings. The best approach for escalation is based on a thorough integration of the monitoring process into the IRP, as you learned in Chapter 4. The monitoring process has three primary deliverables:

- Specific warning bulletins issued when developing threats and specific attacks pose a measurable risk to the organization. The bulletins should assign a meaningful risk level to the threat to help decision makers in the organization formulate the appropriate response.
- Periodic summaries of external information. The summaries present statistical results, such as the number of new or revised CERT advisories per month, or itemized lists of significant new vulnerabilities.
- Detailed intelligence on the highest risk warnings. This information prepares the way for detection and remediation of vulnerabilities in the later steps of vulnerability assessment. This intelligence can include identifying which vendor updates apply to specific vulnerabilities and which types of defenses have been found to work against the specific vulnerabilities reported.

Data Collection and Management Over time, the external monitoring processes should capture information about the external environment in a format that can be referenced throughout the organization as threats emerge and then referenced for historical use. This data collection can use e-mail, Web pages, databases, or even paper-and-pencil recording methods, as long as the essential facts are communicated, stored, and used to create queries when needed. In the final analysis, external monitoring collects raw intelligence, filters it for relevance to the organization, assigns it a relative risk impact, and communicates these findings to decision makers in time to make a difference.

Monitoring the Internal Environment

The primary goal of the **internal monitoring domain** is an informed awareness of the state of the organization's networks, information systems, and information security defenses. This awareness must be communicated and documented, especially for components that are exposed to the external network. Internal monitoring is accomplished by:

- Building and maintaining an inventory of network devices and channels, IT infrastructure and applications, and elements of information security infrastructure.

- Leading the IT governance process within the organization to integrate the inevitable changes found in all network, IT, and information security programs.

- Monitoring IT activity in real time using IDPSs to detect and respond to actions or events that introduce risk to the organization's information assets.

- Monitoring the internal state of the organization's networks and systems. To maintain awareness of new and emerging threats, this recursive review is required of network and system devices that are online at any given moment and of any changes to services offered on the network. This review can be accomplished through automated difference-detection methods that identify variances introduced to the network or system hardware and software.

The value of internal monitoring is increased when knowledge gained from the network and systems configuration is fed into the vulnerability assessment and remediation maintenance domain. However, this knowledge becomes invaluable when incident response processes are fully integrated with the monitoring processes.

Figure 12-6 shows the component processes of the internal monitoring domain, which are discussed in the sections that follow.

Network Characterization and Inventory Organizations should have and maintain a carefully planned and fully populated inventory of all their network devices, communication channels, and computing devices. This inventory should include server hardware, desktop hardware, and software, including operating systems and applications. The inventory should also include *partner interconnections*—network devices, communications channels, and applications that may not be owned by the organization but are essential to its continued partnership with another company. The process of collecting this information is often referred to as *characterization*.

 As reported by journalist Brian Krebs, the high-profile data breach at Target stores in December 2013 was traced back to network credentials that were stolen from a refrigeration, heating, and air conditioning subcontractor. Read more at https://krebsonsecurity.com/2014/02/target-hackers-broke-in-via-hvac-company/.

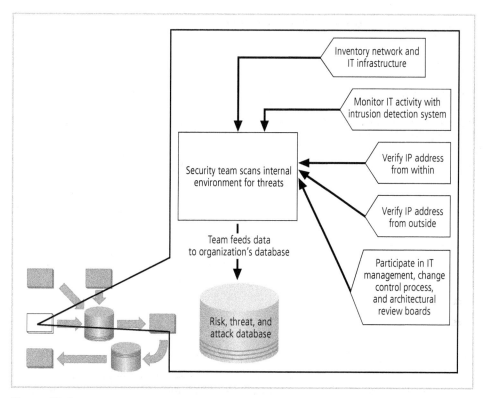

Figure 12-6　Internal monitoring

Once the characteristics of the network environment have been identified and collected as data, they must be carefully organized and stored using a manual or automated mechanism that allows for timely retrieval and rapid integration of disparate facts. For all but the smallest network environments, this requires a relational database. The attributes of network devices, such as systems, switches, and gateways, were discussed in earlier chapters. In contrast to the attributes collected for risk management, which are important for economic and business value, the characteristics collected here—manufacturer and software versions—relate to technical functionality, so they should be kept accurate and up to date. Also, the technology needed to store this data should be stand-alone and portable because if the data is needed to support incident response and disaster recovery, server or network access may be unavailable.

Making IDPSs Work　To be used most effectively, the information that comes from an IDPS must be integrated into the maintenance process. An IDPS generates a seemingly endless flow of alert messages that often have little bearing on the immediate effectiveness of the information security program. Except for an occasional real-time alert that is not a false positive, the IDPS reports events that have already occurred. Given this, the most important value of raw intelligence provided by the IDPS is that it can be used to prevent future attacks by indicating current or imminent vulnerabilities. Whether the organization outsources IDPS monitoring, staffs IDPS monitoring 24/7, staffs IDPS monitoring during business hours, or merely ignores the real-time alerts from the IDPS, the log files from the IDPS engines can be mined for information that can be added to the internal monitoring knowledge base.

12

Another element of IDPS monitoring is traffic analysis. Analyzing the traffic that flows through a system and its associated devices can often be a critically important process because the traffic identifies the most frequently used devices. Also, analyzing attack signatures from unsuccessful system attacks can help identify weaknesses in various security efforts. An example of the type of vulnerability exposed by traffic analysis occurs when an organization tries to determine if all its device signatures have been adequately masked. In general, the default configuration setting of many network devices allows them to respond to any request with a device signature message that identifies the device's make and model and perhaps even its software version. In the interest of greater security, many organizations require that all devices be reconfigured to conceal their device signatures. Suppose that an organization performs an analysis of unsuccessful attacks and discovers that lesser-known UNIX attacks are being launched against one of its servers. This discovery might inform the organization that the server under attack is responding to requests for OS type with its device signature.

Detecting Differences   One approach that can improve the awareness of the information security function uses a process known as **difference analysis** to quickly identify changes to the internal environment. Any unexpected differences between the current state and the baseline state could indicate trouble. Table 12-8 shows how several kinds of difference analyses can be used. Note that the table lists suggestions for *possible* difference analyses; each organization should identify the differences it wants to measure and its criteria for action.

Suggested Frequency	Method of Analysis	Data Source	Purpose
Quarterly	Manual	Firewall rules and logs	To verify that new rules follow all risk assessment and procedural approvals; identify illicit rules; ensure removal of expired rules; and detect tampering
Quarterly	Manual	Edge router rules and logs	To verify that new rules follow all risk assessment and procedural approvals; identify illicit rules; ensure removal of expired rules; and detect tampering
Quarterly	Manual	Internet footprint	To verify that public Internet addresses registered to the organization are accurate and complete
Monthly	Automated	Fingerprint all IP addresses	To verify that only known and authorized devices offering critical services can be reached from the internal network
Weekly	Automated	Fingerprint services on critical servers on the internal network	To verify that only known and approved services are offered from critical servers in the internal network
Daily	Automated	Fingerprint all IP addresses from the outside	To verify that only known and approved servers and other devices can be reached from the public network
Hourly	Automated	Fingerprint services on critical servers exposed to the Internet	To enable e-mail notification of administrators if unexpected services become available on critical servers exposed to the Internet

Table 12-8   Types of Difference Analysis

The value of difference analysis depends on the quality of the baseline, which is the initial snapshot portion of the difference comparison. The value of the analysis also depends on the degree to which the notification of discovered differences can induce action.

Planning and Risk Assessment

Key Term

planning and risk assessment domain The component of the maintenance model that focuses on identifying and planning ongoing information security activities and identifying and managing risks introduced through IT information security projects.

The primary objective of the **planning and risk assessment domain** is to keep lookout over the entire information security program, in part by identifying and planning ongoing information security activities that further reduce risk. In fact, the bulk of the security management maintenance model could fit in this domain. Also, the risk assessment group identifies and documents risks introduced both by IT projects and information security projects. It also identifies and documents risks that may be latent in the present environment. The primary objectives of this domain are:

- Establishing a formal review process for the information security program that complements and supports both IT planning and strategic planning

- Instituting formal project identification, selection, planning, and management processes for follow-up activities that augment the current information security program

- Coordinating with IT project teams to introduce risk assessment and review for all IT projects so that risks introduced by the launches of new IT projects are identified, documented, and factored into decisions about the projects

- Integrating a mindset of risk assessment throughout the organization that encourages other departments to perform risk assessment activities when any technology system is implemented or modified

Figure 12-7 illustrates the relationships between the components of this maintenance domain. Note that there are two pivotal processes: the planning needed for information security programs and evaluation of current risks using operational risk assessment.

Information Security Program Planning and Review An organization should periodically review its ongoing information security program and any planning for enhancements and extensions. The strategic planning process should examine the future IT needs of the organization and their impact on information security.

A recommended approach is to take advantage of the fact that most larger organizations have annual capital budget planning cycles. Thus, the IT group can develop an annual list of project ideas for planning and then prepare an estimate for the effort needed to complete them, the estimated amount of capital required, and a preliminary assessment of the risks associated with performing each project or not. These assessments become part of the organization's project-planning process. When capital and expense budgets are made final, the projects to be funded are chosen using the planning information on hand. This allows

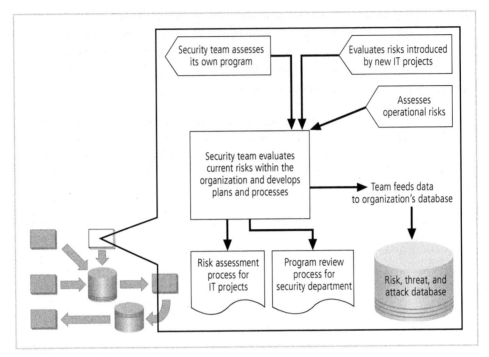

Figure 12-7 Planning and risk assessment

executives to make informed decisions about which projects to fund. The IT group then follows up with quarterly reviews of progress, which include an updated project risk assessment. As each project nears completion, an operational risk assessment group reviews the impact of the project on the organization's risk profile. The sponsors of the project and perhaps other executives then determine if the risk level is acceptable, if the project requires additional risk remediation, or if the project must be aborted.

Projects that organizations might fund to maintain, extend, or enhance the information security program will arise in almost every planning cycle. Larger information security projects should be broken into smaller, incremental projects, which is important for several reasons:

- Smaller projects tend to have more manageable impacts on the networks and users. Larger projects tend to complicate the change control process in the implementation phase.

- Shorter planning, development, and implementation schedules reduce uncertainty for IT planners and financial sponsors.

- Most large projects can easily be broken into smaller projects, giving the security team more opportunities to change direction and gain flexibility as events occur and circumstances change.

Security Risk Assessments A key component in the engine that drives change in the information security program is a relatively straightforward process called a risk assessment (RA), which was described in detail in Chapter 5. The RA is a method of identifying and documenting the risk that a project, process, or action introduces to the organization, and it may also offer suggestions for controls that can reduce the risk. The information security group coordinates the preparation of many types of RA documents, including the following:

- Network connectivity RA: Used to respond to network change requests and network architectural design proposals. It may be part of a business partner's RA or be used to support it.

- Business partner RA: Used to help evaluate a proposal for connectivity with business partners. Note that business partner risks extend beyond the direct contractual relationship to include the partner's vendors, landlords, and other clients. For instance, a cloud vendor may outsource some or all data center operations to a third party, which in turn may lease physical space in part of a building. In such an arrangement, part of physical security may be managed by a simple leasing arrangement, not by a professional data center security team.

- Application RA: Used at various stages in the life cycle of a business application. Its content depends on the project's position in the life cycle when the RA is prepared. Usually, multiple RA documents are prepared at different stages. The definitive version is prepared as the application is readied for conversion to production.

- Vulnerability RA: Used to help communicate the background, details, and proposed remediation as vulnerabilities emerge or change over time.

- Privacy RA: Used to document applications or systems that contain protected personal information that must be evaluated for compliance with the organization's privacy policies and relevant laws.

- Acquisition or divesture RA: Used when planning for reorganization as units of the organization are acquired, divested, or moved.

- Other RA: Used when a statement about risk is needed for any project, proposal, or fault that is not contained in the preceding list.

The RA process identifies risks and proposes controls. Most RA documents are structured to include the components shown in Table 12-9. Most training programs on information security include training sessions for the preparation of RA documents.

Component	Description	When and How Used
Introduction	A standard opening description to explain the RA to readers who are unfamiliar with the format. The exact text varies for each RA template. Here is an example: "The primary purpose of the security risk assessment is to identify computer and network security risks to information assets that may be introduced to the organization by the issue described in this document. This security risk assessment is also used to help identify security controls planned or proposed. Further, the sections below may identify risks that are not adequately controlled by the planned controls."	Found in all RA document templates
Scope	A statement of the boundaries of the RA. Here is an example: "To define the security and control requirements associated with project X running application Y with access via Internet and the migration of that application into the organization's environment."	Found in all RA document templates

Table 12-9 Risk Assessment Documentation Components (*continues*)

Component	Description	When and How Used
Disclaimer	A statement that identifies limits in the risk assessment based on when the report was developed in the project life cycle. The information that was available at different times during the project affects the comprehensiveness and accuracy of the report. Often, risk assessments are the most imprecise at the earliest stages of a project, so decision makers must be made aware of this lack of precision when the risk assessment is based on incomplete information. This statement is sometimes removed from the final RA when all information about the project is available, but it may be left in to provide awareness that some imprecision is inherent in the process. Here is an example: "The issues documented in this report should not be considered all-inclusive. A number of strategic and tactical decisions will be made during the development and implementation stages of the project, and therefore the security control deliverables may change based on actual implementation. Any changes should be reassessed to ensure that proper controls will still be enacted."	Found in all draft RA document templates; some issues may remain in the disclaimer in some final RA templates
Information security resources	A list of information security team members who collected information, analyzed risk, and documented the findings.	Found in all RA document templates
Other resources	A list of other organization members who provided information, assisted in analyzing risk, and documented the findings.	Found in all RA document templates
Background	Documentation of the proposed project, including network changes, application changes, and other issues or faults.	Found in all RA document templates
Planned controls	Documentation of all controls that are planned in the proposed project, including network changes, application changes, and other issues or faults.	Found in all RA document templates
IRP and DRP planning elements	Documentation of the incident response and disaster planning elements prepared for this proposed project, including network changes, application changes, and other issues or faults.	Recommended in all document templates
Opinion of risk	A summary statement of the risk introduced to the organization by the proposed project, network change, application, or other issue or fault. For example: "This application as it currently exists is considered high risk. IMPORTANT NOTE: Because of the high risk of the current implementation and the potential for harming the organization if system or data is compromised in any way, this notification needs to be escalated to the director or manager who would be held responsible for the added expense or loss of revenue associated with such a compromise. In addition, an acknowledgement of the risk and the urgency of correcting it must be signed and returned to the CISO."	Found in all RA document templates

Table 12-9 Risk Assessment Documentation Components (*continues*)

Component	Description	When and How Used
Recommenda- tions	A statement of what needs to be done to implement controls within the project to limit risk from it. For example: "A project team should be formed to assist the operating unit and technical support team in creating a comprehensive plan to address the security issues within application X. Specific areas of concern are authentication and authorization. The corrections of configuration errors found in the platform security validation process must continue. All user accounts need to be reviewed and scrubbed to determine whether the user or service account requires access. All user accounts need to be reviewed and assigned the appropriate privileges. The Web server of the application needs to be separated from the application and database server."	Found in all RA document templates

Information security controls recommendations summary	A summary of the controls that are planned or needed, using the system's security architecture elements as an organizing method. The following categories of information should be documented in tabular form:
	• Security architecture elements and what they provide.
	  ○ Authentication: The user is verified as authentic.
	  ○ Authorization: The user is allowed to use the facility or service.
	  ○ Confidentiality: Content must be kept secret from unintended recipients.
	  ○ Integrity: Data storage must be secure, accurate, and precise.
	  ○ Accountability: Actions and data usage can be attributed to specific people.
	  ○ Availability and reliability: Systems work when needed.
	  ○ Privacy: Systems comply with the organization's privacy policy.
	• Security requirement written for a general audience in terms of the organization's information security policies, using the following core principles of information security:
	  ○ Authentication: Must conform to the organization's authentication policies.
	  ○ Authorization: Must conform to the organization's authorization and usage policies.
	  ○ Confidentiality: Must comply with the requirement to protect data in transit from interception and misuse by using hard encryption.
	  ○ Integrity: Must process data with procedures that ensure freedom from corruption.
	  ○ Accountability: Must track usage to allow actions to be audited later for policy compliance.
	  ○ Availability and reliability: Must be implemented to assure availability that measures up to the organization's expectations.
	  ○ Privacy: Must process, store, and transmit data using procedures that meet legal privacy requirements.
	• Security controls planned or in place: Identify controls for each architectural element.
	• Planned completion date when the control will be fully operational.
	• Who is responsible: Which group or individual employees are accountable for implementing the control?
	• Status: What is the status of the control implementation?
		Recommended in all document templates

Table 12-9 Risk Assessment Documentation Components (*continued*)

12

A risk assessment's identification of systemic or latent vulnerabilities that introduce risk to the organization can provide the opportunity to create a proposal for an information security project. When used as part of a complete risk management maintenance process, the RA can be a powerful and flexible tool that helps identify and document risk and remediate the underlying vulnerabilities that expose the organization to risks of loss.

Vulnerability Assessment and Remediation

Key Terms

Internet vulnerability assessment An assessment approach designed to find and document vulnerabilities that may be present in the organization's public network.

intranet vulnerability assessment An assessment approach designed to find and document selected vulnerabilities that are likely to be present on the organization's internal network.

penetration testing A set of security tests and evaluations that simulate attacks by a hacker or other malicious external source.

platform security validation (PSV) An assessment approach designed to find and document vulnerabilities that may be present because misconfigured systems are used within the organization.

remediation The processes of removing or repairing flaws in information assets that cause a vulnerability or removing the risk associated with the vulnerability.

vulnerability assessment (VA) The process of identifying and documenting specific and provable flaws in the organization's information asset environment.

vulnerability assessment and remediation domain The component of the maintenance model focused on identifying specific, documented vulnerabilities and remediating them in a timely fashion.

war driving The use of mobile scanning techniques to identify open wireless access points.

wireless vulnerability assessment An assessment approach designed to find and document vulnerabilities that may be present in the organization's wireless local area networks.

The primary goal of the **vulnerability assessment and remediation domain** is to identify specific, documented vulnerabilities and remediate them in a timely fashion. This is accomplished by:

- Using documented vulnerability assessment procedures to safely collect intelligence about internal and public networks; platforms, including servers, desktops, and process control; and wireless network systems
- Documenting background information and providing tested remediation procedures for reported vulnerabilities
- Tracking vulnerabilities from the time they are identified until they are remediated or the risk of loss has been accepted by an authorized member of management
- Communicating vulnerability information, including an estimate of the risk and detailed remediation plans to the owners of vulnerable systems
- Reporting on the status of vulnerabilities that have been identified
- Ensuring that the proper level of management is involved in deciding to accept the risk of loss associated with unrepaired vulnerabilities

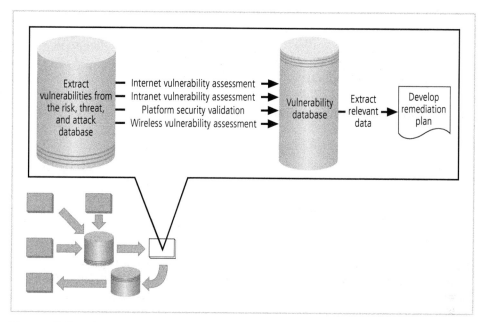

Figure 12-8 Vulnerability assessment and remediation

Figure 12-8 illustrates the process flow of the vulnerability assessment and remediation domain. Using the inventory of environment characteristics stored in the risk, threat, and attack database, the vulnerability assessment identifies and documents vulnerabilities. They are stored, tracked, and reported in the vulnerability database until they are remediated.

As shown in Figure 12-8, there are four common **vulnerability assessment (VA)** processes: Internet VA, intranet VA, platform security validation, and wireless VA. While the exact procedures associated with each can vary, these four processes can help many organizations balance the intrusiveness of vulnerability assessment with the need for a stable and effective production environment. Some organizations pursue a strategy of monthly vulnerability assessments that involve all four processes. Others perform an Internet vulnerability assessment every week and rotate the other three processes on a monthly or quarterly basis. These choices depend on the quantity and quality of resources dedicated to vulnerability assessments.

 For a list of the "top 125 security tools," including vulnerability assessment tools, visit sectools.org, a Web site hosted by insecure.org.

Penetration Testing **Penetration testing** is a level of sophistication beyond vulnerability testing. A penetration test, or *pen test*, is usually performed periodically as part of a full security audit. In most security tests, such as vulnerability assessments, great care is taken not to disrupt normal business operations, but in pen testing the analyst tries to get as far as possible by simulating the actions of an attacker. Unlike the attacker, however, the pen tester's ultimate responsibility is to identify weaknesses in the security of the organization's systems and networks and then present findings to the system's owners in a detailed report.

While vulnerability testing is usually performed inside the organization's security perimeter with complete knowledge of the networks' configuration and operations, pen testing can be

12

conducted in one of two ways—black box pen testing and white box pen testing. In black box pen testing, or blind testing, the "attacker" has no prior knowledge of the systems or network configurations and thus must investigate the organization's information infrastructure from scratch. In white box testing, also known as full-disclosure testing, the organization provides information about the systems to be examined, allowing for a faster, more focused test. White box pen testing is typically used when a specific system or network segment is suspect and the organization wants the pen tester to focus on a particular aspect of the target. Variations of black box and white box testing, known as grey box or partial-disclosure tests, involve partial knowledge of the organization's infrastructure.

Organizations often hire private security firms or consultants to perform penetration testing for a number of reasons:

- The "attacker" would have little knowledge of the inner working and configuration of the systems and network other than that provided by the organization, resulting in a more realistic attack.

- Unlike vulnerability assessment testing, penetration testing is a highly skilled operation, requiring levels of expertise beyond that of the average security professional.

- Also unlike vulnerability assessment testing, penetration testing requires customized attacks instead of standard, preconfigured scripts and utilities.

- External consultants have no vested interest in the outcome of the testing and are thus in a position to offer more honest, critical reports.

A common methodology for pen testing is found in the Open Source Security Testing Methodology Manual (OSSTMM), a manual on security testing and analysis created by Pete Herzog and provided by ISECOM, the nonprofit Institute for Security and Open Methodologies. The methodology itself, which covers what, when, and where to test, is free to use and distribute under the Open Methodology License (OML). The OSSTMM manual is free for noncommercial use and released under a Creative Commons license.

 For more information on OSSTMM, including manual and software downloads, visit www .isecom.org/research/osstmm.html.

A number of penetration testing certifications are available for people who are interested in this aspect of security testing. For example, the Information Assurance Certification Review Board (IACRB) offers a pen testing certification known as the Certified Penetration Tester (CPT). The CPT requires that the applicant pass a multiple-choice exam as well as a take-home practical exam that includes a penetration test against live servers. Subject areas on the multiple-choice exam include:

- Penetration testing methodologies
- Network protocol attacks
- Network reconnaissance
- Vulnerability identification
- Windows exploits
- UNIX/Linux exploits

- Covert Channels and rootkits
- Wireless security flaws
- Web application vulnerabilities

Other penetration testing exams and approaches use the term *ethical hacking*. While these penetration testing certifications and efforts are valid, the use of the term is problematic, as described in the nearby Offline feature.

OFFLINE

Ethical Hacking
An Etymological View of Ethical Hacking[14]

How we describe something defines it. A specific choice of words can cause irreparable damage to an idea or immortalize it. Part of the foundation of the field of information security is the expectation of ethical behavior. Most modern certifications and professional associations in information security, and to a lesser extent information technology in general, require their members to subscribe to codes of ethics. These canons ("a body of rules, principles, or standards accepted as axiomatic and universally binding in a field of study or art"[15]) provide guidance to the members and associates of an organization. They also represent an agreement between the members and their constituencies to provide service that is ethical ("being in accordance with the rules or standards for right conduct or practice, especially the standards of a profession"[16]).

If there is any doubt about the validity of these ethical codes or the conduct of professionals who subscribe to them, the entire discipline suffers. One such dubious area that has gained notoriety in the field of computing is the concept of the "hacker."

When the computer era began, *hacker* was a term for a computer enthusiast, someone who enjoyed pushing the boundaries of computer technologies and who frequently applied unorthodox techniques to accomplish his goals. In the mid-1950s, the term *hacker* was reportedly associated with members of the MIT Model Railroad Club—"one who works like a hack at writing and experimenting with software, one who enjoys computer programming for its own sake."[17]

Today, the term has a much more sinister definition. According to the *American Heritage Dictionary*, to hack is:

a. "*Informal* To alter (a computer program)

b. To gain access to (a computer file or network) illegally or without authorization"[18]

The problem with hacking isn't merely that some people actively seek to gain unauthorized access to others' information assets; the problem is much deeper. The problem is the inexplicable fascination that society has with the disreputable.

(continues)

12

This phenomenon is widespread, and one has only to reflect on our popular culture to find "felonious heroes" like Jesse James, Al Capone, and Bonnie and Clyde. We are enthralled by their apparent disregard for authority, many of whom are portrayed as wrongfully accused. Some argue that we live vicariously through those who display no apparent regard for proper behavior or society's bonds. Others seek the attention afforded to "public enemies" and made notorious by the media. Whatever the psychological attraction, the result is that some segments of our society turn a blind eye to certain crimes. A notable example in recent generations is the growing notoriety of computer hacking.

Computer hacking in the media is portrayed with a mixed message. Movies like *Ferris Bueller's Day Off*,[19] *WarGames*,[20] and *Hackers*[21] portray teenage hackers as idols and heroes. Unfortunately, this mixed message is being perpetuated into the modern information security society. We as the stoic guardians of information assets should condemn the entire hacker genre and culture.

This brings us to the point—the *ethical hacker*. The phrase itself is an oxymoron ("a figure of speech by which a locution produces an incongruous, seemingly self-contradictory effect"[22]). The MIT/Stanford "hacker ethic" written by Stephen Levy attempted to justify the actions of the hacker, and stated that "access to computers should be unlimited and total; all information should be free; authority should be mistrusted," further promoting the concepts that hacking "promotes the belief of individual activity over any form of corporate authority or system of ideals."[23] Yet it is unlikely that Mr. Levy is willing to make his personal financial information "free" to everyone. This manifesto that "information wants to be free" seems to encourage an environment designed to promote and encourage illicit activity. Even in the information security community, there is some dissent over the true meaning of hacking. However, it is generally accepted that a hacker does not intend to follow the policies, rules, and regulations associated with fair and responsible use of computer resources.

Therefore, a distinction exists between hacking and *penetration testing*, or simply *pen testing*—the actions taken by an information security professional to thoroughly test and assess an organization's information assets and their security posture, including gaining access to the root information by bypassing security controls. Most professional information security organizations offer pen testing, and many information security professionals receive training in the craft.

Some will argue that the mindset of the penetration tester is sufficiently different from that of, say, the firewall administrator, because they say different skills are needed to break into a server or network as opposed to protecting it. They argue that people with a "hacker mentality" have a unique perspective on this activity, regardless of whether they have acted on their abilities illegally. This begs the question: Are hackers the only people who can master such skills? Is it not possible to undergo professional training, building upon the ingenuity and natural curiosity of the human psyche, to investigate and solve these puzzles? Or must one "walk on the dark side" to gain this knowledge? To follow the logic of this argument, must all law enforcement professionals "serve time" to better understand the mindset of the criminal? Far too many information security professionals perform penetration testing to claim that they are "reformed" or "converted" hackers.

The heart of the distinction between the pen tester and the hacker is really the issue of *authorization*. With authorization ("permission or power granted by an authority; sanction"[24]), pen testers are able to identify and recommend remediation for faults in the organization's information protection strategy. They are able to determine the presence of vulnerabilities and exposures and demonstrate the techniques used by hackers to attack them. But, at the day's end, pen testers are responsible for documenting their actions and making recommendations to resolve these flaws in the defense posture. The hacker, being irresponsible, has no expectation of obligation or responsibility, only motives that are dubious at best. Some will argue that this is a futile semantic debate, and that what matters is the intent, not the title, when defining the difference between the white hat and the black hat, the hacker and cracker. Yes, the business world judges harshly on the face value of a professional.

For information security professionals, the (ISC)[2] Code of Ethics is their version of the Hippocratic oath ("I will prescribe regimens for the good of my patients according to my ability and my judgment and never do harm to anyone."[25]) The code includes the following:

The safety and welfare of society and the common good, duty to our principals, and to each other, requires that we adhere, and be seen to adhere, to the highest ethical standards of behavior.

- *Protect society, the common good, necessary public trust and confidence, and the infrastructure.*

- *Act honorably, honestly, justly, responsibly, and legally.*

- *Provide diligent and competent service to principals.*

- *Advance and protect the profession.*[26]

The fundamental assertion of this discussion is that any professional—"a person who belongs to one of the professions, especially one of the learned professions; a person who is expert at his or her work"[27]—should be held to higher moral standards than the average employee. Information security professionals are expected to be above reproach as the true guardians of the organization's information assets. Any doubt as to our true beliefs, motives, and ethics undermines the efforts of us all. Adopting the juvenile moniker and attitude of a "hacker" is a cry for attention, to belong to a group of social outcasts. Even though an information security professional may not be a member of the (ISC)[2], the fundamental lesson is what is important: Above all else, do no harm...

12

Internet Vulnerability Assessment The **Internet vulnerability assessment** is designed to find and document vulnerabilities that may be present in the organization's public network. Because attackers from this direction can take advantage of any flaw, this assessment is usually performed against all public addresses using every possible penetration testing approach. The steps in the process are as follows:

- Planning, scheduling, and notification of penetration testing: To execute the data collection phase of this assessment, large organizations often need an entire month, using nights and weekends but avoiding change control blackout windows—periods when changes are not allowed on the organization's systems or networks. This testing yields vast quantities of results and requires many hours of analysis, as explained in the following section. A rule of thumb is that every hour of scanning results in two to three hours of analysis. Therefore, scanning times should be spread out so that analysis is performed on fresh scanning results over the course of the assessment period. Also, the technical support communities should be given the detailed plan so they know when each device is scheduled for testing and what tests are used. This makes disruptions caused by invasive penetration testing easier to diagnose and recover from.

- Target selection: Working from the network characterization elements stored in the risk, threat, and attack database, the organization selects its penetration targets. As previously noted, most organizations choose to test every device that is exposed to the Internet.

- Test selection: This step involves using external monitoring intelligence to configure a test engine (such as Nessus) for the tests to be performed. Selecting the test library to employ usually evolves over time and matches the evolution of the threat environment. After the ground rules are established, there is usually little debate about the risk level of the tests used. After all, if a device is placed in a public role, it must be able to take everything the Internet can send its way, including the most aggressive penetration test scripts.

- Scanning: The penetration test engine is unleashed at the scheduled time using the planned target list and test selection. The results of the entire test run are logged to text files for analysis. This process should be monitored so that if an invasive penetration test causes a disruption to a targeted system, the outage can be reported immediately and recovery activities can be initiated. Note that the log files generated by this scanning, along with all data generated in the rest of this maintenance domain, must be treated as highly confidential.

- Analysis: A knowledgeable and experienced vulnerability analyst screens the test results for possible vulnerabilities logged during scanning. During this step, the analyst must perform three tasks:

  - Classify the risk level of the possible vulnerability as needing attention or as an acceptable risk.

  - Validate the existence of the vulnerability when it is deemed to be a significant risk—that is, the risk is higher than the risk appetite of the organization. This validation is important because it establishes the reality of the risk; the analyst must therefore use manual testing, human judgment, and a large dose of discretion. The goal of this step is to tread lightly and cause as little disruption and damage as possible while removing false positive candidates from further investigation. Proven cases of real vulnerabilities can now be considered vulnerability instances.

- Document the results of the verification by saving a trophy (usually a screenshot) that can be used to convince skeptical systems administrators that the vulnerability is real.

- Record keeping: In this phase, the organization must record the details of the documented vulnerability in the vulnerability database, identifying logical and physical characteristics and assigning a response risk level to differentiate the truly urgent vulnerability from the merely critical. When coupled with the criticality level from the characteristics in the risk, threat, and attack database, these records can help systems administrators decide which items they need to remediate first.

As the list of documented vulnerabilities is identified for Internet information assets, confirmed items are moved to the remediation stage.

Intranet Vulnerability Assessment The **intranet vulnerability assessment** is designed to find and document selected vulnerabilities that are likely to be present on the organization's internal network. Intranet attackers are often internal members of the organization, affiliates of business partners, or automated attack vectors, such as viruses and worms. This assessment is usually performed against critical internal devices with a known, high value and thus requires the use of selective penetration testing.

Many employees and others are now allowed to access an organization's networks using their own devices. This type of environment is often referred to as "bring your own device" (BYOD). BYOD implies that all devices connected to the network, whether owned by the organization or individual workers within it, are in scope for the vulnerability assessment.

The steps in the assessment process are almost identical to those in the Internet vulnerability assessment, except as noted below:

- Planning, scheduling, and notification of penetration testing: Most organizations are amazed at how many devices exist inside even a moderately sized network. Bigger networks contain staggering numbers of networked devices. To plan a meaningful assessment, the planner should be aware that any significant degree of scanning will yield vast quantities of test results and require many hours of analysis. The same rule of thumb for Internet vulnerability assessment applies: every hour of scanning results in two to three hours of analysis, so organizations must plan accordingly. As in Internet scanning, the technical support communities should be notified, although they are probably different from those notified for Internet scanning. The intranet support teams use this information to make any disruptions caused by invasive penetration testing easier to diagnose and recover from. In contrast to Internet systems administrators, who prefer penetration testing to be performed during periods of low demand, such as nights and weekends for commercial operations, intranet administrators often prefer that penetration testing be performed during working hours. The best process accounts for the systems administrator's planning needs when the schedule is built.

- Target selection: Like the Internet vulnerability assessment, the intranet scan starts with the network characterization elements stored in the risk, threat, and attack database. Intranet testing has so many target possibilities, however, that a more selective

12

approach is required. At first, penetration test scanning and analysis should focus on the most valuable and critical systems. As the configuration of these systems is improved and fewer possible vulnerabilities are found in the scanning step, the target list can be expanded. The list of targeted intranet systems should eventually reach equilibrium so that it scans and analyzes as many systems as possible, given the resources dedicated to the process.

- Test selection: The testing for intranet vulnerability assessment typically uses different, less stringent criteria from those for Internet scanning. Test selection usually evolves over time and matches the evolution of the perceived intranet threat environment. Most organizations focus their intranet scanning efforts on a few critical vulnerabilities at first, and then expand the test pool to include more test scripts and detect more vulnerabilities. The degree to which an organization is willing to accept risk while scanning and analyzing also affects the selection of test scripts. If the organization is unwilling to risk disruptions to critical internal systems, test scripts that pose such risks should be avoided in favor of alternate means that confirm safety from those vulnerabilities.

- Scanning: Intranet scanning is the same process used for Internet scanning. The process should be monitored so that if an invasive penetration test causes disruption, it can be reported for repair.

- Analysis: Despite the differences in targets and tested vulnerabilities, the intranet scan analysis is essentially identical to the Internet analysis. It follows the same three steps: classify, validate, and document.

- Record keeping: This step is identical to the one followed in Internet vulnerability analysis. Organizations should use similarities between the processes to their advantage by sharing the database, reports, and procedures used for record keeping, reporting, and follow-up.

By leveraging the common assessment processes and using difference analysis on the data collected during the vulnerability assessment, an organization can identify a list of documented internal vulnerabilities, which is the essential information needed for the remediation stage.

Platform Security Validation

Platform Security Validation The **platform security validation (PSV)** is designed to find and document vulnerabilities that may be present because misconfigured systems are used in the organization. These misconfigured systems fail to comply with company policy or standards that are adopted by the IT governance groups and communicated in the information security and awareness program. Fortunately, automated measurement systems are available to help with the intensive process of validating the compliance of platform configuration with policy. Two products known to provide this function are Symantec Enterprise Security Manager and NetIQ VigilEnt Security Manager. Other products are available, but the approach and terminology presented here are based on the NetIQ product.

- Product selection: Typically an organization implements a PSV solution when deploying the information security program. That solution serves for ongoing PSV compliance as well. If a product has not yet been selected, a separate information security project selects and deploys a PSV solution.

- Policy configuration: As organizational policy and standards evolve, the policy templates of the PSV tool must be changed to match. After all, the goal of any selected approach is to be able to measure how well the systems comply with policy.

- Deployment: All systems that are mission critical should be enrolled in PSV measurement. If the organization can afford the associated licensing and support costs and can dedicate sufficient resources to the PSV program, it should enroll all of its devices. Security personnel should remember that attackers often enter a network using the weakest link, which may not be a critical system itself but a device connected to critical systems.

- Measurement: Using the PSV tools, the organization should measure the compliance of each enrolled system against the policy templates. Deficiencies should be reported as vulnerabilities.

- Exclusion handling: Some provision should be made for the exclusion of specific policy or standard exceptions. For instance, one measurement identifies user accounts that never expire. Some organizations assume the risk of having service accounts that do not expire or that have longer change intervals than standard user accounts. If the proper decision makers have made an informed choice to assume such risks in an organization, the automated PSV tool should be able to exclude the assumed risk factor from the compliance report.

- Reporting: Using the standard reporting components in the PSV tool, most organizations can inform systems administrators of deficiencies that need remediation.

- Remediation: Noncompliant systems need to be updated with configurations that comply with policy. When the PSV process shows an outstanding configuration fault that has not been promptly remedied, the information should flow to the vulnerability database to assure remediation.

The ability of PSV software products to integrate with a custom vulnerability database is not a standard feature, but most PSV products can provide data extracts that an organization can import to its vulnerability database for integrated use in the remediation phase. If this degree of integration is not needed or cannot be justified, the stand-alone reporting capabilities of the products can generate sufficient reports for remediation functions.

Wireless Vulnerability Assessment The **wireless vulnerability assessment** is designed to find and document vulnerabilities that may be present in the organization's wireless local area networks. Because attackers from this direction are likely to take advantage of any flaw, this assessment is usually performed against all publicly accessible areas using every possible approach to wireless penetration testing. This process can sometimes be described as **war driving** because it could be done with a laptop while an attacker drives around. Most often it is done using a cart, but an attacker can just as easily walk around discreetly with any type of portable device. The steps in the process are as follows:

- Planning, scheduling, and notification of wireless penetration testing: This is a noninvasive scanning process that can be done almost any time without notifying systems administrators. Even if company culture requires that administrators be notified, the organization should still consider scheduling some unannounced scans, as administrators have been known to turn off their wireless access points on scheduled test days to avoid detection and the resulting remediation effort. Testing times and days should be rotated over time to detect wireless devices that are used for intermittent projects.

- Target selection: All areas on the organization's premises should be scanned with a portable wireless network scanner, with special attention to the following: all areas that are publicly accessible; all areas in range of commonly available products, such as 802.11b; and areas where visitors might linger without attracting attention. Because the radio emissions of wireless network equipment can act in surprising ways, all locations should be tested periodically.

- Test selection: Wireless scanning tools should look for all wireless signals that do not meet the organization's minimum level of encryption strength.

- Scanning: The walking scan should survey the entire target area and identify all wireless local area network (WLAN) access points that are not cryptographically secure.

- Analysis: A knowledgeable and experienced vulnerability analyst should screen the test results for WLANs that have been logged, as previously described. During this step, the analyst should do the following:

  - Remove false-positive candidates from further consideration as vulnerabilities while causing as little disruption or damage as possible.

  - Document the results of the verification by saving a screen shot or other documentary evidence (often called a trophy). This serves a double purpose: It can convince skeptical systems administrators that the vulnerability is real, and it documents wireless access points that are transient devices and thus may be off the air later.

  - Record keeping: Good reporting makes the effort to communicate and follow up much easier. As in earlier phases of the vulnerability assessment, effective reporting maximizes results.

At this stage in the process, wireless vulnerabilities are documented and ready for remediation.

Now that each group of vulnerability assessments has been described, a discussion of the record keeping process is in order.

Documenting Vulnerabilities The vulnerability database, like the risk, threat, and attack database, both stores and tracks information. It should provide details about the vulnerability being reported and link to the information assets characterized in the risk, threat, and attack database. While this can be done through manual data storage, the low cost and ease of use associated with relational databases makes them a more realistic choice.

The data stored in the vulnerability database should include the following:

- A unique vulnerability ID number for reporting and tracking remediation actions

- Linkage to the risk, threat, and attack database based on the physical information asset underlying the vulnerability; the IP address is a good choice for this linkage

- Vulnerability details, which are usually based on the test script used during the scanning step of the process. If the Nessus scanner is used, each test script has an assigned code (NASL, or Nessus attack scripting language) that can identify the vulnerability effectively.

- Dates and times of notification and remediation activities

- Current status of the vulnerability, such as found, reported, or repaired

- Comments, which give analysts the chance to provide systems administrators with detailed information for fixing the vulnerability

- Other fields as needed to manage the reporting and tracking processes in the remediation phase

The vulnerability database is an essential part of effective remediation because it helps organizations keep track of specific vulnerabilities as they are reported and remediated.

Remediating Vulnerabilities The final process in the vulnerability assessment and remediation domain is the remediation phase. The objective of **remediation** is to repair the flaw that caused a vulnerability or remove the risk associated with the vulnerability. Alternatively, informed decision makers with the proper authority may decide to accept the risk as a last resort.

When approaching the remediation process, it is important to recognize that the key to success is building relationships with those who control the information assets. In other words, success depends on the organization adopting a team approach to remediation in place of push and pull between departments or divisions.

Vulnerabilities can be remediated by accepting or transferring the risk, removing the threat, or repairing the vulnerability.

Acceptance or Transference of Risk In some instances, risk must either simply be acknowledged as part of an organization's business process or the organization should buy insurance to transfer the risk to another organization. The information security professional must assure the general management community that the decision to accept the risk or buy insurance was made by properly informed decision makers. Further, these decision makers must have the proper level of authority within the organization to assume the risk. In reality, however, many situations in which risk is assumed violate the preceding conditions:

- Decisions are made at the wrong level of the organization. For example, systems administrators should not be allowed to skip using passwords on a critical application server just because it creates more work for them.

- Decisions are made by uninformed decision makers. For example, a project manager should not convince an application sponsor that database-level security is not needed in an application and that all users need unlimited access to all data. The sponsor may not realize the implications of this decision.

In the final analysis, the information security group must make sure the right people make risk assumption decisions and that they are aware of the potential impact of those decisions and the cost of the available security controls.

Threat Removal In some circumstances, threats can be removed without requiring a repair of the vulnerability. For example, if an application can only run on an older desktop system that cannot support passwords, the system can be removed from the network and stored in a locked room or equipment rack for use as a stand-alone device. Other vulnerabilities may be mitigated by inexpensive controls—for example, disabling Web services on a server that provides other important services instead of taking the time to update the Web software on the server.

Vulnerability Repair The best solution in most cases is to repair the vulnerability, often by applying patch software or implementing a workaround. Many recent vulnerabilities have exploited Web servers on Windows operating systems, so simply updating the version of the installed Web server removes the vulnerability. Simple repairs are possible in other cases, too. For instance, if an account is flagged as a vulnerability because it has a password that has not been changed within the specified time interval, changing the password removes the vulnerability. Of course, the most common repair is the application of a software patch; this usually makes the system function in the expected fashion and removes the vulnerability.

Readiness and Review

Key Term

war game A type of rehearsal that seeks to realistically simulate the circumstances needed to thoroughly test a plan.

The primary goal of the readiness and review domain is to keep the information security program functioning as designed and improve it continuously over time. This goal can be accomplished by doing the following:

- Policy review: Policy needs to be reviewed and refreshed from time to time to ensure its soundness—in other words, it must provide a current foundation for the information security program.
- Program review: Major planning components should be reviewed on a periodic basis to ensure that they are current, accurate, and appropriate.
- Rehearsals: When possible, major plan elements should be rehearsed.

The relationships among the sectors of the readiness and review domain are shown in Figure 12-9. As the diagram indicates, policy review is the primary initiator of this domain. As policy is revised or current policy is confirmed, the planning elements are reviewed for compliance, the information security program is reviewed, and rehearsals are held to make sure all participants are capable of responding as needed.

Policy Review and Planning Review Policy needs to be reviewed periodically, as you learned in Chapter 4. The planning and review process for incident response, disaster recovery, and business continuity planning (IRP, DRP, and BCP) were also covered in Chapter 4.

Program Review As policy needs shift, a thorough and independent review of the entire information security program is needed. While an exact timetable for review is not proposed here, many organizations find that the CISO should conduct a formal review annually. Earlier in this chapter, you learned about the role of the CISO in the maintenance process. The CISO uses the results of maintenance activities and the review of the information security program to determine if the status quo is adequate against the threats at hand.

If the current information security program is not up to the challenges, the CISO must determine if incremental improvements are possible or if it is time to restructure the information security function within the organization.

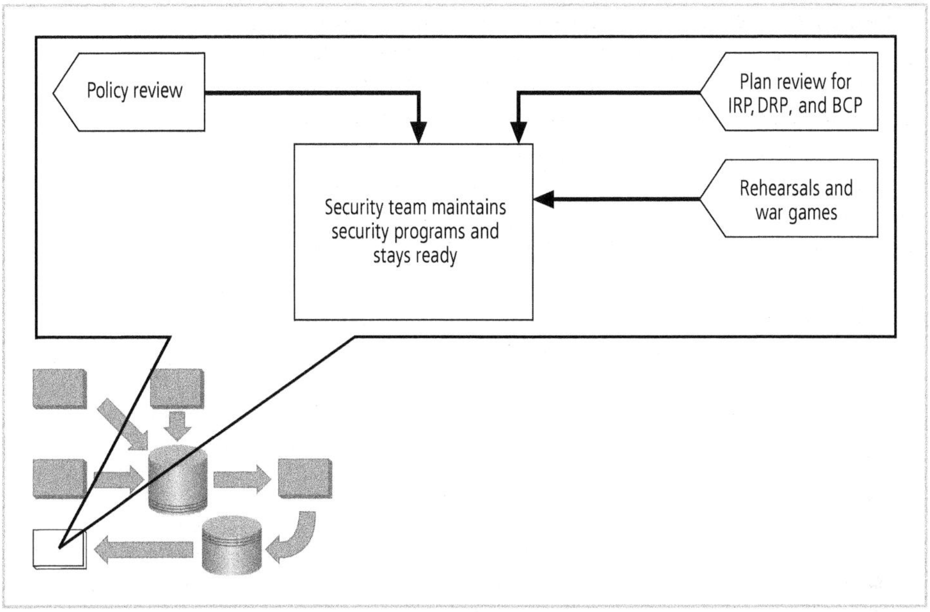

Figure 12-9 Readiness and review

Rehearsals and War Games Whenever possible, major planning elements should be rehearsed. Rehearsal adds value by exercising procedures, identifying shortcomings, and providing security personnel with the opportunity to improve the security plan before it is needed. In addition, rehearsals make people more effective when an actual event occurs. A type of rehearsal known as a **war game** or simulation exercise puts a subset of plans in place to create a realistic test environment. This adds to the value of the rehearsal and can enhance training.

Digital Forensics

Key Terms

digital forensics Investigations that involve the preservation, identification, extraction, documentation, and interpretation of computer media for evidentiary and root cause analysis. Like traditional forensics, digital forensics follows clear, well-defined methodologies but still tends to be as much an art as a science.

digital malfeasance A crime against or using digital media, computer technology, or related components; in other words, a computer is the source of the crime or the object of it.

evidentiary material (EM) Also known as "items of potential evidentiary value," any information that could potentially support an organization's legal or policy-based case against a suspect.

forensics The coherent application of methodical investigatory techniques to present evidence of crimes in a court or similar setting. Forensics allows investigators to determine what happened by examining the results of an event—criminal, natural, intentional, or accidental.

Whether due to a character flaw, a need for vengeance, a profit motive, or simple curiosity, an employee or outsider may attack a physical asset or information asset. When the asset is the responsibility of the CISO, he or she is expected to understand how policies and laws require the matter to be managed and protected. To protect the organization and possibly assist law enforcement in an investigation, the CISO must document what happened and how an incident occurred. This process is called **digital forensics**.

Digital forensics is based on the field of traditional forensics. Made popular by scientific detective shows that focus on crime scene investigations, **forensics** involves the use of science to investigate events. Not all events involve crimes; some involve natural events, accidents, or system malfunctions. Forensics allows investigators to determine what happened by examining the results of an event. It also allows them to determine how the event happened by examining activities, individual actions, physical evidence, and testimony related to the event. However, forensics might not figure out the *why* of the event; that's the focus of psychological, sociological, and criminal justice studies. Here, the focus is on the application of forensics techniques in the digital arena.

Digital forensics involves the preservation, identification, extraction, documentation, and interpretation of digital media, including computer media, for evidentiary and/or root-cause analysis. Like traditional forensics, it follows clear, well-defined methodologies, but it still tends to be as much an art as a science. In other words, the natural curiosity and personal skill of the investigator play a key role in discovering potential **evidentiary material** (**EM**). An item does not become evidence until it is formally admitted by a judge or other ruling official.

Digital forensics investigators use a variety of tools to support their work, as you will learn later in this chapter. However, the tools and methods used by attackers can be equally sophisticated. Digital forensics can be used for two key purposes:

- To investigate allegations of **digital malfeasance**. Such an investigation requires digital forensics to gather, analyze, and report the findings. This is the primary mission of law enforcement in investigating crimes that involve computer technologies or online information.

- To perform root-cause analysis. If an incident occurs and the organization suspects an attack was successful, digital forensics can be used to examine the path and methodology used to gain unauthorized access, and to determine how pervasive and successful the attack was. This type of analysis is used primarily by incident response teams to examine their equipment after an incident.

Some investigations are undertaken by an organization's own personnel, while others require the immediate involvement of law enforcement. In general, whenever investigators discover evidence of a crime, they should immediately notify management and recommend contacting law enforcement. Failure to do so could result in unfavorable action against the investigator or organization.

The organization must choose one of two approaches when employing digital forensics:

1. Protect and forget. This approach, also known as patch and proceed, focuses on the defense of data and the systems that house, use, and transmit it. An investigation that takes this approach focuses on the detection and analysis of events to determine how they happened and to prevent reoccurrence. Once the current event is over, who caused it or why is almost immaterial.

2. Apprehend and prosecute. This approach, also known as pursue and prosecute, focuses on the identification and apprehension of responsible parties, with additional attention to the collection and preservation of potential EM that might support administrative or criminal prosecution. This approach requires much more attention to detail to prevent contamination of evidence that might hinder prosecution.

An organization might find it impossible to retain enough data to successfully handle even administrative penalties, but it should certainly adopt the latter approach if it wants to pursue formal administrative penalties, especially if the employee is likely to challenge them.

 For more information on digital forensics, visit the American Society of Digital Forensics and eDiscovery at www.asdfed.com.

⟩ The Digital Forensics Team

Most organizations cannot sustain a permanent digital forensics team; such expertise is so rarely called upon that it may be better to collect the data and then outsource the analysis component to a regional expert. The organization can then maintain an arm's-length distance from the case and have additional expertise to call upon if the process ends in court. Even so, the information security group should contain members who are trained to understand and manage the forensics process. If the group receives a report of suspected misuse, either internally or externally, a group member must be familiar with digital forensics procedures to avoid contaminating potential EM.

This expertise can be obtained by sending staff members to a regional or national information security conference with a digital forensics track or to dedicated digital forensics training, as mentioned in Chapter 11. The organization should use caution in selecting training for the team or a specialist, as many forensics training programs begin with the analysis process and promote a specific tool rather than teaching management of the process.

⟩ Affidavits and Search Warrants

Key Terms

affidavit Sworn testimony that certain facts are in the possession of an investigating officer and that they warrant the examination of specific items located at a specific place. The facts, the items, and the place must be specified in the affidavit.

search warrant Permission to search for evidentiary material at a specified location and/or to seize items to return to an investigator's lab for examination. An affidavit becomes a search warrant when signed by an approving authority.

Most investigations begin with an allegation or an indication of an incident. Whether via the help desk, the organization's sexual harassment reporting channels, or a direct report, someone alleges that a worker is performing actions explicitly prohibited by the organization or that make another worker uncomfortable in the workplace. The organization's forensics team or other authorized entity must then request permission to examine digital media for potential EM. In law enforcement, the investigating agent would create an **affidavit** requesting permission to search for and confiscate related EM. The affidavit summarizes the facts of the case, items relevant to the investigation, and the location of the event. When an approving authority signs the affidavit or creates a synopsis form based on the document, it becomes a **search warrant**. In corporate environments, the names of these documents may change, and in many cases written authorization may not be needed, but the process should be the same. Formal permission is obtained before an investigation occurs.

› Digital Forensics Methodology

Key Terms

chain of custody See *chain of evidence*.
chain of evidence The detailed documentation of the collection, storage, transfer, and ownership of evidence from the crime scene through its presentation in court.

In digital forensics, all investigations follow the same basic methodology once permission for search and seizure has been obtained:

1. Identify relevant EM.
2. Acquire (seize) the evidence without alteration or damage.
3. Take steps to assure that the evidence is verifiably authentic at every step and is unchanged from the time it was seized.
4. Analyze the data without risking modification or unauthorized access.
5. Report the findings to the proper authority.

This process is illustrated in Figure 12-10.

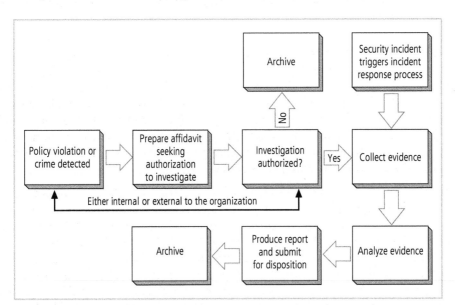

Figure 12-10 The digital forensics process

To support the selection and implementation of a methodology for forensics, the organization may want to seek legal advice or consult with local or state law enforcement. Other references that should become part of the organization's library are:

- Electronic Crime Scene Investigation: A Guide for First Responders, July 2001 (*www.ncjrs.gov/pdffiles1/nij/187736.pdf*)
- First Responders Guide to Computer Forensics (*https://resources.sei.cmu.edu/asset_files/Handbook/2005_002_001_14429.pdf*)
- First Responders Guide to Computer Forensics: Advanced Topics (*http://resources.sei.cmu.edu/asset_files/handbook/2005_002_001_14432.pdf*)
- Searching and Seizing Computers and Obtaining Electronic Evidence in Criminal Investigations (*www.justice.gov/criminal/cybercrime/docs/ssmanual2009.pdf*)
- Scientific Working Group on Digital Evidence: Best Practices for Computer Forensics (*www.oas.org/juridico/spanish/cyb_best_pract.pdf*).

Identifying Relevant Items The affidavit or warrant that authorizes a search must identify what items of evidence can be seized and where they are located. Only EM that fits the description on the authorization can be seized. These seizures often occur under stressful circumstances and strict time constraints, so thorough item descriptions help the process function smoothly and ensure that critical evidence is not overlooked. Thorough descriptions also ensure that items are not wrongly included as EM, which could jeopardize the investigation.

Because users have access to many online server locations via free e-mail archives, FTP servers, and video archives, and could have terabytes of information stored in offsite locations across the Web or on their local systems, investigators must have an idea of what to look for or they may never find it.

Acquiring the Evidence The principal responsibility of the response team is to acquire the information without altering it. Computers and users modify data constantly. Every time someone opens, modifies, or saves a file, or even opens a directory index to view the available files, the state of the system is changed. Normal system file changes may be difficult to explain to a layperson—for example, a jury member with little or no technical knowledge. A normal system consequence of the search for EM could be portrayed by a defense attorney as harmful to the EM's authenticity or integrity, which could lead a jury to suspect it was planted or is otherwise suspect.

Online Versus Offline Data Acquisition There are generally two methods of acquiring evidence from a system. The first is the offline model, in which the investigator removes the power source and then uses a utility or special device to make a bitstream, sector-by-sector copy of the hard drives on the system. By copying the drives at the sector level, you can ensure that any hidden or erased files are also captured. The copied drive then becomes the image that can be used for analysis, and the original drive is stored for safekeeping as true EM or possibly returned to service. For the purposes of this discussion, the term *copy* refers to a drive duplication technique, whereas an image is the file that contains all the information from the source drive.

12

This approach requires the use of sound processes and techniques or read-only hardware known as write-blockers to prevent the accidental overwriting of data on the source drive. The use of these tools also allows investigators to assert that the EM was not modified during acquisition. In another offline approach, the investigator can reboot the system with an alternate operating system or a specialty boot disk like Helix or Knoppix. Still another approach involves specialty hardware that connects directly to a powered-down hard drive and provides direct power and data connections to copy data to an internal drive.

In online or *live* data acquisition, investigators use network-based tools to acquire a protected copy of the information. The only real difference between the two methods is that the source system cannot be taken offline, and the tools must be sophisticated enough to avoid altering the system during data acquisition. Table 12-10 lists common methods of acquiring data.

The creation of a copy or image can take a substantial amount of time. Users who have made USB copies of their data know how much time it takes to back up several gigabytes of data. When dealing with networked server drives, the data acquisition phase can take

Method	Advantages	Disadvantages
Use a dedicated forensic workstation to examine a write-protected hard drive or image of the suspect hard drive.	No concern about the validity of software or hardware on the suspect host. Produces evidence most easily defended in court.	Inconvenient, time-consuming. May result in loss of volatile information.
Boot the system using a verified, write-protected CD or other media with kernel and tools.	Convenient, quick. Evidence is defensible if suspect drives are mounted as read-only.	Assumes that hardware has not been compromised because it is much less likely than compromised software. May result in loss of volatile information.
Build a new system that contains an image of the suspect system and examine it.	Completely replicates operating environment of suspect computer without running the risk of changing its information.	Requires availability of hardware that is identical to that on the suspect computer. May result in loss of volatile information.
Examine the system using external media with verified software.	Convenient, quick. Allows examination of volatile information.	If a kernel is compromised, results may be misleading. External media may not contain every necessary utility.
Verify the software on the suspect system, and then use the verified local software to conduct the examination.	Requires minimal preparation. Allows examination of volatile information. Can be performed remotely.	Lack of write protection for suspect drives makes evidence difficult to defend in court. Finding sources for hash values and verifying the local software requires at least several hours, unless Tripwire was used ahead of time.
Examine the suspect system using the software on it, without verifying the software.	Requires least amount of preparation. Allows examination of volatile information. Can be performed remotely.	Least reliable method. This is exactly what cyberattackers are hoping you will do. Often a complete waste of time.

Table 12-10   **Summary of Methods Employed to Acquire Forensic Data**

many hours to complete, which is one reason investigators prefer to seize drives and take them back to the lab to be imaged or copied.

Other Potential EM Not all EM is on a suspect's computer hard drive. A technically savvy attacker is more likely to store incriminating evidence on other digital media, such as smart phones, removable drives, CDs, DVDs, flash drives, memory chips or sticks, or on other computers accessed across the organization's networks or via the Internet. EM located outside the organization is particularly problematic because the organization cannot legally search systems it doesn't own. However, the simple act of viewing EM on a system leaves clues about the location of the source material, and a skilled investigator can at least provide some assistance to law enforcement when conducting a preliminary investigation. Log files are another source of information about the access and location of EM, as well as what happened and when.

Some evidence isn't electronic or digital. Many suspects have been further incriminated when passwords to their digital media were discovered in the margins of user manuals, in calendars and day planners, and even on notes attached to their systems.

EM Handling Once the evidence is acquired, both the copy image and the original drive should be handled properly to avoid legal challenges based on authenticity and preservation of integrity. If the organization or law enforcement cannot demonstrate that no one had access to the evidence, they cannot provide strong assurances that it has not been altered. Such access can be physical or logical if the device is connected to a network. Once the evidence is in the possession of investigators, they must track its movement, storage, and access until the resolution of the event or case. This is typically accomplished through **chain of evidence** (also known as **chain of custody**) procedures. The evidence is then tracked wherever it is located. When the evidence changes hands or is stored, the documentation is updated.

Not all evidence-handling requirements are met through the chain of custody process. Digital media must be stored in a specially designed environment that can be secured to prevent unauthorized access. For example, individual items might need to be stored in containers or bags that protect them from electrostatic discharge or magnetic fields. Additional details are provided in the nearby Offline feature.

Authenticating the Recovered Evidence The copy or image is typically transferred to the laboratory for the next stage of authentication. Using cryptographic hash tools, the team must be able to demonstrate that any analyzed copy or image is a true and accurate replica of the source EM. As you learned in Chapter 8, the hash tool takes a variable-length file and creates a single numerical value, usually represented in hexadecimal notation, that functions like a digital fingerprint. By hashing the source file and the copy, the investigator can assert that the copy is a true and accurate duplicate of the source.

Analyzing the Data The most complex part of an investigation is analyzing the copy or image for potential EM. While the process can be performed manually using simple utilities, two industry-leading applications dominate the market for digital forensics:

- Guidance Software's EnCase (*www.guidancesoftware.com*)
- AccessData Forensics Tool Kit (FTK, at *www.accessdata.com*)
- OSForensics (*www.osforensics.com/*)

12

Open-source alternatives to these rather expensive tools include Autopsy and The Sleuth Kit, which are available from *www.sleuthkit.org*. Autopsy is a stand-alone GUI interface for The Sleuth Kit, which uses a command line. Each tool is designed to support an investigation and assist in the management of the entire case.

OFFLINE

General Procedures for Evidence Search and Seizure

At the crime scene, complete the following tasks:

1. Secure the crime scene by clearing all unauthorized personnel, delimit the scene with tape or other markers, and post a guard or other person at the entrance.

2. Log into the crime scene by signing the entry/exit log.

3. Photograph the scene beginning at the doorway and covering the entire room in 360 degrees. Include specific photos of potential evidentiary material.

4. Sketch the layout for the room, including furniture and equipment.

5. Following proper procedure, begin searching for physical, documentary evidence to support your case, including papers, media such as CDs or flash memory devices, or other artifacts. Identify the location of each piece of evidence with a marker or other designator and cross-reference it on the sketch. Photograph the item in situ to establish its location and state.

6. For each computer, first check for the presence of a screen saver by moving the mouse. Do not click the mouse or use the keyboard. If the screen is active, photograph the screen. Pull the power on permitted systems. Document each computer by taking a photograph and providing a detailed written description of the manufacturer, model number, serial number, and other details. Using sound processes, remove each disk drive and image it using the appropriate process and equipment. Document each source drive by photographing it and providing a detailed description of the manufacturer, serial number, and other details. Package and secure the image.

7. For each object found, complete the necessary evidence or chain of custody labels.

8. Log out of the crime scene by signing the entry/exit log.

9. Transfer all evidence to the lab for investigation or to a suitable evidence locker for storage. Store and transport all evidence, documentation, and photographic materials in a locked field evidence locker.

Analyze the image:

1. Build the case file by entering background information, including investigator, suspect, date, time, and system analyzed.

2. Load the image file into the case file. Typical image files have .img, .e01, or .001 extensions.

3. Index the image. Note that some systems use a database of known files to filter out files that are known to be applications, system files, or utilities. The use of this filter improves the quality and effectiveness of the indexing process.

4. Identify, export, and bookmark related text files by searching the index.

5. Identify, export, and bookmark related graphics by reviewing the images folder. If the suspect is accused of viewing child pornography, do not directly view the images. Some things you can't "un-see." Use the database of known images to compare hash values and tag them as suspect.

6. Identify, export, and bookmark other evidence files.

7. Integrate all exported and bookmarked material into the case report.

The first component of the analysis phase is indexing. During indexing, many investigatory tools create an index of all text found on the drive, including data found in deleted files and in file slack space. This indexing is similar to that performed by Google Desktop or Windows Desktop Search tools. The index can then be used by the investigator to locate specific documents or document fragments. While indexing, the tools typically organize files into categories, such as documents, images, and executables. Unfortunately, like imaging, indexing is a time- and processor-consuming operation, and it could take days on images that are larger than 20 gigabytes.

In some cases, the investigator may find password-protected files that the suspect used to protect the data. Several commercial password cracking tools can assist the investigator. Some are sold in conjunction with forensics tools, like the AccessData Password Recovery Tool Kit.

Reporting the Findings As investigators examine the analyzed copies or images and identify potential EM, they can tag it and add it to their case files. Once they have found a suitable amount of information, they can summarize their findings with a synopsis of their investigatory procedures in a report and submit it to the appropriate authority. This authority could be law enforcement or management. The suitable amount of EM is a flexible determination made by the investigator. In certain cases, like child pornography, one file is sufficient to warrant turning over the entire investigation to law enforcement. On the other hand, dismissing an employee for the unauthorized sale of intellectual property may require a substantial amount of information to support the organization's assertion. Reporting methods and formats vary among organizations and should be specified in the digital forensics policy. A general guideline is that the report should be sufficiently detailed to allow a similarly trained person to repeat the analysis and achieve similar results.

〉 Evidentiary Procedures

In information security, most operations focus on policies—documents that provide managerial guidance for ongoing implementation and operations. In digital forensics, however, the focus is on procedures. When investigating digital malfeasance or performing root-cause analysis, keep in mind that the results and methods of the investigation may end up in criminal or civil court. For example, during a routine systems update, assume that a technician finds objectionable material on an employee's computer. The employee is fired and promptly sues the organization for wrongful termination, so the investigation of the objectionable material comes under scrutiny by the plaintiff's attorney, who will attempt to cast doubt on the ability of the investigator. While technically not illegal, the presence of the material may have been a clear violation of policy, prompting the dismissal of the employee. However, if an attorney can convince a jury or judge that someone else could have placed the material on the plaintiff's system, the employee could win the case and potentially a large financial settlement.

When the scenario involves criminal issues in which an employee discovers evidence of a crime, the situation changes somewhat. The investigation, analysis, and report are typically performed by law enforcement personnel. However, if the defense attorney can cast reasonable doubt on whether the organization's information security professionals compromised the digital evidentiary material, the employee might win the case.

How do you avoid these legal pitfalls? Strong procedures for handling potential evidentiary material can minimize the probability that an organization will lose a legal challenge.

Organizations should develop specific procedures, along with guidance for their effective use. The policy document should specify the following:

- Who may conduct an investigation
- Who may authorize an investigation
- What affidavits and related documents are required
- What search warrants and related documents are required
- What digital media may be seized or taken offline
- What methodology should be followed
- What methods are required for chain of custody or chain of evidence
- What format the final report should take and to whom it should be given

The policy document should be supported by a procedures manual and developed based on the documents discussed earlier, along with guidance from law enforcement or consultants. By creating and using these policies and procedures, an organization can best protect itself from challenges by employees who have been subject to unfavorable action from an investigation.

Selected Readings

- *Fighting Computer Crime: A New Framework for Protecting Information*, by Donn B. Parker. 1998. John Wiley and Sons.
- *Digital Evidence and Computer Crime*, Third Edition, by Eoghan Casey. 2011. Academic Press.
- *Guide to Computer Forensics and Investigations*, Fourth Edition, by Amelia Phillips and Christopher Steuart. 2010. Course Technology.

Chapter Summary

- Change is inevitable, so organizations should have procedures to deal with changes in the operation and maintenance of the information security program.

- The CISO decides whether the information security program can adapt to change as it is implemented or whether the macroscopic process of the risk management program must be started anew.

- The maintenance model recommended in this chapter is made up of five subject areas or domains: external monitoring, internal monitoring, planning and risk assessment, vulnerability assessment and remediation, and readiness and review.

- To stay current, the information security community of interest and the CISO must constantly monitor the three components of the security triple—threats, assets, and vulnerabilities.

- To assist the information security community in managing and operating the ongoing security program, the organization should adopt a security management maintenance model. These models are frameworks that are structured by the tasks of managing a particular set of activities or business functions.

- NIST SP 800-100, *Information Security Handbook: A Guide for Managers*, outlines managerial tasks performed after the program is operational. For each of the 13 areas of information security management presented in SP 800-100, there are specific monitoring activities:

  1. Information security governance
  2. Systems development life cycle
  3. Awareness and training
  4. Capital planning and investment control
  5. Interconnecting systems
  6. Performance measures
  7. Security planning
  8. Information technology contingency planning
  9. Risk management
  10. Certification, accreditation, and security assessments
  11. Security services and products acquisition
  12. Incident response
  13. Configuration and change management

- The objective of the external monitoring domain in the maintenance model is to provide early awareness of new and emerging threats, threat agents, vulnerabilities, and attacks so that an effective and timely defense can be mounted.

- The objective of the internal monitoring domain is an informed awareness of the state of the organization's networks, information systems, and information security

12

defenses. The security team documents and communicates this awareness, particularly when it concerns system components that face the external network.

- The primary objective of the planning and risk assessment domain is to keep an eye on the entire information security program.

- The primary objectives of the vulnerability assessment and remediation domain are to identify specific, documented vulnerabilities and remediate them in a timely fashion.

- The primary objectives of the readiness and review domain are to keep the information security program functioning as designed and keep improving it over time.

- Digital forensics is the investigation of wrongdoing in the arena of information security. Digital forensics requires the preservation, identification, extraction, documentation, and interpretation of computer media for evidentiary and/or root-cause analysis.

Review Questions

1. List and define the factors that are likely to shift in an organization's information security environment.

2. Who decides if the information security program can adapt to change adequately?

3. List and briefly describe the five domains of the general security maintenance model, as identified in the text.

4. What are the three primary aspects of information security risk management? Why is each important?

5. What is a management maintenance model? What does it accomplish?

6. What changes need to be made to the model in SP 800-100 to adapt it for use in security management maintenance?

7. What ongoing responsibilities do security managers have in securing the SDLC?

8. What is vulnerability assessment?

9. What is penetration testing?

10. What is the difference between configuration management and change management?

11. What is a performance baseline?

12. What is the difference between vulnerability assessment and penetration testing?

13. What is the objective of the external monitoring domain of the maintenance model?

14. List and describe four vulnerability intelligence sources. Which seems the most effective? Why?

15. What does CERT stand for? Is there more than one CERT? What is the purpose of a CERT?

16. What is the primary objective of the internal monitoring domain?

17. What is the objective of the planning and risk assessment domain of the maintenance model? Why is this important?

18. What is the primary goal of the vulnerability assessment and remediation domain of the maintenance model? Is this important to an organization with an Internet presence? Why?

19. List and describe the five vulnerability assessments described in the text. Can you think of other assessment processes that might exist?

20. What is digital forensics, and when is it used in a business setting?

Exercises

1. Search the Web for the Forum of Incident Response and Security Teams (FIRST). In your own words, what is the forum's mission?

2. Search the Web for two or more sites that discuss the ongoing responsibilities of the security manager. What other components of security management can be adapted for use in the security management model?

3. This chapter lists five tools that can be used by security administrators, network administrators, and attackers alike. Search the Web for three to five other tools that fit this description.

4. Using a Web browser and the names of the tools you found in Exercise 3, find a site that claims to be dedicated to supporting hackers. Do you find any references to other hacker tools? If you do, create a list of the tools along with a short description of what they do and how they work.

5. Using the components of risk assessment documentation presented in the chapter, draft a tentative risk assessment of a lab, department, or office at your university. Outline the critical risks you found and discuss them with your class.

Case Exercises

Remember from the beginning of this book how Amy's day started? Now imagine how it could have gone with better planning:

For Amy, the day began like any other at the Sequential Label and Supply Company (SLS) help desk. Taking calls and helping office workers with computer problems was not glamorous, but she enjoyed the work; it was challenging and paid well enough. Some of her friends in the industry worked at bigger companies, some at cutting-edge tech companies, but they all agreed that technology jobs were a good way to pay the bills.

The phone rang, as it did about four times an hour and 28 times a day. The first call of the day, from a user hoping Amy could help him out of a jam, seemed typical. The call display on her monitor showed some of the facts: the user's name, his phone number and department, where his office was on the company campus, and a list of his past calls to the help desk.

"Hi, Bob," Amy said. "Did you get that document formatting problem squared away?"

"Sure did, Amy. Hope we can figure out what's going on this time."

"We'll try, Bob. Tell me about it."

"Well, I need help setting a page break in this new spreadsheet template I'm working on," Bob said.

Amy smiled to herself. She knew spreadsheets well, so she would probably be able to close this call on the first contact. That would help her call statistics, which was one method of measuring her job performance.

Little did Amy know that roughly four minutes before Bob's phone call, a specially programmed computer at the edge of the SLS network had made a programmed decision. This computer was generally known as postoffice.seqlbl.com, but it was called the "e-mail gateway" by the networking, messaging, and information security teams at SLS. The decision was just like many thousands of other decisions it made in a typical day—that is, to block the transmission of a file that was attached to an e-mail addressed to Bob.Hulme@seqlbl .com. The gateway had determined that Bob didn't need an executable program that had been attached to the e-mail message. The gateway had also determined that the message originated from somewhere on the Internet but contained a forged reply-to address from Davey Martinez at SLS. In other words, the gateway had delivered the e-mail to Bob Hulme, but not the attachment.

When Bob got the e-mail, all he saw was another unsolicited commercial e-mail with an unwanted executable that had been blocked. He had deleted the nuisance message without a second thought. While she was talking to Bob, Amy looked up to see Charles Moody walking calmly down the hall. Charlie, as he liked to be called, was the senior manager of the server administration team and the company's chief information security officer. Kelvin Urich and Iris Majwubu were trailing behind Charlie as he headed from his office to the door of the conference room. Amy thought, "It must be time for the weekly security status meeting."

She was the user representative on the company information security oversight committee, so she was due to attend this meeting. Amy continued talking Bob through the procedure for setting up a page break, and decided she would join the information security team for coffee and bagels as soon as she was finished.

Discussion Questions

1. What area of the SP 800-100 management maintenance model addresses the actions of the content filter described here?

2. What recommendations would you give SLS for how it might select a security management maintenance model?

Ethical Decision Making

Referring back to the opening case of this chapter, suppose Charlie had just finished a search for a new job and knew that he would soon be leaving the company. When Iris came in to talk about the tedious and time-consuming review process, he put her off and asked her to schedule a meeting with him "in 2 or 3 weeks," knowing full well that he would be gone by then.

Do you think this kind of action is unethical because Charlie knows he is leaving soon?

Endnotes

1. "Configuration Management." Wikipedia. Accessed 12 October 2016 from *en.wikipedia .org/wiki/Configuration_management.*

2. Bowen, P., Hash, J., and Wilson, M. National Institute of Standards and Technology. *Information Security Handbook: A Guide for Managers.* SP 800-100. Accessed 10 October 2016 from *http://nvlpubs.nist.gov/nistpubs/Legacy/SP/nistspecialpublica tion800-100.pdf.*

3. Ibid.

4. Kissel, R., Stine, K., Scholl, M., Rossman, H., Fahlsing, J., and Gulick, J. National Institute of Standards and Technology. *Security Considerations in the System Development Life Cycle.* SP 800-64, Rev. 2. October 2008. Accessed 10 October 2016 from *http://nvlpubs.nist.gov/nistpubs/Legacy/SP/nistspecialpublication800-64r2.pdf.*

5. Hash, J., Bartol, N., Rollins, H., Robinson, W., Abeles, J., and Batdorff, S. National Institute of Standards and Technology. *Integrating IT Security into the Capital Planning and Investment Control Process.* SP 800-65. January 2005. Accessed 10 October 2016 from *http://nvlpubs.nist.gov/nistpubs/Legacy/SP/nistspecialpublication800-65.pdf.*

6. Grance, T., Hash, J., Peck, S., Smith, J., and Karow-Diks, K. National Institute of Standards and Technology. *Security Guide for Interconnecting Information Technology Systems.* SP 800-47. August 2002. Accessed 10 October 2016 from *csrc.nist.gov /publications/nistpubs/800-47/sp800-47.pdf.*

7. Chew, E., Swanson, M., Stine, K., Bartol, N., Brown, A., and Robinson, W. National Institute of Standards and Technology. *Performance Measurement Guide for Information Security.* SP 800-55, Rev. 1. July 2008. Accessed 10 October 2016 from *csrc.nist .gov/publications/nistpubs/800-55-Rev1/SP800-55-rev1.pdf.*

8. Bowen, P., Hash, J., and Wilson, M. National Institute of Standards and Technology. *Information Security Handbook: A Guide for Managers.* SP 800-100. Accessed 10 October 2016 from *http://nvlpubs.nist.gov/nistpubs/Legacy/SP/nistspecialpublica tion800-100.pdf.*

9. Grance, T., Hash, J., Stevens, M., O'Neal, K., and Bartol, N. National Institute of Standards and Technology. *Guide to Information Technology Security Services.* SP 800-35. October 2003. Accessed 10 October 2016 from *csrc.nist.gov/publications/nistpubs /800-35/NIST-SP800-35.pdf.*

10. Grance, T., Stevens, M., and Myers, M. National Institute of Standards and Technology. *Guide to Selecting Information Technology Security Products.* SP 800-36. October 2003. Accessed 10 October 2016 from *csrc.nist.gov/publications/nistpubs/800-36 /NIST-SP800-36.pdf.*

12

11. Cuff, Jeanne. "Grow Up: How Mature Is Your Help Desk?" *Compass America, Inc.* Accessed 10 October 2016 from *fsz.ifas.ufl.edu/HD/GrowUpWP.pdf.*

12. Kissel, R., Stine, K., Scholl, M., Rossman, H., Fahlsing, J., and Gulick, J. National Institute of Standards and Technology. *Security Considerations in the System Development Life Cycle.* SP 800-64, Rev. 2. October 2008. Accessed 10 October 2016 from *http://nvlpubs.nist.gov/nistpubs/Legacy/SP/nistspecialpublication800-64r2.pdf.*

13. Join Task Force Transformation Initiative. National Institute of Standards and Technology. *Security and Privacy Controls for Federal Information Systems and Organizations.* SP 800-53, Rev. 4. April 2013. Accessed 10 October 2016 from *nvlpubs.nist.gov/nistpubs/SpecialPublications/NIST.SP.800-53r4.pdf.*

14. *Readings and Cases in the Management of Information Security: Legal and Ethical Issues.* 2010. Course Technology.

15. "Canon." Accessed 10 October 2016 from *www.dictionary.com/browse/canon.*

16. "Ethical." Accessed 10 October 2016 from *www.dictionary.com/browse/ethical.*

17. Multiple references, including *www.edu-cyberpg.com/Technology/ethics.html.* Accessed 10 October 2016.

18. "Hacking." Accessed 10 October 2016 from *www.dictionary.com/browse/hacking.*

19. © 1986 Paramount Pictures.

20. © 1983 Metro-Goldwyn-Mayer Studios Inc./United Artists.

21. © 1995 Metro-Goldwyn-Mayer Studios Inc.

22. "Oxymoron." Accessed 10 October 2016 from *www.dictionary.com/browse/oxymoron.*

23. Levy, S. *Hackers: Heroes of the Computer Revolution.* 1984. Putnam, NY: Penguin.

24. "Authorization." Accessed 10 October 2016 from *www.dictionary.com/browse/authorization.*

25. "Hippocratic Oath." Accessed 10 October 2016 from *en.wikipedia.org/wiki/Hippocratic_Oath.*

26. (ISC)^2 Code of Ethics. Accessed 10 October 2016 from *www.isc2.org/ethics/default.aspx?terms=code%20of%20ethics.*

27. "Professional." Accessed 10 October 2016 from *www.dictionary.com/browse/professional.*

10.4 password rule An industry recommendation for password structure and strength that specifies passwords should be at least 10 characters long and contain at least one uppercase letter, one lowercase letter, one number, and one special character.

acceptance risk control strategy The risk control strategy that indicates the organization is willing to accept the current level of risk. As a result, the organization makes a conscious decision to do nothing to protect an information asset from risk and to accept the outcome from any resulting exploitation.

access A subject or object's ability to use, manipulate, modify, or affect another subject or object. Authorized users have legal access to a system, whereas hackers must gain illegal access to a system. Access controls regulate this ability.

access control The selective method by which systems specify who may use a particular resource and how they may use it.

access control list (ACL) Specifications of authorization that govern the rights and privileges of users to a particular information asset. ACLs include user access lists, matrices, and capabilities tables.

access control matrix An integration of access control lists (focusing on assets) and capabilities tables (focusing on users) that results in a matrix with organizational assets listed in the column headings and users listed in the row headings. The matrix contains ACLs in columns for a particular device or asset and capabilities tables in rows for a particular user.

accountability The access control mechanism that ensures all actions on a system—authorized or unauthorized—can be attributed to an authenticated identity. Also known as *auditability*.

accreditation The process that authorizes an IT system to process, store, or transmit information.

accuracy An attribute of information that describes how data is free of errors and has the value that the user expects.

active vulnerability scanner An application that scans networks to identify exposed usernames and groups, open network shares, configuration problems, and other vulnerabilities in servers.

address restrictions Firewall rules designed to prohibit packets with certain addresses or partial addresses from passing through the device.

Advanced Encryption Standard (AES) The current federal standard for the encryption of data, as specified by NIST. AES is based on the Rijndael algorithm, which was developed by Vincent Rijmen and Joan Daemen.

advance-fee fraud (AFF) A form of social engineering, typically conducted via e-mail, in which an organization or some third party indicates that the recipient is due an exorbitant amount of money and needs only a small advance fee or personal banking information to facilitate the transfer.

adverse event An event with negative consequences that could threaten the organization's information assets or operations. Sometimes referred to as an incident candidate.

adware Malware intended to provide undesired marketing and advertising, including pop-ups and banners on a user's screens.

affidavit Sworn testimony that certain facts are in the possession of an investigating officer and that they warrant the examination of specific items located at a specific place. The facts, the items, and the place must be specified in the affidavit.

after-action review A detailed examination and discussion of the events that occurred, from first detection to final recovery.

agent See *sensor*.

aggregate information Collective data that relates to a group or category of people and that has been altered to remove characteristics or components that make it possible to identify individuals within the group. Not to be confused with *information aggregation*.

air-aspirating detector A fire detection sensor used in high-sensitivity areas that works by taking in air, filtering it, and passing it through a chamber that contains a laser beam. The alarm triggers if the beam is broken.

alarm clustering and compaction A process of grouping almost identical alarms that occur nearly at the same time into a single higher-level alarm. This consolidation reduces the number of alarms, which reduces administrative overhead and identifies a relationship among multiple alarms. Clustering may be based on combinations of frequency, similarity in attack signature, similarity in attack target, or other criteria that are defined by system administrators.

alarm filtering The process of classifying IDPS alerts so they can be more effectively managed. An IDPS administrator can set up alarm filtering by running the system for a while to track the types of false positives it generates and then adjusting the alarm classifications. For example, the administrator may set the IDPS to discard alarms produced by false attack stimuli or normal network operations. Alarm filters are similar to packet filters in that they can filter items by their source or destination IP addresses, but they can also filter by operating systems, confidence values, alarm type, or alarm severity.

alert message A scripted description of the incident that usually contains just enough information so that each person knows what portion of the IR plan to implement without slowing down the notification process.

alert or alarm An indication or notification that a system has just been attacked or is under attack. IDPS alerts and alarms take the form of audible signals, e-mail messages, pager notifications, or pop-up windows.

alert roster A document that contains contact information for people to be notified in the event of an incident.

algorithm The mathematical formula or method used to convert an unencrypted message into an encrypted message.

annualized cost of a safeguard (ACS) In a cost-benefit analysis, the total cost of a control or safeguard, including all purchase, maintenance, subscription, personnel, and support fees, divided by the total number of expected years of use.

annualized loss expectancy (ALE) In a cost-benefit analysis, the product of the annualized rate of occurrence and single loss expectancy.

annualized rate of occurrence (ARO) In a cost-benefit analysis, the expected frequency of an attack, expressed on a per-year basis.

anomaly-based detection Also known as *behavior-based detection*, an IDPS detection method that compares current data and traffic patterns to an established baseline of normalcy.

application firewall See *application layer proxy firewall*.

application header (AH) protocol In IPSec, a protocol that provides system-to-system authentication and data integrity verification, but does not provide secrecy for the content of a network communication.

application layer proxy firewall A device capable of functioning both as a firewall and an application layer proxy server.

application protocol verification The process of examining and verifying the higher-order protocols (HTTP, FTP, and Telnet) in network traffic for unexpected packet behavior or improper use.

asset The organizational resource that is being protected. An asset can be logical, such as a Web site, software information, or data; or an asset can be physical, such as a person, computer system, hardware, or other tangible object. Assets, particularly information assets, are the focus of what security efforts are attempting to protect.

asset exposure See *loss magnitude*.

asset valuation The process of assigning financial value or worth to each information asset.

asymmetric encryption A cryptographic method that incorporates mathematical operations involving both a public key and a private key to encipher or decipher a message. Either key can be used to encrypt a message, but then the other key is required to decrypt it.

asynchronous token An authentication component in the form of a token—a card or key fob that contains a computer chip and a liquid crystal display and shows a computer-generated number used to support remote login authentication. This token does not require calibration of the central authentication server; instead, it uses a challenge/response system.

attack An intentional or unintentional act that can damage or otherwise compromise information and the systems that support it. Attacks can be active or passive and direct or indirect.

attack protocol A logical sequence of steps or processes used by an attacker to launch an attack against a target system or network.

attack success probability The number of successful attacks that are expected to occur within a specified time period.

attack surface The functions and features that a system exposes to unauthenticated users.

attribute A characteristic of a subject (user or system) that can be used to restrict access to an object. Also known as a *subject attribute*.

attribute-based access control (ABAC) An access control approach whereby the organization specifies the use of objects based on some attribute of the user or system.

auditability See *accountability*.

auditing The review of a system's use to determine if misuse or malfeasance has occurred.

authentication The access control mechanism that requires the validation and verification of an unauthenticated entity's purported identity.

authentication factors Three mechanisms that provide authentication based on something an unauthenticated entity knows, something an unauthenticated entity has, and something an unauthenticated entity is.

authenticity An attribute of information that describes how data is genuine or original rather than reproduced or fabricated.

authorization The access control mechanism that represents the matching of an authenticated entity to a list of information assets and corresponding access levels.

availability An attribute of information that describes how data is accessible and correctly formatted for use without interference or obstruction.

availability disruption An interruption in service, usually from a service provider, which causes an adverse event within an organization.

avoidance of competitive disadvantage The adoption and implementation of a business model, method, technique, resource, or technology to prevent being outperformed by a competing organization; working to keep pace with the competition through innovation, rather than falling behind.

back door A malware payload that provides access to a system by bypassing normal access controls. A back door may also be an intentional access control bypass left by a system designer to facilitate development.

back hack The process of illegally attempting to determine the source of an intrusion by tracing it and trying to gain access to the originating system.

badge An identification card typically worn in a visible location to quickly verify an authorized member. The badge may or may not show the wearer's name.

baseline An assessment of the performance of some action or process against which future performance is assessed; the first measurement (benchmark) in benchmarking.

baselining The process of conducting a baseline. See also *baseline*.

bastion host A device placed between an external, untrusted network and an internal, trusted network. Also known as a *sacrificial host*, a bastion host serves as the sole target for attack and should therefore be thoroughly secured.

behavioral feasibility See *operational feasibility*.

behavior-based detection See *anomaly-based detection*.

benchmarking An attempt to improve information security practices by comparing an organization's efforts against practices of a similar organization or an industry-developed standard to produce results it would like to duplicate. Sometimes referred to as external benchmarking.

best business practices Security efforts that are considered among the best in the industry.

biometric access control The use of physiological characteristics to provide authentication for a provided identification. Biometric means "life measurement" in Greek. Sometimes referred to as *biometrics*.

biometric lock A lock that reads a unique biological attribute such as a fingerprint, iris, retina, or palm and then uses that input as a key.

bit stream cipher An encryption method that involves converting plaintext to ciphertext one bit at a time.

blacklist A list of systems, users, files, or addresses that have been associated with malicious activity; it is commonly used to block those entities from systems or network access.

blackout A long-term interruption (outage) in electrical power availability.

block cipher An encryption method that involves dividing the plaintext into blocks or sets of bits and then converting the plaintext to ciphertext one block at a time.

boot virus Also known as a boot sector virus, a type of virus that targets the boot sector or Master Boot Record (MBR) of a computer system's hard drive or removable storage media.

bot An abbreviation of *robot*, an automated software program that executes certain commands when it receives a specific input. See also *zombie*.

bottom-up approach A method of establishing security policies and/or practices that begins as a grassroots effort in which systems administrators attempt to improve the security of their systems.

brownout A long-term decrease in electrical power availability.

brute force password attack An attempt to guess a password by attempting every possible combination of characters and numbers in it.

buffer overrun (or buffer overflow) An application error that occurs when more data is sent to a program buffer than it is designed to handle.

build A snapshot of a particular version of software assembled or linked from its component modules.

build list A list of the versions of components that make up a build.

bull's-eye model A method for prioritizing a program of complex change; it requires that issues be addressed from the general to the specific and focuses on systematic solutions instead of individual problems.

business continuity plan (BC plan) The documented product of business continuity planning; a plan that shows the organization's intended efforts to continue critical functions when operations at the primary site are not feasible.

business continuity planning (BCP) The actions taken by senior management to develop and implement the BC policy, plan, and continuity teams.

business impact analysis (BIA) An investigation and assessment of the various adverse events that can affect the organization, conducted as a preliminary phase of the contingency planning process, which includes a determination of how critical a system or set of information is to the organization's core processes and recovery priorities.

business resumption planning (BRP) The actions taken by senior management to develop and implement a combined DR and BC policy, plan, and set of recovery teams.

capabilities table A lattice-based access control with rows of attributes associated with a particular subject (such as a user).

centralized IDPS control strategy An IDPS implementation approach in which all control functions are implemented and managed in a central location.

certificate authority (CA) In PKI, a third party that manages users' digital certificates.

certificate revocation list (CRL) In PKI, a published list of revoked or terminated digital certificates.

certification In information security, the comprehensive evaluation of an IT system's technical and nontechnical security controls that establishes the extent to which a particular design and implementation meets a set of predefined security requirements, usually in support of an accreditation process.

chain of custody See *chain of evidence*.

chain of evidence The detailed documentation of the collection, storage, transfer, and ownership of evidence from the crime scene through its presentation in court.

change control A method of regulating the modification of systems within the organization by requiring formal review and approval for each change.

chief information officer (CIO) An executive-level position that oversees the organization's computing technology and strives to create efficiency in the processing and access of the organization's information.

chief information security officer (CISO) Typically considered the top information security officer in an organization. The CISO is usually not an executive-level position, and frequently the person in this role reports to the CIO.

C.I.A. triad The industry standard for computer security since the development of the mainframe. The standard is based on three characteristics that describe the utility of information: confidentiality, integrity, and availability.

cipher When used as a verb, the transformation of the individual components (characters, bytes, or bits) of an unencrypted message into encrypted components or vice versa (see *decipher* and *encipher*); when used as a noun, the process of encryption or the algorithm used in encryption, and a term synonymous with *cryptosystem*.

ciphertext or cryptogram The unintelligible encrypted or encoded message resulting from an encryption.

clean agent A fire suppression agent that does not leave any residue after use or interfere with the operation of electrical or electronic equipment.

clean desk policy An organizational policy that specifies employees must inspect their work areas and ensure that all classified information, documents, and materials are secured at the end of every work day.

clipping level A predefined assessment level that triggers a predetermined response when surpassed. Typically, the response is to write the event to a log file and/or notify an administrator.

closed-circuit television (CCT) A video capture and recording system used to monitor a facility.

code The process of converting components (words or phrases) of an unencrypted message into encrypted components.

cold site A facility that provides only rudimentary services, with no computer hardware or peripherals. Cold sites are used for BC operations.

command injection An application error that occurs when user input is passed directly to a compiler or interpreter without screening for content that may disrupt or compromise the intended function.

communications security The protection of all communications media, technology, and content.

community of interest A group of individuals who are united by similar interests or values within an organization and who share a common goal of helping the organization to meet its objectives.

competitive advantage The adoption and implementation of an innovative business model, method, technique, resource, or technology in order to outperform the competition.

competitive intelligence The collection and analysis of information about an organization's business competitors through legal and ethical means to gain business intelligence and competitive advantage.

computer forensics The process of collecting, analyzing, and preserving computer-related evidence.

computer security In the early days of computers, this term specified the need to secure the physical location of computer technology from outside threats. This term later came to represent all actions taken to preserve computer systems from losses. It has evolved into the current concept of information security as the scope of protecting information in an organization has expanded.

confidence value The measure of an IDPS's ability to correctly detect and identify certain types of attacks. The confidence value an organization places in the IDPS is based on experience and past performance measurements. The confidence value, which is based on *fuzzy logic*, helps an administrator determine the likelihood that an IDPS alert or alarm indicates an actual attack in progress. For example, if a system deemed 90 percent capable of accurately reporting a denial-of-service (DoS) attack sends a DoS alert, there is a high probability that an actual attack is occurring.

confidentiality An attribute of information that describes how data is protected from disclosure or exposure to unauthorized individuals or systems.

configuration A collection of components that make up a configuration item.

configuration and change management (CCM) An approach to implementing system change that uses policies, procedures, techniques, and tools to manage and evaluate proposed changes, track changes through completion, and maintain systems inventory and supporting documentation.

configuration item A hardware or software item that will be modified and revised throughout its life cycle.

configuration management (CM) See *configuration and change management (CCM)*.

configuration rules The instructions a system administrator codes into a server, networking device, or security device to specify how it operates.

contact and weight sensor An alarm sensor designed to detect increased pressure or contact at a specific location, such as a floor pad or a window.

content filter A software program or hardware/software appliance that allows administrators to restrict content that comes into or leaves a network—for example, restricting user access to Web sites from material that is not related to business, such as pornography or entertainment.

contingency plan The documented product of contingency planning; a plan that shows the organization's intended efforts in reaction to adverse events.

contingency planning (CP) The actions taken by senior management to specify the organization's efforts and actions if an adverse event becomes an incident or disaster. This planning includes incident response, disaster recovery, and business continuity efforts, as well as preparatory business impact analysis.

contingency planning management team (CPMT) The group of senior managers and project members organized to conduct and lead all CP efforts.

control, safeguard, or countermeasure Security mechanisms, policies, or procedures that can successfully counter attacks, reduce risk, resolve vulnerabilities, and otherwise improve security within an organization.

corporate governance Executive management's responsibility to provide strategic direction, ensure the accomplishment of objectives, oversee that risks are appropriately managed, and validate responsible resource use.

cost avoidance The financial savings from using the defense risk control strategy to implement a control and eliminate the financial ramifications of an incident.

cost-benefit analysis (CBA) Also known as an economic feasibility study, the formal assessment and presentation of the economic expenditures needed for a particular security control, contrasted with its projected value to the organization.

covert channels Unauthorized or unintended methods of communications hidden inside a computer system.

cracker A hacker who intentionally removes or bypasses software copyright protection designed to prevent unauthorized duplication or use.

cracking Attempting to reverse-engineer, remove, or bypass a password or other access control protection, such as the copyright protection on software. See *cracker*.

crisis management An organization's set of planning and preparation efforts for dealing with potential human injury, emotional trauma, or loss of life as a result of a disaster.

crossover error rate (CER) Also called the equal error rate, the point at which the rate of false rejections equals the rate of false acceptances.

cross-site scripting (XSS) A Web application fault that occurs when an application running on a Web server inserts commands into a user's browser session and causes information to be sent to a hostile server.

cryptanalysis The process of obtaining the plaintext message from a ciphertext message without knowing the keys used to perform the encryption.

cryptography The process of making and using codes to secure information.

cryptology The field of science that encompasses cryptography and cryptanalysis.

cultural mores The fixed moral attitudes or customs of a particular group.

cyberactivist See *hacktivist*.

cyberterrorist A hacker who attacks systems to conduct terrorist activities via networks or Internet pathways.

cyberwarfare Formally sanctioned offensive operations conducted by a government or state against information or systems of another government or state. Sometimes called information warfare.

data Items of fact collected by an organization. Data includes raw numbers, facts, and words. Student quiz scores are a simple example of data.

data classification scheme A formal access control methodology used to assign a level of confidentiality to an information asset and thus restrict the number of people who can access it.

data custodians Individuals who work directly with data owners and are responsible for storage, maintenance, and protection of information.

data loss prevention A strategy to gain assurance that the users of a network do not send high-value information or other critical information outside the network.

data owners Individuals who control, and are therefore responsible for, the security and use of a particular set of information; data owners may rely on custodians for the practical aspects of protecting their information, specifying which users are authorized to access it, but they are ultimately responsible for it.

data security Commonly used as a surrogate for information security, data security is the focus of protecting data or information in its various states—at rest (in storage), in processing, and in transmission (over networks).

data users Internal and external stakeholders (customers, suppliers, and employees) who interact with information in support of their organization's planning and operations.

database A collection of related data stored in a structured form and usually managed by a database management system.

database security A subset of information security that focuses on the assessment and protection of information stored in data repositories like database management systems and storage media.

database shadowing A backup strategy to store duplicate online transaction data along with duplicate databases at the remote site on a redundant server. This server combines electronic vaulting with remote journaling by writing multiple copies of the database simultaneously to two locations.

de facto standard A standard that has been widely adopted or accepted by a public group rather than a formal standards organization. Contrast with a *de jure standard*.

de jure standard A standard that has been formally evaluated, approved, and ratified by a formal standards organization. Contrast with a *de facto standard*.

decipher See *decryption*.

decryption The process of converting an encoded or enciphered message (ciphertext) back to its original readable form (plaintext).

defense in depth A strategy for the protection of information assets that uses multiple layers and different types of controls (managerial, operational, and technical) to provide optimal protection.

defense risk control strategy The risk control strategy that attempts to eliminate or reduce any remaining uncontrolled risk through the application of additional controls and safeguards. Also known as the avoidance strategy.

deliverable A completed document or program module that can either serve as the beginning point for a later task or become an element in the finished project.

delta conversion online UPS An uninterruptible power supply (UPS) that is similar to a double conversion online UPS except that it incorporates a delta transformer, which assists in powering the inverter while outside power is available.

deluge system A fire suppression sprinkler system that keeps all individual sprinkler heads open and applies water to all areas when activated.

demilitarized zone (DMZ) An intermediate area between two networks designed to provide servers and firewall filtering between a trusted internal network and the outside, untrusted network. Traffic on the outside network carries a higher level of risk.

denial-of-service (DoS) attack An attack that attempts to overwhelm a computer target's ability to handle incoming communications, prohibiting legitimate users from accessing those systems.

dictionary password attack A variation of the brute force password attack that attempts to narrow the range of possible passwords guessed by using a list of common passwords and possibly including attempts based on the target's personal information.

difference analysis A procedure that compares the current state of a network segment against a known previous state of the same network segment (the baseline of systems and services).

differential backup The duplication of all files that have changed or been added since the last full backup.

Diffie-Hellman key exchange A hybrid cryptosystem that facilitates exchanging private keys using public-key encryption.

digital certificates Public-key container files that allow PKI system components and end users to validate a public key and identify its owner.

digital forensics Investigations that involve the preservation, identification, extraction, documentation, and interpretation of computer media for evidentiary and root cause analysis. Like traditional forensics, digital forensics follows clear, well-defined methodologies but still tends to be as much an art as a science.

digital malfeasance A crime against or using digital media, computer technology, or related components; in other words, a computer is the source of the crime or the object of it.

Digital Signature Standard (DSS) The NIST standard for digital signature algorithm usage by federal information systems. DSS is based on a variant of the ElGamal signature scheme.

digital signatures Encrypted message components that can be mathematically proven as authentic.

direct changeover The conversion strategy that involves stopping the old system and starting the new one without any overlap.

disaster An adverse event that could threaten the viability of the entire organization. A disaster may either escalate from an incident or be initially classified as a disaster.

disaster recovery plan (DR plan) The documented product of disaster recovery planning; a plan that shows the organization's intended efforts in the event of a disaster.

disaster recovery planning (DRP) The actions taken by senior management to specify the organization's efforts in preparation for and recovery from a disaster.

discretionary access controls (DACs) Access controls that are implemented at the discretion or option of the data user.

disk duplexing An approach to disk mirroring in which each drive has its own controller to provide additional redundancy.

disk mirroring A RAID implementation (typically referred to as RAID Level 1) in which the computer records all data to twin drives simultaneously, providing a backup if the primary drive fails.

disk striping A RAID implementation (typically referred to as RAID Level 0) in which one logical volume is created by storing data across several available hard drives in segments called stripes.

distributed denial-of-service (DDoS) attack A form of DoS attack in which a coordinated stream of requests is launched against a target from many locations at the same time using bots or zombies.

Domain Name System (DNS) cache poisoning The intentional hacking and modification of a DNS database to redirect legitimate traffic to illegitimate Internet locations. Also known as DNS spoofing.

double conversion online UPS A UPS in which the protected device draws power from an output inverter. The inverter is powered by the UPS battery, which is constantly recharged from the outside power.

downtime The percentage of time a particular service is not available; the opposite of uptime.

dry-pipe system A fire suppression sprinkler system that has pressurized air in all pipes. The air is released in the event of a fire, allowing water to flow from a central area.

due care Measures that an organization takes to ensure every employee knows what is acceptable and what is not.

due diligence Reasonable steps taken by people or organizations to meet the obligations imposed by laws or regulations.

dumb card An authentication card that contains digital user data, such as a personal identification number (PIN), against which user input is compared.

dumpster diving An information attack that involves searching through a target organization's trash and recycling bins for sensitive information.

dynamic packet-filtering firewall A firewall type that can react to network traffic and create or modify configuration rules to adapt.

electromagnetic radiation (EMR) The transmission of radiant energy through space, commonly referred to as radio waves.

electromechanical lock A lock that can accept a variety of inputs as keys, including magnetic strips on ID cards, radio signals from badges, personal identification numbers (PINs) typed into a keypad, or some combination of these to activate an electrically powered locking mechanism.

electronic vaulting A backup method that uses bulk batch transfer of data to an off-site facility; this transfer is usually conducted via leased lines or secure Internet connections.

electrostatic discharge (ESD) The release of ambient static electricity into a ground.

encapsulating security payload (ESP) protocol In IPSec, a protocol that provides secrecy for the contents of network communications as well as system-to-system authentication and data integrity verification.

encipher See *encryption.*

encryption The process of converting an original message (plaintext) into a form that cannot be used by unauthorized individuals (ciphertext).

enterprise information security policy (EISP) The high-level information security policy that sets the strategic direction, scope, and tone for all of an organization's security efforts. An EISP is also known as a security program policy, general security policy, IT security policy, high-level InfoSec policy, or simply an InfoSec policy.

enticement The act of attracting attention to a system by placing tantalizing information in key locations.

entrapment The act of luring a person into committing a crime in order to get a conviction.

ethics The branch of philosophy that considers nature, criteria, sources, logic, and the validity of moral judgment.

evasion The process by which attackers change the format and/or timing of their activities to avoid being detected by an IDPS.

evidence A physical object or documented information entered into a legal proceeding that proves an action occurred or identifies the intent of a perpetrator.

evidentiary material (EM) Also known as "items of potential evidentiary value," any information that could potentially support an organization's legal or policy-based case against a suspect.

exclusive OR operation (XOR) A function within Boolean algebra used as an encryption function in which two bits are compared. If the two bits are identical, the result is a binary 0; otherwise, the result is a binary 1.

exit interview A meeting with an employee who is leaving the organization to remind the employee of contractual obligations, such as nondisclosure agreements, and to obtain feedback about the employee's tenure.

expert hacker A hacker who uses extensive knowledge of the inner workings of computer hardware and software to gain unauthorized access to systems and information. Also known as elite hackers, expert hackers often create automated exploits, scripts, and tools used by other hackers.

exploit A technique used to compromise a system.

exposure A condition or state of being exposed; in information security, exposure exists when a vulnerability is known to an attacker.

exposure factor (EF) In a cost-benefit analysis, the expected percentage of loss that would occur from a particular attack.

external monitoring domain The component of the maintenance model that focuses on evaluating external threats to the organization's information assets.

extranet A segment of the DMZ where additional authentication and authorization controls are put into place to provide services that are not available to the general public.

facilities management The aspect of organizational management focused on the development and maintenance of its buildings and physical infrastructure.

fail-safe lock An electromechanical device that automatically releases the lock protecting a control point if a power outage occurs. This type of lock is used for fire safety locations.

fail-secure lock An electromechanical device that stays locked and maintains the security of the control point if a power outage occurs.

false accept rate The rate at which fraudulent users or nonusers are allowed access to systems or areas as a result of a failure in the biometric device. This failure is also known as a Type II error or a false positive.

false attack stimulus An event that triggers an alarm when no actual attack is in progress. Scenarios that test the configuration of IDPSs may use false attack stimuli to determine if the IDPSs can distinguish between these stimuli and real attacks.

false negative The failure of an IDPS to react to an actual attack event. This is the most grievous IDPS failure, given that its purpose is to detect and respond to attacks.

false positive An alert or alarm that occurs in the absence of an actual attack. A false positive can sometimes be produced when an IDPS mistakes normal system activity for an attack. False positives tend to make users insensitive to alarms and thus reduce their reactions to actual intrusion events.

false reject rate The rate at which authentic users are denied or prevented access to authorized areas as a result of a failure in the biometric device. This failure is also known as a Type I error or a false negative.

fault A short-term interruption in electrical power availability.

fingerprinting The systematic survey of a targeted organization's Internet addresses collected during the footprinting phase to identify the network services offered by the hosts in that range.

fire suppression systems Devices that are installed and maintained to detect and respond to a fire, potential fire, or combustion danger.

firewall In information security, a combination of hardware and software that filters or prevents specific information from moving between the outside network and the inside network.

fixed-temperature sensor A fire detection sensor that works by detecting the point at which the ambient temperature in an area reaches a predetermined level.

flame detector A fire detection system that works by detecting the infrared or ultraviolet light produced by an open flame.

footprinting The organized research and investigation of Internet addresses owned or controlled by a target organization.

forensics The coherent application of methodical investigatory techniques to present evidence of crimes in a court or similar setting. Forensics allows investigators to determine what happened by examining the results of an event—criminal, natural, intentional, or accidental.

full backup The duplication of all files for an entire system, including all applications, operating systems components, and data.

fully distributed IDPS control strategy An IDPS implementation approach in which all control functions are applied at the physical location of each IDPS component.

gap analysis The process of comparing measured results against expected results, then using the resulting "gap" as a measure of project success and as feedback for project management.

gaseous (or chemical gas) emission systems Fire suppression systems that operate through the delivery of gases rather than water.

goals Sometimes used synonymously with *objectives*; the desired end of a planning cycle.

governance "The set of responsibilities and practices exercised by the board and executive management with the goal of providing strategic direction, ensuring that objectives are achieved, ascertaining that risks are managed appropriately and verifying that the enterprise's resources are used responsibly."

ground fault circuit interruption A special circuit device designed to immediately disconnect a power supply when a sudden discharge (ground fault) is detected.

guidelines Nonmandatory recommendations the employee may use as a reference in complying with a policy. If the policy states to "use strong passwords, frequently changed," the guidelines might advise that "we recommend you don't use family or pet names, or parts of your Social Security number, employee number, or phone number in your password."

hacker A person who accesses systems and information without authorization and often illegally.

hacktivist A hacker who seeks to interfere with or disrupt systems to protest the operations, policies, or actions of an organization or government agency.

hash algorithms Public functions that create a hash value, also known as a message digest, by converting variable-length messages into a single fixed-length value.

hash functions Mathematical algorithms that generate a message summary or digest (sometimes called a fingerprint) to confirm message identity and integrity.

hash value See *message digest*.

hierarchical roster An alert roster in which the first person calls a few other people on the roster, who in turn call others. This method typically uses the organizational chart as a structure.

honeynet A monitored network or network segment that contains multiple honeypot systems.

honeypot An application that entices people who are illegally perusing the internal areas of a network by providing simulated rich content while the software notifies the administrator of the intrusion.

host-based IDPS (HIDPS) An IDPS that resides on a particular computer or server, known as the host, and monitors activity only on that system. Also known as a system integrity verifier.

hot site A fully configured computing facility that includes all services, communications links, and physical plant operations. Hot sites are used for BC operations.

hot swap A hard drive feature that allows individual drives to be replaced without powering down the entire system and without causing a fault during the replacement.

humidity The amount of moisture in the air.

hybrid VPN A combination of trusted and secure VPN implementations.

identification The access control mechanism whereby unverified or unauthenticated entities who seek access to a resource provide a label by which they are known to the system.

identification (ID) card A document used to verify the identity of a member of an organization, group, or domain.

identity theft The unauthorized taking of personally identifiable information with the intent of committing fraud and abuse of a person's financial and personal reputation, purchasing goods and services without authorization, and generally impersonating the victim for illegal or unethical purposes.

incident An adverse event that could result in loss of an information asset or assets, but does not currently threaten the viability of the entire organization.

incident candidate See *adverse event*.

incident classification The process of examining an incident candidate and determining whether it constitutes an actual incident.

incident damage assessment The rapid determination of how seriously a breach of confidentiality, integrity, and availability affected information and information assets during an incident or just following one.

incident response plan (IR plan) The documented product of incident response planning; a plan that shows the organization's intended efforts in the event of an incident.

incident response planning (IRP) The actions taken by senior management to develop and implement the IR policy, plan, and computer security incident response team.

incremental backup The duplication of only the files that have been modified since the previous incremental backup.

industrial espionage The collection and analysis of information about an organization's business competitors, often through illegal or unethical means, to gain an unfair competitive advantage. Also known as corporate spying, which is distinguished from espionage for national security reasons.

information Data that has been organized, structured, and presented to provide additional insight into its context, worth, and usefulness. For example, a student's class average can be presented in the context of its value, as in "90 = A."

information aggregation Pieces of nonprivate data that, when combined, may create information that violates privacy. Not to be confused with *aggregate information*.

information asset The focus of information security; information that has value to the organization, and the systems that store, process, and transmit the information.

information assurance The affirmation or guarantee of the confidentiality, integrity, and availability of information in storage, processing, and transmission. This term is often used synonymously with *information security*.

information extortion The act of an attacker or trusted insider who steals or interrupts access to information from a computer system and demands compensation for its return or for an agreement not to disclose the information.

information security Protection of the confidentiality, integrity, and availability of information assets, whether in storage, processing, or transmission, via the application of policy, education, training and awareness, and technology.

information security blueprint In information security, a framework or security model customized to an organization, including implementation details.

information security framework In information security, a specification of a model to be followed during the design, selection, and initial and ongoing implementation of all subsequent security controls, including information security policies, security education and training programs, and technological controls. Also known as a security model.

information security governance The application of the principles of corporate governance to the information security function.

information security model See *information security framework*.

information security policy Written instructions provided by management that inform employees and others in the workplace about proper behavior regarding the use of information and information assets.

information system (IS) The entire set of software, hardware, data, people, procedures, and networks that enable the use of information resources in the organization.

inline sensor An IDPS sensor intended for network perimeter use and deployed in close proximity to a perimeter firewall to detect incoming attacks that could overwhelm the firewall.

integer bug A class of computational error caused by methods that computers use to store and manipulate integer numbers; this bug can be exploited by attackers.

integrity An attribute of information that describes how data is whole, complete, and uncorrupted.

intellectual property (IP) The creation, ownership, and control of original ideas as well as the representation of those ideas.

internal monitoring domain The component of the maintenance model that focuses on identifying, assessing, and managing the configuration and status of information assets in an organization.

Internet vulnerability assessment An assessment approach designed to find and document vulnerabilities that may be present in the organization's public network.

intranet vulnerability assessment An assessment approach designed to find and document selected vulnerabilities that are likely to be present on the organization's internal network.

intrusion An adverse event in which an attacker attempts to gain entry into an information system or disrupt its normal operations, almost always with the intent to do harm.

intrusion detection and prevention system (IDPS) The general term for a system that can both detect and modify its configuration and environment to prevent intrusions. An IDPS encompasses the functions of both intrusion detection systems and intrusion prevention technology.

intrusion detection system (IDS) A system capable of automatically detecting an intrusion into an organization's networks or host systems and notifying a designated authority.

ionization sensor A fire detection sensor that works by exposing the ambient air to a small amount of a harmless radioactive material within a detection chamber; an alarm is triggered when the level of electrical conductivity changes within the chamber.

IP Security (IPSec) The primary and now dominant cryptographic authentication and encryption product of the IETF's IP Protocol Security Working Group. A framework for security development within the TCP/IP family of protocol standards, IPSec provides application support for all uses within TCP/IP, including virtual private networks.

issue-specific security policy (ISSP) An organizational policy that provides detailed, targeted guidance to instruct all members of the organization in the use of a resource, such as one of its processes or technologies.

jailbreaking Escalating privileges to gain administrator-level or root access control over a smartphone operating system (typically associated with Apple iOS smartphones). See also *rooting*.

job rotation The requirement that every employee be able to perform the work of another employee.

jurisdiction The power to make legal decisions and judgments; typically an area within which an entity such as a court or law enforcement agency is empowered to make legal decisions.

Kerberos An authentication system that uses symmetric key encryption to validate an individual user's access to various network resources by keeping a database containing the private keys of clients and servers that are in the authentication domain it supervises.

key or cryptovariable The information used in conjunction with the algorithm to create the ciphertext from the plaintext; it can be a series of bits used in a mathematical algorithm or the knowledge of how to manipulate the plaintext.

keyspace The entire range of values that can be used to construct an individual key.

knowledge-based detection See *signature-based detection*.

known vulnerability A published weakness or fault in an information asset or its protective systems that may be exploited and result in loss.

lattice-based access control (LBAC) A variation on the MAC form of access control, which assigns users a matrix of authorizations for particular areas of access, incorporating the information assets of subjects such as users and objects.

laws Rules that mandate or prohibit certain behavior and are enforced by the state.

least privilege The data access principle that ensures no unnecessary access to data exists by regulating members so they can perform only the minimum data manipulation needed. Least privilege implies a need to know.

liability An entity's legal obligation or responsibility.

likelihood The probability that a specific vulnerability within an organization will be the target of an attack.

line-interactive UPS A UPS in which a pair of inverters and converters draw power from the outside source both to charge the battery and provide power to the internal protected device.

link encryption A series of encryptions and decryptions between a number of systems, wherein each system in a network decrypts the message sent to it and then reencrypts the message using different keys and sends it to the next neighbor.

log file monitor (LFM) An attack detection method that reviews the log files generated by computer systems, looking for patterns and signatures that may indicate an attack or intrusion is in process or has already occurred.

long-arm jurisdiction The ability of a legal entity to exercise its influence beyond its normal boundaries by asserting a connection between an out-of-jurisdiction entity and a local legal case.

loss A single instance of an information asset suffering damage or destruction, unintended or unauthorized modification or disclosure, or denial of use. When an organization's information is stolen, it has suffered a loss.

loss frequency The calculation of the likelihood of an attack coupled with the attack frequency to determine the expected number of losses within a specified time range.

loss magnitude Also known as event loss magnitude, the combination of an asset's value and the percentage of it that might be lost in an attack.

macro virus A type of virus written in a specific macro language to target applications that use the language. The virus is activated when the application's product is opened. A macro virus typically affects documents, slideshows, e-mails, or spreadsheets created by office suite applications.

mail bomb An attack designed to overwhelm the receiver with excessive quantities of e-mail.

maintenance hook See *back door*.

major release A significant revision of a version from its previous state.

malicious code See *malware*.

malicious software See *malware*.

malware Computer software specifically designed to perform malicious or unwanted actions.

managerial controls Information security safeguards that focus on administrative planning, organizing, leading, and controlling, and that are designed by strategic planners and implemented by the organization's security administration. These safeguards include governance and risk management.

managerial guidance SysSP A systems-specific security policy that expresses management's intent for the acquisition, implementation, configuration, and management of a particular technology, written from a business perspective.

mandatory access control (MAC) A required, structured data classification scheme that rates each collection of information as well as each user. These ratings are often referred to as sensitivity or classification levels.

man-in-the-middle A group of attacks whereby a person intercepts a communications stream and inserts himself in the conversation to convince each of the legitimate parties that he is the other communications partner. Some man-in-the-middle attacks involve encryption functions.

mantrap A small room or enclosure with separate entry and exit points, designed to restrain a person who fails an access authorization attempt.

maximum tolerable downtime (MTD) The total amount of time the system owner or authorizing official is willing to accept for a mission/business process outage or disruption, including all impact considerations.

McCumber Cube A graphical representation of the architectural approach widely used in computer and information security; commonly shown as a cube composed of 3×3×3 cells, similar to a Rubik's Cube.

mean time between failure (MTBF) The average amount of time between hardware failures, calculated as the total amount of operation time for a specified number of units divided by the total number of failures.

mean time to diagnose (MTTD) The average amount of time a computer repair technician needs to determine the cause of a failure.

mean time to failure (MTTF) The average amount of time until the next hardware failure.

mean time to repair (MTTR) The average amount of time a computer repair technician needs to resolve the cause of a failure through replacement or repair of a faulty unit.

mechanical lock A physical lock that may rely on either a key or numerical combination to rotate tumblers and release the hasp. Also known as a manual lock.

media As a subset of information assets, the systems and networks that store, process, and transmit information.

media access control layer firewall A firewall designed to operate at the media access control sublayer of the network's data link layer (Layer 2).

memory-resident virus A virus that is capable of installing itself in a computer's operating system, starting when the computer is activated, and residing in the system's memory even after the host application is terminated. Also known as a resident virus.

message authentication code (MAC) A key-dependent, one-way hash function that allows only specific recipients (symmetric key holders) to access the message digest.

message digest A value representing the application of a hash algorithm on a message that is transmitted with the message so it can be compared with the recipient's locally calculated hash of the same message. If both hashes are identical after transmission, the message has arrived without modification. Also known as a *hash value*.

methodology A formal approach to solving a problem based on a structured sequence of procedures.

metrics-based measures Performance measures or metrics based on observed numerical data.

milestone A specific point in the project plan when a task that has a noticeable impact on the plan's progress is complete.

minor release (update or patch) A minor revision of a version from its previous state.

minutiae In biometric access controls, unique points of reference that are digitized and stored in an encrypted format when the user's system access credentials are created.

mirror port See *monitoring port*.

misuse detection See *signature-based detection.*

mitigation risk control strategy The risk control strategy that attempts to reduce the impact of the loss caused by a realized incident, disaster, or attack through effective contingency planning and preparation.

monitoring port Also known as a switched port analysis (SPAN) port or mirror port, a specially configured connection on a network device that can view all the traffic that moves through the device.

monoalphabetic substitution A substitution cipher that only incorporates a single alphabet in the encryption process.

motion detector An alarm sensor designed to detect movement within a defined space.

mutual agreement A continuity strategy in which two organizations sign a contract to assist the other in a disaster by providing BC facilities, resources, and services until the organization in need can recover from the disaster.

need to know The principle of limiting users' access privileges to the specific information required to perform their assigned tasks.

Network Address Translation (NAT) A technology in which multiple real, routable external IP addresses are converted to special ranges of internal IP addresses, usually on a one-to-one basis; that is, one external valid address directly maps to one assigned internal address.

network security A subset of **communications security**; the protection of voice and data networking components, connections, and content.

network-based IDPS (NIDPS) An IDPS that resides on a computer or appliance connected to a segment of an organization's network and monitors traffic on that segment, looking for indications of ongoing or successful attacks.

Next Generation Firewall (NextGen or NGFW) A security appliance that delivers unified threat management capabilities in a single appliance.

noise The presence of additional and disruptive signals in network communications or electrical power delivery. Also, noise can be alarm events that are accurate and noteworthy but do not pose significant threats to information security. Unsuccessful attacks are the most common source of IDPS noise, although some noise might be triggered by scanning and enumeration tools run by network users without harmful intent.

nondiscretionary access controls (NDACs) Access controls that are implemented by a central authority.

non-memory-resident virus A virus that terminates after it has been activated, infected its host system, and replicated itself. NMR viruses do not reside in an operating system or memory after executing. Also known as a non-resident virus.

nonrepudiation The process of reversing public-key encryption to verify that a message was sent by the sender and thus cannot be refuted.

novice hacker A relatively unskilled hacker who uses the work of expert hackers to perform attacks. Also known as a neophyte,

n00b, or newbie. This category of hackers includes script kiddies and packet monkeys.

objectives Sometimes used synonymously with *goals;* the intermediate states obtained to achieve progress toward a goal or goals.

operational controls Information security safeguards focusing on lower-level planning that deals with the functionality of the organization's security. These safeguards include disaster recovery and incident response planning.

operational feasibility An examination of how well a particular solution fits within the organization's culture and the extent to which users are expected to accept the solution. Also known as *behavioral feasibility.*

operational plan The documented product of operational planning; a plan for the organization's intended operational efforts on a day-to-day basis for the next several months.

operational planning The actions taken by management to specify the short-term goals and objectives of the organization in order to obtain specified tactical goals, followed by estimates and schedules for the allocation of resources necessary to achieve those goals and objectives.

organizational feasibility An examination of how well a particular solution fits within the organization's strategic planning objectives and goals.

packet monkey A script kiddie who uses automated exploits to engage in denial-of-service attacks.

packet sniffer A software program or hardware appliance that can intercept, copy, and interpret network traffic.

packet-filtering firewall A networking device that examines the header information of data packets that come into a network and determines whether to drop them (deny) or forward them to the next network connection (allow), based on its configuration rules.

padded cell system A protected honeypot that cannot be easily compromised.

parallel operations The conversion strategy that involves running the new system concurrently with the old system.

partially distributed IDPS control strategy An IDPS implementation approach that combines the best aspects of the centralized and fully distributed strategies.

passive mode An IDPS sensor setting in which the device simply monitors and analyzes observed network or system traffic.

passive vulnerability scanner A scanner that listens in on a network and identifies vulnerable versions of both server and client software.

passphrase A plain-language phrase, typically longer than a password, from which a virtual password is derived.

password A secret word or combination of characters that only the user should know; a password is used to authenticate the user.

pen register An application that records information about outbound communications.

penetration tester An information security professional with authorization to attempt to gain system access in an effort to identify and recommend resolutions for vulnerabilities in those systems.

penetration testing A set of security tests and evaluations that simulate attacks by a hacker or other malicious external source.

performance gap The difference between an organization's observed and desired performance.

permutation cipher See *transposition cipher*.

personally identifiable information (PII) Information about a person's history, background, and attributes that can be used to commit identity theft. This information typically includes a person's name, address, Social Security number, family information, employment history, and financial information.

pharming The redirection of legitimate user Web traffic to illegitimate Web sites with the intent to collect personal information.

phased implementation The conversion strategy that involves a measured rollout of the planned system; only part of the system is brought out and disseminated across an organization before the next piece is implemented.

phishing A form of social engineering in which the attacker provides what appears to be a legitimate communication (usually e-mail), but it contains hidden or embedded code that redirects the reply to a third-party site in an effort to extract personal or confidential information.

photoelectric sensor A fire detection sensor that works by projecting an infrared beam across an area. If the beam is interrupted, presumably by smoke, the alarm or suppression system is activated.

phreaker A hacker who manipulates the public telephone system to make free calls or disrupt services.

physical security The protection of physical items, objects, or areas from unauthorized access and misuse.

pilot implementation The conversion strategy that involves implementing the entire system into a single office, department, or division, and dealing with issues that arise before expanding to the rest of the organization.

plaintext or cleartext The original unencrypted message that is encrypted and is the result of successful decryption.

planning and risk assessment domain The component of the maintenance model that focuses on identifying and planning ongoing information security activities and identifying and managing risks introduced through IT information security projects.

platform security validation (PSV) An assessment approach designed to find and document vulnerabilities that may be present because misconfigured systems are used within the organization.

plenum A space between the ceiling in one level of a commercial building and the floor of the level above. The plenum is used for air return.

policy Guidelines that dictate certain behavior within the organization.

policy administrator An employee responsible for the creation, revision, distribution, and storage of a policy in an organization.

political feasibility An examination of how well a particular solution fits within the organization's political environment—for example, the working relationship within the organization's communities of interest or between the organization and its external environment.

polyalphabetic substitution A substitution cipher that incorporates two or more alphabets in the encryption process.

polymorphic threat Malware (a virus or worm) that over time changes the way it appears to antivirus software programs, making it undetectable by techniques that look for preconfigured signatures.

Port Address Translation (PAT) A technology in which multiple real, routable external IP addresses are converted to special ranges of internal IP addresses, usually on a one-to-many basis; that is, one external valid address is mapped dynamically to a range of internal addresses by adding a unique port number to the address when traffic leaves the private network and is placed on the public network.

port scanners Tools used both by attackers and defenders to identify or fingerprint active computers on a network, the active ports and services on those computers, the functions and roles of the machines, and other useful information.

possession An attribute of information that describes how the data's ownership or control is legitimate or authorized.

practices Examples of actions that illustrate compliance with policies. If the policy states to "use strong passwords, frequently changed," the practices might advise that "according to X, most organizations require employees to change passwords at least semi-annually."

pre-action system A fire suppression sprinkler system that employs a two-phase response to a fire. When a fire is detected anywhere in the facility, the system will first flood all pipes, then activate only the sprinkler heads in the area of the fire.

predecessors Tasks or action steps that come before the specific task at hand.

pretexting A form of social engineering in which the attacker pretends to be an authority figure who needs information to confirm the target's identity, but the real object is to trick the target into revealing confidential information. Pretexting is commonly performed by telephone.

privacy In the context of information security, the right of individuals or groups to protect themselves and their information from unauthorized access, providing confidentiality.

Privacy-Enhanced Mail (PEM) A standard proposed by the Internet Engineering Task Force (IETF) that uses 3DES symmetric key encryption and RSA for key exchanges and digital signatures.

private-key encryption See *symmetric encryption*.

privilege escalation The unauthorized modification of an authorized or unauthorized system user account to gain advanced access and control over system resources.

procedures Step-by-step instructions designed to assist employees in following policies, standards, and guidelines. If the policy states to "use strong passwords, frequently changed," the procedure might advise that "in order to change your password, first click the Windows Start button, then...."

process-based measures Performance measures or metrics based on intangible activities.

professional hacker A hacker who conducts attacks for personal financial benefit or for a crime organization or foreign government. Not to be confused with a penetration tester.

project management The process of identifying and controlling the resources applied to a project as well as measuring progress and adjusting the process as progress is made toward the goal.

project plan The documented instructions for participants and stakeholders of a project that provide details on goals, objectives, tasks, scheduling, and resource management.

project scope A description of a project's features, capabilities, functions, and quality level, used as the basis of a project plan.

project team A small functional team of people who are experienced in one or multiple facets of the required technical and nontechnical areas for the project to which they are assigned.

project wrap-up A process of bringing a project to a conclusion, addressing any pending issues and the overall project effort, and identifying ways to improve the process in the future.

projectitis A situation in project planning in which the project manager spends more time documenting project tasks, collecting performance measurements, recording project task information, and updating project completion forecasts in the project management software than accomplishing meaningful project work.

protection profile or security posture The entire set of controls and safeguards, including policy, education, training and awareness, and technology, that the organization implements to protect the asset. The terms are sometimes used interchangeably with the term *security program*, although a security program often comprises managerial aspects of security, including planning, personnel, and subordinate programs.

protocol stack verification The process of examining and verifying network traffic for invalid data packets—that is, packets that are malformed under the rules of the TCP/IP protocol.

proximity reader An electronic signal receiver used with an electromechanical lock that allows users to place their cards within the reader's range and release the locking mechanism.

proxy server A server that exists to intercept requests for information from external users and provide the requested information by retrieving it from an internal server, thus protecting and minimizing the demand on internal servers. Some proxy servers are also cache servers.

public key infrastructure (PKI) An integrated system of software, encryption methodologies, protocols, legal agreements, and third-party services that enables users to communicate securely through the use of digital certificates.

public-key encryption See *asymmetric encryption*.

qualitative assessment An asset valuation approach that uses categorical or non-numeric values rather than absolute numerical measures.

quantitative assessment An asset valuation approach that attempts to assign absolute numerical measures.

rainbow table A table of hash values and their corresponding plaintext values that can be used to look up password values if an attacker is able to steal a system's encrypted password file.

ransomware Computer software specifically designed to identify and encrypt valuable information in a victim's system in order to extort payment for the key needed to unlock the encryption.

rate-of-rise sensor A fire detection sensor that works by detecting an unusually rapid increase in the area temperature within a relatively short period of time.

recovery point objective (RPO) The point in time prior to a disruption or system outage to which mission/business process data can be recovered after an outage (given the most recent backup copy of the data).

recovery time objective (RTO) The maximum amount of time that a system resource can remain unavailable before there is an unacceptable impact on other system resources, supported mission/business processes, and the MTD.

redundancy The use of multiple types and instances of technology that prevent the failure of one system from compromising the security of information.

redundant array of independent disks (RAID) A system of drives that stores information across multiple units to spread out data and minimize the impact of a single drive failure. By storing the data redundantly, the loss of a drive will not necessarily cause a loss of data. Also known as RAID.

reference monitor Within TCB, a conceptual piece of the system that manages access controls—in other words, it mediates all access to objects by subjects.

registration authority (RA) In PKI, a third party that operates under the trusted collaboration of the certificate authority and handles day-to-day certification functions.

remediation The processes of removing or repairing flaws in information assets that cause a vulnerability or removing the risk associated with the vulnerability.

Remote Authentication Dial-In User Service (RADIUS) A computer connection system that centralizes the management of user authentication by placing the responsibility for authenticating each user on a central authentication server.

remote journaling The backup of data to an off-site facility in close to real time based on transactions as they occur.

request for proposal (RFP) A document specifying the requirements of a project, provided to solicit bids from internal or external contractors.

residual risk The risk to information assets that remains even after current controls have been applied.

resources Components required for the completion of a project, which could include skills, personnel, time, money, and material.

restitution A legal requirement to make compensation or payment resulting from a loss or injury.

reverse firewall See *content filter*.

reverse proxy A proxy server that most commonly retrieves information from inside an organization and provides it to a requesting user or system outside the organization.

revision date The date associated with a particular version or build.

risk The probability of an unwanted occurrence, such as an adverse event or loss. Organizations must minimize risk to match their risk appetite—the quantity and nature of risk they are willing to accept.

risk appetite The quantity and nature of risk that organizations are willing to accept as they evaluate the trade-offs between perfect security and unlimited accessibility.

risk assessment A determination of the extent to which an organization's information assets are exposed to risk.

risk control The application of controls that reduce the risks to an organization's information assets to an acceptable level.

risk identification The recognition, enumeration, and documentation of risks to an organization's information assets.

risk management The process of identifying risk, assessing its relative magnitude, and taking steps to reduce it to an acceptable level.

risk tolerance See *risk appetite*.

role-based access control (RBAC) An example of a nondiscretionary control where privileges are tied to the role a user performs in an organization, and are inherited when a user is assigned to that role. Roles are considered more persistent than tasks. RBAC is an example of an LDAC.

rooting Escalating privileges to gain administrator-level control over a computer system (including smartphones). Typically associated with Android OS smartphones. See also *jailbreaking*.

sacrificial host See *bastion host*.

sag A short-term decrease in electrical power availability.

screened host architecture A firewall architectural model that combines the packet filtering router with a second, dedicated device such as a proxy server or proxy firewall.

screened subnet architecture A firewall architectural model that consists of one or more internal bastion hosts located behind a packet filtering router on a dedicated network segment, with each host performing a role in protecting the trusted network.

script kiddie A hacker of limited skill who uses expertly written software to attack a system. Also known as skids, skiddies, or script bunnies.

search warrant Permission to search for evidentiary material at a specified location and/or to seize items to return to an investigator's lab for examination. An affidavit becomes a search warrant when signed by an approving authority.

secret key A key that can be used in symmetric encryption both to encipher and decipher the message.

Secure Electronic Transactions (SET) A protocol developed by credit card companies to protect against electronic payment fraud.

secure facility A physical location that has controls in place to minimize the risk of attacks from physical threats.

Secure Hash Standard (SHS) A standard issued by the National Institute of Standards and Technology (NIST) that specifies secure algorithms, such as SHA-1, for computing a condensed representation of a message or data file.

Secure HTTP (S-HTTP) An extended version of Hypertext Transfer Protocol that provides for the encryption of protected Web pages transmitted via the Internet between a client and server.

Secure Multipurpose Internet Mail Extensions (S/MIME) A security protocol that builds on the encoding format of the Multipurpose Internet Mail Extensions (MIME) protocol and uses digital signatures based on public-key cryptosystems to secure e-mail.

Secure Sockets Layer (SSL) A security protocol developed by Netscape to use public-key encryption to secure a channel over the Internet.

secure VPN A VPN implementation that uses security protocols to encrypt traffic transmitted across unsecured public networks.

security A state of being secure and free from danger or harm. Also, the actions taken to make someone or something secure.

security clearance A personnel security structure in which each user of an information asset is assigned an authorization level that identifies the level of classified information he or she is "cleared" to access.

security domain An area of trust within which information assets share the same level of protection. Each trusted network within an organization is a security domain. Communication between security domains requires evaluation of communications traffic.

security education, training, and awareness (SETA) A managerial program designed to improve the security of information assets by providing targeted knowledge, skills, and guidance for an organization's employees.

security information and event management (SIEM) A software-enabled approach to aggregating, filtering, and managing the reaction to events, many of which are collected by logging activities of IDPSs and network management devices.

security perimeter The boundary in the network within which an organization attempts to maintain security controls for securing information from threats from untrusted network areas. The advent of mobile and cloud information technologies makes the security perimeter increasingly difficult to define and secure.

sensor A hardware and/or software component deployed on a remote computer or network segment and designed to monitor network or system traffic for suspicious activities and report back to the host application. For example, IDPS sensors report to an IDPS application.

separation of duties The information security principle that requires significant tasks to be split up so that more than one individual is required to complete them.

sequential roster An alert roster in which a single contact person calls each person on the roster.

server fault tolerance A level of redundancy provided by mirroring entire servers to provide redundant capacity for services.

service bureau A continuity strategy in which an organization contracts with a service agency to provide a BC facility for a fee.

service level agreement (SLA) A document or part of a document that specifies the expected level of service from a service provider. An SLA usually contains provisions for minimum acceptable availability and penalties or remediation procedures for downtime.

session hijacking See *TCP hijacking*.

session keys Limited-use symmetric keys for temporary communications during an online session.

shoulder surfing The direct, covert observation of individual information or system use.

signals intelligence The collection, analysis, and distribution of information from foreign communications networks for intelligence and counterintelligence purposes and in support of military operations. In recent years, the debate around the collection and use of signals intelligence has grappled with the integration of domestic intelligence gathering.

signature-based detection Also known as *knowledge-based detection* or *misuse detection*, the examination of system or network data in search of patterns that match known attack signatures.

signatures Patterns that correspond to a known attack.

single bastion host See *bastion host*.

single loss expectancy (SLE) In a cost-benefit analysis, the calculated value associated with the most likely loss from an attack. The SLE is the product of the asset's value and the exposure factor.

site policy The rules and configuration guidelines governing the implementation and operation of IDPSs within the organization.

site policy awareness An IDPS's ability to dynamically modify its configuration in response to environmental activity. A so-called dynamic IDPS can adapt its reactions in response to administrator guidance over time and the local environment. A dynamic IDPS logs events that fit a specific profile instead of minor events, such as file modifications or failed user logins. A smart IDPS knows when it does *not* need to alert the administrator—for example, when an attack is using a known and documented exploit from which the system is protected.

smart card An authentication component similar to a dumb card that contains a computer chip to verify and validate several pieces of information instead of just a PIN.

smoke detection system A category of fire detection systems that focuses on detecting the smoke from a fire.

sniffer See *packet sniffer*.

social engineering The process of using social skills to convince people to reveal access credentials or other valuable information to an attacker.

software assurance (SA) A methodological approach to the development of software that seeks to build security into the development life cycle rather than address it at later stages. SA attempts to intentionally create software free of vulnerabilities and provide effective, efficient software that users can deploy with confidence.

software library A collection of configuration items that is usually controlled and that developers use to construct revisions and issue new configuration items.

software piracy The unauthorized duplication, installation, or distribution of copyrighted computer software, which is a violation of intellectual property.

spam Undesired e-mail, typically commercial advertising transmitted in bulk.

spear phishing Any highly targeted phishing attack.

spike A short-term increase in electrical power availability, also known as a swell.

spoofing A technique for gaining unauthorized access to computers using a forged or modified source IP address to give the perception that messages are coming from a trusted host.

sprinkler system A fire suppression system designed to apply a liquid, usually water, to all areas in which a fire has been detected.

spyware Any technology that aids in gathering information about people or organizations without their knowledge.

standard A detailed statement of what must be done to comply with policy, sometimes viewed as the rules governing policy compliance. If the policy states that employees must "use strong passwords, frequently changed," the standard might specify that the password "must be at least 8 characters, with at least one number, one letter, and one special character."

standby (or offline) UPS An offline battery backup that detects the interruption of power to equipment and activates a transfer switch that provides power from batteries through a DC to AC converter until normal power is restored or the computer is shut down.

standby ferroresonant UPS A UPS in which the outside power source directly feeds the internal protected device. The UPS serves as a battery backup, incorporating a ferroresonant transformer instead of a converter switch, providing line filtering and reducing the effect of some power problems, and reducing noise that may be present in the power as it is delivered.

state table A tabular record of the state and context of each packet in a conversation between an internal and external user or system. A state table is used to expedite traffic filtering.

stateful packet inspection (SPI) firewall A firewall type that keeps track of each network connection between internal and external systems using a state table and that expedites the filtering of those communications. Also known as a stateful inspection firewall.

stateful protocol analysis (SPA) The comparison of vendor-supplied profiles of protocol use and behavior against observed data and network patterns in an effort to detect misuse and attacks.

static electricity An imbalance of electrical charges in the atmosphere or on the surface of a material, caused by triboelectrification.

static packet-filtering firewall A firewall type that requires the configuration rules to be manually created, sequenced, and modified within the firewall.

steganography The process of hiding messages; for example, hiding a message within the digital encoding of a picture or graphic so that it is almost impossible to detect that the hidden message even exists.

storage channels TCSEC-defined covert channels that communicate by modifying a stored object, such as in steganography.

strategic plan The documented product of strategic planning; a plan for the organization's intended strategic efforts over the next several years.

strategic planning The process of defining and specifying the long-term direction (strategy) to be taken by an organization, and the allocation and acquisition of resources needed to pursue this effort.

strong authentication In access control, the use of at least two different authentication mechanisms drawn from two different factors of authentication.

subject attribute See *attribute*.

subjects and objects of attack A computer can be either the subject of an attack—an agent entity used to conduct the attack—or the object of an attack: the target entity, as shown in Figure 1-8. A computer can also be both the subject and object of an attack. For example, it can be compromised by an attack (object) and then used to attack other systems (subject).

substitution cipher An encryption method in which one value is substituted for another.

successors Tasks or action steps that come after the specific task at hand.

sunset clause A component of policy or law that defines an expected end date for its applicability.

surge A long-term increase in electrical power availability.

switched port analysis (SPAN) port See *monitoring port*.

symmetric encryption A cryptographic method in which the same algorithm and secret key are used both to encipher and decipher the message.

synchronous token An authentication component in the form of a token—a card or key fob that contains a computer chip and a liquid crystal display and shows a computer-generated number used to support remote login authentication. This token must be calibrated with the corresponding software on the central authentication server.

systems development life cycle (SDLC) A methodology for the design and implementation of an information system. The SDLC contains different phases depending on the methodology deployed, but generally the phases address the investigation, analysis, design, implementation, and maintenance of an information system.

systems-specific security policies (SysSPs) Organizational policies that often function as standards or procedures to be used when configuring or maintaining systems. SysSPs can be separated into two general groups—managerial guidance and technical specifications—but may be written as a single unified SysSP document.

tactical plan The documented product of tactical planning; a plan for the organization's intended tactical efforts over the next few years.

tactical planning The actions taken by management to specify the intermediate goals and objectives of the organization in order to obtain specified strategic goals, followed by estimates and schedules for the allocation of resources necessary to achieve those goals and objectives.

tailgating The process of gaining unauthorized entry into a facility by closely following another person through an entrance and using the credentials of the authorized person to bypass a control point.

task rotation The requirement that all critical tasks can be performed by multiple individuals.

task-based access control (TBAC) An example of a nondiscretionary control where privileges are tied to a task a user performs in an organization and are inherited when a user is assigned to that task. Tasks are considered more temporary than roles. TBAC is an example of an LDAC.

TCP hijacking A form of man-in-the-middle attack whereby the attacker inserts himself into TCP/IP-based communications. TCP/IP is short for Transmission Control Protocol/Internet Protocol.

technical controls Information security safeguards that focus on the application of modern technologies, systems, and processes to protect information assets. These safeguards include firewalls, virtual private networks, and IDPSs.

technical feasibility An examination of how well a particular solution is supportable given the organization's current technological infrastructure and resources, which include hardware, software, networking, and personnel.

technical specifications SysSP A type of systems-specific security policy that expresses technical details for the acquisition, implementation, configuration, and management of a particular technology, written from a technical perspective. Typically the policy includes details on configuration rules, systems policies, and access control.

technology governance A process organizations use to manage the effects and costs of technology implementation, innovation, and obsolescence.

telecommuting A work arrangement in which employees work from an off-site location and connect to an organization's equipment electronically. Also known as *telework*.

telework See *telecommuting*.

TEMPEST A U.S. government program designed to protect computers from electronic remote eavesdropping by reducing EMR emissions.

termination risk control strategy The risk control strategy that eliminates all risk associated with an information asset by removing it from service.

theft The illegal taking of another's property, which can be physical, electronic, or intellectual.

thermal detection system A category of fire detection systems that focuses on detecting the heat from a fire.

thermal detector An alarm sensor designed to detect a defined rate of change in the ambient temperature within a defined space.

threat Any event or circumstance that has the potential to adversely affect operations and assets.

threat agent The specific instance or a component of a threat.

threat assessment An evaluation of the threats to information assets, including a determination of their potential to endanger the organization.

threat event An occurrence of an event caused by a threat agent.

threat source A category of objects, people, or other entities that represents the origin of danger to an asset—in other words, a category of threat agents.

threats-vulnerabilities-assets (TVA) triples A pairing of an asset with a threat and an identification of vulnerabilities that exist between the two. This pairing is often expressed in the format $TxVyA_z$, where there may be one or more vulnerabilities between Threat X and Asset Z. For example, T1V1A2 would represent Threat 1 to Vulnerability 1 on Asset 2.

threats-vulnerabilities-assets (TVA) worksheet A document that shows a comparative ranking of prioritized assets against prioritized threats, with an indication of any vulnerabilities in the asset/threat pairings.

threshold A value that sets the limit between normal and abnormal behavior. See also *clipping level*.

time-share A continuity strategy in which an organization co-leases facilities with a business partner or sister organization. A time-share allows the organization to have a BC option while reducing its overall costs.

timing channels TCSEC-defined covert channels that communicate by managing the relative timing of events.

top-down approach A methodology of establishing security policies and/or practices that is initiated by upper management.

transference risk control strategy The risk control strategy that attempts to shift risk to other assets, other processes, or other organizations.

transport mode In IPSec, an encryption method in which only a packet's IP data is encrypted, not the IP headers themselves; this method allows intermediate nodes to read the source and destination addresses.

transposition cipher A cryptographic operation that involves simply rearranging the values within a block based on an established pattern. Also known as a *permutation cipher*.

trap door See *back door*.

trap-and-trace application An application that combines the function of honeypots or honeynets with the capability to track the attacker back through the network.

trespass Unauthorized entry into the real or virtual property of another party.

triboelectrification The exchange of electrons between two materials when they make contact, resulting in one object becoming more positively charged and the other more negatively charged.

Trojan horse A malware program that hides its true nature and reveals its designed behavior only when activated.

true attack stimulus An event that triggers an alarm and causes an IDPS to react as if a real attack is in progress. The event may be an actual attack, in which an attacker is attempting a system

compromise, or it may be a drill, in which security personnel are using hacker tools to test a network segment.

trusted computing base (TCB) Under the Trusted Computer System Evaluation Criteria (TCSEC), the combination of all hardware, firmware, and software responsible for enforcing the security policy.

trusted network The system of networks inside the organization that contains its information assets and is under the organization's control.

trusted VPN Also known as a legacy VPN, a VPN implementation that uses leased circuits from a service provider who gives contractual assurance that no one else is allowed to use these circuits and that they are properly maintained and protected.

tuning The process of adjusting an IDPS to maximize its efficiency in detecting true positives while minimizing false positives and false negatives.

tunnel mode In IPSec, an encryption method in which the entire IP packet is encrypted and inserted as the payload in another IP packet. This requires other systems at the beginning and end of the tunnel to act as proxies to send and receive the encrypted packets and then transmit the packets to their ultimate destination.

two-person control The organization of a task or process so that at least two individuals must work together to complete it. Also known as dual control.

Unified Threat Management (UTM) Networking devices categorized by their ability to perform the work of multiple devices, such as stateful packet inspection firewalls, network intrusion detection and prevention systems, content filters, spam filters, and malware scanners and filters.

untrusted network The system of networks outside the organization over which the organization has no control. The Internet is an example of an untrusted network.

uptime The percentage of time a particular service is available; the opposite of downtime.

utility An attribute of information that describes how data has value or usefulness for an end purpose.

Vernam cipher A cryptographic technique developed at AT&T and known as the "one-time pad," this cipher uses a set of characters for encryption operations only one time and then discards it.

version The recorded state of a particular revision of a software or hardware configuration item. The version number is often noted in a specific format, such as "M.N.b." In this notation, "M" is the major release number and "N.b" can represent various minor releases or builds within the major release.

vibration sensor An alarm sensor designed to detect movement of the sensor rather than movement in the environment.

Vigenère cipher An advanced type of substitution cipher that uses a simple polyalphabetic code.

virtual organization A group of people brought together for a specific task, usually from different organizations, divisions, or departments.

virtual password The derivative of a passphrase. See *passphrase*.

virtual private network (VPN) A private, secure network operated over a public and insecure network. A VPN keeps the contents of the network messages hidden from observers who may have access to public traffic.

virus A type of malware that is attached to other executable programs. When activated, it replicates and propagates itself to multiple systems, spreading by multiple communications vectors. For example, a virus might send copies of itself to all users in the infected system's e-mail program.

virus hoax A message that reports the presence of a nonexistent virus or worm and wastes valuable time as employees share the message.

vulnerability A potential weakness in an asset or its defensive control system(s). Some examples of vulnerabilities are a flaw in a software package, an unprotected system port, and an unlocked door. Some well-known vulnerabilities have been examined, documented, and published; others remain latent (or undiscovered).

vulnerability assessment (VA) The process of identifying and documenting specific and provable flaws in the organization's information asset environment.

vulnerability assessment and remediation domain The component of the maintenance model focused on identifying specific, documented vulnerabilities and remediating them in a timely fashion.

war dialer An automatic phone-dialing program that dials every number in a configured range (for example, 555-1000 to 555-2000) and checks whether a person, answering machine, or modem picks up.

war driving The use of mobile scanning techniques to identify open wireless access points.

war game A type of rehearsal that seeks to realistically simulate the circumstances needed to thoroughly test a plan.

warm site A facility that provides many of the same services and options as a hot site, but typically without installed and configured software applications. Warm sites are used for BC operations.

water mist sprinkler A fire suppression sprinkler system that relies on ultra-fine mists to reduce the ambient temperature below that needed to sustain a flame.

waterfall model A type of SDLC in which each phase of the process "flows from" the information gained in the previous phase, with multiple opportunities to return to previous phases and make adjustments.

wet-pipe system A fire suppression sprinkler system that contains pressurized water in all pipes and has some form of valve in each protected area.

whitelist A list of systems, users, files, or addresses that are known to be benign; it is commonly used to expedite those entities' access to systems or networks.

wireless vulnerability assessment An assessment approach designed to find and document vulnerabilities that may be present in the organization's wireless local area networks.

work breakdown structure (WBS) A list of the tasks to be accomplished in the project, the skill sets or individual employees needed to perform the tasks, the start and end dates for tasks, the estimated resources required, and the dependencies among tasks.

work factor The amount of effort (usually expressed in units of time) required to perform cryptanalysis on an encoded message.

work recovery time (WRT) The amount of effort (expressed as elapsed time) necessary to make the business function operational after the technology element is recovered (as identified with RTO). Tasks include testing and validation of the system.

worm A type of malware that is capable of activation and replication without being attached to an existing program.

zero day vulnerability An unknown or undisclosed vulnerability in an information asset or its protection systems that may be exploited and result in loss. This vulnerability is also referred to as *zero day* (or *zero hour*) because once it is discovered, the technology owners have zero days to identify, mitigate, and resolve the vulnerability.

zero-day attack An attack that makes use of malware that is not yet known by the anti-malware software companies.

zombie See *bot*.

Index

Note: Page numbers followed by *f* and *t* indicate figures and tables, respectively.